The Government and Politics of the
Middle East and North Africa

The Government and Politics of the

MIDDLE EAST AND NORTH AFRICA

Sixth Edition

Edited by

David E. Long
Bernard Reich
Mark Gasiorowski

WESTVIEW
PRESS
A Member of the Perseus Books Group

Published by Westview Press,
A Member of the Perseus Books Group

Find us on the World Wide Web at www.westviewpress.com.

Every effort has been made to secure required permissions to use all images, maps, and other art included in this volume.

Westview Press books are available at special discounts for bulk purchases in the United States by corporations, institutions, and other organizations. For more information, please contact the Special Markets Department at the Perseus Books Group, 2300 Chestnut Street, Suite 200, Philadelphia, PA 19103, or call (800) 810-4145, ext. 5000, or e-mail special.markets@perseusbooks.com.

Designed by Jeff Williams

Library of Congress Cataloging-in-Publication Data
The government and politics of the Middle East and North Africa / edited by David E. Long, Bernard Reich, Mark Gasiorowski. — 6th ed.
    p. cm.
  Includes bibliographical references and index.
  ISBN 978-0-8133-4449-2 (alk. paper)
    1. Middle East—Politics and government—1945- 2. Africa, North—Politics and government. I. Long, David E. II. Reich, Bernard. III. Gasiorowski, Mark J., 1954-

DS62.8.G68 2010
956—dc22

2010017176

10 9 8 7 6 5 4 3 2

Contents

Preface, vii
About the Book and Editors, ix
About the Contributors, xi

1   INTRODUCTION: MIDDLE EASTERN AND
NORTH AFRICAN STATES IN COMPARATIVE PERSPECTIVE
David E. Long, Bernard Reich, and Mark Gasiorowski 1

2   REPUBLIC OF TURKEY
Henri J. Barkey and Omer Taspinar 15

3   ISLAMIC REPUBLIC OF IRAN
Mark Gasiorowski 49

4   KINGDOM OF SAUDI ARABIA
Sebastian Maisel 91

5   REPUBLIC OF IRAQ
Judith S. Yaphe 123

6   EASTERN ARABIAN STATES: KUWAIT, BAHRAIN,
QATAR, UNITED ARAB EMIRATES, AND OMAN
Jill Crystal 161

7   REPUBLIC OF YEMEN
Robert D. Burrowes 205

8   REPUBLIC OF LEBANON
William Harris 233

9   SYRIAN ARAB REPUBLIC
David W. Lesch..267

10   HASHIMITE KINGDOM OF JORDAN
Curtis R. Ryan..297

11   STATE OF ISRAEL
David H. Goldberg and Bernard Reich......................................321

12   THE PALESTINIANS
Glenn E. Robinson..365

13   ARAB REPUBLIC OF EGYPT
Marius Deeb...397

14   GREAT SOCIALIST PEOPLE'S LIBYAN ARAB JAMAHIRIYA
Mary-Jane Deeb..423

15   KINGDOM OF MOROCCO
Gregory W. White...447

16   DEMOCRATIC AND POPULAR REPUBLIC OF ALGERIA
Azzedine Layachi..479

17   REPUBLIC OF TUNISIA
John P. Entelis..509

Index, 537

PREFACE

This sixth edition of *The Government and Politics of the Middle East and North Africa* updates the earlier editions and seeks to introduce the reader to the growing challenges facing the countries of the region in the twenty-first century. Substantial change has occurred since the last edition, including the emergence of several new leaders, changes in regional alignments, and efforts to achieve peace and stabilize the region. The consequences of the September 11, 2001, attacks on the United States continue to play out, focusing especially on Afghanistan and Iraq but affecting all states in the region. There has also been continuing technological change in the electronic, telecommunications, and computer sectors, with far-reaching impact on the politics and economics of the region. Our authors have considered all of these factors and taken into account the latest themes and methods of the disciplines used in this book.

In this edition, all authors from the fifth edition have returned to update their country chapters. In addition, David Goldberg has joined Bernie Reich as coauthor of the Israel chapter, which has been thoroughly revised. All of our authors are leading scholars on their respective countries, bringing a wealth of expertise to the book.

In recent decades, laymen, journalists, students, and policy makers have devoted considerable attention to the Middle East and North Africa. Books and articles by scholars exist in large number and cover many aspects of the region, especially its history, politics, and economics. Despite this increased attention and interest, the present volume remains the only work on the politics of the states of the region that is comprehensive in geographic and subject matter coverage, up-to-date, and written by well-known and respected country experts. This was the idea behind the first edition, which appeared in 1980, and it inspired this sixth edition. Therefore, we sought the assistance of a diverse group of Middle East specialists with academic and often policy-related experience to produce a current, comprehensive, and general book that focuses on the politics (and especially the political dynamics) of the Middle East and North Africa. This book is also unique in that it includes North Africa in its broad definition of the area.

Multiple authorship has the advantage of providing greater depth of expertise on the individual countries and political systems than any single author can provide. To facilitate the comparative study of the countries, all of the contributors have followed a common outline, but each chapter differs according to the peculiarities of the political system being examined and the style of the individual author.

In any work of this type, it is impossible to capture all the details of continuing changes in the governmental systems and political process and dynamics of the states and region as they remain constantly in flux. However, the method employed since the initial edition permits the scholars to deal with eternal verities and broad concepts rather than rely on daily current events. The latter events provided the examples that are readily explained and analyzed within the political framework provided in the several chapters.

There are, of course, scores of people to whom we are indebted. As we do not want to leave anyone out inadvertently, we would like to acknowledge them all collectively. A number of our students have been especially helpful, including Lauren Nyman, who assembled the country fact sheets, and Karen Hopkins and Timothy Joyner, who created the maps. And most of all, we wish to acknowledge that without the assistance and understanding of our wives, Barbara, Madelyn, and Mary, this volume would not have been possible.

ABOUT THE BOOK AND EDITORS

The countries of the Middle East and North Africa have been tense and unstable for decades. In recent years the rise of radical Islamist movements, the collapse of the Israeli-Palestinian peace process, the terrorist attacks of September 11, 2001, and the wars in Iraq and Afghanistan have raised tensions in the region even further and touched almost every corner of the globe. These events highlight the importance of understanding the region's history, culture, geography, economics, and—most importantly—politics.

In this sixth edition of *The Government and Politics of the Middle East and North Africa*, David E. Long, Bernard Reich, and Mark Gasiorowski bring together many leading scholars of the region to provide a detailed overview of its domestic and interregional politics. The book includes chapters covering the politics of every country in the region and a chapter on the Palestinians. Each chapter follows a common format, examining a country's historical background, the factors that shape its domestic politics, and its foreign policy. The chapters also contain maps detailing each country and bibliographies with numerous references for further reading. The country chapters provide a comprehensive portrait of domestic politics and interregional relations in the Middle East and North Africa, giving readers a good basis for understanding contemporary events in the region.

David E. Long is an author, teacher, and former diplomat specializing in the Middle East and international terrorism. He served with the US Foreign Service in Washington, DC, Jordan, Morocco, Saudi Arabia, and Sudan. His Washington assignments included deputy director of the State Department's Office of Counter Terrorism for Regional Policy, member of the Secretary of State's policy planning staff, and chief of the Near East Research Division in the Bureau of Intelligence and Research. He has written extensively on the Middle East and terrorism, authoring, among other publications, *The United States and Saudi Arabia: Ambivalent Allies*, *The Anatomy of Terrorism*, *The Kingdom of Saudi Arabia*, and *The Culture and Customs of Saudi Arabia*.

Bernard Reich is professor of political science and international affairs at George Washington University in Washington, DC. He is a member of the board of advisory editors of *The Middle East Journal* and of the international editorial board of *Israel Affairs*. He has authored *Quest for Peace: United States–Israel Relations and the Arab-Israeli Conflict*, *The United States and Israel: Influence in the Special Relationship*, *Israel: Land of Tradition and Conflict*, *Historical Dictionary of Israel*, *Securing the Covenant: United States–Israel Relations After the Cold War*, *Arab-Israeli Conflict and Conciliation: A Documentary History*, *Political Dictionary of Israel*, and *Brief History of Israel*, as well as numerous articles, book chapters, and monographs on Middle East politics, international politics, and US foreign policy.

Mark Gasiorowski is professor of political science and international studies at Louisiana State University. He was a visiting professor at Tehran University in 1994, 1996, and 1998 and a visiting fellow at the Middle East Centre of St. Antony's College, Oxford University, in 2001 through 2002. The author of *U.S. Foreign Policy and the Shah*, he coedited *Neither East nor West* with Nikki Keddie and *Mohammad Mosaddeq and the 1953 Coup in Iran* with Malcolm Byrne.

About the Contributors

Henri J. Barkey is the Bernard and Bertha Cohen Professor of International Relations at Lehigh University. He served on the US State Department's policy planning staff (1998–2000), working on issues related to the eastern Mediterranean and the Middle East. His works include *Turkey's Kurdish Question* (with Graham Fuller), *Preventing Conflict over Kurdistan*, and "Turkey's Transformers," in *Foreign Affairs* (with Morton Abramowitz).

Robert D. Burrowes holds a PhD from Princeton University. He recently retired from the political science department and Henry M. Jackson School of International Studies of the University of Washington. He has authored *The Yemen Arab Republic: The Politics of Development* and *The Historical Dictionary of Yemen*, 2nd ed. His recent articles include "Yemen: Political Economy and the Effort Against Terrorism," in *Battling Terror in the Horn of Africa*, ed. Robert I. Rotberg.

Jill Crystal is a professor of political science at Auburn University. She received a PhD from Harvard University and has authored *Oil and Politics in the Gulf: Rulers and Merchants in Kuwait* and *Qatar and Kuwait: The Transformation of an Oil State*, as well as several articles and book chapters.

Marius Deeb holds a PhD in politics from Oxford University. He teaches Islamic and Middle Eastern studies at the Paul Nitze School of Advanced International Studies at Johns Hopkins University. His publications include *Party Politics in Egypt: The Wafd and Its Rivals 1919–1939*, *Libya Since the Revolution: Aspects of Social and Political Development* (with Mary-Jane Deeb), and *Syria's Terrorist War on Lebanon and the Peace Process*.

Mary-Jane Deeb is chief of the African and Middle Eastern Division at the Library of Congress. She was the editor of *The Middle East Journal* from 1995 to 1998 and taught at American University for a decade. Deeb is the author of *Libya's Foreign Policy in North Africa* and coauthor with Marius K. Deeb of *Libya Since the Revolution: Aspects of Social and Political Development*.

John P. Entelis is professor of political science and director of the Middle East Studies program at Fordham University. He has been a senior Fulbright professor at the University of Tunis and edited the volume *Islam, Democracy, and the State in North Africa*. Entelis is editor of the *Journal of North African Studies* and publications officer of the American Institute for Maghrib Studies.

David H. Goldberg is a Toronto-based policy analyst specializing in Israel. He holds a PhD in political science from McGill University. He has taught at York University and was the publisher of *Middle East Focus*. He has authored or edited seven books, including (with Bernard Reich) *Historical Dictionary of Israel*, 2nd ed.

William Harris holds a PhD from the University of Durham and is a professor in the department of political studies, University of Otago, New Zealand. He is author of *The Levant: A Fractured Mosaic*, 2nd ed., which won a Choice Magazine Outstanding Academic Title award, and *The New Face of Lebanon: History's Revenge*, 2nd ed. He is currently working on a history of Lebanon for Oxford University Press.

Azzedine Layachi is a professor of politics and former associate director of the Center for Global Studies at St. John's University. He received a PhD and MA in politics from New York University and a BA from the Institut des Études Politiques of the University of Algiers. He is the author of numerous books, chapters, and articles on North Africa, including *Economic Crisis and Political Change in North Africa*, *State, Society and Liberalization in Morocco*, *The United States and North Africa: A Cognitive Approach to Foreign Policy*, and *Global Studies: The Middle East*.

David W. Lesch is professor of Middle East history at Trinity University, Texas. He has a PhD in history and Middle Eastern studies from Harvard University. Among his authored books are *The Arab-Israeli Conflict: A History*, *The New Lion of Damascus: Bashar al-Asad and Modern Syria*, and *1979: The Year That Shaped the Modern Middle East*; he also edited *The Middle East and the United States: A Historical and Political Reassessment*, 4th ed.

Sebastian Maisel is an assistant professor of Arabic language and Middle Eastern studies at Grand Valley State University. He holds a PhD in Arabic and Islamic studies and anthropology from the University of Leipzig. Among his publications are *The Customary Law of the Bedouins in Arabia*, *Saudi Arabia and the Gulf States Today: An Encyclopedia of Life in the Arab States* (with J. Shoup), and *The Kingdom of Saudi Arabia* (with David Long). He was the program researcher for the Saudi Arabian National Arts Foundation and has taught at King Saud University.

Glenn E. Robinson holds a PhD from the University of California, Berkeley, and is associate professor of defense analysis at the Naval Postgraduate School. He has written extensively on the Palestinian issue; his publications include three authored or coauthored books: *Building a Palestinian State: The Incomplete Revolution*, *The Arc: A Formal Structure for a Palestinian State*, and *Building a Successful Palestinian State*.

Curtis R. Ryan is an associate professor of political science at Appalachian State University in North Carolina. He holds a PhD from the University of North Carolina, Chapel Hill. He served as a Fulbright scholar at the Center for Strategic

Studies in Jordan (1992–1993) and was twice named a peace scholar by the United States Institute of Peace. He has authored *Inter-Arab Alliances: Regime Security and Jordanian Foreign Policy* and *Jordan in Transition: From Hussein to Abdullah*, as well as articles in *The Middle East Journal, Middle East Insight, Arab Studies Quarterly, Israel Affairs, Southeastern Political Review, Journal of Third World Studies, Middle East Policy*, and *Middle East Report*.

Omer Taspinar is director of the Turkey program at the Brookings Institution's Center on the United States and Europe and an adjunct professor at the Johns Hopkins University, School of Advanced International Studies (SAIS). Prior to joining Brookings, he was assistant professor in the European Studies Department of SAIS and a consultant at the Robert F. Kennedy Center for Justice and Human Rights.

Gregory W. White is a professor of government at Smith College, Northampton, Massachusetts. He is a former Fulbright scholar to Morocco and Tunisia and author of *On the Outside of Europe Looking In: A Comparative Political Economy of Tunisia and Morocco*. He is also a member of the board of the American Institute for Maghrib Studies and an associate editor of the *Journal of North African Studies*.

Judith S. Yaphe is Distinguished Research Fellow for the Middle East in the Institute for National Strategic Studies at National Defense University and a professorial lecturer at the George Washington University. She has authored many articles on Iraqi history and politics and US policy.

1

INTRODUCTION

Middle Eastern and North African States in Comparative Perspective

David E. Long, Bernard Reich, and Mark Gasiorowski

The first decade of the twenty-first century witnessed several major crises originating in the Middle East and North Africa. The terrorist attacks of September 11, 2001, in New York and Washington, DC, were carried out by al-Qa'ida, an Islamist terrorist organization whose ideology and leaders come from the region. In response, the United States invaded and occupied Afghanistan, where al-Qa'ida was based, and unleashed a "global war on terrorism" intended to transform global security. The United States then invaded and occupied Iraq in 2003, triggering a bloody insurgency and enflaming anti-Americanism throughout the region. Many smaller crises originated in the region as well during the decade, including additional al-Qa'ida attacks, severe tension between Israel and the Palestinians, Israeli armed confrontations with Hizballah in Lebanon and Hamas in the Gaza Strip, a major diplomatic confrontation over Iran's nuclear program, sharply fluctuating oil prices, and domestic instability in several countries.

Although some observers view these crises as consequences of recent events, they are, in fact, a continuation of long-standing trends. In the wake of World War II, the Arab-Israeli conflict and Cold War rivalry became endemic, severely destabilizing the region. Political Islam emerged as a major force in the 1970s, deeply affecting domestic and regional politics. Iraq invaded Iran in 1980 and Kuwait in 1990, producing brutal wars and instability in nearby countries. Oil prices have fluctuated sharply since the early 1970s, roiling regional economies and triggering global recessions.

These dramatic events highlight the importance of studying the politics of the Middle East and North Africa. This book aims to contribute to a greater understanding of the region by presenting concise overviews of the history and politics of each of its countries, as well as a similar overview for the Palestinians. It is intended

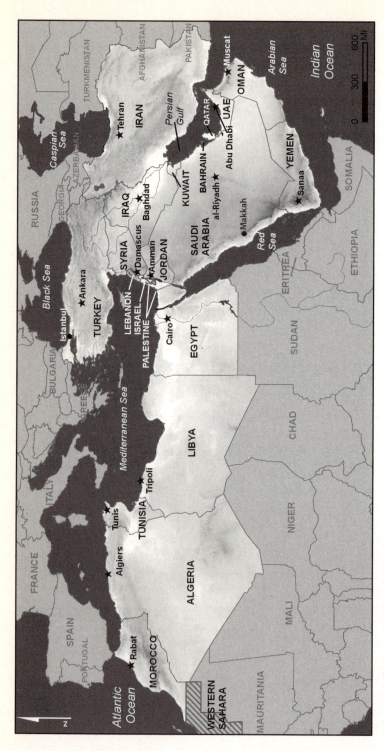

The Middle East and North Africa

to serve as a textbook for university-level classes on Middle East politics and a general reference work for people interested in the region.

The book contains a separate chapter on each of the fourteen larger countries in the region, a single chapter covering the five small Persian Gulf Arab countries (Bahrain, Kuwait, Oman, Qatar, and United Arab Emirates), and a chapter on the Palestinians. Each chapter begins with a historical overview, focusing especially on trends in the modern period that affect politics today. The chapters then examine the broad environment within which politics plays out in each country, considering geographic, social, cultural, economic, and geopolitical factors. Next, they discuss each country's political structure and dynamics, surveying their political institutions and the main factors that animate their politics. Each chapter also includes an overview of the country's foreign policy, as well as a country map, table of facts and figures, and annotated bibliography.

The main purpose of this chapter, therefore, is to present a broad perspective of the entire Middle East–North African area as a single political region, despite the many differences that will be noted throughout the book. It begins with a brief overview of the region's geography, history, and ethnic and religious groups, then sketches the main economic and social trends affecting the entire area, and concludes with a discussion of the main types of political regime that have existed in the region since independence.

PHYSICAL AND SOCIAL GEOGRAPHY

Nomenclature in the geographic area covered in this book can be confusing. Coined in the nineteenth century, the term *Near East* was used mainly by archeologists to distinguish northeastern Arab states and Iran from the Far East. An older term, *Fertile Crescent*, generally applies to the lands extending in an arc from the eastern Mediterranean littoral states to the Tigris-Euphrates valley and Persian Gulf. The term *Middle East* was adopted for this study as a broader term to cover all the states listed. The term *Maghreb* (from *Maghrib*, the Arabic word for "west") includes the North African states of Algeria, Libya, Morocco, and Tunisia. The terms *Middle East* and *North Africa* were chosen for this book to encompass all the states from Morocco east to Iran and from Turkey south to Yemen in the Arabian Peninsula. (See Map 1.)

Most of the Middle East and North Africa is hot and arid, consisting of deserts or grassy steppes. The biggest desert is the Sahara, comprising large portions of the four North African countries, Egypt, and the countries immediately to their south. The Sinai and Negev deserts adjoin each other in Egypt's Sinai Peninsula and southern Israel. The Syrian Desert includes large portions of Iraq, Jordan, Syria, and the far north of Arabia. The Arabian Desert includes al-Nafud in northern Arabia, the Rub' al-Khali ("Empty Quarter") in southern Arabia, and a narrow strip of desert called al-Dahna running north to south in central Arabia and connecting the two. The Dasht-e Kavir and Dasht-e Lut deserts are located in north-central and eastern Iran. These deserts vary considerably in soil composition, elevation, and other features. The Rub' al-Khali, for example, is the largest quartz sand desert in the world with giant dunes reaching hundreds of meters in height and twenty-five kilometers in length. Nearly all are marked by occasional oases, where geological conditions provide enough water for plants and animals to live. Some of these oases are inhabited; others are visited by the small number of nomads who still populate the region, raising sheep and other livestock. By contrast al-Hasa Oasis in eastern Saudi Arabia stretches for about 120 kilometers and has an estimated population of around three-quarters of a million people.

The steppes are transition zones between deserts and well-watered areas, with enough moisture to support scrub grasses, bushes, and some small trees. Many are located in or near mountain ranges, where rain and springs provide varying amounts of water. These include the Atlas Mountains of northern Morocco, Algeria, and Tunisia; the Western and Eastern mountains of Lebanon; the Taurus and Pontic mountains of Turkey; the Zagros and Alborz mountains of Iran; and the Hejaz, Asir, Yemeni, and al Hajar mountains of western, southern, and eastern Arabia. Temperatures are quite moderate in some of these mountains, permitting winter snow in some areas. Other steppes are located in the hinterlands of rivers, seas, and oceans. These steppes support scattered sedentary populations, who raise livestock and cultivate grain and other crops, as well as small nomadic pastoral groups.

Most of the region's population is concentrated in cities and towns in coastal areas and along rivers, where agriculture, industry, and commerce are much more feasible. The most populated part of the region historically has been the Fertile Crescent, stretching from the Nile River Delta area in Egypt northward along the Mediterranean coast, east across northern Syria and southern Turkey, and south through the Tigris-Euphrates river valley in Iraq to the Persian Gulf. Many Middle Eastern cities—including Alexandria, Baghdad, Beirut, Cairo, Damascus, Fez, Jerusalem, Istanbul, Mecca, and Tunis—date back over 1,000 years and have great historical and cultural importance.

NATIONAL, RELIGIOUS, ETHNIC, AND TRIBAL LOYALTIES AND DIVISIONS

It is difficult for many people who are products of Western cultures to imagine that state nationalism is not the premier loyalty of a country and the glue that holds together the social contract between the governed and those who govern in a given country. Yet, state nationalism is a Western concept that first appeared in Europe in the seventeenth century. It did not appear in the Middle East and North Africa until the nineteenth century, when Napoleon first invaded Egypt. Prior to then, the

Islamic world, which included the entire area under study, classified people by their religious affiliations. Those recognized as "peoples of the book" were Christians, Jews, and Zoroastrians, all monotheists. State nationalism, by contrast, is secular.

Every state has multiple loyalties and divisions, which even in stable states have the potential to threaten national, regional, and even global political stability. In the Middle East and North Africa, these include age-old ethnic, tribal, and religious loyalties and divisions.

Numerically, the greatest number of loyalties are linguistic and religious. Some 62 percent of the residents of the Middle East and North Africa speak Arabic as their primary language and consider themselves Arabs. They live throughout the area. There are, of course, numerous other linguistic groups, including Turkish and Persian speakers, who comprise the majority in Turkey and Iran, respectively. Some 92 percent of the region's population is Muslim; roughly two-thirds are Sunnis and one-third are Shi'as. Omanis follow the ancient Ibadi branch of Islam.

The overwhelming number of Arabs and Muslims might seem a major source of both national and regional solidarity; however, although the Islamic faith does indeed preach peace among all believers, and the pan-Arab movement has created an element of solidarity among all Arabs, both inter-Arab conflicts and conflicts in the name of Islam have historically been divisive as well as unifying.

Ethnic differences have also been a major source of past discord and account for the major conflicts today. But probably the greatest threat domestically and regionally arises when religious and ethnic differences are combined as sources of conflict.

Finally, although in earlier times tribal loyalties and divisions were major elements of government and politics, urbanization and modernization have greatly reduced their importance. Nevertheless, they still play a reduced role in some of the countries under study, particularly in the Arabian Peninsula, Iraq, Syria, and, to a lesser extent, some of the North African states. From a societal stand point, extended-family loyalties, be they tribal or not, remain an important element in commercial as well as political networking, particularly in monarchial political systems.

ECONOMIC CONDITIONS

The economies of Middle Eastern and North African countries are very diverse, as Table 1.1 shows.

The most striking pattern in Table 1.1 is that gross domestic product (GDP) per capita—a common measure of the average income of a country's population—varies tremendously across the region, with the richest country (Qatar) having an average income forty-three times higher than that of the poorest (Yemen). While these two countries are atypical, income levels in the region nevertheless vary substantially, with seven countries having 2008 GDP per capita levels above $20,000,

Table 1.1   Selected Economic Indicators

Country	GDP per Capita (US $)	Net Fuel Exports per Capita (US $)	Arable Land (%)	Agriculture (% of GDP)	Services (% of GDP)	Industry (% of GDP)
Algeria	7,000	1,598	3	8	29	63
Bahrain	37,200	5,393	3	0	56	44
Egypt	5,400	57	3	13	51	38
Iran	12,800	892	10	11	45	44
Iraq	4,000	N/A	13	5	27	68
Israel	28,200	−1,104	15	3	66	32
Jordan	5,000	−486	3	4	86	10
Kuwait	57,400	6,561	1	0	48	52
Lebanon	11,100	−510	16	5	76	19
Libya	14,400	N/A	1	2	37	62
Morocco	4,000	−154	19	15	47	39
Oman	20,200	7,605	0	2	61	37
Palestinian territories	2,900	N/A	18	8	79	13
Qatar	103,500	37,548	2	0	21	79
Saudi Arabia	20,700	8,101	2	3	35	62
Syria	4,800	67	25	23	50	28
Tunisia	7,900	−69	17	11	61	28
Turkey	12,000	−230	30	9	63	29
United Arab Emirates	40,000	21,134	1	2	37	62
Yemen	2,400	265	3	9	38	52

Notes: Net fuel exports data are from World Bank, *World Development Indicators Online.* All other data are from *CIA World Factbook.* All data are for 2008 or the most recent year available.

four more having levels above $10,000, three reaching between $5,000 and $10,000, and six others (including the Palestinian territories) at or below $5,000. The comparable figure for the United States is $47,000.

The most important factor driving these income disparities is the huge variation in oil wealth across the region. The second column in Table 1.1 shows each country's net fuel-export revenue per capita (i.e., oil and gas exports minus imports, divided by population size). These data show that six of the seven countries with GDP per capita above $20,000 are major fuel exporters; all those with GDP per capita at or below $5,000 have small or negative net fuel exports; and those in between have modest, small, or negative net fuel exports.

A closer look at these figures shows that the region's main oil and gas exporters fall into three categories: two with net fuel exports per capita above $20,000 (Qatar and the United Arab Emirates), four between $5,000 and $10,000 (Bahrain, Kuwait, Oman, and Saudi Arabia), and two others between $800 and $2,000 (Algeria and Iran). Iraq and Libya, for which comparable data are not available, probably fall in the lower and middle categories, respectively. These levels correlate closely with the GDP per capita data.

The disparity in per capita income between major oil producers and those with little or no oil production, however, does not tell the whole story. Politically, great wealth can be as difficult for governments to deal with as poverty. It is not how much money a person does have but the individual's expectations about what he or she should have that is the crucial question. Virtually all the major oil-producing states seek ways to trickle down public-sector wealth to their citizens, but not only can that undermine the work ethic, which can marginalize a sense of personal fulfillment, but it can create unrealistic and unattainable expectations. An old man who grew up with no transportation other than his feet could be more content with an old, used car than his grandson who drives a new sedan but believes he should have a luxury vehicle. From a political standpoint, political stability is thus based more on fulfilled expectations than actual wealth.

DEMOGRAPHIC CONDITIONS

Demographic and social conditions also vary substantially among the countries of the Middle East and North Africa. As Table 1.2 shows, these countries differ widely in population size, with three having populations of more than 60 million, six having above 20 million, and seven less than 5 million. Moreover, the second column in Table 1.2 shows that all of the small Persian Gulf oil-producing countries host large numbers of immigrant workers, implying that several actually have fewer than a million citizens (Bahrain, Kuwait, and Qatar). The third column shows that most countries in the region have fertility rates well above the population-replacement rate of just over two babies per woman. These high fertility rates have produced rapid population growth in many of these countries in recent decades. Moreover, as shown in the fourth column, countries with high fertility rates and few immigrant workers (who are mainly adult males) have very youthful populations, often creating youth-unemployment problems and potentially volatile political unrest. A few countries (Algeria, Iran, Lebanon, and Tunisia) have brought fertility rates down substantially with family-planning programs, partially mitigating these problems.

The last column of Table 1.2 shows that all countries in the region except Yemen and Egypt are very urbanized, with at least half of their population living in cities. While cities like Dubai and Tel Aviv in the region's wealthier countries boast glittering skyscrapers and broad boulevards, those in poorer countries are often deeply dysfunctional, with severe overcrowding, inadequate physical and social infrastructure, serious pollution problems, and vast impoverished shantytowns. The urban poor in these cities have very difficult lives and are susceptible to Islamist appeals, forming the backbone of radical Islamist movements in Egypt, Iran, Morocco, and elsewhere.

Table 1.2   Selected Demographic Indicators

Country	Population (thousands)	Immigrants (% of population)	Fertility (births per woman)	People Under 15 (% of population)	Urban (% of population)
Algeria	34,178	1	1.8	25	65
Bahrain	728	38	2.5	26	89
Egypt	83,083	0	2.7	31	43
Iran	66,429	3	1.7	22	68
Iraq	28,946	N/A	3.9	39	67
Israel	7,234	38	2.8	28	92
Jordan	6,343	43	2.4	31	78
Kuwait	2,691	74	2.8	26	98
Lebanon	4,017	18	1.9	26	87
Libya	6,310	10	3.1	33	78
Morocco	34,859	0	2.5	30	56
Oman	3,418	27	5.5	43	72
Palestinian territories	4,013	48	3.9	40	72
Qatar	833	90	2.5	22	96
Saudi Arabia	28,686	27	3.8	38	82
Syria	20,178	7	3.1	36	54
Tunisia	10,486	0	1.7	23	67
Turkey	76,806	2	2.2	27	69
United Arab Emirates	4,798	70	2.4	20	78
Yemen	23,823	2	6.3	46	31

Notes: Data on immigrants are from World Bank, *World Development Indicators Online.* All other data are from *CIA World Factbook.* All data are for 2008 or the most recent year available.

Table 1.3 shows several indicators of poverty in the region. Israel and the wealthy Persian Gulf countries have infant-mortality and life-expectancy rates rivaling those in Europe, reflecting the modern health and sanitation systems that now exist in these countries. By contrast, infant mortality and life expectancy are much worse in Yemen and, to a lesser extent, Morocco and Iraq (following decades of war and economic sanctions), reflecting the grinding poverty and inadequate infrastructure in these countries. Adult literacy is very high in Israel and fairly high in the wealthy Persian Gulf countries, where sharp increases in educational availability in recent decades have left almost all young and middle-aged people literate today. Moreover, the fourth column in Table 1.3 shows that female literacy is almost as high as male literacy in these countries, indicating that women have benefited almost as much as men from these increases, despite the conservative character of these cultures. By contrast, male and especially female literacy are much lower in Yemen and Morocco, where poverty severely limits educational availability.

Table 1.3   Selected Social Indicators

Country	Infant Mortality (per 1,000 births)	Life Expectancy (at birth)	Adult Literacy (%)	Adult Female Literacy (%)	Telephones (per 100 people)	Internet Users (per 100 people)
Algeria	28	74	70	60	90	10
Bahrain	15	75	87	84	149	33
Egypt	27	72	71	59	55	14
Iran	36	71	77	70	75	32
Iraq	44	70	74	64	53	N/A
Israel	4	81	97	96	162	28
Jordan	15	79	90	85	94	20
Kuwait	9	78	93	91	117	34
Lebanon	22	74	87	82	48	38
Libya	21	77	83	72	48	4
Morocco	37	72	52	40	73	21
Oman	17	74	81	74	106	13
Palestinian territories	17	74	92	88	37	10
Qatar	13	75	89	89	180	42
Saudi Arabia	12	76	79	71	134	26
Syria	26	71	80	74	49	17
Tunisia	23	76	74	65	89	17
Turkey	26	72	87	80	109	16
United Arab Emirates	13	76	78	82	209	52
Yemen	55	63	50	30	18	1

Notes: Telephone and Internet data are from World Bank, *World Development Indicators Online.* All other data are from *CIA World Factbook.* All data are for 2008 or the most recent year available.

The last two columns in Table 1.3 show that the availability of telephones (including mobile phones) and the Internet varies widely across the region, being highest in Israel and the wealthy Persian Gulf countries, fairly high in Iran, Jordan, Tunisia, and Turkey, and lowest in Libya, the Palestinian territories, Syria, and especially Yemen. The availability of these media gives a good indication of how isolated or connected people in these countries are, both in terms of their fellow citizens and globally. These media also have become crucial means of domestic and international communication and therefore important tools for organizing mass political activity, making some of these countries potentially much more volatile than others.

POLITICAL SYSTEMS

The countries of the region have very diverse political systems, reflecting widely varying historical, socioeconomic, and other conditions. Most of the region's political systems can be divided broadly into two main categories: monarchies and the successors of radical Arab nationalist regimes.

As Table 1.4 shows, Jordan, Morocco, Saudi Arabia, and the five eastern Arabian states (Bahrain, Kuwait, Oman, Qatar, and the United Arab Emirates) all have monarchical regimes of some sort. Egypt, Iraq, Yemen, Libya, and Iran also had monarchies that were overthrown in 1952, 1958, 1962, 1969, and 1979, respectively. Most of these monarchies were established upon independence, based on a precolonial ruling family (the eastern Arabian states, Egypt, Morocco, and Yemen), a prominent family that had led anticolonial resistance (Libya), or a powerful family from a neighboring region (Jordan and Iraq). The Saudi monarchy dates back to the eighteenth century, when the House of Saud ruled in Najd in central Arabia. It was overthrown twice but regained power in the early twentieth century and renamed the country the Kingdom of Saudi Arabia in 1932. Persia, renamed Iran in 1935, had always had a monarchial government until the Pahlavi dynasty, which came to power in the 1920s, was overthrown in 1979 and replaced by an Islamic republic.

These monarchies are similar in many ways, though important differences also exist among them. In each case executive power is concentrated in the hands of the monarch, known formally as the king, amir, shaykh, or sultan. As Table 1.4 shows, the monarchs rule directly as heads of government, although some are constitutional monarchs who rule indirectly through appointed prime ministers. The degree of public participation in the political process, however, is not determined solely by the monarch or by a written constitution. To a great degree, public participation is determined by the political culture of the general population.

Thus, for example, all the monarchies in Arabia have traditional, premodern political systems, whether or not they have Western-style constitutions. As such, they bear a closer resemblance to the political system of republican Yemen than that of monarchial Morocco. Yemen, like virtually all countries under study here, was historically under monarchial rule; unlike most other republics, however, it never experienced European colonialism. Moreover, tribalism is still a major political element there. As a result, its political system resembles traditional monarchial authoritarianism more than virtually any other regime, monarchial or republican, throughout the Middle East and North Africa. On the other hand, Morocco, while it has ancient Islamic monarchial traditions, has been influenced by Western political culture more than other Arab monarchies, including those of the smaller Gulf states that were under British colonial protection until the 1970s. The monarchial regime in Saudi Arabia is unique in that it has never been under colonial rule and, since its founding in the eighteenth century, has always based its equivalent of constitutional law on the Qur'an.

All the Middle East and North African republics have written constitutions based to a great degree on European models. Public participation in the political

Table 1.4 Selected Political Indicators

Country	Year of Independence	Executive System	Written Constitution, Year Adopted	Suffrage, Minimum Voting Age	Public Participation in the Political Process
Algeria	1962	Presidential republic	1963	Universal, 18	Highly limited
Bahrain	1971	Constitutional monarchy	2002	Universal, 20	Limited
Egypt	1922	Presidential republic	1971	Universal, 18	Highly limited
Iran	1501	Presidential theocracy	1979	Universal, 18	Highly limited
Iraq	1932	Parliamentary republic	2005	Universal, 18	Highly limited
Israel	1948	Parliamentary republic	None	Universal, 18	Selectively high
Jordan	1946	Constitutional monarchy	1952	Universal, 18	Selective
Kuwait	1961	Constitutional monarchy	1962	Universal, 21	Selective
Lebanon	1943	Presidential republic	1926	Universal, 21	Selective
Libya	1951	Presidential republic	None	Universal, 18	Highly limited
Morocco	1956	Constitutional monarchy	1972	Universal, 18	Selective
Oman	1650	Traditional monarchy	None	Universal, 21	Limited
Palestinian territories	N/A	Semipresidential under Israeli occupation	2002	Universal, 18	Highly limited
Qatar	1971	Constitutional monarchy	2005	Universal, 18	Limited
Saudi Arabia	1932	Islamic monarchy	None	Men, 21	Limited
Syria	1946	Parliamentary dictatorship	1973	Universal, 18	Highly limited
Tunisia	1956	Presidential republic	1959	Universal, 18	Limited
Turkey	1923	Parliamentary republic	1982	Universal, 18	Selective
United Arab Emirates	1971	Presidential federation of traditional monarchies	1971	None	Limited
Yemen	1918/1967	Presidential republic	1991	Universal, 18	Limited

Notes: Statistical data are from *CIA World Factbook* and Wikipedia.org, July 2009. It should be noted that the term *absolute monarchy* was not used. This is a European term in which the monarch is above the law. In virtually all Middle Eastern–North African countries there are varying degrees of public participation in public consensus making, legitimizing public policy, and in Islam, the ruler is, at least technically, not above the law. On the other hand, Egypt and Libya both qualify as dictatorships, and Algeria and Iran qualify as authoritarian.

process, however, is far more heterogeneous than is the case with monarchies. It ranges from dictatorial regimes (such as those in Egypt, Libya, and Syria) and authoritarian regimes (such as is in Algeria and Iran) to selective and limited public participation in the political process in most of the other countries.

Israel does not have a written constitution but a series of basic laws dealing with various elements generally included in a constitution.

All the countries, monarchial and republican, have in common the fact that the rapid pace of modernization has forced them to evolve toward more institutionalism in their various political processes. The mix of different traditional political cultures and modern Western political acculturation, however, has produced a wide variety of political evolutionary processes, as will be seen throughout this book.

BIBLIOGRAPHY

For introductory works on the history of the Middle East, see Philip K. Hitti, *History of the Arabs,* 10th ed. rev. (New York: Palgrave MacMillan, 2002); Mehran Kamrava, *The Modern Middle East: A Political History Since the First World War* (Berkeley: University of California Press, 2005); and Arthur Goldschmidt Jr. and Lawrence Davidson, *A Concise History of the Middle East*, 9th ed. (Boulder, CO: Westview Press, 2009). For general overviews of the region, see Beverly Milton-Edwards, *Contemporary Politics in the Middle East*, 2nd ed. (Malden, MA: Polity Press, 2006); Michael G. Roskin and James J. Coyle, *Politics of the Middle East: Cultures and Conflicts*, 2nd ed. (Upper Saddle River, NJ: Pearson Education, 2008); and Jillian Schwedler and Deborah J. Gerner, eds., *Understanding the Contemporary Middle East*, 3rd ed. (Boulder, CO: Lynne Rienner, 2008).

On the regional and international politics of the Middle East, see L. Carl Brown, *Diplomacy in the Middle East: The International Relations of Regional and Outside Powers* (London: I. B. Tauris, 2004); Fred Halliday, *The Middle East in International Relations: Power, Politics, and Ideology* (Cambridge: Cambridge University Press, 2005); Karl Yambert, ed., *The Contemporary Middle East* (Boulder, CO: Westview Press, 2006); and Louise Fawcett, ed., *International Relations of the Middle East*, 2nd ed. (New York: Oxford University Press, 2009). On terrorism, see Marc Sageman, *Understanding Terror Networks* (Philadelphia: University of Pennsylvania Press, 2004); Bruce Hoffman, *Inside Terrorism*, rev. enl. ed. (New York: Columbia University Press, 2006); and Bruce Riedel, *The Search for al Qaeda: Its Leadership, Ideology, and Future* (Washington, DC: Brookings Institution Press, 2008).

For introductory works on Islam and political Islam, see Ira M. Lapidus, *A History of Islamic Societies*, 2nd ed. (Cambridge: Cambridge University Press, 2002); John Esposito, *Islam: The Straight Path* (New York: Oxford University Press, 2005); and Peter Mandaville, *Global Political Islam* (New York: Routledge, 2007). On Middle Eastern culture, see Lila Abu-Lughod, *Veiled Sentiments: Honor and Poetry in a Bedouin Society* (Berkeley: University of California Press, 1986); Halim Barakat, *The Arab World: Society, Culture, and State* (Berkeley: University of California Press, 1993); and Lawrence Rosen, *The Culture of Islam: Changing Aspects of Contemporary Muslim Life* (Chicago: University of Chicago Press, 2002). See also classic works of modern Middle Eastern literature such as Abdel Rahman Munif, *Cities of Salt* (London: Cape, 1988); and Naquib Mahfouz, *The Cairo Trilogy: Palace Walk, Palace of Desire, Sugar Street* (New York: Everyman's Library, 2001).

On the geography of the Middle East, see Ewan Anderson, *The Middle East: Geography and Geopolitics*, 8th ed. (New York: Routledge, 2000); and Colbert C. Held, *Middle East Patterns: Places, Peoples, and Politics*, 4th ed. (Boulder, CO: Westview Press, 2006). For the region's economics, see Clement M. Henry and Robert Springborg, *Globalization and the Politics of Development in the Middle East* (Cambridge, MA: Harvard University Press, 2001); and Alan Richards and John Waterbury, *A Political Economy of the Middle East*, 3rd ed. (Boulder, CO: Westview Press, 2007). For an overview of social conditions, see United Nations Development Programme, *Arab Human Development Report 2009* (New York: United Nations Publications, 2009).

For useful websites on the Middle East, see www.mei.edu, http://mepc.org/resources/resources.asp, http://gulf2000.columbia.edu, http://arab.net, mideastweb.org, www.hrw.org/en/middle-east/n-africa, middle-east-pages.com, and lib.utexas.edu/maps/middle_east.html.

2

REPUBLIC OF TURKEY

Henri J. Barkey and Omer Taspinar

HISTORICAL BACKGROUND

The history of the Turkish people goes back to pre-Islamic Central Asia, where shamanism defined the religious context. Their conversion to Islam came in the ninth and tenth centuries as a result of westward territorial expansion. The new religion played a crucial role in consolidating central state power, mainly by legitimizing sultanic rule in the name of protecting and expanding the Islamic realm.

Among the new Muslim-Turkic states, the Seljuks rapidly stood out with their territorial expansion into Persia and further west. In 1071 the Seljuks defeated the Byzantine armies in the eastern Anatolian province of Manzikert. This historic victory opened the gates of Anatolia to the Turks. With their new capital in Konya, the Seljuks conquered a large swath of Anatolia, where they established a great civilization. The Ottomans emerged from the Seljuks after their demise.

The Ottomans continued the Turkish tradition of westward territorial expansion. Their spectacular rise from a small principality to a legendary empire took less than two centuries. After taking Constantinople in 1453, they conquered the Balkans and most of eastern Europe, and by the mid-sixteenth century, Ottoman armies had reached the gates of Vienna. During these centuries the image of the "terrible Turk" symbolized a sort of religious "other," consolidating Europe's own Christian identity. Yet, a long and agonizing Ottoman decline had already started by the late seventeenth century. During the empire's last century, the Ottoman ruling elite sought salvation in one of the earliest projects of Westernization. During the nineteenth century the Young Ottoman and Young Turk movements emerged in an attempt to arrest the empire's decline by introducing reforms modeled after European military, political, and legal systems.

A flair for bureaucratic organization distinguished the Ottomans from their earliest days. Initially the armed forces dominated the government apparatus, but once the era of conquest ended, the problems of administering the huge Ottoman territories demanded increased attention. In response, the civilian hierarchy expanded

Republic of Turkey

in prestige, size, and complexity. Thus, though the army always played an important role, the Ottoman Empire was far more than a praetorian state run by a dominant military caste. It was a bureaucratic empire in which the state enjoyed political legitimacy in the eyes of its subjects.

This deeply rooted state tradition also meant that reforms were state led and promulgated "from above." This tradition duly continued under the Young Turks and Mustafa Kemal Ataturk, the founder of modern Turkey, with greater secularist zeal.

At the same time, the effort to keep the Ottoman state competitive triggered severe intra-elite conflict. On the one hand, secular modernizers, who emerged in the nineteenth century, saw the adoption of European technology as the way to cope with Western intrusions. On the other hand, traditionalists advocated a return to religious purity and a rejection of Western materialism as the recipe for staving off Europe.

By the time the empire collapsed after World War I, however, the religious class was in full retreat. The need to embrace European technology was generally accepted, but dispute centered on whether wholesale cultural Westernization was essential to complement Western technology. This debate continued into the republican era.

Organization by religious community proved a cost-effective method of rule in the centuries before national consciousness was awakened among the subject peoples. But the persistence of communal identity provided fertile ground for separatist movements once nationalism's seeds had been planted. These ethnic separatists threatened to dismember the empire from within while the European powers were pressing from without.

Turkish nationalism did not emerge full-blown until the Ottoman Empire disintegrated. But as early as the Young Turk period, proponents of Turkism were in evidence. After the 1908 Young Turk revolution, forces of economic nationalism emerged, mainly in reaction to the financial controls imposed by European creditors. Yet, although Enver Pasha, one of Turkey's triumvirs in World War I, urged that the world's Turks be assembled in a single state, neither he nor his fellow Young Turks ever abandoned their hope of maintaining the empire, especially its Arab and Islamic elements.

Modern Turkey was built upon the political structures erected by the Young Turks. The Ottoman parliament that had been restored in 1908 continued on as the Grand National Assembly in Ankara, and the Committee of Union and Progress served as the model for Ataturk's own political vehicle, the Republican People's Party.

The First Republic

Ataturk is rightly credited with having established Turkey out of the ruins of the Ottoman state. Yet, he built on local "defense-of-rights" organizations in Anatolia and Thrace that the Committee of Union and Progress had set up to resist the European effort to carve up the Turkish heartland after World War I. Ataturk served as a critical rallying point against the invading Greeks, who landed in Izmir in May 1919. Under his charismatic leadership, Turkey regained its independence, expelled the Greeks, and convinced the Western powers to end their occupation.

Ataturk then began extensive modernization of Turkish society. One of his major contributions was to recognize the folly of trying to retain Arab dominions. But he insisted on keeping a Kurdish-inhabited segment of the Anatolian core area, which he considered essential for modern Turkey. To boost Turkish pride, he tried to translate religious attachment into patriotic fervor for the new state. Ataturk sought to transform Turkey quickly and radically. His reforms ran the gamut, from establishing modern dress codes to replacing the Arabic alphabet with the Latin one. Turkey, he declared, had to join "contemporary civilization."

The new Turkish state was a parliamentary republic in form, though an autocracy in practice. The basic slogan of the republic was "sovereignty belongs to the people"—a sovereignty formally exercised by a unicameral parliament. Ataturk used his Republican People's Party to dominate politics. Backed by a handpicked parliamentary majority, he shut down rival political groups, starting with supporters of the caliph in the 1923 elections, the Progressive Republican Party in 1925, and even his own tame "opposition" Free Party in 1930. Thereafter he attempted to fuse his single party with the government. This effort at a corporate state, however, led the party to atrophy and government organs to become dominant.

Following Ataturk's death in 1938, the regime became even more authoritarian, lashing out at domestic minorities. Ataturk's successor, Ismet Inonu, though a

TURKEY

Capital city	Ankara
Chief of state	President Abdallah Gul
Head of government	Prime Minister Recep Tayyip Erdogan
Major political parties (share of most recent vote)	Justice and Development Party (46.7%), Republican People's Party (20.8%), Nationalist Movement Party (14.3%), Motherland Party, Democratic Party, Democratic Left Party, Democratic Society Party, Felicity Party, Freedom and Solidarity Party, Grand Unity Party, People's Rise Party, Social Democratic People's Party, Young Party
Ethnic groups	Turkish (70%–75%), Kurdish (18%), other minorities (7%–12%)
Religious groups	Muslim, mostly Sunni (99.8%), other (0.2%)
Export partners	Germany (11.2%), United Kingdom (8.1%), Italy (7%), France (5.6%), Russia (4.4%), Spain (4.3%)
Import partners	Russia (13.8%), Germany (10.3%), China (7.8%), Italy (5.9%), United States (4.8%), France (4.6%)

respectable former comrade in arms, lacked his charisma and natural authority. In their search for legitimacy, his successors transformed Ataturk into a cultlike figure. Following the Allied victory in World War II, the Inonu regime sought to align itself with the victors and secure their support against the Soviet Union. Inonu decided to liberalize the regime to gain favor with the West.

Inonu allowed four prominent defectors from the Republican People's Party to form the Democrat Party in 1946. Although the Republicans prevented a free and fair contest in the July 1946 elections, the Democrats won handily in 1950, capitalizing on widespread discontent generated by years of Republican People's Party rule.

The Democrats had the support of rural areas as well as the private sector they had championed. By contrast, the old state elite remained ensconced in the civilian and military bureaucracy, suspicious of the Democrats' willingness to relax Ataturk's reforms, especially regarding religion. Military officers perceived themselves as losers in the new economy, and some as early as the mid-1950s began secretly to agitate for a coup. The absence of a tradition of tolerance engendered a climate of oppression. The Democrats, while winning the 1953 and 1957 elections, feared Inonu and the Republicans and sought to muzzle the opposition.

The Second Republic

Upset with the Democrats, middle-level officers executed a coup in 1960. The officers' reign was short. They banned the Democrat Party, executed three of its leaders after a sham trial, and introduced a new constitution that was surprisingly liberal and progressive. They created a new upper chamber and Constitutional Court and organized new elections. By the end of 1961, they had transferred power to a new parliament that chose Inonu as prime minister. Inonu formed a series of weak and unstable coalitions that nonetheless served to reassure the officers that there would be no retaliation for their coup.

The new rising star of Turkish politics was Suleyman Demirel and his Justice Party. Ironically, the party was nothing but an extension, or reincarnation, of the Democrat Party. It successfully challenged Inonu and the Republicans by winning an overwhelming electoral victory in 1965. Economically, it benefited from the beginning of import-substituting industrialization and workers' remittances from Europe. The Justice Party scored a second electoral victory in 1969.

Demirel was challenged, however, by growing extremism. Government indecisiveness toward mounting student and labor disorder led senior military commanders in March 1971 to issue an extraordinary public demand for more effective rule. Otherwise, they warned, the armed forces would seize power.

Demirel was forced to resign, and parliament voted into power a series of technocratic cabinets under nonpartisan prime ministers. Under the military's tutelage these governments imposed martial law, narrowed some of the more liberal facets of the 1961 constitution, banned Turkey's only legal Marxist party, and made widespread arrests to suppress terrorism. Intellectuals, journalists, and labor leaders filled the jails.

Satisfied with these changes, the military allowed new elections in 1973. These were indecisive, as the Justice Party's right-of-center constituency fragmented, and the Republicans, under a new leader, Bulent Ecevit, won a plurality of seats. Noteworthy was the emergence of Necmettin Erbakan and his National Salvation Party, which appealed to Islamic activists.

The next seven years were marked by a series of coalition governments, with Ecevit and Demirel alternating as prime minister. Each in turn relied on support from the National Salvation Party. Ecevit's first coalition sent Turkish troops into

Cyprus in July 1974, following a Greek-inspired putsch against President Makarios. But when Ecevit resigned, hoping to force early elections to cash in on the popularity of sending troops, he was outmaneuvered and blocked by Demirel.

Elections in 1977 failed to resolve the political impasse. Bitter personal rivalry between Ecevit and Demirel exacerbated political paralysis. Turkey was buffeted by one economic crisis after another, producing shortages of foreign currency that left it unable to import basic necessities. Violence among left- and right-wing student groups increased dramatically. Although a Justice Party minority government in early 1980 was able to take bold economic departures to satisfy the International Monetary Fund (IMF) and shore up Turkey's external creditworthiness, parliament remained deadlocked. It failed to elect a president. The opposition ignored repeated warnings from top generals to cooperate with the government in granting additional authority to the military to impose order. Instead, the National Salvation Party demonstrated open disrespect for the constitutional provisions against exploiting religion, Kurdish unrest began to grow in the east, and no-confidence motions against cabinet ministers challenged the government's existence.

The Third Republic

Once again the military acted to resolve the political paralysis, ousting the civilian government in September 1980, shutting down parliament, and arresting thousands of people. On the economic front the generals initially co-opted Demirel's financial team, led by Turgut Ozal, who had been the architect of a wide-ranging economic-stabilization program. Coup leader Gen. Kenan Evren and the ruling generals promised a return to civilian rule but made it clear they intended to transform Turkey's political system.

It would be three years before a new constitution, election law, and political parties' act could be put in place and elections held. During the first two years of this period, party propaganda was prohibited, the old parties were abolished, and institutions such as universities and unions were fundamentally restructured. The generals then banned all officials of the previously existing parties from political participation for ten years before permitting new parties to be established. The 1982 constitution was approved in a referendum—no one was allowed to campaign against it—that also ratified General Evren's seven-year term as president. The military also decided to create a two-party system and fashioned the new parties to serve its interests. Much to their surprise, Ozal formed his own party, the Motherland Party, and decided to challenge the generals.

In a clear rebuff to the generals, the Motherland Party won a solid majority in parliament in the November 1983 elections. Ozal used his parliamentary majority to enhance economic liberalization and continued to challenge military prerogatives. Within a few years, the two military-created parties disappeared, and the old parties reemerged under different names and guises. All the banned politicians—Ecevit, Erbakan, and Demirel—would also resurrect themselves.

One change introduced by the generals had a lasting impact: A 10 percent electoral threshold prevented smaller parties from entering parliament and strengthened larger ones. In 1987, for instance, Ozal's Motherland Party won 36 percent of the vote and commanded an absolute majority in parliament.

The late 1980s saw the emergence of Kurdish unrest in the southeast, renewed religious agitation, and difficult inflationary pressures. Ozal's reforms, while improving Turkey's economy, fed corruption and a general dissatisfaction with the new class of rich entrepreneurs who made their fortunes thanks to the liberalized foreign-exchange system.

Recognizing the downward spiral in his party's popularity, Prime Minister Ozal used his parliamentary majority to secure election as president in 1989. Although he resigned from the Motherland Party, as required under the constitution, he remained a power behind the scenes in both the party and the government. In April 1991, at Ozal's initiative, restrictions were eased on use of the Kurdish language, and prohibitions on the right to espouse class or religious ideologies were dropped from the penal code.

Ozal could not stem his party's slow decline. The Motherland Party came in second to Demirel's True Path Party in the October 1991 elections. Turkey again faced coalition politics in which personal rivalries played a major role. Not surprisingly, Demirel reached across the philosophical divide to bring the Social Democrat Populist Party into the cabinet rather than seeking Ozal's support, despite their similar views on many issues.

Demirel's coalition faced almost immediate challenges from domestic insurrection and foreign pressures. The aftermath of the 1991 Gulf War enflamed Turkey's own deepening Kurdish unrest. Forceful government retaliation, including thrusts into northern Iraq against Kurdish Workers' Party (PKK) bases, led the Kurdish wing of the Social Democrat Populist Party to split off, narrowing the coalition's parliamentary majority.

Against this background, the unexpected death of President Ozal in April 1993 brought about significant change: Demirel was elected president; he then named a newcomer, Tansu Ciller, as Turkey's first woman prime minister. Ciller would disappoint all those who had hoped she would usher in a new era in Turkish politics. Inexperienced, she alienated key constituencies and allowed rampant corruption in her immediate entourage. By the time of the December 1995 elections, Ciller had become just another Turkish politician, and her True Path Party ran slightly behind Necmettin Erbakan's Welfare Party—the successor to the National Salvation Party of the 1970s. Welfare's appeal as untainted by corruption apparently overcame voters' reluctance to support a religiously oriented party.

The Welfare Party's success created shock waves among the secular civilian and military elite. Thus, as an expedient, Motherland Party leader Mesut Yilmaz overcame his strong personal animus toward Tansu Ciller and formed a coalition government in early 1996. This artificial alliance collapsed after only a few months, and Ciller did the unthinkable: She formed a coalition government with the Welfare Party that rewarded Erbakan, the bête noire of Turkish politics, with the prime ministry. Ciller assumed the roles of foreign minister and deputy prime minister.

Tension between the government and the military quickly materialized. In February 1997 the generals issued an eighteen-point set of demands to the government to preserve secularist institutions, directly contradicting the policies espoused by the Welfare Party. So began what some Turkish political observers called Turkey's postmodern coup: The military, working in tandem with and directing civil society groups, engineered the government's downfall in June 1997. It was replaced by a Yilmaz-led left-of-center/right-of-center coalition. This led to a period in which the military appeared to play a much more active role in politics than during the Ozal years.

Under the military's influence, the Constitutional Court banned the Welfare Party and Erbakan from politics. Welfare, however, reconstituted itself as the Virtue Party, a common occurrence in Turkey where, in anticipation of party banning, shell parties are created to absorb members of parliament and activists.

The Yilmaz government did not last long and was replaced by a minority one led by Ecevit. Ecevit's fortunes received an unexpected boost in February 1999 when US officials handed Abdallah Ocalan, PKK leader and Turkey's arch nemesis, to Turkish authorities. Ocalan, who had lived in Damascus since 1980, was forced to go on the run when the Turkish military threatened the Syrian regime. He had found refuge in Kenya when the Americans located him.

Ecevit's personal probity and the capture of Ocalan catapulted Ecevit's party from fourth to first place in the 1999 elections, winning a plurality of the popular vote. Close behind was the extremist Nationalist Action Party. Its leader, Devlet Bahceli, maneuvered the party into a coalition with Yilmaz's Motherland Party. The coalition government was headed by Ecevit's Democratic Left Party. Its policies seemed largely set by Ecevit who, over the objections of the Nationalist Action Party, blocked the execution of Ocalan. This coalition also appeared more serious than its predecessors about budgetary discipline and trying to meet the criteria for inclusion in the European Union (EU).

These promising developments were set back when Ecevit and the president, Ahmet Necdet Sezer, engaged in a public and undiplomatic row over corruption. The February 2001 dispute occurred at a time when the banking sector was reeling from poor management and fictitious loans. Overnight the currency depreciated by half, inflation rose, and credit dried up. To deal with the most serious economic crisis Turkey had ever faced, Ecevit called in World Bank vice president Kemal Dervis to introduce an IMF-approved stabilization program. The Dervis reforms continue to this day; he first helped arrest the decline and then pushed for a series of rapid changes that produced economic recovery.

The Ecevit government eventually fell victim to its internal feuds; some were the result of having strange bedfellows under one roof, and others were due to the uncertainties associated with Ecevit's frail physical condition. As his party splintered, new elections were called for November 2002. For the first time since Ozal's electoral victories, one party, the Justice and Development Party (AKP), captured almost two-thirds of the seats in parliament, although it garnered only 34 percent of the vote. The AKP was an offshoot of the Islamist Virtue Party, which had been banned by constitutional authorities, initiating a major division among Erbakan's followers. Some, such as former mayor of Istanbul Recep Tayyip Erdogan and Abdallah Gul, decided to seek a more conciliatory approach to the secular state. They distanced themselves from—and even repudiated—Erbakan and his hardcore followers, who had elected to form the Felicity Party. Earlier, the authorities had banned Erdogan from politics when he had recited in public a poem by a well-known nationalist poet. Many perceived his removal from the Istanbul mayoralty following his conviction to be a miscarriage of justice, augmenting his popularity. In 2002, with the ban on Erdogan still in place, the AKP entered the elections under Gul's leadership. The party's success was electrifying. This time an Islamist party, though a much more moderate one, had come to power on its own and would not need to rely on coalition partners to form a government. Gul became prime minister, and the party worked successfully to reverse the ban on Erdogan. By March 2003 he had assumed the reins of power.

The Erdogan government's first priority was to deepen the reforms needed to advance Turkey's EU candidacy. The AKP quickly introduced a series of reforms that began to curtail some of the powerful military's constitutional prerogatives. It continued the Dervis economic reforms and introduced a series of wide-ranging political changes designed to improve political conditions, especially those of the minorities. Erdogan also engineered an about-face in Turkey's Cyprus policy. As a result, the EU in December 2004 announced that Turkey had become a candidate for membership and in October 2005 officially initiated accession negotiations. While there is still a long way to go, the Erdogan government has made far more progress in this area than its predecessors.

The 2003 Iraq War overshadowed many developments in Turkey. It has made Turks of all stripes and ideologies uncomfortable with the United States, especially because it led to an autonomous Kurdish entity in northern Iraq. The war has strained relations between the two countries, and dealings between the military and the governing party have also been tense at times. Secular elites have no confidence in the AKP government and believe it has a hidden agenda to undermine secularism and further an Islamist agenda that will enable women to cover their heads in public spaces, a practice hitherto proscribed by the courts.

The AKP in 2006 was still the dominant party. Its only opposition in parliament, the Republican People's Party, has been woefully ineffective, failing to address the shortcomings of the ruling party—corruption and cronyism—or offer a coherent alternative vision. As a result, the military once again has emerged as the sole de facto opposition to the government, although under Chief of Staff Hilmi Ozkok many crises have been averted before getting out of control. Finally, Turkey's Kurdish problem has reemerged, as Kurds have started to openly challenge the state.

POLITICAL ENVIRONMENT

Turkey is a land of pronounced physical contrasts and sharp economic disparities. Extending 780,576 square kilometers (301,380 square miles)—40 percent larger than France—it ranges from sea level to the 5,165-meter (16,945-foot) peak of Mount Ararat, which is higher than any European mountain. The western part of the country, bordering on the Aegean and Marmara seas, is a region of developed communication and easy access to the inland plateau. Well-watered farming areas produce cash crops, such as cotton, tobacco, and raisins. Eastern Turkey, abutting the Caucasian republics, Iran, and Iraq, is mountainous, cut by rivers into more or less isolated valleys. Income disparity between relatively wealthy western Anatolia and underdeveloped eastern Anatolia is highly visible.

The population of Turkey is about 70 million and increasing at a rate of somewhat under 1.5 percent a year—significantly lower than in recent decades. Demographers project that Turkey's population might stabilize at about 90 to 95 million by 2050.

Istanbul, the former Ottoman capital, remains Turkey's largest city, with a rapidly growing population of over 12 million. Ankara, the capital, is a magnet second only to Istanbul, with 5 million inhabitants. Izmir, on the Aegean coast, Adana, on the Mediterranean (some 3 million each), and newly industrializing Anatolian cities, such as Denizli, Mersin, Kayseri, and Gaziantep, complete the roster of major urban foci.

With a 99 percent Muslim population, modern Turkey is far more homogeneous than the multiethnic and multireligious Ottoman Empire. Sunni Islam predominates, while the heterodox Alevi-Shi'a interpretation of Islam amounts to a sizable minority. Although census data does not distinguish between Sunni and Alevi Islam, the Alevis are estimated to represent about 15 to 20 percent of the total population.

The Alevi-Sunni cleavage remains one of the most important divisions in Turkish society. Under the Sunni supremacy of the Ottoman Empire, Alevis were a persecuted minority. Their Shi'a proclivity and heterodox practice of Islam turned Alevis into a perennial fifth column in the eyes of imperial Istanbul. The Ottomans' historic rivalry with the Shi'a Safavid Empire further complicated the status of Alevis and put in question their loyalty to the Sunni-led Ottoman government.

It was therefore with great enthusiasm that the Alevis supported the secularist reforms of Ataturk that led to the abolition of the Sunni religious establishment in Turkey. Yet the peculiar nature of Turkish secularism, where the state recognizes, controls, and administers the Sunni branch as the only legitimate practice of Islam, is an ongoing source of disappointment for Turkey's Alevi minority. Perhaps more problematic is the anti-Alevi societal and political bias in Turkey, based mainly on the grounds that Alevis do not attend mosques and have their own community centers and religious rituals. To this day intermarriage between Alevis and Sunnis remains quite exceptional.

Kurds constitute the most significant ethnic minority in Turkey. Inspired by France, Turkey's official understanding of citizenship does not recognize ethnic minorities. This is why precise data once again is missing. Yet, it is commonly estimated that about 20 percent of Turkey's population is of Kurdish origin. Kurds represent a clear majority in Turkey's southeast provinces and speak a distinct Indo-European language with several different dialects. Due to conflict-induced migration, over half of Turkey's Kurdish population inhabits the western and southern regions of the country. Istanbul, for instance, is today home to the largest urban concentration of Kurds in the world.

Most Kurds in Turkey used to have tribal connections, but the influence of traditional leaders has been waning rapidly. These chiefs frequently also head branches of dervish orders (Nakshibandi and Kadiri) or belong to religious sects (such as the Nurcular, to which Kurds seem particularly drawn). Especially in eastern Turkey, this social organization historically both perpetuated an identity separate from that of the rest of the Turkish population and divided the various tribes and clans into rival units. This fragmentation caused the Kurdish ethnic uprisings in the 1920s and 1930s to remain limited in scope.

Without endorsing Kurdish separatism, Turkey's political parties have often tacitly exploited Kurdish ethnicity in the past to expand their bases of support in the southeast. A popular tactic has been to offer tribal leaders prominent places on the ticket to capitalize on the propensity of their followers to vote for their chiefs. Such policies are part of populist electoral politics in Turkey, where patronage networks matter greatly.

By Middle Eastern standards, Turkey is a vibrant democracy and model of capitalist economic development. The country has a complex political environment characterized by peculiar historical and socioeconomic circumstances. Perhaps the most important underpinnings of the Turkish political environment are the following:

- a deeply rooted imperial state tradition
- a politically intrusive and highly secular military
- a heartfelt personality cult built around Ataturk
- democratic elections since 1950 that confirm conservative political tendencies
- severe income and regional disparities
- an increasingly robust private sector driving economic growth
- a strong European vocation

Such complexity makes for a rapidly changing society in an increasingly urban context. By 2006 the urbanization rate of Turkey had reached 70 percent. Over the last thirty years, the rapid influx of traditionally oriented, religiously observant peasants has given urban areas a bifurcated appearance, where the modern and traditional chaotically coexist. On the gender front, the picture is also quite mixed. Turkey has brought urban women into the mainstream of political, professional, and cultural life. The educational level of women has risen steadily, and the literacy rate of school-age girls is approaching that of boys. Male literacy is around 95 percent, while female literacy is at 80 percent. Although social barriers still exist, females have not faced legal obstacles hindering employment opportunities since the 1930s. In the villages, however, the traditional male-dominated pattern of life persists, as it does to some extent in the urban ghettos, where new migrants from the countryside have settled.

Economic development has been a major engine of political transformation in Turkey. Until the early 1980s, the public sector and import-substitution industrialization dominated the Turkish economy. Market dynamics and the private sector remained secondary forces. A state-led industrialization drive characterized most of the 1960s and early 1970s. Starting in the 1950s, Turkey also witnessed significant improvements in agricultural productivity thanks to improved mechanization and large-scale irrigation. Yet, more than agricultural productivity, industrialization behind protective walls fueled Turkish economic growth, particularly throughout the 1960s. Public investment in heavy industry and the creation of state-owned enterprises created a manufacturing base targeting the local market.

Yet, there were also clear limits to economic growth during the 1960s and 1970s. Turkey, unlike Korea and other East Asian models, never managed to switch from import-substitution to export-led growth. The vagaries of electoral democracy, major labor disputes, populist economic policies, and systemic fiscal deficits negatively affected economic performance. By the late 1970s, the surge in oil prices, growing trade deficits, an overvalued currency, and high inflation paralyzed the economy. To cope with this challenge, Turkey had to adopt IMF-led liberalization packages in the early 1980s. Under Prime Minister Ozal, the Turkish economy dismantled its subsidies on energy and other basic commodities, devalued its partially privatized public enterprises, and stimulated exports.

Despite considerable structural reform between 1983 and 1987, by the end of the decade Turkey was still unable to control its fiscal deficit and public debt. In the absence of strict fiscal and monetary restraint and because of populist economic policies during electoral cycles, Turkey failed to deal efficiently with rampant inflation.

In addition to serious economic problems, by the 1990s serious "identity" issues with ethnic and religious dimensions also plagued Turkey. In fact, since the end of the Cold War, two major issues have sharply polarized Turkish politics: Kurdish dissent and political Islam. Neither Kurdish nationalism nor political Islam was totally new in Turkish politics. Both issues have their roots in the country's difficult transition from a cosmopolitan Muslim empire to a secular nation-state.

During the first two decades of the republic, nationalism and secularism emerged as the "twin principles" of Ataturk's republic. These two fundamental principles of Kemalism have rapidly generated "twin threats," namely, Kurdish rebellions and Islamic reaction during the 1920s and 1930s. It took the military suppression of a long series of Kurdish and Islamic rebellions for a sense of Kemalist stability to be established after the foundation of the republic.

Turkey's transition to multiparty democracy during the Cold War significantly altered its identity problems and political environment. As the nation was a NATO member with Soviet borders, left-right political divisions came to characterize Turkish politics. Yet, under the new ideological divide, the Kurdish question and political Islam never totally disappeared from Turkey's agenda. Political Islam was part of the anti-Communist Right, while Kurdish dissent was part of the socialist Left. Kurdish dissent was therefore expressed in terms of "class conflict" rather than ethnic grievances. Such dynamics enabled Kurdish political assimilation within Turkey's leftist movements.

Ideological polarization and the democratic process were punctured by short-term military interventions in 1960, 1971 and 1980. Each intervention had different causes: The 1960 coup was instigated by young officers unhappy with their economic lot and diminished importance in society. They, in the process, opened the door for future interventions as groups in society often turned to the military to resolve difficult and stalemated situations. It also gave the military an expectation that, as the self-declared guardian of the republic, it would have undue influence on the management of the Turkish polity. In fact, in 1971 a group of senior generals decided to overthrow the government for failing to deal with growing political violence and immobility. Unwilling to see a repeat of the 1960 coup, when the military hierarchy was ignored, the service chiefs and chief of staff outmaneuvered the generals. The 1980 coup was triggered by political paralysis stemming from the left-right divide, increasing unrest in Kurdish provinces, and Islamist flouting of Kemalist principles.

However, the real threat of Kurdish nationalism or Islamic activism would not materialize fully until after the end of the Cold War and the reemergence of identity problems. Ironically, many of the Kurds who escaped the post-1980 military dragnet found an opening in the repressive years of military rule to launch an insurgency in the southeast. The PKK-led insurgency, which had gained considerable regional support by the end of the 1980s, proved a substantial challenge to the Turkish military. Between 1984 and 1999, the Kurdish conflict caused some 35,000 deaths among insurgents, the local population, and security forces, costing the Turkish economy an estimated $120 billion. Perhaps more importantly, the Kurdish conflict completely derailed Turkey's European agenda. To the dismay of Ankara, the EU—to which Turkey had officially applied for membership in 1987—saw in the Kurdish conflict the rebellion of an ethnic group whose cultural and political rights were denied by an authoritarian regime.

By the mid-1990s, things went from bad to worse. In addition to the Kurdish conflict, political Islam came to haunt the Kemalist republic as well. The Islamist Welfare Party triumphed in local elections (1994), controlled important municipalities such as Istanbul and Ankara, and won a plurality in national elections (1995). By 1996 the secular republic had its first Islamic coalition government. With Kurdish separatism and political Islam on the rise, the political environment was ripe for a military backlash. The counteroffensive by the secular establishment came first with the ousting of the Welfare Party coalition government in June 1997. In February 1999 Kurdish separatism received a more severe blow with the incarceration of PKK leader Abdallah Ocalan.

With political Islam subdued and Kurdish nationalism defeated, the sense of siege that characterized the 1990s slowly came to an end. Interestingly, this costly restoration of Kemalist stability facilitated democratization from a position of strength rather than weakness. Democratization, one could now argue, was intentional rather than imposed. In the meantime, Turkey's improved relations with the EU after the 1999 Helsinki Summit provided much-needed external incentives for difficult reforms.

The EU's impact became particularly clear in the November 2002 elections when a moderate Islamist political party, the newly established AKP, won in a landslide, largely thanks to its pro-EU campaign platform. The fact that a major financial crisis in 2001 had completely discredited Turkey's corrupt and bankrupt political establishment greatly contributed to the AKP victory. In short, the political environment of Turkey in 2003 was radically different than in the 1990s.

So was the global environment. In the wake of the September 11 terrorist attacks, the "clash-of-civilizations" scenario turned into a self-fulfilling prophecy. In such a polarized global context, the symbolism of a Muslim country seeking membership in an exclusive European club gained unprecedented civilizational relevance. The fact that Turkey was pursuing its European vocation under an Islamically oriented government was even more significant.

The AKP's European vocation also helped domestically. The party gained much-needed legitimacy in the eyes of the Kemalist establishment. The military was much more willing to give the benefit of the doubt to a political party with a European vocation rather than to one with anti-Western proclivities, like the banned Welfare Party. The Kemalist backlash against the Welfare Party in 1997 created a genuine sense of appreciation among moderately Islamic politicians for the benefits of liberal democracy. This, in itself, explains why the leadership of the AKP supports pro-EU democratization. Thanks to its pro-EU stance, the AKP also became much more appealing to the business community, the middle class, and liberal intellectuals.

In power, the AKP remained strongly committed to its reformist agenda. It undertook radical reforms in the judicial system, civil-military relations, and human rights practices. The party also attacked corruption and continued to implement an IMF-led structural-reform package. By 2005 the Turkish economy had stabilized, and inflation fell to levels that allowed lopping six zeros off the currency. Such political and economic reforms, combined with the AKP's constructive approach in Cyprus, convinced the EU that Turkey had fulfilled the criteria necessary to begin accession talks. Despite considerable enlargement fatigue in the EU and reform fatigue in Turkey, Ankara's European journey still seems to be on track.

The AKP, however, also lost steam after the EU's decision to start accession negotiations, becoming distracted by other issues discussed below. Commensurate with the AKP's ascent, one particular moderate Islamist movement, that of Fethullah Gulen, though unaffiliated with the AKP, began to gather momentum. An offshoot of the Nurcu movement, it was created by a charismatic preacher who, fearing prosecution, sought asylum in the United States. Gulenists made great efforts to build up their support base by primarily guiding their followers to engage and invest in civil causes, such as building schools in Turkey and elsewhere. They also created a formidable media operation designed as much to expand their influence as to protect themselves from the secular establishment that came to loathe them and fear them as a mortal threat, despite Gulen's moderate message.

POLITICAL STRUCTURE

Turkey is a unitary republic and a parliamentary democracy. Cabinet ministers are "jointly responsible" for the execution of the government's general policy and personally liable for their ministries' acts. The prime minister, as the top executive, heads the Council of Ministers and can dismiss ministers at will.

The 1982 constitution, as amended, centers on a 550-seat unicameral legislature. The senate of the Second Republic was abolished in an effort to strengthen and improve the efficiency of the executive at the expense of the legislative branch. The president of the republic is elected by the Grand National Assembly for a seven-year term. As a result of constitutional amendments, the people will elect future presidents for five-year terms, and assembly members will serve for four years instead of five. Elections, however, can be held earlier by consent of parliament.

One of the most important objectives of the 1982 constitution was to strongly reassert the authority of the state, partly as a reaction to the 1961 constitution, which was perceived as too liberal. Drafted after the 1980 military intervention, the 1982 constitution prioritized law and order and set up state security courts, where military judges served with civilian judges. These courts were abolished in 2004 under the AKP's pro-EU democratization program.

Although superior administrative and military courts have final jurisdiction over cases within their competencies, the Turkish judicial system provides for the Constitutional Court to rule on the constitutionality of laws and decrees. The Constitutional Court functions as the Supreme Court and therefore decides all cases relating to political parties.

Understanding Turkey's political structure requires a basic grasp of the republic's foundational principle. Unlike most other Western democracies, Turkey has an official state ideology. This ideology, Kemalism, is named after Mustafa Kemal Ataturk, the founding father of modern Turkey. In the context of the 1930s, Kemalism represented a secularist, nationalist, and progressive political agenda based on establishing a Turkish nation-state. Modernization and Westernization thus became the main traits of Kemalism.

More problematic, however, is what Kemalism exactly represents as a contemporary political project. There is, in fact, no consensus among Kemalists themselves on what Kemalism stands for in the twenty-first century. This difficulty is understandable because Kemalism is in many ways already a success story. Modern Turkey is a secular nation-state and a democratic republic. There is certainly room for improvement in terms of establishing a truly "liberal" democracy in Turkey; however, as liberalism was never on the Kemalist political agenda, it would be unfair to blame Kemalism for this. After all, liberalism was not on the global agenda of the 1930s. It is therefore possible to argue that Kemalism, as a secularist-nationalist political project aimed at nation building, modernization, and Westernization, achieved its monumental mission.

Today, in modern Turkey, it is this success that transforms Kemalism into a conservative ideology. Turkey's official state ideology, in other words, displays an understandable urge to conserve and protect the republic's historic achievements. Especially for Turkey's politically powerful military, Kemalism represents a defensive political reaction against the "enemies" of the secular republic. In that sense, more than a coherent ideology, Kemalism has become a secularist and nationalist reflex against Kurdish nationalism and political Islam.

The military is the main institution serving as the ultimate guardian of the republic's Kemalist legacy. In that sense, unlike in other Western democracies, the armed forces have a special position in Turkey. Their political weight enters into a broad range of government calculations. This influence comes partly from the centrality of the military in the nineteenth-century Ottoman reform movement. At the end of the Ottoman Empire, the armed forces, with their secular schools, were the main window on the West. As a result, officers were the reformists par excellence. Ataturk himself and his chief lieutenants were career officers who represented the Young Turk tradition of positivism, nationalism, and secularism with great reformist zeal.

After the foundation of the republic, Ataturk wanted to separate military and political tracks, mainly to protect the military's professionalism and keep the armed forces out of day-to-day politics. Abiding by this civilian-military divide, he and his loyal associates gave up their own active-duty status. Yet, Ataturk and Inonu maintained close ties with the armed forces, and Ataturk continually cited the army as the ultimate guardian of the republic, making clear that its role was to defend the cultural and political revolution in addition to protecting the country against foreign foes.

In that sense the Turkish military effectively functions as the guardian of the Kemalist system. No matter what happens in the "realm of politics," the "realm of the Kemalist state" is always defended by the armed forces. This is why the Turkish military is associated with the state rather than with "politics" in the eyes of the Turkish public. The Turkish army, in that sense, serves as a sort of deus ex machina. Whenever it intervenes in the realm of politics, it does so on behalf of the republic. Unlike Latin American militaries, the Turkish army does not stay in power for long. To preserve its professionalism and clean image, it restores the realm of the state and goes back to the barracks. This is why none of the three major military interventions in Turkish politics (1960, 1971, and 1980) lasted more than three years. In the post–Cold War era, the pattern of military interventions changed. Instead of directly overthrowing governments, the military used a variety of means to dislodge or pressure elected governments, sometimes through pronouncements, as in February 1997 and April 2007.

While the 1960 military coup had strong Kemalist undertones, it is important to note that the second and third interventions had unmistakable anti-Left tendencies. In a country bordering the Soviet Union, it was not particularly surprising that the military had serious concerns about the appeal of socialism. In the early twenty-first century, however, the real threat to the Kemalist republic is no longer communism but Kurdish nationalism and political Islam.

As far as these threats are concerned, there is no room for ambiguity in the Kemalist position of the military. The Kurdish problem, whether in the form of political violence or political activity calling for minority rights, is viewed as an existential threat. Hence any assertion of Kurdish ethnic identity, no matter how minor, is perceived as a major security problem endangering Turkey's territorial and national integrity. A similarly alarmist attitude characterizes the military's approach to Islam. Islamic sociopolitical and cultural symbols in the public sphere— such as head scarves in public schools—are seen as harbingers of a fundamentalist revolution.

Especially for the military, Kemalism amounts to "protecting" the republic from its "perceived enemies": Kurdish nationalism and political Islam. Therefore, any deviation from the Turkish character of the nation-state and the secular framework of the republic presents a daunting challenge to Kemalist identity.

Finally, it is also important to note that the French model deeply influenced the Turkish republic's political structure and especially Kemalism's understanding of "secularism" and "nationalism." Turkish secularism was modeled after anticlerical French *laïcité* rather than the less confrontational Anglo-Saxon secularism. According to Kemalist secularism, Islam had to become part of private life. As in France after the 1789 revolution, the state came to control and administer the religious establishment in order to prevent political threats of a conservative and religious nature. The Kemalist state banned religious sects and brotherhoods. Religious activities not controlled by the state had to operate underground.

France proved to be the model for nationalism as well. The Turkish republic refused to recognize ethnic minorities and multiculturalism. All citizens were to be assimilated into Turkish citizenship. The only officially recognized minorities were non-Muslims. In short, all Muslims were to become Turks. With the benefit of hindsight, one can argue that behind the facade of a successful nationalist-secularist revolution, the repression of Kurdish and Islamic identities remained the Achilles' heel of the Kemalist project.

POLITICAL DYNAMICS

Political patterns in Turkey show remarkable continuity, despite frequent military interventions. On the one hand, that continuity reflects the longevity of political figures in Turkey, where tenures of thirty or even forty years for major political leaders are not uncommon. On the other hand, voting blocs themselves have changed little in proportion over the years, which would give the right-of-center a marked edge were it not torn by such intense personal rivalries. Another major aspect of continuity has been the tenacious commitment to elective parliamentary rule, which all political elements, including the military, see as the principal legitimizing process. Turkey's political parties operate with relative efficiency in mobilizing voters. Participation in elections has generally been high, involving between 64 and 94 percent of eligible voters.

The predominance of right-of-center votes in the Third Republic convincingly shows that Turks do not cast ballots on a class basis. Rather, the ups and downs in party performance appear to confirm that Turkish voters seek successful leaders who keep their promises and avoid the appearance of corruption—an image that has proven difficult to maintain. This pattern was visible in the multiparty era of the First Republic; it continued in the Second Republic and has repeated itself in the Third.

The AKP government, which won elections in 2002 and 2007, appears to challenge these dynamics. The AKP has proven exceptionally successful so far in maintaining its grasp on power. The origins of political Islam in Turkey date back to the 1970s, when an anti-Western, antisecular, antiliberal political movement first emerged. Despite their orientation, Turkish Islamist parties have always played by the electoral rules. Thus, compared to its Middle Eastern counterparts, Turkish political Islam was much more moderate and inclined toward gaining electoral legitimacy. Yet, the political ambitions of Turkish Islamists clearly surpassed their competence. In 1996, when political Islam came to power under its third incarnation as the Welfare Party, it failed to rise to the challenge of running a complex and diversified country. The military's forcing the resignation of the Welfare Party–led coalition government in 1997 created a generational and ideological rift in the ranks of the movement. As the patrimonial structure of the old guard broke up, Turkish Islamists split into two parties, the AKP and the Felicity Party, with the latter representing the small, traditional, hard-line wing of the movement.

The AKP first came to power in November 2002. It won an unprecedented victory in 2007, increasing its share of the vote from 34 to 47 percent—the first time an incumbent government had increased its vote share since 1954. Both victories amounted to political earthquakes in Turkish politics, with the party winning comfortable majorities in parliament and thus, for the first time, enabling a moderate Islamist government to come to rule alone.

From very early on, the AKP pursued with growing zeal and determination a pro-EU reform process initiated in the summer of 2002 by the previous government. While more progress still must be made, the reforms passed by parliament have achieved significant progress toward securing human rights and democracy, paving the way for accession negotiations with the EU. Key areas of reform included the following:

Civil-Military Relations. New laws have substantially reduced the military's role in politics. As of August 2004, the National Security Council (NSC)—a platform through which the military traditionally has exerted influence over the government—is no longer headed by a general. NSC meetings are not as frequent and are more transparent. The removal of military representatives from the boards that oversee broadcasting and higher education also has enhanced civilian control. New limits on the jurisdiction of military courts over civilians have been enacted. Nevertheless, the military continues to exert a great deal of influence. Typically, military pronouncements are given extensive coverage by all media outlets. Both the public and the political class continue to view the military as the ultimate source of authority on issues relating to secularism, ethnicity, and foreign security policy. However, starting with an April 2007 military pronouncement aimed at preventing the AKP's choice for president from assuming power, the Erdogan government has made a concerted effort to narrow the military's influence in politics. In 2008, the military's reputation was further tarnished by a criminal investigation of the Ergenekon organization that revealed coup plots among high-ranking retired officers.

Human Rights. Provisions on the rights of detainees and prisoners have been improved. Pretrial detention periods have been shortened and detainees are guaranteed immediate access to an attorney. Legislation also has broadened freedom of expression, the press, association, assembly, and demonstration. The repeal of Article 8 of the Anti-Terror Law, which prohibited the dissemination of separatist propaganda, has led to a significant reduction in the number of political prisoners. However, there remain important shortcomings in the Turkish penal code, such as Article 301, which punishes free thought. The AKP has been reluctant to repeal this provision; as a result, many authors, journalists, and others, including Nobel laureate Orhan Pamuk, have been prosecuted for "denigrating Turkishness."

Cultural Rights. Under the leadership of AKP, the Turkish republic reluctantly has acknowledged the existence of minorities based on "racial, religious, sectarian, cultural, or linguistic differences" and repealed laws curtailing their rights. Recent reforms introduced the right to broadcast, publish, and receive instruction in languages other than Turkish, in effect officially allowing the use of the Kurdish language. In practice, however, the use of Kurdish in the broadcast media remains strictly controlled. In fact, the only nationwide Kurdish TV station is run by the state.

Judicial Reform. The Turkish judicial system has been significantly reformed, and criminal and antiterrorism laws have been amended, in line with EU requirements. The death penalty was abolished in August 2002. Reforms also allow for the retrial of legal cases invalidated by the European Court of Human Rights, although this policy has been implemented sporadically.

Cyprus Policy. Turkish efforts to find a solution to the division of Cyprus were never explicitly made a precondition for EU accession, but the political reality has always been that Turkey's opposition to a Cyprus settlement would undermine its chances of joining the EU. Reversing the course of the hard-line Ecevit government, the Erdogan government made a Cyprus settlement a high priority, largely in the name of removing the issue as an obstacle to EU accession. Erdogan invested significant political capital and defied Turkish nationalists in urging Turkish Cypriots to approve a UN plan for political settlement. In the April 2004 referendum on the plan, 65 percent of Turkish Cypriots supported it, whereas 75 percent of Greek Cypriots rejected it. The Turkish government's strong support for the plan (in contrast to the Greek Cypriot leadership's opposition) earned it much political credit with the EU and has helped Turkey's case for membership. However, Greek Cypriot opposition to the plan did not prevent the Greek part of Cyprus from becoming an EU member in 2005. As a result, a solution to the Cyprus problem remains elusive, and Turkey's own prospects for EU accession have been negatively affected.

Economic Reform. Turkey experienced its most severe economic crisis since World War II in 2001, forcing it to adopt painful, wide-ranging structural reforms. The most important of these reforms included a restructuring of the banking sector. These reforms paid off and helped the Turkish economy post significant growth rates throughout 2002 to 2008. Thanks to its fiscal discipline, mostly dictated by the IMF, Turkey has succeeded in containing its high inflation rate and attracting significant foreign investment. When the 2008 global financial crisis came about, Turkey's economy was not immune, although its banking sector weathered the crisis better than most. The sharp fall in Turkey's exports following the global crisis has endangered macroeconomic stability and employment prospects for Turkish youth.

FOREIGN POLICY

Ataturk was determined to transform and modernize Turkey and make it an integral member of what he termed "contemporary civilization." His most famous adage about foreign relations, "peace at home, peace abroad," also implied a degree of introversion and autarky. To the Kemalists, Ataturk's legacy would be a mixture of Westernization with isolation. Effectively, this would mean that Ataturk and his followers would turn their backs on the Middle East and the emerging Arab world.

World War II was a particularly trying time for the new republic; bereft of its strong leader, who had passed away in 1938, Ankara was caught between the entreaties of the Allied and Axis powers. Its military weakness prevented it from entering the conflict, save for during the last months of the war. With the Allied victory in 1945, Turkey hitched its future to an alliance with the United States and

Europe. It joined NATO and later applied for membership in the EU. Even after the demise of the Soviet Union, Turkey's Western alliance has a solid foundation in the modern Turkish state. Ankara had little choice after the war but to align itself with the West. The Soviet Union was decidedly interested in enlarging its zone of influence, as Stalin tried to make the most of Turkey's wartime neutrality to extract concessions ranging from territory in Turkey's east to privileged access to the Turkish straits. In some respects this was a continuation of nineteenth-century Russo-Ottoman rivalry and therefore conjured up unpleasant memories in Turkey. The Truman Doctrine—enunciated on March 12, 1947, to support Turkey and Greece in the face of continuing Soviet pressure—heralded the beginning of both countries' active participation in the Cold War.

The Truman Doctrine notwithstanding, Washington had reservations about the utility of Turkey and Greece as alliance members and therefore initially resisted their inclusion in NATO. By contrast, Ankara did its utmost to convince the United States to accept it as a member, since it viewed NATO as the ultimate shield against an aggressive Soviet Union. The ruling Democrat Party even sent a contingent of troops to fight in Korea as a means of proving its bona fides. Finally, in 1952, three years after the inception of NATO, Turkey and Greece joined the alliance. Turkey under the Democrat Party became a close US ally; it helped set up the Baghdad Pact, a defense alliance among Great Britain, Iraq, Iran, Pakistan, and Turkey. Military cooperation between the United States and Turkey enabled Ankara to revamp its creaky armed forces. Turkey, as the sole NATO member bordering the Soviet Union, became an important asset in the US policy of containment.

The military leaders who overthrew the Democrat Party in 1960 were too preoccupied with domestic problems to devise major foreign initiatives. In any case, because they came out of Turkey's military tradition, they were for the most part satisfied with US-Turkish relations. Yet, the broader political debate permitted in the Second Republic, especially with the rise of the socialist movement in the early 1960s, set the stage for problems in Turkey's Western orientation. Like Europe, Turkey experienced an upsurge in student activism that contributed to increased pressure on the US-Turkish relationship.

Turks were astounded to learn at the conclusion of the 1962 Cuban Missile Crisis that the Kennedy administration had decided to remove nuclear-tipped Jupiter missiles from Turkey in exchange for the removal of Soviet missiles from Cuba. Although the Jupiters had been scheduled for removal, the lack of consultation upset Turkish authorities. From Ankara's perspective it would be the first important instance of discord between the two countries.

Cyprus was the main foreign policy issue to confront Turkey in the mid-1960s. In December 1963, violence between the small Turkish and much larger Greek Cypriot communities led Ankara to send planes over the island to demonstrate its commitment to the Turkish minority. Continuing communal troubles caused

Turkish Cypriots to group themselves in enclaves and the Turkish government to consider landing troops to protect Turkish Cypriots' rights, a remedy provided in the Treaty of Guarantee that had established the Cypriot state in 1960. In June 1964 Turkey threatened to dispatch forces to the island. This elicited a harsh warning from US President Lyndon Johnson. The Johnson letter, as it came to be known, warned Prime Minister Inonu that NATO might not protect Turkey from Soviet intervention if it took military action on Cyprus, and it categorically forbade the use of American-made weapons in Cyprus. Ironically, it is unclear whether Turkey could have followed up on its threat in view of the fact that it lacked the wherewithal to mount an invasion, not having even a single landing craft. Yet, the appearance of Turkish capitulation in the face of US pressure provoked intense public resentment toward the United States. The Johnson letter henceforth would come to represent an act of perfidy in the annals of US-Turkish relations and mark the beginning of an era of unquestioning Turkish cooperation with Washington.

The 1974 Cyprus crisis was a real turning point in US-Turkish relations. Turkey felt obliged to respond to a coup against the legitimate government of Archbishop Makarios in Cyprus by Greek Cypriot nationalist elements supported by the military junta in Athens. Although the coup was not directed against the Turkish community per se, the man who seized power, Nicos Sampson, was known as a longtime advocate of unification with Greece and a dedicated foe of Turkish Cypriots. On July 20 Turkey landed troops on Cyprus, claiming that it was exercising its treaty rights to repair a clear violation of the Cypriot constitution. Under strong international pressure, however, the Turks halted their military action after two days, having secured merely a foothold in the Kyrenia region, north of Nicosia. During the ensuing peace talks, when the Turks thought the new regime in Athens was stalling, Turkey resumed military operations and speedily secured control over slightly more than the northern one-third of the island.

Despite its insistence that these actions were sanctioned by the Treaty of Guarantee, Turkey found itself largely isolated in the international community. The US Congress in February 1975 imposed a complete embargo on all arms deliveries to Turkey, which lasted until September 1978. In retaliation, Turkey closed all US installations (leaving the NATO air base in Incirlik open, however) and abrogated the 1969 Defense Cooperation Agreement. The embargo, whose origins had more to do with infighting between the executive and legislative branches of government in the United States, nonetheless left a deep imprint on the Turkish psyche regarding the reliability of the United States.

In this context, Turkey's relations with Greece took a decided turn for the worse. Tensions generated by Cyprus were further enflamed by an emerging dispute over the continental shelf and air rights in the Aegean Sea. The geography of the Aegean, with numerous Greek islands hugging the Turkish coast, presented complex problems in apportioning the seabed. Behind its difficulties in dealing with Greece and Cyprus in the 1970s lay a new and painful fact for Turkey: The US Congress, not the executive branch, had become the articulator of Turkish-US problems. Whereas American presidents understood the compulsions that led Turkey to act in Cyprus, Congress was far less willing to credit Turkish arguments. This contest of wills in Washington slowed renegotiation of defense cooperation arrangements. But after the Carter administration finally convinced Congress to lift the arms embargo in September 1978, US facilities were reopened, and a new Cooperation on Defense and Economy Agreement was signed in March 1980.

This was followed by a new challenge: the 1980 military coup. Most Europeans, who were critical of military rule as well as of the treatment of former Turkish politicians, received the advent of the generals in Turkey badly. By contrast, the United States was alarmed by the increasing domestic violence and instability in Turkey just after the shah of Iran lost his throne to anti-American clerics and the Soviets invaded Afghanistan. Turkey's strategic importance once again became crystal clear to Washington, which decided to support the regime.

Economically Turkey was on the mend. Ozal's reforms had made the economy more competitive, especially in the Middle East. In fact, the Iran-Iraq War turned out to be a boon for Turkey, the only country to border both belligerents. Short on foreign exchange and in need of various finished goods, Iran and Iraq became large consumers of Turkish exports, facilitating Turkey's economic transformation in the early 1980s. To cement these favorable trends, Turkey deepened its involvement in the politics of the Islamic world and for a while reduced its diplomatic ties with Israel.

In the 1980s, Cyprus once again became a problem in Ankara's relations with its allies. Turkey's encouragement of Turkish Cypriot independence dismayed the United States and Europe. Faced with concerted European and American pressure, no one, save for Turkey, would recognize the Turkish Cypriot Republic of Northern Cyprus. In the United States, congressional critics of Turkey, especially those with close ties to diaspora Greek and Armenian communities, were able to propose or push through punitive resolutions, including one commemorating the 1915 Armenian genocide.

Steady moves toward democracy improved Turkey's image in both the United States and Europe, and the country was allowed to resume its seat on the Council of Europe. Under Ozal's premiership, Ankara renewed its demand for EU membership. This proved to be the beginning of a long and difficult struggle, marred in part by accusations of human rights violations. Coupled with intransigent Greek opposition, human rights problems doomed Ozal's EU bid.

By 1991, Turkey's strategic environment had been radically transformed by the Soviet Union's disintegration. Unlike that of its long-term rival Greece, Turkey's strategic importance to the West did not decline, despite the vanished Soviet border. Turkey assumed a new, and quite different, role in the post–Cold War era. For Washington, whose relations with Tehran were highly acrimonious, Ankara represented a perfect foil for Iran's ambitions in Central Asia—an area freed from direct Soviet control. Turkey's linguistic and cultural affinity toward Azerbaijan, Turkmenistan, Kazakhstan, and Uzbekistan, several of which had extensive energy reserves, was an asset. US Secretary of State James Baker publicly supported Ankara's fledgling ambitions to become an agent of Western and secular influence and a conduit for hydrocarbon riches, which otherwise would be transported through either Russian or Iranian pipelines. Russia wanted these pipelines to pass through its territory to ensure its sustained financial and diplomatic importance in this region. Turkey equally wanted these routes to pass through its territory and adamantly opposed increasing Bosporus traffic, especially by oil tankers whose passage through the straits posed a safety threat to Istanbul. Such Turkish concerns and US support for non-Russian transportation routes led to construction of the Baku-Tbilisi-Ceyhan pipeline, which has been transporting Caspian Sea oil to Turkey's Mediterranean coast since 2006.

Ataturk wanted to distance Turkey from the Middle East; in fact in 1926, after defeating a Kurdish insurrection, he agreed to cede the mostly Kurdish-inhabited region of Mosul to Iraq, which was under a British mandate. Some sixty years later, Turkey found itself again mired in the affairs of its southern neighbors. The Kurdish insurrection in Turkey meant that Ankara could no longer be immune to developments in neighboring countries with Kurdish populations. This was especially true of Iraq, where Iraqi Kurdish groups, long active in a struggle to free themselves from Baghdad's rule, took advantage of every opportunity to rebel against the central government. The 1980–1988 Iran-Iraq War was no exception. During this war the PKK benefited from the absence of Iraqi government authority in the north to establish bases there. In response, Turkey conducted hot-pursuit operations with the Baghdad government's consent. At the end of that war, when Saddam Husayn took revenge on his rebellious Kurdish population by massacring tens of thousands, many Iraqi Kurds fled to Turkey.

Iraq's 1990 invasion of Kuwait and the resulting war further complicated Turkey's relations both with its neighbors and with its main ally, the United States. Initially President Ozal backed the UN sanctions against Iraq and closed the oil pipeline running from northern Iraq to the Mediterranean. Although Ozal wanted to support, and perhaps even participate in, the war against Iraq, he found that not only the public but also his military chiefs opposed this. For the first time in Turkish history, the armed forces chief of staff resigned rather than execute his orders. More than half a million Kurdish refugees streamed toward the Turkish border during the turmoil following Iraq's 1991 expulsion from Kuwait.

Faced with a humanitarian crisis and a world riveted by the plight of these refugees (1 million others fled to the Iranian border), Turkey, the United States, and Britain helped establish a no-fly zone over northern Iraq and pushed Iraqi troops back from the Kurdish regions. This enabled the refugees to return home and restart their lives. However, Iraqi Kurds, protected by a US-UK air umbrella and no longer under the tutelage of Saddam Husayn, began to manage their own affairs. Because the air assets enforcing the no-fly zone were based at Incirlik airbase, Turkey unwillingly became the midwife to an autonomous Kurdish entity in northern Iraq. Especially at a time when Turkey was facing a severe Kurdish insurrection, it feared that an autonomous Kurdish entity in Iraq would have spillover effects among its own Kurdish population. Operation Provide Comfort (OPC), as this endeavor was called, caused tensions between Turkey and the United States because of the uncertainty that surrounded its periodic renewal by the Turkish parliament. The conundrum for Ankara was that Iraqi Kurds—divided among themselves—were incapable of exercising complete authority over their territory and controlling PKK activities. Ankara, sometimes with the cooperation of the two Kurdish groups and sometimes on its own, conducted cross-border operations against PKK camps near the border in its efforts to end the Kurdish insurgency at home. Ankara made no secret of its preference for a return of Saddam Husayn's regime to the north and an end to the sanctions regime, putting it at odds with Washington's containment of Baghdad. Thanks to OPC, Turkey became an indispensable element of US policy toward Iraq, enabling Washington both to protect the Kurds and to ensure that Husayn's regime was kept on a tight leash. OPC was a double-edged sword, binding the United States to Turkey, heightening the latter's importance, and enabling Ankara to extract concessions from Washington. Washington rewarded Ankara by unconditionally supporting its bid for EU membership, providing help against the PKK (including the delivery of PKK leader Ocalan to Turkish authorities), and assisting it economically whenever necessary. On the other hand, Ankara, despite its misgivings, felt compelled to maintain OPC for fear of a backlash in Washington.

Perhaps the greatest success for US diplomacy came after the EU's 1999 decision to reverse its earlier rejection of Turkey's candidacy for EU membership. The United States, despite its own criticism of Turkey's human rights shortcomings, aggressively lobbied the Europeans to give Turkey a chance at membership. Ironically, it was a change of heart by Greece that helped pave the way for EU consideration. The Greeks, while continuing to disagree with Ankara on a number of fronts, made a strategic calculation that Turkey would constitute less of a threat as an EU candidate or member than if it were kept outside.

Iraq once again would come back to haunt US-Turkish relations. In the run-up to the 2003 war against Iraq, the United States wooed the new AKP-led Turkish government and secured its agreement for the United States to open up a second front against Iraq from Turkish territory. Turkish troops were supposed to follow the Americans and establish a cordon sanitaire, ostensibly to prevent a repeat of the

1988 and 1991 refugee outflows. Washington also promised to put together an economic aid package to protect Turkey from the turbulence the war was expected to cause. The AKP government, then led by Gul with the support of Erdogan as party leader, decided to endorse the second front. With almost 90 percent of the Turkish public adamantly opposed to this venture, the AKP sought to share the political burden with the military. But the Turkish general staff, which had reluctantly concluded to allow the operation in the face of American pressure, was unwilling to offer the AKP political cover. As a result, the army's apparently noncommittal approach confused both the public and politicians. Still, on the morning of March 1, 2003, with the Turkish parliament set to debate and vote on the matter, the AKP estimated it commanded a comfortable margin to pass it. To everyone's surprise, however, the proposal to approve the deployment of US troops failed narrowly.

The invasion of Iraq went ahead without the northern front. Ankara did allow US Special Forces and agents to infiltrate Iraq from its territory. The March 1 vote was hailed as an example of democracy in action, but it had long-term repercussions for US-Turkish relations. The next crisis was not long in coming. On July 4, 2003, US troops raided the offices of the Turkish-affiliated Iraq Turkmen Front (ITC), where they arrested a number of party officials and Turkish Special Forces personnel on suspicion of plotting the assassination of the governor of Kirkuk. The Turkish personnel, who were in northern Iraq with US permission, were handcuffed and hooded and sent to Baghdad for interrogation. The Turkish press, public, and political class erupted with indignation. This was seen as the worst kind of insult by a trusted ally. No one paid much attention to the underlying reason; within a year, and very quietly, the Turkish military high command sidelined three generals who were in charge of the Special Forces personnel, signaling that this was probably a rogue operation.

The reaction to this incident had much to do with the unease Turks felt with US intentions in Iraq. Having dealt themselves out of the Iraq War, they watched the rapprochement between Iraqi Kurds and Americans with increasing anxiety. The Kurdish north turned out to be immune from the Iraqi insurrection and the slow descent into chaos. This enabled the Kurds to consolidate their power and enhance their role in Iraq as Jalal Talabani, the leader of the Patriotic Union of Kurdistan, was elected president of Iraq, and his longtime rival, Massoud Barzani of the Kurdish Democratic Party, became the president of the federal autonomous region of Iraqi Kurdistan. Turks feared that an Iraqi civil war might lead to the division of the country and an independent Kurdish state. Making matters worse was the US reluctance to fight some 3,500 PKK fighters in northern Iraq as many Turks expected them to do. The US unwillingness reflected the refusal of CENTCOM, the military command in charge of Iraq, to divert the already insufficient US forces away from battling the insurgency in the Sunni areas to fight an organization that had hitherto kept its head down.

Turkey also found out that its ability to influence events in Iraq was limited: Initially it opposed an Iraqi federal state, preferring a unitary one. When Turkey agreed to a US request to deploy peacekeeping forces in central Iraq, Iraqi Kurds and Shi'a vetoed their deployment. Similarly, the Turks' main client in Iraq, the ITC, which they hoped would represent the 900,000 Iraqi Turkmen, did poorly in Iraqi elections. Turkey's desire to keep the oil-rich city of Kirkuk out of Kurdish hands also is proving difficult. Ankara has stated on many occasions that Kurdish control of Kirkuk is unacceptable. However, many displaced Kurds have managed to return to the city with the help of Kurdish political parties, as Turkey has watched helplessly.

All these developments have strained US-Turkish relations. Anti-Americanism in Turkey has increased considerably, and in response Turkey has lost much support in Washington. Following a number of spectacular PKK raids on Turkish military outposts, the Bush administration, under pressure from Ankara and facing the prospect of Turkish military intervention into northern Iraq, decided to increase US military and intelligence cooperation with Turkey significantly. This helped avert a potentially crippling crisis and improved US-Turkish relations.

Although the Iraq War is the main source of deteriorating US-Turkish relations, the AKP's attempt to develop a more self-confident and activist foreign policy also has helped increase tensions. The AKP government strongly believes, with significant justification, that Turkey has traditionally punched well below its weight. Its presence in international organizations has been limited, and it has not made enough of its geostrategic location and material strengths to exert influence in the immediate region and beyond. Turkey's difficulties with the United States have come about not because of the change of approach but rather because of its implementation. Erdogan, for instance, undermined the Western consensus on two occasions. When Europe and the United States agreed on a strategy to isolate Syria to force it to evacuate Lebanon, Turkey initiated a visible diplomatic campaign to reduce Syria's isolation. More importantly, when the United States and Europe attempted to devise a strategy against the Palestinian Islamic group Hamas, Turkey invited the most radical Hamas leader to Ankara. This was a poorly thought-out invitation because it also undermined Turkey's antiterrorist stance in Europe and the United States.

The AKP, intent on projecting its influence in areas where Turkey has traditionally played a minor or secondary role, successfully lobbied to win a seat on the UN Security Council for the first time since the early 1960s. Under the leadership of the AKP and Ahmet Davutoglu, the éminence grise of Turkish foreign policy who became foreign minister in 2009, Turkey sought to become more influential in its immediate region. It sent troops to Lebanon and acted as an intermediary between Syria and Israel at a time when the Bush administration had created a vacuum in the Middle East.

Another interesting factor in Turkish foreign relations has been its rapprochement with Russia. Russia has become Turkey's main trade partner, thanks mainly to Turkey's dependence on Russian natural gas. Beyond growing economic relations, Ankara and Moscow have also improved their military and intelligence cooperation on issues related to terrorism. There seems to be more active collaboration between the two countries in the Black Sea region and on the Kurdish and Chechen questions. Despite such enhanced partnership, however, it is too early to speak of a strategic convergence between Russian and Turkish national interests. In fact, a major factor behind Ankara's rapprochement with Moscow was its frustration with the policies of the Bush administration, especially in Iraq and the greater Middle East.

Turkish American relations appear to have improved significantly with the arrival of the Obama administration and the April 2009 presidential visit. Ironically, the same cannot be said of Turkish-EU relations. The opposition of French president Nicholas Sarkozy and his German counterpart, Chancellor Angela Merkel, to full Turkish EU membership has jeopardized both the future of reforms in Turkey and Turkish confidence in Europe. In turn, this does not augur well for resolution of the Cyprus question.

POLITICAL PROSPECTS

The 2007 elections confirmed that the AKP is the dominant political force in Turkish politics. If in 2002 it achieved the impossible, removing from power a whole generation of politicians, some of whom had been there since the 1950s, in 2007 it reaffirmed its hold on the political center. The combination of a majority government, better economic performance, and a determined effort to join the EU has provided Turkey with the kind of stability unseen since the mid-1980s. However, the country remains polarized over identity issues, especially the secular-religious and Turkish-Kurdish divides. The first serious crisis emerged when the AKP decided to promote its then-foreign minister, Abdallah Gul, to the presidency. Gul, whose wife wears a head scarf, was bitterly opposed by the Turkish secular establishment, which went to great lengths to block his nomination. On April 27, 2007, the military issued a midnight memorandum on its official website threatening the government if it went ahead. With the resulting political paralysis, the government called early elections that secured Gul's presidency following a landslide victory.

Unbowed, the establishment pursued a punitive legal offensive by seeking to ban the party and its leaders, including the president and prime minister, from politics. The prosecutor charged the AKP with fostering an Islamic agenda because it sought to open universities to women who wear an Islamic head scarf. Although the court case ended with the Constitutional Court imposing a fine but refusing to close the governing party, it nonetheless created a great deal of uncertainty and partly undermined AKP's self confidence in domestic policy making.

These tensions will continue to distract the political agenda as the arch-secularists and a coalition of moderate Islamists and liberal democrats continue to confront each other as opportunities present themselves. As the Ergenekon investigation drags on, it is bound to further complicate civil-military relations and undermine some of the institutions that hitherto had managed to isolate themselves from the political vagaries, including the judiciary.

Turkey's perceived difficulties with the EU, including the EU's insistence that Turkey open its ports to Greek Cypriot shipping, as called for by its customs union agreement with the EU, have reduced the EU's influence as the main driver of Turkish reforms. This has enabled the AKP to pursue a more multidimensional foreign policy. Europe has become one factor among many that determines Turkish foreign policy.

The Caucasus and the Middle East, especially Iraq, have emerged as important arenas of Turkish contestation. The AKP has concluded that it needs to change its Iraq policy to co-opt the Iraqi Kurds rather than confront them militarily and diplomatically. This change has deep repercussions for Turkey's domestic Kurdish question. At one level, it opens the door to a peaceful resolution to the twenty-year-old PKK-led Kurdish insurrection. Iraqi Kurds are determined to have better relations with Ankara and are seeking ways to demilitarize PKK units based in their territory. For the first time in modern Turkish history, there is talk of a historic compromise in Turkey on the Kurdish question. This said, there remain many potential complicating factors that could derail an internal reckoning over the Kurdish minority. Among them is the future disposition of the northern oil-rich Iraqi city of Kirkuk as well as the threat of a nationalist backlash against the AKP.

On April 22, 2009, Turkey and Armenia agreed on a comprehensive framework for reconciliation. The first steps toward reconciliation could be accomplished by late 2009, with the opening of the Turkish-Armenian border, the establishment of diplomatic relations, and the creation of bilateral commissions to deal with various issues. Yet, a couple of weeks after the agreement was made public, Turkey backtracked in the face of a mounting nationalist reaction in both Turkey and Azerbaijan.

Ankara thus once again linked its Armenia policy to the resolution of the conflict in Nagorno-Karabakh, an enclave within Azerbaijan occupied by Armenian forces since 1993. Failure to improve relations with Armenia is likely to hamper Turkey's Caucasus policy. As Ankara's vision of a "Caucasus Stability and Cooperation Platform" makes clear, Turkey wants to cooperate as equal partners with Russia in the South Caucasus. Despite enjoying good relations with both Georgia and Russia, Turkey is in the awkward position of blockading one of the countries that should normally have its place in this Caucasus platform. Turkey's leadership ambitions in the Caucasus are therefore highly problematic because it is not seen as evenhanded.

Despite Turkey's growing regional ambitions in the Caucasus and Middle East, the EU remains a strategic priority for Turkish foreign policy. The complicating factors on that front are the unresolved question of Cyprus, enlargement fatigue in the EU, and diminishing public hope and support within Turkey for EU membership.

Some in the EU, especially the German Christian Democrats, France, and Austria, would prefer to have Turkey seek a privileged partnership instead of full membership. If the EU were to renege on its commitment to a fair accession process, Turkey's diminishing enthusiasm could turn into a backlash against Europe and the West. Nonetheless, the backlash itself would be contained by the very fact that the bulk of Turkish trade is with Europe.

Moreover, Turkey's strategic importance for Europe is likely to increase in parallel with the EU's quest for energy diversification and a supplier more reliable than Russia. In that sense, the Nabucco pipeline, which would transport natural gas from the Caspian Sea to Central Europe via Turkey, would radically alter Turkey's strategic relationship with the EU.

Hence, Turkey's economic relationship with the EU will likely remain intact. All things considered, Turkey has come a long way; it has managed to overcome difficult situations, albeit sometimes quite slowly. The dynamism and flexibility of Turkish society and its workforce point to a potential yet to be realized.

BIBLIOGRAPHY

Bernard Lewis's *The Emergence of Modern Turkey* (New York: Oxford University Press, 1961) remains the classic volume on Turkey. Feroz Ahmad's *The Making of Modern Turkey* (London: Routledge, 1993) covers Turkish politics up to the 1990s. Erik J. Zurcher, *Turkey: A Modern History* (New York: Tauris, 1994), gives a good overview. Stanford J. Shaw's two-volume *History of the Ottoman Empire and Modern Turkey* (London: Cambridge University Press, 1976–1977) contains a mine of data on the events it chronicles. Andrew Mango, *Ataturk: The Biography of the Founder of Modern Turkey* (Woodstock, NY: Overlook Press, 2000), gives a somewhat more reliable account of Turkey's great leader than Lord Kinross (Patrick Balfour) did in *Ataturk: A Biography of Mustafa Kemal, Father of Modern Turkey* (New York: William Morrow, 1965).

The political system of the Third Republic is analyzed in Ergun Ozbudun, *Contemporary Turkish Politics: Challenges to Democratic Consolidation* (Boulder, CO: Lynne Riener Publishers, 2000). For an earlier view, see George S. Harris, *Turkey: Coping with Crisis* (Boulder, CO: Westview Press, 1985). Hugh Poulton's *Top Hat, Grey Wolf and Crescent: Turkish Nationalism and the Turkish Republic* (London: Hurst & Company,

1997) is a detailed study of the nationalist roots of modern Turkey. For the evolution of political parties up to 1989, consult Metin Heper and Jacob M. Landau, eds., *Political Parties and Democracy in Turkey* (London: I. B. Tauris, 1991). Andrew Finkel and Nukhet Sirman, eds., *Turkish State, Turkish Society* (London: Routledge, 1990), offer a broad analysis of political trends and ethnicity in the Third Republic.

Peter A. Andrews, ed., *Ethnic Groups in the Republic of Turkey* (Wiesbaden: Dr. Ludwig Teichert Verlag, 1989), gives a magisterial treatment of Turkey's cultural geography.

Z.Y. Herslag's *The Contemporary Turkish Economy* (New York: Routledge, 1988) examines the Turkish economy through the post–1980 period of export orientation. Anne O. Krueger and Okan A. Aktan provide an analysis of Turgut Ozal's reforms in the 1980s in *Swimming Against the Tide: Turkish Trade Reform in the 1980s* (San Francisco: Institute for Contemporary Studies Press, 1992).

For an excellent series of articles on Kemalist modernization, see Resat Kasaba and Sibel Bozdogan's *Rethinking Modernity and National Identity in Turkey* (Seattle: University of Washington Press, 1997).

The role of the military in politics is well depicted by William M. Hale, *Turkish Politics and the Military* (London: Routledge, 1995). For an anthropological approach to civil society relations in Turkey, see Ayse Gul Altinay, *The Myth of the Military Nation: Militarism, Gender, and Education in Turkey* (New York: Palgrave, 2004).

Morton Abramowitz, ed., *Friends in Need: Turkey and the United States After September 11* (New York: The Century Foundation, 2003), is a comprehensive approach to US–Turkish relations. Philip Robins's *Suits and Uniforms: Turkish Foreign Policy Since the Cold War* (Seattle: University of Washington Press, 2003) is a novel approach to Turkish foreign policy. Alvin Z. Rubinstein and Oles M. Smolansky, eds., *Regional Power Rivalries in the New Eurasia: Russia, Turkey, and Iran* (Armonk, NY: M. E. Sharpe, 1995), covers the early stages of Turkey's relationship with the newly independent states of the former Soviet Union. Heinz Kramer performs a tour de force on Turkey's role in Europe and its neighborhood in *A Changing Turkey: The Challenge to Europe and the United States* (Washington, DC: Brookings Institution, 2000). On the Cyprus issue, see Michael Emerson and Nathalie Tocci, *Cyprus as Lighthouse of the East Mediterranean: Shaping Re-unification and EU Accession Together* (Brussels: Center for European Research, 2002), and Tozun Bahcheli, *Greek-Turkish Relations Since 1955* (Boulder, CO: Westview Press, 1990).

Richard Tapper, ed., *Islam in Modern Turkey: Religion, Politics, and Literature in a Secular State* (London: I. B. Tauris, 1991), gives the background to recent religious developments. A more specialized treatment is in Jenny White, *Islamist Mobilization in Turkey: A Study in Vernacular Politics* (Seattle: University of Washington Press, 2002). Serif Mardin's *Religion and Social Change in Modern Turkey: The Case of Bediuzzaman Said Nursi* (Albany: State University of New York Press, 1989) is a sophisticated sociological study of the role of religion in Turkey viewed through an analysis of one of the most influential Turkish religious leaders of the twentieth century. On the Gulen movement, see Berna Turam, *Between Islam and the State: The Politics of Engagement* (Stanford, CA: Stanford University Press, 2007). Women's issues are treated in Sirin Tekeli, ed., *Women in Modern Turkish Society: A Reader* (London: Zed, 1995). The Kurdish challenge is covered in David McDowall, *A Modern History of the Kurds* (New York: I. B. Tauris, 1996). See also Henri J. Barkey and Graham E. Fuller, *Turkey's Kurdish Question: An Example of a Trans-State Conflict* (Lanham, MD: Rowman & Littlefield, 1998), and Kemal Kirişçi and Gareth Winrow, *The Kurdish Question and Turkey* (London: Frank Cass, 1997). See also Omer Taspinar, *Kurdish Nationalism and Political Islam in Turkey: Kemalist Identity in Transition* (New York: Routledge, 2005), and Henri J. Barkey, *Preventing Conflict over Kurdistan* (Washington, DC: Carnegie Endowment for International Peace, 2009).

The latest twists and turns of Turkish developments are well reported by the *Hurriyet Daily News* (Ankara). See www.HurriyetDailyNews.com/FrTDN/latest/heads.htm for a daily Internet edition.

3

Islamic Republic of Iran

Mark Gasiorowski

Iran has preserved its unique identity since the dawn of history, despite the Arab, Turkish, and Mongol invasions that once swept through the region. Known as Persia until 1935, it boasted major empires that rivaled those of the ancient Greeks, Byzantines, and Ottomans. It was one of the few countries in the Middle East that was not colonized in the modern era, though European powers exerted considerable influence there in the early twentieth century. Iran is heir to one of the richest cultures in the Middle East, renowned for its poetry, visual arts, music, and cuisine. It is also the birthplace of the Zoroastrian and Baha'i faiths and is the main bastion of the Shi'a branch of Islam.

Iran was convulsed by a popular revolution in 1978 and 1979, replacing 2,500 years of monarchical rule with an Islamic republic. Its new Islamist leaders were very radical during their first decade in power, thoroughly transforming political and cultural life inside the country and engaging in bitter confrontation with the West and with most neighboring countries. Iran then became increasingly moderate in the 1990s, easing cultural restrictions, initiating extensive political reform, and improving relations with its neighbors and with Europe, though not with the United States. However, the momentum behind these reforms faded, and hard-liners swept the parliamentary and presidential elections of 2004 and 2005, establishing a new era of radicalism. Hard-line president Mahmoud Ahmadinejad was reelected in June 2009 in a vote that was widely considered fraudulent, sparking large protests that plunged the country into crisis. These protests continued through December, leaving the future of the Islamic regime very uncertain.

Historical Background

The Great Persian Empires

The ancestors of modern Iranians migrated into the Iranian plateau, in the center of today's Iran, in the eleventh and tenth centuries BCE. The region was

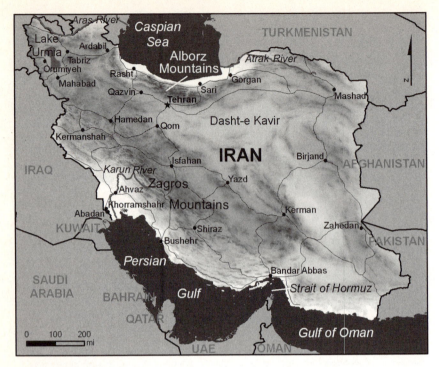

Islamic Republic of Iran

occupied at the time by other ethnic groups, mainly Assyrians, Elamites, and Urartians. In the sixth century BCE, Cyrus the Great united two Iranian tribes, the Medes and the Persians, to form the first great Persian empire, known as the Achaemenian Empire. Cyrus and his descendants conquered vast areas, including much of what are now Egypt, Syria, Iraq, Turkey, and Central Asia. Their efforts to conquer Greece were stopped at the battle of Marathon in 490 BCE. The Achaemenian Empire was finally defeated by Alexander the Great in 330 BCE.

The next great Persian empire was established in 224 CE, when Ardeshir Babakan, a local ruler in what is now southern Iran, conquered the neighboring areas. Ardeshir and his son Shahpour established the Sassanian dynasty, which ruled Iran until the seventh century. Shahpour attacked the Roman Empire's Middle Eastern provinces, seizing the city of Antioch and even capturing the Roman emperor Valerian. During the next few centuries the Sassanians were frequently at war with Rome and its successor, the Byzantine Empire, eventually capturing

Jerusalem and Egypt and even laying siege to Constantinople, the Byzantine capital. The Byzantines then achieved a series of victories in the early seventh century, severely weakening the Sassanian Empire.

Following the death of Mohammad, the great prophet of Islam, in 632 CE, Muslim armies attacked the weakened Sassanian Empire and achieved major victories at Qadisiya in modern-day Iraq in 637 and at Nahavand in central Iran in 641, seizing control over the Iranian heartland. Many Arabs settled in Iran in the following decades, introducing Islam and the Arabic alphabet and vocabulary. Iran's new Arab rulers adopted the Sassanians' advanced administrative techniques and many aspects of Iranian culture, strengthening and enriching the vast empire they were creating during this period.

From the seventh to the eleventh centuries, Iran was ruled either as part of the Arab Empire or by local dynasties. During the next two centuries a series of Turkic military commanders ruled Iran at the behest of local elites and caliphs. This was a rich period in Iran's cultural life, with a flourishing of poetry, the visual arts, and urban development. This period ended in 1251, when Mongol invaders swept into Iran from Central Asia, destroying almost everything in their path and leaving Iran in a state of near anarchy for many decades.

Iran's last great empire, ruled by the Safavid dynasty, was established in 1501 by Shah ("King") Ismail, who made the Shi'a branch of Islam the state religion and united territory roughly comprising the boundaries of today's Iran. The Safavid dynasty was at its height during the reign of Shah Abbas I (1587–1628), who conquered much of Central Asia and parts of the Ottoman Empire. Shah Abbas established his capital in Isfahan, building superb palaces, mosques, bridges, and gardens that make this city one of the most beautiful in the world. The Safavid Empire gradually fell into decline and was conquered by Afghans in 1722, initiating decades of instability.

In the late eighteenth century, the Turkic-speaking Qajar tribe defeated the other tribes and warlords of Iran and recreated much of the Safavid Empire. They also moved the capital to Tehran, which was then merely a village. The Qajar dynasty ruled until 1925. This was an era of decline for Iran, with the Qajars losing substantial territory in the Caucasus and Central Asia to imperial Russia and becoming increasingly indebted to European bankers and entrepreneurs. Internally, Qajar Iran was shaken by the Babi and Baha'i movements in the 1840s and 1850s, the tobacco boycott of 1891–1892, and the constitutional revolution of 1906, which brought Iran the first constitution in the non-Western world. Iran's decline under the Qajars culminated during World War I, when foreign armies occupied parts of the country and famine was widespread, and immediately after the war, when Ahmad Shah Qajar signed a treaty with Britain that made Iran virtually a British protectorate.

IRAN

Capital city	Tehran
Chief of state	Supreme Leader Ali Khamenei
Head of government	President Mahmoud Ahmadinejad
Major political parties	Executives of Construction Party, Islamic Iran Developers' Coalition, Islamic Iran Participation Front, Islamic Labor Party, Militant Clerics' Society, Mojahedin of the Islamic Revolution Organization, National Trust Party, Solidarity Party
Ethnic groups	Persian (51%), Azeri (24%), Gilaki and Mazandarani (8%), Kurd (7%), Arab (3%), Baloch (2%), Lur (2%), Turkmen (2%), other (1%)
Religious group	Shi'a Muslim (89%), Sunni Muslim (9%), other (2%)
Export partners	China (15%), Japan (14.3%), Turkey (7.4%), South Korea (7.3%), Italy (6.4%)
Import partners	China (14.2%), Germany (9.6%), United Arab Emirates (9.1%), South Korea (6.3%), Russia (5.7%), Italy (5%)

The Pahlavi Era

In 1921, Reza Khan Pahlavi, the commander of one of Iran's few effective military units, led a coup against the current government. During the next four years, he gradually consolidated power by eliminating his rivals, defeating various tribal forces, and packing the *majles* (parliament) with his supporters. He then had the *majles* vote to depose the last Qajar shah and name him the new shah. He was crowned in April 1926, establishing the Pahlavi dynasty.

Reza Shah Pahlavi was a modernizing despot, laying the basis for a modern economy and society in Iran but also severely repressing political activity. Like his Turkish contemporary, Mustafa Kemal Ataturk, he did much to develop Iran's economic and social infrastructure, building roads and a large rail network, a modern banking system, a professional civil service, modern educational institutions, and the country's first modern factories. Much of this activity was financed by proceeds from Iran's rapidly growing oil industry, which had been established in 1901 and was controlled by the British-owned Anglo-Iranian Oil Company. Reza Shah also took steps to increase Iran's independence, rescinding the treaty with Britain and reorganizing and strengthening the armed forces. At the same time he was very repressive, brutally suppressing his opponents, preventing the establishment of political parties and other civil society institutions, and taking steps to weaken the Shi'a clergy and its influence in Iranian society.

Britain and the Soviet Union jointly occupied Iran during World War II to establish a supply route for Soviet forces, which were fighting desperately against German invaders in areas to the northwest of Iran. Reza Shah opposed this and was promptly deposed and sent into exile. The occupying powers then installed Reza Shah's twenty-one-year-old son, Mohammad Reza Pahlavi, in his place. The young shah at this time was a weak and timid figure with no political experience. His installation on the throne therefore produced a flourishing of political activity, with various traditionalist, Islamist, nationalist, tribal, and leftist tendencies emerging. During the last years of World War II, the Soviet Union and its close allies in Iran's Communist Tudeh (Masses) Party began to encourage Azeri and Kurdish separatist movements in Iran, producing an incipient crisis. These movements collapsed in 1946, however, as a result of the skillful diplomacy of Prime Minister Ahmad Qavam and support from the United States.

Political activity continued to flourish in Iran in the late 1940s. Nationalist, leftist, and Islamist forces agitated increasingly against British influence in Iran, especially against British control over the oil industry. In 1949, several moderate nationalist parties and assorted individuals created an umbrella organization called the National Front to promote nationalization of the oil industry. Most National Front leaders also wanted to establish democracy in Iran, which entailed wresting power from the pro-British traditional upper class and weakening the monarchy. The National Front was led by Mohammad Mosaddeq, a venerable politician who had long campaigned for oil nationalization and opposed the Pahlavi monarchy since Reza Shah's accession.

As the oil-nationalization movement grew, the shah felt compelled to appoint Mosaddeq prime minister in late April 1951. Mosaddeq then nationalized the oil industry, triggering a confrontation with the British government. The British organized a worldwide embargo of Iranian oil exports and began covert efforts to undermine Mosaddeq's government. They also began preparations to invade Iran, which ended in September 1951 when US President Harry Truman refused to support an invasion. The United States made extensive efforts to negotiate a solution to the oil dispute, but Britain and Iran could not reach an agreement. As the crisis dragged on during 1952, Mosaddeq's coalition began to weaken, with key

Islamist and nationalist allies joining the opposition. US officials increasingly feared that Mosaddeq would become dependent on the Tudeh Party, giving the Soviet Union growing influence in Iran. Soon after US President Dwight Eisenhower was inaugurated in January 1953, the United States agreed to a British proposal to stage a joint coup d'état against Mosaddeq. The US Central Intelligence Agency then organized and carried out the coup, overthrowing Mosaddeq in August 1953.

The 1953 coup initiated a dramatic shift in Iran's political evolution, ending the flourishing of political activity that had occurred since 1941 and beginning a long period of authoritarian rule. Mosaddeq's successor, Fazlollah Zahedi—who had been handpicked by the United States and Britain—declared martial law, arrested thousands, and closed down all opposition parties and newspapers. Mosaddeq was put on trial, imprisoned for three years, and then kept under house arrest until he died in 1967. Most of Mosaddeq's key associates were imprisoned as well, and his foreign minister was executed. An extensive Tudeh Party network in the armed forces was discovered and dismantled in September 1954, severely crippling the party. The United States made extensive efforts to prop up the Zahedi government, giving it extensive economic and security assistance and working tirelessly to negotiate an end to the oil dispute. An oil agreement was finally signed in October 1954 under which a consortium of foreign oil companies purchased Iranian oil produced by the state-owned National Iranian Oil Company.

The shah dismissed Zahedi in April 1955 and appointed a loyalist in his place, beginning a long period in which the shah gradually consolidated power in his own hands. Political unrest continued to simmer, especially among the rapidly growing urban middle class. The shah finally lifted martial law in April 1957. He also authorized the creation of two political parties, the Nationalists' (*Melliyun*) Party and the People's (*Mardom*) Party, but he put loyalists in charge of them. In addition, the Central Intelligence Agency during this period established and trained a new Iranian intelligence agency, *Sazeman-e Ettela'at va Amniyat-e Keshvar* (SAVAK), which soon became a key pillar of the shah's authoritarian regime.

By 1960, political unrest had grown considerably. In January, Tehran high school students staged the first public demonstrations since 1953. Soon after, the shah announced that *majles* elections scheduled for the summer would be completely free, prompting a wide range of politicians to announce their candidacy, including several members of the newly reconstituted National Front. The elections were held in August and featured widespread irregularities and violence, forcing the shah to cancel them. New elections were scheduled for January 1961. Many candidates again emerged, and the elections again were rigged. The National Front, students, and teachers organized large protest demonstrations. US officials began discreetly pressuring the shah to initiate liberalization measures. As a result, the shah fired several unpopular officials and appointed the US-backed moderate reformer Ali Amini as prime minister.

Amini quickly took steps to appease the shah's critics, announcing a series of reforms, including a much-needed land reform program and measures aimed at stimulating the sluggish economy. In addition, the shah announced that new elections would be held. The National Front rejected these measures and organized large demonstrations in the months after Amini's appointment. Amini responded by arresting all of the National Front's leaders and many supporters; he did not schedule new elections. More demonstrations occurred in January 1962. The demonstrators were attacked by the security forces, leaving hundreds injured and hundreds more arrested. Under severe pressure, the National Front began to split into moderate and radical factions during this period.

With his opponents growing weaker, the shah dismissed Amini in July 1962. He then announced his own package of reforms in January 1963, dubbed the "White Revolution," which included a major land reform program, the enfranchisement of women, and efforts to improve literacy and public health. These measures mollified many of the shah's urban middle-class critics, and the land-reform program greatly weakened the traditional upper class. However, many members of the traditional middle and lower classes were angered by the modernizing thrust of the White Revolution. Ayatollah Ruhollah Khomeini and other Islamists organized a series of strikes and demonstrations to protest the White Revolution. Khomeini was arrested after delivering a critical speech in June 1963, triggering huge demonstrations by his traditional middle- and lower-class followers. The security forces viciously attacked these demonstrations, leaving hundreds dead and thousands injured. Khomeini was soon released but was arrested again and sent into exile in October 1964 after denouncing an arrangement giving US military personnel immunity from prosecution.

After the events of 1963, the shah tolerated no opposition. His security forces, especially the notorious SAVAK secret police, effectively suppressed all overt political activity. He replaced the Nationalists Party with the New Iran (*Iran Novin*) Party in late 1963 and later replaced both official parties with a single party, the Resurgence (*Rastakhiz*) Party. These parties failed to attract significant popular support, serving merely as mechanisms of co-optation. Iran's oil revenues grew rapidly during this period and skyrocketed after the huge price increases of the early 1970s, producing a long period of rapid economic growth that helped defuse unrest. The United States stopped pressuring the shah for reform after the early 1960s, and its strong support for him led many opponents to believe he was invincible. Viewed from afar, Iran appeared to be an "island of stability," as US President Jimmy Carter famously remarked on New Year's Eve of 1977.

Nevertheless, despite the appearance of calm, several opposition currents existed in Iran in the late 1960s and 1970s. The National Front, with its aging leadership and moderate rhetoric, became increasingly irrelevant. The Liberation Movement of Iran (*Nezhat-e Azadi-ye Iran*), an Islamic modernist offshoot led by Mehdi Bazargan, had broken off from the National Front in 1961 and remained active during this period, though it had only a narrow base of support. Both the National Front and the Liberation Movement spawned important student organizations among the many Iranians studying in the United States and Europe during this period, creating powerful opposition networks among this crucial segment of society.

More importantly, several leftist guerrilla organizations were established in the late 1960s and early 1970s by young Iranians who had become disillusioned with the moderate positions of the National Front and Liberation Movement and the weakness of the Tudeh Party. The most important of these were the *Mojahedin-e Khalq* (People's Warriors), which had a radical Islamic-leftist ideology, and the *Cherikha-ye Fedayan-e Khalq* (People's Guerrilla Warriors), which had a Third World–oriented Marxist-Leninist ideology. These organizations sent some of their members to Lebanon and other countries for guerrilla training and maintained contact with the student movements in the United States and Europe. They launched an armed uprising against the shah's regime in 1971, attacking police stations and other targets and assassinating government officials and six American military and civilian advisors. The security forces responded with severe repression, torturing and executing many of their members. By 1975 these organizations had been severely weakened.

Finally, a variety of Islamist movements emerged in the 1960s and 1970s. The most important was a network of Shi'a clerics, most of whom had studied under Ayatollah Khomeini. Khomeini lived in the Shi'a holy city of Najaf, Iraq, from 1965 until 1978 and communicated with this network through a series of emissaries who relayed messages back and forth and brought tapes of his fiery sermons to be played in Iran's mosques. He also wrote his seminal book *Islamic Government* during this period, providing a blueprint for the Islamic regime he hoped to establish. Closely affiliated with this clerical network was a small cell of Islamist laymen called the Coalition of Islamic Societies (*Jamiat-e Motalafeh-ye Islami*), which assassinated Prime Minister Hassan Ali Mansur in January 1965. The Islamic modernist intellectual Ali Shariati developed a large following before he died mysteriously in 1977, drawing many students and middle-class Iranians toward political Islam. Inspired by the Mojahedin-e Khalq and Fedayan-e Khalq, many small Islamist guerrilla cells emerged in the mid-1970s and began to stage attacks on the shah's regime. These various Islamist movements were loosely connected with one another, with the Liberation Movement, and with Islamist movements in Lebanon and other countries.

The 1978–1979 Revolution

Several factors created growing popular unrest in Iran in the 1960s and 1970s. The absence of political freedom and high levels of repression alienated many Iranians, especially among students and the urban middle class. Inequality remained high, despite the huge influx of oil revenue in the 1970s, creating unrest among the lower classes. The shah drew even closer to the United States in the early 1970s, buying large quantities of US arms, signing lucrative contracts with US corporations, and bringing tens of thousands of Americans to Iran to administer these projects. He also maintained close relations with Israel in this period. In addition, the shah promoted rapid Westernization in Iran by fostering the growth of Western culture, creating a new Westernized elite, and deemphasizing traditional Persian and Islamic values. These various trends angered not only traditionalist Iranians but also many modernists, who believed that the shah was compromising Iran's rich cultural identity and creating a growing chasm between the traditional and modern segments of society.

In 1976 and 1977, several new conditions emerged that further increased this unrest and made it easier for opposition activists to capitalize on. The mid-1970s oil boom had a number of painful consequences, including higher inflation, shortages, unparalleled corruption, and extensive rural-urban migration, which placed severe strains on public services. The oil boom also forced the shah to take steps that further angered certain segments of society, such as implementing price controls, higher interest rates, an antiprofiteering campaign, and spending cuts. During the 1976 US presidential campaign, candidate Jimmy Carter stated that he would promote human rights if elected president and specifically mentioned Iran as a likely focus. Although in practice Carter made little effort to promote human rights in Iran, the shah anticipated that he would and eased up on his opponents. Finally, the shah was secretly diagnosed with lymphatic cancer in 1974 and began to take powerful medication, forcing him to consider his legacy and probably clouding his judgment.

Under these conditions, opposition leaders began to test the limits on political activity during 1977. Secular activists circulated open letters calling for political reform. Several new civil society organizations were established and began to hold public meetings. The National Front and Liberation Movement, which had been dormant for years, reemerged and began to agitate. These organizations became increasingly active in the fall of 1977, holding rallies and issuing public statements. After Ayatollah Khomeini's son Mostafa died suddenly in October, Khomeini's Islamist allies organized a series of memorial services around the country, which were widely attended. Responding to these pressures, the shah replaced his docile prime minister, Amir Abbas Hoveida, with a respected technocrat and permitted the Resurgence Party and other official bodies to discuss matters more openly.

The security forces did not crack down on opposition activity until November 1977, leading many Iranians to believe that a new era of openness had begun.

Encouraged by these events, Khomeini's allies organized large demonstrations in the holy city of Qom in January 1978 to protest a slanderous newspaper article about Khomeini. The security forces attacked the demonstrators, killing seven and arresting over a hundred. Following traditional Shi'a mourning practices, the Islamists then organized more demonstrations throughout the country forty days later to commemorate those killed in January. Mobs attacked government buildings, theaters, and stores selling liquor and again clashed with the security forces, leaving nine more dead and hundreds arrested. More violent demonstrations then occurred at forty-day intervals in the following months, leaving more dead and filling the country's prisons. By the summer of 1978 Iran had become dangerously unstable.

The shah responded erratically to this challenge, trying to suppress these demonstrations but also making important concessions. This ambiguous approach merely encouraged the opposition, which was now dominated by Khomeini's allies. Islamist guerrillas began to provoke the security forces by shooting at them from crowds and carrying out arson and bombing attacks. Khomeinist clerics called on members of the security forces to defect.

A key turning point came in mid-August 1978, when unknown arsonists set fire to a crowded theater in Abadan, killing hundreds. Huge demonstrations then spread throughout the country, fanned by rumors that SAVAK had burned the theater. The shah tried to end the chaos by again replacing his prime minister, releasing hundreds of political prisoners, calling for free elections, and making other conciliatory gestures. Moderate opposition leaders appealed for calm. These measures failed to stop the crisis. The shah declared martial law. On September 8, army units opened fire on a crowd demonstrating at Zhaleh Square in eastern Tehran, killing scores and injuring hundreds.

Martial law kept demonstrators in check during the following weeks. However, labor unrest began to spread throughout the country, crippling the oil industry and other sectors of the economy. In addition, both Islamist and leftist guerrillas increased their violent attacks against the shah's regime. Khomeini moved from Iraq to Paris in October, enabling him to exercise better leadership over events. Islamist and secularist leaders traveled to Paris to meet with Khomeini, further strengthening his leadership. The shah tried unsuccessfully to persuade moderate opposition leaders to form a government that would carry out reforms but preserve the monarchy. He also continued to release political prisoners and make other conciliatory gestures.

A new wave of violent demonstrations swept through Tehran in early November, leading the shah again to replace his prime minister, this time with a military government. Massive demonstrations, guerrilla activity, and strikes continued in the following weeks, leaving hundreds dead and paralyzing the economy. During Shi'a holy days in early December, millions of demonstrators appeared in the streets of Tehran and other cities. The armed forces began to disintegrate. The shah continued to meet with moderate opposition leaders about forming a new government. He finally persuaded National Front leader Shahpour Bakhtiar to head a new government, but only on condition that the shah leave the country, release all political prisoners, and meet other demands. Bakhtiar became prime minister on December 30. The shah left Iran on January 16, 1979, never to return.

Bakhtiar quickly took a number of conciliatory steps, lifting press restrictions, freeing all remaining political prisoners, promising to dissolve SAVAK, and canceling foreign arms purchases. The United States backed Bakhtiar and sent Gen. Robert Huyser to Iran to strengthen support for him among military officers. These actions did little to calm the situation. Khomeini declared Bakhtiar's government illegal and appointed a Revolutionary Council to oversee the transition to a new regime. The National Front expelled Bakhtiar. Huge demonstrations and strikes continued. Khomeini returned to Tehran on February 1 and was greeted by millions of jubilant supporters. He then appointed Liberation Movement leader Mehdi Bazargan to head a new provisional government. Revolutionary committees sprang up in many neighborhoods and towns, taking over public services and administering "revolutionary justice." Air force technicians mutinied in Tehran on February 9, distributing large stocks of weapons and clashing with loyalist army units. Islamist and leftist guerrillas attacked military and police bases, seizing more weapons and leaving hundreds dead. On February 11 military commanders declared that the armed forces would remain neutral in the fighting, ending their support for Bakhtiar's government. Bakhtiar went into hiding the next day.

The Radical Phase of the Islamic Regime

From February until early November 1979, the moderates in and around Bazargan's provisional government were harshly attacked by radical Islamists and radical leftists. In addition, radical Islamists dominated the Revolutionary Council and several other revolutionary institutions that emerged during this period. These institutions became a kind of parallel government that increasingly marginalized the Bazargan government. Ayatollah Khomeini acted as an arbitrator in the tense struggle among these factions, but he generally backed the radical Islamists. As a result, Iran moved steadily in a radical Islamist direction during this period.

The first major dispute between moderates and radicals emerged when members of the revolutionary committees began to arrest top officials from the shah's regime, bring them before hastily created revolutionary courts, and execute them. Bazargan and other moderates protested but were unable to stop the executions, which numbered over six hundred by November. Another dispute emerged in

March over the wording of a referendum on Iran's new regime. Bazargan pushed for a "democratic republic" or "democratic Islamic republic," but Khomeini and his allies demanded that the referendum offer a simple choice for or against an "Islamic republic." The referendum was held in late March and produced a resounding victory for the radical Islamists. Additional disputes occurred over freedom of the press and women's rights. During the spring of 1979, Iranian Kurds, Arabs, and other ethnic minorities began to rebel, Islamist extremists assassinated several prominent moderates, and the radical leftist guerrilla organizations became increasingly powerful. Radical Islamists therefore created the paramilitary Islamic Revolutionary Guard Corps to protect the new Islamic regime against these various threats. Iran's relations with the United States and neighboring Iraq deteriorated during this period as well.

Tensions also emerged over efforts to write a new constitution. Bazargan appointed a commission that produced a draft constitution providing extensive democratic rights and giving the Shi'a clergy only a limited role in government. Khomeini supported this draft constitution, but radical Islamists, leftists, and ethnic leaders attacked it. Radical Islamists then made extensive efforts to gain control over the constitutional assembly that was to finalize the constitution, organizing huge rallies and harshly attacking their opponents. When elections for the assembly were held in August, radical Islamists intimidated and manipulated voters and managed to achieve a decisive victory. They continued their attacks in the following weeks, closing newspapers, banning demonstrations, and outlawing two major secularist parties. Heavy fighting also occurred in Iran's Kurdish and Arab regions. The constitutional assembly convened in mid-August. In the following months, radical Islamists used their control over this body to enact major revisions of the draft constitution, creating the institutional foundations for a clergy-dominated Islamic state. (See "Political Structure," below.) Bazargan and other moderates despaired about their inability to stop the radicals; many fled into exile.

On November 4, hundreds of radical Islamist students stormed the US embassy compound in Tehran and took sixty-one Americans hostage. After Bazargan and Foreign Minister Ibrahim Yazdi tried unsuccessfully to persuade Khomeini to have the hostages released, Bazargan and his cabinet resigned. Some of the hostages were soon released, but fifty-two were held until January 1981. The students had wanted to humiliate the United States and push Iran in a more radical direction. They succeeded on both counts.

The Revolutionary Council temporarily succeeded Bazargan's government. The council oversaw a December 1979 referendum that overwhelmingly approved the new constitution. It then held presidential elections in January that were won by Abol Hassan Bani-Sadr, a relatively moderate Islamist intellectual who had lived in Paris for many years and became a key aide to Khomeini in 1978. The students holding the US embassy considered Bani-Sadr too moderate and soon began to attack him. Radical Islamists associated with the recently created Islamic Republican Party (IRP) swept the March 1980 parliamentary elections and soon began to attack Bani-Sadr as well, demanding that he accept their nominees for cabinet positions. Led by IRP head Ayatollah Mohammad Beheshti and Speaker of Parliament Akbar Hashemi Rafsanjani, they eventually forced Bani-Sadr to accept their nominee for prime minister, Mohammad Ali Raja'i. Disputes over other cabinet positions continued for months. Bani-Sadr became increasingly dependent on support from the Mojahedin-e Khalq, whose large cadre of urban guerrillas posed a serious threat to the radical Islamists.

Following more than a year of clashes along their common border, Iraq invaded Iran in September 1980. Iraqi forces soon seized some 4,000 square miles of Iranian territory, including much of the oil-producing region in southwestern Iran. The Iranian government began a massive effort to mobilize resistance to the invasion, producing a huge outpouring of volunteers and a groundswell of support for the Islamic regime. Bani-Sadr and his radical opponents both tried to take advantage of the situation by identifying themselves with the war effort and using the war as a pretext to attack one another.

Clashes between Bani-Sadr and the radical Islamists became increasingly tense in the first half of 1981. Bani-Sadr's moderate backers and the Mojahedin organized a series of rallies that were attacked by radical vigilantes. The radicals held rallies of their own, which were generally much larger than the pro–Bani-Sadr rallies. By April violent clashes were occurring almost daily. Parliament and other institutions controlled by the radicals began to strip Bani-Sadr of his powers and close down moderate newspapers, leading Bani-Sadr to call for a popular referendum to resolve the confrontation. Frustrated by the factional infighting, Khomeini in late May began to criticize Bani-Sadr publicly. With Khomeini apparently on their side, the radicals moved to eliminate Bani-Sadr, filing frivolous legal charges against him, arresting many of his associates, assaulting his supporters, and finally calling for his execution. Khomeini dismissed Bani-Sadr on June 22, leading him to flee underground with help from the Mojahedin.

With the radical Islamists now poised to consolidate control, the Mojahedin tried to initiate a counterrevolutionary uprising. They organized a huge rally on June 20 that was brutally attacked by the radicals, leaving dozens dead and over 1,000 arrested. Arrests continued on the following days, and large numbers of Mojahedin and secular leftist guerrillas were executed. The Mojahedin then carried out a series of bombings and assassinations aimed at killing off the radical Islamist leadership and bringing down the Islamic regime. The most dramatic was a June 28 bombing that killed seventy-four IRP leaders, including Beheshti, four cabinet ministers, and twenty-seven members of parliament. The radicals reacted with fury, arresting thousands and executing hundreds. Additional bombings and assassinations occurred in the following months. Raja'i was elected president in late July, but he and the new prime minister were soon killed in another bombing. The arrests and executions continued for many months, leaving thousands dead and decisively weakening the Mojahedin. Most of its surviving members fled to Iraq, where they were armed by the Iraqi government and carried out occasional cross-border attacks. The remnants of the Mojahedin were still based in Iraq in 2009.

In October 1981, Ali Khamenei, a radical cleric, was elected president and Mir Hossein Musavi, a radical lay Islamist, was appointed prime minister. These men, together with Speaker of Parliament Rafsanjani, worked under the general guidance of Ayatollah Khomeini to consolidate the radical Islamists' control and bring order and stability to Iran. After defeating the Mojahedin, their most urgent priority was to drive Iraqi forces out of Iran. They accomplished this in May 1982. Iran then carried the war into Iraqi territory, hoping to bring down the government of Saddam Husayn and establish an Islamic state in Iraq. Iran's forces soon became bogged down, producing a brutal war of attrition that lasted until 1988. Khamenei was reelected in August 1985, and Musavi was reappointed in October 1985.

Having defeated their various opponents, the radical Islamists began to feud among themselves in the mid-1980s. The most important dispute was between the Islamic leftists associated with Prime Minister Musavi, who favored a radical redistribution of wealth and statist economic policies, and Islamic conservatives associated with the traditional clerical and business elite, who favored laissez-faire economic policies. This dispute persisted throughout the mid- and late 1980s, preventing the government from carrying out effective economic policies.

Another dispute surfaced in November 1986, when it emerged that the United States had been selling arms to Iran in exchange for the release of US hostages held in Lebanon by Iran-backed guerrillas. US officials then used the profits from these arms sales to assist Nicaraguan guerrillas in what became known as the Iran-Contra Affair. Information about these arms sales was made public in October 1986 by Mehdi Hashemi, a radical cleric and son-in-law of Ayatollah Hossein Ali Montazari, Khomeini's designated successor. Most of Iran's leaders had backed the arms-for-hostages deal and were deeply embarrassed by the revelation, so Hashemi was imprisoned and executed. Yet another dispute emerged in the late 1980s, when Montazari and others began to call for greater liberalization. Khomeini tried to slow this trend in early 1989 by dismissing Montazari and issuing a death sentence for British author Salman Rushdie, whose book *The Satanic Verses* had offended many Muslims.

The Moderate Phase

Several key changes in 1988 and 1989 initiated a trend toward moderation in Iran. In July 1988, after its ground forces had been severely weakened and driven out of Iraq and much of its navy had been destroyed by the United States, Iran finally agreed to a UN proposal to end the Iran-Iraq War. Ayatollah Khomeini died in June 1989, after a long illness. In July, Rafsanjani, who had emerged as a leading advocate of moderation, was elected president. At the same time, Iran's voters approved a package of constitutional reforms designed to reduce the gridlock that had largely paralyzed the political system since the mid-1980s. The most important of these reforms was a measure to eliminate the position of prime minister and concentrate executive power in the hands of the president.

President Rafsanjani assembled a government dominated by centrist technocrats. His highest priority was to reform the economy, which had deteriorated sharply as a result of the war and years of ideologically driven policy making. Rafsanjani's economic reforms met with strong opposition in parliament, which was dominated by Islamic leftists. He therefore drew closer to the conservatives, who vetoed many leftist candidates for the 1992 parliamentary elections. Most of the remaining leftists were defeated at the polls, giving the conservatives a large majority in parliament, which they retained in the 1996 elections. The conservative-controlled parliament soon turned against Rafsanjani and the centrists, however, blocking most of the reforms they sought to implement.

The leftists' defeat in the 1992 elections demonstrated that they had lost most of their popular support, leading many to become more moderate. In the run-up to the May 1997 presidential election, the leftists established a pro-reform coalition with the centrists, who were disillusioned with the conservatives' opposition to their economic reforms. This reformist coalition backed Hujjat al-Islam Mohammad Khatami, a moderate leftist cleric, in the presidential election. Khatami won a landslide victory, demonstrating that the reformists' views were much more popular than those of the conservatives.

Khatami's election temporarily threw the conservatives off balance and gave the reformists a chance to carry out their program of reforms. The reformists' highest priority was to promote democracy, since free elections would likely give them control over parliament and thus stop the conservatives' efforts to block their other planned reforms. They therefore began to pursue political reform, liberalizing the press, loosening restrictions on political activity, and challenging the conservatives' control over state institutions. The conservatives soon responded, assaulting and arresting reformist leaders, closing their newspapers, and attacking them with demagogic rhetoric. Ayatollah Khamenei largely backed the conservatives, using the broad powers of his office to block many reformist initiatives. By the summer of 1998, the two factions were locked in a bitter power struggle, bringing the reform process largely to an end.

The reformists won another landslide victory in the 1999 municipal council elections. The conservatives continued their attacks, however, focusing especially on the reformist press. In July 1999 they closed a popular reformist newspaper, triggering six days of severe rioting that shook the foundations of the Islamic regime. The reformists then won yet another landslide victory in the February 2000 parliamentary elections, gaining control over this crucial body. The conservatives reacted bitterly, arresting reformist leaders, shooting a key reformist strategist, and closing down most remaining reformist newspapers. Rumors circulated that hard-liners in the security forces might carry out a coup. Once the new parliament was convened, the conservative-dominated Guardian Council vetoed much of its legislation. The reformists pursued a strategy of "active calm," pressing for reform but avoiding confrontational actions that might give the conservatives a pretext for cracking down even further.

As the June 2001 presidential election approached, tensions began to emerge in the reformist camp, with radical reformists calling for a more confrontational approach and some even breaking away from the reformist movement. President Khatami publicly admitted that he was powerless and delayed for many months announcing whether he would run for reelection. In the end, Khatami entered the race and won another landslide victory, indicating that the reformists remained very popular, despite growing unease.

The conservatives continued to attack the reformists and block their reform initiatives during Khatami's second term. In addition, the terrorist attacks of September 11, 2001, the subsequent US declaration that Iran was part of an "axis of evil," and the US invasion of Iraq in March 2003 created growing fear that the United States might attack Iran, strengthening the conservatives' determination to stop the reformists. Fissures continued to grow in the reformist camp during this period, and Khatami openly threatened to resign.

Municipal council elections were held again in February 2003. The conservative Islamic Iran Developers' Council (*Etelaf-e Abadgaran-e Iran-e Islami*), which claimed to be pragmatic and apolitical, ran candidates in Tehran and other major cities and won a sweeping victory. The voter turnout rate fell dramatically from the 1999 level, sharply undermining support for reformist candidates and demonstrating that the Iranian public had become disillusioned with the reformists.

In the run-up to the February 2004 parliamentary elections, many reformists talked openly about staging an election boycott, though most finally chose to participate. The conservatives were determined to control these elections. Accordingly, they vetoed almost all prominent reformist candidates, including eighty incumbent members of parliament. Reformist members of parliament staged a sit-in strike and threatened to resign if the vetoes were upheld, and protest demonstrations occurred in many cities. Although some minor reformist candidates were reinstated, the conservatives remained firm. Most reformist leaders eventually backed down, giving up their strike and their threats to resign. They were then punished by the voters, winning only 17 percent of the seats filled in the first round, compared with 68 percent for conservative candidates, led by the Developers' Council. Turnout was higher than expected, indicating that many Iranians had become disillusioned with the reformists and backed conservatives instead.

As the June 2005 presidential election approached, the conservatives continued to attack the reformists and block their initiatives, despite the Developers' Council's claims to be pragmatic and apolitical. With Khatami ineligible for a third term and most popular reformists likely to be vetoed, the reformists did not have a strong candidate for the election. In the end, Speaker of Parliament Mehdi Karrubi and Mostafa Moin, a little-known former cabinet minister, were the main reformist candidates. Several prominent conservatives entered the race as well, together with former president Rafsanjani, a centrist. Rafsanjani led the first round of voting, followed by Tehran mayor Mahmoud Ahmadinejad, a little-known hard-liner whose populist campaign and humble demeanor proved attractive to many voters. Ahmadinejad then won the second round, shocking most observers and ending, at least temporarily, the moderate era that had prevailed since 1989.

Radical Resurgence

Ahmadinejad's election signaled the beginning of a shift back toward the radicalism of the 1980s. During Ahmadinejad's first term, this resurgent radicalism was manifested mainly in Iran's foreign policy, as discussed below. Domestically Ahmadinejad pursued populist economic policies and governed in a very cronyistic manner, alienating not only his reformist and centrist opponents but also many conservatives. Opposition to Ahmadinejad had become widespread by the end of his first term, though Supreme Leader Khamenei continued to support him.

Ahmadinejad was inaugurated in August 2005 and nominated a cabinet dominated by hard-liners, including several of his close associates. The conservative-led parliament then voted down four of Ahmadinejad's nominees on the grounds of incompetence, beginning a series of clashes over presidential appointments that continued throughout Ahmadinejad's tenure. As they settled into office, Ahmadinejad's cabinet members began to purge reformists and centrists from their ministries and to appoint hard-liners. Ahmadinejad also began to implement some of the populist economic policies he had campaigned on, increasing public spending and driving down interest rates. These actions produced sharp criticism from economists and additional clashes with parliament.

Ahmadinejad's cronyism, partisanship, and controversial policies sparked growing criticism from members of all political factions. Even Khamenei seemed concerned, creating two new mechanisms to oversee Ahmadinejad's performance. As the December 2006 elections for municipal councils and the Assembly of Experts approached, most centrists gravitated to the reformist camp, and Rafsanjani and

Khatami made a series of joint campaign appearances. The new reformist-centrist coalition did fairly well in the election, while conservatives backed by Ahmadinejad did poorly. Rafsanjani was the big winner, taking the largest number of votes in the Assembly of Experts election and later becoming chairman of this powerful body. Students, women, and labor leaders staged frequent demonstrations during this period, often criticizing Ahmadinejad. Another important trend was the emergence of new, ethnically based terrorist movements in Iran's Arab, Kurdish, and Baluch regions, which killed hundreds of people. Iran charged that the United States, Britain, and Israel were behind these movements.

In the months leading up to the March–April 2008 parliamentary election, the conservative camp split into pro- and anti-Ahmadinejad factions. The anti-Ahmadinejad faction was led by Ali Larijani, a Khamenei protégé who had emerged as a major critic of Ahmadinejad. This faction produced its own list of candidates, though many also were backed by the pro-Ahmadinejad faction. Two reformist factions also produced lists of candidates, though many were vetoed by the Guardian Council. The reformists did quite poorly in the election, though this was due partly to the vetoing of candidates and other restrictions. In May the new parliament overwhelmingly elected Larijani as its speaker, indicating that the anti-Ahmadinejad conservatives had done quite well and setting up a new round of confrontation between this body and President Ahmadinejad.

Factional tension continued to grow after the parliamentary election, fueled by mounting inflation, scandals involving cronies of Ahmadinejad, and a harsh crackdown on violations of Islamic cultural restrictions. As the June 12, 2009, presidential election approached, speculation grew about which reformists would run and whether a prominent conservative would challenge Ahmadinejad. In October, Mehdi Karrubi, who had placed third in the 2005 election, announced his candidacy. After publicly encouraging former prime minister Musavi to enter the race, Mohammad Khatami announced his candidacy in January, energizing the reformist camp and alarming conservatives. Musavi then announced his candidacy in March, leading Khatami to withdraw and support Musavi. Despite widespread opposition to Ahmadinejad, no strong conservative candidate emerged to challenge him.

In the weeks leading up to the election, hard-liners repeatedly harassed Karrubi and Musavi and undermined their efforts to campaign. Khamenei made several comments clearly encouraging Iranians to vote for Ahmadinejad. Nevertheless, popular support for the two reformist candidates visibly surged before the election. However, when official results were announced, Ahmadinejad had 62 percent of the vote, Musavi had 34 percent, the pragmatic conservative Mohsen Rezaie had only 2 percent, and Karrubi had only 1 percent.

Reformists and their supporters erupted in fury. Reformist leaders charged that the election had been flagrantly rigged. Thousands of protesters poured into the streets, chanting anti-Ahmadinejad slogans. Much larger demonstrations occurred in the following days, with hundreds of thousands protesting and clashing with the security forces on June 15 and 18. People also began chanting "God is great" and other slogans from their rooftops in the evenings in support of the protests. On June 19, Khamenei made a speech lauding the election as a "divine assessment" and warning that further protests would not be tolerated. The security forces brutally attacked protesters on the following day, killing at least ten, injuring dozens, and arresting hundreds. Additional protests and violent clashes occurred during the following week but then gradually died down. Reports soon emerged that imprisoned protesters were being tortured, raped, and killed. Estimates of the death toll during these events ranged from thirty-two to seventy-three. Some 4,000 were arrested, including many leading reformists, journalists, and intellectuals. Hard-liners began a campaign to blame the unrest on foreign forces.

Although protests over the election results gradually died down, a series of broader protests occurred in the following months at regime-sponsored events, when the security forces could not easily ban marches or disperse crowds. The first of these occurred on July 17, when Rafsanjani gave a Friday prayer sermon that was attended by tens of thousands of people—far larger than the usual crowd. Rafsanjani thereafter was prevented from leading Friday prayers. Additional protests of this sort occurred in the following months on Ahmadinejad's inauguration day, Jerusalem Day, the anniversary of the US embassy seizure, and Students' Day. Reformist leaders played a minimal role in organizing these protests, and the protesters increasingly chanted slogans denouncing Supreme Leader Khamenei and the Islamic regime itself. In late December this political crisis remained unresolved and Iran's future was very uncertain.

POLITICAL ENVIRONMENT

Geography

Iran is located in southwest Asia, bounded to the north by the Caucasus region, the Caspian Sea, and the steppes of Central Asia; to the south by the Persian Gulf and the Gulf of Oman; to the west by Turkey and Iraq; and to the east by Afghanistan and Pakistan. It is bisected by two high mountain ranges: the Zagros, running from the northwestern part of the country to the southeast; and the Alborz, running from west to east, looping below the Caspian Sea. The Zagros range creates natural borders in western and southern Iran, marking the boundary between Iran's predominantly Persian population and its Arab neighbors. The Alborz range and the Caucasus Mountains create natural borders in northern and northwestern Iran, separating it from the various ethnic groups that inhabit the Caucasus and Central Asia. These natural borders have helped preserve Iran's unique identity through the ages, despite its vulnerable location at the crossroads of Central Asia, South Asia, and the Middle East. Today they offer ample protection to the large majority of Iran's population located in the northern and central parts of the country from the various hostile powers located to the west and south.

The central region of Iran, bordered by the Zagros and Alborz ranges, is a high, arid plateau. The eastern part of this plateau features two large, barren deserts. The remainder supports a limited amount of agriculture and includes Tehran, Isfahan, and Mashad, three of Iran's largest cities. North of the Alborz lies the lush Caspian coastal region, where rainfall is plentiful enough to support extensive rice cultivation, along with many other crops. Across the Zagros to the southwest lies Iran's Khuzestan Province, a hot coastal plain that features Iran's only large river (the Karun), marshes, and most of the country's oil and gas reserves. The Caspian and Persian Gulf coastal regions support fishing, shipping, and tourism. Most of Iran's border areas are lightly populated and have rough terrain, so smuggling is common in these areas.

Ethnicity and Religion

Iranian society is ethnically diverse. Persians are the largest ethnic group, comprising 51 percent of the total population and dominating the central and eastern parts of the country. Persians are an Indo-European people whose language is based on Sanskrit, making it distantly related to most European languages. Most Iranians speak the Farsi dialect of Persian, which contains many Arabic and Turkish loanwords but nevertheless is closely related to Tajik, Dari, and other Persian dialects spoken in Central and South Asia. Iran's Kurdish, Lur, and Baluch minorities are related to Persians and speak their own Persian dialects. Kurds comprise 7 percent of the population and live in the mountainous northwestern part of the country, bordering on the Kurdish regions of Turkey and Iraq. Lurs comprise 2 percent and live south of the Kurds, mainly in Luristan Province. Baluch comprise another 2 percent and live in the southeastern province of Sistan and Baluchestan, bordering on the Baluch regions of Afghanistan and Pakistan.

Iran's remaining population consists mainly of Turkic peoples. The second-largest ethnic group is Azeri Turks, who comprise 24 percent of the population and speak the Azeri Turkic dialect. Iran's Azeris live mainly in the northwestern provinces of East and West Azerbaijan, which border the country of Azerbaijan, whose population also is largely Azeri. In recent decades, many Iranian Azeris have moved to Tehran and other cities outside of the northwest, and there has been considerable intermarriage between Azeris and Persians. Another 2 percent of the population are Turkmen, who live in northeastern Iran in areas bordering on Turkmenistan. Qashqai Turks comprise about 1 percent of the population and live in southern Iran, around the city of Shiraz.

Iran has a small ethnic Arab population that comprises about 3 percent of the total population and lives in the southwestern province of Khuzestan and along the Persian Gulf coast. Another 2 percent of Iranians are Armenian, and 1 percent are Assyrian, living mainly in Tehran and other major cities.

Some 89 percent of Iranians are Shi'a Muslims—adherents of a minority branch of Islam who believe that leadership of the Islamic community should have passed from Mohammad to his son-in-law, Ali, and his descendants. Shi'a Islam differs from the majority Sunni branch in having an elaborate clerical hierarchy, following a different school of Islamic law, and observing somewhat different rituals and practices. Iran's Safavid rulers made Shi'a Islam the country's official religion in the 1500s, establishing a close connection between this sect and Iran that continues today. Iraq and Bahrain also have Shi'a majorities, and the most important Shi'a holy sites are located in Iraq. Lebanon, Saudi Arabia, Pakistan, and several other nearby countries have significant Shi'a minorities, which maintain close religious and political ties with their coreligionists in Iran. Thus, Iran's Shi'a identity sets it apart from most other countries in the region and creates suspicions—which are sometimes justified—that it is meddling in its neighbors' internal affairs.

Almost all of Iran's Persian and Turkic population are Shi'a. Some 9 percent of Iranians are Sunni Muslims, including the Baluch and most Kurds. Iran's Armenian and Assyrian populations are Christian, mainly following the Armenian, Nestorian, or Chaldean rites. Iran has had a small Jewish population for over 2,500 years, though most have emigrated to Israel or the United States in recent decades. Iran also has a small population of Zoroastrians, whose faith was predominant in the country before the introduction of Islam. Finally, a small number of Iranians follow the Baha'i sect, which emerged in Iran in the mid-1800s. Baha'is are considered apostates by many Shi'a, producing frequent persecution and leading many to emigrate. By contrast, Iran's Christians, Jews, and Zoroastrians are free to practice their faiths and follow their own customs in matters of family law, and the constitution reserves several seats in parliament for them. Almost all Iranian Jews, Zoroastrians, and Baha'is are ethnic Persians.

Social Change

Driven mainly by economic development, the structure of Iranian society has changed tremendously since the mid-nineteenth century.

Roughly half of Iran's population consisted of tribal nomads in the early nineteenth century, typically living in tents, tending flocks of sheep and goats, migrating between summer and winter pastures, and maintaining distinctive tribal customs, dress, and folklore. Most nomads lived in extended-family groups organized into loose tribal federations headed by *khans* (chiefs), which protected and exercised authority over their members and maintained considerable independence from the central government. A large majority of Iran's nomads gradually became sedentary in the late nineteenth and twentieth centuries, as economic development provided better opportunities for them in agriculture or in towns and cities and as the Pahlavi shahs forcibly disarmed and settled them. In the early twenty-first century, only about 2 percent of Iranians are fully nomadic, though considerably more maintain cultural ties to their tribal origins.

Most other Iranians were landless peasants in the early nineteenth century, generally working on agricultural estates and living at, or near, the subsistence level. As Iran's economy developed and provided new employment opportunities, many of these peasants moved to towns and cities seeking better living standards. This rural-urban migration was especially rapid in the 1960s and 1970s, when oil revenue transformed the economy and the shah's land-reform program pushed many peasants off the land. As a result, Iran's urban population grew from about 20 percent of the total in 1900 to 34 percent in 1960, 50 percent in 1980, and 66 percent today. About 10 percent of the country's population—some 7 million people—live in Tehran, the capital; another 10 percent live in the Tehran metropolitan area; and the cities of Mashad, Tabriz, Isfahan, and Shiraz each have more than 2 million residents.

Economic development also has thoroughly transformed the structure of urban society in Iran. Modern industrial plants began to emerge in Iran's major cities and in the oil-producing areas of Khuzestan Province in the first few decades of the twentieth century, creating an industrial working class. In the same era, the expansion of the state bureaucracy, the creation of a modern educational system, and the growth of services such as journalism and banking began to create a modern middle class, which differed from the traditional middle class of shopkeepers and artisans in having Western-style education and a more cosmopolitan outlook. In the post–World War II era, a modern upper class of businessmen, investors, and cronies of the shah emerged, distinguished from the traditional upper class of wealthy landowners also by its Western education and relatively cosmopolitan outlook.

These changes in the structure of Iranian society shaped the main contours of Iranian politics during the twentieth century. The gradual emergence of a modern middle class propelled the constitutional movement of 1906, Reza Shah's modernization efforts, and the various secular nationalist and leftist movements that emerged from the 1940s through the 1960s. The industrial working class also helped propel these nationalist and leftist movements. The modern upper class became the shah's main base of support in the 1960s and 1970s, though it was not strong or loyal enough to keep him in power. The emergence of these modern classes and their prominent role in both the shah's regime and the secular opposition increasingly aggravated Iran's traditional classes, creating tensions that led to the 1978–1979 revolution and gave the revolution its Islamist character. The extensive rural–urban migration of the 1960s and 1970s brought large numbers of poorly educated, deeply religious people into Iran's cities, providing a large mass of foot soldiers for the revolution and further strengthening its Islamist character. Many members of the modern upper and middle classes emigrated to Western countries after the revolution, creating a large, very successful Iranian diaspora community.

Two other social trends have had a big impact on Iranian politics in recent decades. First, a sharp drop in Iran's infant mortality rate and a persistently high birth rate created a large "baby boom" generation born in the 1970s and 1980s, before Iran's leaders embraced family planning, that came of age in the 1990s and 2000s. These young Iranians generally are better educated than older Iranians and better connected to the outside world through the Internet and contacts with Iranians living abroad. They are also too young to have been caught up in the idealism of the 1978–1979 revolution and the early years of the Islamic regime, experiencing instead the economic stagnation and cultural restrictions that followed; so they are generally less loyal to the Islamic regime and more interested in reforming or abolishing it than older Iranians. This large cohort of young Iranians provided the main social base for the reformist movement that emerged in the late 1990s. Second, rapid increases in educational opportunities for women both before and after the revolution have led women to become increasingly involved in politics in recent years. Many Iranian women resent the restrictions imposed on them under the Islamic regime, so women also strongly supported the reformist movement in the late 1990s.

Political Culture

Iran's history and social structure have shaped its political culture in several important ways.

First, Iran's long, rich history and the many instances of foreign intervention during the nineteenth and twentieth centuries have made most Iranians deeply nationalistic and wary of foreign interference. These sentiments produced strong support for nationalist movements in Iran from the late 1940s through the early 1960s and led many Iranians to oppose the last shah on the grounds that he was a puppet of foreign powers. The Islamist movements that emerged in the 1960s and 1970s emphasized similar themes, expressing their opposition to foreign influence and the shah's foreign connections in language that ranged from the anti-imperialism of the Mojahedin-e Khalq to the culturally oriented, often xenophobic statements of many traditionalists. These themes have remained central to Iran's foreign policy discourse ever since the establishment of the Islamic republic.

Second, Shi'a Islam's strong emphasis on martyrdom and social justice has been a recurring theme in Iran's modern history. Even before the upsurge of Islamist movements in the 1970s, figures like Mohammad Mosaddeq were widely revered by secularists and Islamists alike for their willingness to make sacrifices for a just cause. Martyrdom and morality then became central motifs in the discourse of the 1978–1979 revolution and the Islamic regime it spawned, leading many Iranians willingly to sacrifice their lives during the revolution and in the Iran-Iraq War.

Another recurring theme in Iran's modern history has been an emphasis on political pluralism, reflecting not only the growing importance of the modern middle class but also the country's Shi'a traditions, which include a tendency to support multiple religious leaders and norms of legalism, inclusiveness, and consensus building among the clergy. This emphasis on pluralism has led all major popular movements in modern Iran to claim to speak in the name of the Iranian people and to advocate political freedom, constitutionalism, and representative institutions. These pluralistic themes have been stressed not only by avowedly democratic, secularist movements like the National Front but also by Islamist movements like the Liberation Movement, Khatami's reformist movement, and even the revolutionary Islamist followers of Ayatollah Khomeini. As a result, before the election crisis of 2009, Iran's Islamic regime featured an unusual mixture of authoritarian and democratic features, including a powerful repressive apparatus and institutions that ensure clerical control but also relatively free elections, a fairly open political climate, and frequently intense contestation among the diverse factions of the Islamist elite.

Despite the many pressures on Iranian society since the early nineteenth century, family bonds remain very strong and have a substantial impact on patterns of social and political organization. As Iran's economy has developed and its citizens have become more mobile, these family bonds have been replaced in part by connections based on childhood friendships or relationships established in universities or seminaries. These family bonds and other close connections have a considerable impact on Iranian politics. Politicians often rely heavily on their children, siblings, and old friends for assistance, and the latter benefit considerably from these connections. Political organizations also rely heavily on connections of this sort, giving them a personalistic character. Iranians judge politicians very much on the basis of family background and other personal connections and rely on their own relatives and close friends for connections and advice. As a result, Iranian politics has strong patrimonial and clannish tendencies, and the country's civil society institutions are fairly weak.

Finally, political culture often differs considerably from one segment of Iranian society to another, making it difficult to speak of a single Iranian political culture. Most importantly, the political culture of the modern segment of Iranian society differs substantially from that of traditionalists, who are generally more religious, less educated, less cosmopolitan, more reliant on personal connections, and often deeply concerned about the decline of Islam and the spread of Western culture and values in Iran. The sharply different outlooks of the modern and traditional segments of society were a fundamental cause of the 1978–1979 revolution and have remained the most important theme in Iranian politics since the revolution, underlying the clashes between Islamic leftists and conservatives in the 1980s, centrists and conservatives in the early 1990s, and reformists and conservatives in the late 1990s and 2000s. The large Iranian diaspora community that emerged after the revolution is especially modernist in its outlook and very antagonistic toward the conservatives.

Another important political cultural division exists between younger and older Iranians. As discussed above, Iranians born during the baby boom of the 1970s and 1980s are better educated, more cosmopolitan, less committed to the Islamic regime, and more deeply affected by the economic stagnation and cultural restrictions of recent decades. These young Iranians strongly favor increased political and cultural freedom and greater economic opportunity. While many are quite religious, they generally oppose extensive clerical involvement in government. They also have little interest in socialism and other secular ideologies. Most young Iranians are strongly attracted to Western culture, which they follow avidly on the Internet and satellite television. A large majority at first enthusiastically supported President Khatami but then grew disillusioned with the reformists' failures. Consequently, while most young people strongly favor reform, many are apathetic and cynical about politics. Indeed, in one of the great ironies of the Islamic regime, many young Iranians today dream of emigrating to the West.

Economic Conditions

Iran's economy was based mainly on agriculture before the 1920s, though trade and the manufacture of textiles, carpets, and other handicrafts were important activities as well. Iran's large nomadic population produced most of the country's meat and dairy products, using land unsuitable for farming. Oil was first discovered in Iran in 1901 and began to play an important role in the economy in the 1920s and 1930s, when it helped finance Reza Shah's development efforts. Reza Shah's key economic achievements during this period included building a nationwide network of roads and railroads; establishing factories to produce textiles, sugar, shoes, cement, and other products; creating a modern banking system; and establishing a modern educational system that produced a new class of modern businessmen, managers, and public officials.

Iran's oil revenue began to grow rapidly in the late 1950s as a result of production increases and the higher profits resulting from the 1954 oil agreement. Oil prices then increased eightfold from 1970 to 1974, creating another huge increase in oil revenue. Iran's oil revenue went into the state treasury, where it helped finance both the state's normal operating budget and a series of five-year development plans. Through these mechanisms, oil revenue generated a huge expansion of Iran's economy, with real gross domestic product (GDP) growing by an average of 9.8 percent annually in the 1960s and 12.1 percent in 1970 to 1976, after which it stagnated for several years and then declined sharply as the revolution unfolded. Although much of this growth was in the oil and gas sector, the manufacturing sector grew by an average of 11.5 percent annually in the 1960s and 16.4 percent in 1970 to 1976, when large steel mills, copper mills, automobile assembly plants, and other factories were built. The service sector grew by an annual average of 8.1 percent in the 1960s and 18.3 percent in 1970 to 1976, while the agricultural sector grew by an average of only 3.6 percent and 7.3 percent annually in these periods. As discussed above, the oil boom also had several adverse consequences that helped fuel the 1978–1979 revolution, including higher inflation, shortages, corruption, and rural-urban migration.

The revolution and the 1980–1988 war with Iraq together had a devastating impact on Iran's economy. Oil production fell sharply and domestic consumption of oil products grew substantially. As a result, by 1981 Iran's oil revenue had fallen to 16 percent of its prerevolution high—reached in 1976—despite much higher oil prices, and it remained below 43 percent of this high throughout the 1980s and below 61 percent of it in the 1990s. This sharp decline in oil revenue and higher wartime military spending substantially reduced public investment. The revolution and the war also sharply reduced private investment, damaged production facilities and infrastructure, disrupted foreign borrowing and imports of critical goods, and led many entrepreneurs and skilled workers to emigrate. These factors produced a 21 percent decline in Iran's real GDP from its peak in 1976 to its level in 1988. With the high birth rates of the 1980s, Iran's real GDP per capita fell by 48 percent between 1976 and 1988. In 2009 it finally returned to its 1976 level.

Since the late 1980s, Iran's leaders have carried out a series of five-year development plans whose main goal has been to stimulate economic growth and employment by liberalizing the economy and expanding non-oil industries. None of these plans have been very successful.

The first plan covered the period from 1989 to 1993 and was drawn up in consultation with the International Monetary Fund. It faced strong opposition from Islamic leftists in parliament, who feared that privatization, subsidy cuts, exchange-rate liberalization, and tight monetary policy would hurt the poor. Most of its key goals were never achieved. In addition, the Rafsanjani government undertook massive foreign borrowing and a sharp expansion of imports in conjunction with the first plan, putting severe pressure on Iran's exchange rate and foreign reserves and driving inflation higher.

The Islamic leftists lost control of parliament in 1992, raising hopes that economic reform might move forward. The second development plan (1994–1999) had very ambitious objectives, including exchange-rate liberalization, banking reform, fiscal and monetary restraint, subsidy cuts, and privatization. However, opposition from the conservative-controlled parliament and lower world oil prices prevented implementation of many of the second plan's objectives. As a result, Iran's economy stagnated during the second-plan period, barely growing in per capita terms.

Most Islamic leftists became much more moderate during the mid-1990s, embracing not only political liberalization but also economic reform. Consequently, after his election in 1997, President Khatami continued to implement the reforms embodied in the second plan. His main economic achievement was to adopt a unified, floating exchange-rate system. The Khatami government also drew up a third development plan (2000–2004), which called for further privatization, subsidy cuts, increased foreign investment, an expansion of non-oil exports, and efforts to increase tax collection and reduce bureaucracy. However, conservatives blocked key elements of the third plan before the reformists gained control over parliament in 2000 and worked to undermine the plan as it was being implemented. Moreover, many of the plan's goals were unrealistic. As a result, the third plan also failed to achieve most of its objectives. Nevertheless, due partly to increased oil revenue, Iran's economic performance was substantially better during the third-plan period than in previous years, with real per capita growth averaging 3.8 percent and inflation averaging 16 percent during 2000 to 2004. However, unemployment remained close to 12 percent of the workforce.

President Ahmadinejad had campaigned on an economic populist platform before the June 2005 election. Once in office he quickly began to implement this platform, sharply increasing public spending, cutting interest rates far below the inflation rate, maintaining huge consumer subsidies, and financing these efforts by drawing down Iran's rapidly growing oil windfall. He fired several top officials who warned that his policies would cause inflation and dismantled the Management and Planning Organization, which had overseen Iran's macroeconomic and development policy for decades. As predicted, Ahmadinejad's actions produced sharply higher inflation, which grew from 13 percent in 2005 to a peak of 29 percent in the fall of 2008. In an effort to rein in subsidies, Ahmadinejad unveiled a gasoline rationing plan in 2007 that sparked nationwide rioting, forcing him to withdraw the plan. When oil prices dropped sharply in late 2008 and early 2009, Ahmadinejad was forced to cut back his spending programs, adding to popular unrest.

POLITICAL STRUCTURE

The 1978–1979 revolution swept away Iran's monarchy and most other political institutions of the shah's regime. Ayatollah Khomeini then appointed Mehdi Bazargan to head a transitional government, whose main responsibilities were to

oversee the development of a new constitution and govern Iran until this constitution could be implemented. However, radical Islamists created a series of additional institutions during this period that overshadowed the transitional
government to such an extent that many observers began to describe them as a
"parallel government." These additional institutions included the Revolutionary
Council, revolutionary courts, revolutionary committees, and the Islamic Revolutionary Guard Corps. Bazargan resigned largely because these parallel institutions
made it impossible for him to govern effectively.

The radical Islamists gained control over the constitutional assembly and used
it to write a constitution that embodied the principle of *velayat-e faqih* (guardian-
ship of the jurist), which Khomeini had developed in his seminal book *Islamic
Government*. Under this principle, high-ranking Shi'a clerics would oversee the
state apparatus to ensure that public policy conformed with Islamic law, though
they would not necessarily serve in executive positions. The new constitution was
approved in a December 1979 popular referendum. The Revolutionary Council
was soon dissolved. The revolutionary courts and committees were integrated into
the new judicial and security apparatuses. The Revolutionary Guard Corps was
greatly expanded, eventually including its own navy and air force and a large paramilitary force, the *Basij* (Mobilization).

The 1979 constitution created two key institutions that enabled Shi'a clerics to
oversee the state, as envisioned by Khomeini. First, it created the office of *faqih*
(jurist), commonly known as the (supreme) leader (*rahbar*), which would be occupied by a *marja-e taqlid* (source of emulation), the highest rank of the Shi'a clergy.
The leader would be chosen and overseen by the Assembly of Experts (*Majles-e
Khobregan*), a popularly elected council of Shi'a clerics. The leader was empowered
to set general policy guidelines, supervise policy implementation, appoint the
head of the judiciary and the six clerical members of the Council of Guardians
(see below), dismiss the president, oversee the armed forces, and declare war and
peace. This position was created for Khomeini, who was succeeded by Ayatollah
Ali Khamenei in June 1989. Khomeini and Khamenei gradually built up a large
staff, including senior policy advisors, representatives in all significant government
and religious bodies, an office to oversee Friday prayer sermons, and the heads of
various parastatal foundations and organizations. Second, the constitution created
the Council of Guardians (*Shura-ye Negahban*), consisting of six Shi'a clerics and
six laypeople empowered to interpret the constitution, judge the compatibility of
legislation with Islamic law and with the constitution, and supervise elections. The
six lay members are selected by parliament from nominees proposed by the head
of the judiciary.

The constitution also created a directly elected president and unicameral parliament, whose seats are allocated to Iran's provinces in proportion to population
size. In addition, five seats are reserved for Iran's Christian, Jewish, and Zoroastrian

minorities. As mentioned above, the Council of Guardians is empowered to oversee presidential and parliamentary elections, which are held every four years. In practice, the council vetoes many minor candidates for the presidency and parliament and all candidates who do not fully support the Islamic regime, but it generally leaves enough candidates for each position to ensure genuine competition among the main factions that support the regime. It also generally has not interfered in the voting process itself, though the 2009 election seems to have been manipulated extensively. In addition, the Council of Guardians is empowered to veto parliamentary legislation and does so quite often, limiting the influence of parliament and often creating severe tensions. Finally, the constitution also created the position of prime minister, who would be chosen by parliament, and it left unresolved many issues regarding the division of responsibility between the president and prime minister.

During the 1980s, it became increasingly apparent that the many checks and balances embodied in the constitution were producing governmental paralysis. Ayatollah Khomeini tried to eliminate one source of this paralysis in February 1988 by creating the Council for the Discernment of Expediency (*Majma-e Tashkhis-e Maslehat-e Nezam*), which was empowered to resolve disputes over legislation between parliament and the Guardian Council. Although the Expediency Council proved fairly effective, disputes continued to emerge between these two bodies; and several other checks and balances continued to hinder effective government. Another problem that became increasingly apparent as Khomeini's health deteriorated in the late 1980s was that none of the Assembly of Experts' preferred candidates to succeed Khomeini met the constitutional criterion that the leader must be a *marja-e taqlid*.

To resolve these problems, Khomeini created a panel in April 1989 to study and revise the constitution. This panel made several major changes. It eliminated the position of prime minister, concentrating executive authority in the hands of the president. It spelled out the responsibilities of the Expediency Council. It eliminated the leader's ability to dismiss the president and the requirement that the leader be a *marja*. It also created a Supreme National Security Council to oversee foreign policy. These changes were approved in an August 1989 popular referendum.

The head of the judiciary, who is appointed by the leader, has far-reaching powers, including the power to appoint the prosecutor-general, all judges, and all Supreme Court justices; the power to draft legislation affecting the legal system; and oversight over all aspects of the judicial system. The minister of justice, who is chosen by the president from a list of nominees provided by the judiciary head, is responsible mainly for administrative matters. The constitution bans torture; it guarantees freedom of the press and assembly, except when this violates "the principles of Islam"; and it allows Sunni Muslims and the Christian, Jewish, and Zoroastrian communities (though not Baha'is) to practice their own faiths freely and be governed by their faiths in divorce, probate, and other personal-status matters. There are special courts for cases involving the security forces, government officials, the clergy, the press, and political or national security cases.

Iran's security forces include the regular armed forces, the Revolutionary Guard Corps, the Basij, the Ministry of Intelligence and Security (MOIS), and the Law Enforcement Forces (LEF), which consist of the national police, prison guards, border guards, and rural paramilitary forces. The MOIS is responsible to the president; the other branches of the security forces are responsible to the leader. The Revolutionary Guard and Basij have specialized units for crowd control, and their personnel are specially selected and indoctrinated to strengthen their loyalty to the Islamic regime. After MOIS personnel were implicated in a series of murders in 1998, the Khatami government purged many hard-liners from this ministry, though under Ahmadinejad many have been reinstated and reformists have been purged from this body. The Revolutionary Guard, Basij, and LEF units sometimes work with informal gangs of conservative-backed thugs to attack reformists or opponents of the Islamic regime.

The 1979 constitution created five levels of regional and local government: provinces, subprovinces, districts, cities, and villages. It also called for popularly elected councils to govern these bodies. This latter provision of the constitution was not implemented until 1999, after Khatami and the reformists pressed for it in the hope that these councils would serve as training and recruitment mechanisms for the democratic regime they hoped to establish. Since that time, elections have been held every four years for municipal councils in cities and villages. These councils appoint mayors for their jurisdictions and representatives to provincial, subprovincial, and district councils. Provincial governors-general are appointed by the Interior Ministry and, in turn, appoint the heads of subprovinces and districts.

The constitution also allowed for the establishment of political parties, provided they support and conform to the principles of the Islamic regime. This provision also was not implemented until the late 1990s, though several partylike organizations were allowed to operate. Legislation authorizing the creation of parties was adopted in 1998, and many parties emerged in the following years. In 2009 the main reformist parties were the Islamic Iran Participation Party (*Hezb-e Mosharakat-e Iran-e Islami*), Combatant Clerics Association (*Majma-e Ruhaniyun-e Mobarez*), National Trust Party (*Hezb-e Etemad-e Melli*), Mojahedin of the Islamic Revolution Organization (*Sazman-e Mojahedin-e Enqelab-e Islami*), and Executives of Construction Party (*Hezb-e Kargozaran-e Sazendegi*), which had close ties to former president Rafsanjani. The main conservative parties were the Militant Clerics Association (*Jameh-ye Ruhaniyat-e Mobarez*), Islamic Iran Developers' Council, and Coalition of Islamic Societies. The Liberation Movement and several other Islamic modernist and secular nationalist parties were officially outlawed but

allowed to operate on a limited basis, though their members were frequently harassed. None of these parties are particularly popular or effective.

In addition to these parties, several other important civil society organizations
exist in Iran. The Office for Consolidating Unity (*Daftar-e Takhim-e Vahdat*) is a reformist student organization. The Labor House (*Khaneh-ye Kargar*) is a pro-
reformist, government-sponsored labor federation. The Supporters of the Party of
God (*Ansar-e Hezbollah*) is a hard-line conservative vigilante group created in the
early 1990s mainly to attack the reformists. In addition, a variety of other professional, student, women's, and religious organizations exist, with some supporting
either the reformists or conservatives and others remaining aloof from politics.

In addition, a wide range of parties and civil society organizations exist among
the large Iranian exile communities living in North America, Europe, and elsewhere. The most important is the Mojahedin-e Khalq, which had several thousand
guerrillas living in a base guarded by Iraqi forces in 2009, as well as secret networks inside Iran and a large network of supporters in other countries. Various exile monarchist, nationalist, and leftist organizations exist as well, though none are
very important. Another aspect of civil society in Iran is the news and entertainment media. From mid-1979 through the 1980s, Iran's newspapers were heavily
restricted, providing one-sided news coverage and a narrow range of opinions.
This began to change in the early 1990s, when the Rafsanjani government allowed several critical newspapers and magazines to appear. The print media flourished during the first few years of Khatami's presidency, with some newspapers
going so far as to accuse top officials of complicity in murder. However, hard-liners in the judiciary began to crack down on the press, closing the most critical
newspapers and imprisoning or assaulting editors and journalists. This crackdown
increased sharply after the February 2000 parliamentary elections, when dozens of
newspapers were closed. Since then the judiciary has generally allowed one or
more mildly critical newspapers to appear at any given time but shuts them or arrests staff members if they go too far.

The domestic radio and television media are controlled by Islamic Republic of
Iran Broadcasting, a state agency based in the leader's office. Its programming is
narrow and dull and generally reflects the views of the leader. However, many Iranians listen to Persian-language radio broadcasts beamed to Iran by Britain,
Israel, the United States, and several other countries or watch the many Persian-
language satellite television stations broadcast to Iran from abroad. These broadcasts provide a wide range of programming, giving many Iranians access to diverse
sources of news, commentary, and entertainment. The government makes some
effort to block these foreign broadcasts by jamming them and outlawing satellite
antennas, but these measures have little effect. Iranians also increasingly use the Internet through Internet cafes or computers in their homes or offices. This gives

them access to the many Persian-language websites featuring news, commentary, and entertainment, as well as e-mail contact with friends and relatives living abroad. The government tries to regulate access to the Internet, with little success.

Before the 2009 election crisis, Iran's Islamic regime contained some democratic elements and was more representative than many other regimes in the region. The Council of Guardians sharply restricted elections for the presidency, parliament, and other bodies, but these elections offered voters considerable opportunity to express their preferences, both by voting and by abstaining. The formal powers of these elected bodies were constrained by the Guardian Council and other institutions and their authority was overshadowed by that of the leader, but they nevertheless exercised substantial influence, both formally and informally. The judiciary and much of the security apparatus were not responsible to popularly elected bodies, but repression was not severe. Political parties, the media, and other civil society institutions could not express opposition to the Islamic regime and were restricted in other ways, but they were more open and more numerous than in many neighboring countries. Indeed, Iranians could express their views quite openly, and the country's leaders clearly were concerned about, and responsive to, trends in public opinion.

These democratic features of the Islamic regime were suspended and perhaps permanently eliminated during the crisis that began with the 2009 presidential election. This election seems to have been manipulated extensively, raising strong doubts about the prospects for future elections. Repression had increased substantially by late 2009, with thousands of protesters languishing in prison, torture widespread, all reformist and centrist leaders still in prison or severely restricted in their actions, and civil society organizations rendered largely impotent. A climate of fear gripped many Iranians. The country's conservative leaders seemed intent on imposing their vision of an Islamic regime on the populace. Above all, Supreme Leader Khamenei was orchestrating this process, relying heavily on the security forces and his bickering allies in the executive and legislative branches of government. It remained unclear what sort of political structure would emerge from this crisis.

POLITICAL DYNAMICS

Iran has changed substantially since the Islamic regime was established in 1979.

The early 1980s was a period of revolutionary social transformation. The radical Islamist leadership undertook a comprehensive effort to "Islamicize" Iranian society in this period, restructuring the country's laws and political institutions; turning schools, religious institutions, and the media into instruments of indoctrination; and forcing all Iranians to observe strict Islamic standards of dress and behavior. To accomplish this transformation, the radicals sought to mobilize their supporters with inflammatory rhetoric and dramatic actions like the US embassy hostage crisis and the war with Iraq. They also had to neutralize not only their political opponents but also many secularized Iranians, who strongly opposed their efforts. As a result, repression was fairly high during this period, though it did not approach the levels reached in Russia and China after their revolutions. Although many Iranians opposed the Islamic regime, many others supported it, giving it a populist character.

Much of the revolutionary fervor that animated this period disappeared in the mid-1980s, and popular unrest grew considerably as a result of the war with Iraq, continuing repression, and economic deterioration. When Rafsanjani became president in 1989, he responded to these changes by initiating a period of moderation. His strategy was to reduce unrest by revitalizing the economy and loosening cultural restrictions while keeping the political system largely intact. As discussed above, opposition first from Islamic leftists and then from conservatives blocked many of Rafsanjani's economic reforms, producing anemic economic growth in the early and mid-1990s.

Rafsanjani's failure to revitalize the economy led many Iranians to conclude that more extensive change was necessary, though relatively few wanted to eliminate the Islamic regime altogether. In 1997 this discontent led many Iranians to support the candidacy of Mohammad Khatami, who advocated fundamental change in the nature of the regime. In addition, two important societal changes helped pave the way for Khatami's victory. First, the baby-boom generation mentioned above had begun to come of age by the mid-1990s, producing a large cohort of young people who were more sophisticated than their elders and had not developed strong personal attachments to the Islamic regime by participating in the revolutionary upheaval or the war with Iraq. Second, Iranian women, who had made greater sacrifices than men under the Islamic regime and whose education levels had increased sharply, had become more politicized. The emergence of large numbers of young people and women favoring extensive reform produced a huge constituency for Khatami's reforms in 1997.

Khatami's landslide victory, the reformists' overwhelming success in the 2000 parliamentary elections, and Khatami's strong reelection in 2001 demonstrated that a large majority of Iranians wanted fundamental change. However, the conservatives still controlled key political institutions, including the position of leader, the Council of Guardians, the judiciary, and much of the security apparatus, and they used these institutions to block most of Khatami's reform efforts. As a result, many Iranians became disillusioned with Khatami and the reformists, regarding them as ineffective or even insincere in their promises of reform. The ramifications of this discontent first emerged in the 2003 municipal council elections, when sharply lower turnout by pro-reformist voters led to the defeat of most reformist candidates. Much the same happened in the 2004 parliamentary elections.

The final blow came in 2005, when Ahmadinejad defeated his reformist and centrist opponents. In the first round of voting, the three reformist candidates together took 35 percent of the vote, the centrist (Rafsanjani) took 21 percent, and the three conservatives together took only 39 percent, indicating that Ahmadinejad's victory did not signal a sharp increase in support for the conservatives. Rather, his victory was due to continuing popular discontent with the reformists, widespread opposition to Ahmadinejad's second-round opponent (Rafsanjani), and his own populist appeal.

The 2006 municipal council and Assembly of Experts elections and 2008 parliamentary elections demonstrated both that discontent with the reformists remained high and that Ahmadinejad's hard-line views and style were not very popular. The probable manipulation of the 2009 election results and the absence of reliable polls in Iran make it difficult to assess the implications of this election and the resulting political crisis. However, the country clearly was deeply polarized in late 2009, with a large bloc of Iranians strongly opposed to the views of Ahmadinejad and Supreme Leader Khamenei and increasingly opposed to the Islamic regime itself, while another large bloc continued to support the Islamic regime and the supreme leader, if not the president. It was impossible to judge the size and strength of these two blocs, leaving Iran's future quite uncertain.

FOREIGN POLICY

Before the 1978–1979 revolution, Iran was closely allied with the United States and was becoming increasingly Westernized. The various factions that seized power in 1979 generally opposed these trends but nevertheless held very different views on how Iran's foreign policy should be conducted. Consequently, disputes over foreign policy were a major focus of the power struggles that emerged after the revolution, and the character of Iran's foreign policy has closely paralleled its domestic political dynamics.

Iran's foreign policy was highly confrontational during the first decade of the Islamic regime. Although Prime Minister Bazargan wanted to change Iran's pro-Western orientation, he wanted to do so in ways that would avoid confrontation with the United States and its allies. Most of Bazargan's radical Islamist opponents were intensely anti-Western and wanted to break off relations with the United States, and many wanted violent confrontation with the West. Moreover, the radical Islamists were encouraged by their radical leftist rivals, whose anti-Western views were equally intense. As a result, the radical Islamists and radical leftists opposed Bazargan's nonconfrontational foreign policy and undercut him at every opportunity. This struggle culminated in the November 1979 seizure of the US embassy by radical Islamist students. The radical Islamists used the resulting hostage crisis to drive Bazargan from power and push Iran's foreign policy in a more confrontational direction, hoping to humiliate the United States, position Iran as the leader of a regionwide radical Islamist movement, and mobilize additional support for their efforts to carry out revolutionary social change at home.

The central focus of Iran's confrontational foreign policy during this period was hostility toward the United States, which was manifested not only in the hostage crisis, which lasted more than a year and drove US President Jimmy Carter from office, but also in harsh anti-American rhetoric and indirect attacks on US targets. Iran's leaders routinely called the United States the "great Satan" and chanted "death to America" at meetings and rallies. Realizing that Iran was too weak to attack the United States directly, its leaders undertook a variety of indirect assaults. Most importantly, they encouraged and assisted radical Islamist terrorists in Lebanon who bombed a US marine base and the US embassy (twice) in Beirut, killing some three hundred US and Lebanese citizens and taking thirteen Americans hostage, two of whom died in captivity. They also assisted terrorists who hijacked US airliners and a cruise ship, killing several Americans, and laid mines targeted at US naval vessels and US-flagged commercial ships in the Persian Gulf. The United States responded by backing Iraq in the Iran-Iraq War, attacking Iranian naval vessels in the Gulf, and presumably undertaking covert operations against the Islamic regime.

Iran also carried out or facilitated attacks against various regional and European allies of the United States during this period. Its leaders made extensive efforts to export their Islamic revolution, especially in Lebanon, where they created and assisted the radical Islamist Hizballah group, and in Bahrain, Kuwait, and Saudi Arabia. Although Iran's allies in these countries did not manage to trigger revolutions, they caused severe problems for their US-backed governments and carried out frequent attacks against Iran's enemies. In particular, Hizballah and other radical Shi'a forces attacked not only US targets in Lebanon but also Israeli occupation forces and British and French peacekeeping forces, killing hundreds, and they seized many hostages. Iranian officials repeatedly fomented unrest during the annual Hajj pilgrimage to Mecca in the mid-1980s, leaving hundreds dead and severely embarrassing the Saudi government.

Iran's biggest efforts to export revolution and foment unrest were directed at Iraq. Iranian officials made extensive efforts to trigger a Shi'a uprising in Iraq, both before and after the September 1980 Iraqi invasion, and their July 1982 invasion of Iraq was aimed at toppling its secularist government and establishing an Islamic republic. Although Iraq certainly was not a US ally, Iran claimed that it was and portrayed its invasion of Iraq in part as an effort to drive the United States and Israel out of the region.

Iran's confrontational, anti-Western posture during the 1980s left it very isolated and desperately in need of allies who could sell it arms and provide other forms of assistance. This led Iran's radical Islamist leaders to establish close relationships with several very unlikely countries. During the first few years of the Islamic regime, Iran purchased large quantities of weapons from Israel, which was the only country willing to flaunt US efforts to block the flow of US-made arms to Iran at this time. These Israeli arms sales eventually led to the 1985–1986 Iran-Contra Affair, in which Iran bought arms directly from the United States. Iran also established close relations in the early 1980s with Syria, giving it an important ally in the Arab world. This left Iran's leaders in the uncomfortable position of being closely allied with a country ruled by the same secularist Ba'th Party they were trying to overthrow in Iraq and remaining silent while Syria's leaders carried out a brutal crackdown on their Muslim Brotherhood opponents in 1982. Iran also bought large quantities of arms during this period from China and North Korea, whose Communist regimes were avowedly atheistic.

As the radical phase of the Islamic regime ended, Iran's foreign policy became increasingly contradictory, with radicals seeking to maintain a confrontational, anti-Western posture and moderates hoping to ease the country's isolation in order to concentrate on reconstruction. Iran's July 1988 agreement to stop the war with Iraq ended its most ambitious effort to export revolution and produced considerable optimism that its foreign policy would become more moderate. However, in February 1989 Ayatollah Khomeini denounced Salman Rushdie and called for Muslims to kill him. This created severe tension between Iran and Europe that lingered for many years. After Khomeini died in the summer of 1989, Iran again disrupted the Hajj pilgrimage and began a more concerted effort to assassinate Iranian exile opposition activists, which ultimately claimed dozens of victims in Europe and neighboring countries. Nevertheless, despite these hostile actions, President Rafsanjani began to make overtures to the West, apparently hoping this would facilitate his economic-reform program. Most importantly, he indicated that Iran would help gain the release of US and other hostages still being held in Lebanon in exchange for better relations with the West. The last of these hostages was released in 1992. Iran also stayed out of the 1990–1991 Gulf War and reestablished diplomatic relations with Morocco and Saudi Arabia during this period.

Iran's foreign policy remained contradictory during the mid-1990s. It maintained its close connections with Hizballah, which continued to attack Israeli occupation forces in Lebanon. Iran and Hizballah apparently cooperated in bombing the Israeli embassy and a Jewish cultural center in Argentina in 1992 and 1994 and the Khobar Towers US military complex in Saudi Arabia in 1996, killing many in each case. Iran also helped foment Shi'a unrest in Bahrain and cooperated closely with radical Islamist Palestinian organizations and the radical Islamist government in Sudan during this period. In addition, Iran's campaign of assassinating exile activists continued, and it worked to develop nuclear weapons and medium-range missiles in the mid-1990s. Nevertheless, Rafsanjani at the same time continued to make overtures to the United States, most notably by reaching an agreement in 1995 with the US oil company Conoco to develop a large Iranian natural gas field. The Clinton administration rejected Rafsanjani's overtures, blocking this agreement and expanding US economic sanctions on Iran.

An important turning point in Iran's foreign policy came in late 1996 and early 1997. After the Khobar Towers bombing, US and Saudi officials confronted Iran with evidence of its involvement and exposed a large number of Iranian intelligence officers operating abroad, making clear that they would take even harsher steps if Iran carried out additional attacks of this sort. In early 1997 a German court ruled that top Iranian officials had been involved in the 1989 assassination of four Kurdish Iranian dissidents in Germany, greatly embarrassing Iran and leading most European Union (EU) countries to withdraw their ambassadors from Iran. These two events seem to have enabled the moderates to wrest control over foreign policy from the radicals: Iran's direct involvement in terrorist attacks against Western targets and its assassinations of Iranian exiles stopped altogether in early 1997 and had not resumed by late 2009.

By the time President Khatami was elected in May 1997, many of Iran's reformists had concluded that Iran should normalize its relations with the United States and most other countries, though not with Israel. Accordingly, during his first few months in office, Khatami repeatedly called for better relations with the United States. These statements culminated in an extraordinary television interview in January 1998 in which Khatami expressed "great respect" for the American people, condemned terrorism, and again called for better ties with the United States. Most conservatives still opposed the United States and were alarmed by Khatami's actions. Supreme Leader Khamenei therefore publicly denounced Khatami's televised statement and reiterated that the United States was Iran's "enemy," indicating that he opposed rapid movement toward rapprochement. US officials at first reacted cautiously to Khatami's overtures, waiting until June 1998 to reciprocate. By this time opposition from Khamenei and his allies made it impossible for Khatami to move forward. Nevertheless, until the end of the Clinton administration, US officials made concerted efforts to improve relations with Iran.

Although Khatami did not succeed in improving Iran's relations with the United States, he did forge better relations with many other countries, continuing trends that had begun under Rafsanjani. Khatami soon negotiated an agreement with the EU under which all EU members returned their ambassadors to Iran. In September 1998 his government promised Britain it would not enforce the death threat against Salman Rushdie, eliminating a major source of tension in Iran's relations with Europe. Iran's economic ties with Europe grew rapidly, and it soon began negotiating a major trade and investment agreement with European firms.

Iran's relations with most of its neighbors improved substantially as well. In December 1997 Crown Prince Abdullah of Saudi Arabia visited Iran to attend the

Organization of the Islamic Conference summit. Iran then sent former president Rafsanjani to visit Saudi Arabia a few months later and the two countries signed agreements essentially normalizing their relations. Iran also forged better ties with most of the other Persian Gulf Arab countries, though its relationship with the United Arab Emirates remained strained over their conflicting claims to three strategically important islands in the Gulf. Iran's relations with archfoe Iraq also improved, with the two countries holding talks and exchanging their remaining prisoners of war. Iran continued to enjoy good relations with Pakistan, Turkey, and most of the countries to its north, though its relations with Azerbaijan remained strained over the latter's claims to Iran's Azeri region. The only neighbor that Iran had hostile relations with during this period was Afghanistan, which was ruled by the hard-line Sunni fundamentalist Taliban faction. The anti-Shi'a Taliban were fighting bitterly against factions in northern and western Afghanistan that had close ethnic and political ties to Iran. In August 1998 the Taliban killed several Iranians who were working with these factions, bringing the two countries to the brink of war.

Elsewhere in the region, Iran maintained its close relationship with Syria, Hizballah, and the radical Islamist Palestinian organizations Hamas and Islamic Jihad. However, at the same time it worked diligently to improve relations with Egypt, which had been severely strained since the early days of the Islamic regime, and with other moderate Arab countries. Iran's relations with Sudan became much more distant after the radical Islamist leaders of that country were deposed in 1999. Iran's relations with Israel even thawed slightly, with Khatami making several conciliatory statements and secret meetings occurring between the two sides.

Iran also continued to develop close relations with Russia and various East Asian countries under Khatami. Russia agreed to finish building a nuclear reactor in Bushehr and sold Iran large amounts of military equipment. The two countries also worked closely to support anti-Taliban guerrillas in Afghanistan. Iran expanded its commercial relations with China, Japan, and other East Asian countries as well during this period.

As the reformists grew weaker in 2000 and 2001, Ayatollah Khamenei seems to have decided that Iran could begin to improve its relations with the United States, since the reformists would no longer benefit. Accordingly, Iran made several important gestures toward the United States. Iranian officials expressed deep sympathy toward the victims of the September 11, 2001, terrorist attacks in New York and Washington. When the United States then attacked Afghanistan in an effort to destroy al-Qa'ida and its Taliban allies, Iran provided assistance to US forces. Iran also played a key role in helping the United States establish a post-Taliban government in Afghanistan.

However, as these events were unfolding, Israel intercepted a freighter carrying weapons from Iran to the Palestinian Authority, creating a strong outcry in the

United States. Soon after, US President George Bush bitterly denounced Iran, describing it as part of an "axis of evil." Iran's leaders were deeply angered by this statement, especially after the conciliatory gestures they had made, and ended most cooperation with the United States. The Bush administration kept up its harsh criticism of Iran.

Another crisis began to unfold in 2002, when evidence emerged that Iran's nuclear program was more advanced than previously known and included activities aimed at building nuclear weapons. Britain, France, and Germany then began talks with Iran over the matter, and the EU suspended negotiations on trade and investment. In 2003 Iran agreed to suspend temporarily its efforts to enrich uranium and accept other demands made by the International Atomic Energy Agency (IAEA). However, additional concerns soon emerged, and Iran announced it would resume work on enrichment. The Europeans then negotiated a second temporary agreement with Iran to suspend enrichment activities in 2004.

The election of President Ahmadinejad in June 2005 produced yet another turning point in Iran's foreign policy. In August, Iran rejected a major European proposal on the nuclear dispute and resumed enrichment work. In April 2006 Iran announced that it had mastered the enrichment process, and by late 2008 it had produced enough low-enriched uranium to make a single nuclear weapon, if enriched further. Iran also had deployed dozens of missiles capable of hitting Israel and southeastern Europe by this time, though apparently it could not yet produce nuclear warheads for these missiles. After referral by the IAEA, the UN Security Council in late 2006 voted to impose economic sanctions on Iran. It then approved additional sanctions in 2007 and 2008. Following revelations that Iran was secretly building a second enrichment facility, the Western powers began to push for a fourth set of UN sanctions in late 2009.

Iran's foreign policy became more aggressive in other ways as well during this period. Ahmadinejad and other Iranian officials regularly denounced the United States and other Western countries, and Ahmadinejad made a series of statements calling for the destruction of Israel and expressing doubt about the Holocaust. Iran continued to give extensive financial assistance and weapons to Hizballah and radical Palestinian factions. More ominously, beginning in early 2007, US officials charged that Iran had been supplying roadside bombs and other assistance to insurgents in Iraq, resulting in the deaths of hundreds of US soldiers. US personnel also arrested several Iranian operatives inside Iraq. During this same period, Iranian officials repeatedly charged that Britain, Israel, and the United States were supporting terrorist attacks inside Iran by Arab, Baluch, Kurdish, and Mojahedin-e Khalq guerrillas, suggesting that Iran's actions in Iraq may have been a response to these attacks. Numerous unconfirmed reports about US support for these guerrillas appeared in the Western press as well. US and Israeli officials repeatedly hinted that they might use military force against Iran during this period, while Iran and its allies vowed to respond severely with missiles and other means to any such attack.

In 2008, both the United States and Iran seemed to step back somewhat from their highly confrontational approach of the preceding years. Diplomats from the two countries held official, bilateral talks for the first time in almost thirty years about conditions in Iraq. Several top US officials stated that they had no intention of attacking Iran. Perhaps coincidentally, attacks on US troops in Iraq and terrorist attacks inside Iran also declined substantially during this period. After his inauguration in January 2009, US President Barack Obama made a series of conciliatory gestures toward Iran, hoping to initiate a bilateral dialog. However, Iranian officials made little effort to reciprocate. By the end of the year, Iran's relations with the West remained very tense, and the United States seemed ready to adopt a tougher approach toward Iran.

BIBLIOGRAPHY

Standard reference works on Iran are the seven-volume *Cambridge History of Iran* (Cambridge: Cambridge University Press, 1968–1991) and *Encyclopedia Iranica* (Costa Mesa, CA: Mazda Publications, 1992–present), also available at www.iranica.com. See also Ali Ansari, ed., *Politics of Modern Iran*, 4 vols. (London: Routledge, 2010). A good general survey is Homa Katouzian, *The Persians: Ancient, Mediaeval, and Modern Iran* (New Haven, CT: Yale University Press, 2009). On Iranian culture, see William O. Beeman, *Language, Status, and Power in Iran* (Bloomington: Indiana University Press, 1986). On modern Iranian politics, see Ali Gheissari and Vali Nasr, *Democracy in Iran* (New York: Oxford University Press, 2006); Fakhreddin Azimi, *The Quest for Democracy in Iran: A Century of Struggle Against Authoritarian Rule* (Cambridge, MA: Harvard University Press, 2008); and Ervand Abrahamian, *A History of Modern Iran* (Cambridge: Cambridge University Press, 2008). Useful Internet sites include http://payvand.com, http://iranmania.com, http://gooya.com, www.world-newspapers.com/iran.html, and http://lib.utexas.edu/maps/iran.html.

On Iran before the Islamic revolution, see Rouhollah K. Ramazani, *Iran's Foreign Policy, 1941–1973* (Charlottesville: University of Virginia Press, 1975); Richard Cottam, *Nationalism in Iran* (Pittsburgh, PA: University of Pittsburgh Press, 1979); Shahrough Akhavi, *Religion and Politics in Contemporary Iran* (Albany: State University of New York Press, 1980); Homa Katouzian, *The Political Economy of Modern Iran* (New York: New York University Press, 1981); Ervand Abrahamian, *Iran Between Two Revolutions* (Princeton, NJ: Princeton University Press, 1982); Asadollah Alam, *The Shah and I* (London: I. B. Tauris, 1991); Mark J. Gasiorowski, *U.S. Foreign Policy and the Shah* (Ithaca, NY: Cornell University

Press, 1991); Janet Afary, *The Iranian Constitutional Revolution, 1906–1911* (New York: Columbia University Press, 1996); Sirus Ghani, *Iran and the Rise of Reza Shah* (London: I. B. Tauris, 1998); Stephanie Cronin, ed., *The Making of Modern Iran* (London: Routledge-Curzon, 2003); and Mark Gasiorowski and Malcolm Byrne, eds., *Mohammad Mosaddeq and the 1953 Coup in Iran* (Syracuse, NY: Syracuse University Press, 2004).

On the revolution and its aftermath, see Shaul Bakhash, *The Reign of the Aya-tollahs* (New York: Basic Books, 1984); Rouhollah K. Ramazani, *Revolutionary Iran* (Baltimore: Johns Hopkins University Press, 1986); Said Amir Arjomand, *The Tur-ban for the Crown* (New York: Oxford University Press, 1988); Misagh Parsa, *Social Origins of the Iranian Revolution* (New Brunswick, NJ: Rutgers University Press, 1989); H. E. Chehabi, *Iranian Politics and Religious Modernism* (Ithaca, NY: Cornell University Press, 1990); Mansoor Moaddel, *Class, Politics, and Ideology in the Ira-nian Revolution* (New York: Columbia University Press, 1993); Ervand Abra-hamian, *Khomeinism* (Berkeley: University of California Press, 1993); Hamid Dabashi, *Theology of Discontent* (New York: New York University Press, 1993); Mehrzad Boroujerdi, *Iranian Intellectuals and the West* (Syracuse, NY: Syracuse University Press, 1996); Baqer Moin, *Khomeini: Life of the Ayatollah* (New York: St. Martin's Press, 1999); Vanessa Martin, *Creating an Islamic State* (London: I. B. Tau-ris, 2000); Nikki Keddie, *Modern Iran: Roots and Results of Revolution* (New Haven, CT: Yale University Press, 2003); Charles Kurzman, *The Unthinkable Revo-lution in Iran* (Cambridge, MA: Harvard University Press, 2004); and Abbas Amanat, *Apocalyptic Islam and Iranian Shi'ism* (London: I. B. Tauris, 2009).

On Iran since the revolution, see Samih K. Farsoun and Mehrdad Mashayekhi, *Iran: Political Culture in the Islamic Republic* (London: Routledge, 1992); Anoushira-van Ehteshami, *After Khomeini* (London: Routledge, 1995); Bahman Baktiari, *Par-liamentary Politics in Revolutionary Iran* (Gainesville: University Press of Florida, 1996); Asghar Schirazi, *The Constitution of Iran* (London: I. B. Tauris, 1997); Ja-hangir Amuzegar, *Iran's Economy Under the Islamic Republic* (London: I. B. Tauris, 1997); Haleh Afshar, *Islam and Feminisms: An Iranian Case-Study* (New York: St. Martin's Press, 1998); Maziar Bahrooz, *Rebels with a Cause* (London: I. B. Tauris, 1999); Fariba Adelkhah, *Being Modern in Iran* (New York: Columbia University Press, 2000); Eliz Sanasarian, *Religious Minorities in Iran* (Cambridge: Cambridge University Press, 2000); Wilfried Buchta, *Who Rules Iran?* (Washington, DC: Washington Institute for Near East Policy, 2000); Daniel Brumberg, *Reinventing Khomeini* (Chicago: University of Chicago Press, 2001); Mehdi Moslem, *Factional Politics in Post-Khomeini Iran* (Syracuse, NY: Syracuse University Press, 2002); Eric Hooglund, ed., *Twenty Years of Islamic Revolution* (Syracuse, NY: Syracuse Univer-sity Press, 2002); Kenneth M. Pollack, *The Persian Puzzle* (New York: Random House, 2004); Anthony H. Cordesman, *Iran's Developing Military Capabilities*

(Washington, DC: Center for Strategic and International Studies Press, 2005); Mehran Kamrava, *Iran's Intellectual Revolution* (Cambridge: Cambridge University Press, 2008); Said Amir Arjomand, *After Khomeini: Iran Under His Successors* (New York: Oxford University Press, 2009); and Ray Takeyh, *Guardians of the Revolution: Iran and the World in the Age of the Ayatollahs* (New York: Oxford University Press, 2009).

4

KINGDOM OF SAUDI ARABIA

Sebastian Maisel

HISTORICAL BACKGROUND

Early History

In 1932, King Abd al-Aziz ibn Abd al-Rahman Al Saud formally united the Hijaz and Najd to form the Kingdom of Saudi Arabia. The Saud regime, however, dates back over 250 years to when its founder ruled a small desert principality in Najd, as central Arabia is called. The story of Saudi Arabia, therefore, is the story of the evolution of a small oasis principality into the mighty oil kingdom of today.

The founder of the Al Saud dynasty, Muhammad ibn Saud (c. 1703/ 1704–1765), was amir of Dar'iyyah. Dar'iyyah is a small oasis town located on the Wadi Hanifah, a usually dry streambed in central Najd. In 1744/1745, he became the patron of Muhammad ibn Abd al-Wahhab (1703–1793), a zealous religious revivalist who had been driven from his home, the neighboring town of Uyainah, because of his strict, puritan religious beliefs. The religious leader and the temporal leader formed a bond that has provided ideological cohesion for the Saudi state to this day.

Muhammad ibn Abd al-Wahhab's revival movement was based on the Hanbali school of Islamic jurisprudence, the most conservative of the four recognized schools of Sunni Islam. Many of the revival's teachings were drawn from the writings of an early Hanbali jurist, Taqi al-Din Ahmad Ibn Taymiyyah (c. 1262–1328). The revival stressed a return to the fundamentals of Islam based on the strict monotheistic doctrine of *Tawhid* (the word literally means "monotheism" in Arabic) and condemned many of the religious practices that had cropped up since the time of the Prophet as heretical and those who followed them as idolators and polytheists.

Outside detractors called followers of the revival "Wahhabis," after Abd al-Wahhab. The followers themselves, however, rejected the term as implying worship of a human being rather than God. They preferred to be called Muwahhidin (literally "Unitarians" or "Monotheists"), expressing adherence to the central

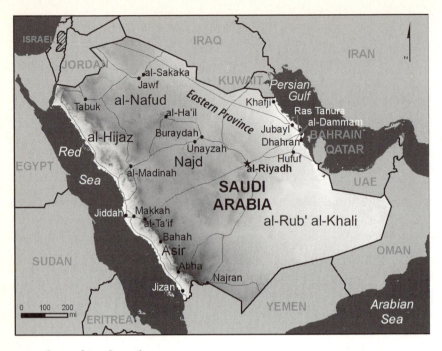

Kingdom of Saudi Arabia

monotheistic doctrine of *Tawhid*. Muhammad ibn Abd al-Wahhab was known as the teacher, or "the Shaykh." His descendants, called Al al-Shaykh (House of the Shaykh), are second in prestige to the Al Saud and still provide religious leadership for the country.

By the end of the eighteenth century, the Al Saud ruled over nearly all of Najd and was preparing to expand even farther. Saudi control of Najd was accomplished with little notice by the outside world, but when in 1801 the Saudis sacked the Shi'a holy city of Karbala in what is now southern Iraq, they came to the attention of the world, particularly the Islamic world. Convinced that pilgrimages to tombs of holy men were idolatry, the Al Saud destroyed the tombs of a number of revered Shi'a "saints," including that of Husayn, the grandson of the Prophet Muhammad. Husayn's tomb is venerated by Shi'as as a site for pilgrimages second in importance only to Makkah and al-Madinah (the official Saudi English spelling for Mecca and al-Madina). In 1806, Muwahhidin forces defeated the Ottoman garrisons in the Hijaz and seized Makkah and al-Madinah. In the east they pushed into Oman, forcing the Sultan of Muscat to pay annual tribute. Persian Gulf mariners, newly converted to the religious revival movement, sent privateers against British and local merchant vessels, deeming the former to be nonbelievers and the latter to be heretics. Thus, in a few short years, Saudi domains had expanded from a small oasis principality to much of the Arabian Peninsula, and Saudi influence extended to the Gulf and the Arabian Sea.

One can speculate how far the forces of the Al Saud might have gone had they not encountered vastly superior military technology from the Ottomans. The capture of the holy places of Makkah and al-Madinah roused the sultan in Constantinople to action. He bade his viceroy in Egypt, Muhammad Ali, to send an army against the invaders. In 1811 Muhammad Ali sent his son Tusun to retake the holy places and invade Najd. Tusun was able to recapture most of the Hijaz but could not defeat the Muwahhidin. In 1816, Tusun's brother Ibrahim Pasha arrived with a well-equipped army and finally captured the Saudi capital at Dar'iyyah in 1818. Ibrahim's forces laid waste to the city, whose ruins can still be seen, and exiled the Saudi amir, Abdallah ibn Saud Al Saud, fourth in the line to Cairo along with other members of the Al Saud and Al al-Shaykh. Abdallah was later sent to Constantinople, where he was eventually beheaded.

During the next four years, the Ottoman-Egyptian occupiers set out to destroy the Al Saud base of power so that it could no longer threaten the holy cities of the Hijaz. They installed Abdallah's brother, Mishari, as a puppet amir and finally withdrew from Najd in 1822 after concluding that the Muwahhidin were no longer a threat to Makkah and al-Madinah.

In 1823/1824, Turki ibn Abdallah, a second cousin, reestablished Saudi rule and moved the capital twenty kilometers down the Wadi Hanifah to Riyadh, where it has remained to this day. He was assassinated in 1834 and succeeded by his son Faisal. In 1837, Egyptians ousted Faisal and installed his cousin, Khalid, but he in turn was overthrown by another cousin, Abdallah ibn Thunayan. Finally, in 1843, Faisal escaped from exile in Cairo, ousted Abdallah ibn Thunayan, and again became undisputed ruler of Najd. During Faisal's second reign (1843–1865), Saudi leadership reached the apex of its power and influence in the nineteenth century. Faisal restored peace, extended his rule to Jabal Shammar in the north, and laid claim to Buraymi Oasis on the Omani frontier.

Faisal's death in 1865 signaled another eclipse in the fortunes of the Al Saud. He was succeeded by his son Abdallah, but Abdallah's leadership was almost immediately challenged by a second son, Saud, who became amir in 1871. After Saud's death in 1875, Abdallah again became amir, but by this time, the Al Saud's grip on Najd was slipping; the Ottomans recaptured Eastern Province (al-Hasa) in the east; the Jabal Shammar tribal area was lost in the north; and Buraymi Oasis was lost in the south. In 1887, the Saudi state again collapsed. This time, Muhammad ibn Rashid, amir of the Shammar, seized Najd and ruled it from the Shammari capital at Hail. Abd al-Rahman, a younger brother of Abdallah and Saud, served briefly as the Rashidi governor in Riyadh, but in 1891, after failing in an abortive revolt, he and his family were forced to flee. He settled for months with

SAUDI ARABIA

Capital city	Riyadh
Chief of state	King and Prime Minister Abdallah bin Abd al-Aziz Al Saud
Head of government	King and Prime Minister Abdallah bin Abd al-Aziz Al Saud
Major political parties	None
Ethnic groups	Arab (90%), Afro-Asian (10%)
Religious groups	Muslim (100%)
Export partners	United States (17.1%), Japan (16.3%), South Korea (9.7%), China (8.1%), Taiwan (4.7%), Singapore (4%)
Import partners	United States (12.6%), China (9.4%), Germany (8.8%), Japan (8.1%), Italy (5%), South Korea (4.9%), United Kingdom (4.5%)

the al-Murrah tribes at the edge of the Rub' al-Khali, or the Empty Quarter, where his son Abd al-Aziz, the future King of Saudi Arabia, learned the Bedouin lifestyle and customs. Later, Abd al-Rahman and his family moved to Kuwait, where they lived off the hospitality of the ruler, Mubarak the Great.

From Desert Principality to Modern Oil Kingdom

The rise of the Al Saud from exile to rulers of the world's foremost oil state was due primarily to Abd al-Rahman's son Abd al-Aziz, known in the West as Ibn Saud. He was an imposing figure. The true measure of his greatness, however, was in his breadth of vision. Even though he did not fully comprehend the revolutionary changes that his acts would ultimately produce, he brought his country from centuries of desert isolation to a place on regional and world political and economic councils.

The first step was the legendary recapture of Riyadh in 1902. It took two decades from that January morning for Abd al-Aziz to complete the conquest of the

Ibn Rashids. His success was greatly facilitated by the fratricidal rivalries that split the Ibn Rashids, much as the Sauds had been split just a generation before. Saudi control continued to expand; in 1912, Abd al-Aziz raised his Najdi state from an emirate to a sultanate, as befitted his growing status. By the time he captured the Rashidi capital of Hail in 1922, he had also recaptured in eastern Arabia the large oasis of al-Hasa from the Ottomans.

In his military campaigns, Abd al-Aziz relied on tribal warriors called the Ikhwan (literally "the Brethren" in Arabic), whom he indoctrinated in the teachings of Ibn Abd al-Wahhab, provided with subsidies and a share of the booty from raids against enemies of the Al Saud, and settled in agricultural communities. The Ikhwan, fighting under the banner of *Tawhid*, might have defeated the Ibn Rashids sooner had not World War I intervened. The war temporarily brought the Arabian Peninsula into the arena of great-power politics, with the British and the Turks in competition for the support of the peninsula's three major rulers, Abd al-Aziz of Najd, Saud ibn Rashid of Jabal Shammar, and Sharif Hussein of Makkah. Ibn Rashid sided with the Turks (and the Germans); the other two chose the British.

During the war period, three Britons came to fame in Arabia: Capt. W. H. I. Shakespeare, Col. T. E. Lawrence (Lawrence of Arabia), and H. St. John B. Philby. Shakespeare, as British political agent in Kuwait, had informally contacted Abd al-Aziz in 1910 and, while on a trek through Arabia in 1913, had visited him in Riyadh. On the eve of the war, Shakespeare was sent back to Riyadh in 1914 as the British political representative to Abd al-Aziz.

In 1916, the British sent Col. T. E. Lawrence to the Hijaz to encourage Sharif Hussein to revolt against the Ottomans. Lawrence subsequently won a place in history by leading Arab raiding parties against Turkish supply routes along the Hijaz Railroad. The following year, the British sent another mission to Abd al-Aziz to persuade him to side with Sharif Hussein and the Allies and to attack the Ibn Rashids. The mission included Philby, who remained in Arabia as an explorer and later became one of the closest confidants of Abd al-Aziz.

With the war's end, Abd al-Aziz finally conquered the capital of Ibn Rashid, but in the meantime, the Al Saud's relations with King (formerly Sharif) Hussein of the Hijaz had begun to deteriorate. Hussein proclaimed himself "King of the Arabs" and claimed precedence over the Al Saud, whom he regarded as mere desert chieftains.

The tide was turning, however. The same year, Abdallah, another of Hussein's sons, set out east of Ta'if to claim the Khurmah Oasis for the Hijaz. While encamped at nearby Turabah, his army was wiped out by the Ikhwan. Only men with horses (including Abdallah) escaped.

Because of British support of the Hijaz, Abd al-Aziz did not press his advantage until 1924, when King Hussein proclaimed himself the caliph after the Ottoman caliphate had been dissolved. This was more than the devout Abd al-Aziz could accept, and he set out to invade the Hijaz. Ta'if surrendered without resistance, but for a still unexplained reason, a shot rang out and the zealous Ikhwan sacked the city. When the rest of the Hijaz learned of the fate of Ta'if, they panicked and forced King Hussein to abdicate in favor of his son, Ali. Ali fared no better, however, and in January 1926, he also set sail from Jiddah into exile.

In a quarter century, Abd al-Aziz, who had started with forty men, had regained the Saudi patrimony. In 1934, he acquired the Wadi Najran after a brief war with the Yemen, completing the present frontiers, pending settlement of remaining boundary disputes. After Abd al-Aziz conquered the Hijaz, he ruled the two countries as the Kingdom of the Hijaz and Sultanate of Najd, then the Kingdom of the Hijaz and Najd. In 1932, the two countries were consolidated as the Kingdom of Saudi Arabia.

With the restoration and consolidation of the kingdom, peace came to Saudi Arabia for one of the few times in recorded history. With no more wars to fight, the Ikhwan became restless, and the king had to put down a tribal uprising at Sibilah in 1929, perhaps the last great Bedouin battle in history. The Ikhwan were subsequently disbanded (except for the brief Yemen campaign), and on the eve of World War II, Saudi Arabia was one of the few countries in the world with no standing army. It did declare war on Germany, however, and became a charter member of the United Nations.

The Postwar Era

The postwar history of Saudi Arabia has been one of unprecedented economic and social development. The enabling factor has been oil, first found in commercial quantities in 1938 but not exported in quantity until after the war. King Abd al-Aziz, by the time of his death in 1953, had constructed a firm foundation on which his successors could build a modern oil state.

He was succeeded by his eldest surviving son, Saud. More at home with tribal politics, Saud lacked the breadth of vision to propel Saudi Arabia from a desert kingdom to a major oil power. Intrigue and lavish spending characterized his reign. Despite growing oil revenues, the treasury was often virtually empty. In 1962, Saud was obliged to turn government operations over to his half brother Faisal, and in 1964, the royal family withdrew its support entirely, forcing him to abdicate. Saud left Saudi Arabia, choosing to remain in exile until his death in Athens in 1969.

King Faisal began his reign with nearly a half century's experience in public affairs. In 1919, at the age of fourteen, he represented his father on an official visit to England. After his father conquered the Hijaz, Faisal was made its viceroy in 1926, and when the Ministry of Foreign Affairs was created in 1930, he became foreign minister, a position he held for the rest of his life, with the exception of a short period during the reign of his half brother, Saud, when Faisal retired to private life.

King Faisal, whose mother was an Al al-Shaykh, was dedicated to the preservation of a conservative Islamic way of life both in Saudi Arabia and throughout the Muslim world, while he at the same time encouraged material and technological modernization. These goals, initiated by his father, were articulated in a ten-point reform program, which Faisal announced in 1962 while he was still heir apparent and prime minister. The measure of his success can be explained by his capacity to introduce modern economic- and social-development programs, but to never be so far out in front that the conservative, Islamic Saudi public would not follow. By balancing tradition and modernization, he was able to win over even the most conservative segments of the population to such innovations as public radio and television and education for women. To dispel religious opposition to radio and television, for example, Faisal ordered large portions of programming time to be devoted to religious instruction and readings from the Qur'an.

Faisal's greatest interest, however, was foreign affairs. As foreign minister, he became one of the most widely traveled Saudi officials of his time. For example, he attended the 1945 San Francisco conference that established the United Nations. Faisal's primary focus was on the Muslim world and the preservation of its values.

His reign coincided with the Cold War, and his strident antipathy toward the Soviet Union was based in large part on his Islamic bipolar worldview (see "The Saudi Worldview," below) that atheistic communism was a threat to the entire Muslim world. Likewise, his strong support of the Palestinian cause was based not only on the political injustice of partitioning Arab lands to create a Jewish state but the Israeli capture during the 1967 Arab-Israeli War of the al-Aqsa Mosque in Jerusalem, the third holiest site in Sunni Islam after Makkah and al-Madinah.

King Faisal was assassinated by a deranged nephew on March 25, 1975, and succeeded by his half brother Khalid. Quiet, retiring, and pious, King Khalid was a very popular ruler. During his reign, in 1979, fanatical followers of Juhayman al-Utaybi and the self-proclaimed Mahdi (Redeemer) Muhammad al-Qahtani seized the Haram Mosque in Makkah, demanding political, religious, and economic reform. With foreign technical support they were killed or captured. King Khalid died of a heart attack in June 1982 and was succeeded by Fahd as king.

Fahd's half brother Abdallah became heir apparent and first-deputy prime minister, also retaining command of the Saudi National Guard, to which he had been appointed by Faisal in 1962. Fahd's full brother Prince Sultan, the minister of defense, became second-deputy prime minister.

King Fahd carried on the evolutionary political and economic policies of his predecessors while continuing to maintain the Islamic nature of the state. In 1992, he promulgated a Basic Law of Government designed to modernize the political process and also promulgated a Consultative Assembly (*Majlis al-Shura*), designed to institutionalize more public participation in the political process commensurate with the Islamic constitutional system. (See "Political Institutions," below.)

In foreign policy, Fahd followed the lead of King Faisal in seeking cooperation with Western as well as moderate regional states to address regional Middle East problems. Radical Arab nationalism had lost its credence after the Arab defeat in the 1967 Arab-Israeli War, and as heir apparent and ultimately king, Fahd could be more active in regional affairs.

Fahd felt vindicated by the failure of the Camp David Accords of 1979 to lead to an Arab-Israeli peace that did not address any Palestinian core issues, and in 1981 he offered the Fahd Plan for an Arab-Israeli peace. It was, however, summarily rejected by Israel and the United States. Succeeding peace negotiations came to naught, and in 2002, the then heir apparent, Prince Abdallah, offered yet another peace proposal that got some support from Israelis but no results. As king, Abdallah offered yet another peace plan, but the newly elected right-wing Israeli government not only rejected it but sought to negate Israeli support of a two-state solution.

COPING WITH MODERNIZATION IN A HOSTILE WORLD

By the end of the 1980s, the collapse of the Soviet Union heralded the end of the Cold War, which for almost a half century Saudi Arabia had considered to be the greatest security threat to the Islamic way of life not only in the kingdom but throughout the Muslim world. It remained concerned about regional threats, however, and its fears were justified in 1990 when Iraq's President Saddam Husayn invaded Kuwait, threatening the rest of the Arabian Peninsula as well. After initial reluctance, King Fahd welcomed a coalition of Arab states and others led by the United States to counter the Iraqi invasion, and in 1991 Operation Desert Storm was launched to drive him out of Kuwait.

Iraq's invasion of Kuwait in 1990 and expulsion by a coalition of Western and Arab military forces in Desert Storm the following year was the greatest crisis for Saudi Arabia of that period. The Saudi military acquitted itself well during the war, particularly the Royal Saudi Air Force.

In the 1980s, many young Saudis volunteered to fight the Soviets in Afghanistan, but returning home after the war was over, many felt more marginalized than ever and turned to militant Islamism to give meaning to their lives, spreading this solution to their pain to younger marginalized youths. In this way, they were drawn to terrorist groups, the most effective of which was Usama Bin Ladin's al-Qa'ida. Thus, modern terrorism, which had never before been a major problem, gradually became the greatest national security problem facing the country.

King Fahd became incapacitated by a series of strokes in 1995 and in 1996 passed the reins of government to his half brother Abdallah, the heir apparent. The next decade was a difficult period for the kingdom in terms of meeting the challenges of social change, measuring up to economic and political expectations, and maintaining national security.

These pressures have been expanding for years, but at such a slow pace that they can best be described as a "creeping crisis." They were mostly unfocused until the 1990s, when the stationing of US troops in the kingdom became a rallying cry for the politically disaffected. But they did not reach a flash point until September 11, 2001, when the country faced fierce hostility, particularly in the United States, for alleged collusion with the terrorists, fifteen out of nineteen of whom were Saudis. (See "Foreign Policies," below.)

But national security really struck home in the kingdom in May 2003 when terrorists attacked residential compounds, killing not only Western expatriates but Muslims as well. Since then, the government has initiated a successful counter-terrorism program, attacking and rounding up terrorists as well as rehabilitating young recruits for reentry into society. It is not possible to eradicate totally all terrorist threats anywhere, but the Saudis have certainly reduced them to more manageable proportions.

When Abdallah became king in 2005 upon the death of Fahd, one of his major concerns was growing public support for more participation in the political process. Adjusting to the challenges and changes of the era of global economy and security, he initiated a reform of the political process and the judicial system as well as the educational sector. For some, the very slow process aims at a renewal and revitalization of the origin of Saudi rule: a balance of politics and religion for the sake not only of the survival but the strong, lasting impact of the "country of the two holy places." He has set about establishing his own personal style of government, though one based on precedent; Saudi domestic and foreign policies will likely continue to follow the lead of Kings Abd al-Aziz, Faisal, and Fahd, emphasizing economic development and social welfare within the framework of Islam and pan-Arabism.

POLITICAL ENVIRONMENT

The Land and People

The Land. Saudi Arabia occupies about 2 million square kilometers (772,000 square miles), but political borders have traditionally been relatively meaningless to Saudi rulers, who have looked on sovereignty more in terms of tribal allegiance. Recognized tribal territories were huge and carefully defined, as Bedouin tribes themselves followed the rains from water hole to water hole and wandered over broad areas. Later, when oil became so important in the region, fixed regional and international borders acquired much more importance. A deviation of a few centimeters from a common point could translate into hundreds of square kilometers when projected for long distances over the desert.

It has taken many years for Saudi Arabia to demarcate its borders. In 1922, the Saudi-Kuwaiti Neutral Zone and the Saudi-Iraqi Neutral Zone were created to avoid tribal border hostilities. The first was abolished in 1966 and the second in 1975, and their territories were divided among the parties. The decades-old Buraymi Oasis territorial dispute among Saudi Arabia, Oman, and Abu Dhabi was settled in 1974 when Saudi Arabia agreed to give up its claim to the oasis and adjacent territory in return for an outlet to the Gulf through Abu Dhabi. Since then, the kingdom has agreed in principle to demarcate the rest of its long border with Oman, and on June 12, 2000, Saudi Arabia and Yemen signed a treaty on their international land and sea borders, ending a dispute that went back to the Saudi invasion of Yemen in 1934.

The same can be said for offshore territorial limits. Saudi Arabia claims a twelve-nautical-mile limit offshore, as well as a number of islands in the Gulf and the Red Sea. With extensive offshore oil discoveries in the Gulf, establishing a median line dividing underwater oil and gas fields among the Gulf states became imperative. Nevertheless, it was not until the 1970s that a median line delineating offshore drilling rights could finally be negotiated.

Because of Saudi Arabia's predominantly desert terrain, a shortage of water is a major concern. In the interior, nonrenewable aquifers are being tapped at an unprecedented rate, particularly as urbanization and population growth expand and as irrigated agricultural development projects have been created in the interior. To augment water supplies, the kingdom has created a massive desalination system.

Despite the arid climate, sporadic rains do fall in Saudi Arabia, and there is occasional snow in the mountains. This water has to run off somewhere, and as a result, there are numerous drainage systems of intersecting wadis, which are usually dry riverbeds and valleys. After local, and occasionally heavy, rains, the wadis can become rushing torrents.

Although nearly all of Saudi Arabia is arid, only a part of it consists of real sand desert. There are three such deserts in the kingdom: the Great Nafud, located in the north (*nafud* is one of several Arabic words meaning "desert"); the Rub' al-Khali (literally, "the Empty Quarter"), stretching along the entire southern frontier; and the Dahna, a narrow strip that forms a great arc from the Great Nafud westward and then south to the Rub' al-Khali. The sand in all three bears iron oxide, giving it a pink color that can turn to deep red in the setting sun.

Excluding the Empty Quarter, the kingdom is divided into four geographical regions: central, western, eastern, and northern. Central Arabia, or Najd, is both the geographical and the political heartland of the country. Najd, Arabic for "highlands," is predominantly an arid plateau interspersed with oases.

Many cities and towns are scattered throughout Najd, the largest being the national capital, Riyadh. The name means "gardens" and refers to the numerous vegetable gardens and date groves that were located there. Riyadh has grown from a small oasis town—about 7,500 in 1900—to a major metropolis with a population of over 3.5 million a century later; by 2000 it was estimated to be approaching 5 million.

Riyadh remained generally closed to Westerners until the 1970s, when the Saudis opened it up to Western development. Between 1969 and 1975, the number of Western expatriates living in the capital rose from fewer than three hundred to hundreds of thousands. Just a few kilometers north, the ruins of Dar'iyyah, ancestral home of the Al Saud, have become a virtual suburb of the capital. Northeast of Riyadh is the district of al-Qasim, with its neighboring and rival cities of Unayzah and Buraydah. The inhabitants of al-Qasim are among the most conservative in the kingdom. Further north is Jabal Shammar and the former Rashidi capital of Hail on the edge of the Great Nafud.

Western Saudi Arabia is divided into two areas, the Hijaz in the north and Asir in the south. The Hijaz extends from the Jordanian border to just south of Jiddah, the kingdom's second-largest city. The economic and social life of the Hijaz has traditionally revolved around the annual Hajj, or "great pilgrimage" to Makkah. With so much attention given to Saudi oil and Middle East politics, few Westerners are aware that to the Muslim world—comprising around 1.4 billion people, or one-fifth of the world's population—the kingdom is even more important as the location of the two holiest cities in Islam, Makkah and al-Madinah. Performing the Hajj once in their lifetime is an obligation for all Muslims who are physically and financially able.

Observed each year by roughly between 2.5 and 3 million of the faithful, the Hajj is not only one of the world's greatest religious celebrations but also one of the greatest exercises in public administration. The Saudi government seeks to ensure that all those who attend do so without incurring serious injury and with a minimum of discomfort.

This requires the concerted effort of health, housing, transportation, security, diplomatic, customs, and finance officials, working with large private-sector guilds to meet, guide, and look after the Hajjis throughout their stay. Over the centuries since the beginning of Islam in the seventh century CE, an extensive service industry has grown up to cater to Hajjis. With the discovery of oil, the Hajj has lost the economic importance it once had, but with an estimated 2.5 to 3 million Hajjis and several million other visitors to Makkah and al-Madinah throughout each year, many staying three to five weeks, it is still a major commercial season, somewhat analogous to the Christmas season in Western countries. Physical infrastructure to accommodate the Hajj is extensive, including one of the largest commercial airports in the world at Jiddah, a modern commercial hub of over 3 million on the Red Sea and the traditional port of entry for the Hajj. The Saudi government has also spent billions of riyals upgrading the Haram Mosque in Makkah and the Prophet's Mosque in al-Madinah, the two holiest sites in Islam.

Asir and southern Tihama (the Red Sea coastal plain) were quasi-independent until the Saudi conquest in the 1920s and 1930s, and they remained relatively isolated until modern roads were built in the 1970s. Its main cities are Jizan, a modest city on the coast; Abha, the provincial capital atop the escarpment; and Najran, located inland on the Saudi-Yemeni border. Not far from Abha is Khamis Mushayt, site of a major Saudi military cantonment area.

Eastern Saudi Arabia is a mixture of old and new. Called the Eastern Province, it includes al-Hasa, the largest oasis in the world, and al-Qatif Oasis on the coast. The primary significance of the region is that underneath it lies the bulk of Saudi Arabia's huge oil reserves, one-fourth of the world's total. The Ghawar field, which stretches over two hundred kilometers from north to south, is the largest single oil field in the world.

The capital and principal city of the province is Dammam, just south of al-Qatif. Once a small pearling and privateering port, it is now a bustling metropolis. South of Dammam is Dhahran, whose name is far more familiar in the West. It is actually not a city but the location of the Saudi Aramco headquarters, King Faisal University, and the US consulate general. Nearby, on the coast, is al-Khobar, which grew from virtually nothing into a major industrial service town.

North of Dammam to the Kuwaiti border are located a number of oil towns and facilities, including Ras Tanura, the principal Saudi Aramco oil terminal, and farther north, Khafji, in what was formerly part of the Saudi-Kuwaiti Neutral Zone. Just north of Ras Tanura is Jubayl, only a tiny village when the first American oil men landed there in 1933 and now a major industrial city and the site of much of Saudi Arabia's petrochemical industry. The largest town in al-Hasa Oasis is the ancient town of Hufuf, now home to many Saudi Aramco workers and the Shi'a minority of the kingdom.

The area extending along the kingdom's northern frontiers with Jordan and Iraq is physically isolated from the rest of the country by the Great Nafud. It is geographically a part of the Syrian Desert, and tribesmen in the area claim kinship with fellow tribesmen in neighboring Jordan, Iraq, and Syria as well as Saudi Arabia, occasionally possessing passports from all four countries. This area was the traditional caravan route for traders from the Fertile Crescent traveling to central and eastern Arabia.

There are no cities in the region. The two principal towns, Dumat al-Jandal (al-Jawf) and Sakaka, the provincial capital, are located in oases just north of the Nafud. Prior to the 1967 Arab-Israeli War, the most important installation in the region economically was the Trans-Arabian Pipeline (TAPLINE), which carried crude oil from the Eastern Province to the Lebanese port of Sidon. With access to Lebanon now closed, TAPLINE has lost much of its economic importance, although oil is still sent through the pipeline to Jordan.

Saudi Arabia has a harsh, hot climate that one would associate with a desert area. There are variations, however. In the interior, the lack of humidity causes daytime temperatures to rise sharply. In the summer, daytime readings can register over 54°C (130°F), then drop precipitously after the sun goes down, sometimes as much as 20°C (70°F) in less than three hours. In the winter, subfreezing temperatures are not uncommon, and the ever-present winds create a windchill that can be very uncomfortable.

The coastal areas combine heat and high humidity. The humidity usually keeps the temperature from exceeding 40°C (around 105°F) in the summer but likewise prevents it from dropping more than a few degrees at night. Winter temperatures, in contrast, are balmier and warmer at night than those in the interior, particularly the farther south one goes. Both along the coasts and in the interior, rainfall is very sporadic. Torrential rains can flood one area and entirely miss areas a few kilometers away. At other times, the same area can go without rain for five to ten years. The sporadic nature of the rains is the main reason desert pastoralists must cover wide areas in search of pasturage for their livestock.

The mountain areas are cooler, particularly in the Asir, where it can get quite cold at night. The Asir also gets the moisture-laden monsoon winds from the south in the winter, when most of its annual rainfall of around five hundred millimeters (twenty inches) occurs.

The People. In 2009 Saudi Arabia had an estimated population of 28.7 million, of which roughly 5.6 million were expatriates. Though the country's population is relatively small in comparison to its great wealth, it has experienced a population explosion in the past quarter century that has radically changed its demography. There are some indications that the population growth rate is stabilizing, declining from over 3.5 percent per year to around 3.2 percent. However, with a median age of about eighteen and a rapidly expanding life expectancy due to vastly improved health care, the kingdom still faces major socioeconomic problems far into the twenty-first century. Every year there are more young Saudis for a finite number of jobs, and more and more of the aged must be supported by their children, with both groups increasingly living off their families' income.

The indigenous Saudi population is among the most homogeneous in the entire Middle East. Virtually all Saudis are Arab and Muslim. Bloodlines, not geography, determine nationality, and being born in Saudi Arabia does not automatically entitle a person to citizenship. The extended family is the most important social institution in Saudi Arabia. If put to the test, loyalty to one's family would probably exceed loyalty to the state. The state has been in existence for a few decades, but most Saudis trace their families back for centuries.

With genealogy so important, there is relatively little social mobility in Saudi Arabia. Not only is Najd the center of Saudi political power, but its tribal affiliations are among the most aristocratic on the Arabian Peninsula. Members of the leading tribal families of Najd are at the top of the social order, and nontribal families are near the bottom.

The Hijazi population is far more cosmopolitan than that of Najd because of centuries of immigration connected with the Hajj. The leading families historically constituted a merchant class that grew up in the Hijaz to serve the Hajj. The Eastern Province, with its concentration of the oil industry, also has a polyglot population, and many families there have close ties in other Gulf states.

The Eastern Province is the home of the only significant minority in the kingdom, the Shi'a community, estimated to number between 500,000 and 800,000. They live mainly in al-Qatif and al-Hasa oases. Unlike much of the rest of the population, the Shi'a are willing to work with their hands and over the years have become the backbone of the skilled and semiskilled workforce in the oil sector. They are members of the predominant Twelver Shi'a sect. Another group of Shi'a is concentrated in the Najran area near Yemen. They are followers of the Isma'ili, or Sevener, sect.

A few families of non-Arabian origin have also become Saudi nationals. Most of them are found in the Hijaz and are descended from Hajjis who never returned to their homelands after the pilgrimage. Some of these families have lived in Jiddah and Makkah for centuries and have attained stature in society and senior government rank. These families came from Java, China, and other, mostly Far Eastern Asian regions. Another group, the Hadhramis, originally came from the Wadi Hadhramawt in what is now western Yemen, particularly in the nineteenth century, and number among the leading merchant families of Jiddah. Also, after the abolition of slavery in 1960, many former slaves stayed in the kingdom and became citizens, often remaining closely allied with their former masters.

The distinction between "foreigners" and "natives" breaks down somewhat when one looks at neighboring states. Many of the old Sunni families of Kuwait and Bahrain migrated from Najd some three hundred years ago. Northern Saudis have close tribal ties in Iraq, Jordan, and Syria. Gulf ties are reflected during the Hajj, when members of the Gulf Cooperation Council (GCC) states are not required to obtain Saudi visas. No matter how long a person's family has resided in the country, however, he is still identified by his family's place of origin.

The foreign community constitutes about one-fifth of the total population. European diplomats, bankers, and merchants have long resided in the Hijaz to service the Hajj trade, but few resided elsewhere. The original function of foreign diplomats and consuls, located in Jiddah, was to look after Hajjis from their home countries, and many countries continue to maintain consulates in Jiddah for that purpose, although all foreign embassies moved to Riyadh in the 1970s.

As the oil-based economy grew, the foreign workforce rapidly expanded. By the 1950s, Aramco employed thousands of foreign workers, from senior American executives to manual laborers from the Persian Gulf states and South Asia. In the 1970s, the oil boom spurred unprecedented economic development throughout the kingdom, and Najd was opened up to Westerners for the first time in a major way. A new diplomatic enclave, separate from the rest of the city, was created in Riyadh by the Saudi government, and many foreign and local businesses moved their headquarters to Riyadh as well. Thus, the capital is not only now the largest city in the kingdom but probably contains most of the kingdom's foreigners. Skilled laborers, clerks, and teachers have come from nearby Arab states, and manual laborers have come from many Arab and South Asian countries. Yemeni workers, for instance, numbered as many as 1 million until many of them were expelled after Desert Storm for security reasons.

Contrary to fears often expressed in the West, the social and political influence of foreign workers on the society has been relatively slight. Not only does the kingdom have a basically closed society, but most foreign workers are there primarily to make as much money as possible before returning home, not to spread some radical political ideology.

In all, with the breathtaking pace of modernization in the past few decades, the miracle of Saudi society is not how it has changed but how resilient it has been in the face of change. The extended-family system is still intact and, indeed, is probably the most stabilizing force in the country. Whatever Saudi Arabia's political or economic future, it is difficult to visualize it without the paramount importance of family ties.

Finally, it is within the context of the extended family that one must view the role of women in government and politics. Although they have "constitutional" rights under Islamic law, which are actually quite detailed, they have no formal participatory political rights in a Western sense. But within the extended family, which is the basic unit of the society, they have tremendous power because women run the family and thus can exercise significant influence over public affairs informally through their spouses and male siblings. King Abd al-Aziz's closest political advisor was his blood sister Nura, and King Faisal's closest political advisor, particularly on women's affairs, was his wife Iffat, called "the Queen" by the people out of respect, although no such title formally existed.

ECONOMIC CONDITIONS

The backbone of the Saudi economy is oil, accounting for 75 percent of revenues and 90 percent of export earnings. The kingdom holds roughly one-fourth of the world's proved oil reserves, the largest reserves in the world.

When one looks at Saudi Arabia's huge oil wealth, it is difficult to imagine that prior to World War II, the country was one of the poorest on earth. Following the incorporation of the Hijaz into the Saudi realm in the 1920s, revenues generated from the Hajj became the major source of foreign exchange. When the world economic depression and political disorders leading to World War II greatly reduced the number of Hajjis in the 1930s, the Saudi economy was badly hit, and although oil had been discovered, revenues were insufficient to fill the gap.

In the pre-oil era, economic activity outside the Hijaz consisted largely of subsistence agriculture in oases and the western mountains, fishing along the Red Sea and Gulf coasts, and pearl diving in the Gulf. Even before oil wealth, Saudi Arabia had one of the most freewheeling market economies in the world. The predominant Hanbali school of Islamic jurisprudence, while ultraconservative on social and political issues, is one of the most liberal schools on economic and commercial matters, and caveat emptor ("buyer beware") is still the order of the day.

The transition of the Saudi economy from subsistence to oil wealth did not occur over night. The first Saudi oil concession was sold in the 1920s but allowed to lapse. Despite his chronic shortage of funds, King Abd al-Aziz feared that granting a concession to European oil companies would lead to imperialist penetration. In 1933, he granted a new concession to an American company, Standard Oil of California (SoCal). This came about in part through the good offices of Philby and Karl Twitchell, an American geologist who had explored for water in the kingdom, and in part because Abd al-Aziz believed the United States had no imperialist designs on Arabia. The company, originally named the California Arabian Standard Oil Company, was later renamed the Arabian American Oil Company (Aramco).

Oil was first discovered in commercial quantities in 1938, but the advent of World War II prevented its export in significant quantities to international markets. Thus, Saudi Arabia did not begin the process of becoming a leading oil state until the late 1940s and early 1950s.

In the 1960s, the kingdom joined the Organization of Petroleum Exporting Countries (OPEC) and quickly became the dominant member, with roughly one-quarter of the world's reserves and most of its production available for export. The original intent of OPEC was to pressure the foreign-owned oil companies to keep prices from collapsing in a buyers' market, but by the late 1960s, the United States, up to then the world's leading exporter, became a net importer, creating a sellers' market. This resulted in a major oil shortage, exacerbated by the 1970s Arab oil embargo; the oil-producing countries, including Saudi Arabia, were able to gain control of production rates from the companies and ultimately to get ownership of the oil itself.

Many OPEC countries simply nationalized the producing companies, but Saudi Arabia acquired ownership of Aramco in a gradual buyout called "participation," a concept developed by Zaki Yamani, then Saudi oil minister. Yamani feared that without extended oil company participation, the oil-producing countries would engage in cutthroat competition that could collapse the entire oil market. By 1980, Saudi Arabia had acquired full ownership of Aramco and renamed the company Saudi Aramco.

The high revenues of the 1970s enabled the Saudis to accelerate their economic and social welfare programs greatly. Ultimately, however, high oil prices also led to increased worldwide energy efficiency and a drop in per capita demand, and in 1980 the market entered a glut from which it did not fully recover for two decades.

Saudi Arabia's evolution from a traditional mercantile state to a major oil-producing state has wrought rapid changes throughout the economy, structurally, institutionally, and operationally. A vivid example is in the area of financial and fiscal transactions. Prior to the oil age, there were no commercial banks except foreign banks in the Hijaz established to handle the Hajj trade. There was no paper currency, which the local population distrusted, and Aramco had to fly in planeloads of silver coins to meet its payroll and royalty payments.

The government turned to Britain, France, and the United States for technical assistance in creating a modern monetary and banking system, and in 1952 it created a central bank, the Saudi Arabian Monetary Agency (SAMA). One of its first tasks was to introduce local paper money. SAMA issued promissory paper notes called "Hajj receipts," ostensibly for use by Hajjis in changing money and payable to the bearer on demand in silver coins. Once the public became accustomed to paper money, the notes were simply identified by denomination.

The evolution of Islamic banking is another creative endeavor, for Islam proscribes charging interest, considered usury. To avoid interest charges and payments, a banking system based on fees has been developed, and there are now a number of Islamic banks in the kingdom.

With advice from Western consultants and following his development philosophy of "modernization without secularization," King Faisal instituted a formal planning process, beginning with the first five-year plan adopted in 1970. The process bears no resemblance to Communist central planning, however, and could better be described as a combination of wish lists and statements of intent. The five-year plans are not intended as detailed instructions for budgetary expenditures and should be viewed impressionistically rather than literally. They are nevertheless fairly accurate indicators of Saudi priorities and the direction in which they believe they should be heading as well as of what lessons they believe are to be learned from the previous five years.

Early plans concentrated on building economic and social infrastructure and on economic diversification, and because of the huge increase in oil revenues in the 1970s, they were very ambitious. With the oil glut of the 1980s and 1990s, revenues dropped drastically, creating deficit financing. Development plans were sharply reduced. The sixth plan (1995–2000) further reflected the need to restructure the economy, stressing human resource development, economic diversification, privatization, and liberalization of trade and investment.

Oil prices have always been cyclical, and the early years of the twenty-first century have witnessed a return of high oil prices. With the global recession beginning in November 2008, prices again declined but recovered to about $70 to $75 per barrel by the summer of 2009, in part due to speculators investing in future production.

In sum, although economic conditions do affect political stability in Saudi Arabia, the kingdom's tight-knit, family-based society continues to be insurance against the kind of political unrest found in many developing countries. But with the demographic problems the kingdom faces and inherent cyclical fluctuations in world oil prices, the end of the latest oil glut is no cause for complacency.

POLITICAL CULTURE

Saudi culture is overwhelmingly Islamic. More than a religion, Islam is a totally self-contained, cosmic system. In assessing the influence of Islam on Saudi political culture, one must emphasize cultural values rather than religious piety. Several characteristics of Saudi culture are basic to Saudi politics. Among the most salient are a heightened sense of inevitability, a compartmentalization of behavior, a high degree of personalization of behavior, and a strong sense of personal honor.

The sense of inevitability derives from the Islamic emphasis on God's will, often expressed in the Arabic phrase "Inshallah," or "God willing." Nothing can happen unless God wills it. Thus, Saudis (and other Muslims) tend to accept situations as inevitable far more quickly than people from Western cultures. Conversely, if convinced that a situation is not God's will, they will persevere against it long after others would give up.

Compartmentalization of behavior, common in non-Western societies, is a tendency to view events from a single context rather than to explore all the ramifications of how it might appear in another context. As a result, a single issue can elicit different, and occasionally incompatible, policy responses, depending on the context in which it is viewed. Because these overlap and cannot be neatly separated, tolerance of major policy inconsistencies is inherent in the Saudi decision-making process.

A third cultural characteristic is the personalization of behavior. In contrast to problem-oriented Western cultures, Saudis are mainly people oriented. Good interpersonal relations are the sine qua non of good political relations, and losing face is to be avoided at all costs.

Two other Saudi cultural characteristics, derived in large part from its desert tribal origins, geographic isolation, and historic insularity, are a strong sense of personal and collective honor (*sharaf*) and a high degree of ethnocentricity. The ancient code of honor is still a guiding principle in interpersonal relations, often more compelling, for example, than contractual obligations, and the desire to avoid the personal and family shame associated with dishonor is very powerful.

Ethnocentricity is also very powerful, particularly in Najd, and Saudis tend to see themselves as the center of their universe. Personal status is conferred more by bloodlines than by money or achievement, and nearly all Saudis claim a proud Arabian ancestry. Having never been under European colonial rule, Saudis have not developed a national inferiority complex, as have many colonized peoples. They see themselves not merely as equals of the West but in fact believe their culture is vastly superior to secular Western culture. Close personal relationships aside, they tend to look on outsiders as people to be tolerated as long as they have something to contribute.

POLITICAL STRUCTURE

Saudi Arabia is one of the few countries without a constitution in the Western political understanding. The country's political system is based on the interpretation and application of divine guidelines from the Qur'an and other primary Islamic sources.

POLITICAL INSTITUTIONS

The creation of modern Saudi political institutions over the past eighty-six years was bred of necessity as the kingdom evolved from a traditional desert principality into a modern oil power. It has made government operations a great deal more orderly, but it has not fundamentally changed the traditional, interpersonal system of government.

The Judicial Branch

Islamic law has always formed the basis of the Saudi constitutional system and is supreme, even over the king. The most recent reaffirmation is Article 1 of the Basic Law of Government, issued by King Fahd on March 1, 1992:

> The Saudi Arabian Kingdom is a sovereign Arab Islamic state with
> Islam as its religion; God's book and the Sunna [which together form

the sources of Islamic law] are its constitution; Arabic is its language; and Riyadh is its capital.

Islam is basically a system of divine law. Islamic theology is quite simple, consisting of five basic tenets, or "pillars," of the faith: profession of faith ("There is no god but God, and Muhammad is the messenger of God"), prayer (five times a day, facing Makkah), alms, fasting (during the Muslim lunar month of Ramadan), and performing the Hajj once during one's lifetime if one is physically and financially able to do so. Another tenet, sometimes called the sixth pillar, is jihad. Often translated as "holy war," it is, in fact, a much broader concept, referring to both the private and the corporate obligation to encourage virtue and resist evil, by force if necessary.

Islamic law, or Shari'a (literally, "the Pathway"), on the other hand, is quite complex. It is the primary area of specialization of Islamic scholars. Despite theological differences among the various branches of Islam (for example, between Sunni and Shi'a), Islamic law is universally respected by all Muslims. The basic sources of the law are the Qur'an and the Sunna, or "Traditions" of the Prophet Muhammad, comprised of Hadiths, his divinely inspired sayings and deeds.

The Saudi legal system is based on Sunni interpretations of Islamic law, principally but not exclusively according to the Hanbali school of Islamic jurisprudence. The most conservative of the schools in social and family law, it reinforces conservative social mores practiced by the desert societies of Arabia for millennia, such as the veiling of women as an expression of modesty.

Saudi courts are presided over by an Islamic judge, or *qadi*. Because Islamic law is considered to be divinely inspired, however, there is no legal precedent based on previous court decisions. Islamic law does provide, however, for binding legal opinions (fatwas), issued without a court case by a mufti. Historically, the principal Saudi judicial official was called the chief qadi and grand mufti. In 1970, the title was changed to the minister of justice, but the functions of the ministry have remained basically the same.

Because the Shari'a is considered divine, legislative or statutory law is proscribed. There is, however, a means for regulating and adjudicating issues that did not exist during the time of Muhammad. Royal decrees (nizams) issued by the king are used to provide regulatory and administrative rules, and special administrative tribunals have been created to adjudicate labor and commercial disputes. In addition, a Board of Grievances (*Diwan al-Mazalim*) adjudicates grievances between citizens and the government.

The Executive Branch

Saudi Arabia is an Islamic monarchy, ruled by the Al Saud. Royal succession is technically legitimized through an ancient Islamic institution, Ahl al-Hall wa'l-

Aqd ("The People Who Bind and Loose"), made up of the elders of the royal family and religious leaders, technocrats, businessmen, and heads of important families not otherwise included in those categories. In reality, however, no king can remain in power without the consensual support of the Al Saud.

The king is both the chief of state and head of government, but he is not above the law. Thus, despite there being no democratically elected representatives of the people, Saudi Arabia is not an absolute monarchy in the historic European sense; the doctrine of "divine right of kings" would be considered heresy. Moreover, despite all the powers residing in the ruler, he cannot act in the face of a contravening consensus. Thus, the king must be more than a chief of state and head of government. In order to legitimize government policies, he must also act as the chief consensus maker through consultation with all those considered part of the national decision-making process.

Prior to the capture of the Hijaz in 1925, the Al Saud regime had few, if any, formal political institutions other than the Islamic judicial system and was ruled by interpersonal consultation with leading members of the royal family and tribal and religious leaders. The Hijaz, in contrast, had a much more formal system of government, including cabinet ministers. When Abd al-Aziz annexed the Hijaz in 1926, he left its political institutions intact. The evolution of Saudi political institutions had no master plan. It can be seen as the expansion of institutions initially found only in the Hijaz to the rest of the country, augmented by creation of new institutions and a bureaucracy to run them as the need arose. Interpersonal relations within the government, as throughout the society as a whole, are still highly personalized, but they are increasingly carried out within the parameters of formal political institutions and more standardized procedures. Moreover, it is still a work in progress.

The first nationwide ministry, the Ministry of Foreign Affairs, was created in 1930, followed by the Ministry of Finance in 1932. Both ministries initially overlapped with separate Hijazi ministries, which continued to exist for a number of years. The Ministry of Finance was initially responsible not only for financial affairs but also for most of the administrative machinery of the entire kingdom, as its predecessor, the Hijazi Ministry of the Interior (abolished in 1934), had been.

Many of the subsequent national ministries thus began as departments under the Ministry of Finance, some becoming independent agencies before being elevated to ministry level. One of Abd al-Aziz's final acts was to create a council of ministers, which he decreed in October 1953, just a month before his death. Nevertheless, because many of the ministries and independent agencies existed before the council of ministers, interministerial and agency cooperation has evolved at a slower pace.

The evolution of local government institutions has faced another set of problems. The country is divided into thirteen provincial regions, all of which have representatives from national ministries who report directly to Riyadh but must also work closely with the regional governors. Each regional governor is responsible for subregional governorates, districts, and local government centers. The Regions Statute, issued by royal decree on March 1, 1992, did not greatly clarify the situation. For example, although the national interior ministry is directly in charge of regional and local government, the decree confers equal ministerial rank on the regional governors. The decree also stipulates a ten-man advisory council for each region.

Consultative Participation

The term *legislative branch of government* is obviously inappropriate for a country that proscribes statuary law. Thus, when King Fahd decreed the creation of an appointed Consultative Assembly (*Majlis al-Shura*) on March 1, 1992, his intent was not to create an embryonic legislature modeled after a Western parliamentary concept. Rather, it was to employ a formal Islamic institution for *shura* ("consultation" in Arabic) with "people of knowledge and expertise and specialists" in order to create a consensus legitimizing public policy. With rapid modernization acquired with oil revenues, it was increasingly obvious that an informal personalized system was no longer adequate to create a true consensus and that public participation in the political process must be expanded.

A Majlis al-Shura existed in the Hijaz when it was annexed by the Saudis. King Abd al-Aziz wished to extend it into a national institution then but met with opposition from Najdi religious authorities, who objected that by in effect dealing with statutory law, the assembly was incompatible with the Shari'a, a wholly self-contained, revealed system of divine law. Thus, in some respects, the 1992 decree completed the process of expanding Hijazi political institutions to the entire country, which had begun in the early years of Abd al-Aziz's reign.

The Majlis al-Shura was inaugurated by the king in December 1993 with 60 members. It was expanded to 90 in 1997 and 150 in 2005. Members are appointed for four-year terms and meet in closed sessions at least every two weeks. They are charged with suggesting new regulatory decrees and reviewing and evaluating foreign and domestic policies.

Members include businessmen, technocrats, journalists, Islamic scholars, and professional soldiers and represent all regions of the country. Breaking with tradition, most members are in their forties and fifties, young by Saudi leadership standards. Thus, although the majority comes from well-known families, they tend not to be the family patriarchs that speculation had suggested would be appointed. Many have doctorates from the United States, Europe, Australia, or the Middle East. Similarly, an ever increasing number of Saudi religious community members are younger men with outside exposure, in contrast with the older generation of

Islamic leaders, many of whom have never been outside the Muslim world or even outside Saudi Arabia. The real test for the Majlis will be the degree to which its members actually participate in the consultative process (*shura*), but whatever its future, it reflects a remarkable vision as an adaptation of a classical Islamic concept to modern government.

In 2005, King Abdallah succeeded his half brother King Fahd, ending a ten-year hiatus during which Fahd was incapacitated due to medical problems and Abdallah headed a caretaker government. As king, Abdallah has reenergized the process of political evolution and increased public participation in the political process. Even before his succession, however, he was seeking new opportunities for more political participation of all Saudi citizens. In response to petitions signed by over 350 intellectuals in 2003, the government, under Abdallah's auspices, initiated the National Dialogue (*al-Hiwar al-Watani*), a forum headquartered in Riyadh to bring together interest groups to discuss topics of public concern such as the role of women, religious tolerance, and future prospects for youth.

Another political concession by Abdallah was for half of the members of the 179 municipal councils to be chosen by popular elections held in 2005. Among the main issues discussed by the candidates were political reform, corruption, environmental issues, and better public service.

The Political Decision-Making Process

Islamic cultural traits have often made the Saudi political decision-making process appear arbitrary and capricious to the untrained eye. There is a systemic logic to the process, however. At the heart of the system are two fundamental concepts, *ijma'* ("consensus" in Arabic), which is derived through *shura* ("consultation"). Consensus has been used to legitimize collective decisions in the Arab world for millennia, whether in government, business, or family, and has been incorporated into Islam.

With the coming of the oil age, government operations have become far too large and too complicated for the traditional, personalized decision-making process that had existed virtually unchanged until the mid-twentieth century. In addition, the advent of the information-technology revolution has increased exponentially the need to expand the number of citizens participating directly in the decision-making process. Evolutionary reform is vital, but to maintain legitimacy, it is more likely to reflect the teachings of Islam than those of Thomas Jefferson.

THE POLITICAL PROCESS

The Saudi political process basically works on three levels: royal-family politics, national politics, and bureaucratic politics. All are separate but highly interrelated.

Royal Family Politics

Few outside the Al Saud know how the royal family actually operates or even its size (estimated in the thousands). It has historically been rife with rivalries and contention, yet assiduously shuns publicity and always seeks an outward appearance of unanimity. Consensus is key, but family, branch, generation, seniority, and sibling ties (particularly siblings of the same mother) are very important. The ruling branch is composed of the surviving sons of King Abd al-Aziz. Some grandsons have been appointed to senior positions—for instance, Prince Saud Al Faisal serves as foreign minister—but they are generally less influential than members of their fathers' generation.

There are also collateral branches of the family, descended from brothers of former rulers. The two leading collateral branches are the Saud al-Kabir, who descend from an older brother of Abd al-Rahman (Abd al-Aziz's father), and the Ibn Jaluwi, who descend from an uncle of Abd al-Rahman, Jaluwi. Technically, the head of the Saud al-Kabir branch outranks all but the king, since the founder was an older brother of Abd al-Rahman; however, the ruling branch has a monopoly on influence.

Among the sons of Abd al-Aziz, seniority of birth is important but not absolute in determining political influence. Older princes not deemed capable of maintaining high government positions are excluded from the decision-making process except with regard to purely royal-family business.

National and Bureaucratic Politics

National politics is played out not in the royal family per se but in the national ministries. The royal family has ensured that family members fill most senior national security–related cabinet posts. However, the regime has consistently named technocrats to ministerial positions not connected with national security. These posts deal mainly with economics and social welfare, and in those areas it may be said that a technocracy has developed.

As the government expanded rapidly over the years, the sheer size and complexity of its operations made it impossible for the king to be personally involved in all but the most pressing national issues. Thus, senior technocrats have considerable powers as principal advisers to the king in their areas of responsibility and as operational decision makers.

In recent years, an increasing number of the younger generation of Western-educated royal-family members, including those from collateral branches, have entered government, creating a new category of "royal technocrats." However, because the more senior positions are occupied, the younger princes join the government in junior positions. It is too soon to know how they will ultimately affect the political equation, but so far the most successful have won respect on merit as much as rank.

On balance, the evolution of public administration in Saudi Arabia has consisted of a gradual shift from the traditional rule of King Abd al-Aziz to a more institutionalized, bureaucratized government. However, the creation of a government bureaucracy has not diminished the personalization of the policy process so much as rechanneled it, and it is within the present structure that bureaucratic politics has grown and flourished.

POLITICAL DYNAMICS

Political Ideology

Saudi political culture is inseparable from Islam. The country is the cradle of Islam and Arabic, the language of the Qur'an, which is indigenous to northern Arabia. Moreover, from the time of the founder of the ruling family 250 years ago, the teachings of Muhammad ibn Abd al-Wahhab, founder of the puritanical Islamic revival movement, Wahhabism, have constituted the political ideology of Saudi Arabia. Those teachings have provided the Saudi regime with an egalitarian, universal, and moral base that has bound rulers and ruled together through many crises and troubles and has been a major factor in the survival of the Saudi state throughout its often turbulent history. One must use care, however, in looking at Saudi political ideology as analogous to secular political ideologies in the West. Considering that there is no separation of church and state in Saudi Arabia, there is no political culture independent of Islam.

Current Political Issues. The government and mainstream establishment in Saudi Arabia are challenged by two internal forms of religious opposition: from Sunnis, who contest the elite's legitimacy and ability to protect the country from Westernization, and from Shi'as, who generally feel rejected by and discriminated against in a Wahhabi-dominated kingdom. After tensions with the Shi'as during the late 1970s and early 1980s had ebbed significantly, a new round of clashes between active Shi'as and government forces broke out in 2003 and continue to flare up, especially during the Hajj or Ashura. King Abdallah, through the National Dialogue and his reform agenda, uses both force and concessions to prevent the conflict from having any impact on the oil industry, which is largely housed in the Eastern Province.

On the other end of the religious spectrum are Sunni scholars, preachers, and activists, who were influenced by the Muslim Brotherhood and started to agitate against the ruling elites. Radical preachers in local mosques called for young Saudis to do something more meaningful with their lives and join the jihad in Afghanistan and Iraq. Some went even further by including corrupt Arab regimes as targets for jihad actions. Al-Qa'ida is a product of this inflammatory speech, and the government is working hard to crack down on those radicals, arresting and reeducating them. Support is provided by the highest religious authorities in the country, who also recognize that more needs to be done on the ideological front to cut the relationship between militants, disillusioned youth, and religious extremists. Some steps, like the ongoing interfaith dialog in Madrid and direct communications with the Vatican, are considered very positive by Western observers but might be counterproductive with the more radicalized ulema.

Foreign Policies

The Saudi Worldview. Saudi foreign and national security policies revolve around four major goals: preserving an Islamic way of life at home and abroad, protecting against external threats to national and regional security, providing for the national economic welfare and extending economic assistance to those in need throughout the Arab and Muslim world, and survival of the regime. How these are translated into relations with other states is largely a product of a uniquely Saudi view of the world.

The Saudi world view conforms closely to the classical, bipolar Islamic theory of international relations that contrasts believers (monotheists) with unbelievers (atheists and polytheists). The believers (who include Christians, Jews, and Zoroastrians as "People of the Book,") inhabit Dar al-Islam, the Abode of Islam (i.e., the land of those who live by God's law), while the unbelievers inhabit Dar al-Harb, the Abode of War (i.e., the land of those who live outside God's law). This world view is a product of three strong, though seemingly contradictory, themes: a strong sense of Arabian self-identity, a deep and abiding allegiance to Islam, and millennia of physical isolation from the non-Islamic outside world until well into the twentieth century, particularly in Najd.

Most Arabs equate their self-identity with pan-Arabism, a relatively recent political movement based on the "rebirth" of secular Arab nationalism. Secular Arab nationalism reached its apogee in the 1950s and 1960s as the idiom for expressing political hostility toward the West after centuries of political domination. The Saudis, while sharing an Arab self-identity, reject secular Arab nationalism as a political ideology, considering it incompatible with Islamic political theory. They base their self-identity on blood lines, equating it with their Arabian tribal genealogy, which they trace back to the beginning of history.

Saudi Arabia takes special pride in being the birthplace of Islam and in the fact that Arabic, the language of Islam's holy book, the Qur'an, is indigenous to northern Arabia. Moreover, the Saudi sense of responsibility for the preservation of the Islamic way of life was substantially strengthened in the 1920s when Abd al-Aziz occupied the Hijaz and the holy cities of Makkah and al-Madinah. As guardians of these two holy sites, the Saudis assumed the responsibility of defenders of the Islamic way of life throughout the Muslim world. It is in this context that one must view the title adopted by King Fahd in 1986, Khadim al-Haramayn al-Sharifayn, meaning "Custodian of the Two Holy Places." The Saudi sense of Arabian self-identity and of their role as custodians of Islamic values has been further reinforced by centuries of isolation from the Western world. Although the oil age has transformed the kingdom into a global oil state, the traditional Saudi worldview has remained largely intact.

The Saudi Approach to Foreign Relations. Saudi foreign and national security policy making is imbued with two strong, though seemingly contradictory, themes: extraordinary cultural self-assurance based on a sense of Islamic heritage and Arabian, tribe-based self-identity and a heightened sense of insecurity based on the historical experience of an insular people eternally surrounded by enemies. A basic tenet of foreign policy, therefore, has always been to avoid confrontations whenever possible and to seek alliances and cooperation in the face of external threats to political, economic, and national security interests.

In accordance with its world view, Saudi Arabia has developed close ties with fellow Arab and Muslim states. It is a member of the Arab League and the GCC, as well as a charter member of and prime mover in the 1969 creation of the Organization of the Islamic Conference (OIC), the premier international organization serving the Muslim world. The OIC Secretariat is located in Jiddah.

Alliance politics with powerful partners sharing mutual interests have traditionally been the major focus of Saudi foreign security and economic policies. In the years leading up to World War I, King Abd al-Aziz relied on the British, the paramount Western power in Arabia, for both protection and economic assistance. Gradually, however, he turned to the United States, in part because he was convinced that they had no imperial designs on the region and also because his earliest experience with Americans was largely positive. American Protestant medical missionaries located in Bahrain began bringing modern medicine to the kingdom in 1913, and in 1933 American oil men began searching for oil in the Eastern Province, establishing what would become important and lasting mutual Saudi-US commercial, and later strategic, oil interests.

Yet, not until World War II did the United States establish a resident diplomatic mission in the kingdom and extend lend-lease economic assistance. Perhaps the cementing of close political relations between the two countries during the reign of King Abd al-Aziz resulted from his meeting with President Franklin D. Roosevelt aboard the USS *Quincy* in the Great Bitter Lake of the Suez Canal on February 14, 1945.

Since then, a special relationship between the two countries has evolved, due not only to mutual interest in reliable supplies of oil flowing to the West but also to their close cooperation in Middle East regional security. During the Cold War, Saudi Arabia considered atheistic Soviet Communist ideology to be the greatest threat to Muslim hearts and minds. Thus, the kingdom also opposed radical Arab leaders such as President Gamal Abd al-Nasser of Egypt, who had established cordial relations with the Soviet Union. Even after the end of the Cold War, Saudi Arabia looked to the United States for military training and for a great proportion of its arms purchases.

US-Saudi relations have not always been smooth, however. The greatest source of stress has been what the Saudis see as the disproportionate US support for Israel. US rejection of Saudi efforts to help in the quest for an Arab-Israeli peace has added to the stress. In general, the most stressful Saudi-US relations have coincided with periods of polarization of the Arab-Israeli conflict, beginning in 1948 with the initial partition of Palestine to create a Jewish state. From the Saudi perspective, not only did the lead US role in the partition of Palestine and the creation of Israel constitute grave injustice, but for President Harry Truman to ignore President Roosevelt's oral and written word to King Abd al-Aziz in 1945 that the United States would not act on partition without first consulting him and other Arab leaders was considered the height of dishonor. Against the advice of the State Department, Truman bowed to US domestic political pressure in engineering the partition and creation of Israel in 1948.

The three periods of greatest polarization since 1948 have resulted from Israel's annexation of Arab East Jerusalem in the wake of the 1967 Arab-Israeli War, the Arab oil embargo led by King Faisal during the 1973 Arab-Israeli War, and a wave of American anti-Arab and anti-Muslim sentiment following the terrorist attacks on the World Trade Center in New York City and the Pentagon in Washington, DC, on September 11, 2001, in which fifteen of the nineteen terrorists were Saudis.

Following the Israeli occupation of the Palestinian West Bank, Gaza, and East Jerusalem in the 1967 Arab-Israeli War, the United Nations Security Council passed Resolution 242, which called for a return of Palestinian territory in return for an end of hostilities (land for peace). Israel ignored the resolution, but particularly egregious from the Saudi perspective was Israel's unilateral "annexation" of Jerusalem. Not only did this violate international law, but it would grant Israeli sovereignty over the Muslim shrines of al-Aqsa, located in East Jerusalem. Al-Aqsa is the third holiest site in Sunni Islam after Makkah and al-Madinah. The US did not recognize the annexation but it did nothing to prevent it, nor did it have the domestic political capital either to push for an Arab-Israeli peace settlement based on UNSC Resolution 242.

The 1973–1974 Arab oil embargo ironically ran counter to the Saudis' estimate of their own economic and security interests. Saudi Arabia has always been moderate on oil prices due to the reality that expansion of alternative sources of energy due to high prices could do irreparable damage to the Saudi oil economy. The embargo also strained Saudi reliance on the United States to deter external military threats against the kingdom that were in neither country's interest.

Apparently, the embargo was the result of King Faisal's anger over what he considered President Richard Nixon's going back on his word. Two days after Nixon had sent a secret message to Faisal assuring him that the United States would be evenhanded during the war, the president announced $2 billion in military aid to Israel, presumably to assuage domestic fears over the heavy equipment losses Israel was sustaining in the war. Faisal had never forgotten President Truman's breaking of Roosevelt's promise on partition in 1948. As Saudi foreign minister at the time, Faisal had urged his father to break diplomatic relations.

The embargo quickly strained Saudi relations with the United States. Not only did it bring economic hardship to the United States, but politically it resulted in a strong anti-Saudi campaign in the US media, exploiting domestic anger at high oil prices and fears that the "Arab oil weapon" could threaten US interests in the region, including Israel's national security. Saudi Arabia originally benefited from high oil prices, but fearing strained relations would undermine its national security interests, which depended heavily on US support, it sought to negotiate a rapid end to the embargo. In the longer run, however, relations returned to normal. The embargo forced the United States and other Western oil consumers to reduce demand by increasing energy efficiency. By the 1980s, the oil shortage was replaced by a glut, keeping oil prices low for a whole generation, and US-Saudi relations based on mutual security as well as petroleum interests normalized.

The September 11, 2001, terrorist attacks traumatized most Americans, who had for years naively believed themselves impervious to such assaults. The fear and anger aroused by the attacks brought broad support for the government's hardline response of all-out global war against terrorism—with the perpetrators identified as chiefly Arabs and Muslims—and Israel was praised as a partner in the war. Saudi businessmen, students, and those seeking medical care were singled out at ports of entry as potential terrorists. The heightened xenophobia was further fueled by another anti-Saudi campaign in the US media, which denounced the kingdom not only as a supporter of terrorism but as thoroughly evil. In Saudi Arabia, American policies and attitudes were in turn met with anger, fear, and a sense of betrayal by a long-time friendly ally, leading to a sharp decline in travel to the United States and a significant flight of Saudi capital investment. As time has passed, mutual fears and feelings of grievance appear again to be receding, and relations have once again begun to normalize. Nevertheless, it is likely that the

Saudis will increase the diversification of their foreign policy, as well as commercial and security relations, to safeguard against a repeat of their post–September 11 experience. Following the military occupation of Iraq by the United States and Britain in 2003, Saudi Arabia rejected the US proposal to use its airfields for attacks on Iraq. US headquarters was thus relocated to Qatar, but the tensions kept growing. The Saudis were against the war due to concerns over growing inter-Arab conflicts. At one point, Abdallah even called it an "illegal foreign occupation," showing his frustration with the dangerous and hazardous directions of the conflict. However, there is also a deep mistrust that a Shi'a-dominated government in Baghdad would become an agent of Iran. The Saudi government long warned about the growing influence of Iran and started to support Sunni tribal militias long before the coalition troops discovered their value.

To challenge the growing security needs of the country, a multileveled and well-equipped security force, headed by the very diverse (for Saudi Arabia) National Security Council, protects the traditional and current form of leadership and government. This gives Saudi Arabia the necessary prowess, strength, and credibility to continue acting like a power broker in broader Gulf and Middle East affairs, and it is utilizing its position to call for a Middle East free of weapons of mass destruction.

Although Iran has for many years been considered a major threat to national and regional security of the Gulf, Saudi Arabia continues to work with the Iranians to solve bilateral issues. While the existence of nuclear weapons in Iran would obviously be seen as a security threat, Saudi Arabia has always accepted the right of other states, including Iran, to develop peaceful uses of nuclear power and retains the right to do so itself at sometime in the future.

As a leading Arab-Islamic state and regional power broker, Saudi Arabia is also committed to mediating in regional conflicts. Following political examples and strategies that have evolved over centuries, the Saudis consider moderation, negotiation, reconciliation, and alliance building the necessary tools to bring together rival fractions in Lebanon, Palestine, and other Arab countries. The level of commitment to, and natural interest in, solving the Arab-Israeli conflict is illustrated by the kingdom's effort to host unity talks between Hamas and Fatah and the Arab League's decision to accept King Abdallah's peace proposal. Also, through the Saudi Fund for Development, the Saudis stretch their influence beyond national borders to deliver help to those countries in need. A balanced foreign policy based on mediation, collaboration, and the building of alliances serves as a tool to lower domestic and international threats to the national security of the kingdom.

BIBLIOGRAPHY

Definitive works on Saudi Arabia are comparatively few. R. Bayly Winder's *Saudi Arabia in the Nineteenth Century* (New York: St. Martin's Press, 1985) is still the standard work in English on earlier history. Any of the several works by H. St. John B. Philby, though not scholarly, captures the feel of Saudi Arabia in the interwar and immediate post–World War II period. Two of his books, *Arabian Jubilee* (London: Robert Hale, 1952) and *Saudi Arabia* (London: Ernest Benn, 1955), written to commemorate the fiftieth year of Abd al-Aziz's reign, would be good places to begin. Another classic is T. E. Lawrence's *The Seven Pillars of Wisdom* (Garden City, NY: Doubleday, 1935), about his exploits in the Hijaz during World War I. For a good study on the earlier history of the Hijaz, see William Ochsenwald's *Religion, Society and the State in Arabia: The Hijaz Under Ottoman Control, 1849–1908* (Columbus: Ohio State University Press, 1984). For a general historical overview, both Alexander Vassiliev's *The History of Saudi Arabia* (London: Saqi, 1998) and Madawi al-Rasheed's atypical *A History of Saudi Arabia* (Cambridge University Press, 2002) are recommended.

There are still relatively few good studies on Saudi society and internal political dynamics. John A. Shaw and David E. Long's *Saudi Arabian Modernization: The Impact of Change on Stability,* vol. 10, Washington Paper No. 89 (New York: Praeger, 1980), though dated, gives a good overview of the impact of social and economic development on the kingdom. A more recent work is Mordachai Abir's *Saudi Arabia: Government, Society and the Gulf Crisis* (London: Routledge, 1993). Mamoun Fandy's *Saudi Arabia and the Politics of Dissent* (New York: St. Martin's Press, 1999) is an analysis of Saudi dissidents in the 1990s, and Joseph Kechichian's *Succession in Saudi Arabia* (New York: I. B. Tauris, 2001) explores a subject that has generated much discussion in the West. Two studies concentrating on Saudi women are Lila Abu-Lughod, *Veiled Sentiments: Honored Poetry in a Bedouin Society* (Berkeley: University of California Press, 1986), and Mona Almunajjed, *Women in Saudi Arabia* (New York: St. Martin's Press, 1997).

For readers interested in the modern Hajj, see David E. Long's *The Hajj Today: A Survey of the Contemporary Makkah Pilgrimage* (Albany: State University of New York Press, 1979). An interesting account of Makkah and the Hajj in the nineteenth century is C. Snouck-Hurgronje's *Mekka in the Latter Part of the Nineteenth Century,* trans. J. H. Monahan (Leiden: E. J. Brill, and London: Luzac and Co., 1931). Natana DeLong-Bas's extensive study on Wahhabism, *Wahhabi Islam* (Oxford University Press, 2004), will be considered the standard in her field. For an example of an ancient Islamic institution being adapted into the Saudi Islamic system, see David E. Long, "The Board of Grievances in Saudi Arabia," *Middle East Journal* 27, no. 4 (winter 1973), 71–75. The impact of the generation gap and new evolving identities are discussed in Mai Yamani's *Changed Identities: The Challenge of the New Generation in Saudi Arabia* (London: The Royal Institute of International Affairs, 2000).

There are a number of good studies on the development of the Saudi oil industry. George W. Stocking's *Middle East Oil: A Study in Political and Economic Controversy*

(Nashville, TN: Vanderbilt University Press, 1970) is a classic. Daniel Yergin's exhaustively researched best seller, *The Prize: The Epic Quest for Oil, Money and Power* (New York: Simon and Schuster, 1990), is must reading. The best scholarly treatment of US–Saudi oil relations is David S. Painter's *Oil and the American Century* (Baltimore: Johns Hopkins University Press, 1986). A fascinating book on the Saudi Arabian Monetary Agency, the Saudi central bank, is *Saudi Arabia: The Making of a Financial Giant* (New York: New York University Press, 1983) by Arthur N. Young, who played a major role in the agency's creation.

Works on political, military, and strategic issues are highly uneven. David E. Long's *The United States and Saudi Arabia: Ambivalent Allies* (Boulder, CO: Westview Press, 1985) is a short but authoritative overview of US–Saudi political, economic, oil, and military relations up to 1985. A good, comprehensive study of military and strategic issues predating the Kuwait invasion is Anthony Cordesman's *The Gulf and the Search for Strategic Stability: Saudi Arabia, the Military Balance in the Gulf, and Trends in the Arab-Israeli Military Balance* (Boulder, CO: Westview Press, and London: Mansell, 1984). A recent study of US relations with Saudi Arabia, Rachel Bronson's *Thicker Than Oil: America's Uneasy Partnership with Saudi Arabia* (New York: Oxford University Press, 2005), documents post–September 11 events.

Two nonscholarly books are worth looking into for their wealth of narrative, if not their interpretative analysis: Robert Lacey's *The Kingdom* (London: Hutcheson, 1981) and David Howarth and Richard Johns' *The House of Saud* (London: Sidgwick and Jackson, 1981). The most recent survey of Saudi Arabia is David E. Long and Sebastian Maisel's *The Kingdom of Saudi Arabia* (Gainesville: University Press of Florida, 2010). Finally, those interested in the Rub' al-Khali should see Wilfred Thesiger's *Arabian Sands* (New York: Dutton, 1959). Finally, David E. Long also provides the most concise study on Saudi Arabian culture in transition: *Culture and Customs of Saudi Arabia* (Westport, CT: Greenwood, 2005), which in combination with Sebastian Maisel and John Shoup's *Encyclopedia of Life in Saudi Arabia and the Arab Gulf States* (Westport, CT: Greenwood, 2009) gives the reader a rare insight into the evolution and functioning of Saudi lifestyles.

5

REPUBLIC OF IRAQ

Judith S. Yaphe

Since the modern state of Iraq was created under a British mandate in 1920, scholars and statesmen have argued over its colonial legacies, identity, and viability. Some saw Iraq as an artificial creation by greedy British and French diplomats eager for booty following the Great War. Iraqis were Arabs or Kurds, Sunnis or Shi'as, Christians or Jews; they were not "Iraqis." For Iraqis, however, Iraqi nationalism was born in the ashes of the Ottoman Empire and was the force that shaped modern Iraq despite British efforts to impose foreign values, government institutions, and rulers on the new country. Iraq has survived three occupations: by the Turks in the sixteenth century, the British in the twentieth century, and the Americans in the twenty-first century. Seven years after liberation, and as it faces its second national parliamentary election, Iraq has an opportunity to showcase its successful transition from dictatorship to democracy. The inability of political factions to agree on the nature of governance, disputed territories, income distribution, and national reconciliation suggests, however, that Iraq as a nation is still more dream than reality.

HISTORICAL BACKGROUND

Iraq is a land rich in resources and history. Known as Mesopotamia ("the land between the rivers," that is, the Tigris and Euphrates) until the twentieth century, it has been a land of strategic importance since ancient times due to geography and the availability of fresh water and in modern times due to significant oil reserves. As a result, it has experienced foreign invasions and occupations, tribal wars, ethnic and sectarian factionalism, violence, and decay. Bordered by deserts in the south and high mountains to the north, Iraq is virtually without natural defenses against invasion. Its occupiers—Arabs, Greeks, Persians, Romans, Turks, and, in modern times, the British and the Americans—have all left their mark on the country's diverse people and cultures, fashioning a society in search of an identity.

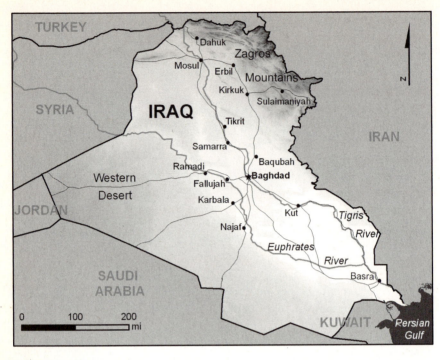

Republic of Iraq

Arab Conquests: 632–1258

The Arab-Islamic conquest of Iraq began in 633 CE, one year after the death of the Prophet Muhammad. It was one of the most decisive events in Iraqi history. Arabic became the predominant language (except among Kurdish speakers in the highlands), and Islam became the religion of virtually all inhabitants. For over a century after the conquest, Iraq was governed as a province from capitals of the Islamic empire, first Medina and then Damascus. Iraqis came to resent the power of Damascus (a theme that persists even in modern times) and often revolted against it. In the process, Iraq acquired a reputation, which it retains, as a territory difficult to govern.

The founding of the Umayyad caliphate, which moved the capital to Damascus in 661, led to a religious schism that still divides the Islamic community. In 680, Husayn, grandson of the Prophet Muhammad and son of Ali, the fourth caliph, challenged the Umayyads and was killed along with a small band of followers near Karbala in Iraq. Ali's followers, known as Shi'a (short for *shi'at Ali*, the "partisans of Ali"), went underground as opponents of the established order. Followers of the Umayyads came to be known as Sunnis, those who adhere to the Prophet's traditions. Gradually, the Shi'as became a distinctive sect within Islam, with different leaders (called imams rather than caliphs) and different doctrines considered heresy by the Sunni victors. As a persecuted minority, the Shi'as acquired a sense of social alienation and feelings of oppression and injustice, characteristics still evident in the twenty-first century.

In 747, Abd al-Abbas, a descendant of Muhammad's uncle, revolted against the Umayyads and in 750 established the Abbasid caliphate. In 762, the Abbasids moved the capital to the new city of Baghdad. The Abbasid period (750–1258) was a great era in Iraqi, Arab, and Islamic history. Iraq became the center of a prosperous empire that stretched from southern France to the borders of China and a brilliant civilization in which science, architecture, and literature flourished.

The decline of the Abbasid caliphate was gradual. Prosperity was concentrated in the urban upper classes, and little filtered down to the rural and urban poor, who often revolted. Turkish captives were used as warriors and administrators, and factionalism within the ruling elite caused economic decline and neglect of the irrigation system. Weakness within encouraged incursion from without, including the invasion of the Seljuk Turks in 1055.

It was the Mongols, however, who caused the ultimate demise of the Abbasid caliphate. In 1258, Hulagu, grandson of Genghis Khan, destroyed much of Baghdad and the irrigation system on which its prosperity depended. Even more devastating to Iraq was the invasion of Timur the Lame in 1401. He so devastated the country that it did not recover until the mid-twentieth century. In addition, Iraq's strategic location astride the major East-West trade routes was greatly undermined by the Portuguese discovery of the sea route around the Cape of Good Hope. Iraqis recall their glorious Abbasid past, but their political and social environment—and much of their psychology—has been shaped mainly by the centuries of stagnation that followed.

Ottoman Rule: 1258–1922

From 1258 until 1534 Iraq was divided into provinces often ruled by Turkish tribal dynasties from capitals in Persian territory. Because of the lack of a central government, neither the irrigation systems nor the urban culture could be revived. The Ottoman conquest of Iraq began in 1514 as an outgrowth of a religious and dynastic war between the Sunni Ottoman sultan and the Shi'a Safavid shah of Persia. Most of Iraq was incorporated into the Ottoman domain and divided into three provinces: Baghdad, Basra, and Mosul.

The Ottomans were unable to bring stability or prosperity to Iraq, primarily for two reasons. The first was a succession of Ottoman-Persian wars that continued until 1818. The wars not only ravaged the Iraqi countryside but also renewed Shi'a-Sunni distrust. Iraqi Shi'as sometimes sided with their coreligionists in Persia, and

IRAQ

Capital city	Baghdad
Chief of state	President Jalal Talabani
Head of government	Prime Minister Nuri al-Maliki
Major political parties	Assyrian Democratic Movement, Badr Organization, Constitutional Monarchy Movement, Da'wa al-Islamiya Party, General Conference of Iraqi People, Independent Iraqi Alliance, Iraqi Communist Party, Iraqi Front for National Dialogue, Iraqi Hizballah, Iraqi Independent Democrats, Iraqi Islamic Party, Iraqi National Accord, Iraqi National Congress, Iraqi National Council for Dialogue, Iraqi National Unity Movement, Islamic Action Organization, Islamic Supreme Council of Iraq, Jama'at al Fadilah, Kurdistan Democratic Party, Kurdistan Islamic Union, Patriotic Union of Kurdistan, Sahawa al-Iraq
Ethnic groups	Arab (75%–80%), Kurdish (15%–20%), Turkoman, Assyrian, or other (5%)
Religious groups	Shi'a Muslim (60%–65%), Sunni Muslim (32%–37%), Christian or other (3%)
Export partners	United States (36.8%), Italy (12.6%), South Korea (9.5%), Taiwan (6.3%), Spain (5.2%), Canada (4.7%), France (4.4%), Netherlands (4.2%)
Import partners	Syria (30.5%), Turkey (19.8%), United States (11.1%), Jordan (5%), China (4.8%)

the Ottomans came to regard them as a potential "fifth column." Eventually the Ottomans came to rely on Sunnis in the army and government, thus perpetuating Sunni political dominance.

Second was the weakness of Ottoman power. As Ottoman society declined in the seventeenth and eighteenth centuries, direct administration ceased in Iraq, and local tribal chiefs held sway in Arab and Kurdish areas. In the late eighteenth century, Ottoman efforts to gain control over Iraq's fractious Arab tribes and restrict the growing influence of Persian Shi'a clerics in southern Iraq hastened the conversion of many Arab tribes from Sunni to Shi'a Islam. By the nineteenth century, the fragmentation was complete. What little Ottoman control remained was inefficient and corrupt. Most of the local population despised the Ottoman Turks as occupiers.

Ottoman administration revived for brief periods. In 1831, Ottoman Sultan Mahmud II reasserted direct control over Iraq, though these gains were frittered away by subsequent rulers. Midhat Pasha, Ottoman governor of Baghdad from 1869 to 1872, extended his authority into the countryside, brought secular education to the cities, and attempted land settlement among the tribes. His schools produced administrators and army officers who went on to become leaders of Iraq after World War I. Almost all these new leaders were Sunni Arabs. The Shi'as shunned the schools, since they were secular and dominated by Sunni Turks.

During the nineteenth century, Iraq was also drawn into international politics and economics. The opening of the Suez Canal in 1869 increased Iraq's trade, and in the south some landlords shifted from subsistence agriculture to cash crops. Printing presses and newspapers were introduced in the 1860s. Contact with new ideas stirred a modest renaissance among religious leaders (Sunni and Shi'a) and Arabic scholars. Because of its strategic location astride overland routes to India, Iraq attracted increasing British concern. Meanwhile, international commerce produced a small class of urban merchants and farmers tied to the new market economy. These benefits, however, could not overcome the centuries of indifferent and often corrupt Ottoman rule. Iraq entered the twentieth century a profoundly underdeveloped country, only marginally touched by the economic, scientific, and political developments that had transformed Europe in the nineteenth century.

The British Mandate: 1920–1932

The impact of the British in shaping modern Iraq has been second only to that of the seventh-century Islamic conquest and the thirteenth-century Mongol invasions. The British created the modern state of Iraq, established its present boundaries, and introduced a monarch with impeccable Arab and Islamic credentials. They also incorporated a diverse ethnic and sectarian population that would be both a source of strength and instability for the new state.

Britain occupied Iraq in stages during World War I, starting with Basra (1914), then Baghdad (1917), and finally Mosul (1918). British control over Iraq was formalized at the San Remo Conference in April 1920, which granted Britain a mandate over the country, subject to supervision by the League of Nations. British control over the territory and its government was constrained by several factors. First, the mandate itself was designed to prepare the country for independence, but the British could not agree among themselves on who should rule Iraq, how it should be ruled, or when Iraqis would meet European standards of political responsibility. Second, Great Britain faced a growing demand at the end of the war to cut back on financial and military commitments to Iraq. This sentiment was hastened by the anti-British revolt of 1920, the suppression of which cost nearly £40 million and hundreds of British lives. Third, a vigorous nationalist movement emerged, which began agitating for removal of British control even before the war had ended. Arabism and nationalism had had a hold on the imaginations of Iraq's Arabs since 1916, when Iraqi Arabs who had served in the Ottoman army joined the Arab revolt against the Turks. In 1920 Sunni and Shi'a Arabs joined together to oppose British occupation, creating a national rite of passage that resonates still.

As a result, the British sought a less expensive means of governing Iraq and found it in three instruments of indirect rule. First, they established a monarchy in Iraq in the person of Prince Faysal, third son of the Hashimite ruler of Makkah, who had cooperated with the British during the war. In 1921, after a carefully controlled election, Faysal became the first of three Hashimite kings to rule Iraq. Under the British-written constitution, the king was given considerable powers, including the right to appoint the prime minister and dismiss parliament. Britain exercised its influence through the king and a network of British advisers in key ministries. Second, the British outlined their mandatory relationship with Iraq through a series of treaties signed between 1922 and 1932. These provided the British with bases and other facilities in return for help, advice, and protection for the new state. Third, they expanded their use of air power to monitor tribal movements and quell threats to security.

Although the British created new Western-style democratic institutions in Iraq, including a parliament, a constitution, and indirect elections, responsibility for government was unclear. King Faysal obeyed British directives but also helped his Iraqi supporters, many of whom had fought with him in the Arab Revolt of 1916, to create an Iraqi and Arab identity in a secular state. The British also relied on this small group of nationalists and on a parliament filled with tribal leaders and wealthy urban elites willing to trade political acquiescence for self-interest and privilege. The British opposed creation of an army and a uniform school system, but Faysal appointed nationalists who built a modern, Sunni-dominated officer corps and an Arab-centric educational system. These became the backbone of the new state.

Not everyone was satisfied with the British distribution of power. The Kurds rebelled against Arab rule and eventually were given special consideration, particularly in the use of their language in schools. Shi'a religious leaders led a rebellion against the mandate and ended up in exile in Iran. For much of the Mandate period, Faysal was able to maintain the balance between British and nationalist in-

terests. In 1929, the British negotiated a treaty that met British and most national-
ist demands. The mandate formally ended in 1932, Iraq was admitted to the
League of Nations as an independent state, and a new Anglo-Iraq treaty gave
Britain air bases and Iraq military protection.

Constitutional Monarchy: 1932–1958

The end of the mandate and the reduction of British control ushered in a period
of instability (1932–1945) that revealed the weakness of the constitutional structure and the fragility of Iraq's sense of nationhood. Several religious and ethnic
groups asserted claims to a greater share of power, and the Iraqi army entered the
political arena and committed its first act of ethnic cleansing.

In 1933 the Assyrian (Nestorian Christian) community demanded the right to
self-government and was put down by the Iraqi army. In the process, a massacre of
Assyrians occurred in northern Iraq that besmirched the reputation of the new
government. In the mid-1930s a rash of rebellions broke out among the Shi'a
tribes of southern Iraq. Shi'a religious leaders used this occasion to demand more
Shi'a representation in government and more recognition of their religion and
culture in the emerging state system. Little heed was paid to these requests, and
both Shi'as and Kurds continued to be underrepresented in cabinets dominated
by Arab Sunnis.

Another source of instability was the untimely death of King Faysal I in September 1933. Faysal was succeeded by his son Ghazi, a young man well liked by
the army and the nationalists but too inexperienced to provide the leadership
needed to balance Iraq's political and social groups. During Ghazi's reign
(1933–1939), the Iraqi army came to play an increasingly dominant role in politics. In 1936, it staged the first of a series of military coups aimed at replacing cabinets but not the monarchy. The increased role of the military indicated its
growing strength as a political force and the fragility of the constitutional system.
The accidental death of King Ghazi in 1939 further weakened the monarchy. He
was succeeded by his four-year-old son, Faysal II, but real power lay in the hands
of his regent, Abd al-Ilah, an unpopular cousin of Ghazi, a pro-British politician,
and a man unable to fill the shoes of Faysal I.

By 1939 the Iraqi political leadership was in disarray. Two factions had emerged:
a pro-British group led by Nuri al-Sa'id, an Ottoman-trained army officer who had
joined the 1916 Arab Revolt, and a pro-German nationalist faction supported by
the army and led by Rashid Ali al-Gaylani, a civilian politician. In 1941, the army
and Rashid Ali led a coup that ousted Abd al-Ilah, Nuri al-Sa'id, and other pro-
British politicians. Fearful that this outcome would alter the balance of power in the
Middle East in the Axis's favor, Britain reoccupied Iraq from 1941 to 1945, restored
Abd al-Ilah and Nuri to power, and encouraged the removal of the anti-British

elements in the army and the bureaucracy. This move restored stability to Iraq and placed the country firmly in the Western orbit, but it also created resentment inside Iraq toward the ruling group and its association with a foreign power. The 1941 coup was a forerunner of the 1958 revolution. It also helped shape the worldview of Saddam Husayn, whose uncle was among those arrested by the British.

From 1945 to 1958 the power structure of Iraq remained relatively stable, with power in the hands of Nuri al-Sa'id, who served as prime minister thirteen times between 1941 and 1958. Stability was enhanced by the development of Iraq's oil resources and the expenditure of oil revenues on dams, roads, health, and education. As education spread to rural areas, more Shi'as and Kurds entered the political establishment, quieting ethnic and sectarian tensions. Between 1945 and 1958 there were two Kurdish and three Shi'a prime ministers. Nuri believed that foreign powers—especially Great Britain and the United States—had a role to play in Iraq's development, and he cooperated closely with them. In 1955, Iraq joined the Baghdad Pact, a Western-oriented, anti-Soviet defense alliance, with Great Britain, Iran, Pakistan, and Turkey and with the United States as an observer.

However, the relative stability of the postwar period could not conceal the flaws of the political and social structure that eventually resulted in the regime's overthrow in a violent revolt. Behind a parliamentary facade, Nuri ruled with a heavy hand. Elections were held periodically, manipulated by Nuri to assure favorable results. Political parties were controlled, and opposition leaders, especially Communists, were jailed; some were executed.

The educated population increasingly resented the regime's close ties with foreign powers. Riots and demonstrations erupted in 1948 (against a proposed new Anglo-Iraq treaty), in 1952 (against establishment of foreign bases, including an attack against a US facility), and in 1956 (against the British, French, and Israeli invasion of Egypt). Nationalist sentiments were fanned by Egyptian president Gamal Abd al-Nasser, who attacked the Baghdad Pact and urged the people of Iraq to overthrow the regime. These antiforeign sentiments took root in the army, where younger officers formed a Free Officers group to plan the overthrow of the regime.

Social reformers also inveighed against the misdistribution of wealth and privilege in the country, pointing to an upper class of landlord-shaykhs and urban entrepreneurs who dominated parliament and blocked land-reform legislation. Rapid urban migration from the countryside created large slum areas in and around the capital, accentuating class divisions. Disaffection with the regime came to a head in 1958. On July 14, troops under the command of Brig. Gen. Abd al-Karim Qasim and Col. Abd al-Salam Arif, both Free Officers, moved on Baghdad and in a violent and bloody coup ended the monarchy, killing the royal family and Nuri al-Sa'id and imprisoning many "old regime" leaders.

Republican Iraq: 1958–1968

The overthrow of the monarchy ushered in a decade of political instability. Between 1958 and 1968 there were four changes of regime, several involving considerable bloodshed. Although a facade of civilian government was maintained, the revolution placed the army in power, with officers assuming the most important political positions.

The republican period began with a military regime headed by Abd al-Karim Qasim (1958–1963). A three-man Council of Sovereignty, consisting of a Sunni Arab, a Shi'a Arab, and a Kurd, replaced the monarchy. Within two weeks of the revolution, a provisional constitution was enacted, placing all executive and legislative authority in the Council of Ministers, with the approval of the Council of Sovereignty. Parliament was abolished. Real power rested in the hands of Qasim, who became prime minister and minister of defense, and Arif, who became deputy prime minister and minister of interior. In the initial euphoria of the revolution, the new government released political opponents jailed under the monarchy, including Communists, and allowed Mustafa Barzani, the leader of a Kurdish rebellion in 1946, to return to Iraq.

The new government moved rapidly to institute social reforms and to change foreign policy. In September 1958 it promulgated an agrarian reform law limiting the size of landholdings and placing a ceiling on rent. Qasim also revised the personal-status law, giving women more rights and security. Finally, in 1961, after a bitter dispute with the foreign-owned Iraq Petroleum Company (IPC), Qasim expropriated 99.5 percent of its concession area. These acts may have brought a measure of social justice, but they were poorly managed and initiated a period of economic decline.

In foreign policy the new regime abrogated the Baghdad Pact and recognized the Soviet Union and the People's Republic of China. In 1959 Iraq signed economic and arms-supply agreements with Moscow. This orientation toward the Communist bloc and the break in treaty relations with the West began a period of isolation from, and increasingly tense relations with, the West, features that persisted long after the end of the Cold War.

Unfortunately, the revolution failed to restrain the power struggle between its two main figures, Qasim and Arif. Their personal differences crystallized around a key policy issue—whether Iraq should move toward union with Egypt or remain independent and concentrate on reform at home. Arif, backed by Nasserists and the Ba'th Party, favored union; Qasim, supported by the Communist Party and the Kurds, opposed it.

In September 1958, Qasim dismissed Arif from office and imprisoned him on a charge of attempting to assassinate Qasim. This provoked the Arab nationalists, who precipitated a rebellion in Mosul in 1959. With the assistance of the Communists and the Kurds, Qasim suppressed the new rebellion, temporarily crushing the Arab nationalists. Their removal from the political scene allowed the ascendancy of the Communists and the Left. It was not long, however, before Qasim turned on these groups as well, removing leftist ministers from office and curtailing their influence. Although Qasim promised a new constitution and a legislature, none appeared. By 1961, Qasim had established a lackluster dictatorship, backed by his supporters in the army. Enemies of the regime were prosecuted in show trials, and dissidents were executed.

The Kurds also turned against the regime. Mustafa Barzani had gradually become disillusioned by Qasim's failure to fulfill his promises for Kurdish self-government, but Qasim was suspicious of Kurdish demands for autonomy. In 1961, a series of tribal clashes in the north manipulated by Qasim degenerated into a full-scale guerrilla war, which did not end until 1975. For the remainder of the Qasim era, the Kurds effectively engaged a large segment of the Iraqi army, intensifying the divisions within the country and eroding Qasim's dwindling support.

The final blow to the regime came with Qasim's inept claim to Kuwait. In June 1961, Qasim refused to recognize Kuwait's newly acquired independence, claiming that it had been part of Iraq under the Ottoman Empire. His position alienated virtually every country in the Arab world and left Iraq hopelessly isolated. These events, together with underground opposition movements, finally precipitated his downfall. On February 8, 1963, Qasim was overthrown in a coup led by the Iraqi Ba'th Party, together with sympathetic army officers and Arab nationalist groups. The overthrow was bloody, resulting in several days of street fighting between Ba'thists and Communists and Qasim's execution.

The Arab Ba'th Socialist Party (*ba'th* means "renaissance" or "awakening" in Arabic) was a militant, anticolonialist, secular pan-Arab party founded in Syria and Iraq in the 1940s. In its early years, it appealed to Sunni and Shi'a Arabs, Christians, and even a few Kurds, providing them with a secular nationalist identity, a political ideology based on Arab unity, and vague theories of economic and social justice. More importantly, it seemed to promise the opportunity to compete on a more equal basis without the advantage or stigma of ethnic, tribal, or sectarian ties.

The regime that succeeded Qasim lasted only nine months. Abd al-Salam Arif was appointed president, but Ba'thists, whether military or civilian, controlled all important positions. These new party leaders were young, inexperienced, and unprepared to govern. Moreover, they were split between moderates who wanted to consolidate power in Iraq and move slowly on union with the United Arab Republic (UAR), comprising Egypt and Syria, and radicals who favored closer unity with the new Ba'th government in Syria and radical domestic reform. Attempts to unite with the UAR failed. So, too, did efforts to heal the breach with the Kurds, who would not countenance any Arab union. Finally, after several internal power struggles, Arif outmaneuvered the Ba'thists and, in a bloodless coup, wrested power from them in November 1963.

Arif governed through a new National Revolutionary Council and a cabinet of military men and technocrats, many of whom favored President Nasser's brand of Arab socialism. In 1964 Iraq took several measures designed to bring the country's political and economic structure into line with that of Egypt. All political parties were asked to join an Arab Socialist Union on the Egyptian model, and laws were passed nationalizing banks, insurance companies, and other key industries except for oil. Iraq was moving in the direction of a socialist economy but was beginning to have second thoughts about the desirability of sharing its oil wealth with a poorer Arab country.

These promising steps were abruptly halted in April 1966, when Arif was killed in a helicopter crash. A new power struggle ensued between the civilians and the military. The military won; Arif's brother, Gen. Abd al-Rahman Arif, was promoted to the presidency, and power gravitated once again into the hands of a small coterie of army officers. However, these elements were unable to control factionalism in the military. The Iraqi military, like its counterparts elsewhere in the Arab world, was humiliated by its defeat in the 1967 Arab-Israeli War. On July 17, 1968, Arif was overthrown in a bloodless coup by Gen. Ahmad Hasan al-Bakr and a group of Ba'thist supporters, in collaboration with non-Ba'thist officers. This time, the Ba'thists were determined not to let power slip from their grasp. Two weeks after the coup, they removed all non–Ba'thist Party members. They then inaugurated their rule with a series of secret trials and brutal executions designed to stamp out dissidents, terrorize the populace, and stabilize the country by force. This modus operandi succeeded in keeping them in power for the next thirty-five years.

Ba'th Party Rule: 1968–2003

The new Ba'th regime ruled through a Revolutionary Command Council (RCC), buttressed by the regional (Iraqi) command of the Ba'th Party and a cabinet. The two leading figures were President Ahmad Hasan al-Bakr, who was also RCC chairman, and the vice chairman of the RCC, Saddam Husayn, who was al-Bakr's kinsman. In July 1970, an interim constitution indicating that Iraq would follow a socialist economic path was promulgated. This constitution, with some modifications, remained in effect until the collapse of the Ba'th regime in 2003. The RCC was given authority to promulgate laws, deal with defense and security, declare war, and approve the budget. The president was given authority to appoint, promote, and dismiss judiciary, civil, and military personnel and members of the party's regional command, thereby ensuring party control of government.

Cabinet ministers were reduced to executing RCC decisions. The constitution provided for the election of a national assembly, but it was not created until 1980.

The first decade of Ba'th rule was notable for increased oil revenue, expanded economic and social development, and sustained stability. Nationalization of oil resources in 1970 and the oil-price rise of 1973 greatly increased the revenue available to the government. As a consequence, the regime embarked on an ambitious economic and social program, mainly in the public sector. Programs to distribute land to the peasants were expanded, as were education and health services, especially in rural areas. Heavy industries—iron, steel, and petrochemicals—were established, mainly in the south. The regime also embarked on a military industrial program that included chemical and nuclear weapons.

The greatest challenge to the regime in the early 1970s came from the Kurds, whose festering war with Baghdad was encouraged by the Shah of Iran. In 1970, after two years of intermittent warfare, the Ba'thist regime negotiated a settlement more comprehensive than any previous agreement. The Kurds were offered autonomy and an elected regional executive and legislative authority, a Kurdish vice president in Baghdad, and a larger share of oil revenues. However, there was to be a four-year delay so that a census could determine the boundaries of the new autonomous zone. When it became clear to the Kurds that they would not receive the degree of autonomy or the extent of territory they desired, Barzani again revolted, this time with military aid from Iran and some financial help from the United States and Israel. The rebellion collapsed in March 1975 when Saddam Husayn, by now vice president of the republic and deputy chairman of the RCC, negotiated the Algiers Accord with the shah. Iran agreed to withdraw its support for Iraq's Kurds in return for Iraqi recognition of Iranian sovereignty over half of the Shatt al-Arab River. Barzani was forced into exile and later died in the United States. That same year, the Kurdish movement split into two factions, the Kurdish Democratic Party (KDP), eventually led by Barzani's son Mas'ud, and the Patriotic Union of Kurdistan (PUK), led by Jalal Talabani.

In the aftermath of the Algiers Accord, Baghdad unilaterally established an autonomous region in the heavily Kurdish north with its own legislative and executive council and budget, named a Kurdish vice president, and appointed at least one Kurd, Jalal Talabani, to the cabinet in Baghdad. Real control over the region, however, remained in the hands of the central government. Baghdad instituted some land reform and economic development in the north. To prevent renewed guerrilla activities, the government razed Kurdish villages along its borders with Turkey and Iran, forcibly resettled Kurds in southern Iraq, and encouraged Arabs to settle in the north, especially in Kirkuk. These activities stirred renewed hostility among the Kurds, and by 1979 the Kurdish opposition had once again begun guerrilla activities.

The Saddam Years: 1979–2003

During the 1970s, Saddam hid his personal ambitions behind the image of Bakr. In July 1979, his patience ran out. He announced Bakr was resigning due to ill health and declared himself president of the republic and head of the party. The fiction of party rule was replaced by personal dictatorship. Saddam purged many of the party faithful, accusing them of plotting with Syria to eliminate him. His tenure would be marked by ruthless suppression of anyone suspected of disloyalty, total concentration of power in his own hands, and elimination of party and military leaders unconvinced of his superiority. He relied increasingly on a coterie of family and clan members and cronies from his home village near Tikrit, a small city north of Baghdad, to maintain power. Saddam's belief in his leadership capabilities, plus the absence of any checks on his power, led to dangerous miscalculations that plunged the country into two devastating wars in little more than a decade.

The Iran-Iraq War began on September 23, 1980, when Iraqi forces invaded Iran. Saddam had mixed motives for going to war. One was defensive. For over a year, the new Islamic government in Iran had incited Shi'a and Kurdish elements in Iraq to overthrow the regime. He feared that if he did not move against the new regime, Iraq would soon face a greater threat. Saddam also had more opportunistic motives. The collapse of the shah's regime provided Saddam with the opportunity to reverse the 1975 Algiers Accord and possibly to seize Iran's oil-rich Khuzistan Province, inhabited largely by Sunni Arabs. Iran was also vulnerable; revolutionary judges were busy purging Iran's American-trained armed forces of anyone deemed politically unreliable, leaving the image of a weak state ripe for plucking.

The war was a profound strategic miscalculation. Saddam expected a quick victory; instead, the war lasted eight years. After an initial thrust into Iranian territory, Iraq was forced into a defensive strategy and soon lost the initiative. Using human waves of suicide troops, Iranian forces counterattacked and by June 1982 had driven Iraq out of Iran. Iran was unable, however, to marshal sufficient forces to win, and the war settled into a long one of attrition. Both sides used long-range missiles to attack major cities. In addition, Iraq used chemical weapons against Iranian troops and on Iraqi Kurds suspected of harboring Iranian military forces. The war ended with Iran's accepting a cease-fire in July 1988 after intensive missile strikes on Iranian cities, attacks into Iran using chemical weapons, and the accidental downing by the United States of an Iranian civilian airliner carrying nearly three hundred people.

The costs of the war were high for Iraq. Its offshore oil-export facilities were destroyed, and the Shatt al-Arab waterway was closed to traffic, filled with sunken ships, chemical weapons, and other ordnance. As a result, Iraq had to turn to the port of Umm Qasr, bordering Kuwait, as its main shipping terminal. Iraqi casualties were an estimated 500,000 including some 150,000 killed. It was also deeply in debt to Europe, the Gulf states, the Soviet Union, and the United States. Nevertheless, Iraq emerged from the war with its territory and its military intact and a sense of national pride for successfully defending its country.

After the war, most observers assumed Saddam would concentrate on domestic reconstruction and debt repayment. He did not. Instead, Saddam looked for a new source of money to continue work on expensive military programs, including acquisition of biological, chemical, and nuclear weapons, while providing expensive subsidies to his support base. In early 1990 he challenged the American military presence in the Gulf, threatened to burn Israel with chemical weapons if it attacked Iraq again, and accused Kuwait of stealing oil from fields that spanned their mutual and contested borders, leaving Iraq unable to meet its debt payments. He demanded new "loans" from Kuwait and the other Gulf Cooperation Council (GCC) states as the price of rescuing them from Iran. When Kuwait refused Iraq's efforts at extortion, he invaded the tiny rich state in August 1990. The invasion was over in less than a day. One week later, Saddam announced that Kuwait had become the nineteenth province of Iraq.

Once again, Saddam had miscalculated. Working through the United Nations, which quickly imposed an embargo on oil sales and sanctions on imported goods except for food and medical supplies, the United States organized a thirty-nation military coalition to force Iraq out of Kuwait. On January 16, 1991, Operation Desert Storm opened with air attacks against Iraqi forces in Kuwait. The ground war began on February 23; it took only one hundred hours to drive Iraqi forces out of Kuwait.

The Kuwait War proved to be even more devastating for Iraq than the war with Iran. Saddam faced two popular rebellions, beginning on March 1 when retreating soldiers started an uprising in Basra. Within days, the Shi'a-inhabited area from the outskirts of Baghdad south to Basra was under rebel control. In the Kurdish-dominated northern provinces, the two Kurdish factions tried to launch a similar rebellion, but their reluctance to coordinate with the rebels in the south or cooperate with each other doomed their efforts. Saddam controlled only three of Iraq's eighteen provinces, but within three months he had regained most of the territory that had rebelled. Both the Kurds and the Shi'as had hoped that the coalition would support them. In the north, the coalition forces created a no-fly, no-drive zone, prohibiting Saddam's ground and air forces to go beyond the thirty-sixth parallel and enabling the Kurds to create a virtually autonomous security zone. In the south, however, Iraqi ground forces were permitted. Saddam sent his Republican Guard force, which had been left untouched by the war, to suppress the Shi'a rebels and anyone showing sympathy for them. Some 60,000 Shi'as were killed and a thousand-year-old Marsh Arab culture destroyed when the marshes were drained.

The rebellions scarcely touched Baghdad and the Sunni-dominated center of the country. By the following year, much of the infrastructure in Baghdad and its environs had been repaired. Saddam's reluctance to adhere to the UN Security Council cease-fire resolutions, particularly those requiring his turning over weapons of mass destruction (WMD), kept sanctions and the oil embargo in place for the next twelve years. Unable to sell its oil or trade except with UN approval, Iraq's economy declined drastically. Saddam's family benefited from oil smuggling and monopolies on goods made scarce by sanctions, but Iraq's once burgeoning middle class was virtually wiped out by high inflation, low salaries, and a dysfunctional political and economic system that rewarded only those loyal to an authoritarian leader out of touch with reality. Iraq's isolation was intense: its sovereignty was curtailed by intrusive international inspections of its weapons facilities, no-fly zones that denied the regime unchallenged access to its northern and southern provinces, and the emergence of a secure zone in the north where regime opponents could operate under coalition protection. From August 1990, when sanctions were first imposed, until April 2003, when the regime fell, sanctions prevented full rehabilitation of the economy and greatly impacted Iraq's economic well-being and social structure. International support for Iraq's isolation and sanctions had begun to erode by 2001, but the long-term damage to the country and its people was done.

Iraq Under American Occupation: 2003–2005

Saddam Husayn's strategy after the end of the Kuwait War was to survive with Iraq's political and territorial integrity intact. He shunned cooperation with the United Nations and the special commission (UNSCOM) established under UN Security Council Resolution 687 to identify and dismantle Iraq's WMD programs. He taunted the coalition; harassed UNSCOM inspectors looking for his nuclear, biological, and chemical weapons; and in general refused to comply with the demands placed on Iraq by the United Nations and the international community. He flirted with the Kurdish factions, who spent much of the 1990s at odds with each other, tried to assassinate former president George H. W. Bush during his visit to Kuwait, and constantly challenged the no-fly zone in southern Iraq. He reinstated tribal law and authority in many areas of the country and rewarded tribal leaders who helped Baghdad maintain a semblance of order in the countryside. He took revenge on those he believed had betrayed him, from Ba'th Party and RCC cronies to his sons-in-law, who defected in 1995 and revealed details of his WMD efforts. And he believed he had won because he had survived.

The American presidential election in 2000 brought to office George W. Bush, son of former president George H. W. Bush, and an administration that seemed determined to reverse policy on Iraq. Their opportunity came after the al-Qa'ida terrorist attacks on New York City and Washington, DC, on September 11, 2001. Administration officials blamed Iraq for the actions of al-Qa'ida and, after the Taliban government in Afghanistan fell (the Taliban had harbored al-Qa'ida and its leader Usama Bin Laden), began to plan for regime change in Iraq. They claimed to have information confirming Iraqi support for al-Qa'ida and plans to produce nuclear weapons. They warned that Saddam would share his new weapons with terrorist groups and raised the specter of a nuclear holocaust, even though the UNSCOM had declared that Iraq had been stripped of virtually all its nuclear components and materiel.

When British general F. S. Maude entered Baghdad in 1917, he said the British came "as Liberators, and not as Conquerors" and that the war "was not about Religion." Unconsciously echoing these sentiments, the Bush administration predicted that the U.S.-led coalition would be welcomed as liberators and Iraq would quickly transition to a democratic government. Iraq, they breathlessly concluded, would become the model to emulate for the entire Middle East. As for the costs of removing Saddam, Iraq's oil would cover all. Saddam's government fell in early April 2003. He did not survive in power; Saddam was pulled out of an underground bunker eight months later, his sons dead and his country in total disarray.

Politics in Saddam's Iraq. Ba'thism was a secular movement founded in the late 1940s in Syria by two Syrians—one Christian and the other Sunni—and an Iraqi Shi'a Arab. It provided a secular nationalist identity and an ideology based on principles of Arab unity and vague theories of economic and social justice. More importantly, it provided the opportunity to compete on a more equal basis without the advantage or stigma of ethnic, tribal, or sectarian ties. At least that was the theory. Under Saddam, party membership became the essential credential for jobs, education, and political security. Membership expanded from a few thousand in the 1950s to more than a million in the early 1970s. Estimates of membership in the 1990s range from a modest 1.2 million to more than 2 million, but only 50,000 may have been actual party activists, leaders, or monitors for political correctness and loyalty. As Saddam tightened his hold on power, the party lost its principles and its theoreticians. In their stead, Saddam fashioned a party of adherents loyal to him and the state. Ba'thist ideology—or what was left of it—became less pan-Arab (which had cost it many of its Shi'a members) and more identified with Iraqi hegemony and Saddam's cult of personality. The party served primarily as a tool through which the government's multiple security services could observe the loyalty of military officers, civilian bureaucrats, and ordinary citizens. Loyalty to Saddam took precedence over political theories and institutional realities.

To many Iraqis, the party represented capability and influence. When Saddam's regime fell in 2003, most members were urban Ba'thists—upper middle class, predominantly Sunni, in their late forties or fifties, Western educated, secular, anti-imperialist, and anti-American. They were administrators, civil servants, and educators with high expectations of power and status. Other Iraqis joined the party as part of their military service or to protect family or tribal interests. They came from the Arab Sunni tribes of the so-called triangle or center, an area bounded by Baqubah, Fallujah, Mosul, and Tikrit and including Baghdad, and provided most of the recruits and personnel for the officer corps of the military, Republican Guard, Special Republican Guard, and other security and intelligence units. They filled the upper ranks of the Ba'th Party and the elite group of advisers around Saddam. Shi'a and Christian Arabs joined the party, but few broke through the glass ceiling of Sunni Arab loyalists. Saddam used the military to police society and the tribes to help maintain control of the country.

Saddam's Ba'thists exhibited elitism and exceptionalism, sentiments that in many Iraqis run deeper than modern political loyalties. In the politics of cultural identity, to be an Iraqi, an Arab, and a Ba'thist was to be one of the best of all Arabs and imparted a sense of entitlement and exclusivity—Iraq was meant to lead the Arab world, and the party was the channel for upward mobility, egalitarianism, modernity, and secularism.

Politics After Saddam. The Bush administration had several goals for post-Saddam Iraq but no plans for governance or reconstruction and no exit strategy. The goals included identifying and removing all WMD sites and programs, purging all Ba'th influence, rebuilding Iraq, creating democratic political institutions, and restoring domestic security. With the collapse of Saddam's regime in April 2003, the United States faced looting and sabotage, ministries ablaze, and a disappeared bureaucracy. One month later, Ambassador L. Paul Bremer established the Coalition Provisional Authority (CPA) under the direction of the Department of Defense.

Bremer issued two controversial orders shortly after arriving in Baghdad. He disbanded the Iraqi armed forces and security forces and banned members of the now outlawed Ba'th Party from serving in any public or official positions. The first announcement put 450,000 military and security personnel out of work with no pay in a country with 75 percent unemployment. The second affected approximately 50,000 of an estimated 2 million party members, many of whom had joined the party to obtain education and employment benefits and were members in name only. The result of both measures was to target the Sunni Arab community's tribes and prominent individuals, who had held most party and government posts and virtually all senior military positions. Few felt great loyalty to Saddam, but they had been well-provisioned and secure, even in times of scarcity and risk. With Bremer's decrees, Iraq's Sunni Arabs began to feel that they were victims of, and not participants in, the new order. On the other hand, the demilitarization and de-Ba'thification decrees were popular with the Shi'a Arab and Kurdish communities, who now demanded justice for their suffering.

De-Ba'thification had other unintended consequences. It put at risk rehabilitation and reconstruction programs by cutting too deeply into government bureaucracies, education, and the military officer corps. Many of Iraq's most competent and experienced managers disappeared, afraid of retribution from people who had suffered under Saddam's rule and from insurgents threatening to kill anyone believed to be collaborating with the occupier. Other unintended consequences included the collapse of vital education, aid, security, and health care systems and exclusion from government employment and public sector jobs. Finally, de-Ba'thification and demilitarization increased the risk of civil war between those marginalized and their victims. In this light, the willingness of disgruntled military officers to join with Saddam loyalists, former Ba'thists, the criminals who comprised Saddam's fedayeen, and Sunni religious extremists becomes more explicable. Elements opposed to the US occupation began terrorist operations against the US military and civilian presence as well as the United Nations, the International Red Cross, governments assisting the occupation (Italy, Jordan, Spain, and Turkey), and Iraqis suspected of collaborating with the United States.

Bremer appointed a governing council of twenty-five exiles to be the public face of Iraq. It was a mathematically correct group—thirteen Shi'a Arabs, five Sunni Arabs, five Kurds, a Turkman, and a Christian—and the presidency rotated monthly among nine of the most prominent members. It was replaced by two interim governments, the first under Iyad Allawi, a secular Shi'a politician, and the second elected in 2005 in Iraq's first transparent election in its eighty-five year history. The prime minister was chosen by the Shi'a coalition party that had won the largest number of seats in the new parliament. Its mission was to write a constitution and prepare for the election of a permanent government.

Bremer's most significant contribution to the new Iraq may have been the interim constitution, referred to as the Transitional Administrative Law. Written by Iraqis with guidance from American advisers, it resonated with protections for individual rights and civil liberties as contained in Western constitutions. It described Iraq as republican, federal, democratic, and pluralistic. Its key sections dealt with issues of federal versus state's rights, the role of Islam in the state, and the structure and nature of governance. Most of its provisions were written into the constitution that was approved in a nationwide referendum in October 2005.

The constitution establishes a weak central authority, with most power residing in the regional or provincial governments. Should a provincial government oppose a law or should an issue be contested by both the federal and provincial governments, then the provincial government's authority is paramount. The federal government has control over defense, security, and foreign policies. It does not have the power to tax.

Iraq's constitution leaves many issues unresolved. The reluctance of Iraqis to support a strong central government is understandable, given the long years of living in a highly centralized state where all decisions were made in Baghdad. Shi'a leaders oppose the provision allowing a majority of voters in three governates the power to veto a new constitution or legislation passed by the majority. Kurds are dissatisfied with the geographic rather than ethnic basis of federalism and probably mistrust the willingness of any Arab-dominated government to share revenues or political offices fairly with them. Sunni Arabs oppose federalism, which they believe could lead to the partition of Iraq. In this, they have Shi'a Arab support. Kurds, Christians, and secular Arabs object to the provision recognizing Iraq as Arab or Muslim. Islamists prefer an avowedly Islamic government with Shari'a (religious) law as the foundation of all law but not with rule by clerics as practiced in Iran.

Prior to the Persian Gulf War of 1991, the three predominantly Kurdish provinces in the north—Dohuk, Irbil, and Sulaymaniyyah—formed a regional authority with a measure of local autonomy. Following that war and the upheaval of the Kurdish rebellion, Baghdad was ordered to withdraw its forces and administrators from the provinces. Under the protection of UN forces, the Kurds then established a Kurdish Regional Government (KRG) independent of Baghdad. Elections were held in 1992 for a regional assembly, and a cabinet was chosen mainly from the two Kurdish parties, the KDP and the PUK. However, the two parties could not maintain the facade of unity for long. A power struggle erupted with frequent military clashes over the next five years. At one point Masud Barzani invited Saddam's forces to cross the no-fly, no-drive zone and help him defeat his rival, Jalal Talabani. In the new Republic of Iraq, there is a Kurdish parliament, but Kurdistan remains divided, with the KDP in control of Irbil and the PUK with its capital in Sulaymaniyyah. In regional elections in July 2009, a third party, *Goran* ("Change"), captured one-quarter of the votes and seats in the KRG. Despite this seeming opening in the political fabric, however, there are few signs of transparency or real democracy, and there is little tolerance for the civil rights of non-Kurds or those heard criticizing the leadership.

Progress on other American goals, especially reconstruction and investment in economic infrastructure, has been slowed by inexperienced American advisers, corruption, contractor greed, and endemic insecurity. A 2006 audit by the US Defense Department Special Inspector General for Iraq Reconstruction lists financial and contractual irregularities in American and other reconstruction projects. The Bush administration's democratization policy intensified rather than moderated sectarian and ethnic animosities. Political stability demands domestic security. A primary mission of the US military forces was to recruit and train a new national integrated security force to combat terrorism and maintain domestic security during the transition from a brutal dictatorship to a stable democracy.

The Transition from Occupation to Independence. Three national elections were held in 2005: January elections for the interim National Assembly, which would write a constitution and prepare for the election of a permanent parliament, an October referendum approving the permanent constitution; and December elections for a permanent parliament. As mandated by the constitution, the new parliament, dominated by the winning Shi'a coalition, chose Ibrahim al-Ja'fari of the Shi'a Da'wa Party as prime minister. He was forced to resign in April 2006 and replaced by Nuri al-Maliki, another Da'wa leader.

POLITICAL ENVIRONMENT

Iraq is a state, but it is not yet a nation. Every Iraqi government since 1920 has attempted to create a single political identity from a diverse population, but none has succeeded in overriding residual ethnic, sectarian, and tribal loyalties or undermining the Arab nationalism fostered by Iraq's Sunni Arab leaders. These factors make Iraq difficult, but not impossible, to govern.

Iraq's People

Iraq's population is approximately 29 million, and its annual growth rate stands at about 2.6 percent. The capital, Baghdad, is the largest city, with 6.5 million people, nearly one-quarter of the country's population. Other urban concentrations include Mosul, Iraq's second largest city; Basra, its port; Kirkuk, an oil center in the north contested by Arabs, Kurds, and Turkmen; Irbil, the capital of the KRG; and Najaf, a major Shi'a religious center in the south.

Iraq has two major demographic fault lines. The first is its ethnic division. The overwhelming majority of the population is Arab (75 to 80 percent); they dominate the western steppe and the Tigris and Euphrates Valley from Basra to the Mosul plain. Kurds are the largest minority (estimated at 20 to 25 percent); their stronghold is in the mountains of northern and eastern Iraq. Saddam killed many Kurds or forced them to migrate to southern Iraq, replacing them with Arabs from the south; since 2003, Kurds have tried to move into Kirkuk, Mosul, and villages in the northeast belonging to Christian, Turkmen, and Yazidi tribes. About one-quarter of Baghdad's population was, and may still be, Kurds. Iraq's Kurds are a portion of the larger Kurdish population inhabiting adjoining regions in Iran, Syria, and Turkey.

Key Provisions of the Iraqi Constitution of October 15, 2005

- *Iraq* is a country of many nationalities, and the Arab people of Iraq are an inseparable part of the Arab nation. An Iraqi citizen is anyone who carries Iraqi nationality.

- *Islam* is the official religion of the country as well as *a* source, but not *the* source, of legislation.

- *Arabic and Kurdish* are the recognized languages, and Iraqis can educate their children in their own language in state and private schools.

- *All Iraqis* have full equality without regard to gender, sect, opinion, belief, nationality, religion, or origin. All are equal before the law and have the right to a fair, speedy, and public trial.

- *The Iraqi government* shall include a national assembly, a president, a council of ministers, a prime minister, and a judiciary. The assembly elects the president and two deputy presidents from its ranks and approves selection of the prime minister, who shall be chosen by the party winning the most votes in the general election. One-quarter of the assembly's 275 representatives shall be women, and all communities are to be fairly represented. There is separation of powers: legislative, executive, and judicial.

- *Federalism* is defined as a system of separation of powers based on geographic and historical realities and not race, ethnicity, nationality, or religious sect. Formulation of national security policy, as well as foreign, diplomatic, economic, trade, and debt policies, lies with the federal government. The management of the country's natural resources and distribution of its revenues fall under federal authority, but a distinction is made between "old" resources (already discovered and exploited), which come under federal authority, and "new" oil and gas resources, which are to come under provincial authority. This is contested by Sunni Arabs in the Shi'a camp. It is, however, a demand of the Kurds, who are signing contracts and selling rights to explore, repair, and exploit fields they do not yet control.

- *The armed forces and the intelligence services* come under civilian control, and all military personnel are banned from political office and activity.

The second demographic fault line is sectarian. Iraqis are divided between the two major divisions in Islam, the Sunni and the Shi'a. Most Kurds are Sunni, but there are also Kurdish Shi'a (*fayli*) Muslims and Christians, as well as a small number of Jewish Kurds. Shi'a Arabs are the majority population from Baghdad south to the Shatt al-Arab. Although some non-Iraqis believe the combination of ethnic and sectarian rivalries is a major stumbling block in restoring a sense of Iraqi identity, Iraqis have a high rate of intermarriage between Sunni and Shi'a and Kurds and Arabs. Until 2003 it also had a large number of integrated communities. The three communities dividing the country—Sunni Arabs, Shi'a Arabs, and Kurds—are not as distinct as some assume.

Sunni Arabs constitute approximately 20 percent of the population. They dominated the government for more than four hundred years of Ottoman, British, and Arab rule. Under Saddam, they constituted a majority of the officer corps and the upper echelons of the Ba'th Party. As an elite, they benefited disproportionately from modernization and education and, in occupation and lifestyles, tended to be more secular than Shi'a Arabs. Since 2003, extremist Sunni Arab religious groups—called *salafis* or *jihadists*, they include elements of the once-banned Muslim Brotherhood—have surfaced to demand Iraq be governed as an Islamic state under Shari'a law.

Shi'a Arabs comprise the majority of the population (55 to 60 percent). Most inhabit the area from Baghdad south to the Shatt al-Arab, the most densely populated section of the country, but like the Kurds and Sunni Arabs, they can be found throughout Iraq. As a result of sectarian violence and ethnic cleansing after the collapse of the Ba'thist regime in 2003, Baghdad has a significantly larger Shi'a majority than it had before the occupation. The heartland of Shi'a Islam, however, has always been the shrine cities of Najaf and Karbala in southern Iraq, where Imams Ali and Husayn are buried. Along with Samarra and Kazimiyyah, a suburb of Baghdad, these shrine cities have long been central to pilgrimage rites, religious education (especially in Islamic law), and burial for religious scholars. Shi'as have rarely held senior political or military positions. This increased their resentment of any highly centralized, Sunni-dominated power structure in Baghdad. Much of the Shi'a population lives in rural and agricultural villages, where lower standards of living and literacy have historically prevailed. This, too, fed Shi'a resentment and spawned an organized, clandestine Shi'a opposition to the increasingly popular Arab secular parties, especially the Ba'th and Communist parties.

The original Shi'a opposition movement was the Da'wa ("Call") Party, founded in Najaf in the 1960s by an Iraqi Arab cleric, Ayatollah Muhammad Baqr al-Sadr. Since the 2005 elections, it is one of the leading political parties in Iraq. The other major opposition faction is the Islamic Supreme Council in Iraq (ISCI)—formerly known as the Supreme Council for the Islamic Revolution in Iraq. It was created by the Iranian Islamic government in 1982 as an umbrella group of anti-Saddam elements and led by another prominent Iraqi cleric, Ayatollah Muhammad Baqr al-Hakim. Saddam may have mistrusted Iraq's Shi'as, and Ayatollah Ruhollah Khomeini may have assumed they would help Iran to defeat Saddam, but most Shi'as remained loyal to the Iraqi state and fought Iran in the eight-year war. They have never desired separation or self-rule, as have Iraq's Kurds, but seek representation commensurate with their majority status in a democratically elected government. Not all clerics are political militants. One of the most revered Shi'a clerics, Iranian-born Grand Ayatollah Ali Sistani, upholds Shi'a political and Iraqi national interests but opposes a role for clerics in government.

The Kurds have long resisted assimilation into Arab Iraq. Traditionally, Kurds lived under the control of the *aghas* (tribal chiefs and landholders), but war, modernization, and land reforms eroded their position. In the twentieth century, a sense of Kurdish identity based on language, close tribal ties, a common history, and a shared sense of victimization by the governments of modern Iraq inspired demands for self-rule. Many Kurds are still engaged in agriculture, but a growing number form an urban, educated elite class. Much of the economy and society of the Kurdish north was drastically disrupted by the razing of over 4,000 villages by Saddam's regime; the death and disappearance of many thousands of Kurds during a concerted campaign against them, called the *Anfal*, at the end of the Iran-Iraq War; and the displacement of large numbers of Kurds as a result of the 1991 rebellion. Protected from Saddam's depredations after 1991, the Kurds made considerable progress in resettling those who had been displaced and in reviving agriculture and industry. Although the major Kurdish parties formed a regional government and have held three elections, real political authority remains in the hands of patriarchal tribal warlords. Most Kurds prefer to keep their current status as an autonomous state within Iraq—or if Iraq fails, then outside it.

Iraq has a number of smaller minority groups, many with bonds to similar peoples across Iraq's borders. In northern cities and towns along the old trade routes from Turkey to Baghdad are Turkish speakers, known as Turkmen. Making up 2 to 3 percent of the population, they are mainly Sunni, middle-class, and urban and have strong ties to Turkey. Until the onset of the Iran-Iraq War, Iraq had a substantial group of Persian speakers, 1 to 2 percent of the population, inhabiting parts of Baghdad and some southern cities, especially Najaf and Karbala. Saddam forcibly expelled this group during the Iran-Iraq War, but many started to return with the reopening of the borders after Saddam's removal. In the south, several hundred thousand Shi'a Arabs, known as Marsh Arabs, inhabited the marshes between the Tigris and Euphrates rivers. For more than one thousand years they dwelled in reed huts, raised water buffalo, and fished. As punishment for their alleged role in the 1991 rebellion and to eliminate a refuge for dissidents, Saddam's army drained most of the marsh territory, dramatically degrading the environment, and ending, possibly forever, their traditional way of life. Efforts since 2003 to restore the marshes and return the population to their traditional homes are failing because of a sharp drop in water levels due to several years of drought and diversion of water by Iraq's upstream neighbors, Iran, Syria, and Turkey.

Finally, roughly 5 percent of the Iraqi population is non-Muslim, including a number of indigenous Christian sects: Armenians, Assyrians (Nestorian Christians who remained independent), Chaldeans (Nestorians who reunited with Rome), Greek Orthodox, and Jacobites. Northern Iraq is also home to small communities of Sabaeans (a pre-Christian group), Shabek, and Yazidis (a Kurdish-speaking group with an eclectic religion drawn in part from Zoroastrianism). Under the Ottoman Empire and the British mandate, Iraq had a large and flourishing Jewish community, but by the early 1950s, most Jews had migrated to Israel.

Iraq's Social Structure

Traditionally, Iraqi society was characterized by a pronounced dichotomy between rural society, organized for the most part by tribes, and urban life. Since 1950, the rural-urban gap has been greatly narrowed by massive rural-to-urban migration, by the spread of education and health services to rural areas, and by the emergence of a sizable middle class. At the end of the monarchy, about 70 percent of the population lived in rural communities; in 2000, 70 percent lived in cities, although many of these people were recent migrants who had not been thoroughly urbanized, a factor that has sharpened class distinctions.

Rural agricultural areas remain much poorer than most cities, but conditions have improved since Mandate times, when a few landlords and tribal leaders controlled large portions of the farmland and the peasants were virtual serfs. Successive land-reform measures eliminated most of this landlord class and gradually extended landownership to a class of small and middle-level farmers. Since the 1958 revolution, agriculture has been neglected, leaving rural sectors poorer than urban areas. Saddam's skewed modernization programs favored industrial development and investment in Sunni Arab areas. The long years of war, sanctions, and economic mismanagement had the most devastating impact on life in rural and urban Iraq.

The growth of education significantly affected Iraq's social structure. Until the Iran-Iraq War, elementary education was available to virtually all Iraqi children. High schools graduated students in the hundreds of thousands; colleges and universities in the tens of thousands. Over time, Iraq produced one of the Arab world's largest professional classes, including a scientific and technocratic elite. Along with a middle class came an urban working class, particularly in the oil and industrial sectors in Baghdad and Basra. Most of Iraq's urban middle and lower classes worked for the government as industrial employees, teachers, bureaucrats, or army officers. Wars and sanctions impoverished Iraq's urban professionals and technocrats, while the violence of occupation, ethnic cleansing, and insurgency have forced many into exile.

One element of Iraq's social structure saw its status improved under Ba'thist rule—women. Encouraged by government legislation, women enjoyed a wider range of freedom and opportunities than did their Arab and Iranian counterparts. They could vote, hold office, receive an education, hold senior positions in the government and the party, and choose whether to follow Western or Islamic dress codes, depending on how tribal and traditional their family culture was. In 1978 a law restricting polygamy and granting women more freedom in the choice of a marriage partner was passed. By the mid-1980s, women comprised 50 percent of the students in elementary schools, 35 percent in high school, and 30 percent in universities. Women taught in universities, worked in government ministries, and could enter any profession.

Women are probably the biggest losers under the 2005 constitution, which mandates that 25 percent of all seats in the National Assembly be held by women; quotas are also applied for minority groups. Personal-status law follows Shari'a law, which does not recognize women's rights to custody of their children in a divorce. Several of the women in the National Assembly are strictly obser-vant Muslims who favor dress and social codes restricting women's clothing and behavior. Iraqi women legislators have been warned that they will no longer en-joy the political power guaranteed them by the Iraqi constitution once the Americans leave Iraq.

Secularism remains strong in the personal lives of Iraq's middle class, but reli-gion plays a much more significant role in the society as a whole, especially in shaping governance, civil society, and education. In post–Saddam Iraq clerics from both sects wield inordinate political influence and fuel political debate as well as insurgency. Religious influence is growing among urbanized Sunni Arabs as well as recent migrants to Baghdad, Basra, and Mosul. In many of Iraq's cities, religious and tribal leaders have assumed significant political roles, eroding the influence secular elites once wielded.

Family, clan, and tribal loyalties have always been strong in Iraq. Saddam, for example, prized traditional tribal values such as courage, honor, and loyalty, and these remain strong. As bureaucratic structures and civil society eroded under the impact of war and sanctions, Iraqis' reliance on tribal and family ties grew even stronger. Despite regime change and the introduction of democratic insti-tutions and processes, political life and social security remain essentially tribal and family centered. Only time will tell if Iraq moves beyond this facade of party politics, but even Western democracies on occasion use traditional patron-age and kinship links.

Iraq's Economic Environment

Iraq is one of the few Middle Eastern countries with the potential for a balanced economy, but its economic infrastructure has been so mismanaged that it has rarely achieved its potential. Since the 1950s, two features have dominated the economy: the preeminence of oil and increased government economic control. These features, plus a sense of entitlement, are complicating recovery from years of a Soviet-style command economy and the devastation of years of war, sanctions, occupation, and civil violence.

Government planning originated during the monarchy when long-range development plans were created to utilize oil revenues. After the 1958 revolution, development plans followed Soviet models, emphasizing heavy industry, collective farming, and state management of the economy. According to government statistics, the share of the public sector in domestic production rose from 31 percent in 1968, when the Ba'thists came to power, to 80 percent a decade later. Under the Ba'thists, the state initially dominated economic decision making and investment policy. In the name of war-time efficiency, Saddam's regime abolished collective farms, loosened government controls, and encouraged the private sector in agriculture, services, commerce, and light industry. The conversion to a market economy was only partial, however. Saddam's government refused to allow foreign private investment, preferring to hire foreign firms to undertake projects that were turned over to the government on completion. Since the collapse of Saddam's regime, political factions vie with each other to control resources and distribute revenues, mostly for their own benefit and that of their supporters. Corruption is pervasive in many ministries, which some politicians in the new Iraq view as their private economic domain.

Iraq's Oil Sector

Oil revenues have long dominated Iraq's economy. Iraq has at least 112 billion barrels of proven reserves, second only to Saudi Arabia, and possibly as much or more in unexplored areas of the north, south, and the western desert. The IPC began commercial export of oil from the Kirkuk field in 1934, but Iraq did not earn substantial oil revenues until the 1950s, when the rich Rumailah field was discovered near the Kuwaiti border. In the early 1960s, Qasim's acrimonious dispute with the IPC and his expropriation of 99.5 percent of its concession initiated a protracted confrontation with the oil companies; as a result, the companies shifted their operations elsewhere in the Gulf. In 1972, the Ba'thist government nationalized the oil industry and, helped by the 1973 Arab oil embargo, saw a fourfold increase in prices and revenues. By 1980, Iraq was exporting 3.2 million barrels a day and earning revenues of $26 billion, more than 60 percent of the gross domestic product (GDP). Iraq used much of this revenue to expand its oil facilities, building new "strategic" pipelines from Kirkuk to the Persian Gulf, through Turkey to the Mediterranean, and through Saudi Arabia to the Red Sea. It built two offshore oil terminals in the Persian Gulf, refineries, and a sophisticated petrochemical industry. Years of war, neglect, underinvestment, embargoes, and terrorism under Saddam resulted in declining oil-production capacity. Iraq's exports fell to three-quarters of pre-1990 levels.

Iraq's long-term oil potential is excellent. If facilities are repaired and expanded, Iraqi production could reach 6 million barrels per day. Realization of this potential, however, will require foreign investment, an end to insurgent attacks on pipelines and facilities, and a stable political climate. Iraq's government will also have to resolve the question of who owns Iraq's oil. The 2005 constitution left control of "old" oil—already discovered and exploited—to the federal government, while the provincial governments "own" all new, undeveloped oil. The Kurds favor this and, expecting to gain control over the Kirkuk fields, have signed contracts with foreign oil companies to repair and explore fields. The contracts have been rejected by the Oil Ministry in Baghdad, which claims that it alone has the right to negotiate contracts. Under sanctions and Saddam's government, the Kurds had been allocated 13 percent of oil revenues. After 2003, they argued that because of their suffering under Saddam and the neglect of successive governments in Baghdad, they were due more. Baghdad agreed to compromise and raised Kurdish revenues to 17 percent, which is dispensed to the KRG.

Raising investment capital remains a problem. In December 2009 Baghdad held an international auction of twenty-year service contracts to develop seven fields. The contracts approved by the government were the first foreign oil contracts since the Iraqi oil sector was nationalized in 1972. The foreign companies were willing to bid on contracts that would pay them a fee per barrel above a set production baseline, despite expected small profit margins, technical obstacles, and continuing security risks.

Iraq's Non-Oil Sectors

Non-oil industries have not played a major role in Iraq's economy. Under the monarchy, indigenous industries consisted almost wholly of food processing, textiles, and cement production. In the 1960s and 1970s, some progress was made in light and intermediate industries. After the oil price rise in the 1970s, there was rapid economic and social modernization, including expansion in heavy industry—petrochemicals, iron, steel, and aluminum plants—as well as intermediate industries like metal working, machine tools, and car and truck assembly. Iraq depended on foreign labor for skilled and unskilled work. In the late 1980s, the industrial sector produced only 10 percent of GDP and employed about 8 percent of the labor force. One area in which the Ba'th invested heavily was military industry, especially chemical and nuclear weapons, and medium- and long-range missile-delivery systems. Like oil, these are not labor-intensive industries and do little to provide employment to native Iraqis.

Under the monarchy, agriculture received the lion's share of the regime's attention. Development programs expanded dams and barrages, and private entrepreneurs introduced pumps to expand production. The amount of land under cultivation in irrigated areas of the south and rain-fed territory in the north increased. Through the 1950s, Iraq was able not only to feed itself but also to export wheat and barley. Unfortunately, most of the surplus profits went to wealthy landlords rather than to cultivators. After the 1958 revolution, land-reform efforts took much of the land away from large landholders but failed to redistribute it in a timely fashion. Efforts were made to improve the land-tenure situation, but agriculture continued to suffer from official neglect.

Farming in the riverain tracts of the south requires intensive investment in drainage, small-scale irrigation systems, and agricultural extension programs. These were never forthcoming. Saddam preferred to invest in flashy military industrial projects rather than agricultural reform. The agricultural share of GDP dropped from 17 percent in 1960 to 8 percent in the 1980s, even though agriculture still employed about 30 percent of the population. Food imports increased until they constituted nearly one-quarter of all imports. Agriculture in the Kurdish area, one of the most fertile in Iraq, was disrupted by war, chemical attacks, ethnic cleansing, and the destruction of villages. In the 1990s, sanctions, plus a Kurdish population haunted by the specter of planes spraying chemicals on villages, prohibited Iraq from using chemicals to spray crops.

It will take years for Iraq's non-oil sector, especially agriculture, to return to pre-Ba'th productivity levels. But Iraq's greatest economic difficulty lies not in the agrarian or oil sectors of the economy. Rather, it is water. All of Iraq's water sources lie outside its boundaries. The Tigris and Euphrates rivers rise in Turkey, and Tigris tributaries flow from Iran. The Euphrates passes through both Turkey and Syria before reaching Iraq. In the past several years, severe drought and the completion of a series of dams in Iran, Syria, and Turkey have drastically reduced the waters of the Tigris and Euphrates. Poor political relations with Syria under Saddam and more recently in 2009 contributed to that country's cutting Iraq's water flow, an act that has dried up Iraqi irrigation and caused severe crop damage.

Iraq's greatest resource is its people. Wars, the oil embargo, and thirteen years of sanctions have taken their toll here, too. Massive inflation fueled by scarcity of goods and corruption reduced the Iraqi dinar to a worthless currency after the Kuwait War, depleting the savings and reserves of both the government and the population. GDP was at a third of what it was in 1989, and per capita income and living standards were drastically reduced. Since 2003, goods have become more plentiful, but unemployment remains high—perhaps 50 percent. Erosion of the infrastructure in health, education, electricity, and water supplies that had produced a serious decline in health standards under Saddam continues. Reconstruction efforts have been slow, with corruption, grandiose planning schemes, and violence undercutting efforts to rebuild. Insurgent attacks on economic infrastructure and on Iraqis alleged to be "collaborating" with the occupiers—meaning the United States, any other foreign country or company in Iraq, and officials in the new post-Saddam governments—made Iraq's cities unsafe places to work under American occupation. Added to this is the high crime rate, with kidnapping, murder, and extortion keeping many in Iraq afraid to leave home and, in some cases, fleeing the country.

Meanwhile, a new class of urban rich and well-to-do has emerged from the wreckage of war and occupation. Exiles and those in a position to seize wealth or carry it over into the new Iraq are thriving, while appointees to the several governments since 2003 have used their ministries to enrich themselves, their families, and their friends. While the hardships of the post-Saddam period are easing, and food and imported consumer goods are available for those who can afford them, the effects of more than a decade of sanctions are still evident and still devastating. Too many Iraqis still lack reliable and available sources of electricity and clean water. The damage wrought by Saddam Husayn's miscalculations on Iraq's economy will take years to repair.

POLITICAL DYNAMICS AND STRUCTURE

Saddam and his Ba'th Party dominated Iraq for more than three decades. Power was concentrated in the hands of one individual who ostensibly governed through the RCC but exercised his authority through a finely tuned cult of personality and with the aid of a multilayered network of intelligence and secret police services. Iraq was a *mukhabbarat* ("police") state. It had a constitution, a parliament, a political party, and elections, and everyone voted, even if the only candidate was Saddam. Nearly 70 percent of Iraqis alive today were born after Saddam assumed the presidency directly in 1979; they have known only wars, sanctions, isolation, terror, and Saddam's overwhelming presence.

A Structured Democracy

Iraq has a popularly elected government dominated by its majority Shi'a political parties. It has a parliament, a constitution, and parliamentary and provincial elections, and much power resides with provincial officials who control their budgets and security forces. Reflecting its diverse populations and the need to balance deeply entrenched ethnic, sectarian, and tribal interests, Iraq is a "structured democracy." The Shi'a prime minister has two deputies, one Sunni Arab and one Kurd; the Kurdish president has two vice presidents, one Sunni Arab and one Shi'a; and the Sunni Arab speaker of the parliament has two subordinates, one Shi'a and one Kurd. Ministry posts were negotiated with the various factions. The Shi'a ISCI party was especially interested in the Ministry of the Interior and, once in control, legitimized its Iranian-trained Badr militia by making them police. The Sunni Arab community felt entitled by history and custom to the Ministry of Defense. Each minister has deputies from the other communities.

The constitution does not guarantee that a Shi'a will always be prime minister, that a Kurd will always be president, or that the speaker will always be a Sunni Arab. In 2010 a new electoral law passed in preparation for the parliamentary election increased the number of seats from 275 to 325, allocated on the basis of an estimated number of voters in each province and abroad. The constitution requires a census be conducted to determine the actual population count, but the political factions cannot agree on when or how it should be conducted.

FOREIGN POLICY

Iraq's leaders have long sought to play a dominant role in regional affairs, choosing and changing alliances based on perceived national interests. A Cold War ally of the West, Iraq was a founding member of the Arab League in 1945 and in 1955 joined the Baghdad Pact, a security arrangement linking Iraq with Great Britain, Iran, Pakistan, and Turkey. Until 1958, Iraq's foreign and security policy and its economy were tied to the West, and diplomatic relations with the Soviet Union were shunned.

This foreign relations orientation changed with the revolution of 1958. Iraq gradually became isolated and anti-Western. As nationalist ideologies, whether Iraqi or pan-Arab, took hold, Iraqis became unwilling to permit any foreign influence in their country. After the 1958 revolution, Iraq turned to the Soviet Union for arms and technical assistance. Moscow sold Baghdad its first nuclear reactor in 1958 and, after Iraq nationalized its oil industry in 1972, provided help in developing Iraq's southern oil fields. In 1972 the two countries signed a friendship treaty. However, Iraq never allowed the Soviet Union to establish bases on its soil, and when oil prices rose in the 1970s, Iraq shifted its purchases to higher-quality Western technology.

Iraq and the Neighbors Before Saddam's Fall

Pan-Arabism notwithstanding, Saddam Husayn's regime had uneasy relations with its Arab neighbors, who feared Iraqi attempts to dominate the region and unseat rival regimes. Saddam, in particular, was involved in a personal and party feud with

Syrian Ba'thist leader Hafiz al-Asad. Their rivalry reached its peak when Syria supported Iran in the Iran-Iraq War and joined the coalition that fought Iraq in Kuwait. Saddam turned Iraq into a state sponsor of international terrorism, primarily to wreck havoc on Asad. Saddam probably envied Asad's ability to make Syria the focus of all Middle Eastern issues, especially those involving Israel, as well as his negotiation and leadership skills. Iraq has been one of the most strident enemies of Israel in its rhetoric, and Iraqi forces contributed to Arab military action against Israel in the wars of 1948, 1967, and 1973.

Saddam may not have been able to rival Hafiz al-Asad's leadership role in the Arab world, but he did contain the ambitions of both the shah and Ayatollah Khomeini. In 1975, Saddam negotiated the Algiers Accord with the shah to end Iranian assistance to Iraq's Kurds. Iraq was in a weak economic and strategic position, and the shah was strong. In exchange for the shah's promise to cut off all support to the Kurds, Saddam recognized Iranian control of the Shatt al-Arab and made some territorial concessions.

Five years later, Iraq was strong, and Iran weak. Iran's Islamic revolution was in disarray, as the clerics purged the shah's unreliable, American-trained armed forces and threatened to export its revolution to Iraq and across the Gulf. Saddam invaded Iran in September 1980. The war was long, costly, and brutal, with combined casualties estimated at nearly 1 million. Pressure on Iraq's oil-rich Gulf neighbors, combined with pleas that he was fighting their war, resulted in approximately $80 billion in loans. Saddam was able to fight Iran and at the same time keep Iraqis fed and build his WMD.

The end of the eight-year war with Iran left Saddam with little to show for his efforts and deeply in debt. Iraq's relations with the GCC states had always been uncertain, ranging from mere unease to outright hostility, regardless of the government in power in Baghdad. Iraq first invaded Kuwait in 1961, but it was Iraq's 1990 invasion and occupation of Kuwait and the 1991 Gulf War that left a legacy of fear and distrust in most Gulf states.

Baghdad and Washington: Rocky Road to War and Liberation

Iraq's invasion of Iran shifted its foreign policy, of necessity, from a somewhat isolated and pro-Moscow orientation to a more pragmatic and pro-Western direction. Relations with the United States that had been cut after the 1967 Arab-Israeli War were renewed in 1984. To offset a possible Iranian victory, and at the behest of Iraq's Arab Gulf neighbors, Washington offered military and financial aid to Baghdad in the form of arms sales, loans, and intelligence on Iranian military dispositions.

This seemingly pragmatic trend did not survive the end of the Iran-Iraq War. Misreading the international climate of détente in the aftermath of the Cold War,

Saddam saw a political vacuum developing in the Arab world and sought to fill it. He renewed his hostile rhetoric against the United States, the Gulf Arab states, and Israel, which cooled relations with America and Europe. His invasion of Kuwait on August 2, 1990, Iraq's defeat in the Kuwait War, and the sanctions imposed by the United Nations and enforced by the U.S.-led coalition after the war left the Iraqi regime too weak to play a significant regional or international role.

Iraq and the Neighbors Since Saddam's Fall

The collapse of the Ba'thist government was greeted with joy inside Iraq and caution outside the beleaguered country. As the U.S.-led coalition sought to reconstruct Iraq's political institutions and introduce democratic processes, Iraq's neighbors urged the installation of a strong—and Sunni Arab—leader in Baghdad who could keep the country united and secure. Democracy, said many Gulf Arabs, could wait until a more propitious time. The neighbors continue to watch developments in Iraq with unease. They fear several kinds of spillover—violence by religious extremists or nationalist-minded insurgents determined to overthrow un-Islamic, corrupt, pro-American rulers as well as the spread of crime, drugs, arms smuggling, and human trafficking. On a deeper level, they fear the side effects of democracy; that is, the idea of a weak central authority with independent provinces and sources of authority generates as much fear as that of having to adopt democratic institutions and processes.

Turkey warns about the dangers from the anti-Turkish Kurdish group, the Kurdish Workers' Party, or PKK, which is based in northern Iraq, and the risk to the small Turkmen community in Iraq from the Kurds and Arab nationalists. Syria and Iran, which share long and virtually open borders with Iraq, encourage and supply insurgent factions that challenge American occupation. Saudi Arabia supports Iraqi Sunni Arab elements, particularly the reemergent Muslim Brotherhood, which Saddam had long banned. Sunni rulers, such as Jordan's King Abdallah II and Saudi Arabia's King Abdallah, deplore a Shi'a-dominated Iraq linked to an Iran that they see building a Shi'a crescent from Lebanon through Syria, Iraq, and Saudi Arabia.

While all the neighbors fear a failed state, none has offered Iraq the kind of assistance it needs to stabilize itself, secure its borders, or become an accepted member of the regional community. Some Gulf Arabs say that Iraq should not look to them for help but should solve its own problems. They certainly see no place for Iraq in the GCC and are wary of competing Iranian and Iraqi ambitions for regional hegemony at some point in the future. They long for a return to the status quo of the years before Saddam invaded anything and American, British, and other Western interests balanced power in the region and shielded them from their neighbors and themselves.

THOUGHTS ON IRAQ'S FUTURE

As this book goes to press in early 2010, Iraq has held its second nationwide parliamentary election. This election could confirm Iraq's future as an institutionalized democracy operating under the rule of law or as a lapsed democracy, where popular participation and public accountability are given lip service and the style of rule has reverted to the ways of the former dictatorship. Life goes on, people go to work and to market, and children go to school. Progress has been made in reconstruction, although many areas of Iraq still lack sufficient power, fuel, or water. The number of terrorist attacks has declined.

This could change quickly and dramatically as political factions prepare for the postelection scramble for power. Some results of the election—what party or individual got how many votes—will be known by mid-March, but it could be months before the new government is named. Parties in the winning coalitions will vie for rewards for themselves and their supporters. How much authority the prime minister will have and whether there will still be deputy prime ministers, deputy ministers, and other officials appointed for their affiliation (the quota system) rather than their abilities or loyalty to the prime minister is uncertain. These decisions could affect the United States as it begins to implement agreements signed with Baghdad in November 2008 calling for the gradual withdrawal of all American combat forces from Iraq by the end of 2011.

Elections in Iraq are an imperfect instrument. They provide a clear sign of the country's limited political progress and at the same time its weakness. Voting is by open lists with parties and candidates clearly identified. A candidate's place on a party's list reflects deals among party leaders rather than local support or issues. In the 2005 elections, Iraqis voted according to sectarian and ethnic interests, reflecting deep-seated fears about their status and futures. In 2010 there seemed to be a shift toward a more nationalist, less sectarian agenda. The Sunni Arabs boycotted the 2005 election and lost their ability to play a role in the new government. In 2005 Shi'a factions, encouraged by Iran, formed a coalition that gave it the majority of seats in parliament and the right to select the prime minister. That alliance broke down in 2010, and leaders of Sunni and Shi'a political factions formed new coalitions that crossed ethnic and religious lines. This does not mean that Iraqi politics and government will no longer be dominated by ethnic and sectarian differences. It does suggest, however, that Iraqi politicians know that issues that worked in the 2009 provincial elections, especially calls for Iraqi nationalism, might work in the next election. Few politicians look beyond the next election.

Iraq has made little progress since 2005 on several key issues: the nature of federalism (defining the power of the state versus the power of the provinces), a hydrocarbon law (determining control of contracts and revenue distribution of Iraq's oil and gas resources), the fate of disputed territories (including Diyala, Kirkuk, and Mosul), and a meaningful de-Ba'thification law that would permit the repatriation and employment of thousands of exiles. Iraq also needs laws against corrupt practices in government, an end to armed militias, and ministries run by a professional civil service and ministers loyal to the state and not personal or private interests. Finally, Iraq needs an election law that will define how parties and lists are formed, how Iraqis vote, and who finances elections.

Time may be running out for reform in Iraq. Prime Minister Maliki in 2008 and 2009 broke with the broad Shi'a coalition favored by Iran and sent troops to end fighting among competing Shi'a militias and clans and to arrest ex-Ba'thists and people he claimed were al-Qa'ida insurgents in Baghdad, Basra, and Mosul. He refused to honor promises to incorporate the Sunni Arab militias who fought against al-Qa'ida—the so-called Sons of Iraq—into the government and military services. He also established a "counterterrorism" special operations force in the military that reports directly to him, rotated senior military officers in disputed provinces to new commands (seen as removing Kurdish officers in the armed forces out of Kurdish-populated areas), and challenged forces loyal to the Kurdish government. He talked about ending the quota system that ensures that all elements of Iraq's population are represented in government. Instead, Maliki said he wanted to establish "true democratic rule," meaning that to the winner will belong all the spoils of victory, all appointments, posts, and assignments. Iraqis, who have only known the extremes of dictatorship or weak federal government, see Maliki either as struggling to restore security, national power, and Iraqi patriotism or as aspiring to be the new Saddam. In an Iraq still reeling from years of authoritarian terror, there can be no middle ground.

Iraq will almost certainly remain an Islamic state and a tribal society in which democratic-sounding institutions and practices are mingled with traditional tribal politics and competing interests. One thing is clear. Iraq's politicians have learned to act as politicians. They talk about Iraqi national identity and secular politics. They argue, make nonnegotiable demands, compromise, cut deals, and try to avoid public scrutiny of their actions—the best and worst behaviors of politicians everywhere. Rather than tackle issues that could lead to military confrontation or civil war—such as Kurdish demands for, and Arab resistance to, resolving Kirkuk's status—both sides have agreed to small compromises to avoid conflict. It is not clear whether former Ba'thists will apologize and be forgiven, how Kirkuk and the disputed territories will be settled, if the constitution will be amended, or if the military and security services can be depoliticized. It is clear that Iraqis are a long way from national reconciliation.

Those who watch Iraq need to keep some basic points in mind:

- *Iraq, if it survives its short-term difficulties, will in the long term be a regional power-house.* It has the potential resources in terms of oil, agriculture, and people, and it may have less of an identity crisis ten years from now than it has in 2010. To get there, Iraqis will need to begin the process of national reconciliation and forgiveness and end their dangerous reliance on family and clan over merit for positions and promotions in government and society.

- *Iraqis will follow policies according to their national interests and not those of Iran or the United States.* Iraq will reject Iranian demands for territory, reparations, resigning the 1975 Algiers Accord, and adherence to policies favored by Iran. It will demand that the United States honor the terms of the agreements signed in 2008: the Status of Forces Agreement, which calls for American combat troops to leave Iraq by 2011, and the Strategic Framework Agreement, which promises American economic, educational, and reconstruction assistance. In the near term, Iraq will need stable relations with its large and powerful neighbor and with the United States. Agreeing to demands set in Tehran or Washington, however, will weaken any government in Iraq, regardless of its strength, popularity, or composition.

- *Iraq's neighbors must stop meddling in Iraq's political and security affairs.* As Iraq grows stronger, it will remember who helped it and who ignored it. If history is a guide, then in twenty years' time, we could see a resurgent and angry Iraq determined once again to claim Kuwait as its nineteenth province and to exercise its lost rights in the Gulf and wider Middle East.

- *Nothing is forever.* Iraq is trying to get Kuwait and the members of the United Nations Security Council to end all Chapter VII sanctions imposed in 1990. These restrictions and the imposed debt will become symbols of unfairness and oppression intended to keep Iraq weak. As Iran progresses with its nuclear plans, including uranium enrichment and weaponization, Iraq is likely to seek to resume its forbidden nuclear programs, only now the argument will be reversed: we in Iraq need nuclear "capability" because Iran has it, instead of we in Iran need nuclear weapons because Saddam is developing them. In the longer term, Iraq could challenge Iran once again for the title of regional hegemon.

NOTE

The opinions expressed in this chapter are the author's and do not reflect the views of the National Defense University or any government agency.

BIBLIOGRAPHY

The most comprehensive studies of Iraq's modern history in one volume are by American historian Phebe Marr, *The Modern History of Iraq*, 2nd ed. (Boulder, CO: Westview Press, 2004), and British historian Charles Tripp, *A History of Iraq*

(Cambridge: Cambridge University Press, 2000). Marr analyzes Iraq's political, social, and economic structure under various regimes with an emphasis on the
emergence of its middle class. Tripp's study focuses on Iraq from the perspective of
those "out of power." Two books by Reeva S. Simon examine the period between
the world wars in Iraq: the first, *The Creation of Iraq, 1914–1921* (New York: Columbia University Press, 2004), is a volume of essays on Basra, Baghdad, and the
Kurds, coedited by Eleanor H. Tejirian; the second is an excellent account titled
Iraq Between the Two World Wars: The Militarist Origins of Tyranny (New York: Columbia University Press, 2004). Toby Dodge's *Inventing Iraq: The Failure of Nation Building and a History Denied* (New York: Columbia University Press, 2003) is a brilliant
study of the mind-set of Britain's imperial overseers in the making of modern
Iraq. A sharply critical study of Iraq under the Ba'th is found in Marion Farouk-
Sluglett and Peter Sluglett, *Iraq Since 1958: From Revolution to Dictatorship* (London: KPI, 1987). Amatzia Baram, *Culture, History and Ideology in the Formation of
Ba'thist Iraq, 1968–1989* (Oxford: Macmillan, 1991), deals with Ba'thist ideology.
Baram has also written an authoritative study of Iraq's political elite: "The Ruling
Political Elite in Ba'thi Iraq, 1968–1986," *International Journal of Middle East Studies*
21, no. 4 (1989). Kanan Makiya, writing under the pseudonym Samir al-Khalil,
wrote two brilliant but polemical depictions of Iraqi society under the Ba'th: *Republic of Fear* (Berkeley: University of California Press, 1989) and *Cruelty and Si-
lence* (New York: Norton, 1993). Among the better biographies of Saddam Husayn
are Said K. Aburish, *Saddam Hussein: The Politics of Revenge* (New York: Blooms-
bury, 2000), and Efraim Karsh and Inari Rautsi, *Saddam Hussein: A Political Biography* (New York: Free Press, 1991).

The most analytical study of Iraq's pre-Ba'th economy is Edith Penrose and E.
F. Penrose, *Iraq: International Relations and National Development* (Boulder, CO:
Westview Press, 1978). On Iraq's social and political structure, no work compares
to Hanna Batatu's monumental study *The Old Social Classes and the Revolutionary
Movements of Iraq* (Princeton, NJ: Princeton University Press, 1978); probably the
most detailed book on Iraq, it covers political and social history, in particular the
history of Iraq's Communist Party, beginning with the monarchy, but it only in-
troduces the Ba'th regime. Elizabeth Fernea draws a compelling picture of life in a
poor southern village in the 1950s in *Guests of the Sheikh* (1965; rpt. New York:
Anchor, 1995), as does Joyce Wiley in *The Islamic Movement of Iraqi Shi'a* (Boulder,
CO: Lynne Rienner, 1992). Two decent histories of Iraq's Kurds are Edmond
Ghareeb's *The Kurdish Question in Iraq* (Syracuse, NY: Syracuse University Press,
1981), and David McDowall's *The Modern History of the Kurds* (London: I. B. Tauris, 1997). The Shi'as are best dealt with in two scholarly works: Yitzhak Nakash,
The Shi'is of Iraq (Princeton, NJ: Princeton University Press, 1994), covers the history, while Faleh A. Jabar, *The Shi'ite Movement in Iraq* (London: Saqi, 2003), deals
with modern Shi'a movements.

The Gulf wars have spawned a huge number of books on Iraq, many of uneven quality. On the Iran-Iraq War, the best are Shahram Chubin and Charles Tripp, *Iran and Iraq at War* (Boulder, CO: Westview Press, 1988), which relates the war to domestic society in both countries; Jasim Abdulghani, *Iran and Iraq* (Baltimore: Johns Hopkins University Press, 1984), which examines the origins of the conflict; and Dilip Hiro, *The Longest War: The Iran-Iraq Military Conflict* (New York: Routledge, 1991), a very good narrative of the conflict. Among the best of the many studies on the Kuwait War are Elaine Sciolino, *The Outlaw State: Saddam Hussein's Quest for Power and the Gulf Crisis* (New York: John Wiley, 1991), which gives a Western point of view, and Ibrahim Ibrahim, ed., *The Gulf Crisis: Background and Consequences* (Washington, DC: Georgetown University Center for Contemporary Arab Studies, 1992), which presents a more Middle Eastern perspective.

Several books have appeared on the impact of sanctions on Iraq after the Kuwait War. The best are Sarah Graham Brown's *Sanctioning Saddam: The Politics of Intervention in Iraq* (London: I. B. Tauris, 1999), which examines the economic and social impact of sanctions, and Anthony Cordesman and Ahmed Hashim's *Iraq: Sanctions and Beyond* (Boulder, CO: Westview Press, 1997), which looks at the security situation. Amatzia Baram, *Building Toward Crisis: Saddam Husayn's Strategy for Survival* (Washington, DC: Washington Institute for Near East Policy, 1998), discusses the relations of family, clan, and power in Iraq in the decade between sanctions and the war for regime change.

The war for regime change in Iraq, from its lead-up after the events of September 11, 2001, through the planning for the war and occupation, to the search for an American exit strategy has produced a veritable flood of studies. Most of the books have been written by military officers who served in Iraq, journalists who were embedded with the military in Iraq, and Bush administration critics and policy pundits in Washington think tanks who know very little about Iraq. Those worth reading include *Night Draws Near: Iraq's People in the Shadow of America's War* (New York: Picador, 2006) by *New York Times* reporter Anthony Shadid; *Naked in Baghdad* (New York: Farrar, Straus and Giroux, 2003) by NPR's Baghdad correspondent Anne Garrels; *Cobra II: The Inside Story of the Invasion and Occupation of Iraq* (New York: Pantheon, 2006) by *New York Times* chief military correspondent Michael R. Gordon and Gen. Bernard Trainer, USMC (ret.); and *The Assassins' Gate: America in Iraq* (New York: Farrar, Strauss and Giroux, 2005) by George Packer. The first account by an Iraqi written in English is Ali Allawi, *The Occupation of Iraq: Winning the War, Losing the Peace* (New Haven, CT: Yale University Press, 2007); it covers the American occupation and the CPA as witnessed by a former minister in the provisional government and is preferable to accounts such as that by the head of the CPA, Paul Bremer, *My Year in Iraq: The Struggle to Build a Future of Hope* (New York: Simon & Schuster, 2006). Books written to advocate for US policy on Iraq or its role in support of Islamic terrorist movements should be avoided.

6

Eastern Arabian States

Kuwait, Bahrain, Qatar, United Arab Emirates, and Oman

Jill Crystal

Historical Background

Archaeological discoveries over the past four decades have revealed much about eastern Arabia's past. An early Gulf trading culture, dating back to the fourth millennium BC, was linked with the ancient civilizations of Mesopotamia to the north and the Indus Valley to the southeast. Centered in the Bahrain archipelago, it came to be known as Dilmun, after its principal urban settlement, the remains of which were discovered in 1953 outside modern Manama. Dilmun extended from Kuwait to Qatar, with a related culture dominating what are now the United Arab Emirates (UAE) and Oman. The fabled kingdom of Magan (or Makan), located in Oman, was a somewhat later culture whose wealth derived from its control of copper sources.

Beginning in about 3000 BC, increasing climatic desiccation greatly reduced the population in the interior of eastern Arabia. In about 4000 BC, oasis date cultivation began providing a vital food source. Highly nutritious and easily transported, dates became a major staple in nomadic life. By 1500 BC, the domestication of the camel became indispensable to Bedouin life in the desert interior.

Peoples on the coast generally turned to the sea for their livelihood. Fishing, pearling, and maritime trade reached their apogee in the eighth and ninth centuries AD, and Arab seafarers sailing in ships much like the present-day dhows created maritime trade networks that reached from East Africa to the coast of China. Arab maritime trade was finally superseded by Spanish and Portuguese merchant ships in the fifteenth and sixteenth centuries.

In the early seventeenth century, the Portuguese yielded maritime primacy to the Dutch and English, whose commercial ambitions were reflected in the estab-

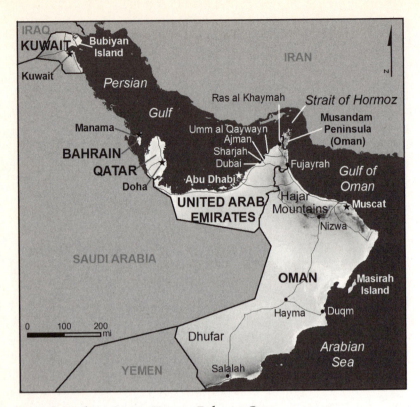

Eastern Arabian States: Kuwait, Bahrain, Qatar, United Arab Emirates, and Oman

lishment of the English and Dutch East India companies in 1600 and 1602, respectively.

The Dutch initially gained the upper hand over the British, but by 1765, the British had become the dominant external power in the region and remained so up to the modern era.

To protect their commercial interests, the British, like the Portuguese and the Dutch, adopted a policy of indirect rule with minimal interference in local affairs.

By the end of the eighteenth century, Napoleonic France had imperial designs on the Middle East. In response, Britain entered into a treaty with Oman in 1788, designed to deny the Gulf to the French and to improve the protection of Britain's lines of communication with its increasingly important Indian possessions.

As the Napoleonic challenge evaporated, another threat presented itself in the form of Arab privateers. Sailing from the shaykhdoms of Sharjah and Ras al-Khaymah, the privateers would strike at commercial maritime shipping, threatening British maritime trade routs to India and beyond. After heavy fighting, Anglo-Indian naval forces decisively defeated the Arab privateer fleet based in Ras al-Khaymah in 1819 and signed a treaty with the local shaykhs that became the cornerstone of Britain's presence in the Gulf area for the next 150 years.

Although the threat of Arab privateering came to an end, tribal warfare continued to threaten stability throughout the shaykhdoms. In 1835, the British prevailed upon all the ruling shaykhs to sign a second treaty prohibiting tribes under the rulers' jurisdiction from raiding each other during the fishing and pearling seasons. In 1838 the treaty was extended throughout the year, and in 1853 it was made permanent in the Treaty of Maritime Peace in Perpetuity.

These treaties formed the basis for British colonial rule in the Gulf. Subsequently, treaties of 1861 and 1880 committed the British to protecting the Al Khalifah rulers of Bahrain, and by the early twentieth century a British political agent resided in that shaykhdom. In 1892 Britain concluded "exclusive agreements" with the Trucial States, assuming responsibility for their defense and foreign affairs. In 1899 a similar relationship, though not then made public, was established with Kuwait, and in 1916 another followed with Qatar. Oman remained outside this treaty system, but the British retained a close relationship with the Al Bu Sa'id sultans of Muscat, who in the nineteenth century lost effective control over Oman's interior.

In addition to taking direct control of these states' external relations, Britain assumed a degree of oversight of their domestic affairs. This control was minimal in some principalities that rarely crossed British interests, such as Kuwait. In others, advice was freely proffered. Most rulers followed the advice; those who refused risked exile, ouster, or British naval bombardment. In this manner Britain brought a degree of stability to the region.

The British left a lasting impact on the Gulf. Their treaty system stabilized political power relationships and led to the establishment of European-style boundaries that largely exist today. In addition, Britain introduced and developed administrative and legal practices, as reflected in the establishment of municipal councils and the application of Western-style legal codes alongside Islamic law (Shari'a). It also launched modest economic- and social-development schemes that pointed the way to much more ambitious postindependence projects. An important consequence of the British imperium in the Gulf was the establishment of English as the area's language of international trade, defense, and diplomacy.

After World War II, British strategic interests in protecting maritime trade routes ceased with the independence of India and Pakistan in 1947. Nevertheless, following the trend of granting full independence throughout the British Empire, Britain granted full independence to Kuwait in 1961, and in 1968 it announced its intention to withdraw completely from the Gulf. In 1971 Britain terminated its special treaty relationships with Bahrain, Qatar, and the Trucial States. It failed to create a federation of the Trucial States, Bahrain, and Qatar when Bahrain and Qatar became separate independent states, but the seven Trucial States federated to form the United Arab Emirates. (Ras al-Khaymah held out but finally joined in 1972.) The 1970s brought both fears and fortunes. The fortunes were the rapid rise in oil revenues due to the Arab oil embargo in the wake of the 1973 Arab-Israeli War. The fears arose as a result of the 1979 Islamic Revolution in Shi'a Iran followed by the Iran-Iraq War (1980–1988). The revolution threatened the domestic security of all the Gulf Cooperation Council (GCC) states, but particularly Bahrain, where a Sunni minority rules a Shi'a majority.

In 1981, Kuwait, Bahrain, Qatar, the UAE, and Saudi Arabia founded the GCC. There had been discussions about creating such an organization to enhance regional security since the British departure, but the idea never materialized, largely because of pressure from Iran and Iraq to be included. The Iran-Iraq War provided both a new incentive and the opportunity to exclude both warring states.

The Iran-Iraq War threatened all the GCC states, whose leaders, fearing Iran more than Iraq, threw their support behind Saddam Husayn. In 1987 Iran initiated regular attacks on Kuwaiti oil tankers in retaliation for Iraqi assaults on Iran's tankers and loading facilities. This led Kuwait to request US naval escorts and the reflagging of some of its tankers. This was a dramatic departure from Kuwait's and the general eastern Arabian states' policy of maintaining security through nonmilitary means, backed by an over-the-horizon US military presence in the Indian Ocean. When Britain left the Gulf, the United States became the only major Western country with a major military presence in the Gulf.

In the 1980s, oil prices that had spiked during the Arab oil embargo following the 1973 Arab-Israeli War collapsed, forcing the Gulf oil-producing states to cut development expenditures and seek new revenue sources. This was a factor leading to the Iraqi invasion of Kuwait in August 1990. The Kuwaiti royal family escaped into exile, but the Kuwaitis suffered through a brutal Iraqi occupation until February 1991, when an allied coalition of military forces led by the United States drove the Iraqis out of Kuwait in Operation Desert Storm. Desert Storm drew the eastern Arabian states closer to the United States in security cooperation. By the mid-1990s GCC states contracted for $36 billion in arms purchases from the United States, a third of US sales worldwide. The Gulf War had domestic reverberations as well, accelerating a nascent political-liberalization process across the Gulf. In Kuwait, the amir agreed to reopen the parliament he had suspended in 1986, holding elections in 1992. In Qatar, Crown Prince Hamad overthrew his father, Khalifah Al Thani, in a bloodless coup in 1995 and in the following years wrote a new constitution and held limited elections. In Bahrain, a government crackdown on Shi'as in the mid-1990s ended with another generational leadership change, as Hamad bin Isa Al

Khalifah became amir after the death of his father in 1999. He took steps to liberalize Bahrain's political system, reinstating an assembly that had been dissolved since 1975. In Oman, Sultan Qabus presided over a more gradual liberalization.

On September 11, 2001, al-Qa'ida launched an attack on US targets in New York and Washington, DC. The attack prompted a sea change in the way US President George W. Bush viewed the world, leading to a more proactive approach to perceived dangers. US policy on Iraq had been at an impasse for a decade. Bush defined his administration's "Global War on Terror" in so expansive a way as to include any unfriendly regime that might develop weapons of mass destruction, then placed Iraq at the top of this list. This contention, although unfounded, was sufficient to forge domestic support for a war in Iraq. In March 2003 the Iraq War began, and in a short time, military victory was achieved. The United States, however, soon became mired in Iraq, fighting an insurgency that by 2005 had turned into a sectarian civil war. The worsening situation in Iraq heightened fears of both regional and domestic instability should Jihadi-Salafis trained in Iraq turn on the GCC's leaders or sectarian tension escalate. By 2009 the sectarian violence had largely ended in a Shi'a victory, and these fears were replaced by concerns about Iraq's stability following an American withdrawal of forces.

All five countries have political commonalities. All are ruled by monarchs, and all but Oman by ruling families who govern through a political form that Michael Herb has called dynastic monarchism, a form of rule adopted first by Kuwait to retain power in a period of rapid economic growth following the arrival of oil revenues, then copied by the other GCC states. Since the Gulf War, these states have undergone a degree of limited political liberalization, typically by creating or expanding elected or partially elected councils that advise the ruler. All five states are largely dependent on oil revenues. All have diversified and liberalized their economies in the past decade in an attempt to mitigate that dependence, yet each Gulf economy remains largely government owned and operated, with a small private sector (more vibrant in Dubai and Kuwait than elsewhere) closely tied to the state.

KUWAIT

Political Environment

Kuwait is a city-state bordering Iraq and Saudi Arabia, with a history shaped by the desert and sea. It was settled in the late seventeenth and early eighteenth centuries when tribes from the central Arabian Unayzah confederation migrated toward the coast. The Bani 'Utub, as they came to call themselves, settled first in Bahrain and then Kuwait. Kuwait's hot, dry climate could sustain little agriculture, so the settlers turned to the sea, developing an economy based on pearling,

KUWAIT

Capital city	Kuwait
Chief of state	Amir Sabah al-Ahmed al-Jabir Al Sabah
Head of government	Prime Minister Nasir al-Muhammad al-Ahmad Al Sabah
Major political parties	None
Ethnic groups	Kuwaiti (45%), other Arab (35%), South Asian (9%), Iranian (4%), other (7%)
Religious groups	Sunni Muslim (60%), Shi'a Muslim (25%), other (15%)
Export partners	Japan (19.9%), South Korea (17%), Taiwan (11.2%), Singapore (9.9%), United States (8.4%), Netherlands (4.8%), China (4.4%)
Import partners	United States (12.7%), Japan (8.5%), Germany (7.3%), China (6.8%), South Korea (6.6%), Saudi Arabia (6.2%), Italy (5.8%), United Kingdom (4.6%)

fishing, and long-distance trade. The tribal structures from their desert past remained largely intact, and Kuwait's ruling elite mainly consisted of descendants of the original Sunni settlers from the Arabian Desert. According to Kuwait's founding myth, these leading families chose one family from among them to rule, the Al Sabah. With time, other groups settled in Kuwait, forming a social hierarchy atop which remained the now urban descendants of these original Sunni families. As the economy shifted from the desert to the sea, the Bani 'Utub became a merchant elite. When oil was discovered and oil revenues had overwhelmed other sources of income, the original economic basis of their wealth vanished, but the entrenched hierarchies remained.

In the early twentieth century, Persian Shi'as migrated to Kuwait, joining the smaller group of Arab Shi'as originally from Bahrain, Iraq, or Saudi Arabia's Eastern Province. These Shi'as formed the next rung in Kuwait's social hierarchy and constitute about one-fifth of Kuwait's population. In the late twentieth century,

Arab Bedouins from the surrounding areas settled in Kuwait, typically on the outskirts of the capital. Those who received citizenship formed the next rung down and now constitute just under half of Kuwait's citizens. In parliamentary elections, their tribal candidates typically win about half the seats, primarily in the outer districts.

With the discovery of oil in commercial quantities in 1938, Kuwait's social structure again changed. As in other GCC states, oil revenues changed the political dynamics of Kuwait by freeing rulers of their financial dependence on the merchants. Oil wealth also brought an influx of expatriate workers who now constitute over half of Kuwait's population. Originally many were Palestinians who fled their country after the partition of Palestine, and many attained high positions in both the government and the private sector. After Desert Storm, however, most Palestinians were expelled from Kuwait due to their to support for the Iraqis.

Since then, most expatriate workers have come from the Indian subcontinent. As a group, expatriate workers form an underclass beneath the Kuwaitis. A hierarchical division also exists within the expatriate community, with Western expatriates at the apex, followed by Arab expatriates, and Asians at the bottom.

A separate group of stateless residents called *bidun* (from *bidun jinsiyyah*, meaning literally "without nationality") constitute a final element of Kuwaiti society. The *bidun* comprise an umbrella category of stateless people, many long-term residents in Kuwait. Many are from the Shammar and Anayzah tribes, which extend into Iraq (as well as Saudi Arabia and Syria). Some have lived in Kuwait for generations, but their ancestors never registered for citizenship when the Nationality Law was introduced in 1959. Others came to Kuwait in the late twentieth century, with the ruler's encouragement, typically to join the police or military, whose ranks before the Iraqi invasion were largely filled by *bidun*. In the decades before the Iraqi invasion, some received nationality; the rest were slowly stripped of many rights. After the Iraqi invasion, the government considered the *bidun* a suspect group because some had collaborated with the Iraqi authorities. The government began an all-out crackdown, firing en masse *bidun* who worked for the government. Those who had fled Kuwait during the occupation were not allowed to return, and those still in Kuwait remain in *bidun* limbo.

The sharpest social divisions in Kuwait remain between citizens and expatriates, Sunnis and Shi'as, and *hadar* (the settled, Sunni, urban elite) and *badu* (the settled Bedouin tribes). Other social identities crosscut these divisions, but none are as salient politically. These affective divisions also reflect differences in wealth; class and communal identities overlap substantially.

Demography is also an important element of Kuwaiti society. Elder generations traditionally dominated the family as well as government and business. They still do to a great extent, but modern health care financed by oil wealth has created a population explosion. Almost two-thirds of the population is under twenty years of age, putting severe pressure on the government to create jobs. Rapid social change has also affected gender relations. The debate over the role of women in society has typically pitted Kuwait's Islamists against its modernists. For years it focused on the issue of women's suffrage. In 2005, however, the amir granted women the right to vote and run for office. In 2009 four women were elected to parliament.

Kuwait's economy is dominated by oil. The Kuwait Oil Company (KOC), originally jointly owned by British Petroleum and (the US-based) Gulf Oil Company, received a concession to search for oil and in 1938 found it in commercial quantities. After World War II, the oil sector expanded dramatically. In 1970 the Kuwaiti government nationalized KOC, becoming the first Arab Gulf state to achieve total ownership of its oil industry. Most of Kuwait's oil comes from the Burgan oil field, the world's second-largest. Burgan, however, has been in production for over fifty years, and some controversy exists over the actual level of remaining reserves.

The Kuwaiti government spent much of the new oil wealth on the public, first in direct handouts of cash and housing (and for the elite, inexpensive land). In time a large welfare state emerged, providing free education, health care, heavily subsidized utilities, and a guaranteed state job to all who wanted one (the constitution guarantees a right to work). Substantial oil revenues were also invested in the Reserve Fund for Future Generations beginning in 1976. By the early 1980s Kuwait was earning more from its overseas investments than from its oil exports. The oil glut of the mid-1980s placed some economic stress on the country, prompting it to pump oil beyond its OPEC quota. In this period, a political storm also arose over the collapse of the Suq al-Manakh, an unofficial stock market, whose bubble burst after many Kuwaitis, including ruling-family members, engaged in massive speculative stock purchases using postdated checks. When the market crashed, the government bailout was so politically charged that it was not finally resolved by Kuwait's National Assembly until 1998.

The Iraqi occupation of Kuwait in 1990 was a financial as well as political and psychological burden on the country. Kuwaiti financial support for the Desert Storm operation that ended the occupation emptied Kuwait's Reserve Fund. The postwar cost of rebuilding Kuwait was high, although the pace of physical recovery of infrastructure was quite swift. These expenses, combined with controversy over the mismanagement of investment funds and lingering issues related to the Suq al-Manakh crisis, provoked public calls for greater government financial accountability. In 1993 Kuwait's National Assembly passed legislation enabling it to examine the financial records of all state-owned companies and investment organizations.

In the 1990s the government embarked on a major economic liberalization initiative to encourage growth, cut government costs, and, it was hoped, create more jobs for younger Kuwaitis, nearly all of whom work for the government. Many restrictions on foreign ownership were lifted in an effort to attract foreign direct investment. Major stakes in state-owned companies were privatized. In the energy sector, the government embarked on Project Kuwait, an ambitious and controversial $8.5 billion plan to invite foreign oil companies to participate in the development of Kuwait's northern oil fields. The Kuwaiti business community, however, was ambivalent about this foreign participation. Much of the tension between the executive and legislature leading up to the 2009 elections turned on the National Assembly's opposition to Project Kuwait, as well as its success in forcing the cancellation of a $27.4 billon joint venture project with Dow Chemical and delaying a government stimulus package.

When oil prices rose in 2005, the government budget went from a deficit to a $9 billion surplus. Much of this was again spent on various direct grants to citizens, rebuilding of infrastructure, and investment in the Reserve Fund (by law, 10 percent of Kuwait's revenues are placed in the fund). Virtually depleted by the Gulf War, by 2006 the fund had grown back to about $100 billion, generating $5 billion in income a year.

Kuwait's economy remains dominated by the state-run energy sector. The majority of the national population works for the state, and the state welfare system remains intact. Of Kuwait's national budget, 40 percent goes to payroll; another 30 percent goes to public subsidies for basic services (such as utilities) and handouts of various sorts. Kuwait benefited from the high oil prices of 2005 and has also suffered from the 2009 recession (it was the only Gulf state in which the government was forced to rescue a bank). Among the contentious issues the new assembly faced was a vote on a multi-billion-dollar stimulus bill.

Political Structure and Dynamics

Kuwait has been ruled since the eighteenth century by members of the Sabah family. The modern history of Kuwait begins in 1899 when Mubarak the Great (ruled 1896–1915) came to power. Fearing pressure from the Ottomans, who exercised nominal suzerainty over the shaykhdom, Mubarak entered into a protected-state relationship with Britain, establishing ties that would last beyond independence.

Britain concerned itself primarily with foreign policy: first with regional security and later with oil. Internal affairs were left largely to the Kuwaitis. On Mubarak's death, a pattern was established of alternation in power between the lines of two of his sons: Jabir (ruled 1915–1917) and Salim (ruled 1917–1921). This alternation held through the twentieth century with one exception: In 1965 Abdallah al-Salim (ruled 1950–1965) was succeeded by his brother, Sabah Al Salim (ruled 1965–1977). Oil revenues began to appear in significant quantities during the reigns of these two amirs (Abdallah and Sabah) and with it the establishment of a welfare state and the rapid expansion of infrastructure and industry.

Like the other Gulf monarchies, Kuwait is ruled by both a public set of officials (ministers and department heads) and a ruling-family council. The two institutions overlap. The most important ministries, called the sovereign ministries (interior, defense, foreign affairs, and energy), are nearly always headed by a ruling-family member. These ministers are also part of a larger family council that decides broad policy matters and handles succession. Its deliberations are secret and normally invisible. From time to time, however, differences appear, as they did in 2006 following the death of Shaykh Jabir (discussed below). Kuwait's ruling family continues to exercise predominant political power in Kuwait. The Kuwaiti citizenry seems generally supportive of the ruling family. No opposition groups call for its removal; rather they seek to preserve and expand the power sharing between the ruling family and society in the National Assembly.

Kuwait has the longest experience of all the GCC states with a written constitution and elected bodies. Kuwait's constitution was adopted in 1962, making it one of the oldest in the region and the oldest in the Gulf. In accordance with this constitution, Kuwait has had an elected unicameral National Assembly (*Majlis al-Umma*) since 1963. It comprises fifty members, elected for four-year terms. The twenty-five districts were gerrymandered in 1981 when the parliament was reconvened after a five-year suspension. These districts were oddly shaped and ranged in population from under 10,000 to under 3,000, making vote buying feasible. Reformist members of parliament (MPs) long called for limiting the number of constituencies, and in 2006 a new election law reduced their number from twenty-five to five. Each voter may vote for up to four candidates.

Elections (with the exception of the 1967 election) have been largely free and open. The assembly also includes fifteen cabinet ministers, one of whom must be elected. The ruler has intervened unconstitutionally twice to suspend the assembly: in 1976 and in 1986. The last assembly elections were held in May 2009, only a year after the previous elections; they followed the amir's suspension of the assembly in March after repeated attempts by MPs to question the prime minister. The 2009 elections were most notable for the election of four female MPs, all of whom held PhDs from US universities.

Also notable was the rise in independent and new candidates (over 40 percent of those elected had not previously served) and the decline of the organized quasi-political parties. Islamists, particularly those formally affiliated with the Muslim Brotherhood and Salafi groups, fell from twenty-one seats in the previous elections to eleven. Seats won by Shi'as and liberal MPs increased slightly. Contention continued in the new assembly, beginning with a walkout by fourteen MPs, some protesting the presence of women in the body (especially of two who did not wear *hijab*), others protesting the government's development plans.

Suffrage is granted to most adult citizens (police and military may not vote) age twenty-one and over whose official ancestry in Kuwait can be traced back to 1921. Naturalized citizens (a very small segment of the population) must have twenty years of Kuwaiti residency before they may vote. Women's suffrage was introduced in 2005, largely through the efforts of the prime minister and over the objections of Sunni Islamists in the assembly.

The assembly's formal powers are limited. However, it does play an important and vocal role in shaping and challenging government policy. The assembly must approve all legislation. It can (and does) interpellate ministers and entertain votes of confidence for individual ministers. Following a confrontation between the government and legislature, nominally over errors in copies of the Qur'an printed by the justice minister, the amir dissolved the assembly in 1999 to prevent the minister's interpellation and possible ouster. In contrast to earlier suspensions, new elections were held within the constitutionally prescribed period of sixty days. However, in the interim the government issued a number of decrees, one of which granted suffrage to women. The new assembly reversed what it saw as an unconstitutionally issued decree; then in 2005 it passed legislation granting women suffrage.

In January 2006 the assembly played an unprecedented role in the succession crisis that occurred upon the death of Kuwait's ruler, Shaykh Jabir. Unusually open discussion followed about the physical and mental fitness of his named successor, Crown Prince Shaykh Sa'd Abdallah. As the ruling family continued to discuss the issue, the country grew impatient. In keeping with a constitutional provision, the assembly voted unanimously to force Shaykh Sa'd's abdication, prompting the ruling family finally to name an appropriate successor, Shaykh Sabah al-Ahmad Al Sabah, prime minister since 2003 (when the posts of crown prince and prime minister were separated). Sabah's accession was also a departure from the pattern of alternation between the Jabir and Salim lines, moving essentially from one Jabir (Shaykh Jabir) to another (Shaykh Sabah). While not entirely unprecedented (an alternation was skipped in 1965), the new amir's selection of his half brother Shaykh Nawaf al-Ahmad al-Jabir al Sabah (another Jabir) as crown prince suggests that the practice of alternation may have come to an end, reflecting a demographic shift toward the Jabir line. The appointment of Shaykh Nasir Muhammad as prime minister continued the separation of the crown prince and prime minister posts that many MPs had demanded. The assembly's active involvement in a succession that might have played out as a bloodless palace coup in other GCC states has emboldened it as an institution. Some MPs even called for the amir to appoint a prime minister from outside the ruling family.

Kuwait's small size precludes significant local government. Administratively, it is divided into five governates. Elected local neighborhood cooperatives are an important element of the Kuwaiti political system and often the springboard to political careers. Kuwait's elected Municipal Council, which predates independence, has the power to approve building, construction, and road projects. In 2006 women voted for the first time in municipal elections, and two ran as candidates.

Political parties are banned in Kuwait. However, partylike blocs (tribal, religious, and ideological) compete in elections and function openly in the assembly. Bedouins in Kuwait organize politically around tribes, often holding tribal primaries (although these are formally banned). The largest group in the assembly consists of pro-government delegates, mostly tribal, with many campaigning as service deputies. Some of them vote with the Islamist bloc at times.

The largest opposition group consists of Islamists. These include Salafis, the Muslim Brotherhood, and independent Islamists. In 2005 the Salafis tried to press for the legalization of parties by founding Kuwait's first openly political party, the Umma Party (*Hizb al-Umma*). The government encouraged the growth of Islamists in the 1960s and 1970s as a counterweight to the Arab nationalists. In 1976 and 1986 the Islamists supported the government when it suspended the assembly. But by the 1981 assembly, the Islamists had clearly eclipsed the Liberals, and as they found their own voice, the government turned increasingly to the tribal deputies for support. In the 2003 election, Islamists were very successful, more in the tribal than the *hadar* districts. But in 2009 their numbers dropped. The Islamist base is the Kuwaiti poor and the upwardly mobile urban middle class shut out of money and power by the old economic elite. The Islamist-Liberal divide is thus a class as well as an ideological conflict. Kuwait has successfully integrated Islamists into its political system. The Islamists, too, have exhibited political flexibility. For example, Islamists opposed women's suffrage, but once it became law, they moved very quickly to campaign for women's votes. As elsewhere, their strength lies in a class base, an ideological agenda, and an ability to organize: to raise funds, take over associations, and form alliances (for example, at times with Shi'a Islamists).

The next largest group in the assembly is the Liberals, whose base is the old, urban, Sunni, *hadar* merchant families. The Liberals began as Arab nationalists in the 1960s, but in the 1970s and 1980s they redefined themselves as a secularist pro-democracy grouping.

Nine Shi'as were elected to the 2009 assembly. With little interest in the predominantly Sunni Arab nationalism supported by the liberal Arab nationalists, they aligned themselves with the ruling family in the 1960s and 1970s and were reliable supporters of government legislation. However, the Iranian revolution prompted the government to view Kuwaiti Shi'as as a potential threat, and the alliance weakened. While some Shi'as are still pro-government, most now identify as Islamist. Kuwait's civil society is vibrant. Kuwaitis feel free to criticize the government and the ruling family. Many civic associations exist, including trade unions, cooperative societies, professional groups, and a human rights group (the nongovernmental Kuwait Human Rights Society was finally granted a license in 2004, after ten years of operating without one). Broadcast media are state owned;

however, print media are privately owned and have, since independence, offered an opportunity for public debate and a lively forum for assembly candidates. In 2006 the assembly passed a new law that expanded press freedoms. Kuwait also has an older institution that plays an important role in shaping debate: the *diwaniyya*, a weekly meeting among men to discuss political and economic issues. At times, for example, during the 1986 suspension, some of these meetings have become extremely politicized.

Kuwait's opposition has largely been a loyal one. However, there have been arrests of people suspected of involvement with militant groups. Kuwaitis, while happy to see Saddam Husayn removed, are concerned about sectarian conflict in Iraq. Some Kuwaitis have gone to fight and train in Iraq.

The Iraqi invasion demonstrated the weakness of Kuwait's army. As a result, in the 1990s the military was restructured with US assistance and rebuilt to about 15,000—nearly the prewar strength. In addition to regular military forces, Kuwait's forces include the paramilitary National Guard. Crown Prince Shaykh Nawaf was a founder of the modern police force and, until his appointment, deputy chief of Kuwait's National Guard. Kuwait's military (and its police) have also undergone significant personnel changes in the last decade in an effort to reduce the dependence on *bidun*, who once constituted the overwhelming majority of military and police recruits. The government has also consolidated its close relationship with the United States. In 2001 Kuwait and the United States renewed a 1991 pact permitting US forces to use Kuwaiti facilities and to station troops and equipment there.

Kuwait has a civil (rather than common) law legal system, administered since 1996 by the Supreme Judicial Council. Unlike many other GCC states, Kuwait has no separate set of Shari'a courts. On personal status matters, Kuwaitis are governed by accepted schools of Islamic jurisprudence (Sunni and Shi'a). Kuwait has a mixed human rights record. As with the other GCC states, its primary weakness concerns maltreatment of foreign laborers. Shi'a Kuwaitis are also subject to discrimination. In addition to a private human rights group operating in the country, the National Assembly has a Human Rights Committee.

BAHRAIN

Political Environment

Bahrain is a small archipelago located between Saudi Arabia and the Qatar Peninsula. The largest island contains the capital, Manama. The second-largest island, Muharraq, is accessible by a four-mile causeway from Manama. It contains the state's second-largest city, also called Muharraq. The four main islands are joined by causeways. The population of Bahrain is the smallest of the GCC states, a bit over

BAHRAIN

Capital city	Manama
Chief of state	King Hamad bin Isa Al Khalifah
Head of government	Prime Minister Khalifah bin Salman Al Khalifa
Major political parties *(seats in lower house)*	al Wifaq (17), al Minbar (7), al Asala (5), al Mustaqbal (4)
Ethnic groups	Bahraini (62.4%), non-Bahraini (37.6%)
Religious groups	Muslim (81.2%), Christian (9%), other (9.8%)
Export partners	Saudi Arabia (3.5%), United States (2.5%), United Arab Emirates (2.5%)
Import partners	Saudi Arabia (37.7%), Japan (7.2%), United States (6.2%), Germany (4.7%), United Kingdom (4.5%), United Arab Emirates (4.2%), China (4.1%)

700,000. This population is primarily Arab. Native Bahrainis account for about two-thirds of the total population, in contrast to other GCC states (except Oman), where expatriates outnumber nationals.

Bahrain's ruling family, the Al Khalifah, is a branch of the Bani 'Utub tribe that rules Kuwait. The Al Khalifah migrated from Kuwait to Zubarah, a settlement at the northwest tip of the Qatar Peninsula, and from there to Bahrain in 1782. There they drove out the Persian-backed rulers, ending Persia's influence along the Arab side of the Gulf.

The Al Khalifah are Sunni; however, some 70 percent of Bahrainis are Shi'a. The Sunnis are divided between those of Arabian tribal origin and, somewhat lower in social status, the Sunni *hawwalah*, descendants of Arabs who migrated to Iran and later returned to Bahrain. The Shi'as are either *baharna*, indigenous to Bahrain, or *ajam*, a smaller group of Iranian origin and somewhat lower in social status. Bahrain's Shi'as, although mostly Twelvers, comprise a varied religious group. They look to many different clerical leaders, including those in Iran, Iraq, and Lebanon. Collectively, the Shi'as have faced significant discrimination from the Sunni elite in housing, education, and employment: The unemployment rate among young Shi'a men is extremely high. The government is torn between its desires to reduce Shi'a unemployment and to placate the demands of its wealthy Sunni constituency, which relies heavily on the low-wage expatriates who constitute a majority of the workforce. Political discrimination has likewise left Shi'as largely out of positions of power. Less than 20 percent of senior government positions are held by Shi'as, and Shi'as are effectively barred from the security forces. From time to time, Shi'a protests have been severely repressed by government forces. Two periods stand out. The first was in the 1980s, during the years after the 1979 Islamic revolution in Shi'a Iran, when Bahrain's rulers, fearing the revolution would spread to their realm, cracked down harshly on all Shi'a dissent. Many Shi'a dissidents took refuge in Iran during this period. The second period was in the mid-1990s when the government responded, again with great harshness and some brutality, to Shi'a demonstrations. The rise to power during the Iraq War of Iraq's Shi'as, once ruled by Sunnis, evoked fears among the Sunni elite reminiscent of the 1980s. Bahraini opposition leaders contend that the government has granted many Sunni Arabs (perhaps as many as 50,000 or more) citizenship under a 2002 revision of Bahrain's citizenship law in order to help shift the country's demographic balance.

Before oil, Bahrain's economy was largely dependent on pearling. Oil was discovered in commercial quantities in the 1930s, but the scope of Bahrain's reserves has always been modest, the lowest in the GCC. Bahrain was both the first Gulf state to develop an oil industry and the first oil producer in the region to begin running out of oil. Production peaked at 76,000 barrels per day (bpd) in 1970 and has been declining since. New recovery methods and the revenues shared with Saudi Arabia from a common offshore field ensure at least modest continuing revenues. Offshore exploration also holds promise for future natural gas production. Bahrain's large oil refinery has, since 1945, processed Saudi oil as well as its own; Saudi oil accounts for 80 percent of the throughput. In 1980 the government acquired 100 percent of the Bahrain Petroleum Company, a subsidiary of Caltex. Despite its depleting reserves, oil production and refining still account for more than half of Bahrain's export and government revenues.

The modest scope of Bahrain's oil made it the first country to make serious efforts to diversify its economy. In the late 1960s Bahrain undertook several industrial projects. The largest was Aluminum Bahrain, which produces over 500,000 tons of aluminum annually and constitutes Bahrain's second major source of exports. Other projects included the Arab Shipbuilding and Repair Yard, designed to accommodate ships of up to 400,000 tons, and the Arab Iron and Steel Company, an ore-pelletizing plant. Another diversification effort was the establishment of offshore banking units, designed originally to capture some of the financial business that had fled Beirut with the outbreak of Lebanon's civil war in 1975. Bahrain's tourism industry benefits from the weekend influx of Saudis across the causeway.

Political Structure and Dynamics

Bahrain's ruling family, the Al Khalifah, has reigned since 1783. Unlike in Kuwait, where the ruling family is generally accepted, in Bahrain it has been opposed by the majority of the Shi'a population. As a result, Bahrain's movements in the direction of political liberalization have been much more cautious.

Bahrain's first attempt at political liberalization was short-lived. From 1961 to 1999, power was shared between the amir, Shaykh Isa bin Salman, and his brother and prime minister, Shaykh Khalifah bin Salman. In an effort to create a degree of legitimacy, Shaykh Khalifah, on independence, drew up a constitution promulgated in mid-1973 and held elections in late 1973 for Bahrain's first National Assembly, a unicameral body. However, continuing protests against the government, led by labor organizations, prompted the ruler to issue the State Security Law in 1975, granting the government wide powers to detain and hold dissidents. The young assembly united in opposition to this law, which was never submitted for assembly approval. In August 1975 the government suspended the assembly and the constitution.

The early 1990s witnessed some efforts to introduce a degree of consultation as demands for political participation grew across the Gulf. In 1992 Bahrain's ruler announced plans for a consultative assembly whose members would be drawn from business, professional, religious, and academic backgrounds. This did little to assuage popular demands, however, and a 1994 petition calling for restoration of the National Assembly, signed by 20,000 Sunni and Shi'a professionals, prompted Shaykh Isa to increase the size and power of the consultative assembly. Shi'a protests over high unemployment and lack of political representation continued, however. Throughout the mid-1990s, large Shi'a demonstrations brought harsh government response, including the arrest and detention of several hundred opposition activists. The violence ebbed and flowed until 1999.

In 1999 Shaykh Isa, who had promoted himself to Amir Isa in 1971, died and was succeeded by his son, Shaykh Hamad bin Isa Al Khalifah. The new ruler released political prisoners, welcomed back pro-democracy activists exiled in the 1990s, and promised a new era of reform. He called on Bahrain to vote on a new national charter that would reinstate an elected legislature, one with real legislative authority. The bicameral National Assembly would consist of an elected lower house and an appointed upper house. He extended suffrage to women and promised to guarantee freedom of the press and religious belief. He won the tentative support of the Shi'a opposition by agreeing to amnesty four hundred political prisoners and repatriate over one hundred exiles. In February 2001 a popular referendum endorsed the new national charter. The State Security Law was abolished, and the state security police, which many blamed for the severity of the crackdowns of the 1990s, was replaced with the National Security Agency.

Then reform stalled. Some signs of the limits to liberalization were visible early on. Despite the new government, the old prime minister (the king's uncle), Shaykh Khalifah bin Salman Al Khalifah, retained his portfolio. Khalifah, a major power center since independence, was a key architect of the crackdown of the 1990s.

In 1999 Shaykh Hamad ibn Isa issued a new Press and Publications Law that expanded the information ministry's censorship powers and mandated fines, publication closures, and even prison terms for journalists. He issued a blanket immunity for officials suspected of human rights violations and declared himself king, designating his son, Salman, crown prince. In place of the national charter, he promulgated a new amended constitution, which deprived the National Assembly of the right to introduce legislation directly, gave preponderant power to an unelected upper house, and gave Hamad nearly limitless powers. In February 2002, he promoted himself to King Hamad.

People protested. Nonetheless, elections went ahead. The first elections, held in May 2002, were for municipal councils. The opposition, with some reluctance, participated. A debate then emerged over the merits of participating in upcoming elections for the Chamber of Deputies in October 2002. In the end, four groups, headed by Bahrain's largest predominantly Shi'a opposition group, al-Wifaq National Islamic Society, boycotted, arguing that more constitutional reforms were needed and that the gerrymandering of districts deprived them of any chance of winning a majority in the lower house. With slightly more than half the eligible voters participating, the outcome of the elections was a body dominated by Sunni Muslims, divided between Islamists and secularists, but leaning toward the former. Six women ran, although none were elected. The king then appointed a new *majlis* and cabinet, retaining his uncle as prime minister.

Despite the limitations on the assembly, the impending collapse of two government-managed pension funds, holding the savings of nearly all Bahrainis, brought out a streak of independence in the body in 2004. The legislature formed a commission, over the government's objection, to investigate the fund's management. In January 2004 the commission submitted a long report to the Council of Deputies detailing the extensive mismanagement and malfeasance of the fund managers and recommended the interpellation of the ministers of finance, labor, and state. To deter more radical steps, the government offered to rescue the pension funds at a cost of nearly $40 million.

In 2006, elections were again held, and this time the Wifaq society and the three other groups that boycotted the 2002 elections participated. This decision led to a break in the Wifaq's ranks, with the minority, which advocated continuing the boycott, leaving to form the al-Haq movement. The forty-member elected lower house included seventeen Wifaq MPs, eight Sunni Salafist al-Asala bloc members, seven Muslim Brothers, four Sunni members of the al-Mustaqbal bloc, and twenty-two pro-government MPs. One woman was among those elected. During the election the naturalization issue emerged as a result of publication of the Bandar Report by a government advisor, alleging a host of government improprieties. Since entering parliament in 2006, Wifaq's main goal has been amending the 2002 constitution. While there have been moments of cooperation, most of the conflict has continued to fall along sectarian lines. In 2008 Wifaq paralyzed parliament in an effort to question the government's grant of nationality to non-Bahraini Sunnis. Political divisions at the top of the ruling family also became public in January 2008 when the king's cancer diagnosis and absence from the country resulted in tension between the crown prince and prime minister. The crown prince publicly protested corruption and other obstacles to economic reform, widely interpreted as criticisms of the prime minister. In the course of the dispute, some allies of the prime minister, including his son, were ousted from positions of power, and the crown prince emerged strengthened.

Civil society in Bahrain functions within limits. Bahrain has several active human rights groups, among them the Bahrain Center for Human Rights. Political parties are banned, but political societies, professional associations, women's groups, and other associations are permitted. Al Wifaq is the largest society with some 65,000 members, nearly all Shi'a. Al-Wifaq is an umbrella organization that emerged from the previously underground group Islamic Enlightenment. It includes Shi'as of many different political slants. The Islamic Action Society, another Shi'a group, is the next largest. It is Islamist in orientation and successor to the Islamic Front for the Liberation of Bahrain, a militant group that advocated the overthrow of the Al Khalifah during the 1990s. A 2005 law on civil and political societies added new restrictions to public associations by limiting the age of members, as well as their association with foreign groups, and banning foreign funding.

The Bahrain Shi'a clergy, as elsewhere, has long maintained independent institutions (mosques and *matams*) and a degree of autonomy unknown to Sunni clergy. However, in 2006 the government began implementing new legislation permitting it to pay salaries to imams, putting some three hundred on salary. This prompted considerable debate in Bahrain about the legitimacy and independence of state-salaried imams.

Shi'a discontent remains. Senior Shi'a clerics, such as Shaykh Isa Qassim, have urged peaceful protest, but demonstrations and confrontation between Shi'as and the national security forces are regular events. The empowerment of Shi'as in Iraq has deepened that frustration. The February 2006 bombing of the Askariyya Mosque in Samarra, Iraq, among the holiest sites in Shi'a Islam, brought out a crowd of over 100,000 in protest in Bahrain. That same Shi'a empowerment in Iraq has made Bahrain's Sunnis more fearful.

Bahrain's military, with about 11,000 members, comprises the smallest forces in the Gulf. The Bahraini military (and police) forces are filled largely with Sunni expatriates from Jordan, Pakistan, Syria, and Yemen. Bahrain also has a police force of 2,000 and a national guard of 1,000 that handles internal security. The security forces consist largely of Pakistani Baluchis under Jordanian and other Arab officers. Bahrainis working for the military, police, and security services are largely Sunni.

Bahrain's judiciary is divided into two branches: the civil law courts and the Shari'a law courts. The civil law courts handle commercial, civil, criminal, and personal-status cases involving non-Muslims. Shari'a courts have jurisdiction over personal-status matters for all Muslims (Bahraini and expatriate), with separate Sunni and Shi'a courts. Women's groups have frequently criticized Shari'a court rulings. The Supreme Court, established in 1989, serves as the final court of appeal for the civil law courts and for personal-status case appeals for non-Muslims. The 2002 constitution gives the Higher Judicial Council (created in 2000) oversight over the courts. It also establishes an appointed constitutional court to rule on constitutional issues. Although nominally independent, the courts have experienced frequent interference from the king.

Bahrain has moved in the direction of economic liberalization in recent years. It is a member of the World Trade Organization. In 2005 it signed a free-trade agreement (FTA) with the United States and created a committee, headed by the chair of the Bahrain Chamber of Commerce and Industry, to oversee its implementation and build public-private partnerships. To diversify, the government has expanded Bahrain's financial sector to include over one hundred offshore banks and twenty-eight Islamic banking institutions. The financial sector accounts for about one-quarter of Bahrain's gross domestic product (GDP). However, Bahrain faces extremely strong competition in this sector from Dubai. Lacking the oil resources its neighbors possess, Bahrain has felt the impact of the global financial crisis and recession more keenly than the other GCC states.

QATAR

Political Environment

Qatar occupies a mitten-shaped peninsula that extends for about one hundred miles northward into the Gulf and measures fifty miles across at its point of greatest width. The land is mostly low-lying and consists largely of sandy or stony desert, with limestone outcroppings and salt flats.

Approximately two-thirds of the population live in the capital of Doha on the east coast of the peninsula. Prior to the production of oil in 1949, the population of Qatar was one of the poorest of any in eastern Arabia. The majority of its inhabitants

QATAR

Capital city	Doha
Chief of state	Amir Hamad bin Khalifa Al Thani
Head of government	Prime Minister Hamad bin Jasim bin Jabir Al Thani
Major political parties	None
Ethnic groups	Arab (40%), Indian (18%), Pakistani (18%), Iranian (10%), other (14%)
Religious groups	Muslim (77.5%), Christian (8.5%), other (14%)
Export partners	Japan (39.9%), South Korea (19.9%), Singapore (9.9%), India (5.1%), Thailand (4.9%), United Arab Emirates (4%)
Import partners	United States (13.3%), Italy (10.8%), Japan (8.9%), France (7.9%), Germany (7.3%), United Kingdom (5.7%), South Korea (5.6%), United Arab Emirates (5.1%), Saudi Arabia (4.3%)

lived at subsistence levels, with most of their income derived from fishing and pearling. By contrast, Qatar's per capita income is currently among the highest in the world, owing largely to the development of its substantial gas reserves. Qatar also has a very small national population: Only about 200,000 of Qatar's population of 833,000 are Qataris; the rest are expatriate workers, mostly South Asians and Arabs. Most of the indigenous population is Arab, some originally from the peninsula; others are *hawwalah*. The Arabs of Qatar are predominantly Sunni Muslims and generally subscribe to the conservative teachings of the same Hanbali school of Islamic jurisprudence as practiced in Saudi Arabia. Wahhabi religious practice is neither as strictly enforced nor as strictly interpreted as in Saudi Arabia. A minority of perhaps 20 percent of Qatari nationals are Shi'a.

Qatar has developed an extensive educational system open to all Qataris. In the nineteenth and early twentieth century, those girls whose parents could afford it typically received a basic education in reading, writing, and religion, typically from a tutor. In 1955 the government opened the first public school for girls; by the early twenty-first century, girls graduated from high school at a higher rate than boys. At Qatar University, the disparity is even more pronounced: Over 70 percent of the students are women. In 2004 a woman, Shaykha bint Ahmad al-Mahmud, was named education minister, and another woman, Dr. Shaykha Abdallah al-Misnad, was appointed president of Qatar University.

Oil production and export, and more recently natural gas exports, have been responsible for much of the dramatic transformation that has taken place in the country's social and economic life. In 1975 the government nationalized the two major oil-producing companies, Qatar Petroleum Company and Shell. Qatar's oil reserves are modest by Gulf standards; however, in the North Dome field, Qatar possesses the world's largest deposit of unassociated natural gas. Its gas reserves are the world's third largest, after those of Russia and Iran. Exploitation of this large gas field began in 1991, and in 1997 the second phase of its development, construction of facilities for production and export of liquefied natural gas, was completed. The government has invested these revenues in a large welfare state that provides Qataris with free education, health care, and guaranteed employment. It has also made continuing investments in infrastructure and taken some steps toward economic diversification, beginning with the manufacture of fertilizer in the 1970s and moving on to building cement and steel plants as well as flour mills and an expanded shrimping industry.

Political Structure and Dynamics

Qatar has been ruled since the nineteenth century by amirs from the Al Thani family. In its basic structure, Qatar's political system is similar to those of the other GCC states. At the top is a ruling family, members of whom hold the sovereign ministries (and, in Qatar's case, usually several other ministries as well). They rule with advice from appointed and elected bodies. In 2000 the amir formally established the Council of the Ruling Family, consisting of thirteen family members. The constitution stipulates that rule be hereditary within the Al Thani family through the line of the current amir's male offspring.

Qatar's political system differs from those of the other GCC states in two important ways. The first is the largely unconsolidated nature of the country's government. While the amir is the country's leader, other powerful family members run governmental fiefdoms with a good deal of independence and often different political agendas. The Al Thani is the largest ruling family in the region, numbering, by some accounts, as many as 20,000. The family has many factions, and some members—among them the very wealthy and powerful prime minister and foreign minister, Shaykh Hamad bin Jasim Al Thani—are nearly as powerful as the ruler. This in part explains why Qatar hosts both US forces and established Al-Jazeera, the controversial satellite station critical of US policy in the Gulf. The second difference, a consequence of the first, is the relative instability the ruling family has experienced in the years since independence. The current amir, Shaykh Hamad, came to power by overthrowing his father, Shaykh Khalifah bin Hamad Al Thani, in a bloodless coup in 1995, then survived a countercoup attempt in 1996. His father, in turn, came to power in a similar manner in 1972 by overthrowing his cousin, Shaykh Ahmad Al Thani. Shaykh Hamad has since reconciled with his father, although not apparently with the entire family. The man believed by some to be behind the 1996 countercoup attempt, former crown prince Shaykh Jasim bin Hamad Al Thani, remains in prison. Upon taking power, Shaykh Khalifah named his son Jasim crown prince, only to change his mind in 2003, passing the title on to his fourth son, Tamim

The pace of political liberalization in Qatar has been slow. The provisional constitution of 1970, which governed political life in Qatar until it was replaced in 2003, provided for a Council of Ministers and an Advisory Council, stipulating that the former was to be appointed by the ruler and that the majority of the latter was to be elected by the general population. However, after taking power in a coup in 1972, the new amir simply appointed an Advisory Council with little authority.

Liberalization reappeared after the Gulf War. In January 1992, fifty leading Qataris petitioned the amir to establish an assembly with legislative powers and to institute economic and educational reforms. His response was only to broaden modestly the Advisory Council's membership.

After Shaykh Hamad took power in 1995, he began tentative steps toward political liberalization. In 1999, 2003, and 2007 Qatar held relatively free and open elections for a twenty-nine-member advisory Central Municipal Council, albeit one with few powers. Suffrage was extended to women, despite modest opposition in the form of a petition signed by twenty-two Islamic scholars. Female candidates ran in the elections, and one woman won a seat in the 2003 and 2007 elections.

In 1999 the amir established a constitutional committee, which submitted a draft constitution in 2002. In April 2003, Qatar's new constitution was adopted by popular referendum, replacing the provisional constitution drawn up with Qatar's independence in 1970. The new constitution came into force in 2005. It called for the creation of a partially elected legislative body and offered protections of civil, political, and social rights. The amir announced in 2006 that in 2007 he would hold for the first time ever the Advisory Council elections stipulated in the constitution (to comprise forty-five members, two-thirds of whom were to be elected by popular vote). These elections were postponed and have been tentatively scheduled for 2010. The Advisory Council will have authority to propose legislation, review budgets, interpellate ministers, and issue no-confidence votes against ministers. Political parties remain banned.

The government also introduced some press freedoms; after taking power, Hamad revoked censorship of the news media and dissolved the Ministry of Information. In 1995 he established Al-Jazeera, a satellite news station, revolutionary at the time because it introduced frank and provocative news reports and commentaries. It was welcomed enthusiastically by a viewing public accustomed to coverage of state visits and broadcasts of official speeches. Al-Jazeera offended many Arab (and non-Arab) governments, but it also inspired a host of other satellite stations in the Gulf. Al-Jazeera, however, has been careful not to criticize the Qatari government or the Al Thani family. While formal censorship was lifted in 1995 and the Ministry of Information abolished, considerable self-censorship by reporters and editors in practice limits the amount of free expression. A new press law, drafted in 2002, was criticized by many journalists because, among other things, it allowed journalists to be imprisoned for their writing.

The right to peaceful public assembly is restricted. Public demonstrations and political parties are banned. Permission is still required for public gatherings and demonstrations, and the government grants these reluctantly. Nongovernmental organizations require government permission to operate, and most groups, from political parties to women's groups to human rights groups, have had license requests refused. In 2004 the government did issue a new labor law, giving Qataris the right to form trade unions and engage in collective bargaining (including the right to strike). It also offered businesses a clearer legal framework for employment. There is a Chamber of Commerce and Industry.

Qatar is divided administratively into ten municipalities (*baladiyat*). However, since the majority of the population lives in the capital, local government is of little practical importance.

Since the early days of oil, when political opposition was frequently sharp and ideological, opposition forces have become much less vocal. There may simply be less simmering discontent in Qatar than elsewhere, but for whatever reason, liberals and even Islamists have not been an important political force. If there is much opposition in Qatar, loyal or otherwise, it has not made its presence known. Aside from a suicide car bomb attack by an Egyptian in 2005 on a theater popular with Western expatriates, neither terrorism nor militant Islam has made an appearance (although there have been reports that Qatar's interior minister hosted some Islamist terrorists in the 1990s). Perhaps preemptively, Qatar does host a number of conservative Islamic clerics, most notably Yusuf al-Qaradawi, known widely from his weekly show on Al-Jazeera.

Social cleavages do exist in Qatar. The old merchant class has historically exerted less influence on government affairs than its larger and older counterparts in Kuwait, Dubai, or even Bahrain. As revenues have accumulated and as many members of the ruling family have become more interested and involved in business themselves, the traditional separation of Al Thani–dominated government and merchant class–dominated business has begun to disappear. The Al Thani and the business community, through a symbiotic process, have increased their collaboration in many areas relating to Qatar's economic growth.

Tribal divisions remain important. Qatar has some twelve major clans linked through marriage. In 2005 the government stripped members of the al-Murrah tribe in southern Qatar of their nationality because of their alleged connection to the 1996 coup attempt; this act was reversed in 2006.

Some older social distinctions have vanished: Slavery, for example, existed into the 1950s. It was not, however, as callous an institution in Arabia as it was in the United States. Other distinctions have appeared with oil revenues, the most important being the division between Qataris and the significantly larger group of foreign workers. The 2004 labor law did not address domestic workers (e.g., drivers and maids) at all and barred all expatriate workers from union activities.

Economic liberalization and diversification have proceeded steadily over the last decade. Shaykh Hamad took power in 1995 with an agenda of economic reform, eager to deal with the lack of transparency and accountability that had led to corruption so massive in the 1980s that it was undermining the country's economy. Shaykh Hamad clamped down on corrupt business practices and introduced standards for transparency and accountability in both the public and the private sectors.

These measures were accompanied by development programs to streamline and expand the economy. A key target was the oil sector. He invited international oil companies to help the country increase oil production by locating and developing new oil fields, investing in advanced oil-recovery systems to extend existing fields, and expanding production of the country's huge natural gas reserves. Qatar's oil exports more than doubled in a decade. Much of the additional income was invested in natural gas projects. As a result, Qatar, which ran deficits in the 1990s, began experiencing some of the highest economic growth rates in the region, earning more from gas than from oil. Qatar has also invested in energy projects abroad, most notably in a $1.5 billion oil refinery in Zimbabwe.

The drop in oil prices in 2008, coupled with the deepening global recession, reduced Qatar's budget surpluses, prompting the head of its sovereign wealth fund, one of the world's largest, to announce a six-month hiatus, a pause for reflection, in March 2009. Nonetheless, Qatar remained in a far better financial situation than many of its neighbors.

Qatar has moved, albeit more cautiously than its neighbors, into other areas, such as tourism. In 2004 the government announced several education reforms, including the inauguration of a new Education City that presently hosts branches of several US universities, among them Cornell's Medical School, Carnegie-Mellon, and Texas A&M.

Qatar's state security forces were merged into one force in June 2003. They remain under the direct control of the amir. Qatar's military of about 12,000 is the second smallest in the region (after Bahrain). Qatar also has a paramilitary royal guard in the Ministry of Defense and a regular police force.

Like many Islamic countries, Qatar's legal system is an amalgam of Islamic law (Shari'a) and Western civil legal procedures. Shari'a, considered the basic legal system, relates mainly to personal and family law based on the conservative Hanbali school of Islamic jurisprudence. Civil law relates to more technical civil and criminal issues, particularly those related to commercial and labor issues.

To introduce legal reform, Shaykh Hamad established the High Judicial Council in 1999. It is tasked with offering advice on judicial appointments and to propose legislation concerning the judicial system. In October 2004, long-promised court reform unified Qatar's dual court system (of Shari'a and civil courts). In 2007 an Administrative Court and a Constitutional Court were established.

Qatar's human rights record is mixed and reflects the clash between, traditional cultural norms and values and modern, secular cultural norms and values. Those most subject to abuse are foreign workers, especially domestic workers. However, in 2003 the amir established a committee on human rights.

UNITED ARAB EMIRATES

Political Environment

The UAE is a loose federation of seven emirates—Abu Dhabi, Dubai, Ajman, Fujayrah, Sharjah, Ras al-Khaymah, and Umm al-Qaywayn—located along the Strait of Hormuz. The emirates vary a good deal in size and wealth. Abu Dhabi is the largest, covering nearly 90 percent of the UAE's territory largely with open desert. It is also the wealthiest, possessing most of the UAE's gas and oil reserves. Dubai, although running out of oil, has become an important business hub for the region and is the second wealthiest emirate.

The most distinctive characteristic of the various shaykhdoms is tribal affiliation. Six principal tribal groups inhabit the country: the Bani Yas, a confederation of nearly a dozen different tribes, two branches of which (the Al Bu Falah and the Al Bu Falasah, respectively) provide the ruling families of Abu Dhabi and Dubai; the Manasir (singular, Mansuri), who range from the western reaches of the UAE to Saudi Arabia and Qatar; the Qawasim (singular, Qasimi), two branches of which rule Sharjah and Ras al-Khaymah; the Al Ali (also Al Mu'alla) of Umm al-Qaywayn; the Sharqiyin in Fujayrah; and the Al Nu'aim in Ajman. All the tribes are Arab and Sunni Muslims. Despite the tribal identification, only a small percentage of the national population is still nomadic.

UNITED ARAB EMIRATES

Capital city	Abu Dhabi
Chief of state	President Khalifah bin Zayid Al Nuhayyan
Head of government	Prime Minister and Vice President Muhammad bin Rashid Al Maktum
Major political parties	None
Ethnic groups	South Asian (50%), other Arab and Iranian (23%), Emirati (19%), other expatriates (8%)
Religious groups	Sunni Muslim (80%), Shi'a Muslim (16%), other (4%)
Export partners	Japan (23.6%), South Korea (9.2%), Thailand (5%), India (4.8%)
Import partners	China (12.8%), India (10%), United States (8.7%), Japan (6.1%), Germany (5.9%), United Kingdom (5.3%), Italy (4.6%)

Other cleavages are politically less salient. Dubai, with its long history as a trading center, has long had a powerful merchant class with a network linked to the Indian subcontinent and Iran. Before the emergence of oil as the dominant factor in the region's economy, Dubai's merchants were major free traders, smuggling gold and other luxury items from picturesque dhows that concealed powerful engines capable of outrunning the coast guard vessels of a half dozen countries.

Political Economy

Oil has transformed the class structure of the UAE as it has those of the other Gulf states. Nearly 10 percent of the world's known oil reserves are located in the UAE, and given the country's relatively small population, it has one of the highest per capita incomes in the world. Despite the global recession, oil production in 2009 was roughly 2.76 million bpd, providing most of the GPD, estimated at $200 billion. The total per capita GPD in 2009 was $42,800.

The most important demographic impact of oil has been the influx of foreign workers. The indigenous inhabitants of the UAE account for less than one-fifth of the total population, with that percentage lower still in the wealthier emirates. The desire for rapid economic development meant bringing in other Arabs, Asians, and Europeans in large numbers to provide the skills needed. Mirroring patterns established elsewhere in the wealthy Arab oil states, Palestinians worked as business managers, filled mid-level positions in the bureaucracy, and were prominent in the nation's press; Egyptians filled teaching positions; and Jordanians served as advisers in the military. After the Gulf War, the Palestinians and Jordanians were replaced, with South Asians forming the largest expatriate community and with Indians, Pakistanis, and Sri Lankans accounting for at least half of the total population, most of them performing skilled or semiskilled tasks or managing small retail enterprises. Of all the GCC states, the distance between expatriates and nationals is perhaps greatest here. The presence of so many nonnationals has created a strong sense of Emirati identity.

The UAE's economy is dominated by its major oil producer, Abu Dhabi. Before the discovery of oil, Abu Dhabi Town was little more than a mud-brick village. Today, however, it is the largest city in the UAE and by far the most advanced in terms of administrative and social welfare services. Dubai and Sharjah have also undertaken extensive development projects. The contrast between these three affluent shaykhdoms and the other four remains substantial, though the gap has decreased somewhat as the federal government, largely financed by Abu Dhabi, has funded numerous development projects in the poorer states. The abundance of new income; the lack, to date, of a strong centralized planning authority with the power to veto or modify individual shaykhdoms' development ventures; and, most importantly, the continuation of intense competition among the various rulers for prestige have resulted in the duplication of many facilities, such as international airports.

Before the discovery of oil in Abu Dhabi in 1958, only Dubai and Sharjah had developed an extensive entrepôt trade. Dubai began to eclipse Sharjah both politically and commercially when Sharjah's harbor began to silt up in the 1940s. The conditions for perpetuating the former's economic edge over the latter were practically ensured when Dubai succeeded in dredging its own inlet (or "creek," as it is called locally). Dubai's merchants have reinvented themselves as modern business executives in a global economy. Dubai remains an entrepôt for goods and services, based on its free market economy. The other emirates have business communities that are tied more closely to the state.

Despite Abu Dhabi's preeminence as the UAE's major oil producer, Dubai has ironically received more attention abroad with its grandiose projects and open market economy. Dubai has also suffered the most from the 2008 recession, which has hurt the financial and investment sectors, caused some dramatic declines in property values, and forced the suspension of many domestic construction projects. But as the global economy begins to recover from the recession, not only are regional oil revenues expected to pick up, but financial activity is also expected to rebound. In the long run, the recession could be a good lesson for the Dubai financial and investment sectors not to become caught up in future economic bubbles that will inevitably burst.

Political Structure and Dynamics

The internal politics of the emirates' ruling families have historically been replete with intrigue and jockeying among contenders for the limited positions of official power. Before the establishment of the UAE, many local rulers fell victim to assassination at the hands of brothers, cousins, or sons. Abu Dhabi, the richest of the emirates, has been ruled by the Al Nuhayyan family for over three centuries. In 1966 a palace coup in Abu Dhabi brought a new ruler, Shaykh Zayid, to power. He had the broad support of many who thought that his brother and predecessor, Shaykh Shakhbut, was not up to the task of ruler of Abu Dhabi. In 1972 the UAE's minister of education, Shaykh Sultan bin Muhammad al-Qasimi, assumed the position of ruler in Sharjah following an abortive palace coup in which his predecessor was murdered. In 1987, Shaykh Abd al-Aziz bin Muhammad al-Qasimi tried to seize power from his brother, the ruler of Sharjah, an event that threatened the union's integrity, both because it raised the question of the legitimacy of all the rulers in the UAE and because Abu Dhabi initially backed the usurper and Dubai backed the incumbent. The UAE's Federal Supreme Council (FSC) temporarily defused the crisis by arranging a compromise sharing of power, with Shaykh Sultan remaining ruler.

Recent successions have been smoother, however. In 2004, Shaykh Zayid, who had ruled Abu Dhabi, was succeeded on his death by Shaykh Khalifah, the crown prince and oldest of his nineteen sons. Even so, Khalifah's brother, Shaykh Muhammad, administers much of the day-to-day business of Abu Dhabi and the UAE. In 1990 the ruler of Dubai, Shaykh Rashid bin Sa'id Al Maktum, was succeeded peacefully on his death by his son, Maktum, who appointed his brother, Muhammad, the de facto ruler, crown prince. When Maktum died in 2006, his brother Shaykh Muhammad took over. The current rulers are Khalifah bin Zayid Al Nuhayyan (Abu Dhabi), Muhammad bin Rashid Al Maktum (Dubai), Sultan bin Muhammad al-Qassimi (Sharjah), Saqr bin Muhammad al-Qassimi (Ras al-Khaymah), Humaid bi Rashid Al Nu'aimi (Ajman), Hamad bin Muhammad al-Sharqi (Fujayrah), and Rashid bin Ahmad Al Mu'alla (Umm al-Qaywayn).

The UAE is ruled as a federation of these families. The UAE's constitution, drafted in 1972 and made permanent in 1996, provides for federal legislative, executive, and judicial bodies. The head of state, the president, is chosen by the seven members of the FSC for a five-year term. The first president and architect of the federation, Shaykh Zayid, served as president from independence until his death in 2004. His son and successor, Shaykh Khalifah, was chosen shortly afterward to be president of the UAE. The ruler of Dubai is the vice president. The FSC meets four times a year. It is charged with formulating and supervising all federal policies, ratifying UAE laws, approving the country's annual budget, ratifying international treaties, and approving several appointments. In procedural matters, a simple majority vote is sufficient for passage of any resolution. However, on substantive issues, Abu Dhabi and Dubai have veto power. Thus, on any substantive vote, five member states, including the two leading shaykhdoms, must approve a resolution in order for the motion to have the force of law. The constitutional allocation of a preponderance of political power to Abu Dhabi and Dubai has been a major point of contention among the other shaykhdoms.

The Federal National Council (FNC) is an appointed consultative assembly with advisory powers. In accordance with the relative size of their constituent populations, eight seats are apportioned to Abu Dhabi and Dubai, six each to Ras al-Khaymah and Sharjah, and four each to the remaining three members. The FNC's duties are limited mainly to discussion and approval of the budget, drafting some legislation, and serving as a forum for discussion and debate of policies and programs under consideration by the government. This last duty is of no small significance because of the absence of political parties, trade unions, and various other kinds of voluntary associations familiar to Westerners. The constitution would permit the FNC's evolution into an elected body exercising real legislative functions.

Although the powers of the presidency are in theory subordinate to those of the FSC, Shaykh Zayid was relatively successful in keeping together what has been the Arab world's foremost example of regional political integration. His success was due in part to Abu Dhabi's preeminence as the most pro-federation state in the union but also to his own strong personal dedication to the UAE's development. Abu Dhabi has thus far been a willing hegemon: Many of the federation's operations are almost completely funded by Abu Dhabi.

Nonetheless, even without Shaykh Zayid's influence, the kinds of economic and security concerns that helped bring the seven shaykhdoms into a federation initially are still present. The habits of working together are well established, and the advantages of doing so are demonstrable. It seems likely, therefore, that the UAE will continue to muddle through as a loose federation for the indefinite future.

Each emirate exercises a degree of independence. Each has its own independent police force. The intelligence services, while formally under one umbrella, operate largely independently. The UAE military is not completely unified. In 1976 several Emirati military forces were formally united and placed under the single command of the Union Defense Force. However, the two principal shaykhdoms, Abu Dhabi and Dubai, did not fully integrate their defense forces into the union force; indeed, the latter has created its own central military region command. Moreover, Fujayrah, Ras al-Khaymah, Sharjah, and Umm al-Qaywayn maintain their own national guard forces. The UAE's military forces number about 65,000. As in other GCC states, many of the nationals working in the police and military are from more recently settled Bedouin families.

The UAE's federal judiciary was established in 1971, but federal judicial structures emerged only slowly. The federal judiciary still does not apply to Dubai and Ras al-Khaymah. In 1973 a Supreme Federal Court was established, and in the following years some judicial matters were transferred from the emirates to the federal level. In 1983 a comprehensive law governing the federal judiciary was issued, although individual emirates retained varying degrees of judicial autonomy. Ras al-Khaymah and Dubai chose not to cede any jurisdiction to the federal courts. The other emirates ceded most, but not all, jurisdiction. All the emirates retained their own Shari'a courts with jurisdiction over personal-status matters. In 1983 a Federal Supreme Judicial Council was created to play an advisory role to the Ministry of Justice, which retains oversight of the court administration. The federal system is three-tiered, with primary courts, appeals courts, and a supreme court. The Supreme Court serves as the highest court of appeal and also adjudicates disputes between individual shaykhdoms as well as those between individual shaykhdoms and the federal government. It also determines the constitutionality of federal or Emirati laws when challenged.

Like the federal bureaucracy, the judiciary has depended heavily on foreign residents' expertise, especially that of Egyptians and Palestinians. Efforts to staff the courts with trained native UAE jurists have been only partially successful. Judges are appointed by the president and serve indefinite terms. Emirati judges may not be dismissed without serious cause. Nonnational judges serve on contract, subject to renewal.

The country's legal system places special emphasis on Islamic law but is drawn from several sources, including Western ones. In February 1994, Shaykh Zayid ordered that a number of serious crimes, including murder, theft, adultery, and drug offenses, be tried in Shari'a courts rather than civil courts. Ras al-Khaymah experienced a flurry of controversy in the 1990s when an Egyptian judge briefly attempted to enforce certain corporal punishments found in Islamic law.

The UAE's record on human rights is mixed. Although foreign workers flock to the Emirates because of the higher wages they can earn there than at home (they comprise over 80 percent of the population and some 90 percent of the private-sector workforce), many are subjected to frequent human rights abuses, including unsafe working conditions, nonpayment of wages, long hours, and poor living conditions. Many of the workers are in virtual debt bondage to recruiting agencies. As in the other Gulf countries, female domestic workers are at particular risk of abuse. Foreign laborers have staged public protests, typically over nonpayment of wages. In 2006 the government announced that it would amend the labor law with the goal of improving the conditions of foreign labor after public protests in Dubai and a Human Rights Watch report critical of the problem brought it unwanted international attention. The abuse of young boys working as camel jockeys was formally banned in 2005. In 2009 an incident involving the videotaped torture, apparently by Shaykh Issa bin Zayid Al Nuhayyan, brother of Abu Dhabi's crown prince, of an Afghan business partner brought the human rights issue to public attention. The government is not a signatory to most human rights treaties and has not responded to repeated efforts by human rights groups to organize inside the country. The UAE has thus far largely resisted regional trends toward political liberalization. Politics within the shaykhdoms traditionally have been tribe based and autocratic, even if tempered by such age-old concepts as social democracy, consultation, consensus, and adherence to the principles and norms enshrined in Islamic law. Considerable debate over the development of a more responsive participatory system of government has been vigorously and extensively covered in the press. In 2003 Dubai formed district municipal councils to encourage a degree of public participation. In 2005 Shaykh Khalifah announced that half the seats in the FNC would be elected at some point in the future. Instead, in 2006 the government allowed an appointed group of fewer than 7,000 Emiratis to vote for half of the members of the consultative FNC.

Most associational life is banned in the UAE. All private associations must be licensed by the government, which rejects most applications. Political parties are illegal in the UAE, and trade unions are banned. In recent years, a handful of professional and student associations have, however, been allowed to emerge. In 2005, the Abu Dhabi Chamber of Commerce and Industry, in an experiment with limited democracy, elected fifteen of its twenty-one seats. The media is relatively free of formal censorship, but considerable self-censorship occurs. The government has blackballed journalists whose views it did not like and has used the Anti-Terrorism Act of 2004 to restrict freedom of expression. A proposed media law in 2009 received criticism from Human Rights Watch and other groups over its press and speech restrictions.

Political Economy

Oil drives the economy of the UAE. Abu Dhabi accounts for more than 85 percent of the UAE's oil production and more than 90 percent of its reserves. Nearly 10 percent of the world's known oil reserves are located in the UAE, and given the country's relatively small population, it has one of the highest per capita incomes in the world. Despite the global recession, oil production in 2009 was roughly 2.76 million bpd, providing most of the GPD, an estimated $200 billion. The total per capita GPD in 2009 was $42,800.

For the past two decades, the UAE has worked to diversify its economy, mainly with light industry, such as food processing, and some heavy industry, such as cement production. The most impressive single example of a non-oil industry is the Dubai Aluminum Smelter (DUBAL), which started production in 1979. An integrated smelter, power plant, and desalination complex, DUBAL, one of the largest facilities of its kind, typifies the spirit of bold enterprise long associated with Dubai. Despite its extreme aridity, the UAE has applied technology to expand its agricultural sector so that it is self-sufficient in dates and nearly so in fresh milk; it also produces the bulk of its vegetable consumption. The fishing industry employs 19,000 men, Emiratis and others, and fully meets local demand for fish.

Of all the GCC entities, Dubai has perhaps the most ambitious and unusual strategy of economic development. Building on its history as a trading entrepôt, Dubai created a niche for itself as a regional banking and tourism center. Dubai began diversifying in the 1950s under Shaykh Rashid Al Maktum, who dredged the creek, allowing larger ships to make Dubai a port of call. In 1979 Shaykh Rashid began building the world's largest man-made harbor at Jabal Ali. In the 1980s Dubai, building on family business ties to Iran, became an important source of connections for that country during the Iran-Iraq War, connections that remain strong, despite a dispute between the UAE and Iran over three Gulf islands. Oil has transformed the class structure of the UAE as it has in the other Gulf states. Nearly 10 percent of the world's known oil reserves are located in the UAE and, given the country's relatively small population, one of the highest per capita incomes in the world. Despite the global recession, oil production in 2009 was roughly 2.76 million bpd, providing most of the GPD, an estimated $200 billion. The total per capita GDP in 2009 was $42,800.

The most important demographic impact of oil has been the influx of foreign workers. The indigenous inhabitants of the UAE account for less than one-fifth of the total population, with that percentage lower still in the wealthier emirates. The desire for rapid economic development meant bringing in other Arabs, Asians, and Europeans in large numbers to provide the skills needed. Mirroring patterns established elsewhere in the wealthy Arab oil states, Palestinians worked as business managers, filled mid-level positions in the bureaucracy, and were prominent in the nation's press; Egyptians filled teaching positions; and Jordanians served as advisers in the military. After the Gulf War, the Palestinians and Jordanians were replaced, with South Asians forming the largest expatriate community and, with Indians, Pakistanis, and Sri Lankans accounting for at least half of the total population, most of them performing skilled or semiskilled tasks or managing small retail enterprises. Of all the GCC states, the distance between expatriates and nationals is perhaps greatest here. The presence of so many nonnationals has created a strong sense of Emirati identity.

The UAE's economy is dominated by its major oil producer, Abu Dhabi. Dubai's oil production has been declining for over a decade. Sharjah produces modest quantities of gas and condensate, and Ras al-Khaymah has small reserves of oil and condensate. While oil continues to underpin the UAE's economic development, a much enlarged role for natural gas is anticipated. Abu Dhabi has 90 percent of the UAE's gas reserves.

Before the discovery of oil in 1958, Abu Dhabi Town was little more than a mud-brick village. Today, however, it is the largest city in the UAE and by far the most advanced in terms of administrative and social welfare services. Dubai and Sharjah have also undertaken extensive development projects. The contrast between these three affluent shaykhdoms and the other four remains substantial, though the gap has decreased somewhat as the federal government, largely financed by Abu Dhabi, has funded numerous development projects in the poorer states. The abundance of new income; the lack, to date, of a strong centralized planning authority with the power to veto or modify individual shaykhdoms' development ventures; and, most importantly, the continuation of intense competition among the various rulers for prestige have resulted in the duplication of many facilities, such as international airports.

In pre-oil times, only Dubai and Sharjah had developed an extensive entrepôt trade. Dubai began to eclipse Sharjah both politically and commercially when Sharjah's harbor began to silt up in the 1940s. The conditions for perpetuating the former's economic edge over the latter were practically ensured when Dubai succeeded in dredging its own inlet (or "creek," as it is called locally). Dubai's merchants have reinvented themselves as modern business executives in a global economy. Dubai remains an entrepôt for goods and services, based on its free market economy. The other emirates have business communities that are tied more closely to the state.

Despite Abu Dhabi's preeminence as the UAE's major oil producer, Dubai has ironically received more attention abroad with its grandiose projects and open market economy. From a small desert port, the city of Dubai has grown into a metropolis with a skyline like a miniature Manhattan. Off shore are manmade islands shaped like palm trees and world continents. On shore there is an indoor ski slope and the world's largest mall. In early 2010, the Dubai Khalifa, the world's largest building, was opened. Its location as a halfway point between Asia and Europe and its wide-open, free market economy have enabled it to become a major upscale winter tourist center. To encourage tourism, Dubai hosts international golf and tennis tournaments and, as of the time of this writing, is building a Dubai Sports City. Dubailand, a theme park twice the size of Disney World, is planned. Dubai has also embarked on a $1.6 billion shopping and entertainment project called Dubai Festival City.

The major factor behind Dubai's renaissance, however, has been its use of its free market economy and accessibility to Gulf oil revenues to develop the emirate as a major global banking and financial investment center. But this could be a two-edged sword. A key to success was to establish Western modern financial standards of transparency and accountability to replace traditional, unregulated free market commercial standards. This has been an evolutionary process. In 2002, the government hired a retired Bank of England regulator to help draw up a financial regulatory system. And in 2004, the Dubai government established the Dubai International Financial Center (DIFC) to attract private investment institutions. Licensed firms operating in the DIFC and other enclave free trade centers benefit from no taxes on profits; no restrictions on foreign ownership, foreign exchange, or repatriation of capital; and access to operational-support and business-continuity facilities. In addition, Dubai aims to become a regional sales, distribution, and trading center for goods sold over the Internet. As a result of its diversification and dwindling oil, Dubai earns less than 10 percent of its GDP from oil revenues.

Dubai initially appeared to be weathering the 2008 recession relatively well. But on November 30, 2009, a Dubai real estate company that insured ambitious projects partly on Islamic bonds asked that $3.5 billion in bonds due on December 14 be suspended. This set off Dubai's $90 billion debt crisis based on speculation that Islamic banking was as susceptible to the recession as hurting financial institutions worldwide. The crisis was averted when Abu Dhabi, the main oil producer in the UAE, proffered $3.5 billion to pay off the debt. Nevertheless, according to the International Monetary Fund, its GDP contracted by 1.3 percent in 2009.

By early 2010, however, there were signs that the global economy would begin to recover. With a balanced financial-growth policy, the chances for Dubai's economy to rebound appeared to be improving. In the long run, the recession could be a good lesson for the Dubai financial and investment sectors not to become caught up in future economic bubbles that will inevitably burst.

Despite its wealth, Abu Dhabi was late in developing modern financial institutions. As late as 1991, it experienced a major financial scandal when regulatory authorities in seven countries without warning terminated the operations of the Bank of Commerce and Credit (BCCI), in which the ruling family of Abu Dhabi held a controlling interest. It was learned that bank authorities had committed major fraud prior to the Al Nuhayyan purchase of the bank's shares. The affair was settled in 1998 when Abu Dhabi authorities made payments of $1.8 billion to compensate the bank's creditors.

The BCCI scandal prompted the strengthening of the UAE Central Bank and stricter regulation of the country's financial sector. In 2005, Abu Dhabi followed Dubai's lead in seeking to attract foreign investment by enacting legislation allowing 100 percent foreign ownership of investments in its Industrial City. One of the most important innovations by the UAE federal government was the establishment of the UAE Offsets Group, which mandates that foreign firms winning defense contracts must invest a percentage of the value of their contracts in joint ventures with local partners. In this way, a number of significant projects, ranging from a shipbuilding company to a health-care center, have been undertaken.

The UAE, with Abu Dhabi in the lead, has also developed a vast network of global investments. Nonetheless the UAE faces economic problems similar to those confronting the other GCC states: unemployment and emiratization, education, and housing shortages (especially given the bubble in real estate prices). The rapid growth and real estate boom dramatically raised the cost of living, even for UAE nationals. While all the emirates were hurt by the economic downturn of 2008, Dubai felt it the most and was in 2009 rewriting its ambitious Strategic Plan for 2015 launched in 2007, having experienced a drop in real estate values, a decline in construction, and an exodus of foreign workers. In 2009 Abu Dhabi began taking steps to rescue financially strapped Dubai.

The other emirates have also drawn up economic and social development plans, albeit on a smaller scale, and for those without oil revenues often with funding provided by Abu Dhabi. For example, Ras al-Khaymah has created plans to develop a mountain resort, a nature park, and a marina. And Sharjah, which has some oil, has concentrated on developing as an educational center.

OMAN

Political Environment

Located on the southeastern reaches of the Arabian Peninsula, the Sultanate of Oman has an area two or three times greater than Kuwait, Bahrain, Qatar, and the UAE combined—82,000 square miles. Perhaps a quarter of Oman's population lives in the Greater Capital Area, which includes Muscat, the capital; Matrah, a major port; and Ruhi, the country's commercial hub. The main city of inner Oman is Nizwa, the traditional religious center of interior Oman. Sur, south of Muscat, is an important fishing port, and Salalah is the largest city and principal port of Dhufar, the southernmost province. Dhufar consists of three ranges of low mountains surrounding a small coastal plain and is separated from the rest of Oman by several hundred miles of desert. Oman proper consists of inner Oman and the coastal plain, known as the Batinah. Inner Oman contains a fertile plateau and the oldest towns in the country. Separating this region from the Batinah is the Hajar mountain range, stretching in an arc from northwest to southeast and reaching nearly 10,000 feet in height at the Jabal al-Akhdar ("Green Mountain"). The

OMAN

Capital city	Muscat
Chief of state	Sultan and Prime Minister Qaboos bin Said al-Said
Head of government	Sultan and Prime Minister Qaboos bin Said al-Said
Major political parties	None
Ethnic groups	Arab, Baluch, South Asian, African
Religious groups	Ibadi Muslim (75%), other (25%)
Export partners	China (26.8%), South Korea (15.2%), Japan (14.3%), Thailand (10.4%), United Arab Emirates (7.6%), United States (4.3%), Iran (4.1%)
Import partners	United Arab Emirates (19.3%), Japan (17.6%), United States (7.4%), Germany (5.2%), India (4.1%)

majority of Oman's population is found along the Batinah coast, which has the country's greatest agricultural potential.

Most Omanis are Arab Muslims. Perhaps half are Ibadhi Muslims, the only remaining branch of Kharijism, Islam's first schism, predating Shi'ism. (The name comes from the Arabic word *kharji*, which means "one who goes out" and refers to seventh-century Muslims who withdrew support from the fourth caliph, Ali ibn Abi Talib.) Most of the remainder of the population is Sunni, including many Baluchis, originally from the coastal area of Iran and Pakistan, who live along the Batinah coast. Many merchants of the capital region and the coast are Indians, either Hindus or Khojas (a community of Shi'a Muslims). There are also Persians and other groups of Shi'a Muslims, including some originally from Iraq or Iran. Dhufar and the surrounding desert are home to several groups whose primary language is South Arabian. Shihuh tribes, a group of mixed Persian–Arab ancestry, inhabit the northern, strategically important exclave of the Musandam Peninsula at the Strait of Hormuz.

Like the other GCC states, Oman has in modern times experienced an influx of migrant labor, principally from other Arab states and the Indian subcontinent. Oman's modest level of wealth has, however, enabled it to avoid the situation of

Kuwait, Qatar, and the UAE, where foreigners outnumber the indigenous population. Omanis constitute over 90 percent of Oman's estimated population of 3.5 million.

Oman has experienced more rapid development than any of the other GCC states in the last few decades owing to its starting point. Economic development was almost totally neglected in Oman until the accession of Sultan Qabus in 1970. Since that time it has progressed steadily. In the early 1980s construction was completed on copper mining and refining facilities, and in 1984 two cement plants began operations. Since the mid-1980s Omani development policies emphasizing light industry (e.g., food processing) have been promoted at industrial zones in Muscat, Sohar, and Salalah. Agriculture generates less than 3 percent of gross national product but employs as much as half the labor force, although official figures are much lower.

Despite some diversification, modern Oman remains largely dependent on its meager and dwindling oil revenues. Oil accounts for some 40 percent of Oman's GDP. Oil exports began in 1967, and in the 1970s the large oil field of Qarn Alam was discovered at the edge of the Empty Quarter. But by the 1980s oil flow had declined significantly. Production fell further from about 800,000 barrels a day at the turn of the millennium to 633,000 in 2006. By some estimates, Oman will run out of oil in less than twenty years. Moreover, oil in Oman is difficult to extract, and so Petroleum Development Oman has invested heavily in enhanced oil recovery. Natural gas production, however, has added to Oman's revenues in recent years. As a result, Oman began economic diversification and Omanization well before the other GCC states. Economic development funds for various projects have been carefully spread across the regions, with industrial poles in Salalah, Sohar, and Sur. A $15 billion tourism project has begun in Madinat al-Zarqa and Vision 2020, Oman's long-term development plan, envisions opening nearly a dozen resorts across the country in coming years, developing a niche in eco-tourism and culture. As part of a broader process of economic liberalization in 2004, the sultan permitted foreign ownership of land in some designated tourist areas. Although the economy was briefly buoyed by the higher oil prices in 2007, the subsequent recession and lowering of prices are expected to have a more notable impact on Oman than its GCC neighbors.

Political Structure and Dynamics

Oman's ruling family, the Al Bu Sa'ids, have ruled Oman since the eighteenth century. In the early twentieth century, a movement to restore an Ibadhi imamate had led to substantial autonomy for the interior of the country. Qabus's father, Sultan Sa'id bin Taimur (ruled 1932–1970), with the assistance of British forces, largely reunified the country in the 1950s. This reunification was completed under Sultan Qabus, who took power in a nearly bloodless coup in 1970 and changed the name of the country from the Sultanate of Muscat and Oman to the Sultanate of Oman.

The southernmost province of Dhufar, annexed in the late nineteenth century after it had been quasi-autonomous for years, became the site of an insurrection in the early 1960s. By 1968 leadership of the rebellion had been seized by the Marxist-oriented Popular Front for the Liberation of the Occupied Arabian Gulf (which changed its name in 1971 to the Popular Front for the Liberation of Oman and the Arab Gulf and in 1974 to the Popular Front for the Liberation of Oman). Supported by Soviet and Chinese aid channeled through South Yemen, the insurrection occupied large areas of the province by the early 1970s. The rebellion was finally put down in 1975, with British advisers and Iranian troops playing key roles in assisting Omani light infantry and tribal militia forces. Sultan Qabus assured Dhufari loyalties thereafter by dispensing generous development funds to the province.

As in the other GCC states, the sultan relies on his relatives, cousins, and uncles who control many (although not always the most important) ministerial and other governmental posts. However, as compared with the other GCC states, the sultan has shared far less power with his family, or indeed with anyone. Qabus himself, in addition to being prime minister, holds the portfolios of defense, finance, and foreign affairs. This may make for a difficult transition, should power remain in the ruling family. The childless sultan has named no heir apparent, leaving Oman alone among the GCC states with no clear successor. He has asked that his family choose a leader from two names he has selected, to be revealed upon his death. They are suspected to be sons of Qabus's uncle, Sayid Tariq bin Taimur, who has played an important role in government for many years.

Over the past twenty years, Oman's political structure has evolved toward increasing popular participation in government. In 1981, Oman established a consultative assembly to advise the sultan on matters of social, educational, and economic policy (defense and foreign policy were excluded). The members, appointed by the sultan, were drawn from the tribal and merchant communities as well as from government. Initially forty-five members served on the council; the total was raised to fifty-five in 1985. This first experiment in representative government lasted for a decade.

In November 1990 the sultan established a new Consultative Assembly (*Majlis al-Shura*) to replace the 1981 body. Regional representatives from each of the fifty-nine districts would nominate three candidates, and the deputy prime minister for legal affairs would select one to serve, subject to the sultan's approval. In 1994 the Consultative Assembly's membership was expanded from fifty-nine to eighty, and women could for the first time be nominated (two were selected in 1995). Although lacking legislative powers, the council was empowered to review social and economic legislation, to help draft and implement development plans, and to propose improvement in public sectors. Ministries were required to submit to the council annual reports on their performance and plans and to answer questions from council members. The council could summon ministers to discuss any issue within the purview of the various ministries. Moreover, the council was required to refer to its appropriate committees questions and suggestions from citizens on public issues and subsequently to inform the correspondents of the actions taken.

In 1996 Sultan Qabus issued a decree establishing a Basic Statute of the State, which defined the system of government and is, in effect, the sultanate's constitution. The document vests substantial authority in the sultan but also sets out a legislative and a judicial branch. In principle, it also guarantees citizens a set of basic civil rights.

The legislature, the Council of Oman, consists of an appointed upper house, the Council of State (*Majlis al-Dawla*), and an eighty-two-member elected lower house (*Majlis al-Shura*). In 1997, 2000, and 2003 the government held elections to the body, expanding suffrage until by 2003 it extended to virtually all adult nationals. Elections, last held in 2007, are scheduled for 2011. The council's mandate remains narrow, primarily restricted to economic and some social matters, but it does enjoy the right to interpellate ministers and provides a forum for public debate. The voting age is twenty-one (lowered from thirty in the 2000 elections). Members of the council are elected to three-year terms and may serve successive terms.

The Ministry of Legal Affairs, established in 1994, oversees the judiciary. A 1999 Judicial Authority Law began a restructuring of the judicial system. Shari'a courts have jurisdiction over personal-status matters; other cases (civil, criminal, and commercial) go to the regular courts. Oman has a three-tiered court system: courts of first instance, six appeals courts, and a supreme court. The sultan is the final court of appeal. State security courts have been used on occasion for political dissidents.

Articles 32 and 33 of the 1996 Basic Statute guarantee free association; however, the 1984 Press and Publications Law allowed the government to censor publications. A new Press and Publications Law was approved by the Consultative Assembly in 2002. Political parties are banned. Candidates for the *majlis* election in 2003 were not allowed to campaign through the media. Some professional and other associations exist, among them the Chamber of Commerce and Industry.

The government has a mixed human rights record. In 1994 state security forces arrested hundreds of regime opponents, including higher-ranking government officials and members of prominent families, alleging they were Islamists (a claim others dismissed, since many of those arrested were Shi'as and Ibadhis). They were charged with sedition but later pardoned.

In early 2005 the government again arrested dozens of dissidents (academics, civil servants, and Islamic scholars). They were convicted of sedition in May 2005 by a state security court. In June 2005 the sultan again pardoned thirty-one of them.

Oman, unlike most of the other GCC states, is large enough for local government. In 1976 the sultan reorganized regional and local governments by establishing thirty-seven (later fifty-nine) districts (*wilayat*), one province (Dhufar, historically a separate sultanate that enjoys more local autonomy than other regions), and a municipality that embraces the capital. The districts are administered by governors appointed by the sultan. They collect taxes, provide local security, settle disputes, and advise the sultan.

Oman has a military of about 43,000. Its domestic forces consist of the Royal Police and a small tribal national guard.

There are four politically important groups in Oman: the ruling family, the tribes, the expatriate advisers, and the merchant class. They occupy a number of key ministerial and other government posts. Traditionally the tribes have also played a significant role in the Omani political process. Under Qabus's father, Sultan Sa'id bin Taimur, manipulation of tribal rivalries was a major element in ruling the country. Qabus, on the other hand, has tried to decrease the power of the tribes through development of local administration such as local government councils. Although the tribes' influence may be reflected in the election of council candidates, especially in rural areas, their power has declined considerably.

EASTERN ARABIAN FOREIGN POLICY INTERESTS

All the eastern Arabian states share much the same major foreign policy interests, regional national security threats, and global economic interests. As a result, there is a degree of coordination among all the states and with Saudi Arabia, by far the largest and most powerful state in the Arabian Peninsula.

At the same time, the differences in the pace and breadth of development in each state far outweigh the similarities. Full political independence and the discovery of oil occurred at different times; there are wide differences in geography, demographics, proved oil reserves, military and security capabilities, and the impact of rapid modernization on traditional social and political values and norms. For example, although Gulf oil policies are carried out based on consensus (*shura*) through OPEC, the GCC as a multilateral institution is little more than a consultative body in the Arabic context of *tashawwar*, which means simply soliciting an opinion with no attempt to reach an overall consensus. For example, although the GCC states have created a multilateral rapid-reaction force of some 5,000 troops, Peninsula Shield, it is in actuality not an operational force.

National Security Foreign Policy Interests

The eastern Arabian states have long understood that their security lies outside their direct control. They are small and militarily weak; yet, their wealth draws the often unwanted attention of the outside world. As a result, they have all looked to larger, more powerful allies for national security. Regionally, that has been Saudi Arabia, also a GCC member. Bilateral relations with Saudi Arabia have been hampered by a great deal of resentment among the smaller states, however, due to what is often seen as its patronizing and domineering attitude toward them. And, at any rate, they have felt the need for a stronger power against potential regional antagonists such as Iraq under Saddam and republican, Shi'a Iran.

Historically, Britain played that role. But with the departure of Britain and advent of the United States as a superpower, the latter has take over that role. It has not been without tensions, however, due in large part to domestic antipathy over the close US relationship with Israel and its lack of political will to create a just settlement of the Palestinian-Israeli conflict. In short, while the eastern Arabian states depend to a great extent on the United States for their national security, they try to avoid being dependent on it. This is done by diversifying military arms purchases and training to include many sources.

At present, the greatest security threat is from Iran, based on a complex set of factors. A major one is sectarian. Iran is Shi'a, which many Sunni Arabs see as heretical and which those states with large Shi'a populations, such as Bahrain, fear could undermine their regimes. A related factor is that the Islamic regime in Tehran is highly xenophobic and entertains ambitions based on the country's historic imperial past to create Iranian hegemony over the entire Gulf area. Furthermore, the US occupation of Iraq and overthrow of Saddam's Sunni Ba'thist regime has provided an opportunity for Iran to seek influence over the Shi'a majority that will dominate the future Iraqi government. Finally, there is concern over Iran's intentions regarding the creation of a nuclear weapon's capability and the possibility that Israel, with or without US support, might seek to prevent its doing so by military force.

All these factors have put a greater strain on relations with the United States for occupying Iraq in the first place and exacerbated the mutual hostility between it and Iran since the overthrow of the Shah three decades ago.

Economic Foreign Policy Interests

As already noted, the global recession of 2008 has hurt all the eastern Arabian states. By and large, however, it has had a positive result in increasing transparency and accountability in the market place. The price of oil has declined, but the price elasticity of oil is high, and as economic recovery proceeds, revenues will recover.

The same should be true for financial markets both at home and abroad. The greatest unknown at the time of this writing is how long it will take.

FUTURE PROSPECTS

The prospects for political stability in the small GCC states are good. All of the states have felt the impact of the global financial crisis, but absent a very deep drop in oil prices, the GCC states are better positioned than most to ride out the storm. Each state has institutionalized a system of family rule that is responsive to the concerns of the major actors in society and manages succession. Bahrain, Qatar, and the UAE have all managed the transfer of power to a new generation relatively smoothly. This challenge still remains for Kuwait and Oman. For Oman, the succession crisis may move the country away from family rule and toward something resembling republicanism. For Kuwait, if the ruling family is seriously divided, the generational succession may again allow some expansion of the National Assembly's role. The prospects for continued political liberalization are best in Kuwait, although even there, the expansion will continue to be gradual.

BIBLIOGRAPHY

A number of useful edited volumes on the Gulf have come out recently, including Annoush Ehteshami and Steven Wright, eds., *Reform in the Middle East Oil Monarchies* (Reading, UK: Ithaca Press, 2007); Joshua Teitelbaum, ed., *Political Liberalization in the Gulf* (New York: Columbia University Press, 2008); and Paul Dresch and James Piscatori, eds., *Monarchies and Nations: Globalisation and Identity in the Arab States of the Gulf* (London: Tauris, 2005). Older overviews worth consulting include Khaldun Al Naqeeb, *Society and States in the Gulf and Arab Peninsula: A Different Perspective* (London: Routledge, 1990); Rosemarie Said Zahlan, *The Making of the Modern: Kuwait, Bahrain, Qatar, the United Arab Emirates, and Oman* (Ithaca, NY: Garnet, 1999); F. Gregory Gause, *Oil Monarchies: Domestic and Security Challenges in the Arab Gulf States* (New York: Council on Foreign Relations Press, 1994); and Liesl Graz, *The Turbulent Gulf: People, Politics and Power* (New York: I. B. Tauris, 1992).

Two books covering multiple countries are Laurence Louer, *Transnational Shi'a Politics: Religious and Political Networks in the Gulf* (New York: Columbia University Press, 2008), focusing on Kuwait, Bahrain, and Saudi Arabia, and Michael Herb, *All in the Family: Absolutism, Revolution, and Democracy in the Middle Eastern Monarchies* (Albany: State University of New York Press, 1999).

Several books offer more detailed treatment on individual states. These include four by Westview Press: Fred H. Lawson, *Bahrain: The Modernization of Autocracy*

(1989), Jill Crystal, *Kuwait: The Transformation of an Oil State* (1992), Malcolm C. Peck, *The United Arab Emirates: A Venture in Unity* (1986), and Calvin H. Allen Jr., *Oman: The Modernization of the Sultanate* (1987). See also Christopher Davidson, *The United Arab Emirates: A Study in Survival* (Boulder, CO: Rienner, 2005), and his *Dubai: The Vulnerability of Success* (New York: Columbia University Press, 2008), which offer more recent treatments of the UAE. Two volumes on the UAE provide thoughtful essays: Joseph A. Kechichian, ed., *A Century in Thirty Years: Shaykh Zayed and the United Arab Emirates* (Washington, DC: Middle East Policy Council, 2000), and Edmund Ghareeb and Ibrahim Al Abed, *Perspectives on the United Arab Emirates* (London: Trident Press, 1997). Frauke Heard-Bey, *From Trucial States to Emirates*, rev. ed. (London: Longman, 1996), is a detailed account of the process by which the UAE emerged.

Joseph A. Kechichian's *Oman and the World: The Emergence of an Independent Foreign Policy* (Santa Monica, CA: RAND, 1995) and his *Political Participation and Stability in the Sultanate of Oman* (Dubai: Gulf Research Center, 2006) add usefully to the literature on that country, as does Francis Owtram, *A Modern History of Oman* (London: Tauris, 2004). Jill Crystal, *Oil and Politics in the Gulf: Rulers and Merchants in Kuwait and Qatar*, rev. ed. (New York: Cambridge University Press, 1995), looks at politics in those two states. Al-Jazeera has generated its own books, among them Hugh Miles, *Al-Jazeera: The Inside Story of the Arab News Channel That is Challenging the West* (New York: Grove Press, 2005), and Mohammed el-Nawawy and Adel Islander, *Al-Jazeera: How the Free Arab News Network Scooped the World and Changed the Middle East* (Boulder, CO: Westview, 2002).

There are several good treatments of the internal politics of Kuwait, in addition to those above. Mary Ann Tetreault's *Stories of Democracy: Politics and Society in Contemporary Kuwait* (New York: Columbia University, 2000) is the thoughtful analysis of a leading scholar on contemporary Kuwait. Pete Moore's *Doing Business in the Gulf: Politics and Economic Crisis in Jordan and Kuwait* (Cambridge: Cambridge University Press, 2004) analyzes the domestic political economy of Kuwait. Anh Nga Longva's *Walls Built on Sand: Migration, Exclusion and Society in Kuwait* (Boulder, CO: Westview, 1999) looks at foreign labor in Kuwait in the context of Kuwaiti politics. A narrower, but interesting, treatment is Deborah Wheeler's *The Internet in the Middle East: Global Expectations and Local Imaginations in Kuwait* (Albany: State University of New York Press, 2005).

Some recent monographs on the Gulf include Paul Salem, "Kuwait: Politics in a Participatory Emirate" (Carnegie Paper No. 3, Carnegie Endowment for International Peace, Washington, DC, June 2007); Edward Burke, "Bahrain: Reaching a Threshold," Working Paper 61 (FRIDE Working Paper 61, May 15, 2009); Steven Wright, "Fixing the Kingdom: Political Evolution and Socio-Economic Challenges in Bahrain" (Occasional Paper No. 3, Georgetown University Center for

International and Regional Studies, Washington, DC, 2008); and Christopher Davidson, "The United Arab Emirates: Prospects for Political Reform," *Brown Journal of World Affairs* 15, no. 2 (spring 2009).

Two very good analyses of the Gulf Cooperation Council, its objectives, and its structure are Erik R. Peterson, *The Gulf Cooperation Council: Search for Unity in a Dynamic Region* (Boulder, CO: Westview Press, 1988), and John Sandwick, ed., *The Gulf Cooperation Council: Moderation and Stability in an Interdependent World* (Boulder, CO: Westview Press, in association with the American–Arab Affairs Council, Washington, DC, 1987). Also recommended is Joseph W. Twinam's *The Gulf, Cooperation and the Council: An American Perspective* (Washington, DC: Middle East Policy Council, 1992).

John E. Peterson's *Defending Arabia* (New York: St. Martin's Press, 1986), although dated, provides an excellent background and introduction to security issues in the Gulf. Anthony H. Cordesman's *The Military Balance in the Gulf* (Washington, DC: Center for Strategic and International Affairs, 2001) presents a detailed analysis of the military balance and force trends in the five countries covered in this chapter, as well as Iran, Iraq, Saudi Arabia, and Yemen. Security issues broadly defined are dealt with in David E. Long and Christian Koch, eds., *Gulf Security in the Twenty-First Century* (Abu Dhabi, UAE: The Emirates Center for Strategic Studies and Research, 1997).

Periodicals are an important source of information on the Arab Gulf states. *The Middle East Journal*, published by the Middle East Institute, Washington, DC, is a quarterly that publishes a very wide selection of book reviews and a chronology of events, as well as articles on the contemporary Middle East. The *International Journal of Middle East Studies*, published quarterly by Cambridge University Press, is the principal academic periodical devoted to the Middle East. *Middle East Report* (quarterly), *Middle East Policy* (quarterly), and *Middle East Insight* (monthly) are Washington, DC, publications that frequently include useful articles on current developments in the Arab GCC states. The International Crisis Group publishes excellent monographs on current issues, including some on the Gulf Arab states.

7

REPUBLIC OF YEMEN

Robert D. Burrowes

The Republic of Yemen (ROY) is the product of the unification in May 1990 of North and South Yemen. It covers an area of 530,000 square kilometers (207,286 square miles), less than three-fourth the size of France, and its population approaches 25 million. The ROY occupies the southernmost corner of the Arabian Peninsula. The location of the two Yemens, on the world's busiest sea-lane at the southern end of the Red Sea where Asia almost meets Africa, gave it strategic significance from the start of the age of imperialism through the Cold War. More relevant today are the facts that Yemen shares a long border with oil-rich Saudi Arabia, serves as a bridge between Arabia and the turbulent Horn of Africa, and is crucially placed to spread or contain global revolutionary Islam.

HISTORICAL BACKGROUND

Arabia felix

Historically Yemen has been dotted with human settlements for several thousand years, perhaps since humans first came out of Africa. Neolithic sites abound, and the surface has barely been scratched regarding these and later prehistoric sites.

Geography largely determined the history of Yemen after the rise of the great ancient civilizations to the north and east, in Egypt, Mesopotamia, and the Mediterranean basin. Roughly from 1000 BCE to 500 CE, this corner of Arabia provided the overland caravan route to these civilizations for highly prized goods, among them spices, myrrh, and frankincense, from South Arabia, East Africa, and India. These were the centuries of the several pre-Islamic trading kingdoms astride the "frankincense trail" along the edge of the desert from the Arabian Sea northwest to the Nabatean capital of Petra and beyond.

These kingdoms included Main and Saba, the latter ruled from Marib by, among others, Bilqis, allegedly the Queen of Sheba (Saba). Farther south and east were the Qataban and Hadhramawt kingdoms. The last of the kingdoms was Himyar, the

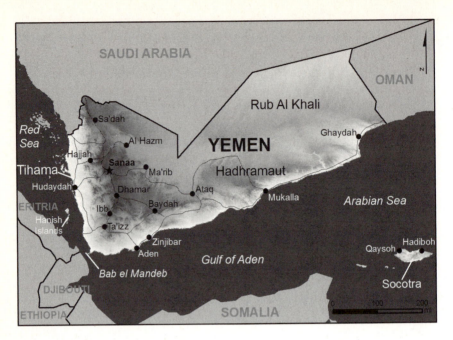

Republic of Yemen

only one ruled from the highlands rather than the desert's edge. At their heights, the Sabean and Himyarite kingdoms embraced much of historic Yemen. Over these early centuries the ideas of Yemen as a place and of a Yemeni people probably emerged.

Occupying what Roman cartographers called *Arabia felix* ("happy Arabia"), these states depended for their prominence and prosperity upon their ability to protect and tax the passage of these luxury goods. When the Romans occupied Egypt in the first century BCE, they soon learned both the secret of the monsoon winds and the true source of the goods they desired. They then made the Red Sea their primary avenue of commerce, causing the interior of Yemen to go into a decline from which it never recovered. Indicative of the decline, weakened indigenous regimes were unable to prevent in the centuries just before the rise of Islam the occupation of Yemen by Christian Abyssinia and the Sassanids of Persia.

The Islamic era, beginning in the seventh century CE, contains many events critical to the making of Yemen and the Yemenis. The force with which Islam exploded out of Makkah in the nearby Hijaz made almost inevitable the early Islamization of adjacent Yemen. Yemen's converts to Islam provided many of the first soldiers of Islam, those who marched north and then west across North Africa. In the late ninth century CE, the founding of an indigenous dynasty in Yemen ended Abbasid rule from distant Baghdad, and this in turn served to free Yemen to develop in relative isolation its own variant of Arab-Islamic civilization. The establishment of the Zaydi imamate in North Yemen, as well as its persistence almost continuously down to the 1962 revolution, forever stamped the northern highlands and their towns and tribes with the Zaydi strand of Shi'a Islam. By contrast, the two-century rule of the Rasulids, beginning in the twelfth century and initially based in Aden, stamped the coast and the south with the Shafi'i form of Sunni Islam.

The occupation of Yemen by the Ottoman Turks in the sixteenth century and their expulsion after a long struggle led by the imamate in the next century served to deepen a sense of Yemeni identity and ushered in another long period of Zaydi rule. Despite the rapid growth of the coffee trade on the coast at al-Mukha (Mocha), the interior highlands of Yemen remained largely cut off from and unknown to the rest of the world from the mid-seventeenth to the mid-nineteenth centuries. During this period western Europe was transformed and came to exercise control over much of the rest of the world. All this passed Yemen by.

The Two Yemens: 1839–1999

The process by which one Yemen and Yemeni people, albeit still vaguely defined, became two Yemens began with both Great Britain's seizure of Aden in 1839 and the start of the second Ottoman occupation of North Yemen in 1849. By the time the Turks and the British delineated the border between their domains in 1904, the bifurcation of Yemen and the development of two polities and political cultures was already underway. Politics in the north turned increasingly on opposition to Ottoman rule and was again led by the imamate. In the south, politics revolved around Britain's position in Aden, its primary concern. Defeat in World War I forced Ottoman withdrawal in 1918, and Britain gradually extended its sway north and beyond Aden's environs.

During the first six decades of the twentieth century, two willful and able imams, Yahya Hamid al-Din and his son Ahmad, acted to forge a monarchical state, much as the kings of England and France did centuries earlier. They strengthened the state, which enabled them to expand their domain and considerably secure the borders and pacify the interior. Their claim to and defense of Yemen fostered a nascent modern Yemeni nationalism.

The two imams used the strengthened imamate to revive and isolate North Yemen's traditional Islamic culture and society. The result was a "backward" Yemen, quite frozen in time, and a tiny but increasing number of Yemenis who, exposed to the outside world, wanted "progress" and blamed the imamate for its absence. This

YEMEN

Capital city	Sanaa
Chief of state	President Ali Abdallah Salih
Head of government	Prime Minister Ali Muhammad Mujawwar
Major political parties (seats in lower house)	General People's Congress (228), Islamic Reform Grouping (47), Yemeni Socialist Party (7), Nasserite Unionist Party (3), National Arab Socialist Ba'th Party (2)
Ethnic groups	Predominantly Arab, but also Afro-Arabs, South Asians, and Europeans
Religious groups	Predominantly Sunni and Zaydi Muslim
Export partners	China (30.9%), Thailand (26.4%), India (17.2%), Japan (5.2%), United Arab Emirates (4.3%)
Import partners	United Arab Emirates (16.4%), China (12.4%), Saudi Arabia (7.8%), Kuwait (5.8%), United States (4.3%)

produced the chain of events that resulted in the 1962 revolution, the abolition of the imamate, and the declaration of the Yemen Arab Republic (YAR).

The brief history of the YAR can be divided into three periods: first, the wrenching first five years under President Abdullah al-Sallal (1962–1967), which were marked by military rule, a long civil war in which an Egyptian military presence backed the republicans and Saudi Arabia backed the royalists, and, above all, the rapid and irreversible opening of the country to the modern world; second, a ten-year period (1967–1977) distinguished by the republican-royalist reconciliation ending the civil war, adoption of the 1970 constitution, the holding of elections under president Abd al-Rahman al-Iryani, and the brief attempt by President Ibrahim al-Hamdi to build the state and turn it to the task of Yemen's development; and third, the twelve-year tenure (1978–1990) of President Ali Abdallah Salih, a soldier and tribesman, and the change from political and economic weakness to political stability, the discovery of oil, and the prospect of oil-driven change and prosperity.

President Salih consolidated his rule by defeating the National Democratic Front rebellion and by creating his ruling party, the General People's Congress (GPC). Important though his era was for the YAR, the period 1967 to 1977 provided a needed breathing space and bought time. The changes that buffeted Yemen in the five years after 1962 had left it both unable to retreat into the past and ill equipped to go forward.

South Yemen's history after the British occupation of Aden in 1839 was quite different. Of critical importance were Britain's focus on Aden and its neglect for decades of the dozen or so statelets in the hinterland. As a consequence, no single polity embraced what soon after independence in 1967 became the People's Democratic Republic of Yemen (PDRY). Instead, by the late 1950s, it consisted of Aden Colony—a partly modern city-state and one of the world's busiest ports— and a vast, mostly distant, and politically fragmented hinterland.

At independence in 1967, the infrastructure, which barely held the country together, consisted of unpaved roads, a number of airstrips, and the telegraph. What little market economy existed mostly centered on Aden and its environs, and, in turn, plugged less into its hinterland than into the international economy via its sea-lanes. This fragile modern sector was dealt devastating blows at independence in 1967. The blocking of the Suez Canal during the 1967 Arab-Israeli War nearly brought port activities to a halt, and Britain's withdrawal months later ended both aid and the economic activity tied to its presence.

The history of independent South Yemen is marked by four periods: first, the period of takeover and consolidation (1967–1969), the initial phase in which the National Liberation Front (NLF) established control in Aden and over the hinterland at the same time that power within it passed from the nationalists to its Marxist left wing; second, the period of uneasy leftist coleadership of Salim Ruba'i Ali and Abd al-Fatah Isma'il (1969–1978), distinguished by the efforts of these two rivals to transform the Yemeni Socialist Party (YSP) into a vanguard party, to organize the country in terms of "scientific socialism," and to align the PDRY with the socialist camp and other liberation movements; third, the era of Ali Nasir Muhammad (1980–1985), the period in which the consolidation of power in a single leader was paralleled by growing moderation in both domestic affairs and external relations, especially with the YAR; and fourth, after the violent end of the Ali Nasir era, a period of collective leadership (1986–1999) in which a weak, decapitated YSP had to cope with worsening economic conditions and the end of aid from the Soviet Bloc.

The era of the PDRY saw considerable conflict and violence (e.g., the execution of Salim Ruba'i Ali and the intraparty bloodbath in which Abd al-Fatah Isma'il and others were assassinated). Nevertheless, the regime had some notable successes: It established order in the country, made progress in bridging the vast gap between Aden and the rest of the country, and made good use of very limited resources to advance such goals as literacy, health care, and women's rights.

The regional relations of both Yemens focused largely on their rich, worried, and overbearing neighbor, Saudi Arabia. Imamate Yemen had fought and lost a short war with the newborn Saudi kingdom in 1934, forcing it to cede control of three northern areas, Asir, Najran, and Jizan. After the Yemeni Civil War, in which the Saudis supported the royalists, their strategy became one of controlling the republicanism on their border by making the YAR dependent on them for aid. For its part, the YAR sought needed aid without forfeiting independence. Although the balance shifted back and forth, the YAR did get a good bit of aid and retained a good bit of independence. As the PDRY moved towards Marxism and gave support to the Dhufar Rebellion in Oman, the Saudis worked to undermine their radical neighbor. Above all, they did what they could to discourage Yemeni unification, especially if dominated by the Marxist south.

During the civil war, the YAR was supported by the Soviet Bloc and not the United States or much of Europe. By 1970, however, the victorious YAR was successfully seeking good relations with—and aid from—the West while maintaining close ties to the Soviet Bloc. As the PDRY moved to the left, it became increasingly dependent economically and politically on the Soviet Bloc. The two Yemens and inter-Yemeni relations were viewed largely in Cold War terms by the two superpowers—and treated accordingly. Both Yemens came to depend heavily on the United Nations and other international and multinational bodies for aid.

Yemeni Unification and the Republic of Yemen

Long desired by many, unification in May 1990 took most Yemenis and non-Yemenis by surprise. The Salih regime took the initiative in the late 1980s, but both sides got caught up in the process in 1989 and 1990. New political parties, organizations, newspapers, and magazines sprang up, and the unification regime came in for unprecedented scrutiny and criticism by these entities as well as in the parliament.

Under the transition terms, Ali Abdullah Salih became president and Ali Salim al-Baydh, YSP's secretary-general, became vice president. The two cabinets were merged, and top positions were shared equally between the two ruling parties, the GPC and the YSP; the parliaments were also merged, supplemented with appointees, and renamed the Council of Deputies (*Majlis al-Nuwab*).

The transition period ended with the 1993 parliamentary elections. The GPC won a little more than twice the number of seats won by either of its main opponents, the YSP and the Yemeni Reform Grouping (Islah), a party formed at unification by anti-YSP tribal shaykhs and conservative Islamists. The GPC, YSP, and Islah formed a "grand coalition" in which cabinet and other top positions were allocated roughly on a 2:1:1 basis. Shaykh Abdullah ibn Husayn al-Ahmar, the head of Islah and long-time ally of President Salih, became parliamentary speaker.

The honeymoon between the GPC and YSP had actually ended in late 1991 and was followed by increasing acrimony and hostility. Their brief closing of ranks for the elections was quickly replaced by bitter conflict between the two parties and their supporters. The conflict rapidly escalated, increasingly punctuated by violence and second thoughts about unification. Many efforts to stop the conflict were made and failed, most notably a reform program endorsed by both sides.

What followed was a brief war of secession in mid-1994. Unified Yemen survived, as largely northern forces loyal to President Salih prevailed over those from the south and led by most of the YSP leaders. Militant Islamists and forces loyal to Ali Nasir Muhammad, PDRY ex-president, supplemented the northern side.

As important as the political competition and hostility, rapidly worsening economic conditions had helped Yemen unravel in the early 1990s. Less than three months after unification, Yemenis caught up in that process were blindsided by Iraq's invasion of Kuwait. Yemen refused to join the effort to expel Iraq by force, and, in reprisal, Saudi Arabia, the United States, and other Gulf Arab states slashed their considerable foreign aid. Far more damaging, the Saudis expelled about 800,000 Yemeni workers, thereby cutting off the remittances upon which Yemen depended and creating for the first time massive unemployment.

From the War of Secession to 2010

With the war of secession over in mid-1994, the Salih regime faced the need both to deal with an economy in free fall and to reintegrate the just-defeated south into the ROY. The regime acted quickly on the latter, granting amnesty to all but the top sixteen leaders in the secession and urging those who had fled abroad to return to Yemen—and most of the latter did.

Addressing the economic crisis, however, involved negotiations with the International Monetary Fund (IMF) and World Bank over a package of economic reforms that led to a complex, demanding agreement in 1995. The costs of unification and the war of secession, but above all the loss of remittances, had halved Yemen's gross domestic product (GDP). Massive unemployment and rising poverty signaled that the economy had ceased to be viable and sustainable. The IMF/World Bank economic package was designed to address this situation by creating an economic environment that would attract domestic and, above all, foreign investment. Sacrifices by the general public (e.g., the elimination of subsidies on necessities) were billed as the price of future jobs and income. Initially, the public seemed prepared to accept this.

On the political side, the multimember executive was abolished, and the parliament elected President Salih to a new term in late 1994. A new coalition government was also approved, which included the GPC and Islah—but not the YSP.

Shaykh al-Ahmar continued as speaker. In 1997, a still-reeling YSP decided to boycott the parliamentary elections. Winning with a huge majority, the Salih regime then chose to rule alone, with the result that Islah became the major opposition party. Shaykh al-Ahmar remained speaker, an indication of his and Islah's unusual relationship to President Salih. Two years later, the GPC used its dominance of parliament to prevent a somewhat revived YSP from running its leader in unified Yemen's first direct popular presidential elections. As a result, President Salih ran virtually unopposed and, with the backing of Islah, was overwhelmingly elected to a new term, one extended by amendment from five to seven years.

The worsening economic conditions probably contributed to increased militant Islamist activity in the late 1990s. Most notably, the kidnapping of twelve tourists in late 1998 ended in the death of four of them. Thereafter, conflict with members of al-Qa'ida and other Salafi groups increased, especially after militants rammed their bomb-laden boat into the destroyer USS *Cole* moored in Aden in October 2000, killing seventeen sailors. These events became more salient politically in September 2001 after the suicide bombings of the World Trade Center and the Pentagon—"9/11"—and the declaration of the War on Terror.

Despite the upsurge in Islamist conflict and worsening economic conditions, the GPC reaffirmed its dominance in the 2003 parliamentary elections. The party increased its majority, taking more than two-thirds of the seats. Islah remained in second place, but with fewer seats than before; the YSP, returning after its boycott in 1997, made a modest comeback, taking seven. Shaykh al-Ahmar remained speaker.

The election results notwithstanding, politics had become increasingly acrimonious and divisive by mid-decade, and behind this lay the effects of the grim state of the economy on most of the people. Unemployment persistently held at about 40 percent, as did the percentages for the malnourished and those below the poverty line. The middle class shrank and was pauperized. On the personal level, most Yemenis were just trying to make ends meet, and more and more were openly expressing their anger.

Against this backdrop, the major opposition parties moved haltingly toward creating a unified opposition to the Salih regime. Largely through the efforts of YSP leader Jarullah Omar, these parties in 2002 created the Joint Meeting Parties (JMP) consisting of five members: the YSP, Islah, the Nasirist Party, the Union of Popular Forces, and al-Haqq ("Truth"). The parties that really counted were Islah and the YSP, and initial tasks were to end the tendencies of the YSP to go it alone and of Islah to form temporary alliances with the GPC. Both parties resisted efforts by the GPC to lure them away from the JMP. Trust and a sense of mutual interest developed fitfully, and the five members of the JMP began to speak and act with one voice.

By late 2005, attention had turned to the 2006 presidential and local council elections. Both the GPC and the JMP drew up reformist programs, the JMP's being very critical of the Salih regime's economic performance. In early 2006, President Salih yielded to "popular demand" and reversed his earlier decision not to run. For its part, the JMP chose a credible candidate who waged a vigorous campaign. Despite this, President Salih again won decisively, and the GPC also swept the local council elections. The JMP remained intact after the elections, pledged to hold the Salih regime to its promises of reform, and began planning for the parliamentary elections in 2009—and the next presidential contest in 2013.

By this time, however, electoral politics were being eclipsed by more confrontational and violent politics. The Houthi Rebellion, named after its founder, Husayn al-Houthi, erupted in June 2004 in Sa'da in the far north. Launched by Zaydi sayyids, the Houthis' chants of "death to the Israelis, death to the Americans" masked a deeper dissatisfaction with their social and political lot during the Salih era. Before a truce in September, many lives were lost and homes and infrastructure destroyed. Partly as a result of the regime's harsh response, the rebellion erupted again and grew more violent in the next four years, defying third-party efforts to reach a truce that would hold. Despite a truce brokered by Qatar in 2008, violence returned in early 2009, erupted into all-out war in August, and continued into 2010. President Salih called the campaign Operation Scorched Earth.

Beginning in mid-2007, and over a period of many months, a rash of protests and demonstrations occurred in several places across the old PDRY, some of them turning violent. They initially involved military officers angered by being forced into retirement on meager pensions after the war of secession. These actions soon broadened to include civil servants, lawyers, teachers, professors, and unemployed youths protesting against what they saw as the north's systematic exploitation of the south since 1994. Southerners' actions and the regime's reactions continued throughout 2008 and became increasingly violent. The pace of the newly proclaimed Southern Movement picked up significantly and grew even more violent in April 2009, only to drop off somewhat over the rest of the year.

The rebellion in the north and the protests in the south came to question the legitimacy of the Salih regime, unification, and even republicanism. Some protesting southerners, moving beyond charges of unfairness, again began asserting that unification was "occupation" and called for secession. Even more fundamentally, some of the Houthis questioned the very idea of republicanism and explicitly called for restoration of the imamate and rule by Zaydi sayyids.

If this were not enough, bombings by al-Qa'ida and its allies occurred in the diplomatic quarter of Sana' in the first half of 2008. This violence spread to Wadi Hadhramawt later in the year, targeting tourists as well as security forces. The massive suicide bombing at the US embassy in September, which claimed nineteen

lives, was the worst of these events. In early 2009, a new al-Qa'ida in the Arabian
Peninsula announced itself, merging the Yemeni and Saudi branches of the organi-
zation. It later declared jihad against the regime and expressed support for the
Southern Movement and the Houthis. The Salih regime's response to the terrorist
acts of 2008 and 2009 was swift and harsh, reaching a peak in the second half of
December 2009.

Thus, by 2009, the legitimacy and continuation of the Salih regime, and even
of the republic itself, were being challenged in the north and south, at the center,
and in the east—that is, from virtually all quarters. Against this background, the
GPC and the JMP had for months negotiated without success on electoral and
other political reforms in advance of the April 2009 parliamentary elections. In
late February, with the violence continuing on all fronts and the threat of a JMP
election boycott looming over the stalled negotiations, the GPC and JMP agreed
to a two-year postponement of the elections. Conflict with the southern secessionists, al-Qa'ida, and the Houthis continued through the year. For his part, President Salih warned that this activity could result in many, not just two, Yemens.

POLITICAL ENVIRONMENT

Geography

Yemen is marked by a high, steep, jagged mountain range that forms the western
and southern edges of a high plateau that descends gradually north and east into
the desert interior, on the border with Saudi Arabia. The mountains rise abruptly
about twenty-five miles inland from a low, flat, coastal desert plain, the Tihama.
They parallel the Red Sea, running north to south the length of North Yemen,
abruptly turn ninety degrees near the old border between the two Yemens, and
then go east parallel to the Gulf of Aden for part of the length of South Yemen.
Averaging several thousand feet—at one place west of Sana' rising to 12,400 feet,
the highest point on the peninsula—the northern highlands have a largely semiarid, but otherwise temperate, climate, despite being well south of the Tropic of
Cancer. By contrast, the southern uplands are quite verdant, and the Tihama and
the southern coast are hot and humid much of the year.

Groundwater and surface runoff are in very short supply in most of Yemen.
However, the annual monsoon winds blow inland after picking up moisture from
the sea; the mountains then force the warm air to rise, cool, and drop its moisture.
It is this considerable, albeit erratic, seasonal rainfall in the mountains and highlands in the early spring and summer that accounts both for intensive cultivation
of crops, much of it in streambeds and on steep, terraced hillsides, and for the relatively dense population in these areas. The highlands in North Yemen are loftier
and more extensive than in South Yemen, which explains its greater rainfall, more

intensive and extensive agriculture, and considerably larger population. By contrast, the eastern two-thirds of South Yemen are all but uninhabitable, except for coastal fishing villages and ports and, deep in the interior, the densely populated Wadi Hadhramawt. Half again larger in area than North Yemen, South Yemen has about one-fourth as many people—roughly 5 million. In the north, nearly all of the population is sedentary, and this is only slightly less the case in the south. What nomads there are mostly live on the edge of the desert near Saudi Arabia.

Regions and Population Centers

Yemen has at least six distinct regions. There are the northern highlands, which include much of the upper half of old North Yemen and are bound on the west by the mountains. The southern uplands consist of the lower half of North Yemen and include most importantly the regions of Taiz and Ibb. The coastal Tihama runs the length of North Yemen between the Red Sea and the mountains. The arid east, on the edge of the desert, consists of the remote regions of Marib, al-Jawf, and Shabwa. Far to the south are Aden and the area running from the Arabian Sea up to the mountains between the two Yemens. To the east is the large, arid Hadhramawt region in which is located an island of habitation, Wadi Hadhramawt. Finally, even farther to the east are the culturally distinct Mahra region, bordering Oman, and the otherworldly island of Socotra.

The country has four major cities, San'a, the capital, and Aden, al-Hudayda, and Taiz. Aden and al-Hudayda are the major ports, Aden being a world-class natural one. There are several large towns: Sa'da, far to the north; Dhamar, Yarim, and Ibb in the middle region; Mukalla on the southern coast; and, in Wadi Hadhramawt, the trio of Shibam, Seiyun, and Tarim. The population of the former PDRY is highly concentrated in a few places—in Mukalla and the towns of Wadi Hadhramawt, in the highlands northeast of Aden, and, above all, in Aden proper and its environs. By contrast, the much larger population of the former YAR is more widely scattered over a great many towns, villages, and hamlets. Still, Taiz and al-Hudayda have experienced considerable growth, and the exploding population of San'a is approaching 2 million.

Economy

Yemen has long been, and remains, a very poor country, the poorest in the Arab world. For centuries its economy was largely self-sufficient, based mostly on subsistence agriculture. Although North Yemen moved quickly from self-sufficiency to dependence on the outside world after 1962, as part of South Yemen had done earlier, farming and animal husbandry remain the chief sources of livelihood for a majority of the population—even though they contribute a small percentage of

total GDP. Fishing, trade and commerce, and traditional artisanship are also important; by contrast, modern industry remains rare, marginal, and small in scale. Finally, the viability of the Yemeni economy after the 1960s increasingly depended
on remittances, and this meant dependence upon the continued employment of
Yemenis abroad; in sharp decline after 1990, remittances still contribute to the
economy. In 2009, Yemen's estimated annual per capita income was about $1,250,
less than $3.50 per day.

Until the mid-1980s, Yemen had no exploited natural resources of consequence other than its fisheries, and these were barely tapped. Modest amounts of
oil were discovered in the north in 1984, and the first oil from Marib was exported in late 1987. At the time of unification in 1990, larger amounts of oil were
discovered in Masila, an area northeast of Mukalla in the Hadhramawt. Yemeni oil
production peaked at 465,000 barrels per day in 2003 and then began to decline;
predictions have reserves depleted by 2020. The development of Yemen's somewhat more substantial gas reserves in Marib got underway in 2005, and the export
of liquefied natural gas began in late 2009.

Culture and Society

The native population of Yemen is almost entirely Arab and Muslim. The Christian communities that existed in pre-Islamic times disappeared early in the Islamic
era. Much of the sizable and important Jewish community migrated en masse to
Israel shortly after its creation in 1948; only several hundred Jews remain, mostly
in the cities and towns from San'a north. The once large and powerful Isma'ili
Shi'a population was reduced through persecution over the centuries to an insignificant though reviving minority in the mountains between San'a and al-
Hudayda.

There remains an old and still politically and socially salient cleavage between
Yemen's two largest Muslim groups, the Zaydi (Shi'a) and the Shafi'i (Sunnis). The
Zaydis of the northern highlands, although only a minority, dominated politics
and cultural life in North Yemen for centuries through the Zaydi tribes and the
Zaydi imamate. With unification and the addition of southern Yemen's almost totally Shafi'i population, the numerical balance has shifted dramatically away from
the Zaydis, who make up little more than 20 percent of the combined population.
Nevertheless, the Zaydis are still vastly overrepresented in the government and
armed forces. While sectarianism has not played a prominent role in Yemeni politics for decades, the Houthi Rebellion that erupted in 2004 suggests that it remains a possibility.

For millennia, tribalism and tribal ties have been the most important basis of
social organization and identity in the highlands of North Yemen, in the mountainous region between the two Yemens, and in remote parts of the Hadhramawt.

Two large tribal confederations predominate in the northern highlands, the Hashid and the Bakil; of lesser importance is the Madhhij confederation, located east of the other two.

While many people in other parts of Yemen claim some tribal affiliation, these ties are less important as bases of identity and solidarity than extended family, locality, class, caste, or occupation. Atop the traditional nontribal social system is the sayyid caste, those Zaydis and Shafi'is who claim descent from the Prophet Muhammad. (The imams must be sayyids.) Beneath the sayyid caste is the *qadi* class, usually learned Zaydis and Shafi'is who serve as judges, administrators, religious figures, and teachers. In the middle is the relatively large and varied class of peasants, merchants, shopkeepers, and artisans. At the bottom are two groups: the *muzayyin* class, which provides the butchers, barbers, bath attendants, and those who perform other "demeaning" tasks, and, at the bottom, the *akhdam* caste of servants, street sweepers, and popular musicians.

Despite great differences in status, North Yemen's economy of scarcity under the imamate fostered a social system that was not marked by great inequality. The imams did live better than most of their fellow Yemenis, but not perceptibly that much better. After the 1962 revolution, inequality increased both within the modern sector and between parts of that sector and traditional Yemen, much as had happened in South Yemen under British rule earlier in the twentieth century. In the PDRY after 1970, the regime's Marxist ideology and economic scarcity served to temper the inequality that usually accompanies the early stages of development. The tendency of entrenched one-party states to widen class divides was countered in the PDRY through the 1980s by relatively wide access to education, health care, and housing and by efforts to integrate the rest of the country into more modern Aden.

Extremely rugged terrain, widely separated population centers, and primitive means of transportation and communication have made for diversity in the considerably homogeneous Yemeni people. Although Arabic is spoken by nearly all, there are several dialectical differences, most notably between the dialect of North Yemen's highlands and that of the southern part of North Yemen and Aden. Beyond language, other sociocultural and regional differences abound. The subtlest and most important one, going beyond dialect and the Zaydi-Shafi'i religious differences, is the cultural difference between "northerners" from the highlands and "southerners" from the southern half of North Yemen and Aden. The former are stereotyped as more likely to have strong tribal ties, claim a warrior tradition, and, at least in the past, be more parochial. The latter are stereotyped as more likely to be of nontribal peasant origins, peaceful or docile, engaged in commercial activities, and more traveled and cosmopolitan. Going to the east, many of the people of Wadi Hadhramawt reflect the cultural influence of Southeast Asia with which they have old social and commercial ties. The people of Mahra and Socotra share a non-Arab language and culture. Finally, the people of the coastal desert and ports reflect the long racial and cultural influences of nearby Africa—Somalia, Ethiopia, and Eritrea—and Aden still hints of the Indian subcontinent, a legacy of the British raj.

POLITICAL STRUCTURE

The 1990 constitution closely resembles the YAR's 1970 constitution and was ratified by the people of both Yemens in 1991. In the absence of a tradition of constitutional government in the Yemens, the constitution neither closely reflects political reality nor tightly constrains or limits the use of power—it is not yet a "living constitution." The system of courts and appointed judges it calls for do not constitute an independent judiciary, and the free speech, right to organize, and other rights it enshrines are largely aspirational.

The constitution originally called for a plural executive, a feature that was changed to a singular presidency in 1994, and for a 301-member Council of Deputies, the members of which were to be chosen by voters in single-member constituencies. The terms of office for legislators and the president were four and five years, respectively, terms that were changed by referendum in 2001 to six and seven years. In addition to its legislative duties, the Council of Deputies selected the president, a provision that was changed in 1994 to direct popular election. In addition, a second chamber, the Shura Council, appointed by the president and with mostly advisory powers, was formed in 1997. The constitution provided for provincial and local council elections and for the appointment of provincial governors by the executive. The first local elections were finally held in 2001. The selection of governors was changed to elective, and the first election of governors was held in 2008.

The opposition to the Salih regime has persistently demanded fundamental constitutional changes that would increase legislative power at the expense of executive power and increase decentralization through greater provincial and local autonomy. Some would give the Shura Council legislative power coequal with that of the Council of Deputies and base elections on proportional representation. Some have called for replacing the presidential system with parliamentary government.

In a break with the YAR's theoretical no-party system and the PDRY's one-party system, the constitution explicitly allows for a multiparty system. The GPC, the "president's party," dominated politics in the YAR and now dominates the Republic of Yemen. Islah, with its organization, cadre, and grassroots support, remains a potential challenge to the GPC. The YSP, with some of the ideology and organization of its glory days, has retained a base of support in the south and in pockets of the north. For their part, the Ba'th and Nasirist parties have little popular support, live in the pan-Arab past, debate irrelevant issues with one another, and separately have been of no real consequence. Other tiny conservative Islamic parties, such as al-Haqq and the Union of Popular Forces, were just that—tiny. With the exception of the Ba'th, these several parties formed the JMP, which showed in the 2006 elections the possibility of credible opposition to the GPC.

Unification witnessed the explosive growth and freedom of newspapers and magazines, while radio and television remained government monopolies. Organized interest groups—civil society organizations or nongovernmental organizations (NGOs)—sprang up by the hundreds and openly voiced their concerns. Although the print media and NGOs continued to be (and remain) outspokenly critical, the Salih regime learned over the years how to subvert them through an array of carrots, sticks, and tricks.

The three parliamentary elections have been to a degree "free and fair." Arguably, the 1993 elections were the most significant because the new Council of Deputies was at that time a focus of attention—even excitement—and, accordingly, of some influence in the newly created ROY. By contrast, the 1997 and 2003 elections were for a legislature that, its formal powers notwithstanding, rarely asserted itself and served largely as a rubber stamp after 1994. Perceiving it as irrelevant, the public dismissed and paid little attention to the legislature, thereby diminishing its role in public discourse and as a shaper of public opinion.

The military played the dominant role in the YAR and an important one in the PDRY. It has come to dominate the present regime. The existence of a ruling "military-tribal-business complex" finds institutional expression in the Military Economic Corporation that dates back to the YAR in the late 1970s. Although falling short of the *makhabarat* (secret police) states elsewhere in the Arab world, both Yemens had security services that were strong and deeply involved in politics. Despite pledges to dismantle them at unification, the security forces have played a strong and growing role since 1994. In particular, the Political Security Organization has become a force of real consequence. Nevertheless, compared to some other countries in the region, there is at present relatively little physical repression in Yemen.

POLITICAL DYNAMICS

Domestic politics since the war of secession, in addition to the imperfect integration of the defeated south, have largely revolved around three issue clusters: the shift from remittances to rents and kleptocracy; economic crisis and failed economic reform; and Yemeni political Islam and global revolutionary Islam.

From Remittances to Rents and Kleptocracy

Many North Yemenis regard the period from the mid-1970s through the mid-1980s as the halcyon years, the best of times. Remittance money flooded into the country from those working abroad, mostly in Saudi Arabia. The remittances were distributed widely—as if magically sprinkled from above—with some of them going directly or indirectly to nearly all families in all parts of the country. In the late 1980s, oil revenues began to flow into North Yemen, at the same time that it continued to receive foreign aid. The situation in the PDRY was very different at this time. Its people benefited from a smaller flow of remittances, its declining Soviet patron had informed it not to expect aid to continue, and prior claims of much oil northeast of Aden proved false.

The creation of the ROY in 1990 held out to most Yemenis hope for a stronger and more prosperous Yemen. These hopes were dashed months later in the wake of Iraq's occupation of Kuwait. Most foreign aid to Yemen was terminated and, more importantly, Saudi Arabia expelled its many Yemeni workers. The latter virtually destroyed Yemen's remittance economy and left it with massive unemployment—having profound implications for its politics.

Claims that Yemen is an emerging democracy notwithstanding, the Salih regime is best described as an oligarchy, an example of rule by the few. Most of the relatively small number of persons and families who get the most of what there is to get—be it political power, economic well-being, or good health—come from the northern highlands of old North Yemen. They have either strong tribal or military (or security) connections, or both. To the military-tribal complex that accumulated power in the YAR in the late 1960s and 1970s was added a northern commercial-business element during the 1980s, the result of an informal "affirmative action" program that favored northern businessmen over their long-dominant colleagues from the southern uplands of North Yemen, especially from Taiz.

From 1990 until 1994, the unification process briefly interrupted this trend toward the concentration of power in the hands of these oligarchs. However, the trend returned after the war of secession, as that event eliminated or weakened politicians from the former PDRY and the YSP. Thereafter, power was further confined to this loose coalition of mostly northern groups. Moreover, late in the 1980s, the decade in which the Salih regime crystallized, the YAR had become the recipient of oil revenues for the first time, as well as of increased economic aid from abroad. The state quickly became a principal source of wealth and private gain for the well-placed and fortunate few. The transformation of the republican state into such a source—something the relatively impoverished imamate had not been—had begun modestly when aid began to flow into the YAR in the mid-1970s. But this trend had been countered by the remittance system under which remittances were spread widely and, most importantly, did not pass through the state.

By the end of the 1990s, the end of the remittance system and the rise in oil (and aid) rents combined to transform the ROY into a special variant of oligarchy, a kleptocracy—government of, by, and for the thieves. The occupants of key government offices through which flow revenues and development aid have been able to use their positions in the state—their "profit centers"—to extract a price for rendering services or granting permissions. The associates, friends, and relatives of occupants of key offices have also been enriched in this manner, the reaping of riches being a matter of connection as well as location.

Graft, bribery, and other forms of corruption pervade all levels of a steeply sided pyramid of patronage. At the base of this pyramid are the hundreds of thousands of government employees and soldiers who are paid extremely low salaries and have to take petty bribes—have to "eat money"—to make ends meet. Perhaps the most visible measures of this corruption high up the pyramid are the growing number of high-end SUVs and new villas—some virtual castles—on the outskirts of San'a, most of which are owned by high government officials on modest salaries. True, many public servants, high and low, choose not to participate in this system, or at least not to participate in it very much. Many other public servants are simply not in offices through which much money flows.

This nouveau aristocracy of shaykhs, officers, and businessmen has a strong sense of entitlement. Its second generation is now slipping into key positions and is even less questioning of its entitlement. This small part of the total population is on the take—and without apology. Some sense that this situation cannot last much longer and that they must get as much as they can while the getting is still good.

The ROY also exhibits arrested statehood, a legacy of North Yemen's history. The Hamid al-Din imamate, as dominant as it was, did not approximate Max Weber's classic definition of a state. It did not have a monopoly on the legitimate use of violence in its territory. In this regard, the description of the Hashid and Bakil tribal confederations as "the wings of the imamate" is suggestive. These tribes and their leaders conceived of themselves, and were perceived by others, as outside and not in or under the imamate, not subject to or subjects of the state.

The YAR's modernists were prevented by events after the 1962 revolution from creating the modern state to which they aspired. The conclusion to the civil war in 1970 dictated that the republic that prevailed would be a conservative one and would preserve much of the traditional order; in particular, it would assure a prominent role for the tribal leaders and tribal system. President al-Hamdi's failed attempt at modern state building allowed arrested statehood to persist into the Salih era.

Reflecting this history, Yemen's state today is in vital ways more like the old imamate than like a modern state. It is severely limited in terms of what it has the power and authority to do and where. Arrested statehood is both cause and effect of the predominantly tribal-military regime that remains firmly in place. The weak state nicely suits a regime inclined to minimize further efforts at state building, especially those that require reining in rampant corruption and incompetence.

Economic Crisis and Reform—and Crisis

By late 1994, Yemen's economy was in free fall and, as then structured, well on its way to becoming nonviable, this despite the steady rise of modest oil revenues. It would be hard to exaggerate the grimness of Yemen's situation. The GDP for 1995 was reduced to less than half its 1990 level; the value of the Yemeni riyal had plunged, raising the cost of goods, especially needed imports. Because of the massive unemployment and loss of remittances, gross inequality and abject poverty were increasing at alarming rates throughout the country.

In mid-1995, the Salih regime agreed with the IMF and World Bank to a program of economic stabilization followed by a program of structural reforms and aid. The premise was that significant IMF/World Bank aid and the major reforms upon which that aid was conditioned would begin to turn the Yemeni economy around. This and the stamp of approval of these bodies would begin to attract other aid donors and, most importantly, private investors, Yemeni and non-Yemeni. The promise was that the belt-tightening initially required of the Yemeni people would produce an economic setting that would attract the investment needed to stimulate business and create jobs.

Yemen's collaboration with the IMF/World Bank on reform followed closely the best-case scenario. In the first year, the Salih regime put in place the stabilization measures and the initial set of structural reforms designed, among other things, to bring inflation under control. Then, in late 1996, the regime took a cautious first step to lift subsidies of essential goods, repeating this process in 1997 and 1998. In return, the IMF/World Bank lent Yemen roughly $1 billion to support reform projects over these years; in addition, they helped organize two donors' conferences that yielded pledges of another $2 billion in aid. IMF commitments also paved the way for a big reduction by the Paris Club of Yemen's foreign debt.

The IMF/World Bank structural-reform program faltered in late 1997, political protests and the sharp decline in oil revenues being major culprits behind the failure. Perhaps more importantly, some of the new reforms reached beyond the poor majority and directly threatened the interests of the privileged and highly placed. Among them were measures designed to fight corruption, increase transparency, make the courts fairer and more efficient, and reform the banking and financial sectors. Many of the well-off simply lost whatever appetite they had had for reform.

Nevertheless, a new IMF/World Bank agreement calling for the broadening and deepening of reform was negotiated in 2000. It required the complete lifting of most subsidies and the loss of many jobs through a downsizing of the civil service and the privatizing of bloated public corporations. Within a year, however, the program was virtually abandoned. Most of the measures agreed to were not implemented or were done so partially and halfheartedly. Reforms of the judiciary and the civil service lagged, and the rampant corruption in the public and private sectors was barely addressed, except verbally.

As a consequence, Yemen failed to attract foreign and Yemeni investors in the late 1990s and later. Wealthy Yemenis who had jumped in early, especially those with origins in Wadi Hadhramawt, quickly retreated after bad personal experiences or hearing the woeful tales of others. Many potential foreign investors decided that the risks were too great relative to gains, based partly on a number of well-publicized cases of corruption, nepotism, and political favoritism.

As with the IMF/World Bank program, major development projects failed to move forward rapidly or fell short of expectations. The Aden free zone and container port project, touted in the early 1990s as Yemen's most important, promised to create thousands of jobs and much wealth. In operation in 2000, after numerous delays, the project failed to meet expectations. In addition to increasing security issues in the region, a big part of the problem had to do with mismanagement and corruption. Similarly, the development of Yemen's natural gas reserves was delayed until 2005 partly by fighting between two groups of Yemeni politicians, each with its own multinational gas developer as client.

Despite higher oil revenues in 2005, due to soaring prices, the overall performance of the economy did not improve. The growth rates of the GDP and job creation were at best barely keeping up with the high population growth rate of about 3.5 percent. Levels of unemployment, malnourishment, and those living below the poverty line persistently held at about 40 percent. The pauperization of the shrinking middle class continued, and the modern institutions in which they worked and had come to place their hopes for a better future were hollowed out. The gap between the rich few and the many poor grew wider—and more visibly so. The education system declined, and medical services were in shorter supply and of poorer quality. On the personal level, most Yemenis had lost hope and were ground down by the effort of trying to make ends meet. More and more people were openly expressing anger and seemed ready to act in terms of it.

Arguably, Yemen's economy and society had ceased to be viable and sustainable by 2009. As importantly, despite public pronouncements, the Salih system clearly seemed to lack the will and capacity to adopt and implement reforms needed to restore Yemen's viability and sustainability. Behind this lack were Yemen's oligarchs—its kleptocrats—and the pyramid of patronage they had come to depend on. The limited capacities of the state made it unlikely that they could do what had to be done, even if they wanted to. They seemed unable to act in terms of their own self-interest—their survival—much less in the interest of Yemen and its people.

Yemeni Political Islam and Global Revolutionary Islam

Modern political Islam came to North Yemen when the Muslim Brotherhood started a branch there in 1947. The brotherhood survived the 1962 revolution and persisted into the republican era; indeed, in the 1970s, it was regarded by successive regimes as a major threat due to its organization and grassroots support. Its top leader in the 1970s was Abd al-Majid al-Zindani, the spiritual leader of Islah since 1990.

The growth of political Islam in Yemen and the role of al-Zindani in that process were largely the result of Saudi Arabia's systematic use of Islam for foreign policy purposes. First, the Saudis tried to influence the YAR in the 1970s and 1980s by promoting their brand of Salafi fundamentalism, Wahhabism, through its schools, or "scientific institutes." Second, the Saudis in the 1980s recruited a disproportionately large number of Yemenis for the jihad against the Soviet forces in Afghanistan, a struggle that served as the incubator for the next generation's global revolutionary Islam. Al-Zindani, working for Saudis, was deeply involved in the promotion of Salafism in Yemen and then in the jihadist project in Afghanistan.

When Soviet forces withdrew at the end of the 1980s, many of the radicalized and battle-hardened Yemeni "Afghani Arabs" came home. Many of them were caught up by 1990 in the politics of both the Gulf War and Yemeni unification, the former causing them to perceive the United States and Saudi Arabia, not the defunct Soviet Union, as Islam's main enemies. Some of them created Yemeni Islamic Jihad (YIJ).

As political conflict between the GPC and the YSP escalated after 1991, President Salih turned a blind eye to the killing of southern leaders by returning militants with old scores to settle. His long-time colleague Ali Muhsin al-Ahmar folded many of the Afghani Arabs into units of the northern army, and many of them participated in the war of secession in 1994, placing the Salih regime in debt to them. Thereafter, when the regime balked at their demands, armed conflict occasionally occurred between them and the security forces.

In the mid-1990s, preoccupied with the YSP, President Salih had viewed militant political Islam largely as a troublesome domestic matter. The bombing of the Goldmur Hotel in Aden at the end of 1992 by YIJ targeted American military personnel staying there. Yemeni forces responded with the arrest of Tarik al-Fadhli, an Afghani Arab leader of YIJ and an heir to one of the sultanates abolished in 1967 by the NLF. Al-Fadhli soon "escaped," and he and some of his followers soon pledged loyalty to President Salih. Some of al-Fadhli's colleagues who refused to go over to the regime created the Aden-Abyan Islamic Army (AAIA), a group with which the Salih regime waged a low-intensity fight over the rest of the 1990s.

In late 1998, the death in Abyan of four tourists kidnapped by the AAIA suggested that the Islamists posed a broader threat to the Salih regime. The sequence of events had started some days earlier with the arrest near Aden of several armed young Muslims from Britain. The AAIA's kidnapping of the mostly British tourists had been requested by Abu Hamza al-Masri, the father of one of those jailed and a militant Muslim preacher in London. Relations between Yemen and Britain became strained and, alarmed by these events, the government quickly tried the kidnappers and executed their leader.

The Salih regime became increasingly concerned with al-Qa'ida after militants bombed the USS *Cole* in Aden in fall 2000. In late 2001, Yemeni troops near Marib failed dramatically in an attempt to eliminate Qaid Sinan al-Harithi, a Yemeni al-Qa'ida leader and alleged mastermind of the *Cole* bombing. Major events rocked the regime in 2002: the suicide bombing of the French oil tanker *Limburg* off Yemen's southern coast; the killing of al-Harithi with a rocket from a US drone in a strike coordinated with a Yemeni regime that had hoped to keep its involvement secret; and the assassination by a militant of YSP's thinker-activist Jarullah Omar and the murder two days later of three American medical missionaries by another militant, a colleague of Jarullah's assassin. In mid-2003, the ambushing by AAIA of a military convoy led to a battle in which several of the dozens of militants were killed. Among the participants were persons involved in the *Cole* and *Limburg* bombings who had recently escaped from prison in Aden.

On another front, President Salih moved in 2002 to bring the Salafi schools—"scientific institutes"—under government control and to close down unofficial religious schools. The state also removed militant ulema from mosques, replacing them with moderates. Both efforts triggered outcries of interference and censorship.

Having pledged full support for the War on Terror after 9/11, President Salih had to balance meeting US demands against a domestic political landscape marked by Yemeni nationalism, strong Islamic sensibilities, and growing anti-American feelings. As importantly, a number of military officers and politicians inside the Salih regime were themselves militant Islamists or politically tied to them (e.g., Ali Muhsin al-Ahmar). From the *Cole* bombing and 9/11 on, President Salih picked his way carefully, but imperfectly and with difficulty, among these often contradictory forces.

Criticized by both secular nationalists and Islamists, President Salih in late 2002 tapped Qadi Hamoud al-Hitar to head the Religious Dialogue Council responsible for reeducating persons charged with terrorist activities. Between then and 2005, some 364 of those who went through the rehabilitation program were released and often provided with no-show jobs in the military. Whatever else it did, this program did lessen some of the domestic political pressure on President Salih.

The coming of the Houthi Rebellion illustrates the complexities Islamic politics in Yemen posed for President Salih. Husayn al-Houthi, who had helped found al-Haqq and was elected to the Council of Deputies in 1993, also founded a network of Zaydi schools in Sa'da and a youth movement, the Believing Youth. President Salih had supported al-Houthi's efforts, concerned as he had become about the assertiveness of the Salafis with whom he had allied himself earlier in his struggle with the YSP. But when the Houthis began challenging the Salih regime, the president responded. He directed the governor of Sa'da to crack down on the movement—and he did. In response, al-Houthi launched his rebellion. Thereafter, the large, indiscriminant military response, which was led by Ali Muhsin al-Ahmar, served to deepen and perpetuate the rebellion.

FOREIGN POLICY

In the face of the escalating conflict with the YSP, President Salih by 1992 saw maintaining external support for unification to be a major concern. During that year, Saudi Arabia approached the YSP and offered support if it sought to secede. During the war of secession that followed, the Salih regime tried to stall implementation of a UN cease-fire until its forces had won; it feared that a cease-fire and troop pullback would mean de facto repartition. Saudi Arabia, which by this time was aiding the secessionists materially, urged the United States to support a quick cease-fire. President Salih's representative shuttled between UN headquarters and Washington, DC, trying to hold the United States off until Aden fell—and he succeeded.

Thereafter, priority was placed on undoing the damage caused by Yemen's failure to join the US- and Saudi-led effort to expel Iraq from Kuwait in 1990. This mainly involved efforts to restore good relations with Kuwait, Saudi Arabia, and the United States. Good relations meant foreign aid and, in the case of Yemen's neighbors, the possibility of jobs, revived remittances, and a neighborhood safe for foreign investment and tourism.

Focused on these concerns, Yemen was taken by surprise in 1995 by armed conflict with newly independent Eritrea over a cluster of tiny Red Sea islands. Although angered by Eritrea's seizure of the islands and capture of Yemeni forces, Yemen dealt in a statesmanlike way with a situation that, if allowed to spin out of control, could have scared off investors and tourists. The dispute was submitted to international arbitration and resolved amicably in 1998, the bulk of the islands going to Yemen.

Among the Arab Gulf states, Kuwait was the most reluctant to forgive, mindful of its long history of aid to Yemen. Yemen's persistence finally resulted in the reestablishment of relations in 2000. Over the second half of the 1990s, relations with Oman, Qatar, and the United Arab Emirates also improved. The Salih regime campaigned hard to join the Gulf Cooperation Council (GCC), but its requests were denied; it was, however, allowed to join some GCC bodies, and full membership was held out as a future probability.

Ambivalent about reconciliation after 1994, Saudi Arabia financed vocal Yemeni dissidents in London and elsewhere. In addition, subsidies paid to the tribes helped make it possible for them to carry out the many kidnappings that made investors and tourists wary. Clearly, however, the biggest obstacle to the restoration of good relations between the two neighbors remained their long undemarcated border, for decades and even very recently the source of violent incidents. Rather suddenly, but after years of negotiations, a June 2000 agreement covering the entire border removed this thorn in the side of Saudi-Yemeni relations. Yemen gave up all claims to the "northern provinces" seized by Saudi Arabia in 1934, and the Saudis made some concessions along the long desert border east to Oman.

Thereafter, some Saudi aid began to flow, and some Yemeni workers were allowed to return to the kingdom. With the May 2003 terrorist bombings in Riyadh, the Saudis increased pressure on Yemen regarding security along their porous border. Over the next few years, the neighbors strengthened their extradition treaty, exchanged dozens of wanted prisoners, and agreed to undertake joint operations to block border infiltration and smuggling. Nevertheless, the Saudis did grow increasingly annoyed in mid-decade as it became apparent that Yemeni frontier forces were sometimes parties to border violations. In early 2006, the escape of twenty-three high-profile terrorists from the main security prison in San'a, apparently with help from security forces, alarmed and angered the Saudis, as did similar, less dramatic events over the next two years.

Late in the decade, however, faced with the worsening Houthi rebellion, the resurgence of al-Qa'ida in Yemen, and the possibility that the growing chaos in Somalia could be replicated next door, the Saudis found themselves in the unfamiliar position of providing major support to the Salih regime and Yemeni unification. It is rumored that Saudi Arabia provided as much as $2 billion in 2009 to cover the budget shortfall caused by declining oil revenues. Beginning in November 2009, moreover, the Saudis took cross-border military action by the Houthis as cause for unleashing sustained aircraft and artillery strikes against the Houthis along that border. Although secondary, ground actions were also carried out. Coordinated with, but separate from, the Yemeni military's ongoing Operation Scorched Earth, the Saudi intervention amounted to part of a major effort to put down the Houthi Rebellion once and for all.

Long concerned about the turmoil in Somalia and the mass exodus of refugees to Yemen, the Salih regime also became concerned about the United States' tendency to view these and other events on the Horn of Africa in terms of its War on Terror. In 2002 President Salih convened a summit with the presidents of Sudan and Ethiopia. This led to the formation of the San'a Forum for Cooperation, which thereafter met annually, later including the president of Djibouti and sometimes the president of Somalia. The forum addressed, with little effect, the worsening situation in Somalia, Ethiopia's major and the United States' limited intervention in that country, and Eritrea's conflicts with both Ethiopia and Djibouti. The dramatic increase in Somali piracy and the international community's response with naval forces were high on the forum's agenda late in the decade.

The United States had drastically reduced relations with and aid to Yemen after the latter failed to support action against Iraq at the United Nations in November 1990. Relations began to thaw in mid-1994 during the war of secession when Washington sided with a unified Yemen. In 1995, the United States strongly backed the IMF/World Bank aid-for-reform package with Yemen and, in something of a first, publicly chastised Saudi Arabia for its attempt to pressure oil companies to refrain from activity near its disputed border with Yemen. Military ties increased modestly in 1997 with, for example, the refueling of US warships in Aden. Still, the rebuilding of strong relations, desired by Yemen, was simply not high on the US list of priorities.

Two events caused the United States to reorder its priorities: the bombing of the USS *Cole* in 2000 and, far more crucial, the suicide bombings in New York City and Washington, DC, on September 11. The latter made US-Yemeni relations much more salient and made global revolutionary Islam and terror the main focus of those relations. Days after 9/11, President Salih flew to Washington and pledged full support for the War on Terror. US aid to Yemen, especially military, was increased significantly. For its part, the Salih regime stepped up its effort against militants in Yemen, arresting many and trying some. The arrest in late 2003 of Muhammad Hamdi Al Ahdal, an al-Qa'ida leader in Yemen, was notable.

Thereafter, the dynamics of US-Yemeni relations were characterized by Washington's insistence on Yemen's full support in the War on Terror and Yemen's attempt to do as much as politically possible to meet this demand. The Salih regime clearly wanted to avoid repeating the punishment meted out in 1990. Still, the new relationship was an uneasy one. President Salih tried to do what Washington wanted, but in a manner the Yemeni public would find politically palatable. When caught in a dilemma, he usually chose to risk angering Washington rather than his domestic audience. Early on, when Washington sought to connect the dots all the way back to Usama Bin Laden in the *Cole* investigation, President Salih balked out of fear that the dots might come uncomfortably close to Yemenis in high places.

The United States has been insensitive to the Salih regime's political situation. When al-Harithi, the Yemeni al-Qa'ida leader, was killed in late 2002 by a Hellfire missile fired from a US Predator drone deep in Yemeni airspace but controlled from Djibouti, Washington's public self-congratulations embarrassed and angered the regime. The response was similar when Muhammad Ali Hassan Al Moayad, a well-known cleric from Sana'a, was entrapped by the FBI in Germany in 2003, extradited to the United States, and then tried and convicted for financing terrorism. In 2004, over Yemeni objections, Washington placed Shaikh Al Zindani, spiritual leader of Islah, on its list of supporters of terrorism; then, in 2006, it asked Yemen to extradite him. Finally, the detaining of many Yemenis at Guantanamo since 2001 has been an affront to Yemenis and hard for the regime to explain to its people. As other detainees were released, leaving a big plurality of Yemenis among those remaining, the issue became a source of growing acrimony. Finally, behind Washington's preference that Yemeni returnees from Guantanamo go for rehabilitation in Saudi Arabia rather than Yemen is the open secret that the United States does not believe that Yemen is up to the task.

The US invasion of Iraq in 2003 was a political nightmare for President Salih. He tried, with difficulty, to distinguish between Washington's action in Iraq and the effort against terror, opposing the former and supporting the latter. He was not helped by President George W. Bush's efforts to equate the invasion with the War on Terror. Nevertheless, beginning in 2003, a stream of senior officials from US Central Command, the Defense Department, and the State Department visited, usually bringing praise and promises of additional aid. The inauguration of the US-trained coast guard with US-supplied gunboats in spring 2004 was accompanied by a pledge of more aid. The lifting of the fourteen-year-old ban on the supply of new military equipment was announced and the possibility of again refueling warships at Aden was raised.

In early 2006, however, questions about Yemen's willingness and ability to do its part in the effort against terrorism were raised anew by the escape of the twenty-three convicted terrorists, including top al-Qa'ida figures in the *Cole* and *Limburg* bombings. US confidence was shaken further when it was learned that, after release from prison, three graduates of Qadi al-Hitar's "dialogue" process had turned up as suicide bombers in Iraq. In addition, convicted terrorists sought by the United States were freed or placed under loose house arrest in 2007 and 2008. Enraged by one of the cases, Washington abruptly called off the ceremony restoring previously canceled aid to Yemen.

On matters of reform, the United States had by 2000 made President Salih a symbol of democratization and economic reform in the Middle East. At the meeting of the Group of 8 countries in the United States in 2004, Salih was a guest and was praised for supporting Washington's call for a new initiative on these issues in the region. Later that year, with US backing, Yemen joined with Turkey and Italy to administer a new political program, the Democratic Assistance Dialogue.

By that time, however, a growing number of donors had begun to criticize Yemen over economic reform and governance—and to act on the criticism. In February 2004, the IMF and World Bank expressed their impatience and displeasure with Yemen's failure to completely lift subsidies and implement civil service reforms designed to address corruption and inefficiency. They warned that continued aid remained contingent on Yemen's keeping its part of the aid-for-reform bargain. In early 2005, the World Bank president repeated the same warning.

The donor community, now joined by the United States, kept up the pressure. In October 2005, the US ambassador to Yemen flatly asserted that the country's progress toward democracy had halted. A month later, President Salih was surprised on a visit to Washington when he was told that Yemen was no longer eligible for a grant under the Millennium Challenge Account because of its failure to control corruption and promote good governance and individual freedom. The following month, the World Bank announced a one-third reduction of its aid to Yemen—from $420 to $280 million—for the same reasons. In February 2006, the ambassadors of Yemen's top donors—the United States, the United Kingdom, Germany, and the Netherlands—met together with President Salih and told him that their countries wanted to see concrete measures quickly taken to address problems with corruption, transparency, and other issues of governance.

Attacks on Western targets in San'a in 2008, especially the US embassy, together with evidence that the new generation of leaders of al-Qa'ida on the Arabian Peninsula (AQAP) were willing to wage jihad in Yemen, restored lagging cooperation between Washington and the Salih regime. High-level visits increased, and projected military assistance in 2009, although still miniscule, was about double that of 2007. By the beginning of 2009, the United States was sending CIA antiterrorism specialists and Special Forces commandos tasked with training and equipping Yemeni forces. In September 2009, Washington revived its moribund aid program with Yemen and signed a three-year $120 million "stabilization program" to create jobs and improve health and other social services.

On December 17, based on intelligence that AQAP was about to launch suicide attacks on Western targets in San'a, Yemen carried out a major air attack on AQAP bases in Abyan and Arhab, aided by US "firepower, intelligence and other support," killing thirty-four. At the same time, arrests were made in San'a. On December 24, another major air strike in Shabwa targeted an alleged meeting of top leaders of AQAP, producing many casualties.

The new collaboration between the United States and Yemen seemed vindicated by the failed attempt to blow up a commercial jet over Detroit on Christmas Day 2009 by a young Nigerian who had studied Arabic and probably been groomed as a suicide bomber in Yemen in 2004 and 2005 and again in August to November 2009. However, collaboration came at the risk of perceptions of Yemeni subservience to an increasingly disliked United States. Civilian casualties threatened to lessen support for both the United States and the Salih regime—and to win support for, and recruits to, AQAP, the Houthis, and the Southern Movement.

PROSPECTS

The performance of the Salih regime since 1995 does not augur well for Yemen's future. Bluntly, the regime has demonstrated the lack of will and capacity, especially political capacity, to do what has to be done to make Yemen viable and sustainable—and to make it again a land of some promise for most of its people.

What makes this so depressing is that Yemen, through its limited oil resources, had by 1990 acquired the means to accomplish what was necessary. Instead of pursuing that goal, the Salih regime has over the past twenty years largely squandered the revenues from its soon-to-be-depleted oil reserves. It has also failed to implement the more demanding reforms—in particular, those called for by the IMF and World Bank—required to make Yemen attractive for investors, Yemeni and non-Yemeni. The main culprits are the kleptocracy that the Salih regime became and the systemic corruption it spawned.

The Republic of Yemen in 2009 qualified as a failing state, its support and legitimacy largely drained away. If it is not very soon to become a failed state in a broken society, then a reformed Salih regime or a successor must institute needed reforms and make better use of modest gas reserves than the government has in the case of Yemen's oil reserves. More important than depleting oil and gas reserves, the rapid depletion of Yemen's water resources makes this a race against time. In the absence of managed water use, the country's ancient and once ample aquifers are being drawn down far more rapidly than they are being recharged. At the same time, its population growth rate is one of the highest in the world. Simply put, Yemen risks running out of the water required to sustain its projected population.

Again, the regime's abysmal stewardship since 1990 provides little cause for hope. The relevant political markers are the parliamentary elections rescheduled for 2011 and the next presidential elections in 2013. Either the Salih regime will rein in the pyramid of patronage and the rampant corruption it supports and depends upon, or it will be replaced or reconfigured by political forces that will try to do what needs doing. If the regime or an elected successor proves unable to do this—if it lacks the required will and capacity—then the door will open to the possibility of state failure, serious violence, and even civil war or chaos. The models of Afghanistan, Lebanon, and even Somalia are relevant to the Yemeni case.

BIBLIOGRAPHY

For background on North Yemen and its political history, see Robert W. Stookey, *Yemen: The Politics of the Yemen Arab Republic* (Boulder, CO: Westview Press, 1978); Manfred W. Wenner, *Modern Yemen, 1918–1966* (Baltimore: Johns

Hopkins Press, 1967); and Robert D. Burrowes, *The Yemen Arab Republic: The Politics of Development, 1962–1986* (Boulder, CO: Westview Press, 1987).

For background on South Yemen and its political history, see Robert W. Stookey, *South Yemen: A Marxist Republic in Arabia* (Boulder, CO: Westview Press, 1982), and Helen Lackner, *PDR Yemen* (London: Ithaca Press, 1985).

On both countries, see Fred Halladay, *Arabia Without Sultans* (London: Penguin Books, 1974), and Robin Bidwell, *The Two Yemens* (Boulder, CO: Westview Press, 1983).

For developments before and since unity, see Sheila Carapico, *Civil Society in Yemen* (Cambridge: Cambridge University Press, 1998); Paul Dresch, *A History of Modern Yemen* (Cambridge: Cambridge University Press, 2000); and Sarah Phillips, *Yemen's Democracy Experiment in Regional Perspective: Patronage and Pluralism* (New York: Palgrave Macmillan, 2008).

On external relations and foreign policy, see Fred Halladay, *Revolution and Foreign Policy: The Case of South Yemen, 1967–1987* (Cambridge: Cambridge University Press, 1989), and F. Gregory Gause III, *Saudi-Yemeni Relations: Domestic Structures and Foreign Influence* (New York: Columbia University Press, 1990).

On the tribes and tribalism, see Paul Dresch, *Tribes, Government and History in Yemen* (Oxford: Oxford University Press, 1989), and Steven C. Caton, *Peaks of Yemen I Summon: Poetry as Performance in a North Yemeni Tribe* (Berkeley: University of California Press, 1990). On law and religion, see Brinkley Messick, *The Calligraphic State: Textual Domination and History in a Muslim Society* (Berkeley: University of California Press, 1993), and Bernard Haykel, *Revival and Reform in Islam: The Legacy of Muhammad al-Shawkani* (Cambridge: Cambridge University Press, 2003). On qat, see John G. Kennedy, *The Flower of Paradise: The Institutionalized Use of the Drug Qat in North Yemen* (Dordrecht, Holland: D. Reidel Publishing Co., 1987).

For an encyclopedia and bibliography on both Yemens, see Robert D. Burrowes, *Historical Dictionary of Yemen*, 2nd ed. (Lanham, MD: Scarecrow Press, 2010). And for good reads, see Steven C. Caton, *Yemen Chronicle: An Anthropology of War and Mediation* (New York: Hill and Wang, 2005), and Tim MacIntosh Smith, *Yemen: Travels in Dictionary Land* (London: John Murray, 1997).

8

REPUBLIC OF LEBANON

William Harris

HISTORICAL BACKGROUND

Lebanon's commercial self-image, sense of history, and even genetic markers trace back to the Phoenician traders who gave the world the alphabet and set out across the Mediterranean from the coast of Mount Lebanon more than 3,000 years ago. Tyre, Sidon, and Jubayl (Byblos) were early Phoenician centers, while Tripoli was a later Phoenician foundation, Baalbek a Hellenistic provincial town, and Beirut a Roman veterans' colony. The Ituraean hill clans of Mount Lebanon proved recalcitrant for many decades after Roman occupation around 60 BCE. The population of both the coastal towns and the hills gradually converted from paganism to Christianity, particularly from the third century CE onward, and there is evidence of Arab tribal infiltration of Mount Lebanon in late Roman times.

Modern Lebanon's character as a conglomerate of sectarian communities dates not from antiquity but from the aftermath of the Islamic conquest of the Roman Levant in 636 to 640. Mount Lebanon and its surrounds witnessed an influx of Muslim Arabs in the seventh and eighth centuries and conversion of part of the local population to Islam. Sidon, Beirut, and Tripoli became citadels of Sunni Islam on the seafront against Byzantium, while dissident Shi'a communities arose in the central and southern hills. The latter reflected the limited ability of the Umayyad (660–750) and Abbasid (750–1258) regimes to exert authority in the Lebanese hills.

Simultaneously, Mount Lebanon continued to host a substantial Christian population. In the late seventh century, a new Christian sect penetrated the area from northern Syria. These Maronites originated around the monastery of Maro in the Orontes Valley and, by the ninth century, represented the predominant Christian group in Mount Lebanon. Orthodox Christians were reduced to minorities in the Sunni ports and to a few rural pockets.

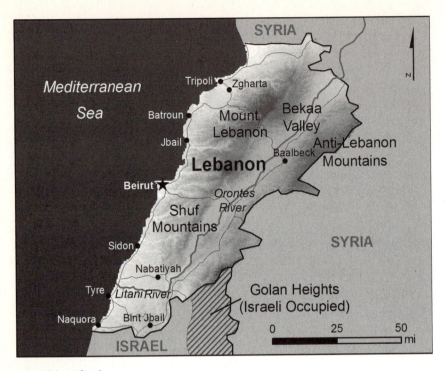

Republic of Lebanon

Like the Christians, the Muslims of Mount Lebanon diversified as Abbasid authority contracted after the mid-ninth century. Twelver Shi'as dominated the coastal hills south of Sidon and much of the Biqa Valley. In contrast, the more mystical Isma'ili version of Shi'ism, with belief in a line of seven imams, gained sympathizers in southern Biqa and the hills near Beirut. When the Isma'ili Fatimid caliph al-Hakim died in Egypt in 1021, a call went out to his followers to give him allegiance as a manifestation of the divine on earth. The Tanukh chiefs of central Mount Lebanon took up the call, thus establishing the Druze sect.

The Seljuk Turks overthrew Twelver Shi'a influence in Iraq and pushed back Isma'ili Fatimid rule in Syria, heralding renewed Sunni Islamic domination of the Levant, later confirmed by the Mamluks of Egypt and the Ottoman Turks. The crusader presence in Mount Lebanon for almost two centuries (1099–1291) gave the mountain communities—Maronites, Druze, and Shi'as—a critical opportunity to consolidate and play between the Frankish coast and the Muslim interior. By the time of Sultan Baybars and the Mamluk ascendancy, the Maronites, Druze, and Shi'as were entrenched.

After capturing Tripoli (1109), Beirut (1110), and Tyre (1124), the Franks dominated Mount Lebanon through the Kingdom of Jerusalem from Beirut southward and the County of Tripoli to the north. The Druze lords were divided in their alliances, those in the Shuf having good relations with the Franks in Sidon and those inland from Beirut leaning toward the emirate of Damascus. The majority of the Maronites sided with the Franks, and their patriarchate entered a de facto union with the Roman Catholic Church. Some Christians in the north even aided Muslim incursions. Despite Salah al-Din's defeat of the Kingdom of Jerusalem in 1187, the crusader revival of the early thirteenth century upheld this pattern of affairs until the Mamluk offensives of 1265 to 1291.

All the mountain communities were subject to Mamluk suspicion and punishments in the late thirteenth century, but the new Sunni Muslim masters of the Levant soon relented regarding the Druze and Maronites. They concentrated their hostility on the Shi'as of the Kisrawan hills, which weakened the Shi'a presence there and facilitated later Maronite immigration.

The Ottoman conquest of the Levant in 1516 did not suit some Druze, particularly the Ma'n lords, and they rebelled through the sixteenth century. The Ottomans sought to manage the Druze, Turcoman, and Shi'a chiefs of Mount Lebanon, Tripoli, and the Beka'a Valley by a mixture of coercion and sharing out administrative appointments. In 1593, they made the Druze leader Fakhr al-Din Ma'n, who pretended to be a Sunni Muslim, governor of the subprovince of Beirut-Sidon. In the early seventeenth century, Fakhr al-Din carved out a personal principality including all of modern Lebanon, at different stages deposing the Ottoman governors of Tripoli and Damascus. After 1607, he hosted refugee relatives of the rebellious Kurdish lord of Aleppo, Ali Janbalad. One of these married into the Druze community to found the Jumblat family, later Druze leaders. Fakhr al-Din also reopened Mount Lebanon to Europe and aligned himself with Tuscany. Most significantly, Fakhr al-Din associated with leading Maronites, particularly the Al Khazens, and encouraged Maronite peasants to move south toward the Druze areas. At the same time, the Vatican restored its relations with the Maronite Church with the 1598 establishment of a college in Rome to train Maronite priests. Fakhr al-Din's ambitions were too much for the Ottomans, who overthrew and executed him in 1635. Nonetheless, Istanbul tolerated the continuation in central Mount Lebanon of the Ma'n family's de facto principality, which became more entrenched after the Shihab relatives of the Ma'ns took it over in 1697.

In the eighteenth and early nineteenth centuries, the balance among the communities of Mount Lebanon and its surrounds changed. The Druze declined vis-à-vis the Maronites, who prospered from silk production and trade with Europe. The Shihabs, as the preeminent Ottoman tax farmers, identified with their Maronite allies. The leading branch of the family converted from Sunni Islam to Maronite

LEBANON

Capital city	Beirut
Chief of state	President Michel Sulayman
Head of government	Prime Minister Fuad Siniora
Major political coalitions and parties (share of most recent vote)	*14 March Coalition* (45.3%); Democratic Gathering Bloc, Democratic Left, Democratic Renewal Movement, Future Movement Bloc, Kataeb Party, Lebanese Forces, Tripoli Independent Bloc; *8 March Coalition* (54.7%); Development and Resistance Bloc, Free Patriotic Movement, Loyalty to the Resistance Bloc, Nasserite Popular Movement, Popular Bloc, Syrian Ba'th Party, Syrian Social Nationalist Party
Ethnic groups	Arab (95%), Armenian (4%), other (1%)
Religious groups	Muslim (59.7%), Christian (39%), other (1.3%)
Export partners	Syria (23.9%), United Arab Emirates (12.4%), Switzerland (7.2%), Saudi Arabia (5.9%), Turkey (4%)
Import partners	Syria (10.7%), France (9.7%), United States (9.5%), Italy (7.4%), China (6.7%), Germany (5%), Saudi Arabia (4.9%), Turkey (4.3%)

Catholicism. Further, in the late eighteenth century, the Ottoman governor of Acre, Ahmad al-Jazzar, devastated Shi'a southern Lebanon. Shi'as were suspect because of their relations with Iran and were at odds with the Sunni Ottomans after the Safavid conversion of Iranians to Twelver Shi'ism with Lebanese Shi'a assistance in the sixteenth century.

After 1820, Bashir II Shihab repressed the Druze chiefs, most prominently Bashir Jumblat, and backed Muhammad Ali of Egypt against Istanbul. The Maronite Church, which flourished under the Shihabs, encouraged Maronite peasants against Maronite and Druze landlords. Bashir II's Egyptian allies occupied

Syria in 1832, and the Shihabi principality collapsed when the British sponsored an Ottoman restoration in 1840. Druze fear of the Maronite advance through the Kisrawan into the Druze districts interacted with Maronite peasant ferment to plunge Mount Lebanon into twenty years of turbulence, exacerbated by Ottoman weakness and manipulation. Sunnis and Shi'as also resented the Christian commercial gains from European penetration. In 1860, the animosities exploded into a Maronite/Druze war in the mountains east and south of Beirut. Despite Maronite numerical superiority, Druze skill and cohesion carried the day. Druze massacred thousands of Christian males, including many non-Maronites. The legacy of the trauma persists to the present.

Ironically, the massacres brought European military intervention and a political settlement to Christian advantage. Most of Mount Lebanon became an autonomous province (*mutasarrifiyya*) with a non-Lebanese Christian governor appointed by the sultan with the consent of the five great European powers. The arrangement involved a prominent role for an elected administrative council, with fixed representation for each major sect and a Christian, but not a Maronite, majority. The police force would be locally recruited. The autonomous province had a Christian majority of over 80 percent, with Maronites alone comprising over half of the population. It did not incorporate the port cities or the Biqa, which remained parts of regular Ottoman provinces. It was not ideal from the Maronite perspective, but it provided a stable environment until 1914 and a platform for more ambitious scenarios.

Contacts between Lebanon and the West intensified between 1860 and 1914. Foreign missionaries spearheaded an educational and intellectual florescence. Presbyterians from the United States founded the American University of Beirut in 1866, and French Jesuits established Saint Joseph University in 1875. Economically, Beirut profited from European trade with the Syrian interior, but Mount Lebanon stagnated and could not support the growing Maronite population, which now had little scope for further territorial expansion. Increasing numbers of Maronites moved into Beirut, where Sunni Muslims were a minority after 1850.

In the late nineteenth century, Lebanese Christians faced greater political and cultural pressure. Ottoman attempts to sustain themselves as the Balkans slipped out of their control became more colored with Islamic overtones and political repression. Economic and political uncertainties caused thousands of Maronites and other Christians to leave for the United States, Latin America, and Australia after 1880.

World War I terminated four centuries of Ottoman rule in the Levant. Allied wartime agreements allocated Mount Lebanon and its surrounds to the French, who in 1920 created the political entity of Greater Lebanon—the modern Lebanese territorial state—under a mandate from the League of Nations. At the insistence of France's Maronite friends, this area encompassed not just the former autonomous province but also Beirut, Tripoli, Sidon, southern Lebanon, the Biqa

Valley, and the Akkar region in the north. France hoped that a larger Lebanon would be more economically and strategically viable. The expansion brought substantial numbers of Sunnis and Shi'as into the new state, reducing the Christian preponderance to a razor-thin majority of 51 percent, according to modern Lebanon's first and last census in 1932. It also stimulated lasting hostility from the new Syrian state founded by the French in the interior.

In Beirut, France sponsored a more complex version of the sectarian power sharing inaugurated in the Ottoman autonomous province. By the 1930s, Sunnis and Shi'as had become reconciled to Greater Lebanon, while many Maronites became less patient with French domination. The French mandatory authorities promulgated a constitution in 1926, allowing the Lebanese to elect a parliament and choose a president, but they suspended the constitution in 1932 and 1939. Friction with the French led many Lebanese to embrace alternative political philosophies, especially socialism and Arab and Syrian nationalism. The French High Commission in Beirut established the economic and bureaucratic infrastructure of modern Lebanon, though they concentrated investment in port facilities, electricity, and roads in Beirut and central Mount Lebanon, neglecting the Sunni and Shi'a peripheries. World War II brought the end of French rule. The British army seized Lebanon in 1941 after the German occupation of France and, in 1943, forced the "Free French" to grant independence to the Lebanese.

POLITICAL ENVIRONMENT

Physical Geography

Lebanon comprises four major geographical elements: a coastal plain, Mount Lebanon, the Biqa Valley, and the Anti-Lebanon Mountains. The coastal plain varies in width from about eight miles (twelve kilometers) in the north to almost nothing in places. Most of the major towns of the country are on this plain, including the three largest—Beirut, Tripoli, and Sidon. Mount Lebanon, from the Akkar in the north to the Barouk range and the hills of Jabal 'Aamil in the south, rises abruptly from the plain. The highest peaks of the coastal massif are inland from Tripoli and Beirut, within fifteen miles (about twenty kilometers) of the coast. These stand between 8,000 and 10,000 feet (2,500 and 3,000 meters) and carry heavy snow in winter and spring.

The fertile Biqa Valley lies between Mount Lebanon and the Anti-Lebanon range. It is a trench with much of the floor about 3,000 feet above sea level, bounded by fault lines that express Lebanon's potential vulnerability to earthquakes. It is widest north of Baalbek, where it gives rise to the Orontes River that flows north into Syria. In most of the valley, however, the Litani River is the main water source. The Litani flows southward, making a right-angle turn west toward the Mediterranean about twelve miles (less than twenty kilometers) north of the Israeli border. To the east, the Anti-Lebanon Mountains are partly in Lebanon and partly in Syria; the boundary between the two countries departs from ridge lines in places and is not well demarcated. These mountains are a little lower than Mount Lebanon and receive much less rainfall. At 9,232 feet (2,900 meters), Mount Hermon on the Syrian-Lebanese-Israeli border is the highest peak.

Mount Lebanon receives the most reliable rainfall in the Levant. Lebanon is the only country in the region fully self-sufficient in water resources, though high population density and poor regulation of use have led to severe pollution problems.

People

In the Middle East, Lebanon represents a unique coalescence of Christian and Muslim communities and of Western and Islamic influences. Its mountains have been a refuge for minority religious groups, and its large Christian population and central coastal position in the Levant have made it a gateway for European cultural and economic penetration since the seventeenth century. Almost all Lebanese identify strongly with their country in its modern territorial configuration, but their interpretation of what it means to be Lebanese varies with communal affiliation. Maronites often emphasize ties with the West as making Lebanon different from the Islamic neighborhood, Sunnis see Lebanon as a distinctive component of a wider Arab and mainly Sunni environment, and Shi'as view Lebanon as a vehicle for their own community, with Iranian as well as Arab ties. About 95 percent of Lebanese have Arabic as their mother tongue, though some speak another language at home. The differences among the confessional groups, however, remain great. In Lebanon, religion is more than a belief system; it is a major element in self- and family identity, apart from influencing interpretation of national identity.

Christians and Muslims comprised roughly equivalent portions of the population through the late Ottoman period until the mid-twentieth century. Maronite dynamism maintained the Christian share, despite the outflow to the wider world after about 1860. Between the 1930s and the 1990s, however, higher Muslim fertility and continued Christian emigration caused a substantial shift. Surveys and estimates indicate that by the 1990s Christians made up less than 40 percent of resident Lebanese. At the same time, strong differentiation between Sunni and Shi'a Muslims meant that Lebanon remained a country without a majority community. Shi'as, trailing Maronites and Sunni Muslims in the 1932 census, had become the largest single community by the 1990s. As for the early twenty-first century, a decline in Shi'a fertility and increases in Muslim emigration imply that population proportions may again be stabilizing. This would leave Shi'as at about one-third of the total, Sunnis above one-quarter, and Maronites below one-quarter within a Christian fraction of 35 to 38 percent. The Druze represent about 5 percent. Translated into numbers, Lebanon's present population of at least 4 million, excluding Palestinians, encompasses roughly 1.3 million Shi'as, 1.1 million Sunnis, and 800,000 Maronites, or in comprehensive terms, 2.4 million Muslims, 1.4 million Christians, and 200,000 Druze. All estimates are speculative, and the communities dispute the details.

The Palestinian refugee population is another problematic factor. This dates back to the major Palestinian influx of 1948 and 1949, accompanying the creation of Israel. There are perhaps 350,000 Palestinians in Lebanon, half of them in squalid refugee camps alongside the main coastal cities. Palestinians, overwhelmingly Sunni Muslim, amount to almost 10 percent of Lebanon's population. Shi'as and Christians, in particular, bitterly oppose citizenship grants and permanent Palestinian settlement because of the implications for communal balances. The impact of grants of Lebanese citizenship to tens of thousands of Syrians and Palestinians in 1992, forced through under Syrian hegemony, is not entirely clear, but it was detrimental to Maronites and Shi'as.

Seven of Lebanon's seventeen officially recognized sectarian communities have what might be termed "political weight." The main poles are of course the three "great" communities, each above 20 percent of the population—Maronite Christians and Sunni and Shi'a Muslims. Then there are four other communities with politically guaranteed ministerial positions in Lebanese governments: the Druze, the Orthodox Christians, the Greek Catholics, and the Armenians.

Among Christians, Maronites represent both the demographic majority and the source of political leadership. Lebanon would not exist without the will of this vigorous mountain Christian community, unique in the modern Middle East, for political separation from its Islamic neighborhood. To a greater degree than the smaller Christian sects, Maronites are extensively represented among poorer and lower-middle-class Lebanese. They have a powerful political, professional, and commercial elite, and they remain the bulk of the population in most of eastern Beirut and the northern half of Mount Lebanon.

Orthodox Christians constitute the second-largest Christian community (around 300,000). Traditionally they are a more urban population than the Maronites, with a dispersed distribution throughout the Levant. Not having a compact home territory like the Maronites, they are more used to being a minority and have had more intense interaction with Sunni Muslims. Orthodox Christians rarely deny Arab ethnicity, in contrast to many Maronites. For example, Orthodox Christians have been in the forefront of those who assert that being an Arab is different from being a Muslim, and some leading late-nineteenth-century Arab nationalists were Orthodox. In the mid-twentieth century, Lebanese Orthodox Christians were active in radical secular movements transcending Middle Eastern political boundaries. In 1932, Antoun Sa'adeh founded the Syrian Nationalist Party, which promoted a greater Syria including Syria, Lebanon, Jordan, and Israel.

Since the 1960s, however, the powerful Islamic emphasis in Arab nationalism has led most Lebanese Orthodox to gravitate together with the Maronites, while still presenting themselves as more open to Muslims and other Arabs. Away from Beirut and Tripoli, Orthodox Christians inhabit the Koura district, parts of the Matn above Beirut, and Marjayoun near the border with Israel.

Greek Catholics in Lebanon (perhaps 150,000) date from the eighteenth century, when a number of Orthodox Christians in Ottoman Syria went into communion with Rome. They have tended to follow the Maronite political lead, though without enthusiasm. They mainly live in eastern Beirut and the Biqa Valley town of Zahle, with a scattering of villages elsewhere, in less defensible locations than the Maronite heartland. Armenians number about 100,000, overwhelmingly in eastern Beirut. As non-Arabs, they are ethnically distinct from other Christians and Lebanese, and they maintain their separate cultural identity. They came to Lebanon during and after World War I, as refugees from Anatolia, and Maronites welcomed them as buttressing the Christian sector. Armenians have kept a distance from Lebanese political factions, supported the forces in power, and looked for freedom to manage their own community. Many left Lebanon in the 1975–1990 war years, when they came under mounting pressure to take sides.

Until the 1980s, the Maronite political advantage in post-Ottoman Lebanon and Muslim resentment of it obscured the divide between Sunnis and Shi'as. Sunni politicians played a double game—they went into partnership with Maronite leaders to command Lebanon in the 1943 National Pact, and they championed Muslim demands for political adjustment, seeking to contain radical elements. This worked as long as they could direct their own community and as long as Shi'as were rural, quiescent, and obedient to their semifeudal chiefs. The game foundered in the late twentieth century when leftist and Palestinian groups attracted Sunni loyalty and as Shi'as moved to Beirut, overtook Sunnis in numbers, and coalesced under new sectarian political movements. Sunnis differ from both Maronites and Shi'as in their long-standing urban concentration in Beirut, Tripoli, and Sidon, with only limited rural extension in the Biqa and northern Lebanon, and in their closer ties with the Arab world. Sunnis have desired that Lebanon play a larger role in Arab affairs, not favored by Maronites, and that Sunni Arab states influence Lebanon's domestic affairs, sometimes against Shi'a as well as Christian interests.

Through the first four decades of Lebanese independence after 1943, the Shi'as were politically underrepresented and economically disadvantaged, compared with Christians, Sunnis, and Druze. For most, migration in the 1960s and 1970s from southern Lebanon and the Biqa to the southern neighborhoods of Beirut—from the periphery of the country to the periphery of the capital—simply meant exchanging rural poverty for urban poverty. Young Shi'as eventually reacted to the coldness of other Lebanese and to manipulation by the Palestinians who cohabited their home areas by turning to their own militant sectarian organizations. In the 1980s, after centuries of isolation, they also acquired foreign patrons to match the Western connections of Maronites and the Arab ties of Sunnis—the new Shi'a Islamic revolutionary regime in Iran and the Alawite/Ba'thist rulers of Syria. The 1989 Ta'if Agreement gave Shi'as parity with Sunnis in parliament and increased the powers of the Shi'a speaker of the Chamber of Deputies. Syrian hegemony over Lebanon in the 1990s provided an umbrella under which Shi'as increased their political, bureaucratic, and hence economic shares, while Iran pumped money into the religious wing of the community. The price was subordination to Syrian and Iranian agendas and the complicity of a new class of bourgeois Shi'a politicians with their Sunni and Maronite equivalents in the corrupt and repressive "second Lebanese republic."

Still politically frustrated, Shi'as buttressed their national influence after 1990 by force of arms. In contrast to other Lebanese militias of the 1975–1990 period, which were disarmed and disbanded in 1991, the "Islamic resistance," the armed wing of Hizballah, enhanced its weaponry. Hizballah's justification was resistance to Israeli occupation of Lebanese land, and the movement took credit for Israel's unilateral withdrawal and the collapse of Israel's ally, the South Lebanese Army, in May 2000. This consolidated Hizballah's standing as Lebanon's largest, most disciplined political movement after 1990, with unrivaled foreign backing. In the 2000, 2005, and 2009 parliamentary elections, Hizballah and the more secular Amal movement commanded the Shi'a population of southern Lebanon, the northern Biqa Valley, and the southern suburbs of Beirut. These elections, however, also emphasized that Hizballah was a sectarian party, stuck in a minority of the population. Its maintenance of its arms after 2000, at the expense of state sovereignty, became controversial for the non–Shi'a majority of Lebanese.

Suspended between the Muslims and Christians, the Druze community is in a peculiar position. The Druze faith derives from Islam but is not really Muslim, and the old Druze mountain partnership with the Maronites came to grief in 1860. Estrangement from Maronites and discontent with the limited prospects for Druze ascent in post-1920 Lebanon led Druze leaders, above all Kamal Jumblat, to champion political revisionism. Here the Druze joined Sunni Muslims, leftists, and Palestinians and forged ties with Soviet Russia. Since Lebanon's independence, the Druze have seemed most comfortable in alignment with Sunnis and the smaller Christian communities, which they perceive as nonthreatening. They feel challenged by the two larger mountain communities, the Maronites and Shi'as. Nonetheless, the historical intimacy of Druze and Maronite clans retains resonance, whereas the Shi'a rise has mainly stimulated fear. Limited Druze numbers are to a degree offset by the strategic location of the community, in the Shuf hills above Beirut, straddling the main road from Beirut to Damascus, and on the slopes of Mount Hermon, between southern Lebanon and the Biqa Valley. The Druze community is the most tightly knit in the country, is generally well educated but not wealthy, and has an impressive warrior reputation.

Even before their religion, Lebanese consider their extended families and villages to be the principal sources of self-identity. Because one does not normally marry outside one's religion, family and religious identification are mutually reinforcing. The extended family in Lebanon remains important to the success of the individual, giving support to its members in exchange for loyalty. Individual achievements reflect well on the whole family, just as disgrace reflects poorly. The family was traditionally the vehicle of political advancement; it plugged into wider clan and patronage networks, with its capability depending on social standing in its community or connection to others with such standing. Family associations have also provided welfare functions elsewhere performed by the state. The war years after 1975 saw a weakening of the family in political affairs, with raw money power, sectarian parties, and obeisance to Syria and the security apparatus becoming the best routes into the regime by the 1990s.

Economic Conditions

Lebanon's legendary entrepreneurial talent, which some date to the Phoenicians, is mainly a product of European commercial influence in late Ottoman times and the maintenance of the country's "merchant economy" while other Arabs indulged in semisocialist experiments. Merchants, shopkeepers, artisans, and the service industries flourished under Lebanon's unfettered free market system until the warfare of 1975 to 1990.

After independence and before 1975, the Lebanese enhanced their regional economic role, benefiting from economic and political developments elsewhere. The independence of Israel cut economic ties between the Arab world and most of the former British Mandate of Palestine, leaving a large gap that the Lebanese filled. For example, the terminal for the Iraq petroleum pipeline was transferred from Haifa to Tripoli. More generally, overland transport and communications that might have traversed the southern Levant were funneled into Beirut. International corporations and banks established regional headquarters in the Lebanese capital, and the economy boomed.

The Lebanese took advantage of the growing wealth of the Arab oil states. Beirut supplied entertainment and investment as well as a transit point for goods and services. Arabs from the Gulf countries flocked to Beirut and the nearby mountain villages each summer to escape the heat. The Lebanese provided their guests with recreation, banking arrangements, and European shopping in an Arab environment. Many Arabs bought homes in the mountains or invested in Beirut. Lebanon's schools and universities educated the children of Arab leaders.

In the decade before the collapse into chaos in 1975, Lebanon experienced rapid industrial growth. The oil refineries at Zahrani and Tripoli had previously been the primary industry. In the 1960s, a manufacturing belt began to grow in the poorer suburbs of Beirut, mostly small enterprises producing light consumer goods, textiles, or processed foods. By 1975, nearly 10 percent of the labor force was involved in such industry. At the same time, the agricultural sector gradually declined as the Lebanese tended more toward urban living. Nonetheless, many people continued to earn part or all of their incomes from their small landholdings or tenant farms. Lebanon's topography offers a wide variety of environments, and apples, citrus fruits, olives, olive oil, and grapes remain significant export items. The Biqa Valley was a breadbasket for the cities. Otherwise, the most interesting aspect of the pre-1975 Lebanese economy was its perennial trade deficit, with imports regularly five times the value of exports. Remittances from Lebanese emigrants, including workers in the oil-producing states, and hard currency from Lebanon's service sector offset the deficit.

Fifteen years of warfare from 1975 to 1990 punctured Lebanon's economic ascent and the status it had achieved as a regional business and media center. Successive rounds of hostilities devastated the commercial and industrial sectors, and crucial middleman functions relocated to Cyprus, the Gulf shaykhdoms, and Jordan, though they remained partially in Lebanese hands. Communications, water supplies, roads, and electricity provision deteriorated. The difficulty of maintaining basic infrastructure did not end with the war years. Israeli air raids up to 2000 damaged electricity facilities, and the Israeli-Hizballah confrontation weakened business confidence.

Rafik Hariri became head of the Council of Ministers in late 1992. Hariri, an extraordinarily successful Lebanese Sunni businessman, had amassed a fortune in Saudi Arabia. Lebanese and international observers hoped that Hariri would entice significant foreign, Arab, and Lebanese diaspora investment to the country and thus restore its former standing. The Syrian regime hoped that Hariri would make its command of Beirut suitably lucrative.

Hariri's government undertook a vigorous program of reconstruction, spending large sums to make up for the years of neglect and destruction. The cost of Hariri's projects far exceeded Lebanon's capacity to pay, and Syrian hegemony, corruption, and political uncertainty contributed to a tepid response from potential investors. As a result, the Lebanese government borrowed large sums of money at inflated interest rates, principally from the domestic banking sector. When Hariri came to office, the national debt was about $900 million; in 1998, it reached $18 billion and had ballooned to $43 billion by 2008, when it stood at 180 percent of gross domestic product. Debt servicing ate up more than half the national budget after the mid-1990s. Despite liberal government deficit spending, economic growth was only modest, unemployment was substantial, income gaps stretched, and the once robust middle class saw its economic status erode. Hariri's reconstruction projects were physically impressive but focused on parts of Beirut, leaving much of Lebanon untouched. Most disturbing was the number of educated and skilled Lebanese workers, from all communities, who emigrated during and after the war years.

By 1998, Hariri's star was under a cloud, and the Syrian leadership shifted its favor to the new Maronite president, Emile Lahoud. Hariri resigned, and through the next two years he and his team endured a cynical campaign of denigration. Nonetheless, the new government had no answers to Lebanon's predicament. Hariri could at least pull some strings in the wider world, and in the fall of 2000 he and his allies won the parliamentary elections, imposing his return as prime minister.

Thereafter, Hariri found himself unable to satisfy the reform requirements of prospective international donors because of conflict with President Lahoud. The state apparatus remained venal and ramshackle. Hariri's achievement in the first five years of the new century was simply to keep Lebanon afloat—his personal standing enabled the government to restructure debt and to keep borrowing. Vigorous support for Lebanon from the UN Security Council mitigated the shock from the assassination of Hariri in February 2005. Syrian military withdrawal and Western backing for Hariri's financial advisor Fuad Siniora as the new prime minister gave hope. On the other hand, political paralysis while Lebanon awaited the outcome of the UN inquiry into Hariri's murder blocked economic improvement, and the July–August 2006 Israel-Hizballah war caused around $4 billion of direct infrastructural damage. Nonetheless, the 2008–2009 global recession did not much disturb Lebanon, at least at first. The Lebanese banks had avoided exposure to risky financial instruments, and regional backers of Shi'a and Sunni factions, principally Iran and Saudi Arabia, directed money into the country to influence the 2009 parliamentary elections.

POLITICAL AND LEGAL STRUCTURE

The system of government bequeathed to Lebanon by the French in 1943 was modeled after that of France but took into account Lebanese sectarian peculiarities. The principal pillars of the system are the 1926 constitution and the 1943 informal National Pact, as modified by the 1989 Ta'if Agreement. Judicial institutions apply French-style civil law. Ordinary courts have criminal and civil wings, with benches of judges at three levels—first instance, appeal, and cassation. There are also administrative courts, military tribunals, a judicial council, and a constitutional court. Legal personnel are competent, but political pressure subverts the theoretically independent legal authorities. They cannot handle political killings, for example.

Beyond the state, each sectarian community has its own religious institutions, with personal-status issues (e.g., marriage, divorce, and inheritance) subject to religious codes—not civil law. Such institutions—for example, the Maronite Church and patriarchate, the office of the Sunni chief mufti, and the Higher Shi'a Islamic Council—control extensive property and their own courts. Spiritual leaders can have significant political influence.

Lebanon's National Pact of 1943, which originated as an understanding between the Maronite Bishara al-Khoury and the Sunni Muslim Riyadh al-Solh, has been the framework of the country's confessional politics. Most prominently, it was an oral agreement about allocation of top posts. Since 1943, the president, chosen by parliamentary vote for a single six-year term, has invariably been a Maronite. The president nominates a Sunni Muslim as prime minister, on the basis of consultation with the parliamentary deputies, and the prime minister forms a cabinet, since 1989 half Christian and half Muslim/Druze. The speaker of the Chamber of Deputies is a Shi'a, and his deputy is an Orthodox Christian. Ministerial portfolios are allocated according to confessional shares, as are many other positions in the executive, legislative, and judicial branches. The army commander is customarily a Maronite, and there is a religious balance among security service chiefs.

Lebanon's legislature, the Chamber of Deputies, elaborates the sectarian political system. Parliamentary seats are distributed on both a confessional and a geographical basis. Deputies come from geographical districts. Each district has a specified number of seats allocated by religion, and all citizens registered in a district vote for candidates for all the seats. As an example, the Shuf constituency used for the 2000 and 2005 elections returned three Maronites, one Greek Catholic, two Druze, and two Sunnis. This was in rough proportion to the demographic distribution of registered voters, a large number of whom no longer lived in the district. Similarly, many Beirut Shi'as vote in southern Lebanon, not Beirut, because they remain registered in their original villages.

Religious sects tend to concentrate sufficiently to justify constituency-based parliamentary seats. Tripoli and Sidon are overwhelmingly Sunni; Zghorta, Kisrawan, and Jubayl are similarly Maronite; Tyre, Nabatiya, and Baalbek have Shi'a majorities; and the Koura is predominantly Orthodox. Even in areas of mixed population, villages tend to belong primarily to a single religious group. In Beirut, Christians, Sunnis, and Shi'as live in separate neighborhoods. The representative system established under the departing French was an attempt to adapt democracy to Lebanese demography.

Apart from confessional political shares, the 1943 National Pact also addressed the conflicting external orientations of the Lebanese. A majority of Christians, particularly Maronites, looked toward Western nations as protectors. Many considered themselves part of the Mediterranean community rather than part of the

Arab world. This "Lebanese" nationalism contrasted sharply with "Arab" national-ism. Muslims often viewed Lebanese nationalism as a denial of Lebanon's Arab face. To Christians, Muslim pan-Arabism seemed to sacrifice Lebanese, particularly Lebanese Christian, interests to Islamic and Arab goals.

The National Pact attempted a compromise between Lebanese and Arab na-tionalists. The Maronite side agreed not to try to alienate Lebanon from the Arab world or to draw Lebanon too close to the West. The Sunni Muslim side recog-nized Lebanon's uniqueness and agreed not to pressure the government to be-come overly involved in the affairs of Arab states. The 1989 Ta'if Agreement upset this aspect of the National Pact, clearly placing Lebanon in the Arab context. Here the Lebanese nationalists suffered a setback, but the new turning of Christians, Sunnis, and Druze toward Western powers in 2005 to throw off Ba'thist Syria in-dicated that the issue remained alive.

In general terms, the Ta'if Agreement recalibrated the political system. Sixty-two of seventy-three surviving members of the 1972 Lebanese parliament, the last elected before the war years, met in Ta'if, Saudi Arabia, from September 30 to Oc-tober 22, 1989, to adjust the constitution to reconcile Muslim grievances with Christian fears. They modified the balance of power while perpetuating most of the 1926 constitution and the National Pact. First, the agreement reduced the ex-ecutive power of the presidency in favor of the Council of Ministers headed by the Sunni prime minister, ultimately dependent on parliamentary confidence. Second, it gave greater influence to the Chamber of Deputies and its Shi'a speaker. For example, the president could no longer veto legislation; he could sim-ply require it to be presented a second time. Third, the agreement changed parlia-ment's composition. It altered the ratio of Christian deputies to non-Christians from 6:5 to equality and established equality between Sunnis and Shi'as. The number of deputies was increased from 99 to 108 and in 1992 to 128. The sixty-four Christian seats became allocated as follows: thirty-four Maronites, fourteen Orthodox, eight Greek Catholics, six Armenians, one Protestant, and one for other Christians. The sixty-four non-Christian seats were to include twenty-seven Sunnis, twenty-seven Shi'as, eight Druze, and two Alawites.

Up to 2005, the Lebanese and Syrian regimes warped implementation of Ta'if. In 1995 and 2004, Syria forced extended terms for Presidents Ilyas Hrawi and Emile Lahoud in defiance of the constitution. On the parliamentary level, the Lebanese authorities set aside the Ta'if provision for using large electorates, instead mixing large and small constituencies to ensure seats for Syria's friends. Elections between 1992 and 2005 made many Christian deputies subject to non-Christian voter majorities. They also undermined traditional leaders in favor of Syrian-aligned political parties, for example, Hizballah and Amal.

Despite abuses, Lebanon's constitution has guaranteed basic rights, including equality before the law, personal liberties, political rights, and freedom of the press, association, speech, and assembly. Beirut remains a regional publishing center, noted for the vigor and diversity of its print media. From 1990 to 2005, Syrian-dominated Lebanon went through a dark period of constricted public freedoms. Senior politicians and the security agencies interfered in elections within the union movement and professional organizations, producing partial state coordination of a dynamic civil society. In 1997 and 1998, such interventions by the parliamentary speaker, the prime minister, and the army command compromised the trade union leadership. The regime also restricted television station licenses. On the other hand, business and banking associations resisted coordination, preserving effective electoral practices. The basic culture of political pluralism provides the platform for a powerful rebound of civil society.

As regards gender in politics, emancipation of women is still not reflected in political participation. Women received the vote in 1953, and the army opened the gate to female officers in 1992. Yet, the number of women in parliament is miserably low: 4 out of 128 deputies in 2009, down from 7 in 2005. In 2009, two female parliamentarians, Nayla Tueni (Orthodox) and Bahiya Hariri (Sunni), owe their prominence to being, respectively, the daughter and sister of murdered male politicians. Strida Ja'ja' (Maronite) is the wife of politician Samir Ja'ja'. Three belong to the pro-Western March 14 bloc, and one, Gilberte Zouein (Maronite), to Michel Aoun's group. One bright spot is female participation in the legal profession; in late 2009 Amal Haddad became president of the Beirut Bar Association and Joyce Thabet became the Lebanese deputy prosecutor of the special international tribunal for the Hariri murder case.

As for the military institution, Lebanon moved from a small Maronite-dominated army, largely neutral in political affairs until the 1960s, to a larger force incorporating militia personnel in the 1990s, with a more representative officer corps. Under Syrian hegemony after 1990, the army command of Gen. Emile Lahoud, military intelligence, and the public security directorate were all politicized in favor of Syria. The restructured army brigades, however, kept popular legitimacy and respect as a nonpolitical armed force. In 2005 and 2009, they could be relied on to uphold elected governments.

POLITICAL DYNAMICS

Lebanon's history since independence from France in 1943 has gone through four phases. From 1943 until 1975, "confessional democracy" prevailed, with little change in the social order and political control in the hands of traditional communal leaders. There were, however, strains with demographic shifts in favor of Muslims in general and Shi'as in particular, combined with intrusion of Middle Eastern regional politics. Between 1975 and 1990, disorder reigned, with hostilities involving local parties and foreign powers. The country disaggregated into sectarian cantons and zones of Syrian, Israeli, and Palestinian occupation, with bare survival of state institutions. Between 1991 and 2004, the Lebanese state resurfaced and calm returned, except on the border with Israel, at the price of Syrian steerage. In 2005, Lebanon entered a new phase of autonomy, though the uneasy coexistence of an inflated Hizballah with a fractured state apparatus after the July–August 2006 Israel-Hizballah war heralded difficulties.

1943–1974

The "confessional democracy" that flourished through the 1950s and 1960s had virtues. It reflected the reality of sectarian allegiances but softened their impact. Relatively small electoral districts gave weight to local and personal ties, often across sectarian lines, which buffered against political radicalism and foreign entanglement. A traditional politician had to provide services for constituents and, to have a national reach, to join a coalition with counterparts from other communities. Competing electoral lists had to be multisectarian because of the design of the multimember electorates, with Maronites pitted against Maronites and Sunnis against Sunnis rather than Christians against Muslims. A Christian elected in a predominantly Muslim area would reflect the winning list's preference for pan-Arabism, whereas a Muslim in the reverse situation would probably be a Lebanese nationalist. The cumulative effect of such circumstances was that votes in parliament rarely broke along religious lines.

Apart from the rigidity of sectarian quotas, the most prominent defect of "confessional democracy" was the discouragement of national parties. Any nationwide bloc of deputies tended to be a factional coalition under a senior politician (for example, the National Bloc of Bishara al-Khoury), not an organized ideological party with a coherent program. Ideological parties, like the Communists, Syrian Social Nationalists, and Ba'thists, had little success unless boosted by family loyalties. Only two parties broke the mold to a limited extent, because they combined ideology with traditional leadership. The Progressive Socialist Party of Kamal Jumblat brought together leftists and a traditional Druze following. The Phalange integrated Lebanese nationalism, a social welfare dimension, and the partisans of the Jumayyil family. Both reached into other sects, but there was no doubting their respective Druze and Maronite foundations.

In consequence, parliaments were highly fragmented. A bloc of fifteen members was considered large, and presidents and prime ministers could never rely on the party backing accepted in the West as a normal underpinning of government. Regimes depended on unstable coalitions, and Presidents Camille Chamoun and Fuad Shihab both fell back on intelligence service manipulation of politics. Nonetheless, most Lebanese were satisfied most of the time that their basic concerns—security and a share of government largesse—were accommodated.

A brief breakdown occurred in 1958, when both Christians and Muslims felt that the National Pact was being violated. President Chamoun feared the pull of Egyptian president Gamal Abd al-Nasser's populist Arab nationalism on Lebanese Sunni Muslims. He wished to move closer to the West to protect Lebanon's independence. Muslims viewed this as a challenge to Lebanon's Arab identity. Chamoun also sought to extend his presidency, which aroused rejection from Christian rivals as well as Muslims. The creation of the United Arab Republic between Egypt and Syria in February 1958 raised the temperature. Fighting ensued between pro- and anti-Chamoun forces, largely but not exclusively intercommunal. US military intervention in July 1958 gave frightened Lebanese leaders a chance to pull back from the brink. Chamoun stepped down at the end of his normal term, and Maronite army commander Fuad Shihab became president. Shihab had a mild reformist agenda and was on good terms with Nasser.

Shihab and his chosen successor, Charles Helou, calmed the political arena amid economic prosperity through the 1960s. Shihab enlarged the state, promoted investment in peripheral areas, and brought more Muslims into the bureaucracy. However, the 1960s saw destabilizing developments in both Lebanon and the wider Levant. Shihab's reforms stimulated Shi'a aspirations at a time when mass migration brought poorer Christians and Shi'as from the countryside to the booming metropolis. Beirut acquired large new suburbs, with Shi'as open to radical leftist influence and Maronites less under the thumb of traditional bosses. The 1960s saw the Shi'a arrival in modern politics, at first under the moderate leadership of Musa Sadr. Beirut's boom sharpened Lebanon's income disparities, producing hostility to the Sunni and Christian bourgeoisie even when many Shi'as found their incomes improving.

The June 1967 Arab-Israeli War introduced critical additional factors. To begin with, the defeat of the Arab states ended the quiescence of Lebanon's Palestinian Arabs, who had come to the country as refugees in 1948 and 1949. For almost two decades the Palestinians had left confrontation with Israel to regular Arab armies and hardly stirred in and around their refugee camps until some paramilitary activity in the early 1960s. The Lebanese army and intelligence agencies, especially the efficient Deuxième Bureau, watched them, and the Lebanese elite discriminated against their middle class in employment and commercial activities. Israel's 1967 triumph provoked the Palestinians into guerilla action along the Israeli border with Lebanon and into militarization and assertion of autonomy in Palestinian strongholds along the Lebanese coast.

In southern Lebanon, the accelerating tempo of Israeli-Palestinian hostilities impelled more Shi'as to move to Beirut and nourished Shi'a discontent with Lebanese realities. In the late 1960s and early 1970s, many younger members of the community joined Palestinian-Lebanese leftist armed groups. More broadly, Lebanese Sunni and Druze activists, most prominently Kamal Jumblat, saw alignment with Palestinian military capability not just as an affirmation of Arabism but also as a weapon to compel the Maronites to accept new political arrangements reflecting Muslim numbers. Traditional Sunni leaders, including prime ministers, did not dare defy the Palestinian-Lebanese leftist alignment. This alignment paralyzed the Lebanese state, meant the Lebanese army could not uphold state sovereignty, and railroaded the Lebanese regime into the 1969 Cairo Accord, giving Palestinian fighters operational freedom in parts of Lebanon.

Christians responded belligerently to what many interpreted as an existential threat. The failure of the Lebanese army to contain the Palestinians led the Phalange and the Chamounists to build up private arsenals. Christian paramilitaries ignored traditional Christian leadership and recruited among Beirut's newer Maronite residents as well as in Mount Lebanon. Events in 1970 and 1971 intensified the crisis. The Jordanian crackdown on Yasir Arafat's Palestine Liberation Organization (PLO) in the Jordanian "civil war" left Lebanon as the only Arab country in which Palestinians could organize freely. The PLO leadership and thousands of fighters shifted from Jordan to Lebanon, further upsetting the Lebanese balance and exciting the Lebanese left against "Maronite hegemony." At the same time, the takeover of Syria by Hafiz al-Asad and stabilization of the Syrian Ba'thist state inaugurated prolonged Syrian interference in Lebanese politics, at first in favor of the Palestinians and the Lebanese Left. In this delicate environment, Lebanon acquired an unpromising new president, Sulayman Franjiyah. President Franjiyah's policies after 1970 were a bewildering mixture of a hard line against the Palestinians; surrender to his old friend Hafiz al-Asad, thereby advantaging the Palestinians; and dismantling Shihab's security apparatus, the eyes and ears of the Lebanese state. This signaled to all sides that they had best look to their own resources and prepare for a showdown.

1975–1990

In early 1975, sporadic incidents between armed Christians and Palestinian militants exploded into fighting in and around Beirut that involved the PLO and the Lebanese leftists. Through 1976, Christian militias carved out a de facto canton in northern Mount Lebanon, and the Palestinians took command of western Beirut and much of southern Lebanon. Despite Christian fears of Syrian Ba'thist designs on Lebanon, President Franjiyah invited Syrian military intervention to forestall PLO advances and Israeli action. Syrian forces, with US and Israeli acquiescence, thereupon deployed through most of Lebanon to contain Syria's Palestinian "allies," except for a zone in southern Lebanon covered by an Israeli "red line."

By 1978, the Christian militias, tired of their brief partnership with Damascus, had compelled the Syrians to retreat from much of the Christian area and turned to Israel. Meanwhile, the Lebanese army fragmented, largely along religious lines, and northern Maronites loyal to the pro-Syrian Franjiyah family split from other Christians. In March 1978, Israel launched a large incursion into southern Lebanon against the Palestinians and established a border strip inside Lebanon under its influence. The latter defied UN Security Council Resolution 425, which demanded Israeli withdrawal.

Between 1978 and 1982, the Palestinians under Arafat's PLO strengthened their position in western Beirut and the south, using their Lebanese allies and their prestige in the Arab world to loosen Syria's grip. The Christian militias in eastern Beirut and its hinterland coalesced into a supermilitia, the Lebanese Forces (LF), under the charismatic Bashir Jumayyil, while the Syrians consolidated their presence in the Biqa Valley and northern Lebanon, Syria's strategic buffers. Within the Shi'a community, the disappearance of Musa Sadr on a visit to Libya, discontent with Palestinian behavior, and the 1979 Iranian revolution stimulated truculence.

The country seemed to be disintegrating, though a battered Lebanese government persisted, shored up by the international community. Only the coffers of the Palestinian "state within the state" averted economic collapse. Lebanon was fundamentally destabilized, with its communities and leaders polarized by domestic quarrels and conflicting external alliances. Its affairs were a free-for-all among the Palestinians, Israel, Syria, and the wider Arab world, and the location on the Arab-Israeli front line raised the stakes. In 1981, a hard-line Israeli government, Maronite wooing of Israel to service Bashir Jumayyil's presidential ambitions, Palestinian bombardment across the Israel-Lebanon border, and Syrian installation of surface-to-air missiles in the Biqa Valley predisposed Israel to an adventure.

Israel's invasion of Lebanon up to Beirut in June 1982, in advance of Lebanon's scheduled 1982 presidential election, certainly changed Lebanese scenery, but mostly away from Israel's wish list. Israel achieved the expulsion of Arafat and his PLO fighters from Beirut and degradation of Palestinian significance in Lebanon. However, although Israel also dealt a military blow to Syria, eliminating the surface-to-air missile batteries and crippling the Syrian air force, subsequent events proceeded in Syria's favor. For Damascus, Bashir Jumayyil's September 1982 election as president with Sunni and Shi'a support, reflecting Muslim disenchantment with the Palestinians and Bashir's distancing of himself from the Israelis, was intolerable. Bashir would divorce Lebanon from Syria, and his cunning only made him a greater menace. Bashir was assassinated before he could take office, removing any chance of a Lebanese order favorable to Israel. Members of Bashir's LF went on a rampage in the Sabra and Shatila Palestinian refugee camps, massacring hundreds of Palestinians and others in an area under Israeli control. Israel was blamed and had to retreat from western Beirut under international opprobrium.

The Lebanese parliament elected Bashir's older brother Amin to the presidency, and Amin turned to the Americans. The United States mobilized a multinational force, including American marines, to buttress Lebanese state authority in western Beirut, but the United States and Amin Jumayyil ran into trouble through 1983. Amin refused to make political concessions to the non-Christians, in particular spurning Nabih Birri's Shi'a Amal movement (founded by Musa Sadr in 1974). This assisted the Syrians in reasserting their influence among Muslims and Druze. Damascus was thus able to block implementation of a May 17, 1983, Lebanese-Israeli agreement, laboriously brokered by the United States, for a conditional Israeli withdrawal.

In September 1983, the Israelis pulled out of the Shuf hills above Beirut, without coordination with the resuscitated Lebanese government and army. Druze forces under Walid Jumblat moved against Christian militiamen who had infiltrated the area, in the process expelling 150,000 Christians. Jumblat also joined the Syrians against the US presence. Lebanese Muslims and Druze viewed the United States as supporting Amin Jumayyil's resistance to reform, while Syria and its Soviet backers determined to remove the "NATO base" in Beirut. The Reagan administration, unwilling to commit more troops, fell back on naval bombardment, and on October 23, 1983, Shi'a suicide truck bombers killed 241 US marines and 60 French soldiers in their Beirut compounds. In February 1984, Shi'a militias overran western Beirut, the Lebanese army again split, and Amin Jumayyil's regime was reduced to the Christian heartland. The US-led multinational force pulled out, and Lebanon returned to decomposition, with the Israelis, Palestinians, and Christians in disarray vis-à-vis the surges of the Syrians, Shi'as, and Druze. Lebanon's Sunnis were in a pathetic situation; before 1975 the leading component of the Islamic sector, in the early 1980s they exchanged subjection to the PLO for subjection to Shi'a and Druze militia bosses.

After September 1983, the Israelis dug in south of the Awali River and across the southern Biqa Valley. This convinced the Shi'as, who had welcomed Israel's defeat of the PLO, that Israel had in mind permanent occupation of southern Lebanon and confiscation of the Litani River waters. Israeli obstinacy interacted disastrously with Shi'a assertiveness. Through late 1983 and 1984, resistance and repression inflated sectarian religious zeal already well fueled by Iran's new Shi'a Islamic revolutionary regime. Various radical tendencies combined to form Hizballah ("Party of God"), which in February 1985 announced its arrival with a manifesto against Israel and in favor of an Iranian-style Islamic state. By June 1985, when the Israelis retreated from most of southern Lebanon to a new border buffer zone south of the Litani River, Israel had acquired a new enemy more tenacious than the PLO.

Elsewhere in Lebanon, the remainder of Amin Jumayyil's presidential term, up to late 1988, was characterized by paralysis. The Syrian recovery stalled in the face of Christian stiffening, intrusion by Iran and Iraq, and local conflicts among Lebanese Muslims and Palestinians. Syria's Hafiz al-Asad, who privately viewed the Israeli expulsion of Arafat from Lebanon as positive and who completed the job by removing the PLO from Tripoli in November 1983, still feared Palestinian autonomy. Through the mid-1980s he supported the Shi'a Amal movement in its sieges of Palestinian camps in Beirut and Sidon. Residual Palestinian forces, no longer a deciding factor in Lebanon, received a dribble of aid from the Christian LF, the Druze, and Hizballah, who all wished for more freedom vis-à-vis Damascus. The ascent of the Shi'a community shuddered to a halt as Amal and Hizballah competed viciously for supremacy. Anarchy engulfed western Beirut, militants linked to Hizballah and Iran kidnapped Westerners, and Israel got a lull in its "security zone."

After 1985, the major issue in Lebanon was Syria's aspiration for hegemony and blockage of that aspiration by the Christian leadership in eastern Beirut. The Maronite "canton" housed the Lebanese presidency, the high command and heavy weaponry of the army, and the LF, Lebanon's largest militia. Its existence also buttressed its smaller Druze counterpart in the Shuf hills. In the late 1980s, Saddam Husayn of Iraq, looking for revenge against Syria for its alliance with Iran in the Iran-Iraq War, shipped arms to both the LF and the army command. The weaknesses of the canton included its multiheaded leadership and its unpopularity even among its 800,000 inhabitants, after the ruinous hostilities of 1982 to 1985 brought collapse of the Lebanese currency and destitution. President Amin Jumayyil and the Maronite patriarchate prevented the mutual jealousies of the militia and army from getting out of hand, but the end of Amin's term in 1988 brought a crisis.

Christian leaders refused a presidential candidate backed by Syria and the United States, which had come to view Ba'thist Syria as a stabilizing force. At the last moment, President Jumayyil reluctantly appointed army commander Michel Aoun as prime minister with executive power until presidential elections could be held. Damascus and Sunni prime minister Salim al-Huss rejected this move, leaving Lebanon with two governments. Aoun had romantic nationalist sentiments and conceived an overthrow of militias, cantons, and foreign occupations in favor of restored state legitimacy spearheaded by his army brigades. This was highly popular, and Aoun boasted a following among Shi'as and Sunnis as well as Maronites. It also guaranteed collisions with the Syrians, the Druze, and, inside eastern Beirut, the LF militia.

In March 1989, General Aoun launched a "war of liberation" against Syrian forces. This comprised destructive artillery exchanges in which the Syrians had the advantage. Aoun hoped to precipitate international intervention. He gained some Arab sympathy and embarrassed Hafiz al-Asad but also alienated the United States, which saw him as a threat to stability in the region. International intervention, therefore, was not to Aoun's benefit. The United States and the Arab states promoted the Ta'if gathering of Lebanese parliamentarians in October 1989,

which agreed on constitutional adjustments, a presidential election, and Syrian assistance to extend the authority of the new regime. The Lebanese deputies elected
Rene Mu'awad president on November 5. Mu'awad, however, was not to Syria's
taste. He was assassinated three weeks later, whereupon parliament reconvened in
the Biqa and voted for Syria's candidate, Ilyas Hrawi.

Only General Aoun now stood in the way of Syrian command of Lebanon.
The LF militia longed to be rid of the general and colluded with Damascus. In
February 1990, Aoun went to war with the LF in eastern Beirut and Mount
Lebanon, a fight that split and weakened the Maronites. In a supreme irony, Asad's
bitter foe Saddam Husayn enabled Syria to administer the coup de grâce. After
Saddam invaded Kuwait in August 1990, the United States felt it needed Syria in
the coalition against Iraq. In exchange, Asad obtained an American "green light"
to suppress Aoun, and the Syrian army overran the Ba'abda presidential palace on
October 13, 1990. Aoun proceeded to the French embassy and exile in France,
and Lebanon fell under Syrian Ba'thist hegemony.

1991–2004

Syria did not waste time tightening its hold on Lebanon. In 1991, all Lebanese
militias apart from Hizballah disbanded, and the Lebanese army began reorganizing under Syrian supervision and its amenable new Maronite commander, Emile
Lahoud. The Treaty of Brotherhood, Cooperation, and Coordination, signed on
May 22, 1991, provided for deep Syrian intrusion into Lebanese policy making. It
established a semifederal Higher Council between the two countries, with committees for "prime ministerial coordination," foreign affairs, security, and economic policy. A Defense and Security Pact followed, banning any activity "in all
military, security, political, and information fields that might endanger or cause
threats to the other country." All American hostages held in Lebanon were released, and Palestinian militants in Sidon and Tyre were limited to the refugee
camps, with subjection to Syrian supremacy. Peace settled over the country, apart
from Hizballah's contest with Israel.

Lebanon's government and post-Ta'if parliament were packed with Syria's allies and clients. Parliamentary elections in 1992 and 1996 produced results pre-
determined by gerrymandering and systematic abuses. In the latter case, the
al-Nahar columnist Sarkis Na'um commented that Damascus deserved an Oscar
for its performance. The LF found itself marginalized, and when its leader, Samir
Ja'ja', declined to join the regime, he was charged with various crimes and imprisoned in the basement of the Ministry of Defense. From 1992 on, the Syrians operated through an executive "troika" of President Ilyas Hrawi, Prime Minister
Rafik Hariri, and Parliamentary Speaker Nabih Birri, who squabbled with one
another while Hariri worked on economic reconstruction, vital for the stability of

Syrian hegemony. Hafiz al-Asad, backed by the Lebanese regime, ignored the Ta'if stipulation for a 1992 redeployment of Syrian forces away from Beirut.

In the late 1990s, Asad patronized domination of Lebanon by a Syrian-style security machine under Emile Lahoud, elevated from the army command to the presidency in 1998. Lahoud, together with the chief of Syrian military intelligence in Lebanon, ran the security machine on behalf of Damascus, closely constraining Hariri, who returned as prime minister in 2000 after spending the first two years of Lahoud's term in opposition. Syria's Alawite overlords found it difficult to circumvent Hariri, especially after his parliamentary election gains in 2000, but suspected his associations with the West, Saudi Arabia, and "old guard" personalities inside the Syrian regime. The distrust intensified when Bashar al-Asad took over as Syrian president after the death of his father. Unlike his father, who floated above the Lebanese arena, Bashar descended into the fray. While preserving correct relations with Hariri, he favored Lahoud and developed a personal rapport with Hizballah secretary-general Hasan Nasrallah.

The presidential change in Syria coincided with Israel's May 2000 abandonment of its "security zone" in southern Lebanon, under Hizballah pressure. The legacy for Syrian hegemony was ambiguous. On the one hand, through the 1990s Israeli bombardments helped to radicalize the Shi'a community to a point where it was hard to imagine Shi'a give-and-take with anyone, including the rest of Lebanon. Syria could therefore still rely on the Shi'as in any problems with Hariri and others. To ensure a common front, in 1996 Syria forced Hizballah and Amal together into a single parliamentary bloc. Despite the friction between the two organizations, general Shi'a resentment encouraged cooperation. Shi'as felt that the Ta'if adjustment of parliamentary seating was only an initial step toward the 40 or more deputies they were worth in the 128-member chamber.

Syria and Hizballah also stirred a fresh border grievance against Israel to justify Hizballah's keeping its weapons and persisting with "resistance." They claimed that a corner of the Israeli-occupied Golan Heights adjacent to Lebanon, the Shebaa farms, was really Lebanese, and so Israeli withdrawal was incomplete. The United Nations, which certified Israel's May 2000 withdrawal as fulfilling Security Council Resolution 425 of 1978, was unimpressed, defining the Shebaa farms as Syrian territory. The United Nations required that Syria confirm Lebanese sovereignty in writing, which the Syrians carefully avoided doing. Nonetheless, the Lebanese government endorsed the claim, thereby also endorsing Hizballah as a private army with command of the border zone facing Israel. Continued trouble with Israel in turn assisted continued Syrian command of Lebanon.

Against all this, the Israeli withdrawal encouraged Lebanese questioning of Syrian hegemony. The Syrian-Lebanese security machine that ran the country and circumscribed Prime Minister Hariri after 2000 was not just a repressive apparatus unprecedented in Lebanon's modern history but also a racketeering combine that siphoned enormous sums, perhaps hundreds of millions of dollars, out of the Lebanese economy. Druze and Sunni voices joined Christian discontent, and Druze leader Walid Jumblat welcomed Maronite patriarch Nasrallah Sfeir, a persistent critic of Damascus, to the Shuf amid excited crowds in August 2001. Bashar al-Asad could keep the lid on the situation, assisted by continued US indulgence of Syria's role in Lebanon, until the George W. Bush administration turned against him after March 2003 because of his encouragement of attacks on US forces in Iraq. This preceded the final months of President Lahoud's six-year term in 2004, when Hariri and Jumblat, backed by the United States and France, expressed their hostility to an unconstitutional extension.

2005 Onward

Syria's president was not to be deterred. He wanted Lahoud, disliked Hariri, and felt the United States was too bogged down in Iraq to take a stand. His security chiefs opposed any change that might disturb their racketeering in Lebanon. Deploying heavy intimidation toward the Lebanese, in late August 2004 he compelled Hariri to assemble the Lebanese parliament to give Lahoud three extra years, sparking an extended crisis. The United States and France mobilized the UN Security Council to pass Resolution 1559 ordering the Syrian army out of Lebanon and demanding dissolution of remaining militias, meaning Hizballah. Hariri, thoroughly alienated from Lahoud and Bashar al-Asad, worked to consolidate a Lebanese majority against Syria in scheduled May 2005 parliamentary elections. On February 14, 2005, Hariri and twenty-two others were killed in a massive explosion in central Beirut. Subsequent competitive demonstrations exposed a dangerous rift in Lebanese society. On March 8, Hizballah brought out half a million to emphasize Shi'a existence and favor Syria. On March 14, 1 million Sunnis, Christians, and Druze gathered to remember Hariri and condemn Syria, widely blamed for the assassination. In April 2005, Bashar bowed with bad grace to the international community, and Syrian uniformed forces departed Lebanon, ending a presence of three decades.

Syria's formal withdrawal in the aftermath of the Hariri assassination terminated Syrian hegemony in an unexpected manner. Syria, however, retained its allies and exerted influence through intelligence personnel and infiltration of weaponry across the border, particularly among Hizballah, radical Palestinian organizations, and Lebanese Sunni Islamists. The Iranian leadership declared that it was in "one trench" with Bashar al-Asad. In April 2005, UN Security Council Resolution 1595 established the international organization's first ever murder inquiry to identify Hariri's assassins. All lines of subsequent investigation pointed to the Syrian-Lebanese security machine and the inner recesses of the Syrian regime.

While the murder investigation ground on, accompanied by further killings of anti-Syrian personalities, Lebanese politics took new twists. Gen. Michel Aoun returned from exile in May 2005 and broke with Hariri's son Saad and Walid Jumblat over their unwillingness to endorse him for the presidency. The May–June parliamentary elections gave the Hariri-Jumblat camp a majority in parliament (72 seats out of 128), but Aoun took the Maronite heartland (21 seats). Together with the Amal-Hizballah bloc and its non-Shi'a clients (35 seats), Aoun blocked the "new majority" drive to remove President Lahoud. In February 2006, Aoun reached an understanding with Hizballah that reflected Maronite and Shi'a suspicions of the Sunni Hariri bloc and its Saudi backers. New prime minister Fuad Siniora, from the "new majority," faced a daunting task in dealing with Aoun and Hizballah, the latter entrenched inside his government. Syria's ruling clique maneuvered vengefully in the background, looking to smash the resurgent Lebanese autonomy backed by the United States and France.

On July 12, 2006, Hizballah raided across the Israel–Lebanon border, kidnapping two Israeli soldiers and killing three in an unprecedented action. Hizballah claimed that this was to compel release of Lebanese and Palestinian prisoners. However, it bore the signs of a bid by the Hizballah-Syria-Iran coalition to turn the tables on opponents inside and outside Lebanon—to rescue Ba'thist Syria, pivot of the coalition, from the Hariri murder inquiry and to enable an effective coup d'état by Hizballah against the "new majority" commanding the Lebanese government. It stretches credulity to suppose that Hizballah did not coordinate with its senior partners in an operation guaranteed to bring a large-scale Israeli response. In the six years after Israel's withdrawal to the international boundary in 2000, Syria and Iran provided Hizballah with up to 15,000 rockets of various calibers, and the party's armed wing turned southern Lebanon into a fortress where the Lebanese state and army had no sway. In 2006, Hizballah was ready to give Israel a military surprise.

Over five weeks, Israel used aerial bombardment and, later, hesitant ground penetration to degrade Hizballah, causing devastation and around 1,000 deaths in the Shi'a areas of Lebanon. Hizballah sent a steady shower of missiles into Israel until the cease-fire and could claim success simply by maintaining itself against a massively larger regular army.

The balance after the August 14 UN-sponsored cease-fire was ambiguous. Hizballah had to accept Lebanese army deployment to the border, stiffened by a more robust UN force. The Lebanese army thus appeared in areas from which it had been absent for decades. UN Security Council Resolution 1701 fingered Hizballah for initiating hostilities, reiterated Resolution 1559 in demanding an end to private armies, and indicated the need to monitor the Syria-Lebanon border. On the other hand, Hizballah could simply conceal weaponry, and Iran supplied cash for Hizballah-led civilian reconstruction, challenging the Lebanese state. Lebanon's Shi'as clustered around Hizballah, but resentment of Hizballah's seizure of decision making for war and peace dominated elsewhere.

Henceforth, Lebanon split between two political camps, named from the demonstrations of March 2005: the anti-Syrian March 14 "new majority" led by Saad Hariri and Walid Jumblat and the March 8 bloc of Hizballah, Amal, and the Aounists, aligned with Syria and Iran. Each bloc was cross-sectarian but with a basic divide of Sunni and Druze (March 14) versus Shi'as (March 8), with Christians fragmented. In November 2006, pro-Syrian ministers resigned from the government to stop endorsement of the UN protocol for a mixed international-Lebanese tribunal to prosecute those responsible for the Hariri murder and associated killings. The government, however, retained its two-thirds quorum, passed the protocol, and persevered as a March 14 rump. The March 8 camp declared it illegitimate and began a street campaign against it.

Prime Minister Siniora's rump cabinet endured from November 2006 until May 2008. It survived more murders of March 14 parliamentarians, an uprising of Sunni Islamists, probably inspired by Syrian military intelligence, in the Nahr al-Bared Palestinian refugee camp near Tripoli, and a six-month vacuum in the Lebanese presidency after Emile Lahoud finally left office in November 2007. Ignoring threats from Bashar al-Asad about violence in Lebanon if the United Nations went ahead with the murder tribunal, the Security Council bypassed the paralyzed Lebanese parliament and unilaterally established the special tribunal in June 2007. The Nahr al-Bared outburst followed promptly, and it took the poorly equipped Lebanese army all summer to crush the Fath al-Islam group. In late 2007, army commander Michel Suleiman received March 14 support to be president. Hizballah, which had positive relations with Suleiman, did not oppose this. The March 8 camp, however, demanded veto power in a new national unity government in exchange for allowing parliament to hold a presidential electoral session. The impasse only ended by violence in May 2008. Hizballah overran mainly Sunni West Beirut after the government tried to shut down its illicit communications system, and the Arab League brokered a political compromise in Doha. Suleiman became president, and March 8 received its blocking capability in a new coalition cabinet under Fuad Siniora.

Thereafter, the approach to the June 2009 parliamentary elections consumed Lebanese politics. Nothing further emerged from the Hariri murder inquiry, although the special tribunal came into physical existence in March 2009. Indictments faded into a hazy future; the hiatus demoralized March 14 and spurred March 8 into a belligerent electoral posture. Hizballah's use of "resistance" weaponry against other Lebanese in May 2008 hung over everyone, and the Aounists hoped small Christian constituencies from the resuscitated 1960 electoral law would facilitate gains. March 14, however, scored an electoral victory on June 7, 2009. Christians hesitated at the brink of the unknown, and Sunnis, smarting from their May 2008 humiliation, mobilized to buttress March 14. Results virtually replicated the outgoing parliament—seventy-one for March 14 and fifty-seven for March 8, with Hizballah retaining its command of the Shi'a.

Saad Hariri received the commission to form a government, but Walid Jumblat decided to break with March 14 and make up with Syria's allies. Jumblat drew his conclusions from "engagement" of the Syrian regime by new US president Barack Obama, lost hope in the special tribunal, and looked to fortify his position by balancing between March 14 and March 8. He hoped to cooperate with Shi'a Amal leader Nabih Berri. This defection from the majority gutted the election result and complicated accommodation of Jumblat, the March 14 rump, Aoun, Amal, Hizballah, and President Suleiman in Saad Hariri's prospective cabinet. In early November 2009, Lebanon still had no government to replace Siniora's caretaker administration.

FOREIGN POLICY

Lebanon matters. The country is located in the core of the Arab world, and Mount Lebanon is the dominant topographic feature of both the coast of the Levant and the land bridge between Eurasia and Africa. The external associations of each of Lebanon's three "great" communities—the Maronites with France and the West, the Sunnis with major Arab states, and the Shi'as with Iran—compound the strategic significance of the mountain. Modern geopolitical fragmentation in the Levant gives the strategic significance special salience. Lebanon offers access to the Arab-Israeli front line and overshadows the Syrian capital. Beyond the Levant, the Lebanese people, with their formidable technical and commercial dexterity and their far-flung diaspora, represent a regional and global human resource. No other Arab country has a reach that remotely compares with the worldwide presence, wealth, and influence of perhaps 10 million overseas Lebanese. Even in its region, Lebanon's smallness is deceptive—the fortunes of democratic politics, a free media, and economic liberalism in Beirut reverberate throughout the Middle East. In the early twenty-first century, Lebanon has the chance to reemerge as a beacon of pluralism and a challenge to autocracy in its Arab neighborhood.

The variety of Lebanon's external connections and the salience of Lebanon for external powers have meant that the country's stability has been constantly at risk. Lebanese governments have often preferred to avoid strong foreign alignments, within or beyond the Arab world. Deviation from this approach has invariably brought trouble, either because of strong opposition within one or more of the country's major communities or because of the hostility of significant external powers exercised through their Lebanese sympathizers. In the 1950s, President Chamoun's relations with the West were suspect to many Muslims, and Egypt's influence on Muslims was in turn suspect to most Christians. After 1967, regime compromises with the Palestinians led Christians to arm themselves, and Maronite relations with Israel and Iraq later contributed to Syrian determination to manipulate its local allies to achieve hegemony. After 1985, Hizballah's ties to revolutionary Iran stimulated a variety of counterpressures on Lebanon from the United States, Israel, and Syria. Lebanese regime leaders of the 1990s had little choice but to bow to Damascus in foreign policy, whatever their private sentiments, but their humiliating subservience could only be sustained through repression. After 2000, the mounting Christian, Sunni, and Druze alienation from Ba'thist Syria was bound to bring a day of reckoning. The reckoning came in 2005, but Syria and Iran were able to operate through the Shi'as to encourage a schism over the convergence of the majority in the new Lebanese government with the United States and France.

As regards Arab-Israeli affairs, Lebanese governments paid lip service to anti-Israeli stands through the 1950s and 1960s but had little taste for activism. Israeli transgressions of Lebanese territory from the 1970s on, however, hardened Lebanese attitudes. Even many Christians viewed Israel as partly responsible for Lebanon's Palestinian problem, for the 1983–1984 Christian disasters in the Shuf hills, and for Shi'a radicalism. In the 1990s, most Lebanese wanted calm on their southern border and resented being coerced by Damascus into serving as Syria's surrogate front line, but they felt little impetus toward an Israeli-Lebanese peace treaty. Syrian pressure to ensure that Lebanon did not seek to emulate the PLO and Jordan in making a separate deal with the Israelis was really unnecessary. In 2006, Walid Jumblat spoke for the non-Shi'a majority when he favored Lebanese army deployment along the border and Hizballah disarmament, with application of the 1949 Lebanese-Israeli armistice agreement, not a formal peace, as long as conditions did not permit a general Arab-Israeli settlement.

Lebanon's principal foreign policy issue in the early twenty-first century stemmed from its principal domestic issue—the Lebanese state's lack of a monopoly of force on much of Lebanese territory. Lebanon could pass as a proper territorial state from independence in 1943 until the early 1970s. Thereafter, for one-third of a century, the procession of sectarian cantons, foreign occupations, and Syrian hegemony meant that Lebanon was simply a territorial shell within which the Lebanese regime was a subordinate actor. The Lebanese state reasserted itself in 2005, but its authority remained partial, dependent on backing from the international community. Syria's grudging military evacuation enabled Lebanon to restore state command of the north and the Biqa Valley, but Syrian aid to various parties and "security islands" continued. Apart from Hizballah's grip on southern Lebanon, these included the Ain al-Helwe Palestinian refugee camp in Sidon, hosting Palestinian and Lebanese Sunni extremists, and outposts of Palestinian militants near the Syrian border. Ba'thist Syria could also liaise with the Shi'a Amal movement, Hizballah's unenthusiastic "partner," which would be valuable if Syria had difficulties with Hizballah and Iran, the Maronite Franjiyahs of Zghorta, and disaffected Sunni and Druze personalities. In December 2008, the discontented Gen. Michel Aoun, holder of the largest bloc of Christian seats in parliament who gave vital cross-sectarian cover to Hizballah's private army, made a reconciliation visit to Syria, his old enemy.

Bashar al-Asad's regime girded itself with its Lebanese allies to confront the UN Security Council, mobilized by the United States, France, and Britain to buttress Lebanon's territorial integrity. Security Council Resolution 1559 of September 2004, which required Lebanese state monopoly of force, led to Resolution 1680 of May 2006, "strongly encouraging" Syria to establish diplomatic relations with Lebanon and to facilitate demarcation of the Lebanese-Syrian border. The novel feature was the Lebanese official demand for embassies, putting aside reluctance to challenge Damascus. The Syrian leadership maintained that diplomatic relations were superfluous between "sister states," but by 2008 Syria had no choice but to concede the embassies.

In 2005, Prime Minister Fuad Siniora, heading a government with an anti-Syrian majority deriving from Lebanon's first free, albeit flawed, parliamentary elections since 1972, returned Lebanon to an Arab and international credibility unknown since the 1960s. Within the constraints of its Western-Arab and Muslim-Christian dualities, Lebanon had played an active role in international affairs from the 1940s to the 1960s. It was a founding member of both the United Nations and the Arab League and had been a respected partner of the conservative, Western-oriented group of Arab states, including the Arabian Peninsula monarchies, Jordan, and Morocco. If it could sustain its escape from the Syrian Ba'thists, it looked to reestablish such a profile, with better democratic credentials and wider connections.

Further, the Hariri murder affair and the 2006 Israeli-Hizballah fighting led to a level of international intervention in the country unique in the world—the UN murder inquiry and the special tribunal, the enlarged UN Interim Force in Lebanon, the UN Border Assessment Team, and special UN envoys to report on implementation of Security Council Resolutions 1559 and 1701, all in addition to the older UN Truce Supervision Organization for the 1949 armistice and the UN Relief and Works Organization for the Palestinian refugees.

Prime Minister Siniora did his best to cement working relations with the US administration, which increased aid to the Lebanese army. He faced intense Shi'a suspicion of US support for Israel. Lebanon's "new majority" also had to cope with French capriciousness after May 2007 as President Nicolas Sarkozy flirted with Damascus, as well as with uncertain support from Saudi Arabia and Egypt while Iran and Syria underwrote the opposition. Siniora scored impressive international financial promises at the Paris III donors' conference for Lebanon in January 2007, but with delivery postponed until the government could implement reforms.

New turns of the wheel in Lebanon's external environment could suddenly nudge the domestic balance. For example, legitimacy issues in Iran after the farcical June 2009 presidential elections for the first time raised a question mark over Hizballah's long-term Iranian backing. This was in addition to other question marks as Syria maneuvered with the West after the February 2008 assassination in Damascus of Hizballah intelligence chief Imad Mughniyeh.

Looking ahead, Lebanon sits on multiple fault lines—Sunni/Shi'a, Arab/Iranian, Arab/Israeli, Christian/Muslim, and Western/Islamic. The domestic and international juggling operations required to secure decent pluralist politics for the long-term are Sisyphean tasks, and the chances of success or failure to a large degree depend on events beyond Lebanon.

BIBLIOGRAPHY

Lebanon is the subject of many excellent books and monographs in several languages; in English and Arabic the range and sophistication for the modern period is great. Important works have appeared since 2000, particularly under the auspices of I. B. Tauris and the disbanded Centre for Lebanese Studies at Oxford. Preexisting gaps for the French mandatory decades and for the 1950s have been largely closed, though social and political developments during the Shihab presidency of 1958 to 1964 deserve more attention. The Syrian hegemony of 1990 to 2005 awaits a definitive overview, which depends on the Hariri murder investigation. The latter may also prompt reexamination of the 1975–1990 war years.

For Lebanon's history before the modern state in 1920, the best starting point remains Kamal Salibi, who offers surveys grounded in Arabic sources. These include *The Modern History of Lebanon* (New York: Praeger Publishers, 1965), *A House of Many Mansions: The History of Lebanon Reconsidered* (London: I. B. Tauris, 1988), and, for the pre-Ottoman centuries, his Arabic monograph *Muntalaq Ta'rikh Lubnan* (*The Opening of Lebanese History*) (Beirut: Caravan, 1979). Abdul-Rahim Abu Husayn gives insights on the sixteenth and seventeenth centuries in *The View from Istanbul: Ottoman Lebanon and the Druze Emirate* (London: I. B. Tauris, 2004), while Ilya Harik's *Politics and Change in a Traditional Society: Lebanon 1711–1845* (Princeton, NJ: Princeton University Press, 1968) and Richard van Leeuwen's *Notables and Clergy in Mount Lebanon: The Khazin Sheikhs and the Maronite Church* (Leiden: E. J. Brill, 1994) provide coverage of the communal developments of the eighteenth century.

Modern Lebanon's emergence from the 1840s on is well covered. Cesar Farah's *The Politics of Interventionism in Ottoman Lebanon, 1830–1861* (London: I. B. Tauris, 2000) and Leila Fawaz's *An Occasion for War: Civil Conflict in Lebanon and Damascus, 1860* (London: I. B. Tauris, 1994) dissect the sectarian turbulence of the mid-nineteenth century. Fawaz also supplies urban social context in *Merchants and Migrants in Nineteenth-Century Beirut* (Cambridge, MA: Harvard University Press, 1983). Engin Akarli's *The Long Peace: Ottoman Lebanon, 1861–1920* (Los Angeles: University of California Press, 1993) and John Spagnolo's *France and Ottoman Lebanon, 1861–1914* (London: Ithaca Press, 1977) analyze the autonomous province of Mount Lebanon.

New books have appeared on Lebanon's transition from French mandatory rule after 1920 to independence after 1943. Kais Firro and Raghid al-Solh investigate the ideological underpinnings of modern Lebanon in *Inventing Lebanon: Nationalism and the State Under the Mandate* (London: I. B. Tauris, 2003) and *Lebanon and Arabism: National Identity and State Formation* (London: I. B. Tauris, 2004), respectively. These supplement Meir Zamir's two-volume study of mandatory Lebanon: *The Formation of Modern Lebanon* (London: Croom Helm, 1985) and *Lebanon's Quest: The Road to Statehood, 1926–39* (London: I. B. Tauris, 1997).

Treatment of Lebanon's progression through the 1950s and 1960s toward breakdown in the mid-1970s is fragmented. An overview benefiting from the new academic perspectives of the post–Cold War era is lacking. Samir Khalaf dissects Lebanese integration of representative politics with sectarian influences and patronage networks in *Lebanon's Predicament* (New York: Columbia University Press, 1987), and Wade Goria reviews political personalities in *Sovereignty and Leadership in Lebanon, 1943–76* (London: Ithaca Press, 1986). Studies of the Khoury and Chamoun presidencies (1943–1958) include Eyal Zisser's *Lebanon: The Challenge of Independence* (London: I. B. Tauris, 2000), Caroline Attié's *Struggle in the Levant: Lebanon in the 1950s* (London: I. B. Tauris, 2004), and Erika Alin's *The United States and the 1958 Lebanon Crisis* (Lanham, MD: University Press of America, 1994). Nasser Kalawoun discusses Lebanon's interaction with Gamal Abd al-Nasser's Egypt in *The Struggle for Lebanon: A Modern History of Lebanese-Egyptian Relations* (London: I. B. Tauris, 2000). The best analysis of Lebanon's difficulties after the 1967 Arab-Israeli War is Farid el-Khazen's *The Breakdown of the State in Lebanon, 1967–1976* (Cambridge, MA: Harvard University Press, 2000).

For the economic and social circumstances of late-twentieth-century Lebanon, consult Caroline Gate's *The Merchant Republic of Lebanon: Rise of an Open Economy* (London: I. B. Tauris, 1998) and Michael Johnson's *All Honourable Men: The Social Origins of War in Lebanon* (London: I. B. Tauris, 2001). Kamal Dib examines the social-economic interface in his *Warlords and Merchants: The Lebanese Business and Political Establishment* (London: Ithaca Press, 2004), while Latif Abul Husn's *The Lebanese Conflict: Looking Inward* (Boulder, CO: Lynne Rienner, 1998) interprets communal affairs and interactions.

As regards individual sectarian communities, the modern emergence of the Shi'as is covered in Fouad Ajami's *The Vanished Imam: Musa al-Sadr and the Shi'a of Lebanon* (Ithaca, NY: Cornell University Press, 1985); Majid Halawi's *A Lebanon*

Defied: Musa al-Sadr and the Shi'a Community (Boulder, CO: Westview, 1992); and Augustus Richard Norton's *Amal and the Shi'a: Struggle for the Soul of Lebanon* (Austin: University of Texas Press, 1987). Chibli Mallat, *Shi'i Thought from the South of Lebanon*, Papers on Lebanon 7 (Oxford: Centre for Lebanese Studies, 1988), discusses Shi'a political concepts. In Arabic, Wadah Sharara's *Dawlat Hizballah: Lubnan Mujtama'an Islamiyan* (*Hizballah's State: Lebanon as an Islamic Society*) (Beirut: Dar al-Nahar, 1997) presents the outlook of a Shi'a critic of the "Party of God." On the Druze, Robert Brenton Bett's *The Druze* (New Haven, CT: Yale University Press, 1988) and Fuad Khuri's *Being a Druze* (London: Druze Heritage Foundation, 2004) deserve note. In contrast, the Maronite and Sunni communities have not received adequate recent attention in the English-language literature, at least since Michael Johnson's brilliant *Class and Client in Beirut: The Sunni Muslim Community and the Lebanese State, 1840–1985* (London: Ithaca Press, 1986).

Much has been written about the war period from 1975 to 1990. For 1975 to 1982, see Samir Kassir's *La guere du Liban: De la dissension nationale au conflit régional, 1975–1982* (*The Lebanon War: From National Dissension to Regional Conflict, 1975–1982*) (Paris: Karthala, 1994) and Itamar Rabinovich's *The War for Lebanon, 1970–1983* (Ithaca, NY: Cornell University Press, 1984). Theodor Hanf's *Co-existence in Wartime Lebanon: Death of a State and Birth of a Nation* (London: I. B. Tauris, 1993) provides an encyclopedic assessment of social and political dimensions. William Harris's *New Face of Lebanon: History's Revenge* (Princeton, NJ: Markus Wiener, 2006) and Elie Salem's *Violence and Diplomacy in Lebanon: The Troubled Years, 1982–1988* (London: I. B. Tauris, 1995) concentrate on the 1980s.

Inevitably, analysis of post-1990 trends remains tentative. In Barry Rubin's *Lebanon: Liberation, Conflict, and Crisis* (New York: Palgrave Macmillan, 2009) various authors survey Lebanon's latest configuration. Nicholas Blanford gives the Hariri story in *Killing Mr. Lebanon: The Assassination of Rafik Hariri and Its Impact on the Middle East* (London: I. B. Tauris, 2006); Oren Barak assesses the changing nature and role of the military in *The Lebanese Army: A National Institution in a Divided Society* (Albany: State University of New York Press, 2009); and Nizar Hamzeh's *In the Path of Hizballah* (Syracuse, NY: Syracuse University Press, 2004) provides data on Lebanon's "state within the state." As regards external entanglements, Robert Rabil's *Embattled Neighbors: Syria, Israel, and Lebanon* (Boulder, CO: Lynne Rienner, 2003) places Lebanon in its regional context.

A number of English-language websites may be mentioned. LebWeb (www.lebweb.com) is the best general Internet guide. It includes links to Lebanese government sites and political factions, as well as Lebanon's Arabic newspapers, for example, *Al-Nahar* (centrist) and *Al-Safir* (leftist/Arabist). Lebanonwire (www.lebanonwire.com) offers a subscriber service with excellent data on a wide range of political and social topics. For current affairs in English, consult Now Lebanon (www.nowlebanon.com), Beirut's *Daily Star* newspaper (www.dailystar.com.lb), and Naharnet (www.naharnet.com). For economic updates, it is hard to beat the quarterly Lebanon country report of the Economist Intelligence Unit, accessible both in hard copy and, for subscribers, at www.eiu.com.

9

Syrian Arab Republic

David W. Lesch

Syria could genuinely be called a "crossroads" of history because of the numerous civilizations that have established themselves in and passed through this ancient territory.[1]

Historical Background

Damascus, the capital of the Syrian Arab Republic, is one of the oldest continually inhabited cities in the world, but the modern identification of Syria as an Arab and Muslim territory began in the seventh century CE. Syria was an important trading destination for Arabs in western Arabia for several centuries before the rise of Islam. The great Islamic conquests began within two years after Muhammad's passing. By 638, Byzantine resistance in greater Syria had been smashed by the Muslim armies, and the second caliph, or successor to Muhammad, Umar, appointed as the first governor of Syria Muawiya ibn Abi Sufyan, who established the Umayyad caliphate based in Damascus in 661. The Umayyads, however, tended to be a regime by the Arabs and for the Arabs. The Abbasid revolution in 750 CE shifted the center of Islam eastward to Baghdad and promised a much more religiously inspired and inclusive leadership. Syria receded to the background as one of many provinces in a growing empire.

The short-lived twelfth- and thirteenth-century Ayyubid dynasty (named after Salah al-Din al-Ayyubi, or Saladin in Western lore) was replaced by the Mamluk Empire, established in Cairo in the second half of the thirteenth century and lasting until 1517. The Mamluks were a Turkish-Circassian dynasty that ruled over Syria. In 1517 the Ottoman Turks entered Cairo, thus extending their domain deep into the Middle East. Syria would become extremely important to the Ottoman sultan based in Constantinople (Istanbul), and it would be one of the few Arab territories that remained under real Ottoman control until World War I. Under Ottoman rule, Syria began to develop modern political and socioeconomic institutions.

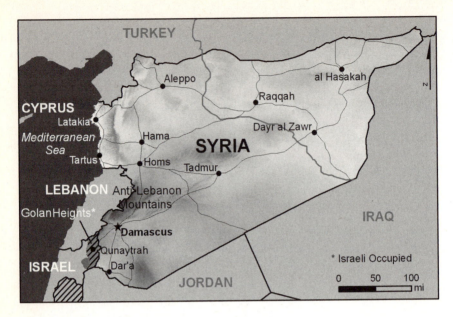

Syrian Arab Republic

As Ottoman power began to decline into the eighteenth and nineteenth centuries, other regional powers and eventually the Europeans began to extend their influence into Syria. Muhammad Ali, the Egyptian dynast, occupied Syria for almost a decade. Only with European assistance did the Ottomans manage to dislodge his forces. In the aftermath of the Ottoman hiatus, a new class of urban notables emerged in Syria that functioned as local authorities and intermediaries with Ottoman officials. This class of notables would become important political players in Syria for the remainder of the nineteenth and well into the twentieth century. In addition, the Ottoman Empire became subject to more pressure from the Europeans to reform along the European model, and modernization—and responses to it—were felt in Syria.

Syria became a focus of a proto-Arab nationalist response to European encroachment and modernization, engendered by a combination of factors, including the rediscovery and new appreciation of Arab heritage and the role the Arabs played in the founding and establishment of Islam, which was bound so tightly with the emergence of the pan-Islamic Salafiyya movement in the late nineteenth century; the so-called Arab awakening spurred on by an Arab literary movement centered in the Levant in the second half of the 1800s; and, finally, the ever-tightening control of the Ottomans while Syria remained one of the few areas to remain under Ottoman rule. This last factor became even more pronounced with the "turkification" policies enforced in Syria before and especially after the Young Turk revolution of 1908 that unleashed a more assertive form of Turkish nationalism upon the shrinking empire. The turkification policies included the prescribed use of the Turkish language at educational levels above primary school, in commercial transactions, in government discourse and correspondence, and in the courts.

Despite the centralization policy emanating from Constantinople, Arab nationalists in Syria tended to agitate for more of a voice in the government and/or more autonomy rather than outright independence. This lasted until World War I. The Ottoman structure had become something of the accepted status quo, one not easily abandoned, especially without the necessary institutional foundation to fill the vacuum. The Arab Muslim majority in Syria, already resentful of the benefits the minority Christians in the area received from sympathetic European powers, avidly supported the pan-Islamism espoused by Ottoman Sultan Abd al-Hamid II; in return for this support, the Sublime Porte continued to assist in the development of Syria's agricultural and commercial sectors, mutually reinforcing the long-standing links between Constantinople and Syrian cities such as Damascus and Aleppo.

When World War I erupted in 1914, the Young Turk regime in power in Constantinople began to fear that Arab nationalism could be used as an ideological wedge to break Syria free from the Ottoman Empire. As a number of Arab nationalists were Christian, known to have close ties with the French, and because the British seemed to be courting Arab nationalists to foment a mass rebellion against Ottoman rule—thereby weakening Ottoman resistance to British military designs in the Middle East, particularly at Gallipoli—the Young Turk leadership began to adopt a more hostile view toward Arab nationalists and other possible malcontents in Syria. As such, one of the Young Turk triumvirs, Jamal Pasha, visited Syria and harshly dealt with the Arab nationalists and Arab secret societies, including ordering scores of executions. The Turks had some reason to be concerned, as an Arab revolt for which a number of Syrians professed support was brewing in the Hijaz in western Arabia—the uprising led by Sharif Hussein, a Hashimite, and his son Faisal. The British had negotiated with Hussein to launch the revolt in return for vague promises (embodied in the Hussein-McMahon correspondence) regarding Arab independence, including a portion of what is now Syria. Although the Arab rebellion was much smaller than the British had desired or anticipated, with Faisal leading the Arab fighters along with British liaison officer T. E. Lawrence ("Lawrence of Arabia"), it did become a disruptive force against the Ottomans alongside the main British column heading up through Palestine from Egypt with Damascus as its ultimate objective.

Damascus had been taken by October 1918, a month before the end of World War I. Faisal's Arab column was allowed by the British to "liberate" Damascus—even though Ottoman troops had already evacuated the city—so that London could have an Arab ally in Syria while preventing the French, at the time ensconced along the

SYRIA

Capital city	Damascus
Chief of state	President Bashar al-Asad
Head of government	Prime Minister Muhammad Naji al-Utri
Major political parties (*seats in parliament*)	Ba'ath Party/National Progressive Front (172) Socialist Unionist Democratic Party (0), Syrian Arab Socialist Union (0), Syrian Communist Party (0), Syrian Social Nationalist Party (0), Unionist Socialist Party (0)
Ethnic groups	Arab (90.3%), Kurds, Armenians, and other (9.7%)
Religious groups	Sunni Muslim (74%), other Muslim, mainly Alawite and Druze (16%), Christian (10%)
Export partners	Iraq (30.2%), Germany (9.6%), Lebanon (9.5%), Italy (6.2%), France (5.4%), Egypt (5.3%), Saudi Arabia (5%)
Import partners	Saudi Arabia (11.8%), China (8.8%), Russia (6.5%), Italy (5.9%), Egypt (5.8%), United Arab Emirates (5.8%), Ukraine (4.6%), Turkey (4.3%), Iran (4.3%)

coast in Lebanon, from acquiring what they thought was their rightful claim to the interior of Syria. As such, the taking of Damascus became enmeshed in postwar diplomacy before the war was even over. Just how much should the British honor French interests as articulated in the wartime Sykes-Picot agreement; just how much should the British honor the pledge given to the Arabs in the Hussein-McMahon correspondence; and how much could the British dictate, and if necessary reshape, the terms of the postwar order in the Middle East with British troops dominant in the region? The first months of Arab rule in Damascus under Faisal were chaotic, amid British and French machinations to secure the interior of Syria through Arab surrogates. But, as British prime minister David Lloyd George commented on one occasion, "France is worth ten Syria's." British troops thus evacuated Syria, leaving Faisal's short-lived Hashimite Kingdom of Syria to fend for itself against French troops. In July 1920, French forces quickly dispatched Arab armed resistance, laying direct claim to what had been formalized earlier in an agreement at San Remo, Italy (i.e., Syria, including Lebanon, would become a French mandate).

With the opposition of the majority Sunni Muslim population in Syria to French rule, mandatory authorities adopted a "divide-and-rule" tactical policy. In this sense the French could utilize Syria's fissiparous ethnic and religious nature against it to prevent any coherent opposition from forming. The Maronite Christians in Lebanon had been the most pro-French element among the various sects; therefore, the French expanded the border of the Ottoman district of Mount Lebanon and administered the area as a separate entity, which ultimately became the core of modern Lebanon. The remainder of French-mandated Syria was then divided into five zones. Each division was chosen to play upon traditional rivalries. Latakia was carved out for the Alawites, Alexandretta for the Turks, and Jabal Druze for the Druze. The Sunni Muslims were divided between Aleppo and Damascus. Moreover, the Alawites were brought into the local military force in numbers far exceeding their percentage of the population. For the traditionally persecuted Alawite sect, joining the military, looked upon with derision by most other Syrians because of the tacit cooperation with the French, was one of the few available avenues for upward social mobility. It turned out to be quite serendipitous following World War II, when the military became politicized and used as a political instrument for acquiring power; the Alawites were then in an advantageous position to advance within the political system, eventually dominating the military-security apparatus and, thus, political power by the middle of the 1960s. The Sunni Arab nationalists, on the other hand, as primarily members of the urban educated classes, were isolated from much of the country during the Mandate years. As such, French rule was generally regarded by Syrians as oppressive. French was introduced in the schools at the expense of Arabic. Singing the French national anthem was required, and the French franc became legal tender. Embittered Syrian nationalists played upon these obvious symbols of the French presence and won widespread support in their opposition to French rule.

Traditional ethnic and religious leaders also opposed French rule, leading to a series of minor rebellions. The most serious rebellion began in the summer of 1925, when rebel Druze tribesmen drove the French out of the towns and villages in Jabal Druze. French military superiority, however, most notably on display with the bombardment of Damascus, had squashed the revolt by the end of the year.

Although Franco-Syrian relations remained tense, differences were generally played out in the political arena. The next decade and a half was marked by slow progress in Syria's attempts to establish a political framework under which it could move toward full independence. One area of controversy was the Syrian insistence that all territories controlled by the French be considered part of Syria, which thus denied the autonomy of Lebanon, Alexandretta, and Jabal Druze. The evolution of

Franco-Syrian relations took a major step in 1936, when a treaty of alliance was worked out. Although the French parliament never ratified the treaty, it served as a basis from which future ties evolved. The cession of the province of Hatay (the Syrian province of Alexandretta) to Turkey in 1939 further incensed the Syrians. The French essentially gave the province to the Turks so that they would remain neutral in the face of World War II. Bashar al-Asad announced Syria's recognition of Hatay as part of Turkey in late 2004; however, an official document on the issue is still being negotiated. Not until recently did Syria recognize the cession of Hatay.

World War II provided the Syrians the opportunity to gain full independence. Some progress was made with the Vichy government, which established partial self-government in 1941 after riots in Damascus. When the Free French arrived in the summer of 1941, they promised full independence in order to win popular support. Actual independence was in fact granted that September, but the French still acted as a mandatory power. Although an elected nationalist government came to power in 1943 under President Shukri al-Quwatli, full independence was not achieved until 1946, when the last French soldiers reluctantly withdrew. Despite the often tense and antagonistic relationship between the French and most indigenous Syrians, the Mandate period significantly influenced Syria for decades and, in some ways, still does today. The Syrian educational system (particularly the private schools), judicial system, and many important sectors of the economy evolved from the French structure imposed during the mandate. Even French language, fashion, cuisine, and architecture are still easily recognizable in Syria, especially as Syrian-French relations became much more cooperative for most of the period following the end of the mandate.

The last contingent of French troops departed in April 1946. The country was now in the hands of a group of politicians who had gained popularity from their long struggle against Ottoman and French suzerainty. The 1947 parliamentary elections gave visible indications of the growing fragmentation of the Syrian polity as well as the increasing public disenchantment with the Mandate-era politicians. The elections of 1947 also introduced interested observers to the Ba'th Party, an ardently nationalistic group operating under a pan-Arab socialist doctrine. It would systematically improve its power position in Syria to the point of virtually dictating by 1955 the government's neutralist and largely anti-West foreign policy.

The Ba'th Party arose primarily from the ideological meeting of the minds of three Syrians: Michel Aflaq, a Christian Arab; Salah al-Din Bitar, a Sunni Arab; and Zaki al-Arzuzi, an Alawite. At first flirting with communism while studying together in Paris from 1929 to 1934, Aflaq and Bitar ultimately rejected Communist doctrine and promoted Arab unity, freedom, and socialism. The Ba'th became the foremost proponent of Arab neutralism. The Communists also opposed the so-called capitalist reactionaries and imperialists, but they were under suspicion from the Ba'th because their ideology was alien and their actions were dictated by another outside power, the Soviet Union. They did, however, share the objective of ridding the country of malevolent outside interference and maintaining Syrian independence. As such, the two groups cooperated from time to time against identical external threats, but as would become apparent into the late 1950s and early 1960s, their latent differences typically manifested themselves in open breaches.

The Ba'th Party might have remained an ideological party of the periphery were it not for its association with the parliamentary deputy from Hama, Akram al-Hawrani. He ultimately provided the muscle for the Ba'th with his close ties with various elements of the Syrian military, which would soon become the final political arbiter in the country. The relationship would prove to be symbiotic, for Hawrani's Arab Socialist Party was in need of an ideological foundation, one that the Ba'th would provide. The formal merger occurred in late 1952 while Hawrani, Aflaq, and Bitar were all in exile in Lebanon. This propitious occurrence had a lasting effect upon the future of Syria, for the new Arab Socialist Resurrection Party, still simply referred to as the Ba'th Party, was now endowed with the political wherewithal to seriously contend for power in Syria by the mid-1950s and thereafter to force upon whatever regime was formally in power the increasingly popular foreign policy edicts of anti-Zionism and neutralist Arab nationalism. The Ba'th became the voice of the opposition to Western imperialism, Israel, and anyone in the government seen as collaborating with either.

The seminal event during this period was the first Arab-Israeli war from 1947 to 1949. The Syrian regime at the time, led by Shukri al-Quwatli and comprising many of the so-called nationalists of the Mandate period, was utterly discredited by its corrupt and inept mishandling of a war that resulted in a humiliating defeat for the Arab combatants, most of whom, including Syria, were more concerned about the strategic designs of rival Arab states than focused on coordinating military strategy against Israel. The discontent among the populace and in the military following the war created an opening for the entrance of the army into Syrian politics with the overthrow of the regime in March 1949 by a military junta led by Gen. Husni al-Zaim. The coup signaled an end to Syria's brief and immature encounter with parliamentary democracy and created the foundation for the alliance between the Ba'th Party and the military.

Syria's political instability was even more evident in the fact that there were two more coups by the end of 1949, ending with Col. Adib al-Shishakli taking power in December. Al-Shishakli would rule from behind the scenes until 1953, when his authoritarian style became more noticeable after his assumption of the presidency. Opposition to al-Shishakli would culminate in yet another military coup in 1954. This political seesaw would continue to rock back and forth as

Syria became subject to a variety of external pressures due to the emerging inter-Arab cold war as well as the imposition of the superpower cold war onto the region. The fissiparous and particularistic nature of Syrian politics made it an attractive political battleground on which external powers could extend influence with money and guns. All the while, the Ba'th Party steadily increased its share of the seats in parliament and disproportionately influenced Syria's foreign policy orientation, veering toward the Soviet Union and pan-Arab nationalism. Both of these foreign policy tendencies led to Syria's ill-fated union with Egypt in February 1958 in the creation of the United Arab Republic (UAR). In essence, the UAR failed because the two countries simply did not fit, economically or politically. Gamal Abd al-Nasser and his Egyptian cohorts came to dominate the "province" of Syria in a manner distasteful to a number of Syrian parties, not least of which was the Ba'th, which had originally pushed for the merger yet soon became marginalized by pro-Nasserist elements. Finally, in September 1961, following yet another coup by parties representing the traditional elite in Damascus, Syria seceded from the UAR. Although anti-Egyptian sentiments ran high for a time, the new regime was not really representative of the direction of Syrian politics, which would soon resume the trajectory it was on prior to the merger with Egypt.

The Ba'th Party formally came to power in Syria in March 1963, a position it holds to this day. Different factions in the Ba'th Party manifested themselves in actual and attempted coups. In 1966 an intra-Ba'th coup brought Salah Jadid to power along with his radical wing of the party. Embracing the Soviet Union and espousing a more assertive anti-Israeli policy, the regime in Damascus consistently compelled Nasser, who had been reluctant to confront Israel directly, to shed his hesitation and adopt measures that heightened tensions at the Arab-Israeli level, especially in late 1966, when Egypt signed a joint defense agreement with Syria, and in May 1967, when the Egyptian president engaged in a series of provocative measures that compelled the Jewish state to launch a devastating preemptive strike in June. The 1967 Arab-Israeli War resulted in Israel's capture of the Sinai Peninsula and Gaza Strip from Egypt, the West Bank (including Arab East Jerusalem) from Jordan, and the Golan Heights from Syria.

Salah Jadid's regime survived the 1967 debacle; however, his continued aggressive policies against Israel and in the inter-Arab arena, particularly sanctioning Syria's intervention in the Jordanian civil war of September 1970 (known also as Black September), compelled more moderate elements in the Ba'th leadership to orchestrate his ouster. This occurred in November, with Hafiz al-Asad, an Alawite military officer who at the time was minister of defense and commander of the air force, taking over the reins of power; he was formally elected president by public referendum in March 1971.

The Political Environment

The Land and Its People

Geographically, Syria is 71,504 square miles (185,170 square kilometers), including the Israeli-occupied Golan Heights. Many Syrians consider the modern boundaries of their country to be an arbitrary European-designed portion of what generally is thought of as Greater Syria, which consists of present-day Lebanon, Jordan, Hatay, and Israel, including the occupied territories. These areas are thought to have been artificially separated from Syria as a result of the mandate system and European manipulation. The Mediterranean Sea is Syria's only natural border, with Tartus and Latakia being the largest cities along the coast north of Lebanon. The border with Lebanon in the west primarily follows the Anti-Lebanon range, while Syria's other borders were for the most part drawn by the European powers at the time of World War I, the longest being that with Turkey to the north (822 kilometers) and Iraq to the east (605 kilometers).

Syria is primarily semiarid and desert plateau, with a narrow coastal plane along the Mediterranean Sea. The eastern four-fifths of Syria constitute a large, mostly semiarid and desert plain that gradually slopes from west to east. The Syrian Desert, in essence the northern extension of the Arabian Desert, abuts deeply into this portion of the country. As such, nearly 80 percent of all Syrians live in the western 20 percent of the country. The bulk of this concentration of people lives in a north-south line of cities (Aleppo, Hama, Homs, Damascus) that generally separates the more fertile areas of the country from the semiarid and desert plain. The borders that became modern Syria cut off many parts of the country from their traditional mercantile and cultural links. A number of cross-cultural affinities and ties exist and are most apparent in the common Syrian mantra regarding Lebanon: "two lands, one people." These cross-cultural identities have had political implications over the years that have at times complicated Syria's relations with its neighbors.

The arable land amounts to about one-quarter of the total, with fertility highest in the Euphrates River valley as well as in the northwest portion of the country toward Aleppo. Cotton is Syria's largest cash crop, accounting for approximately 50 percent of agricultural gross domestic product (GDP). The agricultural sector also produces large quantities of wheat, barley, sugar beets, and olives. Although 80 percent of Syria's agriculture is rain fed, the government in recent years has invested heavily in developing irrigation systems to maintain crop production during drought years. Rainfall is seasonal in Syria, most of it coming in the winter months and falling in the northern and westernmost parts of the country. The semiarid steppe and desert portions of the country receive less than two hundred centimeters (eight inches) of rain per year.

The Golan (*Jawlan* in Arabic) Heights is a piece of territory between Syria and Israel. Geologically, the Golan is part of a plateau formed during the Holocene epoch (i.e., within the last 10,000 years). It is a volcanic field that extends to the east and northeast of the Syrian-Israeli border almost to Damascus—all in all some 1,750 square kilometers in southern Syria. The portion of the Golan Heights captured by Israel in the 1967 Arab-Israeli War covers approximately 1,250 square kilometers, including Mount Hermon at its northernmost point, making up about 1 percent of the total area of Syria. The Golan Heights runs north-south along the Syrian-Israeli extant, bordered on the north by Lebanon and in the south by Jordan. The length of the territory is about sixty-five kilometers, while the width varies between twelve and twenty-five kilometers, the thickest portion almost smack in the middle of the traverse. The average height of the Golan is about 1,000 meters, rising up from 400 to 1,700 meters along the western escarpment overlooking the Huleh Valley in northern Israel, the most fertile agricultural land in the Jewish state. The tallest single point is Mount Hermon (called *Jabal al-Shaykh* in Syria), rising 2,224 meters above sea level. It is of great strategic importance since it peers over much of southern Lebanon, northern Israel, southern Syria, and the Golan Heights itself. At its closest point, Israeli-occupied Golan Heights is only thirty-five kilometers from Damascus. The Golan Heights is geostrategically important for two reasons: Control of the territory would give Syria the strategic advantage of looking down upon northern Israel; while it remains in Israeli hands, the Israeli military can be positioned only a short distance from Damascus on the flat, open Golan plateau. Also, a major water source, particularly for Israel, runs through the Golan Heights as tributaries feeding into the Jordan River, the life-blood of Israel in terms of water capacity, itself running alongside the Golan Heights and feeding into the Sea of Galilee (Lake Tiberius in Syria, Lake Kinneret in Israel) on its northern shore. The three main tributaries of the Jordan River located in the Golan Heights are the Dan, Hasbani, and Banyan rivers, all spring fed by the western and southern slopes of the Mount Hermon massif.

The population of Syria numbers a little over 18 million, 38 percent of which is below the age of fourteen. The capital and largest city in Syria, Damascus, has a population of approximately 5 million, Aleppo has 4.5 million, Homs (Hims) 1.8 million, Hama 1.6 million, and Latakia 1 million. Approximately 90.3 percent of the population is Arab, including some 400,000 Palestinian refugees. As such, Arabic is the official and most widely spoken language. The Kurds make up about 5 to 9 percent of the population depending upon the source. Many of the Kurds still speak Kurdish, and most live in the northeast portion of the country, although sizeable numbers reside in the major cities. Armenians (clustered primarily in and around Aleppo) and a smattering of other ethnicities, such as Turkomans, Circassians, and Jews, make up the remaining small percentage of the population.

Sunni Muslims account for 74 percent of the population, with the Alawites at 12 percent, Christians (of various sects, although the largest is Greek Orthodox) at 10 percent, the Druze at 3 percent (mostly located in southwestern Syria in the Jabal Druze region), and Jews and some other small Muslim sects at 1 percent. The Alawites are an obscure offshoot of Twelver Shi'a Islam. They venerate Ali ibn Abi Talib as the "bearer of divine essence," second in importance only to the Prophet Muhammad himself. Ali was the son-in-law and cousin of Muhammad and the fourth caliph, or successor to the Prophet, as leader of the Islamic community. The name "Alawite" or "Alawi" translates to "those who follow Ali." Also known as Nusayris, a name derived from a ninth-century Muslim prophet, Muhammad ibn Nusayr al-Namiri, the Alawites integrate some Christian and even Persian Zoroastrian rituals and holidays into their faith. For this reason, Sunni Muslims and even most Shi'a Muslims have considered Alawite Islam heretical. The great thirteenth- and fourteenth-century Sunni Islamic scholar Ibn Taymiyya issued a fatwa, or religious ruling, calling the Alawites greater infidels than Christians, Jews, or idolaters, and he authorized a jihad ("struggle" or "holy war") against them. The Alawites in Syria, located in the northwestern reaches of the country, were, until recent times, a persecuted minority in the area for centuries. Although Syria is a highly secularized state in the Middle East, it is still more traditionally oriented than most countries in the West. As such, religious affiliations and sentiments (often times with political overtones) still play an important role in the country.

Modern Political Dynamics and Structure

Hafiz al-Asad's assumption of power between 1970 and 1971 signaled the departure from an ideologically based foreign and domestic policy to a much more pragmatic one prepared to resolve diplomatically the Arab-Israeli conflict but wholeheartedly committed to a full return of the Golan Heights. His primary intent was to bring Syria back within accepted parameters inside the Arab fold, mainly by establishing a working relationship with Egypt and Saudi Arabia in order to coordinate policy toward Israel.

Domestically, Asad's becoming president signaled a retreat from the radical economic policies of Salah Jadid's regime and the opening up of the economy to the private sector. Indeed, Asad's political program upon his ascension to power was called the Corrective Movement (al-Harakat al-Tashishiyya). This first opening, or infitah, paralleled a similar process in Egypt under President Anwar Sadat, one that especially gained steam after the 1973 Arab-Israeli War, among the results of which was the near fourfold increase in the price per barrel of oil. While the profits largely accumulated in the pockets of the oil-exporting Persian Gulf states, the non-oil (or smaller oil-producing) states bordering Israel also benefitted enormously. The only way that countries such as Saudi Arabia and Kuwait could fight the Arab-Israeli conflict and still maintain their "Arab" credentials was to provide healthy amounts of financial aid and grants to the so-called confrontation states. Countries such as Egypt and Syria also reaped the rewards of remittances from their citizens, who were arriving by the tens of thousands in the sparsely populated Gulf countries as laborers.

The 1970s were marked by impressive growth in the Syrian economy. Asad's decision to open up the economy to allow more flexibility for the private sector was designed to find mechanisms to distribute the wealth that was suddenly pouring into the country. The growth was due largely to Arab transfers. In addition, during the oil-boom years of the 1970s, few states did anything to accumulate foreign-exchange reserves or direct remittances toward more productive activity. As such, changes in the regional and/or international economic environment could, and did, have deleterious repercussions for Syria, a country whose prosperity seemed to rely totally on the vagaries of the oil market and, given its primarily agrarian-based economy, seasonal rainfalls.

Hafiz al-Asad soon developed an authoritarian-based regime with a pervasive clientelist network in and outside of the government. It was also a regime that became Bonapartist (i.e., regime maintenance became the most important objective, with domestic and much of foreign policy being but a means to this end). Hafiz al-Asad constructed an alliance of sorts between Alawites and the Sunni business class that some have called the "military-merchant complex," and the Alawites, who came to dominate the military-security apparatus, were not about to relinquish their near-monopolizing hold on power and all of the political, social, and economic benefits that accrued from this; in fact, they were not even about to accept a dilution of that power, which certainly factored into the equation when Asad's son, Bashar, was chosen as president upon the father's death in 2000.

According to the 1973 constitution, Syria is a Socialist Popular Democratic Republic. In actuality, however, for decades it has been an authoritarian polity with only some of the trappings of democracy and still many of the burdens of socialism. Article 2 of the constitution states that Syria's "system of government is republican and sovereignty is exercised by the people," but in practice the people have no avenue or recourse to change the government, and candidates for election to national and municipal institutions are vetted by the Ba'th Party and the government. While the constitution technically allows for a multiparty pluralist system, Syria is in effect a one-party (Ba'th) authoritarian structure.

The constitution establishes the executive, legislative, and judicial branches of government. The unicameral parliament consists of 250 representatives elected by popular vote every four years. The parliament proposes the candidacy of the president, proposes and votes laws (which are generally generated by the executive branch and/or the Ba'th Party), discusses cabinet policy, and approves the budget. The constitution mandates that the Ba'th Party receive at least one-half of the parliamentary seats. Currently the ruling coalition, called the National Progressive Front (NPF)—which is dominated by the Ba'th Party and includes other mostly leftist and Communist parties—holds 169 seats (134 by the Ba'th Party), while non-NPF independents, all of whom are vetted by the government, hold 81 seats. The NPF was established in 1972 by the Hafiz al-Asad regime as a coalition of leftist and Arab nationalist parties that would allow limited participation in government by non-Ba'thist parties. The last parliamentary election was in 2007.

The president is elected to a seven-year renewable term after nomination by the Regional Command of the Ba'th Party and the parliament. Hafiz al-Asad was confirmed by unopposed referenda five times, usually garnering 99 percent of the vote on "yes-no" forms typically bearing only his name. His son, Bashar, ran unopposed following his father's death in June 2000 and received 97.29 percent of the vote in a national referendum. He was reelected to a second seven-year term in a yes–no referendum in 2007, again garnering over 97 percent of the vote. Political opposition to the president is generally not tolerated, except for that of the so-called loyal opposition within parliament. The parliament provides no check on the president.

The sixteen-member Regional Command of the Ba'th Party retains decision-making authority over the cabinet and the ministries. Several members of the cabinet are usually also in the Regional Command, and the president is also typically the head of the Ba'th Party as secretary-general. When Bashar took office the Regional Command was contracted in size and transformed into a more advisory body within the government rather than an entity that interferes with and dictates government policy, as has often been the case since the Ba'th Party rose to power. Since 2000, members of the Regional Command are elected by the Ba'th Party membership at Ba'th Party regional congresses rather than appointed, although all candidates must be approved first by the secretary-general of the party (i.e., the president).

One of the regime's prime weapons against internal dissent over the years has been Decree No. 51 as amended and promulgated on March 9, 1963, one day after the Ba'th Party came to power in Syria. It declared a state of emergency ostensibly designed to thwart the military threat emanating from Israel, but which has instead been used to stifle and eliminate internal challenges to the regime. The Syrian leadership considered the decree a fundamental right as recognized by the International Covenant on Civil and Political Rights, which allows a state to violate its constitutional provisions in a time of public emergency that "threatens the life of the nation." The lifting of the emergency law and the abolition of the associated extraconstitutional Supreme State Security Courts implemented by decree in 1968 have been, and continue to be, two of the prime objectives of humans rights and democracy activists in and outside of Syria. A succession of Syrian regimes, however, have claimed that "living in a dangerous neighborhood" provides ample excuse for keeping the emergency law and security courts in place. The Arab-Israeli conflict, inter-Arab machinations, superpower interference, and a serious Islamist rebellion in the late 1970s and early 1980s, which effectively ended in February 1982 upon the regime's demolishment of the Muslim Brotherhood base in the city of Hama (killing approximately 20,000 people by most estimates), have all contributed to regime paranoia and obsession about security and stability; indeed, even the population, after having experienced coup after coup for two decades, made something of a Faustian bargain (i.e., giving up certain freedoms in return for relative stability), something Hafiz al-Asad did indeed provide for three decades.

Political power ultimately rests upon economic satisfaction, and here the results for Syria have been decidedly mixed. Until the second half of the nineteenth century, Syria had long been a largely self-sufficient agrarian and trade-based economy. The opening of the Suez Canal in 1869, as well as the continuing economic problems of the Ottoman Empire by the 1870s (climaxing with its bankruptcy in 1875), forced a downturn in the Syrian economy for the remainder of the century and into the early twentieth century. Generally speaking, Syrians were (and continue to be) extremely adaptable to changing conditions, and they are resourceful in finding new markets and adopting new techniques when necessary. This did not, however, overcome the general economic malaise in Syria caused by World War I. A pattern of dependence upon Europe emerged in which the rate of economic growth was, for the most part, determined by outside forces. This development only accelerated and deepened with the imposition of the French mandate after the war.

As such, as early as World War I, a strong feeling existed among high-placed Syrians that more state intervention was necessary in order for economic prosperity to return to Syria. Because of the mandate system, Syrians would have to wait until after World War II before they could actually begin to chart a new economic course and promote the state apparatus to a dominant position. This, however, did not preclude change from occurring in other spheres. The older generation of Syrian leaders—primarily the landed aristocratic families of Damascus and Aleppo, which had held the predominant administrative positions, and thus political power, under both the Ottomans and the French—had been largely discredited by World War II in the eyes of the younger generation of Syrians. These younger activists had become politically aware during the Mandate period and saw their elders as corrupt and failing to deliver on their promise of real independence. They also perceived the older generation of leaders as having been co-opted by the French and as leading the nation economically toward what was termed "capitalist exhaustion."

This new generation of leaders, symbolized by such movements as the Ba'th Party, rejected not only the old regimes themselves but also their ideologies based on such Western European imports as liberal constitutionalism and free market capitalism. In a way, the Arab world is still searching for ideological constructs that will establish stable, relatively free political systems characterized by good governance and economic well-being. In the wake of the failure of the (imperfectly applied) socialist and capitalist paradigms, alternative ideologies—particularly Islamic extremism—have risen.

The final factor for the old regimes throughout much of the Arab world was the creation of Israel in 1948 and the humiliating defeat in the first Arab-Israeli war. Within ten years, all of the primary Arab combatants' regimes had been overthrown by movements professing a vehemently anti-imperialist, anti-Israeli, and Arab socialist doctrine. It was this wave that the Ba'th Party rode into the heart of Syrian politics in the 1950s and 1960s.

The shifts in power in the Middle East from foreigners to nationals comprised a well-intentioned process aimed at redistributing wealth and political power more equitably, ending reliance on outside powers, eliminating corruption, and restoring justice. A number of countries in the developing world chose the path of state capitalism. Syria developed a bloated and inefficient public sector that for over four decades has provided the support base for the ruling regime. In the process, it has established a Bonapartist state, wherein regime survival has driven economic policy, especially in a regional environment that has resembled anything but a benevolent capitalist world order. As time went on, the wealth funneled to the state as the capital accumulator became the source of patronage in erecting a pervasive clientelist network, primarily in the military, bureaucracy, and other elements of society tied to the state apparatus.

Because of this dominant public sector tied to the political apparatus, when the Syrian economy faced crisis after crisis in the 1980s and into the 1990s, Hafiz al-Asad embarked on what has been called a program of "selective liberalization." It had to be "selective" because if either Asad (father or son) were to liberalize too much or too quickly, the public-sector patronage system that has maintained the regime in power could be undermined.

Hafiz al-Asad provided stability, something his predecessors were unable to do. He tried to insulate the public sector as much as possible from the effects of incremental liberalization, but ultimately it, too, has been adversely affected. There has been a decrease in real wages from inflation due to currency devaluation, reduction of subsidies, and some privatization. This explains the "zigzag" approach that Hafiz al-Asad took toward economic reform. It also explains the regime's schizophrenia at times, when outdated repressive laws, despite the fact that both the populace and the government all but ignored them, were kept officially on the books just in case they were needed for regime self-interest. Asad thus used arbitrariness as a method of control (the 1986 foreign-currency law, ostensibly intended to crack down on black market foreign-currency exchanges, is a case in point). Furthermore, no outside party is pressuring the regime to accelerate the reform process; indeed, Syria is remarkably independent of any external interference in its economic decision making and is able to avoid the perception of being beholden to outside interests.

In addition to the continuing burden of an overly dominant public sector, a number of other problems inhibit economic growth: a very small and restricted private banking system and, until early 2009, no stock market to organize capital; an inadequate regulatory regime and insufficient transparency related to a corrupt and politicized judiciary that is anything but independent (a major impediment to attracting foreign investment); a private sector that may be too fragmented to lead the way in capital accumulation or to attain sufficient political power in order to accelerate reform; rampant corruption, especially the ubiquitous necessity of *wasta* ("intermediaries"), who in connivance with government officials have established entrances into the Syrian economy that require further investment of time, money, and energy on the part of foreign companies; and the absence of a tradition of large-scale domestic capital investment, as well as intervention by the powerful labor union (a strong remnant of the socialist compact). All of these influences have led to a proliferation of small-scale enterprises and investment in nonproductive areas, such as commerce instead of manufacturing.

Furthermore, economic growth has been hindered over the years by a widespread lack of professionalism within many government ministries, which have generally been unaccustomed to providing the data and services commonly expected by leading multinational corporations. Outdated technologies and techniques make equipment congruency with Western firms difficult. There exists an overall hesitancy to enact policies that could lead to unregulated foreign competition. It is believed that Syrian firms, as latecomers, would be at a disadvantage in such a competitive climate and that the petite bourgeoisie in particular could be overwhelmed by the multinationals. This could then force important sectors in Syria to seek alternative leadership because the social contract made with the people by the state capitalist regime when it came to power would have been broken, and no legitimizing ideology would exist to soften the inevitable inequities and economic dislocation brought about by serious market-oriented reform. Finally, Syria's annual population growth rate is one of the highest in the region, and Syria's population is in danger of outpacing the economy.

Syria's selective liberalization in the 1990s had some success, mostly buoyed by grants and investment from Arab Gulf states, particularly Saudi Arabia and Kuwait. The latter were grateful for Syria's participation in the Gulf War coalition in 1991; affirming this, the Gulf Cooperation Council (GCC) states along with Syria and Egypt formed later in 1991 what came to be called the Damascus Declaration, or GCC+2, a strategic alliance of sorts after the Gulf War that cemented the new direction of the Syrian regime. Domestically, Investment Law No. 10 (May 1991) set the standard for Syria's opening up to outside investment. This law offers the same incentives to local and foreign investors, meaning that companies that obtain licenses receive duty-free privileges for the import of capital goods and materials necessary for a project. At the time, it was hailed as an important step in the economic liberalization of Syria, and it was; however, it was not followed up with other necessary reforms, and the business environment in Syria became typically captive to the deteriorating situation in the Arab-Israeli arena. Indeed, Syria will probably never reach its economic potential until peace with Israel is consummated. Because of this, many Syrians, if not a majority, want peace with Israel and good relations with the United States because they make good business sense. But business and politics in Syria, domestically, regionally, and internationally, are intimately intertwined, and given the state of Syrian affairs, one will not move too far ahead of the other.

The challenges facing Syria today are multifold. The World Bank categorizes Syria as a lower-middle-income country, with per capita income at about $1,200. Its purchasing power parity per capita income is estimated at $4,800. Syria's GDP is highly dependent upon the agrarian and oil sectors. Syria produces approximately 300,000 barrels of oil per day, but this has been on the decline since 2000, when oil production peaked at about 600,000 barrels per day. Smuggling Iraqi oil into Syria contrary to UN oil sanctions against Iraq allowed Syria to reach oil export highs from 2000 to 2003; however, the US invasion of Iraq in 2003 ended the oil smuggling.

Syria needs to expand its labor market consistently to absorb a projected annual labor force increase of 4 percent due primarily to population growth patterns. The country also seems to be in a race against time to diversify and expand its production and export base before oil resources are depleted, as it is forecast that Syria, barring any new significant discovery of oil reserves, will become a net importer of oil within the next few years, with the effective exhaustion of its known oil reserves by the late 2020s. President Bashar al-Asad proposed at the Ba'th Party regional congress meeting in June 2005 the adoption of a "social market economy." While there is still ample room for defining exactly how this is to be applied in Syria, the assumption is that it will follow the post–World War II German model (*soziale marktwirtschaft*), wherein a market economy was adopted but with adequate social safety nets to help those who might fall through the cracks during the transition process and thereafter. The Chinese model is also mentioned frequently in Syria, whereby a strong central government is necessary in order to implement market-oriented economic reform; critics would counter that it is a convenient model to follow in that it will necessitate the regime's remaining in power without associated political reform. It is clear, however, that all Syrians agree on the need for deep, systemic economic reform, although decisions about the pace of change and what changes to implement still lack unanimity. Bashar has spent considerable energy in human resource development because of the recognized deficit in skills that hampers Syria's ability to integrate itself into the globalized economy. Administrative and economic reform has been stressed, and there have been positive developments in both areas in recent years; however, much more structural reform is needed, which itself has been slowed down as much by internal and external political and strategic developments as by the shortcomings of the system itself. The culture of caution and bureaucratic inertia that exists in Syria almost preordains that change will occur at an incremental pace. The country has been able to muddle through in the past, but there is considerable concern that unless serious reform is implemented, it will not be able to do so for much longer before economic deterioration engenders political instability.

FOREIGN POLICY

Syrians have generally considered their country the birthplace of Arab nationalism. As such, Arab nationalist tenets have considerably influenced (some might say hampered) Syria's foreign policy since the country's formal independence from the French. This manifested itself in the ensuing decades in Syria's emergence as a reluctant client-state of the Soviet Union in the Cold War, as the self-proclaimed leader of the anti-Israeli front in the Arab world and the most consistent Arab state proponent of the Palestinian cause, and as the beacon of anti-imperialist pan-Arab neutrality in the region, although this latter character of Syrian foreign policy led to inter-Arab rivalry as much as cooperation, a development that in large measure led to the outbreak of the 1967 Arab-Israeli War.

Hafiz al-Asad adopted a much more pragmatic foreign policy. He improved Syria's relationship with Egypt and Saudi Arabia and teamed up with them to launch the 1973 Arab-Israeli War, which caught the Israelis by surprise, leading to some unexpected battlefield successes in the initial stages of the conflict. With the acceptance of a Syrian-Israeli disengagement agreement in May 1974, brokered by the United States—a separation-of-forces agreement that has been observed assiduously to the present day—Asad tacitly adopted a diplomatic resolution to the Arab-Israeli conflict revolving around the return of the Golan Heights.

Egypt's signing its peace treaty with Israel in March 1979 significantly altered Asad's conception of Syria's role in the region. Faced with losing the leverage and threat posed by Egypt to Israel, Asad searched for allies to confront an empowered Israel that could now focus its attention to the north. The Steadfastness Front, including Algeria, Libya, and the People's Democratic Republic of Yemen—formed in large measure to counter what was feared to be an emerging Egyptian-led consensus of moderate Arab states—diplomatically fortified Syria to a certain degree, but these countries were largely on the fringes of the Arab-Israeli conflict. Asad even briefly flirted with an entente with his Ba'thist rival, Saddam Husayn, in the aftermath of Camp David in order to shore up Syria's eastern front to contain Israel. The association inevitably floundered over continuing differences between the two countries, ranging from persistent Ba'thist elite and ideological quarrels and personal animus between Asad and Husayn to practical matters like water sharing of the Euphrates River and the question of who should be the dominant partner in any planned union. The answer to this question would, in effect, determine who would fill the vacuum of power in the Arab world created by Egypt's departure from the Arab fold after it signed the peace treaty with Israel. Asad, always concerned with flanks and balances, was compelled to meet the strategic challenge.

The culmination of the Iranian revolution in February 1979 and subsequent Iraqi invasion of Iran in September 1980 eliminated whatever hope existed for an Iraqi-Syrian rapprochement. With the arrival of Ayatollah Ruhollah Khomeini and the advent of the new Islamic republic in Tehran as an avowed implacable foe of Israel and United States, Asad saw a definite convergence of interests with Iran, taking steps even before the outbreak of the Iran-Iraq War to develop a relationship that remains intact to this day. From Hafiz al-Asad's point of view, Iran provided some strategic depth now that the multifront approach against Israel was defunct.

Saddam Husayn's invasion of Iran made it easier for Damascus to side openly with Teheran. Not only did Asad believe that Husayn's follies were an untimely and misdirected application of vital Arab resources and assets away from the Arab-Israeli arena, but his actions also created an opportunity to weaken an inter-Arab rival, which would then allow Syria to play a leading role in the region and fill the leadership role abdicated by Egypt. This would not be the first time that Asad would adopt a pragmatic policy that was, on the surface, unexpected—he would do so again ten years later during the 1990–1991 Gulf crisis and ensuing war. Because of its support of non-Arab Iran against Arab Iraq, however, Syria became more isolated in the early 1980s in the Arab world. The Gulf Arab states, on whom Syria depended so much for financial and political support, were more consumed with matters concerning Gulf security and less with the Arab-Israeli arena. In addition, Syria had never quite repaired the damage done to its relationship with the Palestine Liberation Organization (PLO) stemming from its shift to the Maronite side during the 1975–1976 civil war in Lebanon. Despite Syria's frequent efforts to mend fences with the PLO, especially after Sadat engaged in the peace process with Israel, the PLO never totally severed its line to Cairo, much to the consternation of Asad. From PLO Chairman Yasir Arafat's point of view, Syria was trying to turn the PLO into something of a protectorate in order to strengthen its own bargaining power and indispensability so as not to be left out in the cold by another Arab participant in the Arab-Israeli equation.

Nor did Jordan obediently follow Syria. Amman was typically caught between pressures from a variety of sources, including Egypt, Iraq, Saudi Arabia, Syria, and the United States; of these, Jordan had the least to lose with Damascus. With this array of pressures, Jordan naturally gravitated toward the more moderate front within the Arab world, in the process establishing closer ties with Iraq and mending its own fences with the PLO. Iraq, now ensconced in war with Iran, toned down its rhetoric and began cooperating with the moderate Arab states so as to enhance its ability to withstand an Iran that had weathered Iraq's initial attacks and by 1982 was clearly on the offensive. This emerging moderate bloc in the Arab world, due to a significant degree to the Iran-Iraq War, also allowed Egypt to rehabilitate itself and quietly reenter the Arab fold.

By the end of 1980, Syria seemed as isolated as it had ever been in the Middle East. Clearly, Hafiz al-Asad's diplomacy had failed. Egypt had signed a separate peace treaty with Israel, and yet no serious coalition of Arab states would align their positions with Damascus. Worse still, the attention of most Arab states—indeed, of most of the world—was focused on events in the Persian Gulf and South-Central Asia following the December 1979 Soviet invasion of Afghanistan, not on the Arab-Israeli arena.

Syria had to make a tactical change if it was to contain what the Syrian regime perceived as Israeli pressure and carve out a role for itself in the Middle East. Israel's de facto annexation of the Golan Heights (in actuality an extension of Israeli law) in 1981 reinforced Syria's assessment of its own weakened position in the region—it could do nothing about it. Something had to be done, and it seemed from Asad's perspective that Syria would essentially have to go it alone in the region for the time being. Asad began to put forward the possibility of attaining strategic parity with Israel, not so much to defeat the Jewish state as to act as an effective deterrent while Syria at the same time strengthened its bargaining leverage should a peace process develop. To do this, Syria needed massive amounts of military aid from the outside—the Soviet Union.

The Soviet Union and Syria began to build upon what had been a tenuous relationship, exemplified by their 1980 Treaty of Friendship and Cooperation. Moscow also had its policy failures, with Egypt embracing the United States and Iraq invading Iran (against Soviet preferences), then moving toward the moderate Arab Gulf camp to buffer its deteriorating position as the war progressed. In a sense, if not for the virtual disabling of Iraq and Egypt, the Soviets would not have been tempted to invest so much in Syria. For his part, Asad felt he had little choice but to move closer to Moscow.

It was under these conditions that Syria encountered the next challenge to its position: the Israeli invasion of Lebanon in June 1982. Asad was determined to make the best out of a potentially catastrophic situation.

Lebanon gained its independence following World War II as Syria did; however, it developed a confessional democratic parliamentary system that tenuously balanced the various Muslim and Christian factions in the country. The country always seemed to be on the precipice of breaking apart, but the political experiment somehow continued to hold amid internal and external pressures. It seemed inevitable, however, that Lebanon, located between Syria and Israel, would be involved in the Arab-Israeli conflict; this became certain once the PLO relocated its headquarters to Beirut following its expulsion from Jordan in 1970. The added sectarian tensions burst out into open civil war in April 1975. Hafiz al-Asad wanted stability in Lebanon so as to prevent the creation of troubled waters in which the Israelis could fish at Syria's expense or the generation sectarian strife that could spill over into his own country. Lebanon has also been a haven for a variety of Syrian opposition groups over the years, many of them funded by other Arab states, the great powers, or both; therefore, extension of Syrian military-security influence, if not control, in Lebanon has been viewed as something of a strategic necessity. Israel, for instance, developed a relationship with the Maronites in Lebanon, seeing them as another non-Muslim minority in a Muslim-dominated region as well as conduits to advance Israeli interests vis-à-vis Syria. With Sadat heading in his own direction by 1975, Asad saw the situation in Lebanon as an opportunity to gain more control over Lebanese politics and the PLO in order to utilize both as arrows in an increasingly bare quiver against Israel as well as in the inter-Arab arena. He also wanted to prevent these same elements from unwarrantedly precipitating an unwanted conflict with Israel. Asad successfully obtained regional sanction for Syria's military presence in Lebanon at an Arab League summit meeting in Riyadh in October 1976, establishing an all-Arab force, mostly composed of Syrians, stationed in the country ostensibly to maintain stability, a presence that would last for almost thirty years.

From the Syrian perspective, the Israeli invasion of Lebanon in 1982 was the expected repercussion of the Egypt-Israel Peace Treaty. It was thought that Israel, freed up on its southern flank, could now concentrate on securing its position to the north. To Asad, the invasion was an attempt to outflank Syria, something Damascus had been wary of for years, a concern that, of course, precipitated its involvement in Lebanon in 1975 and 1976. Syria seemed to be vulnerable, with its regional isolation and domestic problems, particularly the Muslim Brotherhood's Islamist rebellion and the regime's crushing of it in early 1982. To Asad, the timing of the invasion, coming soon after the return of the final portion of the Sinai Peninsula to Egypt, was not a surprise. One could almost sense that this created something of a last stand for Syria, or at least for Asad's regime; as such, he would fight tooth and nail to prevent an Israeli victory in Lebanon, which would complete Syria's isolation in the region.

Al-stet Asad ended up "winning" in Lebanon. Through his strategic use of various Lebanese factions (particularly Hizballah), rearming by the Soviet Union, and the commitment born of being pressed against the wall, Syria reemerged as the dominant power in Lebanon, its western flank secure. Syria's Arab credentials were somewhat restored for taking on Israel (and even the United States) and not just surviving but emerging as the perceived victor. Syria was the only player that could have provided some semblance of stability, and essentially the playing field was laid open for Damascus to try to do so. The October 22, 1989, Ta'if Accord brokered by the Saudis was an important turning point in ending the civil war, as most of the Lebanese factions finally realized that the National Pact establishing the confessional system of government had to be amended. The 1991 Brother-hood agreement was, in essence, Syria's amendment to the Ta'if Accord, putting its stamp on Lebanon following the Gulf War and the George H. W. Bush administra-tion's de facto acquiescence to Syrian dominance in Lebanon in return for Syrian support of the US-led UN coalition to evict Iraq from Kuwait.

In 1989, Syria's position seemed to take a turn for the worse. Iraq had emerged victorious in the Iran-Iraq War after Tehran reluctantly accepted a UN-brokered cease-fire in August 1988—and it was an Iraq that wanted to reexert its influence in the Middle East. Saddam Husayn remembered Syrian support for his enemy and would make life as difficult as possible for Syria in Lebanon by supporting anti-Syrian groups such as the Christian militia led by Michel Aoun. He would also draw Jordan deeper into Baghdad's orbit through economic incentives. Fur-thermore, the pillar of Soviet support that had braced the Syrian regime for most of the decade virtually crumbled with the ascension to power of Mikhail Gor-bachev in 1985 and the Red Army's exit from Afghanistan by early 1989, both of which led to a dramatic reassessment of Soviet foreign policy that emphasized a drawing down of Soviet commitments abroad, more concentration on domestic restructuring, and improving ties with the United States. This did not bode well for Syria, as Moscow first urged and then backed the PLO's decision to pursue a negotiated solution, and the Kremlin also improved its relations with Israel. Gor-bachev demonstrably made it clear to Asad upon the Syrian president's visit to Moscow in April 1987 that Syria's "reliance on military force in settling the Arab-Israeli conflict has completely lost its credibility," and he went on to suggest that Damascus abandon its doctrine of strategic parity and seek to establish a "balance of interests" to achieve a political settlement in the Middle East.

Because of his position at the end of the 1980s, Asad was again forced to change his policy in a dramatic fashion—he took Gorbachev's advice. In Decem-ber 1988, Asad "acknowledged the importance of Egypt in the Arab arena," the first time he had publicly praised Egypt since before the signing of the Egyptian-Israeli Peace Treaty. By the end of 1989 Damascus had reestablished full diplomatic relations with Cairo. While maintaining the link with Iran—partly to contain the Iraqi threat, continue its relationship with Shi'a groups in Lebanon, and remain a credible military threat to Israel—Syria made a strategic choice to join the Arab-Israeli peace process, the ultimate objective of which was the return of the Golan Heights and a comprehensive peace.

To the rest of the world, the outward manifestation of this policy shift was Syria's participation in the US-led UN coalition to expel Iraq from Kuwait in the 1990–1991 Gulf crisis and war. Not only was it participating in an alliance whose objective was to weaken, if not destroy, the war-making capacity of its archnemesis in the Arab arena, but Syria was clearly situating itself in the Arab world's moderate camp and opening up the economic doors of investment and aid from the West and grateful Arab Gulf states. To the United States, Syria's inclusion in the coalition, although mostly symbolic, was, in effect, the most important of all the Arab states. Since Syria had been at the vanguard of the Steadfastness Front of Arab states arrayed against Israel, its joining up made the coalition seem to consist of the entire Arab world against Saddam Husayn rather than just the usual pro-Western suspects; had the latter been the case, Baghdad could have used that to its own propaganda advantage.

For Asad, establishing a stronger link with Washington was very important, and to do this he had to go through Israel; indeed, some accused Asad of engaging in the peace process not so much to redefine Syria's relationship with Israel as to improve Syria's ties with the United States and the West following the end of the Cold War. Not only would this have economic benefits at a time when Syria desperately needed them, but Asad's engagement in a peace process brokered by the United States was his best defense against Israeli pressure, as Washington, it was thought, would act to curtail Israel in order to maintain Syria's involvement in the process, one that could lead to an entirely new American-dominated Middle East system. It also opened up possibilities of securing his position in Lebanon as a quid pro quo with the United States.

As such, Syria emerged as the key Arab player in the convening of the Madrid peace conference in October 1991, cosponsored by the United States and the Soviet Union and including a Lebanese delegation (clearly acting under the direction of Damascus) and a Jordanian delegation that also consisted of Palestinian representatives from the occupied territories (i.e., not the PLO). For the first time, Syrian officials publicly sat down with Israeli officials to discuss peace. There now existed a window of opportunity to regain the Golan Heights and reposition Syria in the region both economically and politically. The Madrid process consisted of several tracks of peace negotiations between Arab states and Israel.

By 1992 to 1993, Israel's new prime minister, Yitzhak Rabin, and the Clinton administration in the United States preferred to concentrate on the Israeli-Syrian track over the Israeli-Palestinian one, primarily because of the inherently less complex nature of the former in addition to the fact that Israeli leaders simply trusted Asad more than Arafat. But progress with Syria was limited and would soon be overshadowed by the September 1993 Israeli-PLO Declaration of Principles that was largely negotiated in what became known as the Oslo channel. The Jordan-Israel Peace Treaty was signed in October 1994. Asad was furious with both Arafat and King Hussein for doing something very similar to what Sadat had done. It had been an axiom of Syrian foreign policy to maximize Arab bargaining leverage. In essence, Asad's failure to keep Jordan and the PLO within Syria's orbit in the 1980s had become manifest. On the other hand, now that the PLO and Jordan had signed accords with Israel, no longer would Damascus feel obligated to subscribe to the Palestinian or Arab nationalist line, for the PLO itself had compromised its position. Though bereft of some of its bargaining power, Syria as a result felt free to pursue its own interests to a greater extent than it had in the past, first and foremost being the return of the Golan Heights. As such, Syria engaged in serious peace negotiations with Israel throughout the 1990s, and much progress was made on a host of issues separating the two countries. But a peace treaty was never consummated despite the parties' being, according to Syrian officials, 80 percent of the way there. Attempts to bridge the remaining divide in late 1999 and early 2000 before the Clinton administration left office failed. In May 2000, Israel decided unilaterally to withdraw its troops from the Lebanese quagmire without the benefit of the peace treaty with Syria. The following month, Hafiz al-Asad died, bringing to a close any immediate hope of a resumption of Syrian-Israeli negotiations, especially with a relatively young and untested successor in power in Damascus who was more concerned about consolidating his domestic position and was soon caught up in a maelstrom of regional and international events.

BASHAR AL-ASAD IN POWER

Bashar al-Asad took the constitutional oath of office of president and delivered his inaugural speech on July 17, 2000. By Syrian standards, it was a remarkably enlightened speech that deigned even to criticize certain policies of the past, including those implemented by his father. It served to confirm to many that indeed Bashar was a breath of fresh air and would lead the country in a new direction. He focused on economic reform, and while not ruling out democratic reform, he did say that it would have to be "democracy specific to Syria that takes its roots from its history and respects its society."[2]

There was a genuine air of exuberance among many who had longed for change in Syria. Bashar had also nurtured a collaborative relationship with elements in the intelligentsia upon returning from London in 1994, especially in his capacity as chairman of the Syrian Computer Society. A number of people who could legitimately be called reformists, although they were more along the lines of technocrats than pro-democracy elements, were brought into the government. This added to the anticipatory environment. They were tasked with the job of modernizing Syria, implementing administrative reform in the various ministries to which they were assigned, and examining the economic weaknesses of the system and devising ways to correct it; they were not there to enact political reform. Nonetheless, there was noticeably more political openness in the months after Bashar took office, which many have called the Damascus Spring. During the seven to eight months of the Damascus Spring, the political opening was marked by the granting of general amnesties to political prisoners of all persuasions, the licensing of private newspapers, shake-ups of the state-controlled media apparatus, the allowance of political forums and salons in which open criticism and dissent were tolerated, and the discarding of the personality cult that surrounded the previous regime.

The regime was caught off guard by the efflorescence of the civil society organizations combined with the prisoner releases and other measures implemented by Bashar. Some of the stalwart elements in the regime—whom many have termed the "old guard," those who had reached positions of power under and been loyal to Hafiz al-Asad—basically approached Bashar and warned him of the deleterious effects of the evolving situation in Syria. They were certainly detecting clear trends that could soon be harmful to their positions and the regime in general. Serious political reform could jeopardize the predominant position of a number of status quo elements with established sinecures in the system that had brought them economic, social, and political benefits for years. They had witnessed the instability that can befall a country when the center rapidly erodes, and stability remained a priority for the regime and for most Syrians. As such, a Damascus "winter" set in; the salons were closely monitored or closed, private newspapers were shut down, and democracy activists were arrested, although the regime appeared to be engaging in a less brusque form of repression than in the past. Compared to the Damascus Spring, the level of openness had been clearly restricted, but when juxtaposed against Syrian society ten to twenty years earlier, the margins of freedom were indeed wider overall.

The expectations in the West surrounding Bashar al-Asad were unrealistic. Because he belonged to the younger, modernizing next generation in the Arab world, was a licensed ophthalmologist who had studied in London, had an avowed affinity for Western pop music, and was something of a computer nerd as chairman of the Syrian Computer Society and had introduced the Internet to Syria, most concluded that he would immediately make over the country, open it up to the West, and forge peace with Israel. They failed to understand the dilapidated, broken-down country he inherited from his father as well as the tumultuous regional and international environments that constricted his ability to implement reform, starting with the al-Aqsa Intifada that broke out in September 2000, the September 11, 2001, terrorist attacks against the United States, and then the US military response first in Afghanistan in October 2001 and then in Iraq in 2003. In addition, he is the son of Hafiz al-Asad and a child of the Arab-Israeli conflict, the superpower cold war, and the tumult in Lebanon. These relationships and historical events shaped his worldview much more than eighteen months in London studying ophthalmology.

Despite Syrian intelligence cooperation with the United States regarding al-Qa'ida following 9/11, the administration of George W. Bush began to view Syria's traditional support for groups like Hamas and Hizballah as no different from supporting al-Qa'ida. Damascus did not adequately adjust to the changes in American foreign policy as a result of 9/11, symbolized by the Bush Doctrine announced in September 2002. The Syrian regime believed that the old rules of the game in its relationship with the United States were still in place—the "honey-and-vinegar" approach (i.e., despite periods of confrontation in the past, there was always communication as well as other periods of cooperation). And there were mixed messages coming from Washington, with Damascus choosing to believe those voices that tended to advocate continued engagement with Syria. Damascus did not realize that the new rules of the game were being written in Washington—in the halls of Congress, at the Pentagon, and inside influential think tanks—by those who saw Syria as part of the problem rather than the solution. The turning point in this regard came with the US war in Iraq beginning in March 2003, when Washington accused Damascus of a number of different affronts, including aiding a nascent Iraqi insurgency, sheltering Iraqi fugitives, and possibly even hiding the weapons of mass destruction that US personnel could not find in Iraq. Whereas immediately after 9/11 a US State Department official stated that Syria was "saving American lives," the perception after the invasion of Iraq was that it was costing American lives. The relationship between Damascus and Washington continued to deteriorate despite several visits by US officials to Syria as well as some gestures made by the Syrian regime (or certainly what President Bashar considered to be gestures). This deterioration was symbolized by the passage of the Syrian Accountability Act by Congress in October–November 2003; it was signed into law by President Bush in December and activated by the administration in May 2004. Although mostly symbolic, considering the low level of economic interaction between the two countries, the act allows the president to implement a range of sanctions against Syria. President Bush decided to activate sanctions regarding the use of US airspace by Syrian aircraft (which was nonexistent to begin with) and restrictions on US business with Syria.

The pressure on Syria began to mount in the fall of 2004, following what was viewed from the outside as Bashar's blatant intervention in Lebanese politics when Syria forced upon the Lebanese government the extraconstitutional extension of pro-Syrian President Emile Lahoud's term in office. The international community, led by the United States and France, widely condemned the action, which only fed into the waiting hands of those elements in Washington who wanted to tighten the screws on the Syrian regime. The United States and France soon thereafter cosponsored UN Security Council Resolution 1559, calling for the withdrawal of all foreign forces from Lebanon. Not only had Damascus alienated important European friends, but it also emboldened a number of Lebanese figures

to call more openly for the withdrawal of Syria from Lebanon, among them former Lebanese prime minister Rafik Hariri, the billionaire architect of Lebanon's
reconstruction following the destructive civil war.

Syria's position in Lebanon was harmed immeasurably when on February 14,
2005, Rafik Hariri was assassinated in a massive car bomb explosion in down-
town Beirut. Immediate cries rang out in Lebanon and throughout most of the
international community holding Syria responsible, either directly or indirectly.
Vociferous demonstrations spontaneously erupted in Beirut and other Lebanese
cities directly accusing Damascus and its pro-Syrian allies in Lebanon. It was unprecedented open criticism accompanied by calls for Syrian troops and intelligence agents to leave the country. What had been a growing opposition to
Syria's presence and influence in Lebanon before the assassination became that
much more emboldened. As a sign of Washington's displeasure, the US ambassador to Syria was recalled the next day and has yet to return to Damascus as of
this writing.

Despite some pro-Syrian rallies organized primarily by Hizballah, the interna-
tional pressure relentlessly continued, ultimately compelling Bashar al-Asad to
agree to withdraw Syrian forces from Lebanon, which occurred at the end of
April 2005. But the UN investigation continued, and on October 21, 2005, the
UN report on the assassination of Rafik Hariri, compiled by German diplomat
Detlev Mehlis, was submitted to the UN Security Council. The report found
Syria at least indirectly responsible for the murder. The original draft of the report
outlined a trail of names that led directly into the heart of the Syrian regime, particularly Asef al-Shawkat, Bashar's head of intelligence and brother-in-law, and
Maher al-Asad, his younger brother who is a member of the Ba'th Party's central
committee and head of the republican guard. The UN Security Council, however,
could not agree on concerted action by the end of the year, particularly with Russia and China hesitant to accede to US demands that UN sanctions against Syria
be seriously considered.

By mid-2006, the Syrian regime believed it had weathered the storm over the
Hariri assassination. Washington did not receive the support it had hoped for in
the UN Security Council, and at the same time the US quagmire in Iraq continued amid declining domestic support for President Bush and his administration's
policy there. At the same time, the Bush administration's focus seemed to shift to
Iran, with increasing concern that Tehran was in the process of weaponizing its
uranium-enrichment program toward a nuclear weapons capability. Bashar lever-
aged a strong Syrian nationalistic response to the situation in Lebanon and to UN
and US pressure into support for his position and the regime in general. He also
moved aside potential and real impediments to his authority in Syria, particularly
in the summer of 2005 when long-time rival, Vice President Abd al-Halim Khaddam, was compelled to resign. He subsequently went into exile and attempted,

with decidedly mixed results, to become a leading voice of Syria's exiled opposition movement.

The US-led isolation of the Syrian regime began to break down in 2007 and 2008 as US congresspersons and European diplomats visited Damascus on a regular basis to meet with President Bashar. The Syrians also sent a delegation to the Annapolis Conference in the United States sponsored by the Bush administration in late 2007 and intended to jump-start Middle East peace negotiations. Although little progress was made during the remaining year of the Bush administration, the noose around the neck of the Syrian regime was clearly loosening considerably. This became even more manifest when Bashar was invited to Paris by French president Nicholas Sarkozy in July 2008 and attended a meeting of the Mediterranean states to discuss an economic partnership agreement. Although Bashar did not meet with him, Israeli prime minister Ehud Olmert was also in attendance. Concurrent with this gradual opening, Israel and Syria began indirect peace talks brokered by Turkish officials throughout most of 2008, although the talks were suspended in December of that year. There was still plenty of evidence, however, to suggest that Syria had not completely emerged from the cold. The Israelis struck a suspected nuclear site in Syria in September 2007. Hizballah operations mastermind Imad Mughniyeh was assassinated in a fashionable district of Damascus in February 2008 in a very embarrassing incident for the Syrian regime. The United States staged a cross-border raid in October 2008 to kill an alleged Iraqi insurgent with virtual impunity. Israel and the United States understand that Syria cannot do much to retaliate in a tit-for-tat manner. Bashar did not allow these incidents to spiral out of control or to reverse Syria's steady emergence out of isolation. With the election of Barack Obama as US president in November 2008, Bashar also did not want to get off on the wrong foot with an incoming Democratic administration that appeared to be much more favorably disposed to exploring diplomatic engagement with Damascus.

Bashar al-Asad is a more confident leader and more securely in power than at any other time in his presidency—some may say that he is, in fact, overconfident. He is no longer the inexperienced, untested young ruler. He has made mistakes, but he has also shrewdly and cleverly confounded his critics and doubters to survive the onslaught of the Bush administration years and consolidate his position. The Obama administration in early 2009 began to engage Damascus diplomatically. Yet, there exist a network of UN resolutions regarding Syria's influence in Lebanon, a UN tribunal on the Hariri assassination, the Syrian Accountability Act, an International Atomic Energy Agency investigation into the alleged Syrian nuclear site, and Syria's continued inclusion on the State Department's list of states that sponsor terrorism, all of which will complicate any improvement in Syria's relationship with the United States. In addition there is still a significant amount of anti–Syrian inertia in Washington and anti–American inertia in Damascus, breeding a level of mistrust that will take some time to overcome.

NOTES

1. My thanks to Curtis R. Ryan for his contributions to and suggestions for this chapter.

2. This section is based upon the author's work titled *The New Lion of Damascus: Bashar al-Asad and Modern Syria* (New Haven, CT: Yale University Press, 2005). For this book, the author interviewed President Bashar on numerous occasions as well as other leading Syrian figures.

BIBLIOGRAPHY

A good general book on the overall history of Syria is John Devlin's *Syria: Modern State in an Ancient Land* (Boulder, CO: Westview Press, 1983). Also see Moshe Maoz, Joseph Ginat, and Onn Winckler's edited volume, *Modern Syria: From Ottoman Rule to Pivotal Role in the Middle East* (Brighton, UK: Sussex Academic Press, 1999). On the World War I and the French Mandate periods, see Philip S. Khoury's classic *Syria and the French Mandate: The Politics of Arab Nationalism, 1920–1945* (Princeton, NJ: Princeton University Press, 1987). For an insightful examination of domestic political developments and movements during the transition from Ottoman to French rule, see James L. Gelvin's *Divided Loyalties: Nationalism and Mass Politics in Syria at the Close of Empire* (Berkeley: University of California Press, 1999).

On Syria's political development in the twentieth century, particularly the emergence of the Ba'th Party, see the following works: Hanna Batatu, *Syria's Peasantry, the Descendants of Its Lesser Rural Notables, and Their Politics* (Princeton, NJ: Princeton University Press, 1999), and Raymond A. Hinnebusch, *Authoritarian Power and State Formation in Ba'thist Syria: Army, Party, and Peasant* (Boulder, CO: Westview Press, 1990); also see Hinnebusch's *Syria: Revolution from Above* (London: Routledge, 2001); Itamar Rabinovitch's *Syria Under the Ba'th, 1963–1966: The Army Party Symbiosis* (Tel Aviv: The Shiloah Center for Middle Eastern and African Studies, 1972); and Nikolaos Van Dam's *The Struggle for Power in Syria: Politics and Society Under Asad and the Ba'th Party* (London: I. B. Tauris, 1996).

On Syria's regional and international foreign policy in the post–World War II period, see Patrick Seale's seminal *The Struggle for Syria: A Study of Post-War Arab Politics 1945–1958* (New Haven, CT: Yale University Press, 1986); David W. Lesch's *Syria and the United States: Eisenhower's Cold War in the Middle East* (Boulder, CO: Westview Press, 1992); Elie Podeh's *The Decline of Arab Unity: The Rise and Fall of the United Arab Republic* (London: Sussex Academic Press, 1999); Moshe Maoz's *Syria and Israel: From War to Peacemaking* (Oxford: Oxford University Press, 1995); Itamar Rabinovitch's *The War for Lebanon: 1970–1985* (Ithaca, NY: Cornell University Press, 1985); Naomi Weinberger's *Syrian Intervention in Lebanon* (Oxford: Oxford University Press, 1987); Muhammad Muslih's *Golan: The Road to Occupation* (Washington, DC: Institute for Palestine Studies, 2000); and Habib C. Malik's *Between Damascus and Jerusalem: Lebanon and Middle East Peace* (Washington, DC: The Washington Institute for Near East Policy, 2000). Three firsthand accounts (one by a US participant and two by Israeli negotiators) of the Syrian-Israeli peace process in the 1990s are Dennis Ross, *The Missing Peace: The Inside Story of the Fight for Middle East Peace* (New York: Farrar, Straus, and Giroux, 2004); Itamar Rabinovitch, *The Brink of Peace* (Princeton, NJ: Princeton University Press, 1998); and Uri Savir, *The Process: 1,100 Days That Changed the Middle East* (New York: Random House, 1998).

Two good, if more sympathetic, biographies and examinations of Syria under Hafiz al-Asad are Patrick Seale's *Asad of Syria: The Struggle for the Middle East* (London: I. B. Tauris, 1988) and Moshe Maoz's *Asad, the Sphinx of Damascus: A Political Biography* (London: Grove/Atlantic, 1990). A less sympathetic portrayal is Eyal Zisser's *Asad's Legacy: Syria in Transition* (New York: New York University Press, 2001).

On Syria under Bashar al-Asad, see David W. Lesch, *The New Lion of Damascus: Bashar al-Asad and Modern Syria* (New Haven, CT: Yale University Press, 2005), and Flynt Leverett, *Inheriting Syria: Bashar's Trial by Fire* (Washington, DC: Brookings Institution Press, 2005). Both of the preceding books present Bashar in a fairly favorable light, but for a biting critical analysis of the regime under Bashar, see Alan George's *Syria: Neither Bread nor Freedom* (London: Zed Books, 2003).

Syria's economic situation is covered in an excellent work by Volker Perthes, *The Political Economy of Syria Under Asad* (London: I. B. Tauris, 1995). Also see Eberhard Kienle's edited volume *Contemporary Syria: Liberalization Between Cold War and Cold Peace* (London: British Academic Press, 1994). On Syria's culture and society, see Richard T. Antoun and Donald Quataert, eds., *Syria: Society, Culture, and Polity* (Albany: State University of New York Press, 1991); Lisa Wedeen, *Ambiguities of Domination: Politics, Rhetoric, and Symbols in Contemporary Syria* (Chicago: University of Chicago Press, 1999); Umar F. Abdallah, *The Islamic Struggle in Syria* (Berkeley: Mizan Press, 1983); and Sami Moubayed, *Steel and Silk: Men and Women Who Shaped Syria, 1900–2000* (Seattle, WA: Cune Press, 2006).

10

HASHIMITE KINGDOM OF JORDAN

Curtis R. Ryan

Despite its central role in the history of the Arab-Israeli conflict and peace process and its geopolitical importance to major powers from the Cold War era to the present, Jordan remains in many ways a young state with ancient roots. Since its perhaps inauspicious beginnings, Jordan has developed into a modern state that has long defied predictions of its imminent demise. What began as the British Mandate of Transjordan in 1921 evolved into the Emirate of Transjordan at the time of independence from Britain in 1946 and finally into its current form as the Hashimite Kingdom of Jordan since 1949. The Hashimite monarchy has throughout its existence pointedly emphasized its Arab heritage as well as its Islamic lineage, especially the direct Hashimite family line descending from the Prophet Muhammad.

HISTORICAL BACKGROUND

Like many other postcolonial states in the Middle East, the Hashimite Kingdom of Jordan has largely artificial boundaries, drawn by European imperial powers. In the aftermath of World War I, Britain and France divided the territories of the former Ottoman Empire between themselves. As part of the Sykes-Picot wartime agreement between Britain and France, the territory that is modern Jordan came under British tutelage. In 1921, having secured the League of Nations' official mandate for the territories of Palestine, Transjordan, and Iraq, the British government created the Emirate of Transjordan through agreement with its new ruler, Emir Abdallah (later King Abdallah I) of the Hashimite family. Thus, the Hashimites only emerged as rulers in Jordan in the third decade of the twentieth century, having earlier ruled Mecca and the Hijaz territory of western Arabia.

The Hashimites had fought with the British in the Great Arab Revolt against the Turkish Ottoman Empire during World War I. But shortly after the war ended, the Hashimites were defeated and expelled from Arabia by their rivals, the Saudis, who ultimately carved out the modern Kingdom of Saudi Arabia, to which they

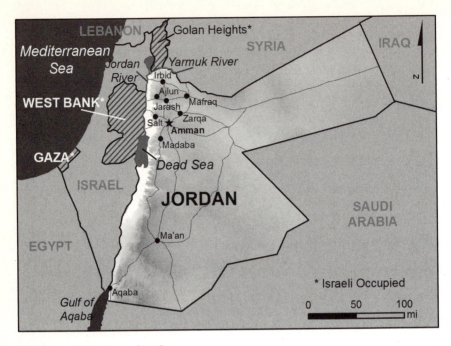

Hashimite Kingdom of Jordan

attached the family name. In the postwar Mandate period, the British government decided to install two brothers of the House of Hashim, Abdallah and Faisal, respectively, in their mandates of Jordan and Iraq. This move was in large part intended as a reward for Hashimite support in the Arab revolt against the Ottoman Empire during World War I. The British thus established new borders and new dynasties for both Transjordan and Iraq. The latter dynasty was overthrown and eliminated in a bloody coup in Baghdad in 1958, but well into the twenty-first century, the Hashimite monarchy continued both to reign and rule in Jordan.

The Kingdom of Jordan is therefore one of the many successor states of the Ottoman Empire, but the territory east of the Jordan River has a history dating back several millennia of being the crossroads between the Mediterranean, the Orient, and Arabia. The ancient biblical kingdoms of Gilead, Moab, and Edom were largely located in present-day Jordan. Because of its relatively remote (albeit strategically important) location, the area was usually the last conquered and the first abandoned as the great ancient empires ebbed and flowed. At various times, Egyptian, Hittite, Assyrian, Persian, Greek, Roman, and Byzantine armies each occupied the region.

Of all the peoples of antiquity, the Nabataen Arabs were most likely the direct ancestors of modern Jordanians. Shortly after 800 BCE, the Aramaic-speaking inhabitants of Petra created their kingdom along the key north–south trading routes, maintaining their independence until they were conquered by the Romans under Pompey in 64 BCE.

In sociological terms, the Islamic conquest of the area had the greatest impact. The battle of Yarmuk in 636 CE expelled the Byzantine Christians and laid the groundwork for the establishment of Islam as the religious and cultural foundation for the majority of the people. At various times, the area was ruled from Damascus, Baghdad, Cairo, Jerusalem, and Istanbul. Under Ottoman rule, southern Jordan was governed as part of the Hijaz while the north was included in the Damascus governorate.

The Emergence of Modern Jordan

The modern Jordanian state emerged following the collapse of the Ottoman Empire during World War I. Arab tribesmen under the leadership of Emir Faisal, son of Sharif Hussein of the Hashimite family of the Hijaz (now Saudi Arabia), and advised by the famous Lawrence of Arabia marched northward against the Ottoman forces. After the war, at the 1919 Paris Peace Conference, Emir Faisal pressed for the complete independence of the Levantine Arabs, basing his arguments on President Woodrow Wilson's Fourteen Points promoting self-determination for all people. Arab leaders also contended that in wartime they had been promised an independent state that included Transjordan and Palestine. Faisal failed, however, to win his point against British and French imperial aspirations and Zionist demands for a homeland. The status of Jordan remained unclear at that time. Emir Abdallah, the brother of Faisal, was in Jordan organizing the tribes to strike the French in Syria. The British, realizing such an attack was not in their best interest, offered Abdallah, who was very popular with the Jordanian tribes, the opportunity to be the emir of Jordan. In this way, Anglo-French difficulties were avoided and British promises to the Hashimites were partially met. Abdallah accepted the British offer because an emirate in Jordan was a tangible gain, and he had little chance of displacing the French from Syria.

The establishment of a governmental system for the new emirate took much time and effort on the part of the British. Being politically cut off from Syria, with whose government its people had been traditionally associated, Jordan lacked a national identity and had practically no economic base. The few Arab administrators in Jordan were those who had fled from the French in Damascus and were generally more concerned with reasserting Arab control in Syria than with making Jordan an independent, self-sufficient state. On the economic side, less than 3 percent of the

JORDAN

Capital city	Amman
Chief of state	King Abdallah II
Head of government	Prime Minister Nader al-Dahabi
Major political parties	Arab Ba'ath Socialist Party, Ba'ath Arab Progressive Party, Call Party, Democratic People's Party, Democratic Popular Unity Party, Islamic Action Front, Islamic Center Party, Jordanian Communist Party, Jordanian National Party, Jordanian United Front, Life Party, Message Party, National Constitution Party, National Movement for Direct Democracy
Ethnic groups	Arab (98%), Circassian (1%), Armenian (1%)
Religious groups	Sunni Muslim (92%), Christian (6%), other (2%)
Export partners	United States (16%), Iraq (13.4%), United Arab Emirates (8.1%), India (7.8%), Saudi Arabia (7.8%), Syria (4.6%)
Import partners	Saudi Arabia (20.3%), China (9.7%), Germany (6.5%), United States (5.6%)

land was under cultivation, and with virtually no other economic assets in the country, the new government was heavily dependent on British economic support.

Thus, when Britain recognized Jordan as a self-governing state on May 15, 1923, Emir Abdallah was in no position to run a country. National borders were ill-defined. His father's kingdom of Hijaz to the south was collapsing before the followers of Ibn Saud, and he lacked the resources to assist his father or to protect his own interests. His nation, moreover, was totally dependent on British subsidies. Therefore, though recognized as self-governing, Jordan was, in fact, governed by the British.

With the assistance of a small group of British officials, Jordan under Emir Abdallah made slow progress toward true independence. At first, the administration

was simple. Abdallah ruled with the advice of a small executive council. British officials handled defense, foreign affairs, and finance. A major step toward real independence came with a new treaty in 1928 that gave greater authority to the emir
and his officials. However, London retained the right to oversee finance and foreign policy, and British officers still controlled the Jordanian Army, known then as
the Arab Legion. The Organic Law of 1928 took the first move toward a representative government by providing for a legislative council to replace the old executive council. In 1946, Jordan and Britain reached a new agreement whereby a
constitution replaced the Organic Law of 1928, and Abdallah was recognized as
king of Jordan. Two years later, London agreed to continue paying a subsidy in return for British access to two military bases.

   The rising crisis in Palestine became the dominant concern of the fledgling
state. Abdallah's policy toward Palestine differed from that of other Arab states. In
fact, he met secretly with Zionist leaders, including Golda Meir, in an attempt to
work out some modus vivendi with the Jews in Palestine. Nevertheless, when Israel declared its independence, Jordan's army—then known as the Arab Legion—
occupied areas of Palestine adjacent to Jordan that had been allocated to the Arabs
in the UN Partition Plan of 1947. Abdallah's forces were the most successful of the
Arab armies. When the fighting halted, the Arab Legion held perhaps 20 percent
of Palestine, including East Jerusalem.

   On April 24, 1950, Abdallah unilaterally annexed the portion of Palestine
called the West Bank. More importantly, most other Arabs joined the Palestinians
in believing that Abdallah had betrayed them by annexing part of Palestine. Jordan
became a pariah among the Arab states, with only the fellow Hashimite regime in
Iraq offering support. At the same time, Abdallah alone among the Arab rulers extended full citizenship rights to the Palestinians. Nevertheless, many Palestinians
detested him for what they perceived to be his self-serving action and betrayal of
their desire to obtain Palestinian national rights. As King Abdallah was leaving the
al-Aqsa Mosque in Jerusalem on July 20, 1951, he was assassinated by a Palestinian
nationalist.

Jordan Under King Hussein

After his death, Abdallah was succeeded by his eldest son, Talal, under whom a
new constitution was promulgated in January 1952. Talal, however, had a long history of mental illness and under his doctor's advice abdicated in favor of his son
Hussein, who was still a minor. A regency council of three was formed to govern
for several months until the young Hussein reached maturity and assumed the
throne in May 1953.

   King Hussein ruled Jordan from 1953 until his death in 1999 and therefore became one of the longest serving monarchs of the twentieth century. The king had

served for so long, in fact, that his imprint remains indelibly marked on the evolution of Jordan as a modern state. For most of the modern history of the Hashimite Kingdom of Jordan, most Jordanians knew only one king as architect of the kingdom's domestic development and foreign policy. King Hussein consolidated the Hashimite regime in Jordan and defended it against internal and external challenges, neither of which were in short supply.

Hussein thwarted attempts by nationalist army officers to overturn the monarchy in the 1950s. In the 1960s, Jordan was drawn into the June 1967 Arab-Israeli War. That military disaster carried even more profound social, economic, and political implications, as Jordan lost control of the entire West Bank—including East Jerusalem and its holy places—to Israeli forces. The 1967 debacle also led hundreds of thousands of Palestinian refugees to flee across the Jordan River, joining the thousands already there since the 1948 Palestine War. The changing demographics and regional tensions soon exploded within the kingdom itself, in the form of the 1970–1971 Jordanian civil war. The internal struggle pitted the guerrilla forces of the Palestine Liberation Organization (PLO) against King Hussein's regular army. The royalists won the war, but at a very high cost, particularly in Palestinian lives. Although PLO forces were thereafter expelled from the kingdom, the scars of that bitter conflict remained many decades later for many Palestinians and Jordanians.

Jordan managed largely to avoid the 1973 Arab-Israeli War, with the regime arguing that another wartime loss would spell the end of Jordan entirely. Token forces were sent to support the Syrian front, but for the most part Jordan remained outside the fighting. The kingdom also remained outside the postwar peace process between Egypt and Israel. In the 1980s, regional tensions and war threatened once again, only this time to the east of Jordan. The 1980–1988 Iran-Iraq War created a new set of challenging circumstances for Jordan. As the war dragged on, Jordan increased its support for Iraq. This policy coincided with the policies of the Gulf states and the US administration. Jordan provided Iraq a safe port, strategic depth, and a good trading partner. But if Iraq was Jordan's strongest regional ally in the 1980s, it seemed to be more of a liability with the onset of the 1990s.

Jordan's most serious international challenge in almost two decades resulted from the August 2, 1990, Iraqi invasion and occupation of Kuwait. The overwhelming majority of Jordanians supported Iraq against the allied coalition. Facing such strong domestic sentiments, the Hashimite regime attempted to bridge the divide between its traditional Western allies and Iraq. King Hussein shuttled between various capitals in a failed effort to avert war. But Jordan's fence-straddling policy alienated virtually all of its local and global allies, at great cost to the kingdom. The United States, Western allies, Gulf Arabs, Egyptians, and Syrians sharply criticized Jordan's actions. Foreign assistance all but evaporated. The Gulf states expelled 300,000 Jordanians, and an allied armada searched ships entering and leaving the port of Aqaba. Despite the international criticism, King Hussein's popularity soared at home.

In the immediate aftermath of the war, the Hashimite regime played on Jordan's vital role in any Arab-Israeli peace settlement by enthusiastically accepting terms for multilateral negotiations to begin in 1991 in Madrid. Jordanians and Palestinians initially formed a joint delegation to the peace talks before eventually shifting to distinct negotiating teams in Palestinian-Israeli and Jordanian-Israeli peace talks. After Israel and the PLO reached a breakthrough in the Oslo Peace Accords in 1993, the Jordanians pushed for a full and formal peace treaty with Israel. Jordan and Israel made their peace official in 1994, and Jordan was able to utilize the peace process to reestablish its warm ties with the United States and Europe. By the late 1990s, Jordan had also restored diplomatic relations and financial aid with each of the Arab Gulf monarchies, including Kuwait and Saudi Arabia.

In February 1999, King Hussein of Jordan passed away after a long battle with cancer. But the king's passing in 1999 and his son, King Abdallah II's accession to the throne actually marked the latest in a series of dramatic transitions in Jordanian politics over the last decade of the twentieth century. These included a process of limited democratization (since 1989), several rounds of economic adjustment and restructuring as the kingdom came to terms with globalization (also since 1989), and the conclusion of a full and formal peace treaty with the State of Israel (in 1994). As the kingdom entered the twenty-first century under King Abdallah II, these three transitions remained the central and most controversial issues in Jordanian politics. Most of the remaining sections of this chapter—on political structure, political dynamics, the economy, and foreign policy—examine in more detail Jordanian politics since Abdullah II's accession to the throne.

POLITICAL ENVIRONMENT

The Land

The Hashimite Kingdom of Jordan sits on part of the north Arabian plateau that Jordan shares with Syria to the north, Iraq to the east, and Saudi Arabia to the south. No natural frontiers exist between Jordan and its Arab neighbors. The western border of Jordan is the Great Rift Valley, through which the Jordan River flows. From an average of 600 to 900 meters (2,000 to 3,000 feet) on the plateau, the landscape plummets to well below sea level in the valley. The Great Rift Valley also includes the Dead Sea and the Gulf of Aqaba to the south. Jordan's only coastline is a nineteen-kilometer (twelve-mile) stretch on the Gulf, including the port of Aqaba. Beyond the Great Rift Valley lie Israel and the West Bank highlands.

More than four-fifths of Jordan is desert or semidesert receiving less than ten centimeters (four inches) of rain annually. Prevailing westerly winds draw winter rains to the northern areas of the country, but in the south, dry winds from the Sahara are the rule. Consequently, Jordan's population is concentrated in the western part of the kingdom where rainfall, averaging about thirty to forty-one centimeters (twelve to sixteen inches) annually, permits some farming. All of Jordan's major cities—Amman, Irbid, and Zarqa—are concentrated in this area. Some attempt has been made to expand the area of settlement and cultivation. Of particular note are reforestation projects north of Amman and the East Ghor irrigation canal project in the Jordan River valley. As part of the terms of its 1994 peace treaty, Jordan began importing water from Israel.

The People

Most Jordanians are of Arab heritage and may be roughly divided into two principal groups: Palestinians and East Bank Jordanians. Palestinians are those Arabs (and their descendants) who lived in the British Mandate of Palestine and have been under Jordanian sovereignty since 1948. These include the refugees who fled from Israel and Palestine in the wars of 1948 and 1967. Palestinians now constitute more than half of the total Jordanian population. Perhaps one-fourth still live in the UN Relief and Works Agency (UNRWA) camps. The others are more assimilated into the general population.

Since 1948 Jordan alone among the Arab states has given full citizenship to all Palestinians, and no official distinction is made between Palestinians and East Bank Jordanians. Palestinians are afforded the same political rights as all Jordanians. Grievances remain, however, particularly among Palestinians who often feel that theirs is a secondary status in Jordanian society. Others, both Palestinian and Jordanian, feel that these distinctions are no longer important. Generally speaking, East Bank Jordanians dominate much of the government, public-sector industry, and military, while Palestinians are heavily represented in private-sector businesses and in the various professions. For many in the regime, however, the East Bank Jordanians remain the rock upon which the Hashimite monarchy was built.

Most East Bankers are Sunni Muslims, although a small Christian minority is also present. Among the Palestinians, the percentage of Christians is higher. Many East Bank Jordanians are members of one of several hundred Arab tribes. Even though Bedouins are a small minority of the overall population, Bedouin values and traditions continue to have an important influence on society. The few who continue to live a nomadic life, as well as those who have settled in towns, maintain these values. In Jordan, more than any other state in the Fertile Crescent, tribal elements provide a disproportionate number of recruits for the military and are guaranteed representation in parliament.

Two minority groups—the Christians and the Circassians—have also provided backing for the Hashimites. Jordan's Christian population is urban and has lived in the area for centuries. Predominantly Greek Orthodox and Greek Catholic, most are the descendants of very early converts to Christianity, whereas others have allegedly descended from the crusaders.

The Circassians settled in Jordan in the last decades of the nineteenth century. They were part of the approximately 1 million Muslims who fled the Caucasus region when the Russians captured it from the Ottomans, and they were given land by the Ottoman sultan in what is now Israel, Jordan, and Syria. The Circassians are Sunni Muslims; they have traditionally been loyal to the monarchy and have held very senior positions in the government. They are particularly numerous in the armed forces as well as in the police force. Jordanian Circassians are divided into two major groups—the Adigah and the Chechen. Both groups of Circassians, like the Bedouins and Christians, are guaranteed representation in parliament.

Economic Conditions

Despite a harsh climate, Jordan historically was an agricultural country. The loss of the West Bank in the 1967 war, however, dealt a harsh blow to Jordan's economy. Before 1967 the West Bank accounted for 60 to 80 percent of the country's agricultural land, 75 percent of the gross national product, 40 percent of the government's revenue, and nearly 33 percent of its foreign-currency income. With the loss of the West Bank, the hope for self-sufficiency all but vanished.

Nevertheless, the East Bank did have significant economic assets, including industry and mining. The national power plants and important phosphate mines were in the East Bank. In addition, most of the larger manufacturing facilities were located between Amman and Zarqa. These included textiles, leather, batteries, food processing, brewing and bottling, and cigarette manufacturing.

Although possessing no oil of its own, Jordan indirectly benefited from the rapid rise in the price of oil during the 1970s. Subsidies from Arab oil-producing states and remittances from Jordanians working in those states helped provide necessary capital. Real gross domestic product (GDP) rose at an average annual rate of 11.7 percent, industrial production increased by 16.6 percent, and construction increased by 23.8 percent annually in the 1970s. This rapid growth transformed the economy. By 1991, the service sector accounted for 63.7 percent of the GDP, industry was 28.2 percent, and agriculture only 7 percent.

With the economic slowdown in the oil industry during the 1980s, the Jordanians experienced a decline in their economic growth rates to less than 5 percent. Remittances from workers abroad, however, remained fairly constant, as Jordanian workers were not as heavily involved in construction and other sectors of the Arab Gulf economies, which were drastically reduced. Subsidies from the Arab states to the Jordanian government were cut in half, contributing to the difficulties. With steadily declining foreign aid, the kingdom faced a series of shortfalls in the government budget in the late 1980s. By 1988, Jordan's debt was twice its GDP.

By March 1989, the government felt it had no recourse but to turn to the International Monetary Fund (IMF) for financial help. That help was forthcoming, but only in return for a severe economic-adjustment program. The IMF program included cutbacks in state subsidies of staple foods and other products, which led to skyrocketing prices and ultimately to political unrest as well. Riots erupted throughout the country to protest the economic measures and government corruption. The regime, caught off guard by the intensity of the unrest, moved to stave it off by sacking the government, restoring some subsidies, and announcing the resumption of elections and more meaningful parliamentary life in the kingdom. Thus, a positive outcome emerged from decidedly negative circumstances, as the kingdom embarked on its program of limited democratization. That program was not even a year old, however, when another external shock jolted the Jordanian economy. On August 2, 1990, Iraqi forces invaded Kuwait, triggering a major regional and global crisis.

By the time the 1991 Gulf War was over, the crisis had created still more challenges for the Jordanian economy. Subsidies from the oil-producing states were eliminated; Iraq, Jordan's largest trading partner and source of petroleum, was in ruins and boycotted by the international community; and 300,000 Jordanian citizens were forced to leave the Gulf states, causing the loss of hundreds of millions of dollars in remittances and a major strain on social services within the kingdom.

The loss of assistance from the Gulf states was partially offset by a $450 million Japanese concessionary loan. The loss of trade with Iraq and the Gulf states forced Jordanian merchants to find new markets in China, Europe, Russia, and elsewhere in the Arab world. They were so successful that exports had reached prewar levels by mid-1992. The return of refugees, moreover, caused a brief but significant stimulus to the economy. Many had significant savings that increased foreign-currency deposits from $1.4 billion in February 1991 to $3.2 billion in July 1992. Furthermore, demand created by the need to provide housing and other services to the former Gulf residents provided a significant stimulus to construction and other industries. Although the Jordanian economy exceeded expectations following the Gulf crisis, serious problems remained. Political estrangement from the Gulf states continued for almost a decade with significant economic repercussions. Iraq remained under the UN embargo, depriving Jordan of a primary market. Large numbers of returnees were unable to find work.

By the time of the royal succession in 1999, however, Jordan had managed to restore diplomatic ties with all six Arab Gulf monarchies and had revived part of the earlier economic partnership between Jordan and the Gulf states. Under King Abdallah II, Jordan strengthened its economic and military ties to both the United States and the European Union by securing a free trade agreement with the United

States and joining the European Free Trade Agreement. In 2000, Jordan joined the World Trade Organization. King Abdallah's regime clearly sees Jordan's economic and political future as closely tied to these powerful Western states and organizations. Ultimately, hopes for an improved economy will rest on these economic relationships, on peace in the region, and on maintaining and expanding the opportunities for Jordan's well-educated population to find employment throughout the region.

King Abdallah II has made clear that economic development is his main priority. His regime has created free trade and investment zones in the area around the port of Aqaba, while encouraging extensive foreign investment and tourism in the kingdom. Abdallah has also been particularly zealous in developing information technology as a key part of Jordan's economic and social development. Unlike many of its neighbors, Jordan has also supported nongovernmental organization (NGO)–oriented sustainable development projects, including protecting nature preserves while also developing these areas for ecotourism. Yet, for all the many development projects, Jordan remains a small and relatively poor country; hence, it remains largely dependent on outside sources of financial aid as well as on concessionary sources of oil. Still, Jordan's influence and approach to world politics has never been limited by its size and relative lack of resources. This is perhaps best illustrated in the fact that the World Economic Forum, an annual global gathering of some of the world's most influential business and political leaders, is now routinely held in Jordan in the kingdom's Dead Sea resort area.

POLITICAL STRUCTURE AND POLITICAL DYNAMICS

Jordan is a constitutional monarchy. Promulgated in 1952 during the brief reign of King Talal, the constitution gives increased authority to parliament. Nevertheless, the monarch retains ultimate authority over the legislative, executive, and judicial branches.

Executive power is primarily vested in the king. He appoints the prime minister and members of the cabinet and has the power to dismiss members of the cabinet. Power to dismiss the prime minister is vested in the parliament. When the parliament is suspended, the king assumes this responsibility. The king's considerable powers include the right to sign and promulgate laws, veto legislation, issue royal decrees (with the consent of the prime minister and four cabinet members), approve amendments to the constitution, command the armed forces, and declare war. In addition, he appoints and dismisses judges. The question of royal succession is also addressed in the constitution. The throne is guaranteed through the eldest male in direct line from King Abdallah I. Should there be no direct male heir, the king's eldest brother assumes the throne. On occasion, the king has altered this formula by decree. If a king is either a minor or incapacitated for more than four months, a regent or regency council is established.

Jordan is divided into five provinces or governates: Amman, Balqa, Irbid, Karak, and Ma'an. Each province is administered by a governor appointed by the king. At the national level, Jordan has a bicameral parliament. The 55 senators in the upper house (*Majlis al-Ayyan*, or "Assembly of Notables") are appointed by the king, while the 110 deputies in the lower house (*Majlis al-Nu'ab*, or "Assembly of Deputies") are directly elected. (These numbers had stood respectively at forty and eighty for several decades, but were increased by royal decree in 2003.) The prime minister originates legislation and submits proposals to the lower house. The approval of the upper chamber is necessary only when the lower house accepts a proposal. Should only one of the houses of parliament pass a bill, the two meet together to resolve their differences. Jordan maintains full adult suffrage, and women have had the right to vote and to run for office since 1973.

There are three sources of Jordanian law: Shari'a (Islamic law), European codes, and tradition. The Jordanian constitution and the Court Establishment Act of 1951 mandate a judiciary to reflect these sources of law. Three categories of courts are outlined in the constitution: regular civil courts, religious courts, and special courts. The civil courts system, which is heavily based on Western law, has jurisdiction in all cases not specifically granted to the others. The religious court system has responsibility for personal status and communal endowment. Shari'a courts have responsibility for Muslims, whereas the various Christian sects have their own councils. The special courts have responsibility for tribal questions and land issues. The king retains the right to appoint and dismiss judges and to pardon offenders.

Parliament, Elections, and Political Change

The 1967 war radically transformed the Jordanian political landscape. Half of the elected representatives in parliament had come from the now Israeli-occupied West Bank. The decision of the Arab states at Rabat in 1974 giving the PLO sole responsibility for the destiny of the West Bank further clouded the issue of West Bank representation in parliament, which King Hussein subsequently dissolved. In 1978, he replaced that body with a sixty-member National Consultative Council. Members of the council were appointed by the king for two-year terms. Powers were limited to reviewing bills, and their views were not binding. The council was reappointed in 1980 and 1982.

By January 1984, King Hussein had determined that circumstances had changed. It was again in Jordan's perceived interest to increase its influence on the West Bank, open the political system to increasingly well-educated and prosperous citizens, and renew the search for peace with Israel. In order to accomplish these objectives, the king recalled the parliament, including representatives from the West Bank. As it was not possible to hold elections on the West Bank, the parliament amended the constitution, allowing elections to be held on the East Bank with West Bank deputies to be chosen by parliament. This flurry of activity, in fact, had less to do with parliamentary development and more to do with determining Jordan's future relationship with the West Bank and the Palestinians. In 1988, the question of West Bank representation was rendered moot when King Hussein and the Jordanian government formally renounced claims to the West Bank.

Within Jordan, however, the need to open the political system was made very clear by the widespread political unrest of April 1989. The first election for a purely East Bank parliament was held in November 1989. These elections underlined the acceptance of the Jordanian leaders that East Bank Jordan was a separate political entity. A temporary election law promulgated in late 1988 allowed for the election of eighty deputies from the five governorates of the East Bank. Parties were not allowed to participate. Although all candidates were officially independent, many were known to be affiliated with one particular party or group.

The results of the election in November 1989 alarmed many regime loyalists, as opposition candidates fared very well. Thirty-four of the eighty seats in the chamber went to candidates identified with the Muslim Brotherhood and to independent Islamists. Together they formed the single largest bloc in parliament. Leftist and Arab nationalist candidates won another thirteen seats.

The Jordanian establishment had to adjust its policies in order to adapt to changes in popular opinion. As a means of establishing a national consensus, the king appointed a sixty-member commission that included leaders from all factions, from leftists to Islamic fundamentalists. The commission wrote a national charter, which was a political compact having in many ways as much authority as the constitution. The charter addressed all aspects of state and society and stressed the importance of political pluralism, equality of women, and education and advocated a social safety net and updated labor laws. In agreeing to the national charter, the political opposition in Jordan had endorsed increasing pluralism and political liberalization. In doing so, the opposition also accepted the legitimacy of the ruling Hashimite monarchy.

The king endorsed the charter in June 1991 and ended the remaining elements of martial law the following month. In the spirit of the national charter, parliament drafted a law legalizing political parties as a preliminary step for national elections. Throughout the early months of 1993, the king called for a national dialogue about an electoral system, similar to the dialogue through which the national charter was written. Subsequently, the king announced basic changes in the law and laid the groundwork for elections to be held in November 1993.

The elections of 1993 resulted in a more moderate parliament. Traditional elements were strengthened, and the Islamic groups and the leftists were weakened, although Islamists and their allies continued to be the single largest bloc. The loss of seats for the opposition, however, was due in large part to the new and controversial electoral law that limited voters to one vote each. The previous electoral law had allowed each voter to vote as many times as the number of representatives for their district. Thus, voters in Irbid in 1989 could vote for up to nine representatives for their city to the national parliament. The Muslim Brotherhood utilized this system to run blocks of candidates up to the exact number of seats in a district. That way, they were able to exploit the plurality-based system to gain representation well above their percentage of the overall national vote. But the 1993 electoral law had virtually the reverse effect. The one-person, one-vote restriction was coupled with adjusted new districts that tended to enhance representation in traditionally pro-Hashimite areas—such as rural rather than urban districts. This electoral law remained a bone of contention between the regime and the opposition long after the 1993 elections.

Prior to the next round of elections, in 1997, the regime imposed more restrictive media rules, cutting back on much of the openness that had been achieved since 1989. In 1997, an eleven-party opposition bloc boycotted the parliamentary elections to protest the electoral law, media restrictions, continuing economic-adjustment policies, and normalization of relations with Israel. The electoral boycott led, naturally, to a relatively pliant pro-regime parliament. In effect, the issues that prompted the 1997 electoral boycott remained the central points of debate in Jordanian politics even more than a decade later.

LIBERALIZATION AND DELIBERALIZATION

Despite the institutional structure of Jordan's constitutional monarchy, political power remains decidedly with the king. Nevertheless, the king is a politician who must have public support for his policies. Although there is little doubt that King Abdallah believes in the benefits of a more representative government, the legislature is only as powerful as the monarch allows it to be. In addition, while the lower house is a directly elected body, the upper house remains royally appointed and amounts to a veritable who's who of Jordanian politics. Liberalization efforts therefore continue to focus on elections to the lower house.

Despite several rounds of parliamentary elections since 1989, Jordan's political party system remains weak, with parties largely associated with particular personalities or charismatic figures. In 1989, the first modern round of parliamentary elections took place in the context of a decades-old ban on political parties. But as political liberalization continued, Jordan promulgated the national charter, repealed martial law, and legalized political parties once again. When the next parliamentary elections were held on November 8, 1993, twenty legal political parties participated. The 1993 elections, however, demonstrated the weaknesses, rather than the strengths, of the parties. Less than one-third of the elected members were party members; the majority comprised independents who supported the king. Even those who were members of political parties often ran without party affiliation. Family membership and local influence remain far more important than party identification.

In 1997, party representation within parliament declined still further when the eleven-party opposition bloc boycotted the elections. Even after the 2003 elections, most Jordanians remained independent of any political party. King Abdallah II, like King Hussein, has called continually for a coalescence of the dozens of opposition parties into a more coherent set of three that would represent leftist, centrist, and rightist ideological tendencies. Yet, no such coalescence appears forthcoming. The sole exception to the rule regarding weak political parties is the Islamic Action Front (IAF), which emerged in the early 1990s as the political party of Jordan's Muslim Brotherhood. The Brotherhood has operated as a largely loyal opposition within Jordan for more than half a century; hence, it remains the best-organized opposition group within Jordanian politics.

Following the 1997 electoral boycott, the IAF and indeed most of Jordan's opposition groups—including most secular leftist parties—found themselves with no representation in parliament. This institutional vacuum was filled as the locus of opposition within Jordanian politics shifted increasingly from the parties to the professional associations (PAs). These organizations—representing engineers, lawyers, pharmacists, and other professionals—held democratic elections for their own leadership posts. More often than not, the PA elections were won by Islamist candidates. Jordanian debates about liberalization and deliberalization therefore came to include not only parties, parliament, and the media but also the professional associations and other aspects of Jordanian civil society.

In 2003, Jordan held national parliamentary elections in an effort to reengage its stalled political-liberalization process. Given this context, the 2003 elections were deemed especially important by both government and opposition. They were the first since 1997, the first since the dissolution of parliament in 2001, and the first under King Abdallah II. In 2003, the political opposition returned to full electoral participation. The regime had postponed the elections for more than two years, initially over a new voter card system that would take some time to prepare. The more pressing reason, however, may have been the return of the Palestinian Intifada, or uprising, against Israeli military occupation of the West Bank and Gaza. After the Intifada began in 2000, however, regional politics only destabilized further with US invasions of Afghanistan (in 2001) and Iraq (in 2003). In each case, new electoral delays were announced.

In June 2003 the elections were finally held under still another electoral law. The new law, announced in July 2001, lowered the age of voting eligibility for men and women from nineteen to eighteen and increased the number of parliamentary seats from 80 to 104, with new (but still uneven) electoral districts. In February 2003, King Abdallah added to the changes with a new decree adding six more parliamentary seats in a specific quota to ensure minimal representation for women. In the previous three elections—1989, 1993, and 1997—only one woman was elected to parliament: Tujan Al Faisal (in 1993). Interestingly, the IAF had originally opposed the women's quota, but then included for the first time a woman, Hayat Al Musayni, among its slate of thirty candidates. No Jordanian woman won a seat outright in 2003, but Musayni turned out to be the top vote-getter among women candidates overall. Thus, in an ironic twist, the first woman seated in the new 2003–2007 parliament was a conservative Islamist activist. The IAF succeeded in getting seventeen of its party members elected (including Musayni). Aside from the IAF, five independent Islamists were also elected. Most of the parliamentary seats, however, went to traditional tribal leaders or former government officials. At least 62 seats out of 110, in short, went to loyalist pro-regime figures.

In 2006, Hamas won a sweeping victory against Fateh in Palestinian legislative elections in the West Bank and Gaza. This seemed to inject a "Hamas factor" into the dynamics of government and opposition in Jordan. For many Jordanian Islamists, the Hamas victory was on the one hand inspiring; on the other, it also demonstrated their comparative limitations. Hamas's electoral win translated immediately into a new Hamas-led government and cabinet. Within Jordan, in contrast, years of Islamist electoral strategies had indeed translated to some success, but at no time did the Muslim Brotherhood or IAF have the opportunity to form a government in Jordan. Still, the Hamas victory seemed to embolden more hawkish elements in the Jordanian Islamist movement, even as it hardened the positions of the state and especially its intelligence services, or *mukhabarat*, against any Hamas-like shift in the politics of Islamism in Jordan. After the Hamas victory, Jordan's IAF reasserted its demand that governments be drawn from parliament rather than royally appointed. The party also continued to emphasize its more standard policy stances, including implementing Shari'a law and abandoning the peace treaty with Israel.

Yet, in the next round of national parliamentary elections in Jordan in November 2007, the Islamists suffered a resounding and controversial defeat. Islamist strength in parliament dropped from seventeen seats to a mere six, and Islamist candidates even lost in such traditional strongholds as Zarqa. The IAF charged the government with vote rigging and announced its withdrawal from the electoral process—but only on election day itself. The government, in contrast, argued that the Islamists were merely trying to save face in the midst of a certain electoral defeat. In the aftermath of the election, a split within the Islamist movement between hawkish and dovish wings became clearer, with the more hawkish elements winning internal elections for leadership of both the Muslim Brotherhood and the IAF. Still, despite the hardened positions of both the state and its largest opposition movement, this remains a struggle between the regime and a loyal opposition—not a militant or revolutionary movement—over the future of Jordanian policy and especially over the liberalization process itself.

Despite differences in ideological or even religious orientation, opposition parties of all types in Jordan actually agree on several things. Most have been sharply critical of the peace treaty with Israel, for example. They demand that the regime cease normalizing relations with Israel, and some even demand the abolition of the treaty itself. Within domestic politics and policy, the opposition parties also insist that future prime ministers and cabinets should be drawn from parliament in a truer model of a parliamentary system, rather than royally appointed pending only the formality of parliamentary approval. Still, whether rooted in Islamic, Pan-Arab nationalist, or secular leftist ideas, political opposition in Jordan has tended to struggle with the regime over policy and the direction of the state (including demands for greater democratization); it has not tended to challenge the nature of the state itself as a Hashimite monarchy.

There was some cause for optimism in the wake of the 2007 elections in terms of efforts at gender equality. Women made up more than 25 percent of the candidates for parliamentary office and amounted to four times the number who had contested the 2003 elections. Still, success has remained hard to come by, aside from the six members of parliament determined by the women's quota. But in 2007, Falak Jamaani became the first woman to win a Jordanian parliamentary seat outright—without any form of quota. Jamaani, a career army dentist who had retired with the rank of major general, had earned a parliamentary seat in 2003 through the quota system. When she ran for reelection in 2007 in her home district of Madaba, she earned an outright victory. Jamaani's victory was hailed by women's empowerment activists throughout the kingdom as the first major crack in a glass ceiling over women's representation.

Overall, since the initiation of the political-liberalization process in 1989, the Jordanian political system took major steps toward pluralism, but then reversed or stalled many of those steps, leaving full democracy an ideal but not a reality. Political parties, NGOs, and independent media are all part of Jordanian society and political life. Yet, tensions remain between the security concerns of the regime and the ambitious reformist agenda of many Jordanian individuals and organizations desiring deeper levels of democratization.

Jordanian media include a plethora of independent newspapers, magazines, and even tabloids, for example; yet, the press and publications laws tend to include ambiguous regulations preventing journalists from harming state security. Since it remains unclear what might be read as "harming" the state, journalists often practice self-censorship in an effort to avoid running afoul of the intelligence services. Similarly, Jordanian civil society has grown so much that one Jordanian NGO, the Al-Urdun al-Jadid Research Center, catalogued no less than 1,800 different civil society organizations operating in the kingdom. These include societies and associations for a variety of purposes, such as educational, cultural, professional, environmental, and, of course, political activism. But here, too, the glass appears both half full and half empty. There is clearly no shortage of civil society organizations in Jordan, but the whole purpose of civil society is to be independent of the state, while these organizations are registered with, and monitored by, government ministries.

In general, Jordan under King Abdallah II has pursued a fairly ambitious program of liberalization, but the regime also favors economic over political liberalization. And the latter tends to be slowed by any perceived threats to the security of the Hashimite regime itself. Thus, regional tensions have at times served to undermine the domestic reform process, but they can also underscore, or even reinvigorate, existing divisions within Jordanian society. The Palestinian uprising against Israeli occupation, for example, revived questions within the kingdom about the nature of Jordanian identity itself. Who, exactly, is a Jordanian? If a Palestinian state were to be established, would Palestinians be loyal to that state or to Jordan? This question, though not of great concern to many Jordanians, is asked by powerful conservative East Bank Jordanians and, hence, matters within domestic politics. Even economic liberalization carries ethnic implications. As the state slowly privatizes various industries, the historically Palestinian-dominant private sector continues to get larger, while East Bank Jordanian dominance of the public sector is under threat.

For its part, the monarchy insists on its stated policy of "Jordan first," arguing that any emphasis on a Jordanian-Palestinian rift is outdated, divisive, and even unpatriotic. King Abdallah and his wife, Queen Rania (who is of Palestinian origin), both argue that intra-ethnic divisions are part of Jordan's past, not its future. Still, Jordan is literally wedged between Israel and Palestine to the west and Iraq to the east; hence, regional crises and violence do still cross the border, carrying with them the threat of inflaming local divisions. The Hashimite monarchy, however, sees economic development as the key to continuing to unify the kingdom, in the way that King Abdallah's "Jordan first" program implies.

Yet, as noted above, Jordan remains vulnerable to regional tensions and crises. On November 9, 2005, al-Qa'ida suicide bombers struck three luxury hotels in central Amman, killing sixty people—mostly Jordanians—and injuring more than one hundred. Jordanians referred to this horrific event as "their 9/11." Since Jordan, like most countries, writes dates in the order of day, month, year, this 9/11 reference is also literal, since the attacks took place (presumably on purpose) on the ninth of November (9/11). Jordanians from all walks of life were understandably outraged. Interestingly, the IAF and the Muslim Brotherhood were among the first to respond to the tragedy by organizing anti-al-Qa'ida demonstrations in the capital. King Abdallah appointed a new government that reflected a regime very much in security mode. The government announced that counterterrorism would be a key policy focus and called for "preemptive war" on militant forms of Islamism. Although the IAF and Muslim Brotherhood remained by no means militant, they nonetheless feared what the new security measures might mean for them.

FOREIGN POLICY

From the foundation of the Hashimite state onward, Jordan maintained close strategic ties to Britain and later the United States. After World War II and with the onset of the Cold War, Jordan also established stronger and stronger links to the United States, as the Western powers came to view Jordan as a conservative bulwark against communism and radical forms of pan-Arabism and as potentially a moderating element in the Arab-Israeli conflict. From the beginning, then, Jordan has held close ties to powerful Western states and has in fact depended heavily on foreign aid from these countries to keep the kingdom afloat. Jordan's very centrality in Middle East politics and geography has also carried with it a real strategic vulnerability.

Given its location, Jordan was from the outset deeply involved in the various dimensions of the Palestinian-Israeli and broader Arab-Israeli conflicts. By the time of Jordanian independence in 1946, tensions were peaking in neighboring Palestine between Jews and Arabs over the issue of Jewish versus Palestinian aspirations to full statehood. When the United Nations voted to partition Palestine between the two peoples in 1947 and Israel declared its independence the following year, Jordan's Arab Legion was one of the Arab armies that fought Israel, joining fighting that had already begun between Jews and Arabs in Palestine. In that hard-fought campaign—a defeat for the Arab forces—Jordan's Arab Legion held on to East Jerusalem and the West Bank. Jordan later lost both territories in the disastrous 1967 Arab-Israeli War.

While tensions continued in the years that followed, Jordanian foreign policy thereafter avoided direct confrontation with Israel and pursued a resolutely cautious and conservative course. The chief architect of this approach to foreign policy was, of course, the late King Hussein. Under Hussein, and afterward under King Abdallah II, Jordanian foreign policy has been driven by regime security above all things.

In the Jordanian context, regime security carries not only military but also economic components. As a small and relatively poor state, Jordan relies on external sources of aid and oil and is further dependent on external labor markets. Tourism and foreign investment are cornerstones of King Abdallah's approach to national development, and both require domestic and regional stability to reach fruition. As a result, King Abdallah has maintained his father's emphasis on cautious foreign policy, while also actively pursuing a regional role as a peacemaker. Despite its small size, Jordan sends its soldiers on UN peacekeeping operations throughout the world.

In regional politics, meanwhile, King Abdallah maintained the kingdom's peace treaty with Israel, while pressing for a peace settlement between Israel and the Palestinian National Authority. Abdallah argued to US officials in particular that the Palestinian issue—not Iraq—is the single most destabilizing issue in Middle East politics. The Jordanian government therefore consistently offered its good offices between the United States, Israel, and the Palestinian authority. But with the second Palestinian uprising (in 2000) and later the 2003 US invasion of Iraq, Jordan's geography alone guaranteed that the kingdom would be wedged between two zones of conflict, both deeply important to the Jordanian people. Public concerns for the welfare of both Palestinians and Iraqis has been an important part of Jordanian politics for some time, but as violence increased and death tolls mounted, so too did public anger. While much of this was vented toward the Israeli, US, or UK governments and the actions of their respective armed forces, some focused also on the Hashimite monarchy.

The close alliance of Jordan with the United States and Britain provided vital strategic and economic support for Jordan in the eyes of the monarchy. But in the eyes of many in the general public, the US and British connection became more and more of a liability. While few felt that these alliances could actually be tampered with, many regarded the peace treaty with Israel as malleable, to say the least. Israeli actions against Palestinians angered virtually all Jordanians; hence, the monarchy faced increasing criticism for maintaining the treaty at all, in addition to a rising tide of domestic criticism. The IAF and a host of opposition parties—as well as most professional associations—had earlier declared a boycott on any interaction with Israel. Their goal was to prevent normalization of relations, despite the treaty, by preventing professional exchanges and interactions and by discouraging any kind of business or economic activity. The antinormalization campaign continued well beyond the transition from King Hussein to King Abdallah and indeed gained strength from the series of regional crises that had served to make the treaty still less popular. Abdallah's regime, however, insisted that the treaty had been completed long ago (1994) and was not negotiable. For the monarchy, then, maintaining the treaty as well as increasingly unpopular alliances with powerful Western countries remained absolutely essential to the regime's goals for stability, international trade and investment, and economic development. For many in the opposition, precisely the reverse was true.

Following the September 11, 2001, terrorist attacks on the United States, Jordan supported the US war against the Taliban regime in Afghanistan and US attempts to eradicate al-Qa'ida. Like most US allies, however, Jordan argued against the US invasion of Iraq. King Abdallah and other top Jordanian policy makers urged the

United States not to invade, arguing that doing so would only destabilize Iraq and the entire region still further, while also eliminating a buffer state against potential Iranian ambitions. While Jordanian predictions all came true, the regime was intent on maintaining its US and British alliances, even if the states had disagreed profoundly on a key foreign policy issue. Jordan refused to allow combat operations to take place from Jordan but did allow the temporary placement of US Patriot missile batteries in the eastern Jordanian desert, near the Iraqi border.

While Jordan had argued against the US war on Iraq, the kingdom nonetheless supported the postinvasion attempt to reconstruct the country, including the provision of extensive training for Iraqi police and security forces at camps in Jordan. Before and after the invasion, however, Jordanian policy makers consistently argued that the real issue in regional politics remained the unresolved question of Palestinian rights and independence. With violence to the west and east of Jordan and al-Qa'ida attacks even within Jordan itself, the kingdom remained focused necessarily on its own security and survival.

Despite the intensity of regional insecurity, Jordan for the most part remained stable and secure within its borders, while the regime continued to emphasize economic development, trade, investment, and an active tourism industry as the ultimate keys to Jordan's present and future. These priorities, in turn, led the monarchy to pursue warm relations with economically influential states, from the Arab Gulf monarchies, to the European Union countries, to the United States. In this vein, Jordan also continued to host the annual meeting of the World Economic Forum. Under King Abdallah II, as under King Hussein before him, Jordan presented itself as a source of regional moderation and stability, and the kingdom continued to play a foreign policy role far beyond what its small size and its limited resources would otherwise suggest.

BIBLIOGRAPHY

For good general histories of Jordan, see Philip Robins, *A History of Jordan* (Cambridge: Cambridge University Press, 2004), and Kamal Salibi, *The Modern History of Jordan* (London: I. B. Tauris, 1998). Robert Satloff's *From Abdullah to Hussein: Jordan in Transition* (New York: Oxford University Press, 1993) examines the emergence of the Hussein regime in the early 1950s. For a detailed analysis of the emergence of Jordan as a country, see Mary C. Wilson's *King Abdullah, Britain and the Making of Jordan* (Cambridge: Cambridge University Press, 1987). On the issues of Jordanian development, national identity, and debates over these issues within Jordanian politics, see Marc Lynch, *State Interests and Public Spheres: The International Politics of Jordan's Identity* (New York: Columbia University Press, 1999), and Joseph Massad, *Colonial Effects: The Making of National Identity in Jordan* (New York: Columbia University Press, 2001).

Several articles have examined various aspects of the democratization process in the kingdom, including Rex Brynen, "Economic Crisis and Post-Rentier Democratization in the Arab World: The Case of Jordan," *Canadian Journal of Political Science* 25, no. 1 (1992): 69–97, and Glenn E. Robinson, "Defensive Democratization in Jordan," *International Journal of Middle East Studies* 30, no. 3 (1998): 373–387. For an analysis of the 1989, 1993, and 1997 elections, see Curtis R. Ryan, "Elections and Parliamentary Democratization in Jordan," *Democratization* 5, no. 4 (1998): 176–196.

On contemporary Jordanian politics, particularly the democratization process, economic reform, peace with Israel, and the succession from Hussein to Abdallah, see Curtis R. Ryan, *Jordan in Transition: From Hussein to Abdullah* (Boulder, CO: Lynne Rienner, 2002). On economic change, see Peter Moore, *Doing Business in the Middle East: Politics and Economic Crises in Jordan and Kuwait* (Cambridge: Cambridge University Press, 2004).

An interesting and challenging discussion of Palestinian-Jordanian relations within the kingdom can be found in Mustafa Hamarneh, Rosemary Hollis, and Khalil Shikaki, *Jordanian-Palestinian Relations: Where To?* (London: Royal Institute of International Affairs, 1997).

On the Islamist movement within Jordan, see Jillian M. Schwedler, *Faith in Moderation: Islamist Parties in Jordan and Yemen* (Cambridge: Cambridge University Press, 2006); Janine A. Clark, *Islam, Charity, and Activism: Middle Class Networks and Social Welfare in Egypt, Jordan, and Yemen* (Bloomington: Indiana University Press, 2004); and Quintan Wiktorowicz, *The Management of Islamic Activism: Salafis, the Muslim Brotherhood, and State Power in Jordan* (Albany: State University of New York Press, 2000).

On Jordan's international relations and foreign policy, see Laurie A. Brand, *Jordan's Inter-Arab Relations: The Political Economy of Alliance Making* (New York: Columbia University Press, 1994); Marc Lynch, *State Interests and Public Spheres* (New York: Columbia University Press, 1999); and Curtis R. Ryan, *Inter-Arab Alliances: Regime Security and Jordanian Foreign Policy* (Gainesville: University Press of Florida, 2009).

Key Websites for Jordan

Website of the Jordanian embassy to the United States, including Jordanian positions on a host of foreign policy issues: www.jordanembassyus.org/new/index.shtml.

Website of the Jordan Times, the main English-language daily newspaper in the kingdom: www.jordantimes.com.

Website of the Center for Strategic Studies (CSS) at the University of Jordan;

the CSS is one of the most extensive and most impressive centers for polling and research in the kingdom and in the Arab world: www.css-jordan.org.

Website of the al-Urdun al-Jadid Research Center, a major research non-governmental organization working on democracy and civil society in the king-dom: www.ujrc-jordan.org.

Website of the American Center for Oriental Research, the largest center in the kingdom for research on Jordan's many archeological sites: www.bu.edu/acor.

Extensive website of the Jordan Tourism Board, with videos, photo galleries, and interactive links to Jordan's many tourist sites: www.visitjordan.com.

Site dedicated to the memory and accomplishments of the late King Hussein: www.kinghussein.gov.jo.

Official website of His Majesty King Abdallah of Jordan, including speeches and photo galleries: www.kingabdullah.jo/homepage.php.

Official website of Her Majesty Queen Rania of Jordan, including links to ex-tensive projects for the rights of women and children: www.queenrania.jo.

11

STATE OF ISRAEL

David H. Goldberg and Bernard Reich

Israel is a product of Zionism (the Jewish national movement). Since biblical days, Jews of the Diaspora (Jewish communities outside Israel) have hoped to return to Zion, the Promised Land. While some Jews always lived in the Holy Land, the overwhelming majority were located in the Diaspora. Over the centuries Zionism developed spiritual, religious, cultural, social, and historical concepts linking Jews to the land of the historical Jewish state in Israel. The political variant of Zionism that saw the establishment of a Jewish state as a logical consequence of its actions developed in the nineteenth century partly as a result of political currents then prevalent in Europe, especially nationalism and anti-Semitism (often referred to as the Jewish question).

HISTORICAL BACKGROUND

In 1897 Theodor Herzl, a Viennese journalist who had proposed establishing a self-governing community for the Jewish people in his book *Der Judenstaat* (*The Jewish State*), organized a conference at Basel, Switzerland, to assemble prominent leaders from the major Jewish communities and organizations throughout the world. This assembly shaped a Zionist political movement and established the World Zionist Organization. The Basel Program, which became the cornerstone of Zionist ideology, enunciated the basic aim of Zionism: "to create for the Jewish people a home in Palestine secured by public law" as a response to the Jewish question.

World War I enabled the Zionist movement to make important gains. As a consequence of the war, the Ottoman Empire, which had ruled Palestine since the sixteenth century, was forced to relinquish the territory. With the aid of Chaim Weizmann, a prominent Zionist leader and a chemist who contributed to the British war effort, the Zionist organization secured from the British government the Balfour Declaration (1917), stating, inter alia, "His Majesty's Government view with favour the establishment in Palestine of a national home for the Jewish

State of Israel

people." By the end of the war, British control had replaced Ottoman rule in Palestine. The League of Nations allocated the Palestine Mandate to Great Britain, which controlled the area between 1920 and May 1948.

During the Mandate period, the British mandatory government entrusted the elected representative body of the organized Jewish community in Palestine (the Yishuv) with the responsibility for Jewish communal affairs—but not foreign policy or defense—and granted it considerable autonomy. The National Council established institutions for self-government and procedures for implementing political decisions; it also controlled the clandestine recruitment and military training of Jewish youth in the defense force (Hagana), which after independence formed the core of Israel's defense forces.

Prototypical political institutions, founded and developed by the Jewish community, laid the foundation for many of Israel's public bodies and political processes. Several of the semigovernmental organizations that were created—most notably the General Federation of Labor (Histadrut), founded in 1920, and the Jewish Agency (legitimized in Article 4 of the League of Nations Palestine Mandate)—continued to play important roles after Israel's independence and contributed to the growth of a highly developed system of Zionist political parties and the consequent prevalence of coalition executive bodies in the Zionist movement and the local organs of Palestine Jewry.

Throughout the Mandate period, the Jewish and Arab communities of Palestine were in conflict over the future of the territory. Arab opposition to Jewish immigration and land purchase was manifested in such actions as the Arab revolts in the 1920s and 1930s. British policy vacillated, but restrictions on Jewish immigration became central elements of the British response to intercommunal violence. Unable to find a solution to satisfy these conflicting views, the British eventually conceded that the mandate was unworkable and turned the problem over to the United Nations, which placed the Palestine issue before its General Assembly in the spring of 1947.

The UN Special Committee on Palestine studied the problem and recommended that the mandate be terminated and that the independence of Palestine be achieved without delay; however, the committee was divided over the future of the territory. The majority proposal recommended partition into a Jewish state and an Arab state linked in an economic union, with Jerusalem and its environs established as an international enclave—a separate body (*corpus separatum*). The minority recommended that Palestine become a single federal state, with Jerusalem the capital and with Jews and Arabs enjoying autonomy in their respective areas. On November 29, 1947, the UN General Assembly, over strong Arab opposition, adopted the majority recommendation by thirty-three votes to thirteen, with ten abstentions. The Zionists reluctantly accepted the decision as the best practical outcome. The Palestinian Arabs and other Arabs rejected the vote.

Thereafter the situation in Palestine deteriorated rapidly. Disorders, reminiscent of those of the 1920s and 1930s, broke out in all parts of the territory, and as the end of the mandate approached, these degenerated into a virtual civil war. Gen. Sir Alan Gordon Cunningham, the last British high commissioner, departed. Israel declared its independence as a Jewish and democratic state on May 14, 1948. Armies of the Arab states entered Palestine and engaged in open warfare with the defense forces of the new State of Israel. The United Nations secured a truce, and the military situation was stabilized in the spring of 1949 by a series of armistice agreements between Israel and the neighboring Arab states, but no general peace settlement was achieved.

Israel

Capital city	Jerusalem
Chief of state	President Shimon Peres
Head of government	Prime Minister Benjamin Netanyahu
Major political parties (share of most recent vote)	Kadima (23.2%), Likud (22.3%), Yisrael Beiteinu (12.1%), Labor Party (10.2%), Shas (8.8%), United Torah Judaism (4.5%), United Arab List–Ta'al (3.5%), National Union (3.4%), Democratic Front for Peace and Equality (3.4%), The Jewish Home (3%), The New Movement–Meretz (3%); Balad (2.6%)
Ethnic groups	Jewish (76.4%), non-Jewish, mostly Arab (23.6%)
Religious groups	Jewish (76.4%), Muslim (16%), Arab Christian (1.7%), other Christians (0.4%), Druze (1.6%), unspecified (3.9%)
Export partners	United States (32.5%), Belgium (7.5%), Hong Kong (6.7%)
Import partners	United States (12.3%), Belgium (6.5%), China (6.5%), Switzerland (6.1%), Germany (6%)

The provisional government of Israel, which was formed at the time of independence and recognized by the major powers, was new in name only. It had begun to function following the adoption of the partition resolution in 1947, and it drew on the experience gained by the Yishuv. After proclaiming Israel's independence, the provisional government repealed the British mandatory restrictions on immigration and the sale of land and converted the Hagana into the Israel Defense Forces (IDF).

Political Environment

Israel's special role as the world's only Jewish state has had a manifold effect on its political system. Israel is interested in the well-being of Jews everywhere and concerned that all Jews who wish to immigrate be free to do so. Israel's Declaration of Independence proclaims that "the State of Israel will be open to the immigration of Jews from all countries of their dispersion." The Law of Return of July 5, 1950, provides that "every Jew has the right to come to this country as an 'oleh' [Jew immigrating to Israel]" and has been reinforced by the programs and actions of successive Israeli governments. The "ingathering of the exiles" has received overwhelming support in the Knesset (Israel's parliament) and from the Jewish population, and it has been implemented almost without regard to the economic costs and social dislocations caused by the rapid and massive influx of people. Immigration serves Israel's needs by providing the manpower necessary for Israel's security and development and for maintaining Israel's unique Jewish character.

The early immigrants laid the foundations for an essentially European culture in Palestine, and subsequent immigration accelerated the trend of Westernization. The Occidental (overwhelmingly Ashkenazi, referring to Jews of central and eastern European extraction) immigrants developed the Yishuv structure of land settlement, trade unions, political parties, and education in preparation for a Western-oriented Jewish national state. Future immigrants (including the massive influxes of the Jewish communities of Muslim states in the Middle East and North Africa) had to adapt themselves to a society that had formed these institutions, and this presented a problem for those who were part of the immigration from non-Western countries.

Economic, social, and cultural assimilation of the immigrants in a short time span would have been a formidable undertaking for a small country even under the most favorable conditions. In Israel, this has been attempted despite the obstacles posed by limited resources, defense needs, and the diverse composition and character of the new immigration. Mandatory military service, which emphasizes education as well as the experience of common living and working and of learning the Hebrew language, facilitates acculturation and encourages evolution in the direction of a unified, multicultural Jewish Israeli society.

The Arabs of Israel (that is, those who have lived in Israel since its independence and their offspring, who are Israeli citizens)—some 22 percent of the population in 2009—are confronted by problems qualitatively different from those facing Jewish immigrants. After the 1949 armistice agreements, most of the areas held by Israel and inhabited by Arabs were placed under military administration. Israel's Arabs were granted citizenship but forbidden to travel into or out of security areas without permission from the military as a means of preventing infiltration, sabotage, and espionage. As evidence developed that Israel's Arab citizens were not a disloyal fifth column, popular pressure for relaxation and then for total abolition of military restrictions grew. The restrictions were gradually modified, and on December 1, 1966, the military government was abolished.

The major long-term challenge for the Arab minority is its social integration. Although Israeli Arabs vote, sit in the Knesset, serve in government offices, have their own schools and courts, and prosper materially, they face difficulties in adjusting to Israel's modern Jewish- and Western-oriented society. The Arabs tend to live in separate villages and separate sections of the major cities. They speak Arabic, attend a separate school system, and, with few exceptions, do not serve in the army. Israel's Arab and Jewish communities have few points of contact, and those that exist are not intimate; the societies are separate and generally continue to hold stereotypical images of each other, often reinforced by the schools, media, and social distance, as well as by the tensions and problems created by the larger Arab-Israeli conflict in its numerous dimensions.

Over time the Arab community has become restive and increasingly politically aware. In the spring of 1976, Israel's Arabs participated in their first general protest and staged the most violent demonstrations to that date in Israel's history. The riots grew out of a general strike that was organized to protest land expropriations. The demonstrations escalated and eventually became broader and more general in their focus.

Israeli Arabs demonstrated greater political activism after the beginning of the Palestinian uprising (intifada) in the West Bank and Gaza Strip in December 1987. They began to identify more strongly with the Arabs in the occupied territories and showed signs of growing nationalism and greater militancy. In October 2000, Israeli Arabs rioted and demonstrated in support of the Palestinians and expressed long-standing grievances. Twelve Israeli Arabs (and one resident of the Gaza Strip) were killed in clashes with Israeli police. The Orr State Commission of Inquiry was appointed to examine the riots. It concluded that specific circumstances had triggered the events, and these were combined with a long-standing sense of grievance in Israel's Arab community concerning unfair treatment and discrimination by the Jewish majority. There was a gap between government plans and decisions on the one hand and their implementation on the other.

Despite the existence of a number of Arab political parties, Israeli Arabs have failed to form a significant independent Arab political party that could represent the Arab minority in the quest for Arab rights and express its opinions and views. In the absence of such an Arab political party, the Arab Democratic Party, the United Arab List, and the Israel Communist Party, in their various incarnations, have played important roles in the articulation of the Arab perspective and in promoting Arab positions. Arab members of the Knesset (MKs) continue to stir controversy by meeting with leaders of terrorist organizations (such as Hamas and Hizballah) and leaders of Arab states not at peace with Israel.

In February 2006, Israel's High Court of Justice held that Israel's Arab citizens are endowed with equal rights and must not be discriminated against in resource allocation and that racism and discrimination must be avoided. The court noted that although Israel is defined as a Jewish and democratic state, it rejected outright any favorable bias in education budgets for Jewish communities. The democratic nature of the state requires that citizens residing in it have equal rights.

RELIGION AND THE STATE

Israel is a Jewish state, but that does not ensure agreement on the appropriate relationship between religion and the state, or that between the religious and secular authorities, or on the methods and techniques to be employed by religious authorities for determining "who is a Jew." Since independence, Israel has had to come to terms with the concept of its "Jewishness" and the question "who is a Jew?" And thus it has had to address the meaning of a "Jewish state." Secular and religious authorities and ordinary citizens have faced the question in connection with issues of immigration, marriage, divorce, inheritance, and conversion, as well as in matters related to registration to secure identity cards and the official collection of data and information. The question relates to the application of laws, such as the Law of Return, the Nationality Law, and others passed by the Knesset, and their interpretation by secular and religious authorities. It remains essential not only to determine "who is a Jew" but to decide who should make such a determination and what criteria should be used.

Although Israel's government is secular, there is no formal wall of separation between religion and state as is common in most Western democracies. The Ministry of Religious Affairs is concerned with meeting Jewish religious requirements, such as the supply of ritually killed (kosher) meat, rabbinical courts, and religious schools (yeshivot), as well as with meeting the religious needs of the non-Jewish communities that enjoy religious autonomy. These functions are noncontroversial. Nevertheless, there is sharp and recurrent controversy concerning the extent to which religious observance or restriction is directly or indirectly imposed on the entire Jewish population. The religiously observant community, through its own political parties and its membership in government coalitions, has been able to secure government agreement to establish separate school systems, to exempt most of its young men and young women from army service, and to curtail almost all business and public activity on the Sabbath. The less-observant and secular Jews of Israel argue that they do not have religious freedom because of governmental acquiescence to demands of the observant Jewish groups and the limitations placed on the role of non-Orthodox Judaism in Israel.

Israel utilizes a modified millet system derived from the Ottoman period for distributing authority among religious communities. The various religious communities exercise jurisdiction in litigation involving personal status and family law and apply religious codes and principles in their own judicial institutions. Matters that are secular concerns in other states often fall within the purview of religious authorities in Israel; even though there is no established state religion, all religious institutions have a special status and authority granted by the state and are supported by state funds.

The political reality that has required coalition governments in Israel from the outset has also necessitated inclusion of political parties of the religious community in virtually all cabinets as coalition partners. They have sought to control the Ministry of Religious Affairs and usually also the Ministry of the Interior and the Ministry of Education. This has given the religious parties substantial political power and thus an ability to enforce many of their demands and perspectives concerning the role of religion in the Jewish state. The role of religion in Israel's everyday life clearly remains a major social and political issue.

ECONOMIC CONDITIONS

Israel's economy has undergone substantial change since independence, and the economic well-being of its people has improved significantly. Israel remains something of an economic "miracle," belying the preindependence prophecies that its troubled economy could not long endure. Instead, a country virtually bereft of natural resources and faced with substantial burdens imposed by massive immigration and Arab hostility achieved a relatively prosperous economic standard. By the beginning of the twenty-first century, Israel had achieved a large economy by regional standards (with a gross domestic product [GDP] of more than $200 billion), and its people generally had become prosperous (with more than $28,000 per capita GDP in 2008). The standard of living in Israel and the productivity of its labor force are comparable to those in western European countries; Israel was admitted to the Organization of Economic Cooperation and Development (OECD) in 2007 and that year led all OECD countries in civilian research and development as a proportion of GDP. Israel's life-expectancy levels are among the highest in the world, and it has maintained extensive social services for its population.

Israel's small size and lack of mineral and water resources profoundly affect its economy. Israel's dearth of energy resources has made it virtually completely dependent on foreign supplies of oil, coal, and natural gas. Since the 1980s Israel's oil imports have contributed significantly to its large balance-of-payments deficit.

Extensive irrigation and intensive farming methods have dramatically increased agricultural production for both domestic consumption and export. The amount of irrigated land and agricultural exports rose substantially between 1948 and the 1980s. Israel exports citrus, cotton, vegetables, and dairy products and is a world leader in developing advanced agricultural technology.

Israel's industrial development can be traced to an investment program financed from outside sources, including US government loans and grants, the sale of Israel bonds, investments, and German reparations and restitution payments. At the same time, charitable contributions from the world Jewish community helped reduce the government's burdens in the social welfare sector, thereby permitting the use of scarce funds for economic projects. Israel's substantial human resources include Nobel Prize winners nurtured by world-class universities.

Israel has maintained growth rates in real gross national product (GNP) exceeding 9 percent for prolonged periods. From 1950 to 1972, real output grew at an average annual rate of nearly 10 percent, and output per worker more than tripled.

During the Labor Party's domination of politics from before independence to 1977, it pursued socialist economic policies in a mixed economy adapted to the special circumstances of Israel. The government played a central and decisive role in the economy, aided by the Jewish Agency, the United Israel Appeal, the Jewish National Fund, and the Histadrut. The government owned and operated the railroads, the postal service, and the telephone, telegraph, and broadcasting facilities, in addition to the usual government public works, such as road and irrigation projects. There was also substantial government investment in public corporations in areas such as oil, electricity, and fertilizer. When the nonsocialist Likud came to power in 1977, the system was altered to reduce the government's role in the economy and increasingly to apply free market principles.

Hyperinflation in the mid-1980s was arrested by an economic-stabilization program adopted in July 1985. The program was successful in reducing the public sector's budget deficit, and aid from the United States eased pressures on the balance of payments. Nevertheless, government involvement in the economy continued at a high level, and the economy was soon buffeted by the Palestinian Intifada that started in December 1987, the mass immigration of Soviet Jews that began in 1989, and the crisis resulting from the Iraqi invasion of Kuwait in 1990.

In the first half of the 1990s, the high-tech sector took off, there was a large influx of immigrants, and prospects for regional peace improved—all combining to fuel the economy's strong performance. The economy slowed temporarily in the second half of the 1990s.

A recovery of economic activity started in the second half of 1999, taking the form of a rapid expansion of GDP driven by industrial exports in high-technology sectors, mainly electronics. Israel had also undertaken important structural reforms (such as privatization and reduced controls on foreign-currency exchanges and profit remittances by foreign companies). Apparent progress in peace negotiations attracted tourism and foreign investment. Israel made progress in the direction of a more open, competitive, market-oriented economy, although public spending remained a significant proportion of the country's GDP, and top marginal income tax rates remained high.

The outbreak of the al-Aqsa Intifada in September 2000 plunged Israel's economy into a recession. GDP shrank for two years, and unemployment reached 11 percent. Tourism all but disappeared. A growing government budget deficit forced an austerity program that, among other factors, cut social welfare benefits. As before, however, conditions began to improve as the violence was contained and security improved.

Beginning in 2004 the effects of the Intifada seemed to have worn off, and investors and businessmen saw the long-term resilience of the Israeli economy despite the absence of peace and continuing (though lessened) terrorist attacks. Israel's economy returned to its robust pre–September 2000 economic expansion. The integration of the Israeli economy into the global economy continued with imports at 40 percent of GDP and exports at more than 35 percent. Israel's economic growth for 2005 was the highest in the Western world. GDP rose by 5.2 percent, and per capita income jumped 3.3 percent. Other statistics showed similar economic strength.

Israel's economy was largely unaffected by the 2006 war in Lebanon, despite the incessant Hizballah shelling that resulted in massive societal disruption affecting more than 1 million citizens as well as the short-term collapse of tourism. From an economic standpoint, the key was that foreign investment continued as if there had been no hostilities.

Like most other countries, Israel was affected by the global recession that began in late 2006. As was the case with the Second Lebanon War (2006), Operation Cast Lead against Hamas (December 2008–January 2009) did not have a great impact on Israel's economic performance or outlook.

POLITICAL STRUCTURE

Constitutional Consensus

Israel's system of government is based on an unwritten constitution. The first legislative act of the Constituent Assembly in February 1949 was to enact the Transition Law (small constitution), which became the basis of constitutional life in the state.

The First Knesset (parliament) devoted much time to a profound discussion of the constitutional issue, and on June 13, 1950, it adopted a compromise that has indefinitely postponed the real debate. It decided, in principle, that a written constitution would ultimately be adopted; for the time being, however, there would not be a formal and comprehensive document. Instead, a number of fundamental or basic laws would be passed dealing with specific subjects, which might, in time, form chapters in a consolidated constitution. Israel has adopted Basic Laws dealing with various subjects: The Knesset; The Lands of Israel; The President; The Government; The State Economy; The Israel Defense Forces; Jerusalem, the Capital of Israel; The Judiciary; The State Comptroller; Freedom of Occupation; and Human

Dignity and Liberty. The Basic Laws (and their amendments) articulate the formal requirements of the system in specific areas of activity, thereby providing a written framework for governmental action.

Several areas of popular national consensus, together with the fundamental laws, define the parameters of Israel's political system. Those disavowing allegiance to these Jewish–Zionist ideals tend to serve as little more than token protest groups. Israel's self-definition as a Jewish state is perhaps the most significant area of consensus, although there is a divergence of views on some of its tenets and their interpretation. Accord centers on the "ingathering of the exiles" and ensuring that Israel is a social welfare state in which all share in the benefits of society and have access to essential social, health, and similar services. Foreign and security policy draws from a wide consensus because of its overriding importance in light of continuing Arab hostility and the resultant conflict, although there is discord concerning methods and techniques employed. The IDF enjoys an enviable reputation and serves as a national unifying institution—despite vilification by Far Left and Far Right activists because of specific actions and events.

Political Institutions

Israel is a parliamentary political system where the government (cabinet) and the parliament (Knesset) are the dominant institutions, and the president serves essentially as a ceremonial/symbolic figure.

The president, the government (cabinet), and the Knesset perform the basic political functions of the state within the framework provided by Israel's constitutional consensus. The president is elected by the Knesset for a seven-year term and may not be reelected. He or she is generally a figure of considerable stature with popularity and support among the population. Until 2000 all presidents completed their terms or died in office. In 2000, President Ezer Weizman resigned over criticism about financial improprieties. Weizman was succeeded by former Likud MK Moshe Katzav, who resigned in disgrace in June 2007 amid accusations of sexual harassment; during a leave of absence from January to June 2007, he was replaced on an interim basis by Knesset Speaker Dalia Itzik. In July 2007 the Knesset chose veteran Israeli parliamentarian and statesman Shimon Peres as Israel's ninth president.

The president is head of state, and his powers and functions are essentially representative. In the sphere of foreign affairs, these include signing treaties ratified by the Knesset, receiving diplomatic representatives, and issuing consular exequaturs. In the domestic sphere, the president has the power to grant pardons and reprieves and to commute sentences. Subsequent to nomination by the appropriate body, he appoints judges, *dayanim* (judges of Jewish religious courts), *qadis* (judges of Muslim religious courts), the governor of the Bank of Israel, and the state comptroller, as well as other officials as determined by law. He signs all laws passed by the Knesset, with the exception of those relating to presidential powers and all documents to which the state seal is affixed.

The president participates in the formation of the government and receives the government's resignation. The president's powers and functions relating to the formation of the government require consultation with the parties in the Knesset and selection of a member of that body to form a government. Although anyone may be chosen, and traditionally the member has been the leader of the largest party in the Knesset, the president can use his discretion to choose the person he feels is most capable of creating a viable coalition government. This occurred after the 2009 elections, when Peres turned to Benjamin ("Bibi") Netanyahu, leader of the Likud Party, holder of twenty-eight Knesset seats, despite the fact that Tzipi Livni's Kadima Party held twenty-nine seats.

In 1996 the election process changed, and the prime minister, as well as the Knesset, was chosen by popular vote. This eliminated the president's function of providing the mandate to the prime minister. The change was short-lived; in March 2001 the Knesset eliminated the direct election of the prime minister and restored the previous system.

The prime minister is the most powerful figure in the Israeli system. The member of parliament entrusted by the president (or, from 1996 to 2001, the individual chosen by direct election) with the task of establishing a government or cabinet, generally with him- or herself as prime minister and a number of ministers who are usually, but not necessarily, members of the Knesset.

The government is formally instituted upon obtaining a vote of confidence from the Knesset. The cabinet is collectively responsible to the Knesset, reports to it, and remains in office as long as it enjoys the confidence of that body. There has been only one successful Knesset vote of no confidence causing the ouster of a government (in March 1990). A government's tenure may also be terminated by the ending of the Knesset's tenure, by the resignation of the government on its own initiative, or by the resignation of the prime minister.

The Knesset is the supreme authority in the state. It is a unicameral body of 120 members elected by national, general, secret, direct, equal, and proportional suffrage for a term not to exceed four years. Voters cast their ballots for parties, rather than individual candidates, and each party presents voters with a list, in order of preference, of up to 120 candidates—its choices for Knesset seats. After ballots are cast, seats in the Knesset are determined. From 1949 to 1988, only those party lists that received at least 1 percent of the total number of valid votes cast were represented in the Knesset. The threshold in 2009 stood at 2.5 percent. Any list failing to obtain this minimum does not share in the distribution of mandates, and its votes are not taken into account when determining the composition of the

Knesset. Each party fills its seats in the order that the candidates are listed on the party's election list.

The main functions of the Knesset are similar to those of most modern parliaments. They include expressing a vote of confidence or no confidence in the government (cabinet), legislating, participating in the formation of national policy, and supervising the activities of the governmental administration. The Knesset must also approve the budget and taxation, elect the president of the state, recommend the appointment of the state comptroller, and participate in the appointment of judges. It is divided into a number of committees, each responsible for a specific area of legislation, where many of the Knesset's activities are performed.

Judicial authority is vested in religious as well as civil courts. The Supreme Court of Israel is unique in that all citizens have the right to direct appeal. The Supreme Court does not formally have the power of judicial review of Knesset legislation, but it has the authority to invalidate administrative actions and interpret statutes it regards as contrary to the law. Each major religious community has its own religious court system that deals with matters of personal status. Rabbinical courts have exclusive jurisdiction over Jews in marriage and divorce, and they may act on alimony, probate, succession, and other similar questions with the parties' consent. The Christian ecclesiastical courts have exclusive authority over marriage, divorce, alimony, and confirmation of wills of Christians, and they may judge other similar matters if the parties agree. The Muslim courts have exclusive jurisdiction in all matters of personal status for Muslims.

POLITICAL DYNAMICS

Political life is intense in Israel, political participation is extensive, and political parties play a central role in the political life of the country. Israel's political system is characterized by a wide range of political and social viewpoints that are given expression not only in political parties but also in newspapers and a host of social, religious, cultural, and other organizations. Numerous minority and splinter factions freely criticize the government. This diversity has been most apparent in the existence of multiple parties contesting Knesset elections (and in the factions within most of the major parties) and in the coalition governments that have been characteristic of Israel since its independence. Because Israelis vote not for individuals but for parties in parliamentary elections, the party determines where individuals will be placed on the electoral list and thus who will represent it in the Knesset and in government. Individuals or groups of individuals, no matter how prominent, generally have not fared well when divested of the support of the established parties. In the several instances in which there has been notable success (such as that of the Democratic Movement for Change in 1977 and the Center

Party in 1999), the success has tended to be ephemeral. Electoral campaigns are controlled by the parties, which make the decisions, wage the campaigns, and spend the money. In the final analysis the voter focuses on the party, the party member looks to it for fulfillment of his or her needs, and the politician needs its leaders and machinery to assure a political future.

Israel's political parties and the blocs they have formed have gone through a substantial number of mergers, splits, disagreements, and reconciliations as a result of the intensity of ideological differences, policy disagreements, and personality clashes. Numerous parties have contested the 120 seats in the Knesset, and many have been successful in winning representation in it. The complex party structure demonstrates various dimensions of cleavage, but socioeconomic, religious-secular, and foreign policy–national security issues tend to be the most significant.

The multiplicity of parties, the diversity of views they represent, and the pro-portional-representation electoral system have resulted in the failure of any one party to win a majority of Knesset seats in any of the eighteen elections between 1949 and 2009, thus necessitating the formation of coalition governments. Prior to the national unity government formed in 1984, only twice had the coalitions been truly broad based. Those were established in times of national stress—the provisional government formed on independence and the government of national unity formed during the crisis preceding the 1967 war and maintained until the summer of 1970. The 1984 national unity government was unique in that it was based on a principle of power sharing between Labor and Likud, the two major political blocs. This experiment was repeated after the 1988 election and lasted until spring 1990. The personal stabilizing influence of David Ben-Gurion, Moshe Sharett, Levi Eshkol, and Golda Meir during their respective tenures as prime minister, as well as the preponderant strength of Mapai (Land of Israel Worker's Party) and the Labor Party until 1977, were important factors in maintaining coalition stability. After the 1977 election, Menachem Begin played a similar stabilizing role in the governments he led, until his resignation in 1983. The rigorous discipline of Israel's parties has curbed irresponsible action by indi-vidual Knesset members. Continuity of policy has also been enhanced by the reappointment of many ministers in reshuffled cabinets and the continuity of bu-reaucratic officeholders.

Notwithstanding the varying views and interests, the coalitions proved remark-ably stable. In the 1990s, systemic changes in Israeli society resulted in the end of the coalition stability in Israeli politics as the Knesset devolved into numerous rel-atively small parties, necessitating extensive negotiations in the formation and maintenance of coalition governments. Only once, despite many efforts, was a government brought down by a vote of no confidence (in the spring of 1990).

The requirements of coalition government have placed limitations on the prime minister's ability to control fully the cabinet and its actions. The prime minister does not appoint ministers in the traditional sense; he or she reaches accord with the other parties, and together they select the individuals who hold the various ministerial portfolios and who share in the cabinet's collective responsibility for governing Israel. Similarly, the prime minister does not have the power to dismiss ministers, although Ariel Sharon did succeed in dismissing right-wing ministers Avigdor Lieberman and Binyamin Elon in 2004 in a dispute over Sharon's Gaza disengagement plan. The prime minister does, however, possess substantial powers that enable him or her to influence the process by which ministers are selected and removed. Cabinets often contain individuals selected because of party loyalty, not qualification, who may well be divided in regard to perspectives and quarrelsome in regard to procedures. The bargaining resulting from the coalition system has permitted the religious parties—NRP/Mafdal, Agudat Israel, Poalei Agudat Israel, and Shas—to gain considerable policy concessions and play strong roles in government decision making because they were essential to secure a majority in the Knesset.

Coalition formation is one of the more interesting and arduous tasks of the prime minister. Each party and each political leader has a complex set of interests and concerns and seeks to maximize its gain from its participation in and support of the prime minister's government. Each party leader wants ministerial slots, concessions on policy matters, and funding for institutions, as well as patronage and positions for party loyalists.

Despite party proliferation and general political intensity and diversity, Israel's political life has been dominated by a relatively small and cohesive Jewish elite that has been mostly homogeneous in background. Most of its early leaders were European in origin, arrived in Israel during the Second Aliyah (1904–1914), and were personally acquainted, if not intimate. The political elite was predominantly civilian in character and background, although, increasingly, high-ranking military officers have become senior political figures and opinion leaders after completing their military careers. Religious elements have exerted strong influence in the cabinet and Knesset as political parties because of their role in government formation. The rabbinate is not considered part of the political elite, and the religious establishment generally does not intervene directly in politics.

The IDF is virtually unique in the Middle East in that it does not, as an entity, play a role in politics, despite its size, budget, and importance. Individual officers and senior commanders have secured important political positions, but they have done so as individuals, after retiring from active military service and joining political parties, and without the backing of the military as an institution. Only after their retirement did Generals Moshe Dayan, Yitzhak Rabin, Yigael Yadin, Ehud Barak, Yigal Allon, and Ariel Sharon play key roles in political life. Their military reputations and popular prestige enhanced their chances for, but did not ensure, significant political careers.

CHANGING POLITICAL DIMENSIONS:
FROM LABOR TO LIKUD TO KADIMA TO LIKUD

The Labor Party, in various incarnations, dominated the political life of the Yishuv and of Israel from the 1920s to the 1970s. The turmoil in Israel's political life at the time of the Yom Kippur War (1973) set in motion forces that created the political "earthquake," or *mahapach*, that led to Likud's replacement of Labor in the 1977 Knesset elections. The effect of the government's controversial handling of the war was not obvious in the elections held at the end of December 1973. Labor won the most seats, and Golda Meir, Israel's prime minister during the war, was charged with creating a new government and did so in early 1974, only to resign a month later, primarily because of dissension within Labor that centered on the question of political responsibility for serious lapses in decision making at the outset of the war.

This situation set the stage for the selection of Yitzhak Rabin—a hero of the 1967 war, former IDF chief of staff, former ambassador to the United States, and scion of a prominent labor-movement family—as Labor Party leader and prime minister. Rabin's government represented a departure from the past and ushered in a new era in which some of Israel's best-known names and personalities moved away from the center of power. Leadership had begun to be transferred from the immigrant-founder generation to the native-born (*sabra*) sons.

Many of the social and political forces set in motion by the Yom Kippur War and its aftermath seemed to coalesce when Israel's electorate went to the polls in May 1977; another "factor" was a scandal over an illegal foreign bank account held by his wife that forced Rabin to cede the Labor Party leadership to Shimon Peres on the eve of the elections. The largest number of votes went to the Likud, led by Menachem Begin, and Labor lost a substantial number of seats, many of which went to the newly established Democratic Movement for Change. This ended Labor's dominance of Israeli politics, which had begun in the Yishuv. This "political earthquake" resulted from Labor failures associated with the Yom Kippur War, the Rabin scandal, and the failure of the party to meet the needs of the Sephardic population. The Likud emerged as the leading political force, formed the government, and took control of Israel's governmental bureaucracy. The parties constituting the Likud bloc (especially Begin's Herut) had been serving as the opposition since independence, with the exception of their joining the "wall-to-wall" government of national unity from 1967 to 1970. Now Likud established the coalition responsible for establishing and implementing programs and policies, and Begin worked toward implementation of Vladimir Zeev Jabotinsky's revisionist vision, developed decades earlier, of a Jewish state in all of the Land of Israel.

The 1981 Knesset election was not conclusive: The electorate virtually divided its votes between the two blocs but awarded neither a majority of votes nor seats in parliament. President Yitzhak Navon granted the mandate to form the new government to Begin, and the latter succeeded in forming a Likud-led coalition.

The election highlighted the political dimension of the ethnic issue in Israeli politics: Likud secured the majority (probably some 70 percent) of the Oriental Jewish vote, following a pattern foreshadowed in the 1977 election. ("Oriental Jews" are non-Ashkenazi Jews, primarily of Afro-Asian origin. In Hebrew they are called collectively *Edot Hamizrach*, meaning "Eastern" or "Oriental communities." Generally the term refers to Jews whose origins are in Muslim lands.) Begin's popularity in the Oriental community was a direct result of previous Oriental failure to secure appropriate representation in the Knesset, his courting of the community even as opposition leader, and his responsiveness to their concerns during his first administration. This support of Begin and Likud—an apparent identification by Orientals of a political home—came in lieu of an effective independent Oriental political organization. Likud was widely seen as the party that would assist the Oriental community in emerging from its second-class status.

Although the second Begin government (1981–1983) came to office with a narrow parliamentary margin, the prime minister was able to maintain control despite the traumatic events associated with the war in Lebanon (1982) and major economic problems. Begin, personally, was a popular politician with strong charismatic appeal, and he was an able and skilled political leader. When Begin resigned in the fall of 1983, his foreign minister, Yitzhak Shamir, a relative newcomer to politics, replaced him. The short-lived Shamir government was virtually the same as its predecessor in personalities and pursued a policy of continuity.

In the 1984 election, fifteen of the twenty-six political parties that participated secured a seat in the Knesset. The Labor Alignment secured forty-four seats and the Likud forty-one. This division in the Israeli body politic contributed to, and complicated the formation of, a government of national unity that was approved by the Knesset in September 1984.

The new government inaugurated an experiment in Israeli politics, at the basis of which was an agreement by the two dominant parties to share power, with the unusual proviso of a "rotation" of their leaders, Shimon Peres and Yitzhak Shamir, in the positions of prime minister and foreign minister. The national unity government, with the power-sharing and rotation concepts, lasted its full term largely because there was strong public support for its continuation, and no politician wanted to be responsible for bringing it down and thereby to be seen as flouting the popular will.

The jockeying for power between the left and the right portions of the center continued in the election campaign of 1988. The results of the election, however, were similar to the inconclusive outcome of the 1984 balloting. Likud emerged with only a slight edge over Labor, winning forty Knesset seats to Labor's thirty-nine. The Oriental Jewish community continued to vote for Likud in greater numbers than for Labor, although there were indications that its support for Likud was weakening and that some were turning more to Shas and other religious parties.

Labor's poor showing in the 1988 election underscored the power of the incumbency of Yitzhak Shamir and Likud. As prime minister during the national unity government's first two years, Shimon Peres established himself as a dominant figure in Israeli politics, transforming his image from that of a widely disliked, unscrupulous politician to that of a dignified, self-confident political figure and statesman and an asset rather than a liability to the Labor Party. During the latter half of the national unity government's term, however, Foreign Minister Peres struggled to pursue an activist foreign policy, trying to revitalize the Arab-Israeli peace process so that he would not be overshadowed by Shamir, who was then prime minister. In the end, Peres's diplomatic maneuvering did not enable him to escape the relative political obscurity of the foreign ministry. Even within the Labor Party, Peres found himself at a disadvantage compared to Labor Party leadership rival Yitzhak Rabin, who benefited from the importance and high visibility of the defense portfolio that he retained throughout the government's term. This became especially important after the outbreak of the Palestinian Intifada in December 1987.

The establishment of a new and different national unity government in December 1988 was a complicated process, but after weeks of maneuvering, Likud's Yitzhak Shamir was able to establish a government in which he would remain prime minister throughout its tenure. Labor's Shimon Peres was appointed finance minister, a position that would give him little international visibility and little opportunity to generate popular support within Israel. Yitzhak Rabin retained the post of defense minister.

In early 1990 Labor quit the Shamir government. This led to the only successful vote of no confidence in the Knesset's history. Peres was granted a mandate from the president to form a successor coalition but was unable to construct a viable government. Shamir ultimately established a narrow coalition (in June 1990) supported by parties and individuals from the political right and from the religious bloc. The political maneuvering associated with the undermining of the Shamir government further tarnished Shimon Peres's image and raised serious doubts about his leadership qualities. This, and the formation of the new Likud-led coalition, led to the emergence within Labor of new questions about Peres's role as party leader. A test of these views took place within the party hierarchy in July 1990, but Peres succeeded in retaining his position.

The Iraqi Scud missile attacks during the Persian Gulf War (1991) soon tested the new government—and Shamir's leadership. The government showed remarkable restraint and did not respond militarily to the attacks, largely in response to US President George H. W. Bush's urging.

After the Gulf War, in October 1991, Israel entered into peace negotiations in Madrid, Spain, to resolve the Arab-Israeli conflict with its Arab neighbors. The opening plenary session soon gave way to separate bilateral meetings between Israel and several Arab delegations. In January 1992, after three rounds of bilateral talks, the right-wing Tehiya and Moledet parties, which together held five Knesset seats, resigned from the government over Shamir's willingness to discuss an interim agreement on Palestinian self-rule in the West Bank and Gaza Strip. The defection of the two parties deprived the coalition of a parliamentary majority, and agreement was reached to schedule national elections on June 23, 1992.

The imminent election provided a new opportunity for Yitzhak Rabin to try to unseat Shimon Peres as Labor leader. In February 1992, Rabin won the Labor Party leadership primary.

The Knesset election of June 1992 was contested by twenty-five political parties, representing virtually all points of the political spectrum.

Commentators called the outcome of the 1992 election another political earthquake in the sense of revolutionary change, as in 1977. This time Labor was the victor, winning forty-four Knesset seats, ending a decade and a half of Likud rule. Likud lost eight seats, falling to thirty-two. The religious parties fell from eighteen to sixteen seats, but more importantly, they lost their traditional role as kingmakers.

Ultimately, ten parties were able to secure the 1.5 percent of the valid vote necessary to secure a seat in parliament. The crucial element in the outcome was the creation of a blocking majority of sixty-one Knesset seats, which meant that Yitzhak Shamir would not be able to reconstruct a Likud-led nationalist-religious right-wing coalition. The election result was a case of voters punishing the incumbent party for years of bad or ineffective government. It also reflected the impact on the electoral system of new immigrants from the former Soviet Union who were voting for the first time. Israeli pollsters estimated that 47 percent of the new immigrants voted for Labor. Yitzhak Rabin moved quickly to forge a coalition that included Meretz (with twelve seats) and Shas. The new government was presented to the Knesset on July 13, 1992, and won its approval by a vote of sixty-seven to fifty-three.

Labor's return to control of the Knesset and government generated an initial euphoria among many in Israel, and external observers, especially in the United States, were hopeful that the peace process might be reinvigorated. This soon proved to be the case, as seen in the signing of the Oslo Accords (in September 2003). Some movement also took place in Israel's negotiations with Syria. But Rabin was assassinated in November 1995 by Yigal Amir, a right-wing, religious student who believed him to be a traitor who had relinquished territory occupied by Israel in the 1967 war that had been promised by God to the Jewish people.

Rabin was succeeded by Shimon Peres, who initially hesitated and then called for elections in May 1996.

The 1996 elections were held under a changed electoral process that allowed Israelis to cast two ballots—one for a party list for the Knesset and one for direct election of the prime minister. Shimon Peres campaigned on the theme of continuity and expansion of the peace process but was defeated by the Likud's Benjamin ("Bibi") Netanyahu, who focused on the need for security as the first imperative, with peace achievable at the same time. Peres lost the direct election of the prime minister by a margin of less than 1 percent, and Netanyahu formed a Likud-led coalition government that included secular-nationalist and religious parties. Netanyahu's tenure in office was marked by a fractioned Knesset and coalition government. He suffered from discord on both domestic and foreign policy issues, especially the peace process. Although negotiations with the Palestinians moved slowly, eventually there were the Hebron Agreement (January 1997) and the Wye River Memorandum (October 1998), which were approved separately by narrow margins in the Knesset. However, Netanyahu could not keep his restive coalition together, and agreement was reached to hold new elections for both the Knesset and prime minister in the spring of 1999.

Ehud Barak—former IDF chief of staff and newly chosen leader of the One Israel bloc comprising Labor and two small parties—was elected prime minister in May 1999, defeating Benjamin Netanyahu by a margin of 56 percent to 44 percent. However, One Israel was able to obtain only twenty-six seats in the Knesset election, and this led to the formation of a broad and disparate coalition. Despite his significant margin of victory over Netanyahu, Barak faced a very divided Knesset. Israel's two traditionally dominant political parties, Labor/One Israel and Likud together held fewer than half the seats in the Knesset, with thirteen parties, representing virtually all points on the political spectrum, initially sharing the remainder. Nevertheless, Barak succeeded in cobbling together a coalition of these diverse political units. Its longevity was questioned from the outset, but it seemed to hold together as Barak began efforts to achieve his goals of peace and security.

After June 2000 the coalition unraveled. David Levy, the leader of Gesher and the minister of foreign affairs, left One Israel in protest of Barak's handling of the peace negotiations, and the National Religious and ultra-Orthodox parties withdrew from the coalition. The most influential of the coalition defectors was Shas, with seventeen Knesset seats. Barak's government was reduced from 75 of the Knesset's 120 seats in July 1999 to only 30 seats as of August 2000, although the prime minister could rely on some support from outside the government for the retention of power. Nevertheless he soon called for a new, special direct election of the prime minister. This time he faced Ariel ("Arik") Sharon, who had replaced Netanyahu as Likud leader.

Election 2001 occurred against the background of weeks of intense Palestinian violence that followed Palestine Liberation Organization (PLO) leader Yasir Arafat's rejection of Barak's diplomatic offer at Camp David II (July 2000). Sharon won, overwhelmingly (receiving 62.3 percent of the vote compared to Barak's 37.6 percent), primarily because he suggested a different way to ensure security for the average Israeli.

The debate, the election, the victory speech, and the new government's program focused on security and peace. Sharon understood Israeli concerns about security. Israelis sought, and Sharon promoted, "security and peace." The political fortunes of Ehud Barak were hurt because he was seen as politically somewhat naive, despite his military experience, and as someone who had too much self-confidence or, perhaps, arrogance. He was attacked for constantly changing his mind and for consulting with few of his advisors. Sharon made clear in his campaign that the Oslo process "was dead" and that the security of Israelis was the central requirement and objective of his administration. The two elements overlapped in his demand that the end to Palestinian violence must precede a return to negotiations that would not be restricted by the Oslo process. For a large number of Israelis, Barak had failed to deliver significant movement on the peace process despite substantial concessions to the Palestinian position, and many saw erosion in their personal security as the al-Aqsa Intifada clearly and adversely affected the situation of the average Israeli.

Sharon's government, approved by the Knesset by a vote of seventy-two to twenty-one on March 7, 2001, was broad based, including Likud, Labor, and Shas, as well as a number of smaller secular-nationalist and religious parties. For the first time, the government included an Israeli Arab as a minister (he resigned in January 2002). Dalia Rabin-Pelossof (Yitzhak Rabin's daughter) became deputy defense minister. The government reflected a broad Israeli national consensus that the time was not ripe to achieve a peace treaty with the Palestinians. Supporters and opponents of the Oslo process joined in a cabinet whose clear first objective was to stop the violence and restore security to the average Israeli.

The coalition unity government collapsed on October 30, 2002, when Labor Party ministers resigned in a dispute focusing on the reallocation of social funding to settlement activity in the West Bank and Gaza Strip. Sharon sought alternative Knesset support for the government from religious and right-wing nationalist parties. He chose not to alter the government's guidelines, believing that such actions might undermine Israel's strategic understandings with the United States, break the budget framework, and cater to narrow political interests.

Sharon retained the leadership of the caretaker government and added new members to it. Former Likud prime minister Benjamin Netanyahu became foreign minister, and Shaul Mofaz became defense minister. Mofaz was a former IDF chief of staff who had advocated sending Yasir Arafat into exile; his inclusion was widely seen as shifting the government more to the right on terrorism and security issues.

The Labor and Likud parties conducted internal elections for party leader. In Likud the choice was between Sharon and Netanyahu and in Labor between Binyamin ("Fuad") Ben-Eliezer, Haim Ramon, and Amram Mitzna (a former IDF general and the popular mayor of Haifa). Sharon remained leader of Likud, while Mitzna was successful in Labor. Agreement was reached to hold new Knesset elections on January 28, 2003.

The 2003 elections resulted in another major victory for Sharon, with Likud taking thirty-eight Knesset seats compared with only nineteen seats for Mitzna's Labor Party. Sharon emerged with a stronger mandate to deal with the Palestinians and the security issue, while Labor suffered its worst election defeat and shrank to its smallest size ever. Clearly, Likud was, again, the dominant power in Israeli political life.

Most saw Labor's significant losses as a direct result of the failure of the party to project a strong image and of Mitzna to match party policy with public preferences on both security and economic performance. During the campaign Mitzna called for negotiations with whatever leaders the Palestinians put forward, even if that was the PLO with Yasir Arafat, and suggested unilateral Israeli separation from the Palestinian population in the West Bank and Gaza if talks failed within a year. Sharon made it clear that peace talks would not resume until the violence stopped, and Arafat was not seen as a viable option. Israeli voters overwhelmingly agreed with Sharon. On May 4, 2003, Mitzna resigned as Labor Party leader, and Shimon Peres was appointed acting chairman.

Sharon presented the coalition government to the Knesset on February 27, 2003, his seventy-fifth birthday. It comprised the centrist Shinui Party (with fifteen Knesset seats) and the Orthodox, right-leaning National Religious Party (six seats). Likud, with Natan Sharansky's Russian immigrant–based Yisrael B'Aliya merged into it, held forty seats. This would give Sharon a narrow but valid parliamentary majority. Subsequently, an agreement with the far-right HaIchud HaLeumi (National Union Party), with seven mandates, gave Sharon a comfortable majority. Sharon noted that his government's mission would be to deal with the worsening economic situation and to resolve the conflict between Israel and the Palestinians.

In a lengthy interview published in *Ha'aretz* in April 2003, Sharon spoke of "painful concessions" to help achieve peace and suggested giving up some Jewish settlements in the occupied territories—"steps that are painful for every Jew and painful for me personally. . . . If we reach a situation of true peace, real peace, peace for generations, we will have to make painful concessions." He suggested, "Look, we are talking about the cradle of the Jewish people. Our whole history is bound up with these places. Bethlehem, Shiloh, Beit El. And I know that we will have to part with some of these places. As a Jew, this agonizes me." He would not make concessions that would jeopardize Israel's security.

On December 18, 2003, Sharon announced that Israel would take unilateral steps to ensure the country's security in the absence of a Palestinian partner for peace. He warned that Israel would end negotiations and take unilateral "disengagement" measures if the Palestinian Authority did not take action to halt terrorism and there was no progress toward a negotiated peace within the next few months.

During a visit to Washington, DC, on April 14, 2004, President George W. Bush essentially recognized Israel's right to retain some West Bank settlements and called Sharon's plan "historic" and "courageous." Bush referred to "new realities on the ground" and suggested that it was unrealistic to expect the outcome of final-status negotiations to be a full and complete return to the 1949 armistice lines and that the so-called right of return of Palestinian refugees to Israel was effectively ruled out.

Sharon moved ahead on his plan for a unilateral Israeli withdrawal from Gaza.

The last months of 2004 and the first months of 2005 focused on the Gaza disengagement plan, which called for dismantling all twenty-one Israeli settlements in the Gaza Strip and four small isolated ones in the northern West Bank beginning in July 2005. It pitted all elements of Israeli society against one another and developed along all of the political and religious fault lines, overshadowing other aspects of national life. Ultimately, Sharon prevailed.

Overshadowing everything was the death of Yasir Arafat on November 11, 2004. On January 9, 2005, the Palestinians went to the polls to elect a successor as head of the Palestinian Authority. Mahmoud Abbas (Abu Mazen), who had already replaced Arafat as chairman of the PLO, won the election handily and seemed to bring a new approach to the conflict with Israel that suggested prospects for new openings and opportunities. Even as he reaffirmed his support for the Intifada as a vehicle of Palestinian resistance against Israel, Abbas implied that violence and the Palestinian resort to arms were counterproductive. This suggested prospects for an improvement in relations with Israel.

Arafat's death and the opportunity presented by Sharon's disengagement proposal led Labor, under Shimon Peres, to rejoin the coalition government on January 10, 2005. Labor was convinced that Sharon's Gaza disengagement plan was a crucial step toward a settlement with the Palestinians and could fail without Labor's support. The Knesset voted approval of a new coalition led by Sharon by a vote of fifty-eight to fifty-six with six abstentions. On January 27, 2005, Sharon said that there was an opportunity for a historic breakthrough with the Palestinians, but he noted the need for comprehensive action by the Palestinians to stop "terrorism, violence and incitement." Sharon and Abbas met in Sharm el-Sheikh,

Egypt, on February 8, 2005, and agreed to suspend the Palestinian attacks and Israeli counterterrorism actions that had marked the al-Aqsa Intifada since 2000.
On February 20, 2005, the Israeli cabinet approved Sharon's plan to withdraw
unilaterally Israeli settlers and soldiers from the Gaza Strip. The cabinet also voted
for a modified route for the security fence in the West Bank (based on a controversial July 2004 ruling of Israel's High Court). The new route would generally
move the fence closer to the 1967 Green Line.

Over the summer of 2005, Israel withdrew fully from the Gaza Strip. The settlers were evacuated, the settlements demolished, the troops withdrawn, and the
military positions abandoned and destroyed. Palestinian control replaced Israeli
(since 1967) and Egyptian (1949 to 1967) control.

The Israeli body politic overwhelmingly supported Sharon's disengagement.

In a speech to the UN General Assembly on September 15, 2005, Sharon
spelled out a critical principle to guide future Israeli policy concerning the territories and the nature of Israeli-Palestinian relations: "The right of the Jewish
people to the Land of Israel does not mean disregarding the rights of others in the
land. The Palestinians will always be our neighbors. We respect them and have no
aspirations to rule over them. They are also entitled to freedom and to a national,
sovereign existence in a state of their own."

Ariel Sharon, one of the principal founders of the Likud, increasingly frustrated
by the rebellion and opposition within the party, decided to leave it (he resigned
on November 12, 2005) and create a new "centrist" political party—Kadima
("Forward")—that he would lead in the forthcoming 2006 Knesset elections and
toward a resolution of the conflict with the Palestinians. Sharon took with him a
number of Likud ministers and MKs and was joined by some leading Labor Party
members (including Shimon Peres) and other prominent Israelis. This political
earthquake set in motion changes within the political system with a new "center"
emerging under Sharon's leadership. Sharon said he left Likud because he did not
want to waste time with political wrangling or miss the opportunities presented
by Israel's withdrawal from Gaza.

Amir Peretz, a Moroccan immigrant and head of the Histadrut Labor Federation, defeated Shimon Peres for leadership of the Labor Party in November 2005
by a margin of 2.4 percent. Peretz appealed to Israel's working class and Sephardic
Jews of Middle Eastern descent and origin.

The Knesset was disbanded officially on December 8, 2005, preparing the way
for the next Knesset election to be held on March 29, 2006. Thirty-one parties
presented lists of candidates.

On the night of January 4, 2006, Sharon suffered a major stroke and fell into a
coma. Unexpectedly, his career was over, and Israel was in search of new political
leadership, as was the peace process.

Sharon's incapacitation, followed by the Palestinian elections of January 25, 2006, posed a major challenge for the Israeli body politic. The election results were as much a repudiation of the PLO mainstream Fatah movement (for corruption and ineffectiveness) as they were a vote for the Islamic fundamentalist Hamas and its stated political objectives. For Israel it raised a basic question—how to deal with a Palestinian government whose dominant party (and prime minister) was Hamas, an organization whose charter calls for the end of Israel.

In early April 2006, with no change expected in Sharon's condition, the Kadima-led cabinet deemed him officially and permanently incapacitated and unable to discharge his duties of office. They chose Ehud Olmert to serve as interim prime minister.

The 2006 election marked the beginning of a new and significant period in Israel's political life. The voter turnout was only 63.2 percent with 3,186,739 (of the 5,014,622 eligible voters) votes cast. Twelve parties gained sufficient votes to pass the 2 percent threshold required to win seats in the Seventeenth Knesset.

The election results were an earthquake that dramatically altered Israel's political landscape. The new Kadima Party, without its founder Ariel Sharon, won twenty-nine seats, and its new leader, Ehud Olmert, was tasked with forming the new government. Labor was the second-largest party, winning nineteen seats. Likud, which had dominated Israeli politics (and was basically the party in power) for more than a quarter of a century (with some brief interludes), shrank in size and influence. The left-right balance and the religious-nonreligious balance in the Knesset seemed to focus on a centrist approach.

On May 4, 2006, Israel's thirty-first government, headed by Ehud Olmert, was approved by the Knesset. It was a coalition comprised of Kadima, Labor, Shas, and the small Pensioners Party (GIL). The cabinet was large and a curious mix of individuals. Olmert served for the first time as prime minister. Tzipi Livni became the second woman (after Golda Meir) to serve as foreign minister. Labor Party leader Amir Peretz became minister of defense, despite a lack of significant military experience.

Olmert noted that he preferred negotiations with the Palestinians for a solution but only with a Palestinian Authority that upheld all previous agreements with Israel and fought terror. If it continued to be led by terrorist factions, it would not be a partner for negotiations; nor would there be practical day-to-day relations. Failing a change—"We will not wait forever"—Israel will act without an agreement to establish defensible borders and ensure a solid Jewish majority. In the government policy guidelines, Olmert noted that major settlement blocs in the West Bank would be part of the sovereign State of Israel forever. The disengagements from the Gaza Strip and northern settlements in the West Bank were a prelude to his "convergence" proposal, which would move tens of thousands from settlements scattered throughout the West Bank to several settlement blocs near the Green Line.

Olmert's tenure in office was beset by crises from the outset. The kidnapping of an Israeli soldier (Gilad Shalit) by Hamas on June 25, 2006, and the failure of the IDF to achieve the release of two Israeli soldiers (Ehud Goldwasser and Eldad Regev) kidnapped by Hizballah on July 12, 2006, or to accomplish Israel's poorly conceived objectives in the Second Lebanon War (July–September 2006) underscored for many Israelis the political and military inexperience of the prime minister and (especially) of the defense minister, Labor Party leader Amir Peretz. A committee of inquiry (headed by retired judge Eliyahu Winograd), established to investigate errors in Israel's prosecution of the Second Lebanon War, issued its interim report in April 2007; the report was strongly critical of the wartime decision making of Olmert and Peretz. However, while finding failings in their management of the war, the Winograd Committee final report (January 30, 2008) determined that concerning the crucial cabinet decisions affecting the IDF's prosecution of the war, Olmert and Peretz had acted on the merits and "on the basis of the facts before them."

Asserting that the mountain of allegations of corruption and financial impropriety rapidly piling up against him had been the product of a "political witch hunt," Olmert on July 31, 2008, announced his decision to resign as prime minister following the Kadima Party leadership primary on September 17, 2008. Stymied by the religious parties in her efforts to form a new coalition, the new Kadima leader, foreign minister Tzipi Livni on October 26, 2008, recommended to Israel's president that new Knesset elections be held. Agreement was reached to hold the elections on February 10, 2009. Under Israeli law, Olmert and the government remained in office, with full authority, pending the formation of a viable successor coalition government. It was in this "caretaker" capacity that the Olmert-led government prosecuted Operation Cast Lead, the twenty-three day IDF counterterrorism operation against Hamas in the Gaza Strip from December 27, 2008, to January 18, 2009.

Much change occurred in Israel's political landscape in the run-up to the 2009 elections. Following Ariel Sharon's dramatic departure, on December 19, 2005, Benjamin Netanyahu was chosen to again lead the Likud Party. Similarly, Ehud Barak was elected to again lead the Labor Party on June 12, 2007, succeeding Amir Peretz; Barak also took over Peretz's position as defense minister in the governing coalition.

The 2009 election campaign focused exclusively on security and peace issues. Kadima leader and foreign minister Tzipi Livni endorsed the basic principles adopted at the Annapolis Conference (November 2007), including expedited bilateral negotiations leading to a viable two-state solution, coupled with a "zero-tolerance" approach to Hamas rocket attacks from the Gaza Strip. By contrast,

Benjamin Netanyahu and Likud were skeptical of the Annapolis efforts, calling instead for a return to the "performance-based roadmap" initially formulated by US President George W. Bush in 2002.

Livni's Kadima Party won twenty-eight seats in the elections, one more than Netanyahu's Likud. Avigdor Lieberman's Russian and right-wing Yisrael Beiteinu party rose to third place in the Knesset with fifteen seats (and was the "big winner" in the elections, pushing a controversial agenda that called on Israeli Arabs to voluntarily take a "loyalty oath" to the Jewish state), while Ehud Barak's Labor Party took thirteen mandates. Shas won eleven seats. A total of twelve parties won seats in the new Knesset.

Having considered the overall configuration of the new Knesset and after consulting the parties, President Shimon Peres invited Netanyahu to form Israel's thirty-second government and it was approved by a Knesset vote of sixty-nine for and forty-five against on March 31, 2009.

FOREIGN AND SECURITY POLICIES

The primary objectives of Israel's foreign and security policies remain the quest for peace through negotiations (with the Arab states and the Palestinians) and the assurance of security in a region of hostility through an effective defense capability. The goals of peace and security derive from the continuing conflict with the Arab states and the Palestinians that remains the preeminent problem confronting Israel; it affects all of Israel's policies and activities—both domestic and foreign. Israel recognizes that peace and cooperation with the Palestinians and the neighboring Arab states is vital for the long-term survival and development of the Jewish state, and this remains the cornerstone of its foreign policy.

During its first thirty-four years of existence (between 1948 and 1982), Israel fought six wars with Arab states and the PLO. Between 1987 and 2006 two intifadas brought violence and terrorism to Israel. In 2006 Hizballah initiated a thirty-four day war that engulfed Israel and Lebanon. From December 2008 to January 2009, Israel fought a twenty-three day war with Hamas in an effort to stop the smuggling of weapons into the Gaza Strip and end rocket attacks on Israeli towns and cities. Wars, countless skirmishes and terrorist attacks, and incessant, vituperative rhetoric, combined with the Holocaust and with Arab hostility during the Mandate period, all left their mark on Israel's national consciousness. Israel spends, on a continuing basis, a major portion of its budget and GNP/GDP on defense and defense-related items and has, by regional standards, a sizable standing army and reserve force widely considered to be of great quality and capability. It is believed to have (undeclared) nuclear weapons. Israel's military power is substantial, but not unlimited, and is constrained by its own demography and economy as well as by international factors.

Israel's quest for peace with its Arab neighbors dates from its establishment. Although Israel accepted the UN Partition Plan (UN General Assembly Resolution 181[II]), the Arabs opposed the partition of Palestine, and the Arab League declared war in response to Israel's declaration of independence upon termination of the British mandate. The armistice agreements of 1949, following the first Arab-Israeli war (Israel's War of Independence, 1948–1949), were intended to facilitate a transition to "permanent peace in Palestine." Negotiations did not begin, and Israelis soon became preoccupied with the need for security. The Suez War of 1956 (the second Arab-Israeli war) reinforced that concern and was waged in response to Egyptian president Gamal Abd al-Nasser's calls for Israel's destruction.

The Six Day War of 1967 generated dramatic change in Israel and Israelis' perceptions of their situation. The realities of Arab hostility, the nature of the Arab threat, and the difficulties of achieving a settlement became more obvious. Belligerent threats from the Arab world, especially Egypt, engendered realistic Israeli concerns of politicide (the destruction of the state). Israel's preemptive military strike proved successful in preventing the imminent threat of an Arab military invasion; Israel staved off defeat and achieved a militarily secure position. The dynamic of the conflict changed with the extent of the Israeli victory: Israel occupied the Sinai Peninsula of Egypt, the Gaza Strip, the West Bank, East Jerusalem, and the Golan Heights of Syria. Israel adopted the position that it would not withdraw from those territories until negotiations with the Arab states had led to peace agreements that recognized Israel's right to exist and accepted Israel's permanent status and borders. The Arab view was articulated in the Palestine National Covenant of 1964, which called the creation of Israel "null and void," and in the "three no's" resolution of the Arab League summit meeting in Khartoum, Sudan, in September 1967: "no peace with Israel, no recognition of Israel, no negotiations with it."

Throughout the period between the Six Day War and the Yom Kippur War (1973), the focal point was the effort to achieve a settlement of the Arab-Israeli conflict and to secure a just and lasting peace. In those attempts, based on UN Security Council Resolution 242 of November 22, 1967, the regional states, the superpowers (and other powers), and the main instrumentalities of the international system were engaged. Israel focused its attention on peace and security objectives and developed positions concerning the occupied territories, the Palestinians, and related questions. Although some of the interwar efforts were promising, peace was not achieved. In 1969 and 1970, Israel and Egypt were engaged in a lengthy and costly war of attrition along the Suez Canal in which Soviet pilots were deployed to fly operational missions over the Canal Zone in support of Egypt.

The Yom Kippur War created a new environment for the quest for peace and the development of Israeli foreign policy. Israel's position deteriorated with the outbreak of the fighting, as the country was condemned by various states and some of them severed diplomatic relations.

In the wake of the Yom Kippur War, modifications of Israel's policy were relatively minor. The primary goals remained the achievement of an Arab-Israeli settlement and the assurance of security in the interim. This constancy resulted, in part, from Israel's collective conception of its fundamental international position—and the limited policy options that flowed therefrom—which was not substantially altered. Israel's view of itself as geographically isolated and lacking dependable allies, its geographical vulnerability, and its need to acquire and produce arms for self-defense were reaffirmed by the Yom Kippur War. Israel believed that it won a military victory and that its strategic concepts were vindicated.

After the 1977 elections, the Begin government maintained Israel's focus on the goal of establishing peace that would include the end of war, full reconciliation and normalization, and an open border over which people and goods could cross without hindrance. On the matter of the territories taken in 1967, the new government could rely on a consensus among Israelis opposing a return to the armistice lines of 1949, thus ruling out total withdrawal, although there was disagreement concerning the final lines to be established and the extent of compromise. The focus of territorial disagreement was the West Bank. There was a substantial difference between the Likud view, which opposed relinquishing any territory, and the compromise views articulated by Labor and others to Likud's left. The Labor-led coalition governments between 1967 and 1977 had generally tried to limit Jewish settlements to those that could serve a security function and had sought to avoid conflict between the settlements and the local Arab populations. The Begin government elected in 1977 altered that policy. Rather than restricting settlements in the West Bank (known by many Israelis as the biblical Judea and Samaria) to those that were primarily security oriented, it supported settlement in that area as a natural and inalienable Jewish right. The broadest and most articulate consensus continued to revolve around the question of a Palestinian state and PLO. Israel's refusal to negotiate with the PLO and its opposition to the establishment of an independent Palestinian state on the West Bank and in the Gaza Strip were reaffirmed.

Israel's national consensus focused on the need for peace, and the main obstacle appeared to be the continuing Arab unwillingness to accept Israel or negotiate with it. This was modified as a result of the November 1977 initiative of President Anwar Sadat of Egypt to visit Israel and inaugurate direct bilateral negotiations between Israel and Egypt. The negotiations culminated in the Camp David summit meeting of September 1978 at which Egypt, Israel, and the United States agreed to two frameworks for continued negotiations. The primary objective of post–Camp David negotiations was to convert the two frameworks into peace treaties. Despite efforts to secure the involvement of other Arab states, none agreed to participate. The parties concentrated their initial efforts on the Egypt-Israel Peace Treaty, which was signed at the White House on March 26, 1979.

The Egypt-Israel Peace Treaty was a significant accomplishment that represented a first step toward a comprehensive Arab-Israeli settlement and regional stability. Peace was established, but it was often a "cold" peace, one in which long-standing mistrust had not been replaced by the warmth of friendly relations.

Begin also fulfilled his government's pledge regarding the Golan Heights. In December 1981, the Knesset adopted the Golan Heights Law, which extended Israel's "law, jurisdiction, and administration" to the area. Begin cited Syrian president Hafiz al-Asad's refusal to negotiate a peace treaty with Israel as the main reason for the decision.

The Egypt-Israel peace process was soon overshadowed by the sixth Arab-Israeli war—the 1982 War in Lebanon. The continued presence in Lebanon of surface-to-air missiles that had been moved there by Syria in the spring of 1981 remained an Israeli concern. So were PLO terrorist attacks in northern Israel from bases in southern Lebanon and terrorist attacks against Israeli and Jewish targets worldwide, despite a US-arranged cease-fire in the summer of 1981. The war's immediate precipitating event was the attempted assassination of Sholmo Argov, Israel's ambassador to Britain. On June 6, 1982, Israel launched a major military action against the PLO in Lebanon (Operation Peace for Galilee). The military objectives were to assure security for northern Israel, to destroy the PLO infrastructure that had established a state within a state ("Fatahland") in southern Lebanon, to eliminate a center of international terrorism, and to eliminate the PLO from Lebanon so that its territory would not serve as a base of operations from which Israel could be threatened. The operation's political objectives were not as precise. The goal was to weaken the PLO so that it would no longer be as significant politically, but there was also the hope that a new political order might lead Lebanon to consider becoming the second Arab state to make peace with Israel.

In many respects the results of the war in Lebanon were ambiguous. Israel's northern border was more secure, but Israeli troops who remained in Lebanon became targets for terrorists and others, and numerous casualties resulted. The achievements were primarily in the military realm: The PLO was defeated, and its military and terrorist infrastructure in Lebanon was destroyed. The political achievements were less tangible. Despite some losses in credibility, the PLO remained the primary representative of the Palestinians, and Yasir Arafat, now operating from Tunis, soon rebounded to his preeminent position. Although an agreement between Israel and Lebanon calling for Israeli withdrawal and for the normalization of relations between the two countries was concluded in May 1983, it was soon unilaterally abrogated by the government of Lebanon under Syrian pressure.

Little occurred in the foreign and security domain until the outbreak of the first Intifada in 1987.

Palestinians in the Gaza Strip began a wave of violent protests and riots in Gaza on December 8, 1987. It quickly spread to the West Bank and Israel. The initial effect of the uprising (intifada) on Israel was to reinforce the sharp cleavages dividing the public between those who believed the Palestinian problem had to be resolved through territorial compromise and those who believed Israel could have both peace and the territories.

Dialogue was opened in December 1988 between the United States and the PLO in the wake of Arafat's acceptance—to US satisfaction—of UN Security Council Resolutions 242 and 338, recognition of Israel and renunciation of terrorism. This development added to the growing internal and external pressures on Israel to work on a constructive policy to deal with the Intifada and to advance the peace process.

In January 1989, Defense Minister Yitzhak Rabin suggested publicly that the government should consider adopting Labor's idea that West Bank and Gaza Palestinians elect their own representatives to peace talks. On May 14, 1989, the cabinet adopted a similar proposal (the "Shamir Plan") as its official policy. Over the months, the United States worked to narrow the differences between Israel and the Palestinians over the election initiative and to start direct negotiations. The diplomatic maneuvering was carried out in the context of political differences in Likud and in the national unity government. In March 1990, the national unity government fell in a Labor-sponsored vote of no confidence over Likud's unwillingness to respond affirmatively to US proposals. Shamir formed a new Likud-led, narrow, right-wing-religious government in June 1990 comprising right-wing and religious parties.

When, in August 1990, Iraq invaded Kuwait, much of the world's attention was diverted from the Arab-Israeli conflict (despite Iraq's firing of thirty-nine Scud missiles at Israeli cities). After the Persian Gulf War ended, on March 6, 1991, President George H. W. Bush announced that "the time had come to put an end to Arab-Israel conflict," and he dispatched Secretary of State James Baker to the Middle East to convene an international peace conference on October 30, 1991, in Madrid, Spain.

The Madrid Conference did not achieve a substantive breakthrough, although it broke the procedural and psychological barriers to direct bilateral negotiations between Israel and its immediate neighbors by having Israeli and Egyptian, Jordanian-Palestinian, Lebanese, and Syrian delegations meet at an opening public and official plenary session and deliver speeches and responses. Bilateral negotiations between Israel and each of the Arab delegations followed.

The Madrid meetings were followed by bilateral talks in Washington in December 1991 and in 1992, 1993, and 1994. Progress was measured chiefly by the continuation of the process rather than by the achievement of a substantive accord on the issues in dispute.

In the bilateral discussions, the Israeli–Palestinian and Israeli–Syrian negotiations proved to be both the most central and the most difficult. In the case of both Jordan and Lebanon, the general perception was that agreements would be relatively easy to achieve, although they would have to await the resolution of the Syrian and Palestinian talks. In the case of Syria, the central issues were peace, security, and the future of the Golan Heights. In the Israeli–Palestinian discussions, the disagreement centered on the Palestinian desire for an independent state in the West Bank and Gaza Strip and the Israeli opposition to that goal.

Labor's victory in the 1992 Knesset elections was widely heralded as a significant and positive factor that would alter the regional situation and the prospects for progress. Secret negotiations between Israel and the PLO began in Oslo in the spring of 1993 and led to an exchange of mutual recognition in September 1993, soon followed by the formal signing on September 13, 1993, of a Declaration of Principles, a first step and a crucial and historic breakthrough. Additional implementing agreements were signed in Paris and Cairo in spring 1994. Israel and Jordan began formal negotiations that summer. In late July 1994, Prime Minister Rabin and King Hussein of Jordan signed the Washington Declaration, formally ending the state of belligerence. In October 1994, Israel and Jordan signed a formal peace treaty, which ushered in an era of peace and normalization of relations between the two states.

The 1996 shift from Labor to Likud brought with it a change in the substance and style of Israel's peace-process strategy and tactics. Under Yitzhak Rabin and Foreign Minister Shimon Peres, Israel made gains in its quest for peace and the normalization of relations with the Palestinians and neighboring Arab countries. Nevertheless, the outcome of the May 29, 1996, election, held against a background of terrorist bombings, indicated that the majority of Israelis perceived Labor's peace strategy as riskier than Likud's and, consequently, voted in favor of what they envisioned to be a more controlled and balanced approach. Benjamin Netanyahu promised Israeli voters that he would achieve a "secure peace" and that, while he accepted the reality of the Oslo framework for Israeli-Palestinian negotiations (and in that context negotiated the Hebron and Wye River agreements), he would never accept a Palestinian state.

When Labor resumed power in July 1999, optimism followed that there could now be renewed progress in the peace process. Ehud Barak transferred some control over territories in the West Bank to the Palestinian Authority. He also hinted that he might return virtually all of the Golan Heights to Syria in exchange for peace, but summit talks in Shepherdstown, West Virginia, in early 2000, with US President Bill Clinton participating, and in Geneva, Switzerland, in March 2000, involving Clinton and Syrian president Hafiz al-Asad, failed to bring an agreement. At the time of al-Asad's death in June 2000, the process had reached a stalemate, despite substantial agreement between al-Asad and Barak negotiating through intermediaries.

In May 2000, Barak unilaterally withdrew Israeli forces from Lebanon back to a United Nations–marked and internationally accepted international border. Despite the fact that this met fully the conditions in UN Security Council Resolution 425 (a point confirmed by the council), Lebanon and Syria continued to stress that Israel's withdrawal was incomplete.

A summit took place at Camp David in the summer of 2000, at which US President Bill Clinton, Barak, and Yasir Arafat focused on a comprehensive peace agreement by which Israel would relinquish territory occupied in the 1967 war and the Palestinians would agree to live alongside Israel in peace. Despite intensive efforts and some areas of accord, no agreement was reached. Arafat rejected Barak's compromise proposals. The failure of the Camp David II summit and the ensuing violence brought the Oslo process to a halt. The Clinton administration was followed by that of George W. Bush; Ariel Sharon replaced Ehud Barak as Israel's prime minister. The peace process that had marked the decade of the 1990s was replaced by violence—the al-Aqsa Intifada broke out in September 2000 and continued in the ensuing years. The problem was further exacerbated in the wake of the al-Qa'ida terrorist attacks in New York and Washington, DC, on September 11, 2001, when Palestinian terrorists escalated their attacks against Israeli civilians. The assassination of an Israeli cabinet minister (Rehavam Ze'evi in October 2001) and large-scale attacks inside Israel targeting Israeli civilians elicited a strong Israeli military response (recognized as legitimate self-defense by the United States). Israel's goal was to rout out the terrorists and force Arafat and the Palestinian Authority to arrest them; they also sought to prevent the support of the terrorists by various Palestinian organizations.

Sharon made it clear in the 2001 election campaign that the Oslo process "was dead" and that the security of Israel (and Israelis) was the paramount concern and central objective of his administration. His demand was that the violence must stop before the negotiations could take place. Given continuous violence and the lack of confidence between Israel and the PLO, the peace process remained moribund.

Despite the unilateral Israeli withdrawals from Lebanon (in 2000) and the Gaza Strip (in 2005) to the international frontiers, no progress was made on the peace process. Despite UN Security Council Resolution 1559 (September 2004) calling for the disarmament and dismantling of Hizballah, Hizballah remained armed. And following Hamas's victory in the Palestinian Authority election of January 25, 2006, and its formation of the Palestinian Authority government, rocket attacks into Israel from Gaza escalated. The lack of movement in the Arab-Israeli peace process and continued tensions along Israel's borders with Lebanon and the Gaza Strip were replaced in the summer of 2006 by conflict. On June 26, Palestinian terrorists tunneled under the international border between Israel and Gaza, attacked an Israeli patrol, killed two soldiers, and kidnapped a third (Gilad Shalit). Israel responded by attacking a series of terrorist and infrastructure targets in the Gaza Strip, but the kidnapped Israeli soldier remained in captivity. Hizballah, on July 12, initiated a cross-border raid from Lebanon into Israel, killing several Israeli soldiers and kidnapping two others (Eldad Regev and Ehud Goldwasser). The Hizballah raid was followed by thirty-four days of fighting that ended on August 14, 2006. Subsequently, Hassan Nasrallah, the leader of Hizballah, said that he had not thought that the capture of the two Israelis would lead to a war of that magnitude at that time.

As with previous wars (1973 and 1982) that ended without clear and overwhelming Israeli success, there developed after the Second Lebanon War (2006) a series of perceptions in Israel concerning wartime "failures." There were protests and demonstrations, as well as calls for inquiries to evaluate the handling of the conflict and the IDF and Israel's political leadership. This was due partly to the substantial attacks on Israeli territory, with more than 3,000 missiles fired by Hizballah into northern Israeli cities and towns, but also to the number of Israeli soldiers wounded and killed and the substantial attacks on, and damage suffered by, the civilian population, as well as the inconclusive results of the war. When the fighting ended, the two kidnapped Israeli soldiers remained in their captors' hands, and Israel's image as an overwhelmingly successful military power seemed diminished. Israel's deterrence capacity was to some extent restored in Operation Cast Lead, the IDF operation against Hamas in Gaza in December 2008 and January 2009; there was almost unanimous public support in Israel for the operation as necessary to end the unrelenting Hamas rocket fire on Israeli population centers in the southern Negev region and the smuggling of weapons into Gaza, and the operation's prosecution suggested that Israel's political leadership and the IDF command had internalized the findings of the Winograd Committee inquiry into the major failings that occurred in the Second Lebanon War (2006). Nevertheless, Gilad Shalit, the IDF soldier kidnapped by Hamas in 2006, remained in captivity, and the evidence uncovered in the Gaza Strip of the increased cooperation between Hamas and Iranian operatives did not portend movement toward greater stability or peace for Israel in the Middle East.

In a major foreign policy speech on June 14, 2009, Prime Minister Benjamin Netanyahu described "the nexus between radical Islam and nuclear weapons" centered in Iran, as "the greatest danger confronting Israel, the Middle East, the entire world and human race." President Mahmoud Ahmadinejad and senior Iranian officials have repeatedly threatened Israel's destruction.

The twenty-first century began with Israeli foreign policy continuing its quest for peace. Many Israelis questioned their situation more than a decade after the promising start of the Madrid Conference and the Oslo peace process. Despite the efforts of eight prime ministers in the 1990s and the first decade of the twenty-

first century (Shamir, Rabin, Peres, Netanyahu, Barak, Sharon, Olmert, and Netanyahu again), Israel's overall acceptance in the region was only marginally advanced (peace was achieved only with Jordan in 1994), security for Israel had
deteriorated, and Israel was far from being accepted as an integral part of the Middle East region in which it was located.

THE SEARCH FOR FRIENDS AND ALLIES

Israel's broader approach to foreign policy began to take shape once it became
clear that peace would not follow the 1949 armistice agreements with the Arab
states that marked the end of its War of Independence. The continuing Arab threat
and Israel's geographical isolation suggested a need for positive relationships with
other states. Israel directed its attention beyond the circle of neighboring Arab
states to the international community in an effort to establish friendly relations
with the states of Europe and the developing world, especially Africa and Latin
America, as well as the superpowers, and to gain their support in the international
arena. These relationships were seen as having a positive effect on Israel's position
in the Arab-Israeli conflict; bilateral political and economic advantages would help
to ensure Israel's deterrent strength vis-à-vis the Arabs through national armed
power and through increased international support for its position.

At the outset Israel held a positive view of the United Nations, fostered by that
organization's role in the creation of the state. With the increasingly large anti-
Israel majority in the General Assembly and the resulting virtually automatic support for Arab and Palestinian perspectives, Israel's views changed markedly, and the
United Nations came to be regarded as an unhelpful and often negative factor in
the quest for peace and security. This changed after the Madrid peace conference
and the consequent bilateral negotiations between Israel and its neighbors and the
multilateral negotiations, which involved a large number of other powers. In addition, the collapse of the Soviet Union and the disintegration of the Soviet Bloc
led to the restoration of Israel's relations with a large number of states that previously had been hostile. All of this contributed to an improved relationship with
Israel in the 1990s. But with the failure of the Oslo process and the resort to the
United Nations for anti-Israel resolutions and decisions by the Palestinians and the
Arab states, this view was again altered. At the onset of the twenty-first century,
Israel's perspective of the United Nations was marked by an ambivalence con-
cerning the role the organization might play in Israel's foreign policy.

The developed and economically advanced industrialized states of Europe, as
well as Australia, Canada, Japan, and Korea, are, and have been, of great significance
to Israel because of their political power and economic significance.

Europe has posed an interesting challenge and presented a significant opportunity for Israeli policy makers. Israel has sought to maintain positive relations with

Europe based on the commonality of the Judeo-Christian heritage (its biblical links to Christianity), democratic tradition, and the memories of, and "guilt complex" surrounding, the Holocaust. With Israel seeking links to significant powers for military (aid and arms acquisition) and economic (trade and economic aid) assistance, Europe has seemed a logical choice. A tacit alliance with France was supplemented by links with Great Britain and Germany and a formalized relationship with the European Economic Community (EEC) and, now, the European Union (EU). Over time Israel has been successful in establishing economic links with the EEC and EU, albeit within limitations, and also with various European states (especially Germany and France) on a bilateral level. France proved a valuable supplier of military aid until the June 1967 Six Day War, while Germany, through its moral and material reparations for World War II crimes, was an indispensable factor in Israel's economic development beginning in the 1950s. Israel has also successfully established positive trade, cultural, and political ties with many of the new members of the expanded EU.

The emergence of the new states of Africa and Asia in the 1950s and 1960s led Israel to pursue a policy in keeping with Afro-Asian aspirations for economic development and modernization. In an effort to befriend these states and to secure their support, Israel's multifaceted program focused on technical assistance, exchange and training programs, loans, joint economic enterprises, and trade. The program grew dramatically and remains an important element of Israeli foreign policy. It had successes in economic and social terms and proved politically beneficial in various international venues. Developing world support helped to prevent the United Nations from adopting anti-Israel measures after the 1967 war, and in the early 1970s a committee of African presidents worked to achieve Arab-Israeli negotiations (albeit without success). The nadir of the policy was reached at the time of the Yom Kippur War, when virtually all the African states with which Israel had established ties broke those relations in support of the Arab effort to regain the territories lost in the Six Day War by attempting to isolate and delegitimize the State of Israel and Zionism. For some Israelis this reflected a policy failure, although some African states have reestablished close links, and some have sustained informal but significant ties despite their official actions (for example, Kenya's link to Israel as demonstrated during Israel's Entebbe hostage rescue operation in 1976).

China and India, with the world's two largest populations and two of the globe's most dynamic economies, have been increasingly important to Israel. Israel was among the first countries in the world to recognize the People's Republic of China in January 1950, but official relations were established only in 1992. Since then substantial links have been created in the areas of trade, aviation, culture, and scientific cooperation. Numerous reciprocal visits have taken place, and there has also been progress in the area of arms sales.

India recognized Israel on September 18, 1950, but established full diplomatic relations only in January 1992. Israel had opened a consulate in Bombay in the early 1950s, but its functions and jurisdiction were extremely limited and restricted. Since the 1990s, India and Israel have developed increasingly strong bonds that are reflected both in commercial and military trade and the sharing of intelligence against global terrorism. India has also become an increasingly popular tourist destination for (especially young) Israelis.

Despite substantial effort in these sectors, the centrality of the Arab-Israeli conflict has enlarged and enhanced the role of the superpowers, particularly the United States, in Israeli eyes.

From World War II to the 1990s, the superpowers (the United States and the Soviet Union) were the major players of the international system. Israel, like all other states, had to operate within the confines of the Cold War. But the cumulative impact of multiple factors was greater on Israel than on most other states. Both superpowers were also significant because they comprised large segments of the world's Jewish population.

Zionism and the "ingathering of the exiles" requires Israel to be concerned for Jewish communities elsewhere—with their well-being and potential to emigrate from imperiled locations to the haven of the Jewish state. Thus, in focusing on the superpowers, an additional concern of Israel was for what was then the world's two largest Diaspora Jewish communities.

Anti-Semitism was, and arguably remains, an endemic feature of Russian (and Soviet) society and history. Not only were Soviet Jews unable to assist the Jewish state in its birth and consolidation, but Israel (during the Cold War) was unable to protect them and could not secure large-scale emigration of those at risk. This began to change in the last years of the Gorbachev era, and immigration to Israel became a continuous flow with the end of the Soviet Union and the Cold War.

The Soviet Union voted for the UN Partition Plan of 1947, accorded de jure recognition to Israel shortly after its independence, supported its applications for UN membership, and gave it moral, political, and material support in the early years after independence. This made it easier for Israel's government, upon attainment of statehood, to proclaim a policy of noncommitment (nonidentification) in the East-West conflict. However, soon after the end of the War of Independence, various factors, including ideological sympathies, the large size and importance of Western Jewry, and Soviet abandonment of support for Israel and denial of loan requests, coupled with a relatively constant flow of economic aid from the US government and American Jewry, contributed to Israel's shift to a pro-Western orientation.

Relations between the Soviet Union and Israel deteriorated rapidly from 1949 to 1953, and Israel's foreign policy no longer reflected belief in Soviet friendship and support. Soviet support for, and expanded relations with, the Arab states by the mid-1950s tended to confirm this perspective. Soviet military and economic assistance to the Arab world, the Soviet Bloc's rupture of relations with Israel in 1967 (in the context of Moscow's contribution to the outbreak of the Six Day War through its circulation of a false rumor concerning Israeli military mobilization), and the continuation of that break led Israel farther into the Western camp, although it continued to seek the restoration of ties to the Soviet Union and its allies and to promote the well-being and emigration of Soviet Jews.

After the Six Day War, the Soviet Union attempted to become a more significant factor in the Arab-Israeli peace process but made limited progress until the advent of the Gorbachev tenure, when more liberal approaches to foreign policy permitted the relationship between Jerusalem and Moscow to improve. Consular contacts and exchanges took place, Soviet Jewish emigration increased substantially, and several East European states restored diplomatic relations with Israel. On October 18, 1991, the Soviet Union and Israel reestablished full diplomatic relations.

Beginning in the early 1990s, some 1 million citizens of the former Soviet Union emigrated to Israel, and there was significant growth in bilateral relations with Russia and several of the former Soviet republics in the cultural and commercial domains. Nevertheless, Israel remains skeptical about Russia's ambitions in the Middle East, as reflected in its relations with militant Arab regimes (including Syria) and its transfer of military and nuclear technology to Iran.

Once a power providing limited direct support for Israel, the United States has become the world's only superpower linked to Israel in a free trade area and a crucial provider of political, diplomatic, moral, and strategic (security) support, as well as economic aid.

The complex and multifaceted "special relationship" with the United States that had its origins prior to the independence of Israel has been centered on the continuing US support for the survival, security, and well-being of Israel. During the first decades after Israel's independence, the US-Israeli relationship was grounded primarily in humanitarian concerns, in religious and historical links, and in a moral-emotional-political arena rather than a strategic-military one. The United States declared an arms embargo on December 5, 1947; there was practically no US military aid or sales of military equipment and no formal, or even informal, military agreement or strategic cooperation between the two states. Extensive dealings in the strategic realm became significant only in the 1970s and 1980s. The concept of Israel as a "strategic asset" was more an outcome of the developing relationship than a foundation for its establishment. US policy on arms supply evolved from embargo to principal supplier, and arms became an important tool of US policy to reassure Israel and to achieve policy modification.

The two states developed a diplomatic-political relationship that focused on the need to resolve the Arab-Israeli dispute, but although they agreed on the general concept, they often differed on the precise means for achieving the desired result. The relationship became especially close after the Six Day War, when a congruence of policy prevailed on many of their salient concerns. Nevertheless, the two states often held differing perspectives on regional developments and on the dangers and opportunities they presented. No major ruptures took place, although significant tensions were generated at various junctures.

Israel's special relationship with the United States—which is based on substantial positive perception and sentiment evident in public opinion and official statements and manifest in political-diplomatic support and in military and economic assistance—has never been enshrined in a formal, legally binding document joining the two states in a formal alliance. Israel has no mutual security treaty with the United States; nor is it a member of any alliance system requiring the United States to take up arms automatically on its behalf, despite Israel's status as a major non-NATO ally. The US commitment to Israel has taken the form of presidential statements that have reaffirmed the US interest in supporting the political independence and territorial integrity of Israel.

The United States is today an indispensable, if not fully dependable, ally. It provides Israel, through one form or another, with economic (governmental and private), technical, military, political, diplomatic, and moral support. The United States was seen as the ultimate resource against the Soviet Union and remains a central participant in the campaign against Islamic terrorism; it is the source of Israel's sophisticated military hardware; it is central to the Arab-Israeli peace process.

The United States and Israel have established a special relationship replete with broad areas of agreement and numerous examples of discord. There was, is, and will be a divergence that derives from a difference of perspective of the environment in which each makes its policies. The United States remains the world's only superpower; Israel is a small regional power. Nevertheless, the two states maintain a remarkable degree of congruence on broad policy goals. Israel continues to focus on the centrality and significance of the ties.

At Israel's birth, the United States seemed to be a dispassionate, almost uninterested, midwife—its role was essential and unconventional but also unpredictable and hotly debated in US policy circles. Decades later, some of the policy debate continues, and there are periods of tension in the relationship, but there is little doubt about the overall nature of US support for its small and still embattled ally.

In remarks at the American Israel Public Affairs Committee annual policy conference on June 4, 2008, then senator Barak Obama summed up the relationship in these terms:

> Our alliance is based on shared interests and shared values. Those who threaten Israel threaten us; Israel has always faced these threats on the front line and I will bring to the White House an unshakable commitment to Israel's security. . . . We know that the establishment

of Israel was just and necessary, rooted in centuries of struggle and decades of patient work, but sixty years later we know that we cannot relent, we cannot yield, and as President I will never compromise when it comes to Israel. Not when there's still voices that deny the Holocaust; not when there are terrorist groups and political leaders committed to Israel's destruction; not when there are maps across the Middle East that don't even acknowledge Israel's existence and government-funded textbooks filled with hatred towards Jews; not when there are rockets raining down on Sderot and Israeli children have to take a deep breath and summon uncommon courage every time they board a bus or walk to school.

BIBLIOGRAPHY

Bernard Reich, *Historical Dictionary of Israel* (Metuchen, NJ: Scarecrow Press, 1992), Bernard Reich and David H. Goldberg, *Historical Dictionary of Israel*, 2nd ed. (Lanham, MD: Scarecrow Press, 2008), and Bernard Reich and David H. Goldberg, *Political Dictionary of Israel* (Lanham, MD: Scarecrow Press, 2000), are convenient reference works. On the Arab-Israeli conflict, the reader is referred to Bernard Reich, ed., *An Historical Encyclopedia of the Arab-Israeli Conflict* (Westport, CT: Greenwood Press, 1996), and Bernard Reich, ed., *Arab-Israeli Conflict and Conciliation: A Documentary History* (Westport, CT: Praeger, 1995).

On the history of Israel, consult Bernard Reich, *A Brief History of Israel*, 2nd ed. (New York: Facts on File, Inc., 2008); Martin Gilbert, *Israel: A History*, rev. ed. (Santa Barbara, CA: McNally and Loftin, 2008); and Howard M. Sachar, *A History of Israel: From the Rise of Zionism to Our Time* (New York: Knopf, 1976) and *A History of Israel*, vol. 2, *From the Aftermath of the Yom Kippur War* (Oxford: Oxford University Press, 1987). The Mandate period is discussed in J. C. Hurewitz's *The Struggle for Palestine* (New York: Norton, 1950) and Christopher Sykes's *Crossroads to Israel* (Cleveland, OH: World Publishing, 1965). Shlomo Avineri's *The Making of Modern Zionism: The Intellectual Origins of the Jewish State* (New York: Basic Books, 1981) and Walter Laqueur's *A History of Zionism* (New York: Holt, Rinehart and Winston, 1972) provide a comprehensive history and examination of the Zionist movement, its origins, and its diverse ideological trends. A useful reference is Charles I. Waxman and Rafael Medoff, *Historical Dictionary of Zionism* (Lanham, MD: Scarecrow Press, 2000).

Studies of Israel's parliament include Asher Zidon, *Knesset: The Parliament of Israel* (New York: Herzl Press, 1967); Eliahu S. Likhovski, *Israel's Parliament: The Law of the Knesset* (Oxford: Oxford University Press, 1971); Gregory S. Mahler, *The Knesset: Parliament in the Israeli Political System* (Rutherford, NJ: Fairleigh Dickinson University Press, 1981); and Samuel Sager, *The Parliamentary System of Israel* (Syracuse, NY: Syracuse University Press, 1985).

Various aspects of Israeli politics and policy have been the subject of specialized studies, including Myron J. Aronoff, *Israeli Visions and Divisions: Cultural Change and Political Conflict* (New Brunswick, NJ: Transaction Books, 1989); Marcia Drezon-Tepler, *Interest Groups and Political Change in Israel* (Albany: State University of New York Press, 1990); Dan Horowitz and Moshe Lissak, *Trouble in Utopia: The Overburdened Polity of Israel* (Albany: State University of New York Press, 1989); Bernard Reich and Gershon R. Kieval, eds., *Israel Faces the Future* (New York: Praeger, 1986); *Israeli Politics in the 1990s: Key Domestic and Foreign Policy Factors* (Westport, CT: Greenwood Press, 1991); and Ehud Sprinzak, *The Ascendance of Israel's Radical Right* (New York: Oxford University Press, 1991). Political parties are the particular focus of Peter Y. Medding, *Mapai in Israel: Political Organization and Government in a New Society* (Cambridge: Cambridge University Press, 1972); Peter Y. Medding, *The Founding of Israeli Democracy, 1948–1988* (London: Oxford University Press, 1989); Jonathan Mendilow, *Ideology, Party Change, and Electoral Campaigns in Israel, 1965–2001* (Albany: State University of New York Press, 2003); Yonathan Shapiro, *The Road to Power: Herut Party in Israel* (Albany: State University of New York Press, 1991); and Yoram Peri, *Generals in the Cabinet Room: How the Military Shapes Israeli Policy* (Washington, DC: United States Institute of Peace Press, 2006).

Studies of the salient domestic, political, economic, and social issues include S. N. Eisenstadt, *The Transformation of Israeli Society* (Boulder, CO: Westview Press, 1985); Yair Aharoni, *The Israeli Economy: Dreams and Realities* (London: Routledge, 1991); and Yoram Ben-Porath, ed., *The Israeli Economy: Maturing Through Crises* (Cambridge, MA: Harvard University Press, 1986). The relationship of religion and the state is discussed in Charles S. Liebman and Eliezer Don-Yehiya, *Civil Religion in Israel: Traditional Judaism and Political Culture in the Jewish State* (Berkeley: University of California Press, 1983). Jacob M. Landau, in *The Arabs in Israel: A Political Study* (London: Oxford University Press, 1969), presents a comprehensive survey and analysis of the role of the Arabs in Israel. An alternative perspective is provided by Sabri Jiryis, *The Arabs in Israel* (New York: Monthly Review Press, 1976). See also As'ad Ghanem, *The Palestinian-Arab Minority in Israel, 1948–2000: A Political Study* (Albany: State University of New York Press, 2001).

For an overview of Israel's foreign policy, see Aaron S. Klieman, *Israel and the World After Forty Years* (Elmsford, NY: Pergamon, 1989), *Israel's Global Reach: Arms Sales as Diplomacy* (Washington, DC: Pergamon-Brassey's, 1985), and *Statecraft in the Dark: Israel's Practice of Quiet Diplomacy* (Boulder, CO: Westview Press, 1988); Ilan Peleg, *Begin's Foreign Policy, 1977–1983: Israel's Move to the Right* (Westport, CT: Greenwood Press, 1987); and Bernard Reich and Gershon R. Kieval, eds., *Israeli National Security Policy: Political Actors and Perspectives* (Westport, CT: Greenwood

Press, 1988). *Israel's Foreign Relations, Selected Documents, 1947–2001,* 18 vols. (Jerusalem: Ministry of Foreign Affairs, 1976–2002) provides the major documents of Israel's foreign policy from its inception through 1999. Gershon R. Kieval, *Party Politics in Israel and the Occupied Territories* (Westport, CT: Greenwood Press, 1983), provides a detailed analysis of Israel's policy. Bernard Reich, in *Quest for Peace: United States–Israel Relations and the Arab-Israeli Conflict* (New Brunswick, NJ: Transaction Books, 1977), deals with Israel's relations with the United States in the context of the efforts to resolve the Arab-Israeli conflict. Bernard Reich, in *The United States and Israel: Influence in the Special Relationship* (New York: Praeger, 1984), examines Israel's crucial links with the United States. Bernard Reich, in *Securing the Covenant: United States–Israel Relations After the Cold War* (Westport, CT: Greenwood Press, 1995), examines the special relationship of these allies.

Specific aspects of Israeli foreign policy are considered in Jacob Abadi, *Israel's Quest for Recognition and Acceptance in Asia: Garrison State Diplomacy* (London: Frank Cass, 2004); Andrea S. Arbel, *Riding the Wave: The Jewish Agency's Role in the Mass Aliyah of Soviet and Ethiopian Jewry to Israel, 1987–1995* (Jerusalem: Gefen Publishing House, 2001); Gadi Ben-Ezer, *The Ethiopian Jewish Exodus: Narratives of the Migration Journey to Israel, 1977–1985* (London: Routledge, 2002); Ofra Bengio, *The Turkish-Israeli Relationship: Changing Ties of Middle Eastern Outsiders* (New York: Palgrave Macmillan, 2004); and Uri Bialer, *Cross on the Star of David: The Christian World in Israel's Foreign Policy, 1948–1967* (Bloomington: Indiana University Press, 2005).

Some recent works on elements of the Arab-Israeli conflict are Michael B. Oren, *Six Days of War: June 1967 and the Making of the Modern Middle East* (New York: Oxford University Press, 2002); Itamar Rabinovich, *Waging Peace: Israel and the Arabs, 1948–2003* (Princeton, NJ: Princeton University Press, 2004); Dennis Ross, *The Missing Peace: The Inside Story of the Fight for Middle East Peace* (New York: Farrar, Straus, and Giroux, 2004); Eytan Bentsur, *Making Peace: A First-Hand Account of the Arab-Israeli Peace Process* (Westport, CT: Praeger, 2001); Mordechai Gazit, *Israeli Diplomacy and the Quest for Peace* (London: Frank Cass, 2002); and Raphael Israeli, *Jerusalem Divided: The Armistice Regime, 1947–1967* (London: Frank Cass, 2002).

Yigal Allon, *The Making of Israel's Army* (New York: Bantam Books, 1971), and Amos Perlmutter, *Military and Politics in Israel: Nation-Building and Role Expansion* (London: Frank Cass, 1969), consider the role of the military. For a general overview of the IDF, its background and development, see Ze'ev Schiff, *A History of the Israeli Army (1870–1974)* (New York: Simon and Schuster, 1974).

The government of Israel is a prolific publisher of high-quality materials, such as the *Israel Government Year Book* and the *Statistical Abstract of Israel,* that would serve the interested reader well.

The websites of the government of Israel are a substantial resource providing access to virtually all official information that a student or researcher could desire. The Israel government portal is www.gov.il. The prime minister's office is found at www.pmo.gov.il. The Knesset site is www.knesset.gov.il. The Israel Ministry of Foreign Affairs website is www.mfa.gov.il. The Ministry of Defense website is www.mod.gov.il. Statistical data for Israel is available through the Central Bureau of Statistics at www.cbs.gov.il.

The daily newspaper *Ha'aretz* (English online edition) may be found at www.Haartez.com. The English-language *Jerusalem Post* publishes its online edition at www.jpost.com.

12

THE PALESTINIANS

Glenn E. Robinson

A predominately Arab-Muslim people ever since the Muslim conquest in the seventh century CE, Palestinians are descendants of the peoples that had conquered the territory over the centuries—including the Jewish tribes who populated the area 2,000 years ago. Palestinians today seek to create a viable and independent state.

HISTORICAL BACKGROUND

Much of the Palestinians' history prior to the Roman conquest 2,000 years ago is more speculation than actual history. The population for many centuries prior to the Roman period was largely tribal and often nomadic, although settled agricultural communities were increasingly common. The Old Testament presents many fascinating stories about the Israelite period, but there are few independent sources to confirm the accuracy of these accounts. Alexander the Great conquered the area in 332 BCE when his forces defeated Persia, but he largely ignored the area later called Palestine. The Roman Empire seized control of the region in 63 BCE, and it was Roman rulers who coined the name "Palestine."

As the Roman Empire collapsed in the fourth century CE, control passed to the Byzantine, or eastern Roman, Empire, which ruled from a distance until the Muslim conquest in 634 CE by tribes from the Arabian Peninsula. The caliph 'Umar's conquest of Jerusalem and Palestine marked the beginning of nearly 1,300 years of continuous Muslim rule, interrupted only by the European Crusades (primarily twelfth century CE). Saladin famously recaptured Jerusalem from the crusaders in 1187.

The Ottoman Empire

The Muslim Ottoman Empire, based in Istanbul, ruled Palestine indirectly for four centuries, from 1516 to 1920. Regional governors and other local elites had wide discretion to wield power in ways they saw fit, allowing local business leaders,

Gaza Strip and West Bank

military commanders, and religious figures to become prominent; these were known collectively as the "notable" (*a'yan*) social class. The authority of local notables increased dramatically during the nineteenth century as a result of a number of reforms enacted by the Ottoman Empire in its bid to fend off growing European power. Ottoman policies helped shape Palestine's social structure, which consisted primarily of a handful of notable families holding sway over a largely illiterate peasant society.

In the latter part of the nineteenth century, Jewish immigration, primarily to escape persecution in Europe, increased.

As early as 1891, a group of Muslim and Christian notables in Palestine cabled Istanbul to urge the government to prohibit immigration and land purchases by European Jews, fearing that large-scale immigration would displace the Arab residents. After the Young Turk revolution of 1908, elite Palestinians expressed their concerns through the parliament in Istanbul, as well as through newly permitted political and cultural societies and newspapers. The experience that Arabs gained in municipalities, district councils, and religious institutions fueled their desire for self-rule. The rural majority—illiterate and relatively isolated—shared the elite's unease at the increasing number of Jewish agricultural villages.

By World War I (1914), the Jewish community in Palestine comprised 11 percent of the total inhabitants (about 75,000 out of 690,000). That was a visible change since 1880, when the Jews made up 6 percent of the population (35,000 out of 485,000). The four historical Jewish communities in Palestine (in the cities of Hebron, Jerusalem, Safad, and Tiberias) were populated primarily by religious, nonpolitical Jews, while most of the new Jewish migrants from Europe after 1880 espoused Zionism. From that point on, two emerging national groups—Jewish and Palestinian—claimed the same land as their own, making conflict inevitable.

The British Mandate

With the defeat of the Ottoman Empire in World War I, Great Britain took control of Palestine. Arab leaders thought that Palestine would be included in the area promised independence by Sir Henry McMahon, the British high commissioner for Egypt, in letters he wrote during 1915 and 1916 to Sharif Hussein of Mecca. Hussein and McMahon had agreed that the British would support Arab independence from the Turks if the Arabs launched a revolt against the Ottoman Empire. In the Balfour Declaration Britain supported "the establishment in Palestine of a national home for the Jewish people." That proclamation, issued on November 2, 1917, and later incorporated into the British Mandate of Palestine, transformed the balance of power between the Arab majority and the Jewish minority, providing the Zionist movement its long-sought legal status.

Arabs in Palestine had assumed that they would gain independence when Ottoman rule disintegrated, either by establishing a separate state or by merging with neighboring Arab lands. They felt betrayed when Britain imposed the mandate and immediately objected to the Zionist organization's privileged status as well as to the continuing alienation of the land. During the 1920s, the nationalist movement was led by Palestinian elites who, for the most part, employed nonviolent tactics. During the 1930s, however, radicalized youth and labor activists goaded the leadership to use strikes and violence to confront both the British and the expanding Jewish population. Palestinian followers of the preacher Iz Al Din Al Qassam launched an armed insurgency in late 1935, leading to a general strike in 1936 that Palestinians sustained for an unprecedented six months. The strike was followed by a widespread rural revolt that lasted nearly two years. The rebellion welled up from the depths of Palestinian society—among unemployed urban workers, displaced peasants crowded into towns, debt-ridden villagers. Most merchants and professionals in the towns supported the uprising, and the elite formed the Arab Higher Committee, which presented Arab demands to the British administration.

The British crushed the uprising, taking advantage of Palestinian political cleavages to do so. The most famous social divide among the political leadership was between the Husseini and Nashashibi notable families. Pitting one family against another, the British effectively weakened Palestinian resistance. Still largely traditional and agrarian, albeit in the midst of upheaval, Palestinian society had few credible nonfamilial institutions able to replace the weakening family-based leadership.

After the British decapitated the Palestinian national movement and forcibly suppressed the revolt, Palestinians had no coherent organizations or skilled leaders with which to press for self-determination. Arab states, for the most part still in the last stages of gaining their own independence, were too involved in domestic issues to be of much support. Jewish violence against the British and Arabs increased. Finally, in 1947, the British announced that they were ending the mandate and turning the Palestine issue over to the United Nations.

In November 1947, the UN General Assembly approved a partition plan that divided the Palestine Mandate into a Jewish state, an Arab state, and an international area of Jerusalem. The Jewish state comprised about 55 percent of the territory, even though Jewish landholdings comprised less than 7 percent of the total land surface or 12 percent of arable land. The Jewish state would have nearly as many Arab as Jewish residents. The Arab state would control only about 40 percent of Palestine; deprived of the best agricultural land and seaports, it would retain Galilee, the central mountains (now primarily the West Bank), and the Gaza coast. The United Nations would administer Jerusalem as an international zone.

The Palestinians rejected the partition plan and tried to defend their homeland, but their village-based militias could not stand up to Jewish forces, which seized control of nearly all the areas assigned to the Jewish state during a five-week campaign in April and May 1948. That campaign forced 300,000 Palestinians (of an eventual 700,000) to flee from their homes in villages and cities such as Tiberias, Haifa, and Jaffa.

Following the British withdrawal on May 14, 1948, and the unilateral declaration of independence by Israel, Arab states sent in troops, and full-scale fighting erupted. The Arab armies were no match for the better trained and better equipped Israeli forces; when armistice agreements were signed in 1949, only 23 percent of Palestine remained in Arab hands, and an additional 400,000 Palestinians had become refugees. The Egyptian army held the Gaza Strip, and Transjordanian forces held the West Bank, including East Jerusalem.

The first Arab-Israeli war was complicated, with different rationales for each actor, especially among the Arab parties. Zionist leaders and King Abdullah of Jordan (with British agreement) had forged a secret, informal arrangement to divide the lands designated for the Palestinian state. This was implemented in the fighting. The suspected collusion led to the 1951 assassination of King Abdullah by a Palestinian nationalist. Egypt's military intervention seemed designed at least as much to thwart Abdullah's ambitions in Palestine as to defeat Israel. At the time, Egypt and Jordan were the main rivals for power in the Arab world.

Fragmentation and Exile: 1948–1967

Some 85 percent of the mandate's Arab population fled during the 1947–1949 conflict. Many Palestinians took temporary flight when war came to their villages; others, such as those in the towns of Lydda and Ramle, were expelled at gunpoint; still others left in fright as word spread of massacres like that in Deir Yassin; and others left expecting to return after the successes of the Arab armies. Palestinian elites who had the means were the first to leave. Displaced Palestinians became permanent refugees on June 16, 1948, when Israel's new government decided not to allow any Palestinian refugees to return to their homes in lands under Israel's control or in lands that would come under Israel's control during the remainder of the war. The departure of Palestinians in 1948 from their homes and villages shattered Palestinian society. Most Palestinian refugees went to makeshift camps established by the United Nations. Over time, these camps evolved into squalid, cinder block encampments housing the world's largest refugee population. Of the 1.2 million Palestinian Arab population, over 700,000 became refugees, dispersed to Egypt, Jordan, Lebanon, and Syria. About 500,000 remained in place, of which 150,000 stayed in Israel (primarily in the Galilee region), with the remainder in the West Bank (annexed by Jordan) and the Gaza Strip (administered by Egypt). The situation facing the Palestinians in the countries to which they fled varied considerably.

Palestinian society was changed profoundly by this trauma, which they call *al-nakba* ("the disaster"). The society was previously highly stratified and largely rural, with a powerful notable social class, a large peasantry, and a small middle class. Palestinian peasants were forced into wage labor, the elite lost the land that underpinned their power, and merchants lost their livelihoods. In time, dispersal transformed Palestinians into a mobile but highly insecure people among whom educational attainment and political activism ranked high as criteria for social standing. The physical dispersion made it difficult to reestablish a coherent political center. Living under different authoritarian regimes and subject to restrictions on political expression, the Palestinians suffered from constant pressure toward fragmentation. Palestinians' political aims evolved significantly. At first they were determined to regain all of Palestine, but beginning in the 1970s an increasing number conceded that territorial partition—the establishment of a Palestinian state alongside Israel—was the most that could be achieved. The concept of partition remains controversial, but for many it seemed the only way to ensure their national survival.

At the political level, the landed and professional political elites lost credibility and legitimacy. Their disunity and ineffectiveness were blamed for *al-nakba*. Only the village-level structures remained somewhat intact, since family and local institutions helped to organize life in the refugee camps. However, the village structure there was severely distorted due to the loss of agricultural land and home ownership.

The refugees underwent profound psychological transformations. At first they felt lost, disoriented, and separated from their familiar ways of life. The humiliation of being landless contributed to their sense of alienation. The older generation succumbed to an ever-lengthening wait for *al-awda* ("the return").

The sense of alienation was increased by the ambivalence of host countries toward the refugees. Although the Arab states initially welcomed the commercial and professional skills of the small Palestinian middle class, they could not absorb the mass of displaced farmers and laborers. Moreover, politically active Palestinians resisted efforts to cancel their refugee status, since that could undermine their perceived right to reclaim Palestine.

Controls imposed by the host countries took different forms. In Israel, Palestinians gained citizenship but lived under strict military administration until 1966. The movement of Palestinian residents was closely regulated, access to education and employment was restricted, and political activities were curtailed. In the Gaza Strip, the Egyptian military government maintained tight control over the restive Palestinians, of whom 80 percent lived in refugee camps. Palestinians living in Syria had the same access to jobs and schools as Syrian citizens, but their ability to travel abroad was curtailed. The Lebanese authorities were especially restrictive, denying Palestinians citizenship and the right either to study in public schools or to obtain permanent employment. Lebanese troops entered the refugee camps to arrest residents. Friction developed between the Palestinians, who were largely Sunni Muslim by religion, and those Lebanese politicians who sought to retain the special status of the Maronite Christian minority.

Life was least disrupted in the West Bank, where most people remained in their original homes. Palestinians staffed the administrative and educational systems in Jordan and developed many of its commercial enterprises. Palestinians also enjoyed citizenship rights in Jordan, which set Jordan apart from its Arab neighbors. But the regime never trusted them with senior posts in sensitive ministries and in the armed forces, and their loyalty to the monarchy remained tenuous. Moreover, the West Bank faced economic hardship as trade through Mediterranean ports was blocked, villages lost valuable agricultural land to Israel, and the Jordanian government favored the East Bank for industrial and agricultural development. Because of these factors, tens of thousands of Palestinians left the West Bank and migrated to Amman, Jordan's capital, in the 1950s and 1960s.

During the 1950s, Palestinians were attracted to the various forms of pan-Arabism that asserted that Palestine could only be regained if the Arab world were united politically. The idea of Arab unity received a blow in 1961 when the union between Egypt and Syria dissolved after less than three years. Moreover, the ideological cold war between Egypt and Saudi Arabia—played out on the battlefields of North Yemen—polarized the Arab world. The belief in Arab military strength was destroyed in June 1967 when the Israeli army defeated the combined Arab forces in a lightning strike and seized the Golan Heights from Syria, the West Bank and East Jerusalem from Jordan, and the Gaza Strip and Sinai Peninsula from Egypt.

That disillusionment accelerated processes that were already under way among Palestinians. Their feeling that they were discriminated against by fellow Arabs and their disappointment with the rhetoric of Arab regimes led many Palestinians to set aside their own passivity and reject their dependence on Arab states. They sought to transform their situation through their own actions rather than wait for Arab governments to rescue them. Small underground guerrilla cells sprang up in the early 1960s. Al-Fatah, founded in Kuwait in 1959 by the young engineer Yasir Arafat and several colleagues, launched its first raid into Israel on New Year's Eve, 1965. The fedayeen ("guerrillas") had a twofold strategy: They asserted that self-reliance was the route to liberation and sought to catalyze popular mobilization that would shame the Arab rulers into fighting Israel. When that war finally came in 1967 and ended disastrously for the Arab states, the Palestinian guerrilla movement was thrust into the leadership position on the issue of Palestine, eclipsing the leading role that had been played by Amman, Cairo, and Damascus.

The Palestine Liberation Organization and the Palestinian Diaspora: 1967–1993

The 1967 war cut the Palestinian community in two: Half of all Palestinians now lived inside the boundaries of old mandatory Palestine under Israeli rule, and half continued to live in the diaspora outside of mandatory Palestine, mostly in various Arab countries. The Palestine Liberation Organization (PLO) was initially created in 1964 by the Arab League—in particular, by Egypt's Gamal Abd al-Nasser to show that he was "doing something" about reclaiming Palestinian rights. In its early years it was an ineffective organization led by Palestinians tied to Arab regimes, especially Egypt. PLO leaders like Ahmad Al Shuqayri gave fiery speeches but did little to change the situation on the ground.

Shuqayri and other well-to-do Palestinians wrote the PLO Charter, amended in 1968, which called for the elimination of Israel, the creation of a secular Palestinian state in its place, and the return to Europe of Jews who had migrated under the banner of Zionism. It was a maximalist document that reflected Palestinian thinking of the time. In the ensuing decades, PLO thinking would evolve substantially.

The humiliating defeat in 1967 provided the opportunity for the Palestinian guerrilla groups to take control of the PLO and transform it into an autonomous and important umbrella organization that came to represent Palestinian interests in the region and internationally. The guerrilla organizations asserted their new-found muscle at the Fifth Palestine National Council meeting of 1969, where they ousted the old PLO leadership and installed Arafat, head of the largest guerrilla faction, as its new leader.

As an umbrella organization, the PLO contained many diverse and competing groups. The largest and most important was Fatah, led by Arafat, which espoused a nationalist ideology typical of national liberation movements everywhere. There was little social content to Fatah's ideology, simply a call to regain lost lands. The two other most important constituent groups of the PLO espoused ideologies that were more hard-line Arab nationalist and Marxist in orientation: the Popular Front for the Liberation of Palestine (PFLP) founded by George Habash, a Greek Orthodox physician, and the Democratic Front for the Liberation of Palestine (DFLP), led by Nayif Hawatmeh, a Jordanian from the city of Salt. While Fatah focused on freeing Palestine, the more radical groups believed that only a more general revolution by the Arabs against their own conservative regimes could lead to the liberation of Palestine. The PFLP's hijacking spree of civilian aircraft in 1970 was intended to launch the revolution.

The PLO began to flex its muscle by creating "states within states." The first ministate was created in Jordan, where King Hussein at first tolerated it. This ended when radical factions within the PLO openly called for the overthrow of his regime and then set about implementing revolution. The hijacking of civilian passenger planes to a desert airfield in Jordan (where they were blown up after the passengers and crew had been released) proved to be the breaking point. The Jordanian army defeated the PLO in a bloody showdown in 1970 (later known as Black September), seized control of the refugee camps, and forced the guerrillas to flee to Syria and Lebanon in July 1971.

While the PLO was establishing a base of operations in Lebanon, high-profile acts of political violence continued in the early 1970s. In retaliation for Black September, Palestinian commandoes assassinated Jordan's prime minister when he visited Cairo in November 1971. In one of the most infamous acts of terror in modern history, Palestinians kidnapped and murdered eleven Israeli athletes at the 1972 Munich Olympics. Operations across the Lebanon-Israel border likewise intensified. Palestinian attacks were matched by Israeli bombardments and special operations in villages and refugee camps in Lebanon. Tit-for-tat violence and assassinations continued between Israel and the PLO in Lebanon until 1982, when

Israel launched an invasion of Lebanon in an operation designed to eliminate the PLO as a political force.

PLO weakness compelled it to reevaluate its strategy. Even during the heady days of revolution between the 1967 war and Black September in Jordan in 1970, the PLO was powerless to reverse Israel's occupation of the West Bank and Gaza Strip, much less to regain all of Palestine. Attempts to organize an armed rebellion in the West Bank failed. Black September demonstrated the futility of taking on Arab regimes that had no interest in furthering the Palestinian cause if it meant the loss of their own power. Recognizing that the balance of power did not favor Palestinian interests, some Palestinians began calling for the establishment of a Palestinian state only in the lands occupied by Israel during the 1967 war: the West Bank, East Jerusalem, and the Gaza Strip.

The October 1973 Arab-Israeli War further consolidated the transformation of PLO policy toward accepting a two-state solution. The 1973 war was a victory for states, both Arab and Israeli. The performance of Egyptian and Syrian militaries was strong enough to dim the memory of their humiliations in 1967. Israel's ultimate triumph on the battlefield in 1973, even after absorbing a devastating initial blow, showed again that the PLO had no chance of defeating Israel militarily. Over the objections of the PFLP and other hard-liners, the 1974 Palestine National Council of the PLO took a major step toward embracing a two-state solution when it pledged to create a "national authority" over any liberated lands of Palestine. Several months later, the Arab League recognized the PLO as the "sole legitimate representative of the Palestinian people," a move that led to the PLO's achieving observer status at the United Nations and Yasir Arafat's speech to the General Assembly in November 1974.

The 1979 peace treaty between Israel and Egypt dramatically altered the geostrategic landscape for the PLO. The PLO rejected Israel's offer (made to Egypt) of autonomy under overarching Israeli control for Palestinians living in the West Bank and Gaza Strip. The rapid expansion of Israel's colonization efforts in the West Bank under Menachem Begin and the Likud Party, in power since 1977, showed clearly to Palestinians that Israel was not interested in withdrawing to the 1967 borders and allowing a Palestinian state to develop. Moreover, the peace treaty effectively removed the Arab world's most powerful state from the Arab-Israeli stage, giving Israel a much freer hand in dealing with other Arabs. Egypt under Anwar Sadat was most interested in gaining the return of the Sinai Peninsula and currying favor with the United States, both cornerstones of its new economic-development strategy.

Having neutralized Egypt politically, Israel turned its eyes toward eliminating the PLO. Leaders of Israel's Likud Party believed that crushing the PLO and its state-within-a-state in Lebanon would deprive Palestinians in the West Bank of political leadership, thus making permanent Israeli control of the West Bank more feasible. Following the October 1981 assassination of Anwar Sadat and the April 1982 withdrawal from the last part of the Sinai Peninsula, Israel made destroying the PLO its first priority.

No longer feeling vulnerable to Arab counterattack, Israel invaded Lebanon in June 1982. Israeli forces easily defeated the Lebanese, Palestinian, and Syrian forces it encountered on its drive to Beirut. Trapped, the PLO negotiated with the United States an exit of their forces to Tunisia and elsewhere in the Arab world. The American promise to protect Palestinian civilians left behind in Beirut proved hollow, as Lebanese forces, with logistical assistance from the Israel Defense Forces, slaughtered hundreds of refugees in the Sabra and Shatilla camps shortly afterward.

Israel's gambit to destroy the PLO by invading Lebanon initially seemed to pay dividends. The PLO had been decimated, its remaining forces scattered throughout the Arab world; its new headquarters was in far-off Tunis, its factions were fighting each other more than Israel, and its prospects for pushing the international community to compel an Israeli withdrawal from the occupied territories seemed remote. Two events proved critical in rescuing the PLO from possible oblivion. First, Palestinians living inside the occupied territories launched their own uprising (intifada) against Israel beginning in 1987. The Intifada showed that Palestinians inside the West Bank and Gaza would actively resist Israel's occupation and confiscation of Palestinian lands, even in the face of a badly weakened PLO in the diaspora. The political mobilization of Palestinians that gave rise to the Intifada was in part a response by West Bank and Gaza Palestinians to Israel's attempt to destroy the PLO.

Ironically, Israel itself helped rescue the PLO from obscurity when it engaged in secret peace negotiations with the PLO in Oslo, Norway, in 1993. At the time, the PLO as an organization was extremely weak. During the 1990–1991 Iraq War, the PLO made a serious strategic miscalculation by backing Iraq in its war against a US-led coalition determined to end Iraq's occupation of Kuwait. Kuwait and Saudi Arabia had long been the PLO's chief financial backers through a tax they collected on Palestinians living in those countries, which was then passed on to the PLO. Yasir Arafat's public embrace of Saddam Husayn during the war caused Kuwait and Saudi Arabia to end their financial support of the PLO. The PLO went bankrupt, closed a number of offices, and cut financial disbursements to Palestinian families and organizations. The PLO also lost political support from much of the Arab world for its stance during this first Gulf war.

Because of its extreme weakness, the PLO offered Israel terms in Oslo that Israel had long demanded and that the PLO had long rejected. These PLO concessions included a long interim period, no guarantee of ultimate statehood, continued Israeli control of all of Jerusalem during the interim period, and no explicit cessation of Israeli colonization of the occupied territories. Indeed, the number of Israeli settlers in the West Bank and Gaza doubled in the decade following the September 1993 signing of the Oslo Accords.

The Israeli Occupation: 1967–1993

After the 1967 war, developments in the occupied West Bank and Gaza Strip were markedly different from those affecting Palestinians elsewhere. The Palestinians in the occupied territories went through a period of relative political quiescence, even experiencing economic growth, while the others were engaging in radical politics, civil war, and displacement. Then, as the PLO gradually moved toward accommodation with its Arab hosts and mainstream nationalism, the "inside" Palestinians increasingly radicalized and mobilized. In particular, three structural changes helped to transform Palestinian society: the opening of Israeli labor markets to Palestinians, the extensive confiscation of Palestinian lands by the Israeli government, and the establishment and expansion of the Palestinian university system.

After the 1967 war, Israel opened its domestic labor market to Palestinians from the occupied territories. Palestinians were recruited to do the unskilled or semi-skilled jobs that Israelis refused to do themselves—primarily in the agricultural and construction sectors. This pool of cheap labor was a boon to Israeli businesses, which grew rapidly in the late 1960s and early 1970s. These jobs appealed to Palestinians both because they paid relatively well in comparison to jobs in the occupied territories and because there was an endemic shortage of local jobs. The Palestinians employed in Israel tended to come from the lower classes, primarily the peasantry and refugee camp dwellers. They came in large numbers: Shortly after Israel opened its labor market, one-third of the Palestinian labor force in the West Bank and Gaza Strip was employed in Israel. By the 1980s, over 120,000 Palestinians—fully 40 percent of the Palestinian labor force—worked in Israel daily. As much as 70 percent of the Gazan labor force worked in Israel or in Israeli settlements. The result was the virtual disappearance of the Palestinian peasantry and the destruction of many patron-client networks, especially in the West Bank, seriously undermining one of the pillars of social power for the Palestinian elite. This pool of recruits proved crucial in the general political mobilization campaign of the 1980s and the subsequent Intifada.

A second change was the massive Israeli confiscation of land. In the immediate wake of the 1967 war, Israel tripled the size of the municipal boundaries of Jerusalem and then annexed it. Large sections contained within the new boundaries of Jerusalem were unilaterally declared state lands and taken by Israel, often for Jewish settlements. Other lands in East Jerusalem were confiscated on "security grounds," while other parcels were awarded to Israelis who had claims dating to the pre-1948 period. Those Palestinian claims on land parcels in West Jerusalem, also dating to the pre-1948 period, were not similarly recognized. Those lands not confiscated were in essence frozen, so that the natural expansion of Palestinian neighborhoods was virtually impossible.

Confiscation of land in the West Bank and Gaza Strip was even more extensive. The most common form was to declare parcels of land as state land or as needed for security reasons; recognized private property was also confiscated outright. Often Jewish settlements would be built on the land seized. While large tracts of land in the West Bank and Gaza were confiscated in the first decade of military occupation, the confiscations were accelerated and were often deliberately provocative after the Likud Party came to power in Israel in 1977. On the eve of the Palestinian uprising in 1987, over half of the West Bank and one-third of the Gaza Strip had been confiscated or otherwise made off-limits to Palestinians.

In addition to antagonizing the Palestinians, such confiscations directly attacked a second pillar of notable power—control over land—further undermining this elite's legitimacy as they were shown to be powerless to stop or slow Israel's land seizures.

The third change was the creation and expansion of a Palestinian university system. Prior to 1972, higher education was a privilege reserved for the Palestinian elite, as only those families could afford to send their children abroad for university. In 1972, the first full-fledged Palestinian university, Birzeit, was established. In subsequent years, more universities were established in Bethlehem, Hebron, Gaza, Jerusalem, and Nablus. In the decade preceding the Intifada, the Palestinian university student population grew from a few thousand to between 15,000 and 20,000 annually. The effect was significant, as tens of thousands of Palestinians went through the university and its concomitant political socialization. The composition of the student population at these new universities was striking: 70 percent of the students came from refugee camps, villages, and small towns. It was from this student population that a new Palestinian elite emerged in the 1970s and 1980s—one that was larger, more diffuse, from lower social strata, more activist, and less urban than the notable Palestinian elite it largely replaced. As a result, Palestinian politics became more confrontational with Israel.

The major strategy of this rising Palestinian elite in the 1980s was to build grassroots organizations designed to mobilize the Palestinian population against the occupation. In turn, these institutions would act as protostate structures, designed to vest authority in Palestinian hands and away from the military government. During this period Palestinians built or expanded most labor unions, student blocs, and women's, agricultural-relief, medical-relief, and voluntary-works committees.

Two international events helped spur the mobilization campaign. First, the Egypt-Israel Peace Treaty shifted the regional balance of power dramatically in Israel's favor. The Palestinians recognized that any positive solution to their dilemma would be a long way off. Thus, the primary objective was to make the West Bank and Gaza difficult for the Israelis to rule and absorb. Second, Israel's 1982 invasion of Lebanon had the unintended consequence of invigorating the emerging elite in the West Bank and Gaza and making it clear that they could no longer rely on the "outside" PLO for salvation—it would have to be accomplished by those Palestinians still living there. While this new elite was widely affiliated with the major factions of the PLO—Fatah, Popular Front for the Liberation of Palestine, Democratic Front for the Liberation of Palestine, and the Palestine Communist Party—it was significant that the political initiative clearly lay with those on the "inside."

The First Intifada: 1987–1993

In December 1987 a mass uprising, or intifada, against Israeli occupation began. It was a spontaneous event; no person or faction planned it, and the earlier social structure could not have produced such a sustained and organized revolt. It was not an armed uprising; nor was it particularly violent. It took the form of thrown rocks, bricks, and occasional Molotov cocktails. Demonstrations, marches, and rallies were employed, especially in the first six months. However, the Intifada was primarily about mass organized disengagement from Israel. In political terms, Palestinians denied Israeli authority on any number of issues and created alternative authoritative bodies to govern Palestinian society. The principal locus of authority for over two years was the Unified National Leadership of the Uprising (UNLU), an ever-changing body of local PLO activists who published periodic leaflets directing the Intifada. The UNLU's first confrontation with the military government came over strike hours demanded of commercial establishments. The UNLU would instruct merchants to close their businesses at certain hours, while the military government commanded that they stay open during those hours and close for other hours. The confrontation went on for weeks, until finally Israel relented, and the UNLU was free to set strike hours and days. Their authority in these matters was recognized and widely obeyed, especially in the first two years of the Intifada.

Political disengagement was not limited to the UNLU. Alternative structures of authority sprang up everywhere in the form of popular and neighborhood committees. These committees would provide social services to meet needs generated by the Intifada, including the distribution of food during curfews, organizing "popular education" when the schools were closed, planting "victory gardens" to diminish dependence on Israeli agricultural products, organizing guard duty to watch for military or settler attacks, ensuring compliance with strike days, and the like. Some committees undertook more violent activities, particularly the interrogation and execution of alleged collaborators.

Economic disengagement was seen in the boycott of Israeli-made goods and the refusal to pay taxes to Israel in a number of communities, especially the town of Bayt Sahur. Institutional disengagement was illustrated by the mass resignation, at the UNLU's urging, of Palestinian policemen employed by the military government. Perhaps most important was the psychological disengagement. The uprising was a vehicle of individual and communal empowerment, where, at least for a time, Palestinians believed they could actually roll back the occupation.

After an initial period of confusion, Israel responded to the Intifada harshly, using, in the words of then defense minister Yitzhak Rabin, "force, might, beatings" to crush it. Well over 1,000 Palestinians were killed by Israeli forces, with many thousands more injured, and tens of thousands were imprisoned—many without charge or trial. Most important was the strategy of collective punishment, where many were punished—through house demolitions, curfews, destruction of crops, and similar means—for the actions of a few. Bringing disproportionate force to bear was a reasonably successful strategy in containing the Intifada.

The Intifada was also responsible for significant changes in Palestinian society. First, the traditional respect for elders was largely lost. Neither the youth throwing stones nor the more important "mid-generation" building popular institutions had much time for what they regarded as the compromises and concessions of their elders. This was seen clearly in the liberalization of family structures, where clan patriarchs lost their influence in decision making.

Second was the antinotable aspect of the Intifada. While Israel was the primary target of the Intifada, the old Palestinian elite was the secondary target. The families that had held local power for generations were largely marginalized, continuing a process begun even before the uprising.

Third, the Intifada produced a rise to prominence of a powerful Islamist alternative to the secular PLO. The largest Islamist group, the Muslim Brotherhood, had been politically discredited in the years before the uprising because of their cooperation with Israeli authorities. The Intifada radicalized the Islamist movement, giving birth in its early days to the Islamic Resistance Movement, or Hamas. Hamas (and the Islamic Jihad group) brought to Palestinian resistance a level of operational violence against Israeli targets that the PLO in the West Bank and Gaza had never employed, gaining converts and splitting Palestinian society. Hamas would continue to grow in strength.

The "outside" PLO in Tunis was as surprised as Israel when the Intifada broke out and was not particularly important to the unfolding of events. Rather, Tunis sought to capture and control the Intifada, something it never managed to do completely. The PLO funneled resources and advice to the occupied territories in support of the Intifada and provided it with greater attention on the world's stage. The PLO had not lost its legitimacy, but Tunis was geographically and situationally too far removed from the course of events in the West Bank and Gaza to matter much.

Clearly, though, the PLO was not enamored of the alternative bodies of authority and viewed them and any autonomous political activity as potential threats to its position. As a rule, the PLO undermined political actions in the Intifada over which it had little control through lack of support, while those activities it could manage were strongly endorsed. Thus, while the PLO supported the Intifada in principle, it often acted to demobilize Palestinian society in the West Bank and Gaza.

The Oslo Accords and Their Failure: 1993–2006

In the aftermath of the Gulf War (1990–1991), the United States launched a major effort to deal with the Arab-Israeli conflict. In October 1991, the Madrid Conference convened with American, Arab, European, Israeli, Palestinian, and Russian participation. It led to a series of bilateral negotiations in Washington, DC, that made little progress. The return to power of Yitzhak Rabin and the Labor Party in the 1992 Israeli elections, combined with a keen PLO interest in moving toward a peace agreement (and thus extracting itself from the political grave it had dug by backing Iraq in the 1990–1991 Gulf War), provided the basis for diplomatic progress. Secret negotiations begun in Oslo in January 1993 between PLO officials and two Israeli academics linked to the dovish Labor politician Yossi Beilin ultimately led to a breakthrough agreement between Israel and the PLO that was signed on the White House lawn in September 1993.

In addition to letters of mutual recognition, the 1993 Oslo Accords—formally known as the Declaration of Principles—established the principles upon which the interim period was to be based and identified the key issues that the parties would need to resolve in a timely manner in order to enter into a final-status agreement. Indeed, the interim period was supposed to have ended in May 1999. The 1993 accord was followed by the Gaza-Jericho Agreement of 1994 that established the Palestinian Authority (PA) in the Gaza Strip and the West Bank city of Jericho. An interim agreement was signed in September 1995. A subsequent agreement that expanded the territory under PA control was signed at Wye River in Maryland in 1998.

The Oslo peace process essentially ended in the summer of 2000. US President Bill Clinton convened a summit meeting at Camp David in July to negotiate a final-status agreement between Israel and the PLO. Accounts vary of what exactly happened there. The dominant Israeli interpretation was that Arafat rejected a generous proposal and returned to prepare for a new round of fighting. The dominant Palestinian understanding was that Israel was not serious about making peace. Israel offered to return all of Gaza and a large portion of the West Bank to

Palestinian control but refused to engage the refugee issue and insisted on control over most of East Jerusalem. Palestinians noted that Israel's proposal for the West Bank left Palestinians with three unconnected cantons (often referred to pejoratively as Bantustans), each surrounded by Israeli territory. Each side came away from Camp David convinced that the other was not interested in a real peace agreement.

The failure at Camp David left both sides simmering in an atmosphere of distrust. Ariel Sharon, then fighting for the leadership of the Likud Party (and a staunch opponent of the Camp David negotiations), made a provocative visit on September 28, 2000, to the site of what Muslims regard as the third holiest mosque in Islam, the Haram al-Sharif, which Jews refer to as the Temple Mount, the site of the Temple in Jerusalem. Scuffles and rock throwing degenerated the next day into large demonstrations and clashes with Israeli police, with deadly consequences. The second Intifada had begun.

Clinton pursued a last effort at peacemaking in December and January, but it failed. Ariel Sharon won a resounding victory to replace Ehud Barak as prime minister and was largely successful in ending the uprising, primarily by reoccupation of the West Bank in March and April 2003. A major criticism of the Oslo Accords is that they never specified, even in broad terms, what peace at the end of the road was supposed to look like. Palestinian opponents of the Oslo Accords—such as Hamas and the PFLP—openly criticized Yasir Arafat for falling into a trap, for agreeing to what would become a never-ending interim period with no Palestinian state ever resulting. The breakdown of the Oslo peace process gave credence to this charge in the eyes of many Palestinians.

From the Palestinian perspective, the fundamental problem with the Oslo negotiations was that the parties were negotiating from two different base points. Israel's negotiating posture, in essence, was that the conflict began in 1967 and, thus, the disposition of the West Bank and Gaza Strip were the items to be negotiated. From this vantage point, returning 100 percent of those lands won in the 1967 war would seem one-sided, and seriously discussing refugees from 1948 would not be in order. The PLO's negotiating posture dated the conflict to 1948. As a result, Palestinians believed they had already ceded 77 percent of historic Palestine, so asking for the remaining 23 percent (all of the West Bank and Gaza) constituted a fair and modest proposal. Moreover, finally settling the refugee issue was essential.

Yasir Arafat, under siege in his Ramallah-based, and mostly destroyed, *muqatama* headquarters, fell ill in October 2004 and died in France a month later. Mahmoud Abbas (Abu Mazen) was elected as the new Palestinian president.

The breakdown of the Oslo peace process led to two major Israeli moves. First, Israel began construction of a large barrier along its border with the West Bank. While its architect, Ariel Sharon, maintained the wall was a security barrier, not a political line, Sharon's successor, Ehud Olmert, quickly pledged that the barrier would represent Israel's border with the western half of the West Bank.

Israel's second step was to withdraw from the Gaza Strip in the summer of 2005. The idea of ridding itself of control of Gaza had long been popular among almost all segments of Israel's population. The withdrawal went relatively smoothly, although, since it was done unilaterally, PA president Mahmoud Abbas could not claim political credit for it. Instead, the Palestinian Islamist group Hamas capitalized on the withdrawal as evidence that its policy of armed resistance was paying off.

Fragmentation and War: 2006–2009

Palestinian frustration with the lack of any real progress in ending the occupation and with PA corruption and inefficiencies led directly to the success of Hamas in the 2006 parliamentary elections. Hamas won 44 percent of the national vote (to 41 percent for Fatah) but was able to parlay that plurality, because of an unusual electoral law, into a commanding majority in the Palestinian Legislative Council. Hamas's victory led to a halt in negotiations to end Israel's occupation. Israel froze relations with the PA as it concerned Hamas (Fatah's Mahmoud Abbas remained president). The United States and Europe also sought to isolate the new Hamas government.

Fatah did not take lightly the end of years of one-party rule and all the benefits and privileges that went along with its dominion over Palestinian society. Fatah conspired to take back what it viewed as its rightful role, instigating significant social turmoil as a result. Combined with the general breakdown of Palestinian institutions of law and order during the second Intifada, lawlessness and factional violence were widespread during 2006 and early 2007. By June 2007, the Hamas government feared that Fatah was planning a coup to take back power. Hamas launched a preemptive putsch in its heartland, the Gaza Strip, routing Fatah in four days of heavy fighting and taking full control over the Gaza Strip. Fatah responded by dismissing the Hamas government and appointing a new government. Palestine was now effectively divided between a Hamas-controlled Gaza Strip and a Fatah-controlled West Bank.

Hamas's seizure of the Gaza Strip immediately led to an Israeli siege, with substantial international support. This wrecked an already fragile economy. General scarcity made those with some resources, such as Hamas, even more important to the population. Hamas's putsch in Gaza also sparked cross-border violence between Israel and Gaza. A July 2008 cease-fire agreement between Israel and Hamas brought four months of relative quiet but no end to the economic strangulation of Gaza, as had been agreed in the cease-fire.

The cease-fire ended on the night of the US presidential election, November 4, 2008. Israel raided Gaza in order to destroy suspected tunnels under the border with Egypt, killing a number of Hamas militants in the process. A cycle of escalating violence ensued, which included Hamas rocket fire into Israel. Matters came to a head on December 27, 2008, when Israel began an aerial bombardment of Gaza, followed on January 3, 2009, by a ground offensive. While far more Palestinians were killed—about 1,400 to 13 Israelis—the nature of warfare has so changed in the modern era that Israel's unquestioned military supremacy cannot be effectively utilized against what are essentially civilian militia ensconced in a general population.

Even after the Gaza war ended, Operation Cast Lead in Israel's parlance, the siege of Gaza remained in place throughout 2009. Palestinian fragmentation and weakness were apparent, as was Israel's inability to determine outcomes in Gaza effectively. The election of a hard-line government in Israel in 2009 further dimmed the prospects for an end to the occupation anytime soon.

Political Environment

The West Bank (including East Jerusalem) and the Gaza Strip constitute 23 percent of historic Palestine and are separated by Israel. Gaza is a small, densely populated area along the Mediterranean Sea largely inhabited by refugees from the 1948 war and their families. Poverty rates are very high and have been exacerbated by frequent closures of the border with Israel, preventing Palestinian laborers from working as day laborers in Israel. Unemployment is extensive and endemic. Saltwater intrusion into Gaza's aquifer has polluted freshwater supplies, a problem that increasingly threatens public health. Gaza's only river, which flows from the Hebron hills in the West Bank out to the Mediterranean through Wadi Gaza, is seasonal only and badly polluted. Beginning in 2000 with the outbreak of the second Intifada, malnutrition in Gaza's children increased sharply. In terms of human misery, the Gaza Strip is one of the most desperate places on earth.

By contrast, the West Bank is larger and less densely populated, with somewhat better health and employment prospects for its residents. The west-facing hills receive significant winter rains that promote agriculture and replenish the western aquifer, a key source of freshwater for both Israel and the Palestinians. A hilly north-south spine separates the relatively lush and populated areas in the western half of the West Bank from the much more arid and sparsely populated eastern half. These hills drop off into the hot and humid Jordan Valley. While the valley is below sea level, it is served by the Jordan River and thus generates some agricultural production.

Even in this small territory with fewer than 4 million Palestinians, there are a number of important social and demographic divisions that characterize modern

Palestinian society. At the top are the remnants of Palestine's old notable social class, consisting of some of the prominent families. Their wealth and property holdings today are a fraction of what they were a century ago. Palestine's merchant class runs the gamut from small store owners to wealthier businessmen. During the rule of the PA, individuals with important political ties to power often were rewarded with lucrative state contracts or monopolies that generated significant wealth in a short time. Such corruption and "leapfrogging" over more established businessmen generated significant resentment in the higher merchant community.

The nonlanded, professional middle class rose to political prominence in the 1980s. Usually from modest origins, members of this socioeconomic class used university education as their stepping-stone to relative success. While Israeli confiscation policies did the most to undermine the notable elite in Palestine, the professional middle class likewise had no love lost for what it collectively viewed as a regressive force in Palestinian society. In many cases, members of declining notable families dropped out and joined the professional middle class.

These old and new elite classes in Palestine sit atop large blue-collar and agricultural working classes. Until recent decades, the peasantry had always constituted the largest class in Palestine. Today, peasants and poor farmers remain, but their number is dwindling. Most Palestinian peasants became wage laborers following the 1967 war. Throughout the 1970s and 1980s, Israeli construction, service, and agricultural sectors became dependent on Palestinian wage laborers, who themselves preferred to leave their small farms in order to get better wages in Israel. Before Israel's closure policy began in 1993, 40 percent of the Palestinian labor force worked in Israel, almost all as wage laborers. As Israel gradually closed its labor market to Palestinians, these workers rarely returned to agriculture. Many became unemployed.

Another important social cleavage is between refugees and nonrefugees. Generally, refugees have lower social status than nonrefugees. A similar cleavage exists between the West Bank and Gazan populations. Given its poverty and abundance of refugees, the Gaza Strip tends to be seen as a lesser place by those in the West Bank. When the Palestinian Authority was first established in Gaza and then spread in 1995 to most West Bank cities, some West Bankers spoke openly of the *ihtilal ghazawi* ("the Gazan occupation"). While that regional resentment was a mostly transitory phenomenon, there is no question that the physical separation of the two geographic parts of Palestine, and Israel's reluctance to allow Palestinians to travel between the West Bank and Gaza, will keep these two islands moving on different social trajectories.

A demographic cleavage of diminishing importance is that between Muslim and Christian Palestinians. Historically, Christians made up about 10 percent of the total Palestinian population. However, given their privileged relations with European colonizers, Arab Christians have had much higher rates of emigration than their Muslim brethren. For example, while a small minority throughout the Arab world, Arab Christians make up about half of all Arabs who have immigrated to the United States. By 2010, Christians made up less than 2 percent of the Palestinian population in Palestine.

Of significant political importance is the cleavage between "insiders" and "outsiders." The signing of the Oslo Accords in 1993 opened the door for some 100,000 Palestinians associated with Yasir Arafat's Fatah movement to move to the West Bank and Gaza. While most were rank-and-file members of police and security forces and their families, they also included the political elite that came to dominate Palestinian politics after Oslo. They were sometimes called "Tunisians" by Palestinians, since so many came from the old PLO headquarters in Tunisia. The efforts of this outside elite to consolidate power "inside" were central to defining Palestinian politics after Oslo. The Oslo elite tangled in complex ways with the homegrown political activists, or new elite, that had developed in the 1970s and 1980s. Some refer to this struggle as being between the "old guard" and the "young guard."

Palestinian social demography is a complex web of relations and divisions. A myriad of other types of social cleavages are not discussed here, including, for example, relations between urban and rural Palestinians and between tribalized and nontribalized Palestinians. But the dominant factor by far in the Palestinian political and economic environment is Israel. More than any other power or factor, Israel controls the facts on the ground in the West Bank and Gaza. Israel decides if the borders are opened or closed, whether goods and services can move between towns or be exported or imported, whether Palestinians can come or go or even travel internally, whether settlements get built and more land gets confiscated. In short, since 1967, there is simply no important sector of Palestinian life that has not been directly impacted by Israel. The post-1993 Oslo period only altered that reality slightly by granting limited autonomy to the Palestinians. Israel and the decisions it makes about Palestinians will remain the dominant feature of Palestine's political environment for decades to come.

POLITICAL STRUCTURES AND DYNAMICS
UNDER THE PALESTINIAN AUTHORITY: 1993–2006

On paper, the Palestinian Authority was constructed as a democratic polity. Its dominant institution was to be its parliament, known as the Palestinian Legislative Council. The executive branch of the PA under the *ra'is* ("president") was designed to be of secondary importance. An independent judiciary, harkening back to the days of British rule, was to play an important role in asserting the rule of law in Palestine.

Palestine also had one of the most active civil societies in the Middle East. In the absence of an actual state and in the face of a hostile occupation, Palestinians mobilized around institutions of civil society, including women's and medical committees, human rights organizations, labor groups, and many others. Political factions seemed poised to transition into political parties, including the major factions of the PLO (Fatah, the Popular Front, the Democratic Front, and the People's Party) and even Hamas.

However, the PA evolved into a soft authoritarian regime marked by both the centralization and personalization of power. Three dynamics in particular contributed to PA authoritarianism: elite conflict, Palestine's political economy, and the imbalance of power between Palestine and Israel. PA authoritarianism and corruption under Fatah rule provided an opening for Hamas to gain popular support.

Elite Conflict

The Oslo Elites. Post-Oslo Palestine contained two distinct political elites. The "Oslo elite" (sometimes referred to as the old guard or the Tunisians) consisted primarily of top PLO officials and their networks of supporters who returned to the West Bank and Gaza Strip from Tunisia with the establishment of the PA in 1994. The Oslo elite was represented most dramatically by Yasir Arafat but also included numerous cabinet ministers, high ministry officials, most of the top leaders of the security and police forces, and a number of leading businessmen. Some of the most recognizable names of the Oslo elite are Mahmoud Abbas (Abu Mazen), Ahmad Qurei' (Abu Ala), and Nabil Sha'th.

The New Elite. The second political elite consisted primarily of "native-born" Palestinians in the West Bank and Gaza who were educated in Palestinian universities and Israeli prisons. These cadres were better educated and more numerous but less wealthy than their Oslo counterparts. This group of political activists has variously been called the "new elite," the "Intifada elite," and the "young guard." The new elite and its heirs led both the first Intifada (1987–1993) and the current uprising (September 2000–present). Activist Marwan Barghouti, imprisoned by Israel for his work with the al-Aqsa Martyrs Brigade, is perhaps the most prominent of the new elite, which also includes the leaders of Hamas.

Both sets of political leaders have strong national and familial ties with each other; however, they are sociologically and philosophically quite distinct and their visions of the proper political "rules of the game" differ significantly. These are not differences in *policies* so much as in how *politics* gets organized and practiced. In a simple sense, the Oslo elite represents more traditional politics, and the new elite is more modern in its political sensibilities. These differences stem in part from diverse life experiences, but they also have a tactical political component.

When Arafat and the Oslo elite returned, their primary political task was to consolidate their power, and to do that they needed to undermine the new elite. Only the new elite had the proven mobilization skills to thwart the Oslo project from within Palestinian society if it so chose.

The PA—an institution primarily of the Oslo elite, or old guard—had some success in co-opting some members of the new elite and intimidating others. The institutional home of the new elite consisted primarily of the organizations of Palestinian civil society. Indeed, the formation of civil society in modern Palestine was largely a result of the efforts of the new elite in the post-1979 period. The domination of civil society organizations by the new elite is the underlying reason for the persistent PA attacks on its own civil society since 1994.

In order to weaken the new elite, the PA engaged in a *politics of antithesis*—the implementation of rules of politics at odds with the strengths of the new elite. Because the new elite based its politics in institutions, the PA emphasized personalism. The cult of personality that was developed around Arafat was the most obvious, but not the only, form of this personalism. In general, one's official office said much less about actual power than one's personal ties to powerful people. Because the new elite practiced diffused, grassroots authority (a practical necessity under occupation), the PA centralized power, deliberately disempowering the grassroots. Because the new elite was more democratic in its political sensibilities, the PA adopted more authoritarian rules of politics.

The al-Aqsa Intifada, the internal Palestinian reform movement, and, most especially, Arafat's death in November 2004 called into question how long the Oslo elite would be the dominant power in Palestine. The Oslo elite bet its political future in Palestine on the success of the Oslo peace process. The failure of that process in Palestinian eyes discredited this elite, opening the door for its rivals to reassume power within Palestinian society. Hamas's electoral victory in the 2006 parliamentary elections was further evidence of the weakening of the Oslo elite in the post-Arafat period.

The tension between these two elite groups is best seen as an *evolving* dynamic. From the establishment of the PA until the al-Aqsa Intifada and concomitant reform movement, the cleavage between these two elites was sharp and formed the decisive component of internal Palestinian politics. The Oslo elite, however, was predominant. The reform movement born of the al-Aqsa Intifada heralded a second stage in the evolution of this elite conflict. The reemergence of the new elite in this period was demonstrated in part by the new prominence of reformers in Palestinian government and the new political alliances that sprang out of the changed circumstances. The sharp and decisive distinction between the Oslo and new elites blurred as the latter reemerged on the political scene, most dramatically with the Hamas victory in 2006. Given the demographic weight of the new elite and the population it represents, the third stage in this evolving dynamic will likely see the consolidation of power by the new elite and the absorption of the remnants of the Oslo elite.

As the new elite consolidates power, cleavages within it will likely emerge. The most obvious cleavage is the ideological one between Islamists and nationalists, Hamas and Fatah. The cadres who lead these movements are sociologically identical in terms of their class origins and educational backgrounds, but they are ideologically divided. That divide evolved into a low-level but fierce civil war between Hamas and Fatah. Conflict between these two elements was not inevitable. Fatah and Hamas cadres went to school together, spent time in Israeli prisons together, and cooperated tactically for many years. This is not to say that relations have always been warm; they clearly have not. But it is useful to remember that Fatah itself emerged from the Muslim Brotherhood organization in Gaza in the 1950s, long before Hamas and Fatah worked together during the al-Aqsa Intifada. They have regularly shared cultural and ideological frames and symbols, with Hamas openly promoting Palestinian nationalism and Fatah embracing Islamic symbols. The emergence of Fatah's al-Aqsa Martyrs Brigade (*Kita'ib Shuhada' al-Aqsa*) is a case in point. Its very name combines words that have nationalist and Islamic connotations.

Political Economy

A second contributing factor to PA authoritarianism and corruption was the basic political economy established since Oslo—one quite similar to that of the oil-rich states of the Persian Gulf.

The Palestinian Authority can be considered a distributive state because a large majority of its budgetary revenues come from direct payments to the PA from international sources. The most important payment has been the transfer by Israel to the PA of various taxes collected by Israel on Palestinian goods, services, and labor. But these transfers proved unstable, as Israel would periodically cut them off, such as during the second Intifada or when Hamas won the 2006 elections. Prior to the uprising, Israeli payments to the PA amounted to about $600 million of the PA's $850 million typical annual budget revenues, or about 70 percent. In terms of their political impact, such direct payments created the same dynamic as oil rents: They helped create and sustain a top-heavy, centralized, and authoritarian political structure. In addition, foreign donors contributed a total of about $3 billion in the period from 1994 to 2000. In some cases, these expenditures took the form of direct subsidies to the PA's budget, although more commonly they supported specific projects, which in turn freed up monies for the PA to spend elsewhere. In sum, of the approximately $8 billion spent by the PA directly or on its behalf by foreign donors prior to the al-Aqsa Intifada, about $6.5 billion, or over 80 percent, came in the form of external transfers to the PA.

The taxes that Israel collects for the PA do belong to the legitimate Palestinian government. But the fact that they are collected by another state and simply transferred as a lump sum to the PA treasury has important consequences. That about three-quarters of all government revenues come to the PA as simple transfers has the same type of political impact as in oil-based distributive states. Creating a democracy out of a consolidated distributive political economy is extremely difficult.

Imbalance of Power

A third factor contributing to authoritarianism in the PA was the vast imbalance of power between Israel and the Palestinians. The negotiating process accurately reflected the imbalance of power to Israel's advantage, including Oslo's focus on interim measures only, the absence of powerful policy levers for keeping Israeli withdrawal from Palestinian territory on schedule (Palestinians fully controlled only about 18 percent of the West Bank at its apex), the doubling of the number of Jewish settlers in the West Bank during the peace negotiations of the 1990s, and Israeli veto power on key issues such as Jerusalem and refugees, which ultimately scuttled negotiations.

As the weaker party, the PA was a "term taker"—it could accept or reject Israeli offers but had little leverage to compel different terms from Israel. Within the Palestinian body politic, this often meant having little choice but accepting—de facto if not de jure—terms and conditions deeply unpopular within Palestinian society. Massive settlement expansion and endemic Israeli "closures" of Palestinian areas while negotiations were ongoing were the most important exemplars of PA impotence vis-à-vis Israel in the eyes of most Palestinians.

The imbalance of power put the PA in a dilemma: In order to continue the peace process, it was forced to accept highly unpopular terms and realities. In turn, the PA had to crack down on the growing public dissent that resulted. Even if Arafat and the PA had been inclined to embrace democracy, the fact that elections would have empowered rejectionist elements from the Islamist Hamas within the democratic mainstream of Haydar 'Abd Al Shafi deterred the Oslo elite from conducting them. For this reason no municipal elections were held from the establishment of the PA in 1994 until 2005, and no parliamentary elections were held between 1996 and 2006.

HAMAS RULE IN GAZA

Fatah's clumsy authoritarian rule and corruption ultimately affected its political situation in the 2006 elections. While Hamas had boycotted the 1996 parliamentary elections, it ran a full slate of candidates in the January 2006 elections. Hamas ran a disciplined election, never having more candidates than available seats. Fatah-oriented candidates, however, ran in far greater numbers, thereby splitting their votes. As a result, Hamas was able to parlay a small 44 to 41 percent popular vote margin into a substantial parliamentary majority—74 seats out of 132. Hamas's Ismail Haniya became the new PA prime minister.

Hamas's victory was not only a reaction to Fatah's ineffective rule but also a result of Hamas's policy of continuing armed resistance to Israel's occupation. Fatah had chosen to follow predominately a political process to end the occupation and create a Palestinian state, and that was seen to have failed. Hamas promised the path of armed resistance, which many Palestinians felt was the only viable means to end the occupation.

Hamas's electoral victory sent shock waves through much of the world. Israel, the United States, and Europe all consequently tried to isolate Hamas, refusing to work with a group they all considered to be a terrorist organization. While some voices in Fatah encouraged dialogue with Hamas, the bulk of Fatah's leaders supported isolating Hamas as well. Fatah was following the path of other once-dominant parties that have suddenly lost the benefits, privileges, and patronage associated with one-party rule. Fatah decided to try to win back power by any means necessary.

Israel ceased transferring taxes and duties owed to the PA, now that Hamas controlled the purse strings, and subsequently imprisoned without charge dozens of Hamas parliamentarians, cabinet ministers, and high officials. Resentment between Hamas and Fatah led to street clashes in the Palestinian territory, especially in Gaza, throughout 2006 and early 2007.

Matters came to a head in June 2007 following the publication of leaked documents that suggested an impending coup attempt by Fatah, backed by the United States. Hamas struck first, routing Fatah forces in Gaza and consolidating its rule. PA president Mahmoud Abbas then dismissed the Hamas government under questionable legal rules and installed a new government under Prime Minister Salam Fayyad. Fayyad's government had effective control over only parts of the West Bank and none in Gaza. The West Bank and Gaza were now formally split, with Fatah ruling the former and Hamas the latter.

Hamas rule in Gaza had mixed results. On the positive side, Hamas was given credit for bringing the era of near anarchy to a close and establishing law and order. As part of this effort, Hamas took on clan militia in Gaza that were operating outside the law, often protecting lucrative black market enterprises, including large-scale tunnel operations linking Gaza to Egypt.

On the negative side, Hamas was largely intolerant of challenges to its rule and ideology, continuing its proxy war with Fatah. The international isolation of Gaza under Hamas rule, including Israel's tight siege, brought even more misery to Gaza, although the Palestinian population largely blamed others, not Hamas, for this condition. The conflict between Hamas and Israel contributed to the war beginning in December 2008.

FOREIGN POLICY

While not a sovereign state, the Palestinian Authority had an active foreign policy during the Oslo period of limited autonomy. Formally, the PA was merely the interim government, and Palestinian foreign policy was conducted by the PLO. In actual fact, the two organizations merged to the point of being indistinguishable.

The PA had different target audiences for its foreign policy. The United States was a key partner, as only the United States had the leverage over Israel essential to achieve Palestinian goals. The European Union was also an important foreign policy partner because it contributed the most aid to the PA and because European powers, especially Britain, could (it was thought) influence Washington on key issues. The Arab states constituted a third target audience because they could help deliver regional support and legitimacy to the Oslo process and Palestinian goals. Finally, there was Israel, the foreign power that held control over all Palestinian lands and must be convinced to relinquish that control. While some Palestinian leaders recognized that it was critical to try to win over domestic Israeli opinion, the PA never was adept at it. Whatever gains and inroads the Palestinians had made were lost entirely with the second Intifada.

The PA had three primary foreign policy goals. It needed financial resources. The PA had as a core function a patronage role of distributing jobs and resources to key supporters and constituencies. It became the largest single employer (by far) in the occupied territories, employing about 160,000 Palestinians and thus supporting about 20 percent of all Palestinian families in the West Bank and Gaza. Organizational survival was essential, and foreign aid was critical to this. The PA was generally successful in meeting this objective; indeed, it typically received the second-most foreign aid per capita of any polity in the world, following only Israel.

A second foreign policy objective was to ensure that the interim period generated the maximum amount of Palestinian sovereignty over the occupied territories. The PA needed a successful interim period in order to sell the Oslo peace process to a skeptical national constituency and to set the stage for final-status negotiations. On this foreign policy objective, the PA was less successful. At its peak, the PA had full control over less than 20 percent of the West Bank; Israel maintained full control over 60 percent of the West Bank, with the remainder being jointly administered. The PA had no control over East Jerusalem at any point. As for Gaza, the PA controlled about two-thirds of the Gaza Strip until 2005, when Israel unilaterally withdrew from all of Gaza. Even after the withdrawal, however, Israel still fully controlled the land and sea borders of Gaza and the airspace above it. The only exception was Gaza's land border with Egypt, where Israel maintained only partial control.

The number of Jewish settlers in the West Bank doubled during the Oslo peace process, further pointing out the PA's failure to secure Palestinian lands. Its failure to gain credible control over the occupied territories during the interim period undermined its legitimacy in the eyes of most Palestinians. The consequences of this failure included the al-Aqsa Intifada and the coming to power of the rejectionist Hamas.

A third foreign policy objective for the PA was to put together enough international support to achieve a good final-status agreement. Winning over the United States when it came to key Palestinian positions was considered central to the overall strategy of securing a legitimate Palestinian state. However, the US administration under Bill Clinton rejected the "right of return" for Palestinian refugees, insisted on significant Israeli sovereignty in East Jerusalem, never pushed Israel to cease its colonization of the West Bank, and advocated Israeli annexation of parts of the West Bank. The US administration of George W. Bush further distanced itself from Palestinian interests by allowing Israeli prime minister Ariel Sharon to implement a series of unilateral measures in the occupied territories that were designed, it was widely believed, to prevent the emergence of a viable Palestinian state. None of the other international support the PA generated could counterbalance the strong US support of Israel.

FUTURE PROSPECTS

The future is bleak for the Palestinians, in large measure because they do not control their own fate. Palestinians in the West Bank and Gaza are essentially powerless in a world of states, and their future will be decided far more by others than by themselves. The fragmentation of Palestine between Hamas rule in Gaza and Fatah rule in the West Bank complicates Palestinian prospects. Palestinians cannot speak with a unified voice in such a situation, which only weakens their ability to affect outcomes and promote their right to self-determination effectively.

BIBLIOGRAPHY

The Palestine problem has been studied exhaustively from different political and analytical perspectives. The best broad historical narratives that give excellent overviews of Palestinian history and the conflict with Israel include Charles D. Smith, *Palestine and the Arab-Israeli Conflict*, 5th ed. (New York: Palgrave MacMillan Press, 2004); Baruch Kimmerling and Joel S. Migdal, *The Palestinian People: A History* (Cambridge, MA: Harvard University Press, 2003); James Gelvin, *The Israel-Palestine Conflict: One Hundred Years of War* (New York: Cambridge University Press, 2005); Benny Morris, *Righteous Victims: A History of the Zionist-Arab Conflict, 1881–1999* (New York: Alfred A. Knopf, 1999); Ilan Pappe, *A History of Modern Palestine: One Land, Two Peoples* (New York: Cambridge University Press, 2004); Mark Tessler, *A History of the Israeli-Palestinian Conflict* (Bloomington: Indiana University Press, 1994); Samih K. Farsoun and Naseer Aruri, *Palestine and the Palestinians*, 2nd ed. (Boulder, CO: Westview, 2007); and Avi Shlaim, *The Iron Wall: Israel and the Arab World* (New York: Norton, 2000). Philip Mattar's *Encyclopedia of the Palestinians* (New York: Facts on File, 2000) is an indispensable resource.

Among the few studies of pre-twentieth-century Palestine, Beshara Doumani's *Rediscovering Palestine: Merchants and Peasants in Jabal Nablus, 1700–1900* (Berkeley: University of California Press, 1995) is outstanding for its insight into the political economy of an important town. Also excellent is Alexander Scholch, *Palestine in Transformation, 1856–1882: Studies in Social, Economic and Political Development* (Washington, DC: Institute for Palestine Studies, 1993). Rashid Khalidi examines the evolution of Palestinian nationalism before and after World War I in *Palestinian Identity: The Construction of Modern National Consciousness* (New York: Columbia University Press, 1997), as does Muhammad Muslih in *The Origins of Palestinian Nationalism* (New York: Columbia University Press, 1988).

For overviews of the British Mandate period, the reader can study Tom Segev, *One Palestine, Complete: Jews and Arabs Under the British Mandate* (New York: Henry Holt, 2000); J. C. Hurewitz, *Struggle for Palestine* (New York: Norton, 1950); Ann Lesch, *Arab Politics in Palestine, 1917–1939* (Ithaca, NY: Cornell University Press, 1979); Yehoshua Porath, *The Emergence of the Palestinian-Arab National Movement, 1918–1929* (London: Frank Cass, 1974); and *The Palestinian Arab National Movement, 1929–1939* (London: Frank Cass, 1977). Walid Khalidi, ed., *Before Their Diaspora: A Photographic History of the Palestinians, 1876–1948* (Washington, DC: Institute for Palestine Studies, 1984), offers visual evidence of family life, culture, and customs in Palestine.

Gershon Shafir emphasizes the centrality of land to the conflict in *Land, Labor and the Origins of the Israeli-Palestinian Conflict, 1882–1914* (New York: Cambridge University Press, 1989). Walid Khalidi, ed., *All That Remains: The Palestinian Villages Occupied and Depopulated by Israel in 1948* (Washington, DC: Institute for Palestine Studies, 1992), lists more than four hundred villages destroyed during and after the 1948–1949 war.

Our knowledge and understanding of the events surrounding the 1948 war have been revolutionized by the work primarily of Israeli scholars who gained access to critical documents once Israel and Britain's thirty-year classification rule expired. Among many excellent books that shed light on 1948 are Benny Morris, *The Birth of the Palestinian Refugee Problem Revisited* (New York: Cambridge, 2004) and *1948 and After* (New York: Oxford Clarendon, 1990); Avi Shlaim, *Collusion Across the Jordan: King Abdullah, the Zionist Movement, and the Partition of Palestine* (New York: Columbia, 1988); Ilan Pappe, *The Making of the Arab-Israeli Conflict, 1947–1951* (New York: I. B. Tauris, 1992); Zeev Sternhell, *The Founding Myths of Israel* (Princeton, NJ: Princeton University Press, 1998); and Eugene L. Rogan and Avi Shlaim, *The War for Palestine: Rewriting the History of 1948* (New York: Cambridge, 2001). For an excellent depiction of the city of Jerusalem during the 1948 war, see Salim Tamari, ed., *Jerusalem, 1948: The Arab Neighbourhoods and Their Fate in the War* (Jerusalem: The Institute of Jerusalem Studies and Badil Resource Center, 1999).

The Jordanian dimension of the Palestine problem is analyzed in Shaul Mishal, *West Bank/East Bank: The Palestinians in Jordan, 1949–1957* (New Haven, CT: Yale University Press, 1978), as well as in the book by Avi Shlaim noted above, *Collusion Across the Jordan*. Highly recommended is Adnan Abu Odeh, *Jordanians, Palestinians and the Hashemite Kingdom in the Middle East Peace Process* (Washington, DC: US Institute of Peace, 1999).

The status of Palestinian citizens of Israel has been examined by Sammy Smooha in his two-volume *Arabs and Jews in Israel* (Boulder, CO: Westview, 1989, 1992) and by Ian Lustick in *Arabs in the Jewish State* (Austin: University of Texas Press, 1980). Highly recommended is David Grossman, *Sleeping on a Wire: Conversations with Palestinians in Israel* (New York: Farrar, Straus and Giroux, 1993, reissued in 2003 by Picador).

Books on the conditions and political struggles in the occupied territories prior to the first Intifada include George Emile Bisharat, *Palestinian Lawyers and Israeli Rule: Law and Disorder in the West Bank* (Austin: University of Texas Press, 1989); Rita Giacaman, *Life and Health in Three Palestinian Villages* (London: Ithaca Press, 1988); and Joost R. Hiltermann's *Behind the Intifada* (Princeton, NJ: Princeton University Press, 1991). Israeli author David Grossman wrote an insightful account of Palestinian life under occupation in the 1980s in *The Yellow Wind* (New York: Farrar, Straus and Giroux, 1988, reissued in 2002 by Picador). A very personal account of growing up under occupation is by the Palestinian lawyer Raja Shehadeh, *Strangers in the House: Coming of Age in Occupied Palestine* (New York: Penguin, 2003).

Moshe Ma'oz, in *Palestinian Leadership on the West Bank: The Changing Role of the Mayors Under Jordan and Israel* (London: Frank Cass, 1984), and Emile Sahliyyeh, in *In Search of Leadership: West Bank Politics Since 1967* (Washington, DC: Brookings Institution, 1988), offer insights into local politics. Sara Roy, *The Gaza Strip: The Political Economy of De-development* (Washington, DC: The Institute for Palestine

Studies, 1995), provides a comprehensive analysis of Israeli policies that stifled Gaza's economy. Details on legal, socioeconomic, and political conditions are contained in Naseer H. Aruri, ed., *Occupation: Israel over Palestine*, 2nd ed. (Belmont, MA: Arab American University Graduates, 1989). The complexities of life under Israeli occupation are depicted by novelist Sahar Khalifeh in *Wild Thorns* (New York: Olive Branch Press, 1989). Raja Shehadeh writes a penetrating critique of how law was used as a tool of occupation, not justice, in *Occupier's Law* (Washington, DC: Institute for Palestine Studies, 1988).

The Intifada of 1987 to 1993 spawned many books, including my own *Building a Palestinian State: The Incomplete Revolution* (Bloomington: Indiana University Press, 1997). While my book covers both the uprising and its political aftermath, other books just focus on the Intifada itself, including Zachary Lockman and Joel Beinin, eds., *Intifada* (Boston: South End Press, 1989); Jamal R. Nassar and Roger Heacock, eds., *Intifada* (New York: Praeger, 1990); Zeev Schiff and Ehud Ya'ari, *Intifada* (New York: Simon and Schuster, 1990); and F. Robert Hunter, *The Palestinian Uprising* (Berkeley: University of California Press, 1993). Helen Winternitz illustrates the impact of the uprising on a West Bank village in *A Season of Stones: Living in a Palestinian Village* (New York: Atlantic Monthly Press, 1991).

Yezid Sayigh has written the most detailed history of the PLO, titled *Armed Struggle and the Search for State* (Oxford: Clarendon Press, 1997). Shorter accounts of the Palestinian movement before 1982 can be found in Helena Cobban, *The Palestinian Liberation Organization* (New York: Cambridge University Press, 1984); Alain Gresh, *The PLO: The Struggle Within* (London: Zed, 1985); and William Quandt et al., *The Politics of Palestinian Nationalism* (Berkeley: University of California Press, 1973). Salah Khalaf (Abu Iyad), in *My Home, My Land* (New York: Times Books, 1981), describes his key role in the establishment and growth of the PLO. Rashid Khalidi details the PLO's withdrawal from Beirut in *Under Siege: PLO Decisionmaking during the 1982 War* (New York: Columbia University Press, 1986).

Laurie Brand considers the circumstances facing Palestinians in exile in *Palestinians in the Arab World: In Search of State* (New York: Columbia University Press, 1988). Rosemary Sayigh, *Palestinians: From Peasants to Revolutionaries* (London: Zed, 1979), focuses on the political awakening of Palestinian refugees in Lebanon. Salma K. Jayyusi's comprehensive *Anthology of Modern Palestinian Literature* (New York: Columbia University Press, 1992) captures the spirit of Palestinians living in exile and under Israeli rule.

The rise to prominence of Hamas has generated several recent works detailing the Islamist movement in Palestine, including Ziad Abu-Amr, *Islamic Fundamentalism in the West Bank and Gaza* (Bloomington: Indiana University Press, 1994); Khaled Hroub, *Hamas: Political Thought and Practice* (Washington DC: Institute for

Palestine Studies, 2000); Shaul Mishal and Avraham Sela, *The Palestinian Hamas: Vision, Violence and Coexistence* (New York: Columbia University Press, 2000); and Glenn E. Robinson, "Hamas as Social Movement," in *Islamic Activism*, ed. Quintan Wiktorowicz, 112–139 (Bloomington: Indiana University Press, 2003).

Prior to the signing of the Oslo Accords in 1993, a number of authors outlined their visions of a two-state solution to the conflict, including Mark A. Heller, *A Palestinian State* (Cambridge, MA: Harvard University Press, 1983); Mark A. Heller and Sari Nusseibeh, *No Trumpets, No Drums: A Two-State Settlement of the Israeli-Palestinian Conflict* (New York: Hill and Wang, 1991); Jerome M. Segal, *Creating a Palestinian State: A Strategy of Peace* (Chicago: Lawrence Hill, 1989); and Ann Lesch, *Transition to Palestinian Self-Government: Practical Steps Toward Israeli-Palestinian Peace* (Cambridge, MA: American Academy of Arts and Sciences, 1992). In 2005, the RAND Corporation prepared a two-volume set on the requirements for creating a successful Palestinian state: Steven N. Simon, C. Ross Anthony, Glenn E. Robinson, David C. Gompert, Jerrold D. Green, Robert E. Hunter, C. Richard Neu, and Kenneth I. Shine, *Building a Successful Palestinian State* (Santa Monica, CA: RAND, 2005), and Doug Suisman, Steven N. Simon, Glenn E. Robinson, C. Ross Anthony, and Michael Schoenbaum, *The Arc: A Formal Structure for a Palestinian State* (Santa Monica, CA: RAND, 2005).

Studies of internal Palestinian politics and problems during the Oslo process include Joel Beinin and Rebecca L. Stein, eds., *The Struggle for Sovereignty: Palestine and Israel, 1993–2005* (Palo Alto, CA: Stanford University Press, 2006), and Amira Hess, *Drinking the Sea at Gaza* (New York: Owl Books, 2000). Edward W. Said pens a scathing critique of the underlying principles and implementation of the Oslo Accords in *The End of the Peace Process: Oslo and After* (New York: Pantheon, 2000).

Scholars are still contemplating the long-term impact of the al-Aqsa Intifada (2000–2005), but early accounts of the impact on Palestinians include Raja Shehadeh, *When the Birds Stopped Singing: Life in Ramallah Under Siege* (South Royalton, VT: Steerforth, 2003); Roane Carey, *The New Intifada* (New York: Verso, 2001); and Baruch Kimmerling, *Politicide* (New York: Verso, 2006).

Key Websites in English on Palestine

Foundation for Middle East Peace: www.fmep.org

United Nations Relief and Works Agency: www.un.org/unrwa

PLO Negotiations Affairs Department: www.nad-plo.org

Badil Resource Center: www.badil.org

Palestinian Authority: www.palestine-net.com

Palestine Central Bureau of Statistics: www.pcbs.gov.ps

Palestinian Democracy Initiative: www.miftah.org

Birzeit University: www.birzeit.edu

Palestinian Non Governmental Organizations: www.pngo.net

Jerusalem Media and Communications Center: www.jmcc.org

Palestinian Center for Policy and Survey Research: www.pcpsr.org

Online daily newspapers in English that cover Palestinian issues include:

Daily Star (Beirut): www.dailystar.com.lb

Jordan Times (Amman): www.jordantimes.com

Ha'aretz (Tel Aviv): www.haaretz.com

13

Arab Republic of Egypt

Marius Deeb

Historical Background

Throughout recorded history, the civilization of the Nile Valley flourished due to a combination of plentiful water, good soil, and climatic conditions, which contributed to a long growing season. The Nile River also provided swift, efficient, and cheap transportation and became the focal point of both ancient and modern civilizations. Starting from 3000 BCE, a series of great kingdoms ruled by pharaohs developed in the valley and made important and long-lasting contributions to civilization in the fields of science, architecture, arts, politics, and economics. From among the seven wonders of the ancient world, only the Pyramids at Giza have survived. In 332 BCE, when Alexander the Great conquered Egypt, he founded the city of Alexandria as its new capital. Under the Ptolemies, Alexandria became the greatest city in antiquity. For over eight centuries, Alexandria, with its famous library, became the center of the sciences and the arts, attracting the best minds during the Ptolemaic, Roman, and Byzantine periods. Egypt had become Christian by the end of the sixth century, and it was in Egypt that Christian monastic orders first appeared.

When the Arab Muslims conquered Egypt in 639, the country began to decline gradually, but the Christian Copts, whose Demotic language combined the old hieroglyphic language of the ancient Egyptians and the Greek language, remained the majority of the population for at least seven more centuries. Arab Muslim political domination led to a gradual Arabization and Islamization as a consequence of discrimination rooted in the second-class status of Copts as *Dhimmis* (recognized monotheists under Islam) or of outright persecution. Under the Mamluks (1252–1517), Egypt enjoyed some prosperity, but it declined again under the Ottomans (1517–1805).

The landing of Napoleon in Egypt in 1798 changed the history of the country. The scientists and scholars who accompanied Napoleon wrote the monumental study *Description de l'Egypte*, and they uncovered the Rosetta stone, which led to

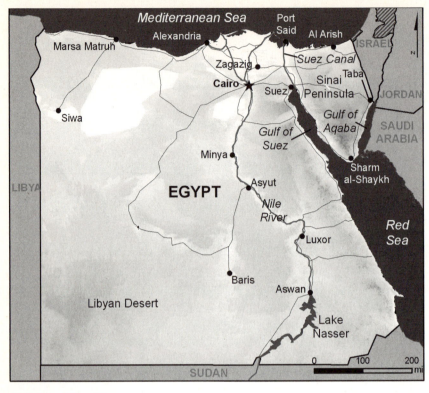

Arab Republic of Egypt

the decipherment of the hieroglyphic language. Napoleon's brief conquest of Egypt led in turn to the rise of Muhammad Ali (1805–1849), known as the founder of modern Egypt.

Muhammad Ali was an Albanian who came to Egypt from Kavala (Greece) as an army commander in charge of a unit of the Ottoman army sent to deal with Napoleon. In 1805 the Ottoman sultan appointed him governor of Egypt with the title of pasha. Muhammad Ali brought significant change to the country and, to a large degree, established its independence from the Ottoman sultan. Under Muhammad Ali, Egypt began to develop the elements of a modern state and a more European cultural orientation. He launched a series of ambitious domestic projects designed to improve the economy and general condition of the state. Agricultural production was improved and reorganized, and a program of industrialization was inaugurated. He forced Egyptian products into the European market and encouraged the production of long-staple cotton. Turks were replaced with Egyptians in the administration. He stressed education and sought to improve its quality. He created a modern national army, organized on European lines, which gained substantial experience in various areas of the Middle East during his reign. He created the base for a modern political system and the conditions for the rise of Egyptian nationalism.

Although European powers had been interested in Egypt for some time, the opening of the Suez Canal to world navigation and commerce in 1869 vastly increased great-power interest in Egypt. England, the greatest sea power of the time, was particularly concerned with the canal because it provided a shorter and more efficient link to much of the British Empire, especially India. Problems associated with the operation of the canal and Egypt's financial mismanagement provided the framework for the British occupation in 1882, although other European powers had also been concerned about the financial situation of Egypt. Foreign creditors, anxious about the funds they had entrusted to Khedive ("Viceroy") Ismail, pressed their respective governments for relief and assistance. As a result, Egyptian finances were controlled by foreign creditors, and Ismail was deposed in 1879. Popular opposition formed against the khedive, his court, and the foreign powers. Khedive Tawfiq, who succeeded Ismail, ruled a country that was heavily taxed and under British and French financial supervision and British political control.

In response to this situation, Col. Ahmed Arabi led a group of Egyptian nationalists who, scorning the weakness of the khedive, protested British and French interference in the sovereignty of Egypt and the lack of indigenous political participation. They sought constitutional reform, liberalization of Egyptian political participation, and an end to foreign interference in the affairs of Egypt. The British and French supported the khedive. In July 1882 British forces landed in Egypt and crushed the Arabi revolt. Although they were originally supposed to leave after the restoration of order, British forces remained in Egypt until June 1956, and real control over the affairs of state resided in British hands for seven decades, thereby giving Britain control over the canal.

World War I added a new dimension to the commercial and strategic importance of the Suez Canal for Britain and the West. In December 1914 Britain proclaimed Egypt a British protectorate, and the title of khedive was changed to sultan.

Opposition among Egyptians to the British intensified during World War I. President Woodrow Wilson's Fourteen Points had engendered some hope. Egyptian nationalists wanted to remove British control and establish indigenous Egyptian rule over the country. In this post–World War I context, a new political organization was formed, al-Wafd al-Misri ("the Egyptian Delegation"), known as the Wafd. Under the leadership of Saad Zaghlul, the Wafd sought independence from the British and self-rule in Egypt. The Wafd hoped to present its position to the great powers at the postwar conferences—especially at the Paris Peace Conference, where the fate of the Ottoman territories was to be determined. British opposition to Egyptian independence prevented the Wafd from achieving its goal.

EGYPT

Capital city	Cairo
Chief of state	President Mohamed Hosni Mubarak
Head of government	Prime Minister Ahmed Mohamed Nazif
Major political parties (*seats in lower house*)	National Democratic Party (311), New Wafd Party (6), National Progressive Unionist Grouping (2), Tomorrow Party (1)
Ethnic groups	Egyptian (99.6%), other (0.4%)
Religious groups	Muslim (90%), Coptic Christian (9%), other Christian (1%)
Export partners	Italy (10.3%), United States (7.7%), Spain (6.7%), Syria (5.1%), Saudi Arabia (5%), Japan (4.9%), Germany (4.9%), France (4%)
Import partners	United States (10.6%), China (10.2%), Italy (7.5%), Germany (7%), Saudi Arabia (5%)

In the aftermath of World War I, a populist revolution engulfed Egypt during March and April 1919. In the face of such pressure, the protectorate was terminated, and in February 1922 the British unilaterally proclaimed Egypt a constitutional monarchy. However, the British formally reserved their freedom of action on four matters: the Sudan, the defense of Egypt against foreign intervention, the security of the canal (which remained the communications link of the British Empire), and the protection of foreign interests and minorities. In March, Sultan Fuad became the king of Egypt.

A constitution was written and promulgated in April 1923. The parliamentary elections of 1923 and 1924 ushered in a liberal democratic system that lasted for almost three decades. During that period there were six free parliamentary elections, in 1923, 1926, 1929, 1936, 1942, and 1950. The Wafd Party, which was a genuine mass political party with support in both the urban centers and the rural areas, won a majority in all these free elections. This was Egypt's liberal era, characterized by the independence of the judiciary; all the basic freedoms of thought, religion, and press; and the right of habeas corpus.

British influence, however, remained paramount. British troops and officials were stationed in Egypt, mostly but not solely concerned with the canal and the security of the imperial communications system. Through them, the British were able to influence political activity and policy decisions. British-Egyptian negotiations continued on a somewhat sporadic basis until 1936. At that time a new Anglo-Egyptian treaty was written that altered, but did not terminate, the British role.

Opposition by the nationalists to the British role in Egypt continued. Negotiations to revise the 1936 treaty, especially those aspects of the agreement relating to the questions of the Sudan and the canal, were unsuccessful. Throughout its existence, the Wafd Party opposed British imperialism and sought Nile unity, with the Sudan as a part of Egypt. Clashes between the British and Egyptian nationalists became increasingly frequent. On October 15, 1951, the government of Egypt, under Prime Minister Mustafa al-Nahhas, unilaterally abrogated the 1936 treaty and proclaimed Farouk king of Egypt and the Sudan.

When mobs, probably instigated by xenophobic parties, attacked foreign establishments in Cairo on January 26, 1952, a day of great violence ensued that came to be known as Black Saturday; it was followed by the ouster, by the king, of democratically elected Prime Minister Mustafa al-Nahhas and the proclamation of martial law.

The Egyptian Revolution of 1952

On July 23, 1952, members of a small clandestine organization within the army, known as the Free Officers Movement, staged a coup d'état and took over power. This group consisted of ninety-four officers whose inner circle numbered about a dozen. Most of them (including Gamal Abd al-Nasser and Anwar Sadat) were at one time or another members of secret cells of the Muslim Brotherhood, which was established in 1928 and became a powerful fundamentalist movement in the 1940s. King Farouk was forced to abdicate and left the country on July 26, 1952.

The Free Officers ruled through what they called the Revolutionary Command Council (RCC). The council was headed by Gen. Muhammad Naguib, who was chosen because he was a popular senior officer although he was not a member of the Free Officers Movement. The new regime declared its opposition to colonialism, imperialism, and monopolies and asserted its support for social justice, a strong military, and a democratic way of life.

Although Farouk was forced into exile, the constitutional monarchy was preserved at first, and a regency council was established to preside in the name of Farouk's infant son, Fuad II. After a period of some uncertainty, the RCC decided, in December 1952, to suspend the constitution of 1923 and the parliamentary form of government. The following January, Gen. Muhammad Naguib announced that all political parties had been banned, that their funds had been confiscated, and that the constitutional government would not operate for a three-year transition period. In February 1953 an interim constitution was proclaimed that provided the terms for the operation of the government during this time. This constitution noted that the people were the source of all authority, but it vested all power in the RCC for the transition period. With the abolition of political parties, the RCC created a new political organization called the Liberation Rally to help mobilize political support for the new regime.

In June 1953 the RCC moved to the next step in the conversion of the political system. The monarchy was abolished. A republic, with Muhammad Naguib as both president and prime minister, was declared. A power struggle within the RCC between the Free Officers Movement's real leader, Col. Gamal Abd al-Nasser, and Gen. Muhammad Naguib went through several stages in which the former emerged as the victor, culminating in the ouster of Naguib on November 14, 1954, and his being placed under house arrest.

The Egyptian revolution of 1952 was launched to deal with a political issue, but almost as crucial were the substantial economic and social problems of Egypt, which were among the earliest problems tackled by the regime. In 1945 it was estimated that 0.5 percent of the landowners owned 36.9 percent of the total land. Already in the late 1940s, there were proposals to levy taxes on large estates in proportion to their size or even to confiscate from large landowners all landed property over fifty *feddans* (approximately fifty acres), but all these proposals were rejected by parliament, which was dominated by large landowners. The large landowners prevented the adoption of reform measures that would diminish their economic and political control. Even before the 1952 revolution, when the price of cotton soared in 1950 and 1951 and the large landowners were amassing huge profits, demands were voiced for "an urgent agrarian reform." The poor, mostly landless peasants constituted more than 75 percent of the population. They were illiterate and had little opportunity to improve their situation. Health standards were deplorable. Education was severely limited in the rural areas.

One of the goals of the revolution, announced shortly after the takeover by the Free Officers, was the achievement of social and economic justice by providing free health care in the countryside. After medical students completed their studies, which were free, they were obliged to work for three years in the rural areas providing the peasantry with the health services that they needed. Drinking water and electricity were no longer confined to urban centers and were extended to the rural provinces. Although lacking a specific ideology and well-developed programs for implementing these goals, the new government attempted to raise the standard of living of the average Egyptian, especially of the *fellahin* ("peasants") of the Nile Valley. Agrarian reform became the first and most significant domestic effort of the new regime, as demonstrated by the Agrarian Reform Law of September 1952. It limited individual landholdings to less than two hundred *feddans* (approximately two hundred acres), reduced the rent paid for land, and increased agricultural wages. In an effort to redistribute existing agricultural land and to divide the wealth of the country more equitably, some lands were expropriated (with compensation) and redistributed.

POLITICAL STRUCTURE

There have been several variations in Egypt's basic political structure since the 1952 revolution. With Nasser at its head, the RCC held the reins of political power. During this transition period, a number of outstanding problems were resolved. The Anglo-Egyptian Treaty, signed in July 1954, called for the final removal of British forces from Egypt and the canal zone by June 13, 1956.

In 1956 Nasser formally inaugurated a new system that consolidated power in his own hands. On January 16, 1956, a new constitution was proclaimed in which extensive powers were concentrated in the hands of the president. The constitution also established a single political party, the National Union, which replaced the Liberation Rally. The party, the National Assembly, and the other organs of government and politics remained under the control of Nasser, who was elected president by more than 99.9 percent of the vote in a plebiscite on June 25, 1956. The inauguration of the new constitution, formally approved in a plebiscite, ushered in a number of changes in the political system: Martial law was terminated, political prisoners were released, and the RCC members became civilians (with the exception of Gen. Abdul Hakim Amer, who was minister of defense) and joined various agencies of the government.

In February 1958 Nasser yielded to the demands of a new government in Syria that the two nations be joined to form the United Arab Republic (UAR). The union of these two dissimilar and geographically noncontiguous political units into a single state called for the creation of a new political structure with, at least theoretically, Nasser sharing power with the Syrian leadership. The provisional constitution of the new UAR was proclaimed, and Nasser became president. Nasser received nearly all the votes cast in the presidential election on February 21, 1958. Both Egyptians and Syrians were represented in the institutions of government, but most of the actual governing was conducted by decree of Nasser and his chief advisers and aides—especially General Amer, who largely controlled the Syrian region. On September 28, 1961, Syria, disenchanted with Egyptian domination and Nasser's growing socialism, severed ties with the UAR and reestablished its independence. Egypt continued to be known as the United Arab Republic until it became the Arab Republic of Egypt in 1971.

With the termination of the union of Egypt and Syria in 1961, there was an intensification of Nasser's socialist programs in Egypt. A new governmental system was again devised and implemented soon thereafter, with a clear socialistic focus. Socialist measures adopted in the early 1960s included further agrarian reform, progressive tax measures, nationalization of business enterprises, and, in general, increased governmental control over the economy. A new charter and constitution were created, and a new political organization, the Arab Socialist Union (ASU), was formed in January 1963. A new constitution was adopted in 1964 that provided the framework for the remainder of the Nasser tenure.

A new phase in Egyptian politics began with the death of Nasser on September 28, 1970, and his replacement by Anwar Sadat. Sadat's consolidation of political control in May 1971 was followed by changes in the political structures and processes of politics. On September 11, 1971, the current constitution was approved by general referendum. It is similar to its predecessor in continuing the strong presidential system extant in Egypt since the revolution. According to the constitution, the president of the republic is head of state. He is empowered to declare a state of emergency in the case of national danger, subject to a referendum within sixty days. Legislative power is vested in the National Assembly, composed of 444 directly elected members and others nominated by the president; members of parliament serve a five-year term. The president may object to laws passed by the National Assembly within thirty days of their passage, but the assembly has the right to override his objection by a two-thirds vote. The president has the power to appoint vice presidents, the prime minister and his cabinet, High Court judges, provincial governors, university presidents, and even some religious leaders. He is the supreme commander of the armed forces. Although the constitution increases the powers of the National Assembly, dominant authority remains with the president, who has the right of temporary rule by decree. Presidential decrees have the power of law. The constitution includes guarantees of freedom of expression, as well as assurance of freedom from arbitrary arrest, seizure of property, and mail censorship. Press censorship is banned except in periods of war or emergency. At first, the Arab Socialist Union was declared the only authorized political party, but this was gradually modified, and the party was virtually defunct by October 1976.

In 1976 Sadat initiated what appeared to be a move toward a multiparty system when he announced that three ideological "platforms" would be organized within the ASU. The centrist group had Sadat's personal support and won a vast majority of the seats in the 1976 parliamentary election. Sadat still refused to allow the formation of independent parties, and the three organizations never took root as genuine vehicles of political participation. Only after the violent clashes over increased prices of basic commodities in January 1977 did Sadat permit political parties to be formed. Members of the formidable old Wafd Party, headed by Fouad Saraj al-Din, formed officially in January 1978 as the New Wafd Party. The popularity of this new party rose dramatically. Within two and a half months after its inception, the New Wafd Party had almost 1 million members. Sadat panicked and, not wanting to share power, let alone relinquish it to the party, decided through a series of laws and decrees to undermine the New Wafd Party.

In July 1978 Sadat created the National Democratic Party (NDP) and later permitted a leftist party to organize as an official opposition. The Arab Socialist Union was abolished in December 1976. The Advisory Council (*Majlis al-Shura*) was established to serve the functions of the old ASU central committee, and in the September 1980 elections for that council, Sadat's new NDP won all 140 seats, with the 70 remaining posts being appointed directly by the president. Sadat, like Nasser before him, wanted to create a political organization but was unable to tolerate the loss of political control that would occur if these "parties" were to become genuine vehicles for mass participation.

Sadat's assassination in October 1981 by Islamic fundamentalists opposed to his peacemaking with Israel changed very little about Egyptian domestic politics. Sadat's successor, Hosni Mubarak, left the basic structure unaltered. He allowed the New Wafd Party to participate in the 1984 parliamentary elections. Those elections were not free and the NDP won the majority of the seats. The party of the president won 384 seats in the November 1990 election, with the main opposition parties boycotting the polls. Mubarak was elected to a third presidential term in October 1993 and a fourth in September 1999. In the parliamentary elections held in October and November 2000, the NDP won 388 seats out of a total of 444.

In late 2004 a secular opposition emerged with the objective of challenging President Mubarak, who had been ruling Egypt autocratically since October 1981, choosing prime ministers and cabinet ministers and changing them at will. After the New Wafd Party was taken over by a leader who gave it an Islamic Nasserist orientation, 3,000 members left in October 2004 and decided to form a new party called al-Ghad ("Future"). The leader of the al-Ghad Party, Ayman Nour, decided to challenge Mubarak in the presidential elections. Nour's popularity rose rapidly, which alarmed Mubarak. Ayman Nour was arrested on January 29, 2005, on fabricated charges, but after pressure by the United States, he was released six weeks later. More American pressure was needed for the Egyptian parliament to amend the constitution to allow a multicandidate presidential election. Although Mubarak was reelected for a fifth term in September 2005, he continued to worry about the new secular opposition, so Ayman Nour was arrested in December 2005 on the same fabricated charges and was sentenced to five years in prison with hard labor.

Fearing that Ayman Nour could challenge him or his forty-one-year-old son, Gamal Mubarak, in the next election, President Mubarak manipulated the parliamentary elections of November and December 2005 to prop up the Muslim Brotherhood, which increased its representation fivefold to 88 seats, while the

NDP won 333 seats. In effect, Mubarak used the Brotherhood as a political "bo-geyman" so that those who called for real democratic change in Egypt would face either "the Mubarak regime or the abyss."

President Mubarak has been able to resist all changes and has kept Egypt a strong presidential system with a facade of elections and party rule. The judiciary is somewhat independent, but the government can, and has, used military courts or the "state-of-emergency" regulations (in force without interruption since 1981) to ignore judicial decisions it does not favor. The Muslim Brotherhood, which only lacks legal recognition, is given full freedom to Islamize Egyptian society, but this has worked against the Christian Coptic community of 10 million people, who are persecuted by the Egyptian authorities as well as by the Muslim militants.

Although the Egyptian authorities give the Muslim Brotherhood the freedom to operate, this is not the case with the more radical Islamic groups that have re-sorted to violence to advance their cause. After the assassination of Sadat, there was a lull in these violent activities. They resumed in the 1990s, and in October 1990 the speaker of the People's Assembly was killed. Leading liberal thinker Farag Fouda was assassinated in June 1992. There was an unsuccessful attempt to assassi-nate the literature Nobel Prize winner Naguib Mahfouz in October 1994. Vio-lence by fundamentalists was also directed against Coptic Christians, government officials, and foreign tourists.

THE CONTINUED LEGACIES OF THE 1952 REVOLUTION

Secularism and Liberalism Undermined

The leaders of Egypt since the 1952 revolution have undermined the territorial secular and liberal Egyptian nationalism of the first half of the twentieth cen-tury. Pan-Arab Nationalism in the Egyptian context has a strong Islamic flavor and thus acted as a bridge to the pan-Islamism of the Muslim Brotherhood. There was not a single Christian Copt among the ninety-four members of the Free Officers Movement, although Copts constituted 15 percent of the total population. Discrimination against the Christian Copts has become prevalent, verging on persecution, especially under Sadat and Mubarak. After the 1952 revolution, enlightened liberalism, the dominant ideology for three decades in the aftermath of the 1919 revolution, was undermined by pan-Arabism and pan-Islamism. Over the past fifty years, political expression by both those in power and the organized politically disaffected has used various combinations of these ideas, beginning with Nasser's Arab socialism and, increasingly, contempo-rary militant political Islamism.

An Aversion to Democracy and a Military-Based Regime

Gamal Abd al-Nasser (1952–1970), Anwar Sadat (1970–1981), and Hosni Mubarak (1981–present) represent continuity in three basic elements. First, all three regimes can be characterized as military based. Second, in the final analysis they also represent the *mukhabarat* ("intelligence services") regime. Third, all three leaders share an aversion to democracy. In the case of Nasser, after the agrarian reform of 1952 and the abolition of the monarchy in 1953, some of his colleagues suggested the return of the army to its barracks and the resumption of civilian rule through free parliamentary elections, but Nasser refused. In a meeting of the RCC on April 4, 1954, as reported by Abd al-Latif al-Baghdadi in his memoirs, Nasser admitted that the 1952 revolution by then had no support among the Egyptians and that only fifty officers of the original ninety-four had continued to support the revolution. In other words, the Free Officers led by Nasser had imposed their rule over the Egyptian people. The Army is the keystone institution of Egyptian society. It has been the backbone of the three regimes since the 1952 revolution. The three leaders of these regimes hailed from the military, so whenever the military was needed they used it. In the bread riots of 1977 in protest against the threatened end of food subsidies, the army intervened, restored order, and withdrew. It was to do this again in 1986 when paramilitary troops rebelled. The segment of the army prepared to carry out this support of the regime and the defense of the constitution has been the army of combat. There is also the army of production, which makes Egypt self-reliant in arms production but also produces consumer goods. The army is free from budgetary accountability, and the "production" army is especially free from scrutiny and is monopolistic in its activities. The *mukhabarat* has played a crucial role in controlling the Egyptian polity. Nasser invented the *mukhabarat* state, and as a result Egypt has become a model to be emulated by other autocrats in the Middle East.

EGYPT'S FOREIGN POLICY SINCE THE 1952 REVOLUTION

Nasser ruled Egypt from 1952 until his death in 1970. During his tenure he captured the attention and imagination not only of the Egyptian people but also of the Arab world, much of the Third World, and other portions of the international community. Egypt ended British control, established a republican form of government, and began extensive political change.

The 1950s were the heyday of Nasser's rule as a charismatic leader. On July 26, 1956, he nationalized the Suez Canal Company. He had unwittingly provoked the Suez War of October–November 1956 in which Britain, France, and Israel invaded Egypt. Although Nasser was militarily defeated, he achieved a political victory with the aid of the United States and the Soviet Union, which both insisted on the removal of foreign troops from Egypt. He secured arms and aid for the Aswan High Dam from the Soviet Union and Soviet Bloc allies after the United States and other lenders decided not to provide the necessary assistance. Nasser became a leader of the Nonaligned Movement, and despite the many difficulties in implementing any form of Arab unity, he mobilized people all over the Arab world to think of themselves as members of a group larger than their own state. Nasser symbolized renascent Arab strength for many of the ordinary citizens of the Arab world.

Nasser's accomplishments in the 1950s were soon followed by difficulties. The United Arab Republic dissolved acrimoniously in 1961, Egypt became involved in the civil war in Yemen in the early 1960s (which turned out to be a quagmire from which it was difficult to withdraw), and there were feuds with other Arab states and challenges to Nasser's role as Arab world leader. Nasser provoked, but did not initiate, the June 1967 Arab-Israeli War, which proved to be disastrous and resulted in the loss of the Sinai Peninsula (one-seventh of Egypt's land area), the closure of the Suez Canal, and the loss of a substantial portion of Egypt's military capability.

Despite these reverses, Nasser was still the preeminent Egyptian and Arab, the most influential figure in the Middle East, and a focal point of regional and international attention. Nasser's role extended beyond that designated in the constitution. He controlled all the main instruments of power and coercion, including the army, the secret police and intelligence agencies, and the Arab Socialist Union. Nasser's central role and his charismatic appeal to the overwhelming majority of Egyptians raised doubts, at the time of his death, about a successor's ability to replace him as the undisputed leader of Egypt and the Arab world. Nasser died of a heart attack on September 28, 1970, following intense negotiations he had brokered between King Hussein of Jordan and Chairman of the Palestine Liberation Organization (PLO) Yasir Arafat, whose forces had been at war in Jordan.

The constitution in force at that time called for Vice President Anwar Sadat to succeed Nasser in office. Sadat initially enjoyed the legitimacy of being the formal successor and of his long association with Nasser (he was virtually the only former Free Officer left in office by this time), but it was generally assumed that he would soon be replaced by one of the powerful rivals maneuvering behind the scene. Although Sadat was elected president in an October 1970 referendum (receiving only 85 percent of the vote, as opposed to Nasser's traditional 99 percent), the long-term stability of his regime was not yet assured.

Sadat sought to consolidate his position but did not make a major overt move until May 1971, when he suddenly purged the government of all senior officials who opposed him. This group included a former vice president, Ali Sabri, a prominent left-leaning figure who had headed the ASU and was regarded as

Moscow's favorite candidate, as well as the minister of war, the head of intelligence, and other senior officials. These officials were later tried for high treason.

Sadat did not enjoy the widespread adulation Nasser had evoked from the masses and had even been derided as Nasser's yes-man. His declaration that 1971 would be a "year of decision" that would result in war or peace in the Arab-Israeli conflict did nothing to improve his popularity, as the year ended with no movement toward achievement of this objective. By 1972 Sadat had become an object of ridicule and cruel jokes that raised doubts about his leadership. In partial response to domestic criticism and to the concerns and complaints of the military, he decided to terminate the role of the Soviet advisers in Egypt in 1972. Sadat soon began to prepare for the October War (the 1973 Arab-Israeli War) because he saw little progress toward a political settlement of the conflict with Israel. He achieved a formidable success in taking the Israelis by surprise and crossing the heavily fortified Suez Canal at the beginning of the war in October 1973. Although he ultimately lost the war in a military sense, with the Egyptian Third Army surrounded by Israeli troops, his initial success in the field and his mobilization of support from the conservative Arab oil producers (who, at his behest, used oil as a political weapon for the first time) made the war a political success. Sadat was able to place Israel on the defensive internationally, to secure further international support for the Egyptian and Arab positions, and to attract increased aid from the oil-rich Arab states. Of the many honorary titles he received, Sadat was said to have favored above all the phrase that came into use after Egyptian troops took the Suez Canal back from the Israeli forces that had held its eastern shore since 1967: "Hero of the Crossing."

In April 1974 Sadat produced a document called the October Working Paper that discussed the new era ushered in by the October War. It called for extensive reform and change in Egypt and suggested that the lot of the average Egyptian would improve. It embodied his new approach to politics and economics, especially the liberalization of politics, the economic "opening" to Western aid and investment, and the restructuring of the Egyptian government toward decentralization and away from the centrally planned economy. Sadat's turn to the West, which actually began with the expulsion of Soviet advisers in 1972, accelerated during the period after the October 1973 war, and culminated with the Egypt-Israel Peace Treaty of 1979, may have been part of a huge economic gamble: By turning to the West, could he attract substantial aid and investment and get rid of the heavy economic burden of the war with Israel (and regain the Sinai Peninsula), while at the same time not totally alienating the oil-rich Arab states that had supported Egypt since 1967 with aid and investment?

By 1980 domestic tension in Egypt had grown, although Sadat's grip on power was in no way diminished. Confessional conflict had occurred between the large Coptic Christian minority and the Islamic fundamentalists, and Sadat placed restrictions on both. In the years after 1979, it became clear that there remained serious opposition to Egypt's move toward the West and its peace with Israel, especially from Islamic fundamentalists. What may have been Sadat's economic gamble was not paying off as well as he might have hoped: There was some Western aid and investment, but it was not substantial, and Arab aid and investment dropped sharply. Egypt had been suspended from the Arab League for making peace with Israel and remained isolated in the Arab world. More pressing yet, there had been no significant economic progress, and the standard of living of the average Egyptian was very low and getting worse. Sadat held his course. The years 1980 and 1981 were marked by increasing political violence, including clashes between Coptic Christians and Islamic fundamentalists. The Sadat government reacted repressively.

Sadat initiated severe repression of his opposition in September 1980, beginning with the formerly tolerated leftist party, but the major move was made almost a year later, in September 1981, when more than 1,500 Egyptian political figures of all political persuasions were arrested. Certain religious groups were banned and their newspapers closed. A number of Muslim Brotherhood leaders were arrested, and Sadat tried to dismiss the Coptic leader, Pope Shenuda III. Many fundamentalist mosques were taken over by the government, and the security apparatus began to clamp down on universities.

On October 6, 1981, Sadat was assassinated by Muslim fundamentalists at a parade celebrating the eighth anniversary of his supreme military achievement: the crossing of the Suez Canal at the opening of the 1973 October War. A state of emergency was declared, and the National Assembly nominated Vice President Hosni Mubarak to succeed Sadat. Although the assassins were quickly arrested, conflict broke out in Asyut between the security forces and Muslim fundamentalists. The anti-Sadat demonstrations were limited in scope and were soon quelled. A presidential referendum was held, and Mubarak was sworn in as president on October 14, 1981.

Although Mubarak cracked down on the religious extremists associated with Sadat's assassination, he released many of the other political figures whom Sadat had had arrested a month before his death. Despite the release of many political detainees, Mubarak kept a tight rein on Egyptian politics. The state of emergency is likely to remain in force, even though the emergency following Sadat's death has long passed. Mubarak made substantial economic progress and managed to put Egypt back into the center of the Arab world without reneging on the Egypt-Israel Peace Treaty of 1979. He faced down serious challenges to his rule, such as the February 1986 uprising by 20,000 conscripts of the Security Force and the challenges that the Islamic fundamentalists continued to pose—all of which were brutally suppressed. As long as Mubarak continues to retain the all-important confidence of the Egyptian military, his regime is stable.

Economic Development and Economic Policies

Historical Background. The great modernizer of Egypt, Muhammad Ali (1805–1849), opened Egypt to the migration of foreigners (both Europeans and Levantines), as he needed them in his factories and enterprises and for their contacts with Europe for the import-export trade. Alexandria, which had declined over the centuries both in population and importance, was revived, and by the end of Muhammad Ali's reign there were so many Europeans in Alexandria that it appeared to have become a European city. The local foreign minorities consisted of Europeans of various nationalities with a large number of Armenians, Greeks, and Italians; European and Levantine Jews; and Lebanese and Syrian Christians. The local foreign communities tied Egypt to the European capitalist market through their economic activities, especially after 1854, when the Egyptian countryside was opened to merchants and creditors. The two main social forces in Egypt between the mid-nineteenth century and the first two decades of the twentieth century were the local foreigners and the large landowners. The 1919 revolution resulted in the emergence of the Wafd Party, which tended to challenge the political dominance of the large landowners because it was plebian in character, based on the *effenidiya* in the urban centers and the resident medium landowners in the rural provinces. Through the alliance of these two classes, the Wafd Party became a mass political party that was able to win the majority of seats in all free parliamentary elections, the last of which was in January 1950. In the aftermath of the 1919 revolution, a nascent Egyptian bourgeoisie emerged. An Egyptian bank called Bank Misr was established in May 1920; its shareholders were predominantly wealthy Egyptian landowners and merchants. Bank Misr was both a credit bank and an industrial bank. In the latter capacity it formed a large number of joint-stock companies in various economic venues, such as paper manufacturing, trading, cotton ginning, silk weaving, fisheries, and cotton spinning and weaving. By the late 1930s the Egyptian bourgeoisie, centered on Bank Misr and its various industrial enterprises, was cooperating with the local foreign bourgeoisie centered on the Federation of Industries originally formed in 1922. Throughout the 1930s and the 1940s, the interests of the local bourgeoisie were frequently at loggerheads with those of the large landowners, but the latter had greater political influence to prevent improvement in the conditions of the peasants in the countryside, let alone limiting the property held by large landowners.

Economic Policies Since the 1952 Revolution. The 1952 revolution abolished the titles of Pasha and Bey that were given by the king to prominent Egyptians, deservedly or not, when it abolished the monarchy. The agrarian reforms limited the power and wealth of large landowners. When Nasser adopted socialism in the early 1960s, he nationalized the major sectors of the economy and created a command economy. The remaining members of local foreign communities who had an important role in the economy were pushed out and forced to leave Egypt; some of them had been in Egypt for two centuries. The class structure, despite the 1952 revolution, is still quite marked, although landed classes of various amounts of wealth do exist in the countryside along with the landless peasantry. In the urban centers, there are the wealthy merchants, industrialists, and financiers; some belong to the families that were rich before the revolution, but others became wealthy after Sadat's economic *infitah* ("open-door" policy). There are also a middle class and a lower-middle class as well as a proletariat. It is estimated that 80 percent of small businesses are free from the payment of taxes; 30 percent of the gross domestic product is located in that economic sector.

Egypt, the "gift of the Nile," has been dependent on that main source of freshwater for the thousands of years of its recorded history. There is a narrow strip of land along the Mediterranean coast where crops can be grown with the limited rainfall available. Except for this area and a few oases, all agriculture is dependent on irrigation from the Nile. The land made inhabitable and cultivable by the river constitutes a small portion of Egypt's overall land area (about 4 percent). In ancient times this rich soil of Egypt was more than sufficient to meet the needs of its population. After all during the time of Roman and Byzantine empires, Egypt was known as the granary of Rome and Constantinople. The inability to feed its population since the 1950s has been due to the government's agricultural policies and to the increase in population. On the eve of the 1952 revolution, the population was estimated at around 25 million. In 2010, it is at around 77 million. The rate of population growth has decreased to 1.78 percent from 3 percent in the mid-1980s. Nasser wanted to increase the land under cultivation by building the Aswan High Dam, which was completed in 1971. Many of the anticipated benefits of the Aswan High Dam have been realized. There has been a significant increase in the cultivated area of Egypt and in net agricultural output; flood control has also fostered productivity gains; additional electric power, primarily for industrial use, has been made available; navigation along the Nile, used as a major transportation artery in Egypt, has been improved; and a fishing industry has been developed in Lake Nasser. There are, however, some problems. For example, the silt that fertilized the lands of the Nile Valley with the annual flood has been trapped behind the dam in Lake Nasser. This makes it necessary to use large amounts of chemical fertilizers. Salinity has increased in the northern portion of the river and in some of the land that was drained by the annual floods.

Sadat began, in the aftermath of the October 1973 Arab-Israeli War, his *infitah* to encourage foreign and domestic private investment. The Suez Canal was reopened in 1975, and the Sinai oil fields were eventually returned to Egyptian control. Economic performance began to improve due to the Suez Canal tolls, the tourism revenues, and the remittances from Egyptians working abroad. Between

1974 and 1981 the gross domestic product increased by an annual average of 9 percent. In 1991, Mubarak embarked on a massive structural-adjustment program with the International Monetary Fund and the World Bank. There was an increase in privatization of the economy but nothing close to what it was before 1952, when the private sector constituted 95 percent of the economy. The Egyptian currency was floated. But subsidies for major staple-food items for the vast majority of Egyptians remained intact. In fact the subsidies increased over the last three years as President Hosni Mubarak has been grooming his son Gamal Mubarak to succeed him.

FOREIGN POLICY

Overview

Napoleon once labeled Egypt "the most important country" because of its central location, providing a gateway to Africa and the Middle East. In the post–World War II period, Egypt became even more significant. The Suez Canal, although it cannot accommodate supertankers, is a prime artery for oil. Egypt is a leader among African, Arab, Islamic, and other developing nations. It is also a major actor for the establishment of peace or the waging of war in the Arab-Israeli conflict. It has been courted by both the United States and the Soviet Union, each in pursuit of its own interests in the region and in the broader international community.

Egypt is the leader of the Arab world in a number of other respects. Its population and military forces are the largest. It has led the Arab world in communications (publishing, arts, literature, films) and other spheres. In the nineteenth century and the early part of the twentieth century, Egypt spearheaded Arab contact with the Western world and helped to develop the intellectual bases for Arab, as well as Egyptian, nationalism. It was a leader in the establishment of the Arab League. Furthermore, its Suez Canal was an important strategic and economic asset.

After the 1952 revolution, Egypt emerged as an important Third World neutralist and nonaligned power, and Egypt and Nasser were increasingly relied upon for leadership in the Arab world and beyond. Egypt's foreign policy was virtually nonexistent prior to the 1952 revolution, since Egypt was largely controlled by non-Egyptians. Major and assertive foreign policy positions developed only after the revolution and seemed to be reactive, responding to events as they developed. Nasser's foreign policy focused, in the first instance, on the need to eliminate the British colonial presence in the canal zone and in the Sudan. In the second instance, there was the problem of Israel. It is in these contexts that Egypt's relations with the United States and the Soviet Union emerged.

Initial successes included the agreement on the withdrawal of the British from their positions in Egypt and the resolution of the Sudan problem (although Sudan eventually chose independence over union with Egypt). On February 12, 1953, Britain and Egypt signed the Agreement on Self-Government and Self-Determination for the Sudan, which provided for the latter's transition to self-government and its choice between linkage with Egypt or full independence. The Suez question was settled in an agreement on October 19, 1954. That agreement declared the 1936 treaty to be terminated and provided for the withdrawal of British forces from Egyptian territory within twenty months.

Relations with the superpowers were different. Although the United States was initially helpful to the new regime and provided technical and economic aid, as well as some assistance in the negotiations with the British, there were difficulties concerning Nasser's requests for arms. Moreover, US Secretary of State John Foster Dulles viewed Egypt's increasingly close ties with Communist China and the Soviet Union with suspicion. The Baghdad Pact, a Western-oriented defense alliance conceived and sponsored by the United States, was not viewed positively by Nasser, who saw it as a threat to Arab independence and autonomy. Raids on Israel by fedayeen and counterraids by Israel into Gaza sparked, in Nasser's view, a need for arms for defense, and his quest led him to establish closer links with the Soviet Bloc, further straining ties with the United States. The Dulles decision that the United States would not fund the Aswan High Dam was a major blow to the plans of the new regime, which decided to continue building and to secure the necessary funding and assistance from alternative sources. The Soviet Union was prepared to assist in the construction and to provide some financial aid. But in Nasser's view, a more demonstrable act was needed. Thus, in July 1956, he nationalized the Suez Canal and stated that the canal revenues would go to the construction of the dam.

While the US-Egyptian relationship was deteriorating, the Soviet role in Egypt (and elsewhere in the Arab world) was improving. Soviet assistance for the Aswan High Dam project, as well as the supply of arms essential to the Egyptian military's continued stature and satisfaction and, ostensibly, to the defense of Egypt against Israel, helped to ensure the positive Soviet-Egyptian relationship.

Then came the Sinai-Suez war of 1956, when Britain, France, and Israel joined in an effort to unseat Nasser and restore the canal to Western control while destroying Egypt's military capability (especially its ability to use the newly acquired arms). The United States opposed the invasion and exerted considerable pressure on its three friends to withdraw from Egyptian territory. In assisting the Nasser regime, the United States won much goodwill in the Arab world, especially in Egypt. But this goodwill was soon dissipated when the United States became involved in the 1958 Lebanese crisis and opposed the Egyptian position.

The chill between the United States and Egypt thawed slightly during the Kennedy administration, but with the death of John Kennedy and the establishment of President Lyndon Johnson's position on foreign policy, the relationship began to deteriorate once again. By the time of the Six Day War of June 1967, relations between the two states were poor, and the war itself precipitated the break of diplomatic relations. The relationship between the United States and Egypt remained antagonistic until the end of the October War, when President Richard Nixon and Secretary of State Henry Kissinger established the policy that led to a rapprochement. A cordial relationship grew in the mid-1970s in virtually all the bilateral spheres, demonstrated by state visits by Sadat to the United States in 1975 and 1977 and a 1974 state visit by Nixon to Egypt.

Relations with the Soviet Union were somewhat different. Beginning in the mid-1950s, Soviet economic and technical assistance were important elements in the Aswan High Dam project and in Egypt's economic development. Military assistance was another element in the developing relations of the two states. Because Nasser felt that Egypt required arms to maintain the regime and to deal with Israel, the Soviet Union became a major factor inasmuch as it was prepared to provide arms under cost and with payment terms acceptable to the Egyptians. The Egyptian military soon had a Soviet arsenal. Soviet equipment provided the arms essential for the Egyptian armies in the 1956, 1967, 1969–1970, and 1973 wars. But despite the consummation of a treaty of friendship between the countries in 1971, the Soviets were never popular with senior members of the Egyptian military.

The rift between Egypt and the Soviet Union began when the Soviet Union attempted to influence the choice of Nasser's replacement after his sudden death in 1970. After Sadat's consolidation of his position following the arrest of his major opponents, Egypt's relationship with the Soviet Union deteriorated further, as the Soviet Union and its Egyptian clients began to differ on the type of equipment the Soviets were willing to provide and on Soviet attempts to constrain Egyptian military plans. This culminated in the expulsion of Soviet advisers in July 1972. Although Egyptian-Soviet relations improved somewhat during the months that followed, they never returned to their former levels. After the October War, Egypt complained that the Soviets were lax in resupplying the Egyptian military forces. Egypt increasingly turned to the West, especially the United States, and Sadat articulated the view that the United States held the crucial cards for peace in the region and could also become the source of essential economic and technical assistance for Egypt. The policy seemed to be a zero-sum game: Better relations with the United States meant poorer relations with the Soviet Union.

Arab nationalism has always been a key concept in Egyptian foreign policy, although its passionate espousal during the Nasser period diminished to lip service under Sadat and Mubarak. In his *Philosophy of the Revolution*, Nasser argued that Arab unity had to be established, for it would provide strength for the Arab nation to deal with its other problems. Arab unity was a consistent theme during his tenure. Sadat retained that general theme but focused much of his foreign policy on the Arab-Israeli conflict and the future of the Palestinians. His signing of the

Camp David Accords and the Egypt-Israel Peace Treaty of 1979 left him open to charges that he had forgotten the Palestinians and the rest of the Arab world in his pursuit of Egyptian interests alone. The brotherhood of the Arab people has not disappeared from the political lexicon of the Egyptian leadership. Even during the early 1980s, when Egypt remained isolated from the Arab world, Mubarak did not disown the concept. The heyday of Arab nationalism, however, had clearly passed for a number of reasons, including perhaps Sadat's willingness to go it alone with Israel and Mubarak's ability to survive the isolation from the Arab world that followed.

Another important theme of Egyptian policy has been its leadership role in the Arab world. Developed as part of the pan-Arab or Arab nationalist approach, this theme acquired added dimensions with Nasser's increasing interests in the Arabian Peninsula and the Gulf region in the 1960s. Increasingly, Egypt became the Arab leader in the conflict with Israel. The Arab-Israeli conflict and the wars of 1956, 1967, and 1970 (the War of Attrition along the Suez Canal) consumed Nasser's attention in foreign policy, and Egypt played the leading role in most aspects of the Arab side of the conflict. After 1967 the radical-conservative split in the Arab world was more or less healed at the Khartoum summit, and Egypt's leadership began to encompass even the more conservative Arab states.

Following the October War, Sadat initiated a dramatic transformation of Egyptian foreign policy. He began with the assumption that the key to both his domestic and his foreign policy problems lay in closer ties with the United States, for he felt that only the United States could push Israel to relinquish territories occupied in the 1967 war (most critical for Egypt, the Sinai) and provide the technical and economic assistance the Egyptian economy desperately needed. The US option thus seemed logical for both political and economic reasons.

The postwar approach began in the months following the war. In January 1974, Kissinger achieved a first-stage disengagement agreement separating Israeli and Egyptian forces along the Suez Canal and in Sinai. Relations between Egypt and the United States began to improve dramatically, and relations with the Soviet Union continued to deteriorate. After further and substantial effort, a second-stage disengagement between Israel and Egypt, known as Sinai II, was signed in September 1975. It provided for further Israeli withdrawals and the return to Egypt of important oil fields in Sinai. Nixon visited Egypt in June 1974, with the Watergate scandal at its height, and Sadat later visited the United States (October to November 1975).

In the wake of the Sinai II agreement, Egyptian policy took on a new cast. Sadat seemed to be interested in maintaining the role of the United States as the power that would help attain peace by pressuring Israel to change its policies. Movement was slowed, however, by regional developments—especially the civil war in Lebanon—and by the US presidential elections. The conclusion of the elections in November 1976 and the temporary winding down of the Lebanon conflict set a new process in motion.

During the initial months of President Jimmy Carter's administration, there was substantial movement toward the establishment of a process to lead toward peace or at least toward a Geneva conference designed to maintain the momentum toward a settlement. But the movement seemed to have slowed substantially by October 1977, leading to Sadat's decision to "go to Jerusalem" and to present his case and the Arab position directly to the Israeli parliament and people. In so doing he set in motion a new approach to the Arab-Israeli conflict in which direct Egyptian-Israeli negotiations became, for the first time, the means to peace in the Middle East. Direct negotiations were continued at the Cairo Conference and Ismailia summit meeting of December 1977 and in lower-level contacts over the ensuing months. Then, in September 1978, Sadat met with President Carter and Prime Minister Menachem Begin of Israel at the Camp David summit, which provided a framework for peace between Egypt and Israel and, ultimately, for a broader arrangement between Israel and the other Arab states. On March 26, 1979, Sadat signed the Egypt-Israel Peace Treaty in Washington, DC. Implementation of the treaty, which normalized relations between the two states, proceeded as scheduled, and diplomatic relations were established. At the same time, various contacts were made, including tourist and communications links. These actions led to Egypt's expulsion from the Arab League and its isolation in the Arab world, which refused to accept Sadat's argument that the treaty and peace with Israel were in the best interests of the Palestinians and the other Arabs. Failure to achieve substantial progress toward implementation of the other Camp David framework providing for arrangements for the West Bank and Gaza further complicated Egypt's and Sadat's position. Despite US efforts, the talks were suspended.

Sadat's assassination in October 1981 raised questions about Egypt's foreign policy direction, particularly its arrangements with Israel. President Mubarak reaffirmed and built upon the policies he inherited from Sadat, emphasizing negotiated solutions to the Arab-Israeli conflict, maintenance of the peace with Israel, and close and positive relations with the United States. The peace treaty's provisions were implemented on or ahead of schedule. Although Mubarak insisted on maintenance of the peace with Israel, he also has been critical of Israel at times. He sharply criticized Israel's June 1982 invasion of Lebanon and withdrew his ambassador from Israel following the Sabra and Shatilla refugee camp massacres in September 1982. (Egypt's embassy remained in Tel Aviv, however, just as Israel's embassy remained in Egypt, and the Egyptian ambassador later returned.) Nevertheless, Mubarak worked to reduce Egypt's Arab world isolation by gradually restoring and improving relations with the Arab states. He succeeded in improving ties with the moderate Arab states, and Egypt was readmitted to the Islamic Conference in early 1984. Mubarak also shrewdly utilized the opportunity presented by the Iran-Iraq War to improve his ties with several Arab moderate states, in part through offers of assistance to Iraq. By 1989 he had succeeded in returning Egypt to the mainstream of the Arab world without making a single concession, and in May 1989 Egypt rejoined the Arab League.

Another inter-Arab conflict gave Mubarak the chance to improve Egypt's situation. Egypt played a key role in pulling together the Arab states opposed to Iraq's invasion of Kuwait. With Saudi Arabia and Syria, Egypt provided the major Arab element of the coalition that joined with US and European forces in the offensive against Iraq in January 1991. Egypt sent the second-largest foreign force in the Gulf after the United States: 27,000 men to Saudi Arabia and some 5,000 to the United Arab Emirates.

After 1989, Egypt's relations with several of the Arab states—Syria and Libya in particular—improved sharply. Libya invited Egypt to mediate in its conflict with the United States and the United Kingdom over the bombing of the Pan Am jet-liner over Lockerbie, Scotland, in 1988. Conversely, Egypt's relations with the Arab supporters of Iraq—Jordan, Sudan, and Yemen—have remained poor. Relations with Sudan deteriorated not only because of a border quarrel but also because of Mubarak's fears that the Islamic fundamentalist government in Khartoum was sponsoring the training of fundamentalist insurgents and their infiltration into Egypt and other moderate Arab states (such as Algeria).

Relations with Israel under Mubarak have been correct, if not warm, but Mubarak has played a strong role in supporting and sponsoring Israeli negotiations with other key players in the Arab-Israeli conflict, principally the PLO and Syria. In Cairo in February 1994 Israeli foreign minister Shimon Peres and PLO Chairman Yasir Arafat signed an agreement that recorded some progress in implementing the breakthrough agreement signed by the PLO and Israel in Washington, DC, in September 1993. The role of mediating between the Israelis and the Palestinians has continued; Mubarak hosted Israeli and Palestinian leaders in February 2005 when they agreed on a cease-fire that virtually ended the second Palestinian Intifada.

Relations with the United States have remained positive since their restoration in 1974. The personal chemistry between Sadat and Carter was an important factor in this development. Mubarak has been able to broaden and strengthen the relationship since his accession to office. Numerous exchanges of visits between US and Egyptian officials (including regular trips by Mubarak to Washington) have allowed the dialogue on Middle Eastern and other issues to continue. US economic and military assistance to Egypt rose to several billion dollars a year in the 1980s, then to about $2.5 billion a year in the late 1980s and early 1990s, and has remained near that level into the twenty-first century. Mubarak obtained an unwritten agreement to have US aid to Egypt tied to the level of aid to Israel, although at a slightly lower level.

Egyptian Foreign Policy: A Net Assessment

One way to look at Egyptian foreign policy is to assess its strengths and weaknesses. A major strength, at least from the viewpoint of foreign policy decision makers, is the centralization of authority in a patrimonial executive supported by an acquiescent political class. On the other hand, Egypt's lack of economic resources severely limits its ability to influence other countries to adopt policies in furtherance of its national interests, either through diplomacy or, indirectly, through force of arms. As a result, Egypt has had to pursue a foreign policy of seeking infusions of foreign financial and military assistance to maintain internal stability and external security and to create economic growth.

During the Cold War, Egypt's ability to play one superpower against the other facilitated this effort, and with tensions running high in the Middle East, it was successful in building up its military, first with Soviet and then, in the 1970s, with American arms. When President Sadat negotiated a peace treaty with Israel in 1979, Egypt exchanged peace for economic assistance, and since that time, Egypt has received the second-largest amount of economic assistance given by the United States worldwide, next to Israel itself.

The apex of Egyptian regional influence in the Arab world occurred in the 1960s under the charismatic Gamal Abd al-Nasser. Sadat became a pariah in the Arab world following his peace treaty with Israel, and though his successor, Hosni Mubarak, engineered Egypt's return to the Arab fold, his foreign policy concentrated on mediating between the Israelis and the Palestinians and Syria or between the United States and some Arab countries like Libya.

BIBLIOGRAPHY

A review of the background of modern Egypt and the nature of its people is essential to an understanding of its political culture. Two particularly important works in this regard are Henry A. Ayrout's *The Egyptian Peasant* (Boston: Beacon Press, 1963) and William Lane's *Manners and Customs of the Modern Egyptians* (New York: Dutton, 1923). For the historical background of modern Egypt prior to the 1952 revolution, the following sources are essential: Marius Deeb, "The Socioeconomic Role of the Local Foreign Minorities in Modern Egypt, 1805–1961," *International Journal of Middle East Studies* 9 (1978):11–22; Marius Deeb, "Bank Misr and the Emergence of the Local Bourgeoisie in Egypt," *Middle Eastern Studies* 12, no. 3 (October 1976): 69–86; Marius Deeb, "Large Landowners and Social Transformation in Egypt, 1940–1952," in *Land Tenure and Social Transformation in the Middle East*, ed. Tarif Khalidi, 425–436 (Beirut: American University of Beirut, 1984); Marius Deeb, *Party Politics in Egypt: The Wafd and Its Rivals, 1919–1939*, St. Antony's Middle East Monograph No. 9 (London: Ithaca Press, 1979); and Nadav

Safran, *Egypt in Search of Political Community: An Analysis of the Intellectual and Polit-ical Evolution of Egypt, 1804–1952* (Cambridge, MA: Harvard University Press, 1961). Jamal Mohammed Ahmed, in *The Intellectual Origins of Egyptian Nationalism* (London: Oxford University Press, 1960), provides an introduction to nationalism as it developed in Egypt.

Among the many studies of Egypt since the revolution are Anouar Abdel-Malek, *Egypt: Military Society—the Army Regime, the Left, and Social Change Under Nasser*, trans. Charles Lam Markmann (New York: Random House, 1968); R. Hrair Dekmejian, *Egypt Under Nasir: A Study in Political Dynamics* (London: University of London Press, and Albany: State University of New York Press, 1972); Peter Mansfield, *Nasser's Egypt*, rev. ed. (Baltimore: Penguin Books, 1969); Georgiana G. Stevens, *Egypt: Yesterday and Today* (New York: Holt, Rinehart & Winston, 1963); P. J. Vatikiotis, ed., *Egypt Since the Revolution* (New York: Praeger Publishers, 1968); Keith Wheelock, *Nasser's New Egypt: A Critical Analysis* (New York: Praeger Publishers, 1960); John Waterbury, *Egypt: Burdens of the Past, Options for the Future* (Bloomington: Indiana University Press, 1978); John Waterbury, *The Egypt of Nasser and Sadat* (Princeton, NJ: Princeton University Press, 1983); Panayotis J. Vatikiotis, *Nasser and His Generation* (New York: St. Martin's Press, 1978); Mohamed Heikal, *Autumn of Fury: The Assassination of Sadat* (New York: Random House, 1983); Raymond Baker, *Egypt's Uncertain Revolution Under Nasser and Sadat* (Cambridge, MA: Harvard University Press, 1978); Elie Kedourie and Sylvia G. Haim, eds., *Modern Egypt: Studies in Politics and Society* (London: Frank Cass, 1980); Hamied Ansari, *Egypt: The Stalled Society* (Albany: State University of New York Press, 1986); and John Waterbury, *Hydropolitics of the Nile Valley* (Syracuse, NY: Syracuse University Press, 1979).

An understanding of revolutionary Egypt is facilitated by the works of three of its presidents: Mohammad Naguib's *Egypt's Destiny: A Personal Statement* (Garden City, NY: Doubleday, 1955); Gamal Abd al-Nasser's *Egypt's Liberation: The Philosophy of the Revolution* (Washington, DC: Public Affairs Press, 1955); and Anwar el-Sadat's *Revolt on the Nile* (New York: John Day, 1957) and *In Search of Identity: An Autobiography* (New York: Harper & Row, 1978).

Studies of particular aspects of politics of Egypt include Iliya Hark, *The Political Mobilization of Peasants: A Study of an Egyptian Community* (Bloomington: Indiana University Press, 1974); James B. Mayfield, *Rural Politics in Nasser's Egypt: A Quest for Legitimacy* (Austin: University of Texas Press, 1971); J. Vatikiotis, *The Egyptian Army in Politics: Pattern for New Nations?* (Bloomington: Indiana University Press, 1961); and Malcolm Kerr and El Sayed Yassin, eds., *Rich and Poor States in the Middle East: Egypt and the New Arab Order* (Boulder, CO: Westview Press, 1982).

Egyptian foreign policy has not engendered many full-length studies. Nevertheless, several works provide a useful beginning. They include Charles D. Cremeans, *The Arabs and the World: Nasser's Arab Nationalist Policy* (New York: Praeger

Publishers, for the Council on Foreign Relations, 1963), and A. I. Dawisha, *Egypt in the Arab World: The Elements of Foreign Policy* (New York: John Wiley, 1976). More specific themes are considered in Karen Dawisha's *Soviet Foreign Policy Towards Egypt* (New York: St. Martin's Press, 1979), and Ismail Fahmy's *Negotiating for Peace in the Middle East* (Baltimore: Johns Hopkins University Press, 1983).

Valuable studies of Egypt's economy are provided in Bent Hansen and Karim Nashashibi, *Foreign Trade Regimes and Economic Development: Egypt* (New York: National Bureau of Economic Research, 1975); Charles Issawi, *Egypt in Revolution: An Economic Analysis* (London: Oxford University Press, for the Royal Institute of International Affairs, 1963); Robert Mabro, *The Egyptian Economy, 1952–1972* (London: Oxford University Press, 1974); Patrick O'Brien, *The Revolution in Egypt's Economic System: From Private Enterprise to Socialism, 1952–1965* (London: Oxford University Press, issued under the auspices of the Royal Institute of International Affairs, 1966); Khalid Ikram, ed., *Egypt: Economic Management in a Period of Transition* (Baltimore: Johns Hopkins University Press, for the International Bank for Reconstruction and Development, 1980); and Alan Richards, *Egypt's Agricultural Development, 1800–1980: Technical and Social Change* (Boulder, CO: Westview Press, 1982).

Finally, more recent studies include Robert Springborg's *Mubarak's Egypt: Fragmentation of the Political Order* (Boulder, CO: Westview Press, 1989); Anthony McDermott's *Egypt from Nasser to Mubarak: A Flawed Revolution* (London: Croom Helm, 1988); and Raymond Baker's *Sadat and After: Struggles for Egypt's Soul* (Cambridge, MA: Harvard University Press, 1990).

14

GREAT SOCIALIST PEOPLE'S LIBYAN ARAB JAMAHIRIYA

Mary-Jane Deeb

Libya is situated in North Africa, bordered by the Mediterranean Sea in the north, the Arab Republic of Egypt and the Sudan in the east, Niger and Chad in the south, and Tunisia and Algeria in the west. It has an area of just under 1.8 million square kilometers (685,000 square miles), more than 90 percent of which is desert. Libya comprises three distinct geographical units: Tripolitania in the west, with an area of about 248,640 square kilometers (96,000 square miles); Cyrenaica in the east, with an area of about 699,300 square kilometers (270,000 square miles); and Fezzan in the south and southwest, with an area of about 826,210 square kilometers (319,000 square miles).

Libya has a small population, estimated at 6.2 million in 2009, of which 90 percent live in less than 10 percent of the total area, primarily along the Mediterranean coast. About 70 percent of the population is urban, mostly concentrated in the two largest cities, Benghazi and Tripoli. The majority of the population is of Arab origin, descending from a number of Arab tribes, including the two powerful tribes of Beni Hilal and Beni Sulaiman, who came originally from the Arabian Peninsula. But Libya is also partly African (in the Fezzan region) and Berber (in the north and central regions). Berbers descend from the original inhabitants of North Africa. Virtually all Libyans are Sunni Muslims.

HISTORICAL BACKGROUND

In the earliest days the area that is now Libya was visited by Phoenician sailors, who established trading posts along the coastline. Later the Greeks landed. Subsequently, control of part of the area fell to Alexander the Great and later to the Egyptian kingdom of the Ptolemies. Rome annexed Cyrenaica and Tripolitania,

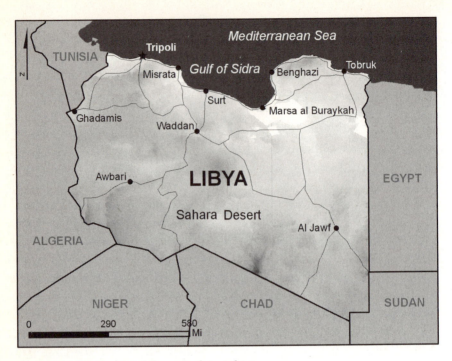

Great Socialist People's Libyan Arab Jamahiriya

and both became part of the Roman Empire. Eventually Pax Romana prevailed, and Libya enjoyed a long period of prosperity and peace. A period of decline began in the middle of the fourth century. In the seventh century Arab invaders arrived from Egypt, and most of the Berber tribes embraced Islam. The Arabs who swept across North Africa in the seventh century ruled for nine hundred years, interrupted by the Normans, the Spaniards, and the Knights of St. John. They were finally replaced in 1551 by the Ottoman Turks, who ruled until 1911. Italy declared war on the Ottoman Empire in September 1911, and Italian troops landed in Tripoli in early October and later that month in Benghazi.

The Italian conquest faced opposition from the powerful Sanusiya movement, led by Muhammad Idris al-Mahdi al-Sanusi, the grandson of the movement's founder. The Sanusiya was a Muslim reformist movement that started in the Hijaz in 1837 and a few years later moved to Cyrenaica. It was primarily a missionary movement whose functions were to spread the call to Islam throughout North Africa and mediate intertribal conflicts. It became a powerful political movement in the last two decades of the nineteenth century, when it sought to curb Ottoman power in the region and later when it tried to push the Italians out of Libya.

In 1929 Italy officially adopted the name "Libya" to refer to its colony consisting of Cyrenaica, Tripolitania, and Fezzan. Until then it had been known by the name of its capital, Tripoli, although the word "Libya" had been used in early times by the Greeks to denote a much larger area in Africa. Colonization along the coast included the settlement of Italian peasants and consolidation of Italian control. Resistance against Italian control continued until 1931, although by 1932, Fascist rule had subdued all opposition.

World War II interrupted Italy's plans: By the end of 1942 British and French forces had swept the Italians out of the country. The North African campaigns of World War II devastated the country, leaving Benghazi partly destroyed. The head of the Sanusiya, Sayyid Muhammad Idris I, who had gone into exile in Egypt in 1922 but continued to support resistance to the Italian occupation, had sided with the British during the war and been promised, at minimum, freedom from Italy. Between 1943 and 1947 the British established a military administration in Tripolitania and Cyrenaica, and the French set up one in the Fezzan on a caretaker basis until the final status of the territories could be settled.

The settlement of the country's future was contained in the Italian Peace Treaty of 1947. Britain, France, the Soviet Union, and the United States were to decide it, with the stipulation that if no agreement was reached, the question would be taken to the United Nations. Each of the powers proposed a different plan (as did Egypt in 1945 and 1946), and it was decided that a four-power commission should ascertain the wishes of the Libyans. In 1947, after visiting Libya, the commission ended in disagreement on many of the specifics; however, the members reached accord on the view that the Libyans wanted independence but were not yet ready to rule themselves. By the summer of 1948, it was clear that the four powers were unable to agree, and the matter went to the United Nations, where it was debated in the General Assembly in spring 1949. Initial sentiment seemed to favor the postponement of independence and the establishment of some form of trusteeship. But agreement could not be reached on this approach, and support for independence increased. On November 21, 1949, the General Assembly adopted a resolution that Libya (composed of three territories) should become an independent state no later than January 1, 1952.

The assembly resolution allowed approximately two years for Libya to prepare for independence. British and French administration continued during much of the period, as Adrian Pelt, the UN commissioner appointed to assist in the transition to independence, helped prepare the institutions of self-government. Pelt was assisted by an international advisory council composed of representatives of several UN member countries and a committee of twenty-one Libyans (seven from each region). A constituent assembly was convened in December 1950, but it encountered difficulties in its efforts to devise a constitution and establish institutions of government. Eventually, Libya was established as a federation in which substantial

LIBYA

Capital city	Tripoli
Chief of state	Revolutionary Leader Col. Muammar Abu Minyar al-Qaddafi
Head of government	Secretary of the General People's Committee al-Baghdadi Ali al-Mahmudi
Major political parties	None
Ethnic groups	Arab-Berber (97%), other (3%)
Religious groups	Sunni Muslim (97%), other (3%)
Export partners	Italy (39.5%), Germany (12.5%), France (7.7%), Spain (7.1%), United States (6.7%), China (4.2%)
Import partners	Italy (22.8%), Germany (8.9%), China (8.5%), Turkey (6.3%), Tunisia (6%), United States (4.2%), France (4.2%)

autonomy was given to each of the three component units. Libya became independent on December 24, 1951, as the United Kingdom of Libya, made up of Fezzan, Cyrenaica, and Tripolitania and with Sayyid Muhammad Idris I as its monarch.

Kingdom of Libya

The 1951 constitution established the United Kingdom of Libya as a constitutional monarchy under Muhammad Idris al-Mahdi al-Sanusi. Sovereignty was vested in the nation but entrusted by the people to Idris and his male heirs. Islam was declared the religion of the state and Arabic the official language. Executive power was granted to the king, whereas legislative power was shared by the king and parliament. King Idris was to exercise his executive power through an appointed prime minister and cabinet, or council of ministers, whereas legislative power was vested in a parliament, which he convened and could adjourn (for up to thirty days) or dissolve. The king sanctioned and promulgated all laws and made the necessary regulations through the relevant ministries for their implementation. In "exceptional and urgent circumstances," when parliament was not in session, the king was permitted to issue decrees, subject to confirmation by parliament when it convened. He could veto legislation, and his veto could be overridden only by a two-thirds vote of both the Senate and the House of Representatives. The king was supreme commander of the armed forces; he could proclaim a state of emergency and martial law, declare war, and conclude peace, with the approval of parliament. In addition, he appointed senators, judges, and senior public servants. The king was supreme head of state, "inviolable," and "exempt from all responsibility."

The cabinet was appointed and dismissed by royal decree on the prime minister's recommendation. Although the cabinet was selected by the king, under Article 86 its members were collectively responsible to the lower house of parliament, and each was individually responsible for the activities of his own ministry. The cabinet was responsible for the direction of all internal and external affairs of state.

Parliament consisted of two chambers. The Senate had twenty-four members (eight from each province), one-half of whom were appointed by the king. The others were elected by the legislative councils of the provinces. Each served for eight years and could be reappointed or reelected. The House of Representatives consisted of deputies elected by popular suffrage on the basis of one deputy for every 20,000 inhabitants or any fraction of that number exceeding half, although each province was required to have at least five members. The deputies served for a maximum of four years. Parliamentary sessions were called by the king in November. During sessions, a bill could be introduced by the king or by one of the chambers; it had to be adopted by both chambers and ratified by the king before becoming law. However, only the king and the House of Representatives could initiate bills involving the budget.

The federal government exercised legislative and executive powers as described in Article 36 of the constitution, which provided a detailed listing of areas for the exercise of its power. In other areas there were provisions for joint powers between the federal and provincial governments. The provinces were to exercise all powers not assigned to the federal government by the constitution. Each province was to have a governor (*wali*) appointed by the king and representing the king in the province. An executive council and a legislative council were established in each province.

The original adoption of the federal system was a necessary compromise in the drafting of the constitution. It allowed for a common political authority while preserving some autonomy for the three provinces of Cyrenaica, Fezzan, and Tripolitania. Local affairs were administered independently in each province, and certain powers were reserved for the federal government. The federal structure was abolished in 1963, when a new constitution established a unitary system that had jurisdiction over all matters within the state. The country's name was changed to the Kingdom of Libya (instead of the United Kingdom of Libya), with Idris I remaining the monarch. The provinces surrendered administrative and financial decision making to the national government, whose authority was exercised through ten administrative districts, or *wilayas*.

The shift from the federal to a unitary system did not alter the government greatly because much of the structure established in 1951 remained intact at the national level. The major changes in the revised constitution related to the federal elements contained in the 1951 constitution. Each of the ten administrative districts was headed by a *wali* appointed by the council of ministers and empowered to execute the policies of the government in his district. The council also had the power to transfer or dismiss the *wali*, whose powers were more limited than those of the governor of a province or state under the 1951 constitution. All matters except those dealing exclusively with local affairs were under the direction of the national government. Another significant change related to parliament. The 1963 constitution empowered the king to appoint all the senators, and he could increase their number. Elections for members of the lower house were opened to universal suffrage.

Although King Idris determined the policies that were implemented by his ministers, whom he appointed and dismissed at will, he often did not appear to be involved in the daily activity of the government. He allowed the prime minister and cabinet to adopt policies they deemed appropriate as long as they had the confidence of parliament and stayed within the broad outlines established by the king.

The political circle Idris led was centered in the palace and in the special ties to Cyrenaica. Political expression was limited, and political parties were disbanded soon after independence. The ministers were close to, and dependent on, the monarchy, despite the constitutional provisions that stated they were collectively and individually responsible to the lower house of parliament. In the governmental structure the only significant potential alternative power center was the House of Representatives. It was the only place in which policies were publicly discussed, evaluated, and frequently criticized, and it provided a forum for the opposition to express its views.

In less than two decades, King Idris managed to unify the Libyan state. By means of political alliances and diplomacy, he protected his very weak country from external aggression and intervention. He was also able to obtain assistance from Western powers to help Libya feed its people and build schools and hospitals at a time when it was one of the poorest countries in the world.

The discovery of oil and the rise of Egyptian president Gamal Abd al-Nasser as a major charismatic figure in the Arab world transformed the Libyan political scene. King Idris was old (he was eighty in 1969, when he was overthrown) and in poor health. He had lost interest in the day-to-day running of the affairs of his country. His entourage had become progressively more powerful, and its conspicuous wealth was creating a great deal of resentment among Libyans. By the late 1960s, significant opposition to the policies and programs of the state was coming from many quarters of Libyan society.

POLITICAL STRUCTURE AND THE REVOLUTION OF 1969

On September 1, 1969, a bloodless military coup d'état overthrew the government of King Idris (who was out of the country at the time). There was little resistance, even by elements loyal to the king, such as the police and the tribes of Cyrenaica. Although the king made an attempt to secure British assistance to restore him to power, he was unsuccessful, and the monarchy was abolished. Little was known about the coup makers except that they called themselves the Free Unionist Officers and advocated "social justice, socialism, and unity."

In the first few weeks, a number of moderate civilians and army officers were appointed to the first postcoup cabinet. Although strongly nationalistic, these people were not antagonistic to the West and were prepared to develop good relations with Western powers after the evacuation of their military bases. Regionally, they were more pro-Arab and spoke more openly of supporting Arab causes, such as Arab unity and the Palestinians. Although socialism and social justice were discussed, the first Libyan cabinet did not plan to nationalize any sector of the economy, and foreigners who lived in Libya would be allowed to keep their property. The Revolutionary Command Council (RCC), however, headed by a young army officer named Muammar al-Qaddafi, advocated radical economic, social, and political change.

The confrontation between the Free Unionist Officers and the cabinet took place in December 1969, when the prime minister and a number of his cabinet ministers were accused of attempting to overthrow the regime and were arrested. The next day all powers were transferred to the RCC, which was made up of the Free Unionist Officers, and it was proclaimed the supreme authority in the land. The direction the political system was to take was decided then.

At the outset Qaddafi attempted to follow in the footsteps of Nasser of Egypt, going as far as to name a party that he created the Arab Socialist Union, like its Egyptian counterpart. In the mid-1970s, however, Qaddafi moved away from Nasserism and invented his own brand of socialism, which he called "natural socialism." He enunciated its principles in his *Green Book*, published in three volumes between 1976 and 1978. He preached complete egalitarianism and the abolition of wage labor and private ownership of land. Trade was portrayed as exploitative and nonproductive and therefore had to be taken over by the state. He strongly upheld the principles of Arab nationalism and called for support of the Palestinians and the creation of a powerful bloc of Arab states to fight Israel.

Religious reform was a very important part of his ideology: He emphasized that the Qur'an was the only source of Islamic law, or Shari'a. He claimed that Muhammad, the Muslim prophet, was just an intermediary between God and man and that since the Qur'an was in Arabic, anyone could read it and understand it and did not need a clergyman or imam to interpret it for him. From the mid-1980s on, he moved even further from the traditional Sunni Muslim position and claimed that religion had nothing to do with politics and that men of religion should focus on the spiritual rather than on the mundane in their Friday *khutba*, or sermon. He cracked down on Islamic militant groups inside Libya and shared intelligence with Algeria, Egypt, and Tunisia on the movements of those groups and their leaders in the region. In February 1994, however, Qaddafi appeared to change course, probably to undermine the rising tide of Islamic fundamentalism, by calling for the implementation of Islamic law in Libya primarily for criminal offenses but also for marriage and divorce. In the same vein, he called for the revival of the tradition of Sufi brotherhoods as a source of Islamic teachings.

Muammar al-Qaddafi was born in 1942 in the area of Sirte on the Mediterranean coast midway between Tripoli and Benghazi. He was the only surviving son of a poor Arabized Berber family belonging to the Qaddafi tribe. At the age of ten, he was sent to elementary school in the town of Sirte, and in 1956 he moved with his family to Sebha, where he attended the Sebha Preparatory School until 1961. It was there that he created the first command committee with many of the people who would become his closest allies and members of the RCC after the revolution. During that period he also learned about the events in Egypt: the 1956 Suez Canal crisis, the evacuation of the British forces, and Nasser's agrarian reforms and nationalizations. But perhaps what would influence him most would be Nasser's call for a united Arab world.

Qaddafi and his family moved to Misrata in Tripolitania, where he completed high school in 1963 and then entered the military academy in Benghazi. Three of his classmates from Sebha and Misrata joined him there, where they formed the nucleus of the Free Unionist Movement that planned the overthrow of the monarchy. After graduating from the academy in 1965, Qaddafi was sent to England to attend an army school at Bovington Hythe in Beaconsfield, where he took a six-month signal course. On his return to Libya, he enrolled in the history department at the University of Benghazi, but he was commissioned in 1966 to the signals corps of the Libyan army and never completed his university education. He remained in regular contact with the large network of fellow officers and friends he had developed over the years and built a secret organization that enabled him to carry out the coup in 1969.

Once firmly in control of the government in Libya, Qaddafi began to build his political power base. The first political organization he built in 1971 was the Arab Socialist Union (ASU), which was supposed to mobilize the population in support of the new regime's policies. Half of its members had to be farmers and workers, and its structure was to have local, regional, and national units headed by the RCC. The ASU, however, failed to mobilize popular enthusiasm for the revolution; consequently, in 1976, at its Third Party Congress, it ceased to exist as a political party.

Earlier, in 1973, Qaddafi had attempted to create a "cultural revolution," this time using the Chinese model, to mobilize popular support for the regime by criticizing the government bureaucracy, the bourgeoisie, the RCC, and the cabinet. He advocated the destruction of the bureaucracy, the suspension of all laws, the arming of the people, and a return to the principles of the Qur'an; he called on the people to take over the responsibilities of government. The outcome of this "cultural revolution" was a period of chaos during which were launched the first "popular committees" that were to involve people directly in the process of governing Libya. Qaddafi claimed that direct democracy was the only real democracy and, therefore, only through such organizations could Libya become really democratic.

Those popular committees were small units (sixteen to twenty people) of directly elected individuals representing people at the level of the workplace, school and university, village community, and city neighborhood. The popular committees selected some of their members to represent them at the district level. District committees sent representatives to the larger provincial committees. Once a year the provincial committees sent members to the General People's Congress. The decisions made at the congress were submitted to the participants so they could be implemented by the popular committees. The General People's Congress was also a vehicle for informing the ruling junta of the basic problems and demands of the people at the grassroots level.

In the second half of the 1970s, when Qaddafi felt that the Libyans were again becoming apathetic about the political system, he came up with new ideas for political reorganization. In 1977, he formed the revolutionary committees (*lijan thawriya*) that became watchdogs over the political activities of the popular committees and the secretariats of the popular congresses. These revolutionary committees became extremely powerful and quite unruly at times. They arrested people arbitrarily on charges of subversive activities, settled personal scores, and acted as spies for the government. The experiment with popular committees was reintroduced in the mid-1990s, when "purification committees" were set up to root out corruption in the private-sector retail trade. These committees, in turn, suffered a similar fate, when "volcano committees" were organized to purge their members accused of corruption in the late 1990s.

Until 1977 government activities were managed by a cabinet appointed by the RCC. The cabinet comprised mainly civilian technocrats, but RCC members held such critical cabinet posts or secretariats as defense and interior. After the attempted coup against Qaddafi by members of the RCC in 1975, the RCC was reduced from its original twelve members to only five. In 1977, in a carefully orchestrated maneuver, a General People's Congress of elected representatives changed the country's name to the Socialist People's Libyan Arab Jamahiriya, proclaimed the establishment of people's power, and vested all official power in the General People's Congress, abolishing the RCC as the supreme authority but naming the five remaining RCC officers as members of the congress's secretariat. Those five, with Qaddafi as the undisputed leader, continued to be the real power in Libya for the next two decades. The cabinet became the General People's Congress Committee.

In November 1988 Qaddafi announced the restructuring of the military and the creation of a new voluntary paramilitary organization under a separate command. He felt that the army that had tried to overthrow him on a number of occasions had become even more threatening after its defeat in Chad in 1987. Consequently, the restructuring of the traditional army was meant to purge its more dangerous elements. Paramilitary organizations, such as the People's Militia and the Jamahiri Guards, had been in existence since the late 1970s.

Opposition to the regime, however, continued unabated. There were reports of mutinies in the military throughout the 1980s, and one took place in 1993. The reaction was always swift and deadly. In the case of the 1993 mutiny, the air force was used to bomb selected military targets. Monarchist organizations, such as the Libyan Constitutional Union established in 1981, called for general elections and the return of the monarchy. The best-known organization opposing the Qaddafi regime is the National Front for the Liberation of Libya (NFSL), also founded in 1981 and headed by a former ambassador to India, Muhammad al-Maqaryaf. This organization succeeded in bringing together Islamists and secular pro-democracy opponents of the regime under one umbrella. Some members of the Muslim Brotherhood left the NFSL in 1982, and some secularists left in March 1994 (forming a new opposition organization calling itself the Movement for Change and Reform). The principal organ of the NFSL is the *Inqadh* ("Salvation"), a publication that appears seven or eight times a year with articles condemning the regime, exposing human rights violations in Libya, and discussing the social, economic, and political conditions in the country. The NFSL also publishes a bimonthly newsletter and has a radio program, *Voice of Libya*, that has been broadcast daily from Cairo since 1982. The NFSL attempted to overthrow the regime in 1984 with a military attack against the barracks of Bab al-Aziziya. The attack failed, but the NFSL subsequently built a paramilitary wing to the party: the Libyan National Army.

In the 1990s the Islamists became another major opposition force in Libya. They have their roots in older movements, such as the Ikhwan, the Muslim Brotherhood, a movement that developed in Libya with the arrival of Egyptian schoolteachers in the 1950s. The Hizb al-Tahrir ("Liberation Party") and Jabhat al-Tahrir al-Islami ("Islamic Liberation Front") are examples of such offshoots. Other Islamic opposition groups include Al-Jama'a al-Islamiyah 'Libya' ("Islamic Group–Libya"), Al-Haraka al-Islamiya 'Libya' ("Islamic Movement–Libya"), and Al-Takfir wa-al-Hijra ("Apostasy and Migration"). Libya has responded to this opposition like other governments in the region, by cracking down on these groups, imprisoning their leaders, and censoring their publications.

The Libyan authorities have also imprisoned and assassinated individuals critical of the government, although they belonged neither to Islamist nor to terrorist groups. For example, Daif al-Ghazal, a prominent Libyan writer and journalist for the London-based online newspaper *Libya al-Yawm*, was abducted from his car in May 2005 and severely tortured; his mutilated body was discovered two weeks later. He had been writing articles critical of the corruption in Libya and called for the formation of a civil society committee against corruption. Abd al-Razaq al-Mansuri, an Internet writer and former bookseller, received an eighteen-month prison sentence because of his Internet articles on www.akhbar-libya.com criticizing the Libyan regime. Libya's best-known prisoner of conscience, Fathi al-Jahmi, was incarcerated in March 2002, without trial, at an internal facility in Tripoli after he gave interviews to the international media criticizing Muammar al-Qaddafi and calling for internal reform. He was released after US Senator Joseph Biden intervened on his behalf in March 2004. A few days later, he was again arrested, this time with his family, and although his wife and son were released six months later, he remained incarcerated. On May 5, 2009, he was released and sent to Amman, Jordan, for medical care. A few days later, on May 21, he died of a heart ailment that had not been treated during his imprisonment in Libya.

POLITICAL AND ECONOMIC ENVIRONMENT

At independence at least 90 percent of the population was illiterate, and no significant educated elite existed. With the best agricultural land held by Italian settlers, there was no indigenous economic infrastructure. Furthermore, the substantial amounts of capital required for development were not internally available. These deficiencies were partially overcome by outside assistance, notably from France, Italy, the United Kingdom, and the United States. To overcome the shortage of qualified personnel, Libya recruited foreign experts in industry, agriculture, education, planning, and development through the United Nations and its specialized agencies and from various governments, primarily from Egypt. Libyans also studied abroad on government fellowships to acquire and refine their knowledge in technical and administrative fields.

The nature and prospects of the Libyan economy changed drastically with the discovery of important petroleum reserves at the end of the 1950s. Although small amounts of oil had been found as early as 1935, it was not until 1955 that the first major oil find was made at Edjeleh, on the border with Algeria. That year the Libyan government passed its first petroleum law, which was designed to encourage diversity among companies wishing to have oil concessions in Libya and to prevent any one country or company from being the sole concessionaire.

Although the first major oil finds were in the western part of Libya, most of the other important discoveries were further northeast, primarily in Sirtica. In 1959 Esso oil wells in the Zelten field in Sirtica yielded 17,500 barrels per day (bpd), and other major oil strikes were made in the same area in that year and the following one. Libya's position was strengthened even further after the June 1967 Middle East war because, with the closing of the Suez Canal, Libyan petroleum exports to Europe had a significant comparative advantage over petroleum from the Gulf area, which had to be either transshipped or routed around Africa. Production and exports continued to increase very rapidly over the next decade, rising from 6 million barrels in 1961 to 1.2 billion barrels in 1970.

After Qaddafi seized power, he decided to exert more control over oil production in Libya. In April 1970, serious negotiations began with the major oil companies over a reduction in production, an increase in prices, and control of the companies' operations in Libya. With expert legal advice, Libya put certain proposals on the table and threatened the companies with nationalization if they did not agree to its terms. Several companies refused to give Libya 51 percent control of their operations and left the country, but the majority agreed to renegotiate the terms of their concessions. The outcome was a decline in production and a tremendous increase in revenue for the Libyan government. Whereas in 1969 Libya was producing 1.12 billion barrels of oil and its oil revenues totaled $1.17 billion, by 1973 production had declined to 794 million barrels, and oil revenues had risen to $2.22 billion. In 1974, after the Arab oil embargo, Libya produced 544 million barrels, and oil revenues increased to $6 billion.

Throughout the 1980s Libyan production hovered around 1.1 million bpd, the quota limit set by OPEC, but rose to 1.5 million bpd in the early 1990s, when world oil prices were very low. By 2005 production was up again, reaching an estimated 1.7 million bpd. Oil revenues declined from $21 billion in 1980 to $10.2 billion in 1991 and $5.7 billion in 1998, after which world oil prices began rising significantly, and Libya's oil revenues grew commensurably. Libya earned an estimated $24 billion from oil exports in 2005 and $35 billion in 2008, as oil prices continued to rise. In the early 1990s Libya's proven reserves of crude oil were estimated at 22.8 billion barrels, but further exploration led experts to raise the estimate to 40 billion by 2005. Most of the oil wells are in the eastern part of the country in the Sirte basin in Cyrenaica, but Libya also has access to major offshore deposits on the continental shelf between Libya and Tunisia, which may contain as much as 7 billion barrels of oil, and near the Maltese coast.

As of January 2007, Libya's proven natural gas reserves were estimated at 52.7 trillion cubic feet. The Western Libyan Gas Project (WLGP), which came online in 2004, has made it possible to transfer this gas to Europe via a 520 kilometer underwater pipeline called the Green Stream. In 2005, 10 billion cubic meters of gas were produced (up from 7 billion the previous year); eight of these were sold to Europe, and two were consumed domestically. The WLGP is a fifty-fifty joint venture between Italy's Ente Nazionale Idrocarburi (ENI) and Libya's National Oil Company.

Libya's major economic activity, before the discovery of petroleum in the 1950s, had been agriculture. However, only 1.2 percent of Libya's land is arable, and of that, less than 1 percent is irrigated. The agricultural sector still retains its importance and, together with forestry and fishing, represented 7.6 percent of the gross domestic product and employed 17 percent of the labor force in 1999. However, the country does not produce enough to feed its own population: Libya imports 75 percent of its food requirements.

Water is scarce, and the supply is very irregular in areas where rainfall is its main source. Water for irrigation has been drawn from aquifers in the Jefara plain at a rate equivalent to six times the amount of rainfall needed to recharge those aquifers. In 1983 a massive water pipeline project, the Great Manmade River, was inaugurated at the Sarir Oasis. When completed it will have cost an estimated $30 billion. The first phase of the project was completed in 1994, and 2 million tons of water a day were supplied to Benghazi via a 1,874 kilometer pipeline from fields at Tazerno and Sarir in the east central region of Libya. The second phase, completed in 1996, provides 2.5 million tons of water daily to Tripoli from three fields in the southern oasis of Kufra via a 1,551 kilometer pipeline. The plan for the third phase is to link the two pipelines with a bidirectional pipeline, flow control, and pump stations that will double daily water capacity. Phase four envisages pipelines to Tobruk and Zuwara. The ultimate goal is not only to provide fresh water to all the main urban centers in Libya but also to irrigate 500,000 hectares, of which 40 percent will be located in the Sirte region in the north-central plains of Libya. Part of the water is to be used for pastureland for sheep and cattle.

The non-oil manufacturing and construction sectors account for 20 percent of the gross national product. The manufacturing sector includes not only the processing of agricultural products but also more complex industries, such as the manufacture of petrochemicals and iron and steel. The only identified non-hydrocarbon mineral deposit in Libya is the iron ore at Wadi Shatti, which has an estimated 2 to 3 billion tons, ranging from 25 to 50 percent iron content. The government plans to use it instead of the iron that is currently imported for the iron and steel complex in Misrata. It is also interested in diversifying the economy and developing tourism based on Libya's Roman ruins and 1,200 miles of pristine beaches.

After the 1969 revolution, the RCC redirected the economy toward rapid economic development, a more equal distribution of income and services, greater government economic control, and independence from foreign influence. An increase in the literacy of the population was sought through compulsory and free elementary education. The literacy rate, which in 1973 was estimated at 40 percent for the Libyan population as a whole, with a lower rate for women, rose to 76 percent in the late 1990s and an estimated 87 percent by 2007. This is considerably higher than any other North African country, including Egypt and Tunisia. Secondary schools, universities, and adult and technical education also became more widely available. The two universities, Al-Fateh in Tripoli and Gar Yunis in Benghazi, have new campuses in Tobruk. A new university opened in Sebha in 1986, and there is a college of science and technology at Marsa Brega with additional facilities in Misrata. There are a number of international schools in Tripoli and Benghazi, most notably three Philippine international schools that serve the Philippine community in those two cities. In 2005, Global Education Management Systems offered a program of education to students in the first six grades of the international school in Tripoli that included both British and Libyan curricula. Until 1982 a large number of Libyan students were sent abroad to study. Since then, deteriorating relations with the West and a decline in financial resources have resulted in a sharp decrease in the number of students studying abroad. With the thawing of US-Libyan relations since 2004, discussions have been underway between the two governments to expand student exchanges and increase the number of Libyan students at American institutions of higher learning.

Upgrading of health standards and other measures to improve the personal situation of the population have also contributed to the improved resource base. The number of medical doctors rose to 1.29 per 1,000 people in 2008. That compares favorably with some industrialized countries, such as the United Kingdom with 1.66 physicians per 1,000 people and Singapore with 1.40 physicians. The infant mortality rate dropped from 160 per 1,000 live births in 1960 to 72 in 1991 and 17 in 2008, and life expectancy rose from 46.7 years in 1960 to 77.3 years in 2009. It is important to note, however, that despite these figures Libyans complain about the quality of health care, and there were several reported cases of bubonic plague in 2009.

Under the Qaddafi regime, the government's role in the economy became predominant. Libya not only took majority control of the oil companies operating in its territory but also nationalized the local assets of some companies completely, such as Shell in 1974. Starting in November 1969, it nationalized all foreign banks, including the Arab Bank, Banco di Roma, and Barclay's Bank. By the end of 1970, the number of commercial banks had been reduced to five, three of which were state owned, and two were state controlled. Insurance companies had been completely nationalized by 1971 and were merged into two state-owned companies. Basic infrastructural facilities, including major airlines, electric power plants, and communications, became state owned and operated.

Large- and medium-sized industries with foreign proprietors—primarily Italians, who owned 75 to 80 percent of all industrial plants in Libya—were taken over by the state. Those included tobacco, tanning and leather, textile, lumber, and construction plants, as well as food industries, including canned sardines and tomatoes and bottled soft drinks. In 1972 agricultural cooperatives were established and gave financial, technical, and marketing assistance to the farmers who joined. The small-business sector prospered at first, as the government adopted a policy of giving contracts to Libyan firms and lending up to 95 percent of the capital to finance indigenous commercial enterprises. Between 1969 and 1976 the government issued 40,000 licenses to new grocery stores in the district of Tripoli alone. Starting in 1971, workers became part owners and were given a larger share of the profits made by the firms that employed them. Free housing was provided to some, and loans were given to others to buy suitable housing.

Although the aim of the government in implementing these policies had been to stimulate Libyan entrepreneurship and develop a strong indigenous middle class that would become a powerful political base for the regime, the policies had different outcomes. Local businesses that were assured of receiving government contracts or loans began to depend more and more on government subsidies and foreign labor and know-how, and many became mere fronts for non-Libyan interests. A number of the large agricultural projects that were meant to modernize and develop the rural sector foundered because of water shortages, poor planning and management, and the small size of the rural labor force. The settlement policy pursued by the government to induce farmers to remain in rural areas was by and large unsuccessful, as the rural population continued to migrate to cities, seeking employment and a higher standard of living. In the industrial sector the policies of the government led to an increase in the importation of capital goods and raw materials. Because of shortages of skilled manpower and administrative personnel, labor had to be imported as well. In 1975, 58 percent of the managerial and professional manpower in Libya was foreign, as were 35 percent of the technical personnel, 27 percent of the skilled and semiskilled workforce, and 42 percent of the unskilled workers. In 2008, the labor force was estimated at 1.8 million people.

The attempt to develop an entrepreneurial middle class failed as well when the Libyan businessmen who had government contracts reaped huge profits and then invested them abroad. What was taking place was not so much the formation of a new middle class of small businessmen supportive of the regime as the consolidation of the economic power of the traditional urban notability, who had the skills, practice, and connections to take advantage of government-sponsored programs to enrich themselves. That process in turn frightened the Qaddafi regime, which perceived the notables as a major potential force of domestic opposition.

Consequently, the policies of the state became more radical in the period from 1976 to 1980. Qaddafi's *Green Book*, expounding his political and economic philosophy, first appeared during that period. He called on workers to take a large number of commercial and industrial enterprises over from their Libyan owners. A law was promulgated in 1978 specifying that every family had the right to own a home of its own and that tenants therefore could take immediate possession of their rented homes. Those two injunctions dealt a very severe blow to the urban notables, who lost both their commercial establishments and their real estate investments. By some estimates the private sector had invested 41 percent of its capital in real estate. Furthermore, all foreign trade was to be conducted by the state, whereas until then the private sector had been allowed to import goods and sell them on the Libyan market.

In the 1980s the confrontation that pitted the United States against Libya because of the latter's support for terrorism resulted in the imposition of economic sanctions banning US import of Libyan oil and export of high technology equipment to Libya. After 1985 the United States stopped importing products derived from Libyan crude, such as naphtha, methanol, and low-sulfur fuel oil. In 1986 Libyan assets in the United States, estimated at $1 to $2 billion, were frozen. These embargoes, bans, and freezes, coupled with a decline in the price of oil, resulted in a major decline in Libya's export revenues.

The outbreak of the Gulf crisis in 1990 led to windfall profits for several months, owing to an increase in crude output and prices. But Libya began facing economic difficulties after 1992, when the UN Security Council imposed major economic sanctions on Libya for its alleged role in the bombing of Pan Am Flight 103 over Lockerbie, Scotland, in 1988. UN Resolution 731 banned flights to and from Libya and prohibited the supply of aircraft or aircraft parts to Libya and the sale or transfer to Libya of military equipment of any kind. It also called on all UN member states to significantly reduce diplomatic personnel and staff in Libyan embassies on their territories. In 1999 the UN sanctions were suspended, after the two bombing suspects were turned in to a Scottish court. Only after Libya officially accepted responsibility for the bombing and agreed to pay $2.7 billion in compensation to the families of the victims did the UN Security Council vote to lift the sanctions in September 2003.

Because of its dwindling resources and international trade problems in the early 1990s, Libya was unable to pay the salaries of government officials and the armed forces regularly or to maintain 1980s levels of expenditure on health and education. To reduce the deficit and deal with the economic crisis, Qaddafi called for privatization in September 1992 and passed Law No. 9 urging Libyans to form joint-stock companies and set up family firms, partnerships, and individual businesses. In March 1993, for the first time since the nationalizations of the 1970s, Libya allowed the establishment of private banks. In July of that year, the government permitted private-sector companies to engage in wholesale trade. In June 2003 Qaddafi announced that Libya's public sector had failed economically and would be abolished, and he once again called for privatization. He appointed an American-trained technocrat, Shukri Ghanim, as prime minister to oversee the process of privatization. The following year, Ghanim announced that 160 publicly owned companies, out of 360 earmarked for privatization, had been privatized. The rest, he claimed, would be transferred to the private sector gradually over the next four years, and some would be open to foreign investors.

FOREIGN RELATIONS

King Idris followed a pro-Western foreign policy. Treaties signed with Britain in 1953 and the United States in 1954 provided for the maintenance of military bases and forces in Libya in exchange for ensuring Libyan security, and both Britain and the United States were the source of development grants and budget-ary subventions. An agreement with France in 1955 provided for communications facilities in the southwestern desert areas. Close ties were also maintained with Turkey and Greece. Libya joined the Arab League in 1953 but remained basically neutral in inter-Arab and Arab-Western conflicts, following the theory that it was in Libya's security interest not to be involved. The king's decisions not to close the British military bases in 1956 during the Suez Canal crisis and not to participate in the 1967 Arab-Israeli War created resentment among young Libyans, who felt the country was being kept out of Arab affairs and marginalized in the Arab world. Under internal and external pressure to close foreign bases, the govern-ment after 1964 publicly supported the early evacuation of these bases but took few practical steps in that direction. The issue was brought up again in 1967, and the process of closing bases began in earnest.

Qaddafi regarded the coup of September 1969 as the starting point of Libyan independence. In order to legitimize its power, the RCC gave priority to remov-ing the foreign bases. It could then claim that the new regime had liberated Libya from foreign imperialism. Agreement was soon reached between the RCC and the US and British governments to evacuate the Wheelus base and the British bases at Tobruk and al-Adam in spring 1970.

Libya's relations with its neighbors have been characterized by numerous at-tempts at unity. Those attempts, however, did not always come from Libya. The first took place in December 1969 when Egypt, Libya, and Sudan attempted to set up a federation. The new Libyan regime's goal was not merely to formalize its ad-herence to the principles of Arab unity but also to boost its questionable legiti-macy domestically through association with Nasser, the most important leader in the Arab world in the eyes of Libyans. The Federation of Arab Republics (with Egypt and Syria), promulgated in September 1971, was an additional attempt by

Libya to cement its alliance with Egypt, especially after Nasser's death. Although Qaddafi's position was somewhat weakened by Nasser's death, he attempted to take Nasser's place and thus enhance his legitimacy at home by becoming the new ideologue of Arab nationalism and Arab unity.

Libya and Tunisia announced the formation of a union in January 1974, following several months of talks between Tunisian president Habib Bourguiba and Qaddafi. The plan called for a single state, the Arab Islamic Republic. The original offer came from Tunisia, in an effort to wean Libya away from Egypt. When Libyan-Egyptian relations deteriorated after the October 1973 Arab-Israeli War, Libya pursued the merger with Tunisia to ensure itself a regional ally. Opposition within Tunisia as well as from Algeria aborted the merger plans. In 1975 Libya and Algeria signed a mutual defense pact, the Hassi Mas'ud Treaty, which ensured Libya a major regional ally. When Egypt attacked Libya in July 1977 and destroyed Soviet radar installations on the Libyan-Egyptian border, Algeria intervened on Libya's behalf, and the bombing was stopped. In return, Libya supported Algeria against Morocco on the Western Sahara issue and supplied the Polisario Front with both financial and military resources for the next six years. In 1981 Libya merged with Chad in an attempt to put an end to the war between the two countries. Libya also wanted to ensure its dominance of northern Chad. That merger worsened relations with Algeria, which turned toward Tunisia and then Mauritania and signed the Treaty of Brotherhood and Concord in 1983, which did not include Libya. The Arab-African Federation, set up between Libya and Morocco in August 1984, was in part a reaction to the renewed regional isolation of Libya and in part a reaction to King Hassan's concern with retaining control of the Western Sahara. The outcome was a significant decline of Libyan support for the Polisario. This support was further eroded by Libya's dwindling resources after the fall of oil prices in the mid-1980s.

In February 1989 Algeria, Libya, Morocco, Mauritania, and Tunisia announced the creation of the Arab Maghrib Union (UMA), meant to foster economic integration on the model of the European community. The countries of the Maghrib wanted to enlarge their markets and find an alternative outlet for their labor. Although they lack economic complementarity, they have set up joint companies and joint projects to increase efficiency and prevent duplication in the manufacturing sector, for instance. Libya has been the only country capable of absorbing some of the regional labor surplus. It has removed trade barriers with its neighbors, enhancing trade and allowing Libyans to shop in Tunisia for goods they cannot find at home. Libya is a major partner in the Arab Maghribi Bank for Investment and Trade and has a large number of joint projects with its neighbors, including Egypt, in the agricultural, transport and communications, industrial, and petrochemical sectors.

Libya's relations with Egypt have been turbulent for the last quarter century. From the early closeness with Nasser during the first year of the Libyan revolution, relations deteriorated progressively under Anwar Sadat, culminating in Egypt's bombing of Libya in 1977, partly in retaliation for Libya's subversive activities in Egypt and partly because Libya allowed the Soviets to survey Egypt's military installations by means of radar based on the Libyan-Egyptian frontier. In the 1980s, however, relations with the regime of Hosni Mubarak improved markedly. Tens of thousands of Egyptians live and work in Libya, and a large number of joint infrastructural, industrial, and agricultural projects were set up between the two countries. Mubarak and Qaddafi have shared intelligence on Islamic fundamentalists on both sides of the border, and Mubarak has personally interceded on Libya's behalf for the lifting of UN sanctions.

Under Qaddafi, the Libyan government has been uncompromising in its stance toward Israel. Qaddafi has condemned Zionism as aggressive nationalism and has supported the more radical groups among the Palestinians, such as the Popular Front for the Liberation of Palestine–General Command. Although the Libyan leader has provided financial, moral, and political support to the Palestine Liberation Organization, he also had strong disagreements with its longtime chairman, Yasir Arafat. After the Camp David Accords of 1978 and the Egypt-Israel Peace Treaty of 1979, Libya became a leader of the "rejection front"—Arab states that denounced any political settlement with Israel. Qaddafi was against the 1993 peace initiative between the Palestinians and the Israelis, but in May 1993 he sent two hundred Libyans on a pilgrimage to Jerusalem and invited Libyan Jews who lived abroad to come and visit Libya. Since the second Palestinian Intifada ("uprising") that began in the fall of 2000, Libya has again become very vocal in its criticism of Israel and of US policy in the region. Qaddafi has also worked actively for over two decades to counter Israeli influence in sub-Saharan Africa.

Libya's relations with the United States deteriorated over the years. Until the 1973 Arab-Israeli War, Qaddafi had merely been critical of US Middle East policies. After the war, Sadat moved closer to the West and to the United States; the Libyan leader, perceiving this as threatening to Libya's security, moved closer to the Soviet Bloc. His support for terrorist groups in various parts of the world caused the United States to stop selling arms and military hardware to Libya. In December 1979 the US embassy in Tripoli was sacked and burned. The Reagan administration then chose Qaddafi as the principal target of its antiterrorist policy and adopted further economic and political measures to isolate Libya regionally and internationally. This culminated in the bombing of Tripoli in 1986 in retaliation for a terrorist bombing later traced to the radical Palestinian Abu Nidal organization.

In 1991 the United States and the United Kingdom formally charged Libya with the bombing of Pan Am Flight 103 over Lockerbie, Scotland, while France issued arrest warrants for four Libyans accused of participating in a 1988 bombing of a French Union des Transports Aériennes (UTA) airliner over Niger. The Lockerbie and UTA charges led to the passing of UN Resolutions 731 and 748 in 1992, imposing sanctions on Libya, including a ban on all flights to and from Libya and a prohibition on the supply of aircraft, aircraft parts, and military equipment of any kind. The United States and Great Britain demanded that Libya extradite two Libyans accused of the Lockerbie bombing. Libya refused. In the mid-1990s the United States passed a law imposing sanctions on non-US firms investing in the oil sectors of Libya and Iran, which became known as the Iran-Libya Sanctions Act (ILSA). The European Union, in turn, strongly objected and passed legislation to block the impact of ILSA, making it illegal for European firms to comply with it.

Due to many factors, including the sharp fall in oil prices at the end of the 1990s, Qaddafi decided to turn in the two Libyan suspects. In April 1999 the men were sent to The Hague to a specially convened Scottish court, where their trial opened a year later. One of the men was found innocent of all charges, but the second was found guilty. Qaddafi promised to appeal the case. The UN sanctions against Libya were suspended when the two suspects were turned over to the Scottish court and were finally lifted in September 2003 after Libya agreed to pay $10 million to the families of each victim of the Lockerbie bombing.

In December 2003 Libya announced it would end all programs aimed at developing weapons of mass destruction. In the following month it ratified the Comprehensive Nuclear Test Ban Treaty and allowed a compliance-monitoring team to be posted on its territory. In response to these initiatives, the US administration lifted its travel ban and unilateral trade and investment sanctions on Libya and ceased application of ILSA. It also unblocked Libya's frozen assets, encouraged people-to-people exchanges in education and health, and welcomed Libya's application to the World Trade Organization. In May 2006 US Secretary of State Condoleeza Rice announced that the United States was restoring full diplomatic relations with Libya, and in 2007 President George Bush appointed Gene Cretz ambassador to Libya, ending a thirty-five-year vacancy for the position. In 2007 Libya was elected to the UN Security Council by the General Assembly; it even assumed the presidency of the council for a month in January 2008 (the position rotates monthly among member states).

Libyan-Soviet relations became closer after the rapprochement between Egypt and the West that began in 1974. Relations were based primarily on mutual interest rather than on ideology, as Qaddafi had been consistently critical of communism. Libya needed a stable supplier of arms and a strong ally to balance US influence in Egypt. The Soviet Union was assured of a client that could pay its bills and was strategically located, with the longest coastline on the southern Mediterranean. The sharp drop in oil prices and Libya's inability to pay its debts later soured relations between the two countries. For a time oil was used to pay some of Libya's debts, estimated at $4.5 billion. Russia respected the sanctions and refused to sell arms to Libya until it handed over the two Lockerbie bombing suspects. After that, Russian-Libyan relations improved significantly, and trade between the two countries resumed. In April 2008 Russian president Vladimir Putin visited Libya, the first such visit by a Russian head of state since 1985. He agreed to suspend Libya's debt in return for signing a number of military and civilian agreements, including a $3.4 billion contract to build a railway between Sirte and Benghazi on the Mediterranean.

Libya's relations with western Europe gradually improved during the 1990s and more rapidly after the lifting of UN sanctions in 2003. Energy was a major determinant in these relations, as Libya exports oil and gas to western Europe and imports foodstuffs, capital goods, medicine, and other commodities. Royal Dutch/Shell, the energy giant, announced an agreement with the National Oil Corporation of Libya in May 2005 to rejuvenate and upgrade the existing liquefied natural gas plant at Marsa Brega on the Libyan coast and to explore for gas in five areas in the Sirte Basin region. Italy's ENI and AGIP oil and gas companies were exploring for and producing oil, as were Austria's OMV 4, France's Total, Spain's Repsol, Greece's Hellenic Petroleum, British Petroleum, and the British Gas Group. As of 2006, Tamoil, an oil-refining, marketing, and distribution company controlled by Netherlands-based Oil Invest and partly owned by Europoil, a group of private Libyan investors, owned 2,967 service stations in Germany, Italy, the Netherlands, Spain, and Switzerland, as well as refineries in Hamburg, Germany, Cremona, Italy, and Collombey, Switzerland.

Qaddafi has supported Muslims in Africa and Asia politically, financially, and culturally. He has aided Muslim insurgents in the Philippines, built mosques and schools in Niger and Mali, and given financial aid to a large number of states, including Burundi, the Central African Republic, Gabon, Indonesia, Malaysia, Pakistan, Togo, and Uganda. The Organization of African Unity (OAU) passed a resolution in June 1998 declaring that its member states would no longer recognize the UN embargo on flights to and from Libya and the UN sanctions against Libya unless the United States and United Kingdom agreed to try the Libyan bombing suspects in a neutral country. The OAU's action and Nelson Mandela's support for Libya were critical in the final negotiations to hold the trial at The Hague.

In the late 1990s Qaddafi declared that a "United States of Africa" should be formed to replace the OAU. He convinced the African heads of state of the importance of this idea, and in September 1999 they issued the Sirte Declaration calling for the establishment of the African Union (AU). The declaration was followed by a summit in Lomé, Togo, in 2000 where the Constitutive Act of the African Union was adopted. Two years later the African Union was launched in Durban, South Africa, by its first president, South African president Thabo Mbeki. The AU has fifty-three member states, including all African states except Morocco (because of its position on the Western Sahara). It is a successor not only of the OAU but also of the African Economic Community. In February 2009 Qaddafi was elected chairman of the African Union at a closed session in Ethiopia.

Since coming to power, Qaddafi has sought to associate Libya with "revolutionary" causes and movements. He has been active in various regions in support of coups and in funding and training guerrilla groups and opposition political movements. He has been implicated in efforts to assassinate rival leaders and opponents of his regime and in support of terrorist groups and movements. Moreover, Libya was involved in military ventures in Uganda in 1979 in support of Idi Amin and has occupied the Aouzou Strip in Chad since 1972. In September 1988 Libya was accused of manufacturing chemical weapons at a plant in Rabta. These and similar activities strained Libya's relations with many European states and the United States over the years. In 1993, in response to UN sanctions, Libya closed down the offices of the notorious terrorist Abu Nidal in Tripoli and issued a statement renouncing terrorism. Libyan officials also met with British officials in Geneva in June 1993 and gave them information about the Irish Republican Army, which had received Libyan assistance.

One of Qaddafi's sons, Sayf al-Islam, is apparently positioning himself to succeed his father and has tried to improve Libya's "terrorist state" image. Educated in Libya and Europe and able to communicate in several languages, he seems less ideologically driven than his father. As chairman of the Al-Qaddafi Foundation for Charity Organization, he helped negotiate the release in 2000 of European and South African hostages held in the Philippines by the Abu Sayaf rebels; in 2001 he was involved in negotiations to help free "Shelters Now" aid workers who had been taken hostage by the Taliban government in Afghanistan; and in 2003 he negotiated an agreement with France on behalf of Libya to provide compensation to the families of victims of the 1989 UTA plane bombing.

Libya today remains under the control of a small group of men led by Muammar al-Qaddafi. Economic and political liberalization are still limited, and democratization has not taken place; nor is it likely to unfold smoothly under the present regime.

BIBLIOGRAPHY

Historical works on Libya include John Wright's *Libya* (New York: Praeger Publishers, 1969), which focuses especially on the period 1911 to 1951. Wright's second volume, *Libya: A Modern History* (Baltimore: Johns Hopkins University Press, 1982), covers the period through 1981. E. E. Evans-Pritchard's *The Sanusi of Cyrenaica* (London: Oxford University Press, 1949) provides an important study of Libya's main religious order and its role in the country's development, as does Nicola Ziadeh's *Sanusiyah: A Study of a Revivalist Movement in Islam* (Leiden: E. J. Brill, 1968). Henry Serrano Villard, the first US minister to Libya after independence, gives a general overview in *Libya: The New Arab Kingdom of North Africa* (Ithaca, NY: Cornell University Press, 1956). The UN commissioner in Libya, Adrian Pelt, describes the transformation of Libya from an Italian colony to an independent state in *Libyan Independence and the United Nations: A Case of Planned Decolonization* (New Haven, CT: Yale University Press, 1970). Lisa Anderson covers the social and political history of Libya for a century and a half in *The State and Social Transformation in Tunisia and Libya, 1830–1980* (Princeton, NJ: Princeton University Press, 1986). Majid Khadduri, in *Modern Libya: A Study in Political Development* (Baltimore: Johns Hopkins University Press, 1963), considers the monarchy in detail.

Studies of Libya's political, social, and economic system and foreign policy since 1969 include J. A. Allan, *Libya Since Independence: Economic and Social Development* (London: Croom Helm, 1982); Omar L. Fathaly and Monte Palmer, *Political Development and Social Change in Libya* (Lexington, MA: Lexington Books, 1979); Harold D. Nelson, *Libya: A Country Study*, 3rd ed. (Washington, DC: American University, Foreign Area Studies, 1979); John K. Cooley, *Libyan Sandstorm* (New York: Holt, Rinehart & Winston, 1982); Marius Deeb and Mary-Jane Deeb, *Libya Since the Revolution: Aspects of Social and Political Development* (New York: Praeger Publishers, 1982); Mary-Jane Deeb, *Libya's Foreign Policy in North Africa* (Boulder, CO: Westview Press, 1991); Ruth First, *Libya: The Elusive Revolution* (Middlesex, UK: Penguin Books, 1974); Ronald Bruce St. John, *Qaddafi's World Design: Libyan Foreign Policy, 1969–1987* (London: Saqi Books, 1987); Lillian Craig Harris, *Qadhafi's Revolution and the Modern State* (Boulder, CO: Westview/Croom Helm, 1986); E. G. H. Joffe and K. S. McLachlan, *Social and Economic Development of Libya* (Cambridgeshire, UK: MENAS Press, 1982); Jonathan Bearman, *Qadhafi's Libya* (London: Zed Books, 1986); J. A. Allan, *Libya: The Experience of Oil* (Boulder, CO: Westview Press, 1981); Mirella Bianco, *Gadafi: Voice from the Desert* (London: Longman Group, 1975); David Blundy and Andrew Lycett, *Qaddafi and the Libyan Revolution* (Boston: Little, Brown, 1987); Edward Haley, *Qadhafi and the United States Since 1969* (New York: Praeger, 1984); and René Lemarchand, *The Green and the Black: Qadhafi's Policies in Africa* (Bloomington: Indiana University Press, 1988).

Recent books include Tim Niblock, *"Pariah States" and Sanctions in the Middle East: Iraq, Libya, Sudan* (Boulder, CO: Lynne Rienner Publishers, 2001); Mansoor El-Kikhia, *Libya's Qaddafi: The Politics of Contradiction* (Gainesville: University Press of Florida, 1997); Dirk Vandewalle, *Libya Since Independence: Oil and State-Building* (Ithaca, NY: Cornell University Press, 1998) and *History of Modern Libya* (New York: Cambridge University Press, 2006); J. Millard Burr and Robert O. Collins, *Africa's Thirty Years War: Libya, Chad, and the Sudan, 1963–1993* (Boulder, CO: Westview Press, 1999); Judith Gurney, *Libya: The Political Economy of Oil* (Oxford: Oxford University Press, 1996); and Ronald Bruce St. John, *Libya and the United States: Two Centuries of Strife* (Philadelphia: University of Pennsylvania Press, 2002).

15

Kingdom of Morocco

Gregory W. White

Historical Background

Precolonial Morocco

What is known today as Morocco remained largely cut off from Roman North Africa, largely because of the Rif and Atlas mountains. The indigenous tribes resisted external imperial incursion. Still, the Roman presence was not insignificant, and important occupations were established in Tingis (Tangier) and Volubilis. In turn, the Vandal activities in the fifth century were similarly incomplete, as was the effort of Byzantium to take control of the territory in the sixth century.

The Islamic campaign in the 660s reached as far as the Atlantic, but in 683 the Berber chieftain Kusayla defeated ʿUqba, sending Islamic forces back east to present-day Libya. By 698, however, Arab forces had recaptured the Byzantine footholds on the North African coast. And by the early eighth century, Arabo-Islamic power had spread back into Morocco, across the Strait of Gibraltar, and onto the Iberian Peninsula.

For centuries, several influential and powerful dynasties dominated the region: the Idrissids, who founded Fez in the 780s; the Almoravids, who established Marrakech in the eleventh century; the Almohads, who reigned during the fall of Muslim Spain; the Merenids; the Wattasids; and the Saadians. The scope of these empires was truly astounding. At its height in 1100, for example, the Almoravid state reached from northern present-day Mauritania, east to Algiers, and north into Spain to include Zaragosa.

The Christian *Reconquista* of Spain changed the political economy of Morocco. The extension of Christian control into North Africa transformed the trans-Sahara slave trade and prompted the emergence of Christian enclaves on the Mediterranean coast: Melilla and Ceuta. In turn, it set the stage for the Ottoman efforts to move into the western Mediterranean in the sixteenth century. Both the Saadians and, in its turn, the Alawite dynasty in the seventeenth century

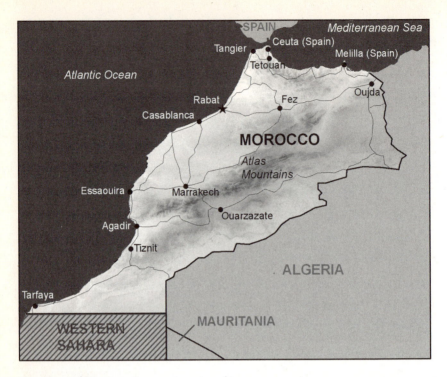

Kingdom of Morocco

avoided Ottoman penetration from the east. The Alawites established Meknes as their capital and have ruled Morocco until this day.

By the late nineteenth century, the country was largely in disarray and decline. The French occupation of Algeria in 1830 was met with virtually no response from the ruling Moroccan monarchy. In 1856, a treaty with Great Britain opened the country to "free trade" and gave Britain control over the Strait of Gibraltar. The Spanish seized control of more coastal islands and rocks in the mid-nineteenth century and occupied Tetouan.

From 1873 to 1894 Mulay Hassan fully established the authority of the Alawi Sharifian Empire. After his death, however, the country fell into immediate difficulties, largely owing to mismanagement by Hassan's son, Abd al-Aziz (1894–1908). Under Abd al-Aziz the country incurred a large external debt, undermining its internal sovereignty. By 1904 Spain and France had effectively divided the country; Britain abandoned its claims in exchange for French recognition of British authority in Egypt. By 1908 Moroccans were in revolt against Abd al-Aziz, and his brother, Mulay Hafid, replaced him.

Formal European Colonialism

Mulay Hafid further indebted the country to European creditors. At the same time, dissident tribes in Fez besieged him, and he turned to France for military, political, and economic assistance. On March 30, 1912, Mulay Hafid signed the Treaty of Fez, establishing a French protectorate.

The French colonial presence in Rabat retained the basic structure of the sultan's government. The administration of Marshall Lyautey ruled through a policy of co-optation; Mulay Hafid signed official decrees in his own name, thereby remaining the ostensible authority. Many have noted that the French colonial presence propped up what had become an increasingly dissolute monarchy. Had Morocco achieved independence in the 1930s, the Alawite monarchy might have given way to a more republican form of government.

In striking contrast to France's extensive colonial occupation of Algeria, colonialism in Morocco left domestic institutions relatively intact. The traditionally privileged classes were preserved, especially the commercially dominant Arab bourgeoisie in the cities of Fez and in the southern Sousse, as well as Berber tribal notables. Similarly, internal social evolution was modest. On the one hand, sectors of the traditional elite were not infused with fresh blood by upwardly mobile lower-status groups. On the other hand, few of these elites either received a French education or gained access to professional careers, as had, for example, some Tunisians.

Often missing from quick characterizations of Morocco as a formerly French colony is the fact that Spain colonized the north. Although the anti-Atlas tribes offered significant opposition, the north exhibited the strongest resistance to European colonialism, with Abd al-Krim al-Khattabi forming a Rifian republic that espoused a mix of nationalism and Salafi (militant Islamist) fervor. His forces delivered a humiliating defeat to a superior Spanish army at the battle of Anoual in 1921. Nonetheless, the Rif population was ultimately suppressed by 1926, with colonial forces (including a young Francisco Franco) making extensive use of mustard gas. The campaign was brutal. Legend has it that Franco once returned from a raid with the bloody heads of Berber tribesmen as trophies. Today Abd al-Krim's resistance is trumpeted as a source of national honor, a complicated deployment of nationalist symbols given the Berber origin of the dynamic.

Emergent Nationalism

Nationalists among the traditional elite eventually capitulated to French demands and reluctantly accepted their status. They retained their national identity, however, and after 1926 their ranks were joined by a small group of populists. Disaffection emerged as well among skilled urban craftspeople who were beginning to

MOROCCO

Capital city	Rabat
Chief of state	King Mohammed VI
Head of government	Prime Minister Abbas El Fassi
Major political parties *(seats in lower house)*	Independence Party (52), Justice and Development Party (46), Popular Movement (41), National Rally of Independents (39), Socialist Union of Popular Forces (38), Constitutional Union Party (27), Progress and Socialism Party (17), Democratic Forces Front (9), Democratic and Social Movement (9), Covenant Party (8)
Ethnic groups	Arab-Berber (99.1%), other (0.7%), Jewish (0.2%)
Religious groups	Muslim (98.7%), Christian (1.1%), Jewish (0.2%)
Export partners	Spain (18.7%), France (17.1%), Brazil (6.9%), United States (4.4%), Belgium (4.3%), Italy (4.2%)
Import partners	France (17%), Spain (14.2%), Italy (6.8%), Saudi Arabia (6.8%), China (6.3%), Germany (5.9%), United States (4.1%)

suffer because of strong competition from colonial imports. The combination of disgruntled traditional elites, radicalized younger elites, and lower-middle-class elements constituted a powerful nationalist front.

The national independence movement gained momentum on May 16, 1930, when the colonial authorities issued an infamous *dahir*, or Berber decree, establishing a separate system of customary-law tribunals in Berber-populated parts of the country. It was part of a French effort to isolate the rural areas from the growing nationalism in urban areas. Empowered to deal with civil matters, these tribunals created an artificial division between Arabs and Berbers by removing the latter from the national system of Muslim jurisprudence on civil matters. Berber, or Tamazight, identity politics remain salient until this day.

Incipient nationalist elements representing traditionalists, such as Allal al-Fassi, as well as pro-French intellectuals, such as Ahmad Balafrej, vigorously protested the decree. Although French authorities sought to dilute the impact of the *dahir*, the damage had already been done.

In May 1932 the Kutla al-Amal al-Watani ("National Action Bloc") was formed as the first overtly nationalist party in the country. The bloc sought a reform plan that called for autonomy and an end to colonial efforts to craft a distinctive Berber identity. Nonetheless, French officials (and Sultan Muhammad Ben Yussuf, or Muhammad V) ignored the plan. The bloc worked peacefully, but in vain, for reforms within the framework of the protectorate until the French dissolved the party in 1937. In 1943 the Istiqlal ("Independence") Party was formed.

After World War II, the Istiqlal enjoyed strong support in the towns and a tacit alliance with the throne. It was challenged, however, by powerful rural chieftains allied with the French, by some traditionalist elements in the cities, and by the heads of some religious brotherhoods. During the late 1940s, the Istiqlal transformed itself into a broad-based independence movement. As the alliance between the Istiqlal and the monarchy became more overt and began to challenge French hegemony, colonial authorities took action. In August 1953, they sent Muhammad V and his family, including his son Hassan, into exile in Madagascar and replaced him with a more docile relative. Once again, however, the French had miscalculated. Muhammad V became a martyr in the eyes of the population, and the nationalist movement was catalyzed into an all-out fight for independence.

In part because of the turmoil in neighboring Algeria, a quick political settlement was achieved. Muhammad V's return from exile in fall 1955 marked the end of colonial rule. On March 2, 1956, the French regions were joined with the Spanish-controlled areas, and France formally granted independence. In 1957, the country was proclaimed a kingdom.

Early Years of Independence

The monarchy emerged as the major beneficiary of independence. Indeed, Morocco is virtually unique in the Arab world in that its struggle for independence revolved around the revival of a monarchy that was rather ineffective prior to colonial rule. The population revered Muhammad V for his *baraka*, or religious blessing. Upon independence the country enjoyed a sufficient level of institutional stability and a reasonably effective political leadership. The political parties, with the Istiqlal in the lead, provided necessary cadres for the new government. The urban resistance forces were incorporated into the police, and the Army of Liberation, one of the last groups to recognize the monarchy, was absorbed into the Royal Armed Forces. Civil servants were recruited from the former protectorate government and from newly trained Moroccan youth. Over this heterogeneous group, Muhammad V ruled as a symbol of Moroccan unity.

Within five years, however, the working relationship between the king and the political parties disintegrated. Muhammad V was unwilling to become a constitutional figurehead, and the internally divided Istiqlal leadership was unwilling to accept the secondary role envisioned by the king. Tension between the conservative and radical wings of the party reached a breaking point in 1959, when Prime Minister Abdallah Ibrahim of the Istiqlal joined a group of secular intellectuals and trade unionists to form a new left-wing party, the National Union of Popular Forces (UNFP), closely allied with the large Moroccan Workers Union. The UNFP charged the Istiqlal leadership with not standing up to the king and with indifference to meaningful reforms. The fragmentation of the Istiqlal and the limited appeal of the UNFP outside urban areas, however, greatly facilitated the king's efforts to expand the powers of the monarchy.

Muhammad V dismissed the government of Prime Minister Ibrahim and his predominantly UNFP cabinet in May 1960, naming himself prime minister and making Crown Prince Hassan his deputy. The king suddenly died the following February after minor surgery and was succeeded by Hassan on March 3, 1961. Hassan, with a law degree from the University of Bordeaux, quickly consolidated power in his own hands and further reduced the political role of the parties. He believed that the role of parties was to organize support for the monarchy, not to represent the electorate in the formulation of public policy. The young king lacked Muhammad V's charisma, however, as well as the advantage of being a nationalist hero.

With a minimum of consultation, but in keeping with his father's public promise, King Hassan introduced a constitution that was approved in a referendum in December 1962. Drawing inspiration from France's Fifth Republic, the new constitution guaranteed political freedoms. Yet, its principal provisions solidified the king's power; the king was given the authority to dissolve the legislature and exercise unlimited emergency powers.

In the first national elections in May 1963, Hassan encouraged the creation of parties loyal to the throne, including the Constitutional Institutions Defense Front (FDIC) and a conservative Berber party, the Popular Movement (MP). The FDIC was unable to win the majority the king hoped for. On June 7, 1965, following a series of bloody riots in Casablanca, Hassan invoked Article 35 of the constitution and assumed full power.

This move only exacerbated the unrest that had existed since Muhammad V's death. The gulf between the throne and the opposition parties widened even more with the abduction in Paris in 1965 of popular UNFP leader Mehdi Ben Barka.

Ben Barka had been sentenced to death in absentia because of his criticism of Hassan's rule; he was living in exile when agents seized him in a Paris café in broad daylight. Although his fate was the subject of speculation for years—with Hassan claiming ignorance in interviews—the release of official documents after Hassan's death in 1999 indicate that Ben Barka was tortured to death with French connivance. Then Ben Barka's body was flown to Rabat, where it was dissolved in a vat of acid.

Throughout the late 1960s, the police seized newspapers and made many arrests, and sanctioned political activity virtually disappeared. In July 1970, however, the king unexpectedly announced that a new constitution would be submitted for a national referendum, an attempt to shore up his faltering legitimacy. Elections for a new single-chamber *majlis* were held immediately after the successful referendum. The Istiqlal and the UNFP—which had joined together in the Kutla Wataniya ("National Front") to oppose ratification of the new constitution—tried to organize a boycott of elections. In both instances, the Kutla's efforts were futile in the face of the regime's campaign to arouse popular support. Nevertheless, by opposing the constitution and the elections, the Kutla did deprive the king of a meaningful popular mandate. In the end, the regime was forced to continue its reliance on loyal "independent" politicians, the internal security forces, and, ultimately, the army.

Coups

The elimination of political opposition failed to prevent—or perhaps prompted—two attempts by military officers to assassinate the king: one in July 1971 at Skhirat and the other in August 1972 in Rabat. Discontent over Hassan's autocratic rule and corruption among many of his associates helped bring on the attempted coups. Hassan emerged uninjured in both instances, more determined than ever to suppress perceived enemies.

The August 1972 coup attempt provided the country with one of its most notorious political episodes: the death of Gen. Mohammed Oufkir. Oufkir, a former defense minister and longtime ally of Hassan, is now known to have been present at Ben Barka's torture and murder. Nevertheless, Oufkir conspired to overthrow the king, ordering fighter planes to strafe the royal jet as it returned from Europe. Hassan survived the attack, and by evening the general was dead. According to official accounts, Oufkir confessed to the plot and promptly committed suicide. It appears to have been an "acrobatic suicide," as bullet holes were found in the back of his head. Security forces imprisoned the general's family. They were released in 1991 after nearly twenty years and allowed to leave the country in 1996.

In 1972 the king announced a third constitution. Executive power was to be vested in the government and a new chamber of representatives. Two-thirds of the chamber's membership was to be elected by universal suffrage, compared with one-half under the 1970 constitution. The Kutla, caught unprepared, urged a boycott of the constitutional referendum and again accused the government of rigging the balloting. With the split between the palace and the opposition as wide as ever, the appointed cabinet was substantially similar to its predecessor. Elections for the new *majlis* were postponed indefinitely.

Once the king felt confident that he had reestablished control of the military, he ignored the demands for more political freedom by the muddled opposition parties. Differences between the Istiqlal and the UNFP had reemerged, ending the Kutla coalition. Moreover, differences within the UNFP—between a wing headed by Ibrahim Ben Siddiq (Casablanca) and Abderrahim Bouabid (Rabat)— had led to a formal rupture in July 1972. The dominant Bouabid faction reconstituted itself as the Union Socialiste des Forces Populaires (USFP), while the Casablanca group gradually declined in influence.

The Controlled Opening of the Economy in the 1970s and the Western Sahara

At the same time, Hassan slowly began to liberalize trade with Europe. In this way he combined his ability to outmaneuver opposition parties with economic liberalization measures that created the impression of change and progress.

In 1973 King Hassan undertook additional economic programs designed to increase support for the monarchy, including the distribution of nationalized land (mostly French) among the peasantry. Further, he introduced an ambitious five-year development plan that called for an annual economic growth rate of 7.5 percent.

Hassan also launched several foreign policy initiatives designed, perhaps, to defuse domestic unrest, including a strong stand in a fishing dispute with Spain in 1973. Conflict with Spain and, in turn, the European Union (EU) over access to Morocco's Atlantic fisheries persists to this day. The king also scored a major political victory in 1974 and 1975 by reasserting his country's historic claim to the former Spanish Sahara. This move mobilized popular support from all segments of society and raised Hassan's political fortunes enormously. Moreover, both the Istiqlal and the USFP, as part of their own nationalist orientations, supported "reintegration" of the Western Sahara, putting them on the defensive.

Spanish withdrawal from the territory also set the stage for a major act of political theater. In November 1975, Hassan organized the *massira*, or "Green March," in which approximately 350,000 civilians assembled on the southern border with the Western Sahara and staged a short symbolic walk into the disputed territory. The event is celebrated annually as a national holiday. Since the northern two-thirds of the territory contained large deposits of phosphate as well as oil and uranium reserves, the victory seemed to portend economic gains. Ostensible political tranquility did not last long, however. An insurgency by the Popular Front for the Liberation of Saguit al-Hamra and Rio de Oro, or Polisario Front, claiming the right to an independent Sahara, broke out in 1976, shortly after Morocco claimed sovereignty. The Western Sahara is discussed more extensively below.

Severe drought frequently ravaged the economy as well, devastating the agricultural sector and encouraging urban migration. World phosphate prices also began their steep decline during this period. After placing strong emphasis on phosphate exports to earn foreign exchange, the rentier state grew increasingly indebted and was forced to reduce public investment in development projects. In the face of such economic difficulties, public discontent reemerged in 1978 and 1979. Unemployment reached as high as 35 to 40 percent of the youth workforce. Labor unrest increased, and militant Islamist groups opposed to the established political order also emerged.

The Moribund 1980s

Major riots broke out in Casablanca in June 1981, with attacks on banks, car dealerships, and other symbols of authority and privilege. Security forces were barely able to regain order in some areas, killing by conservative estimates two hundred protesters. The rioting was followed by numerous arrests, including those of trade union leaders and even some members of the *majlis* belonging to the USFP.

In January 1983, there were reports of another military plot against the king. Officers were arrested, and Gen. Ahmed Dlimi, commander of the Saharan forces, was killed in a mysterious car accident. Following Dlimi's death, Hassan fragmented the military command structure. In 1983, Hassan again postponed the elections to the *majlis* as well as elections for provincial and prefectural assemblies, deepening still further public alienation and cynicism.

Elections for municipal and rural councils finally took place but were accompanied by serious irregularities, rendering meaningless the victory of Hassan's supporters. Widespread intimidation and fraud accompanied the balloting, and many complained about interference in candidate registration and campaign procedures.

January 1984 brought new riots. They began with strikes by students in Marrakech and spread throughout the country. The security forces killed at least 150 people by the time order was restored. The International League of Human Rights estimated that 1,500 to 2,000 were arrested. The courts condemned some individuals to life in prison. Verdicts handed to Islamists were especially harsh, including thirteen death sentences, the first for political crimes since 1972.

In August 1984 Morocco concluded a union with Libya. The union secured Muammar al-Qaddafi's agreement to withdraw support from the Polisario Front. Moreover, it set in motion a series of economic cooperation efforts, including employment opportunities in oil-rich Libya for Moroccan migrant labor, the purchase of Libyan oil at preferential prices, and several trade agreements. But the Moroccan-Libyan union was not bound to last. After Qaddafi denounced Rabat for its support of Reagan administration policies—and after Qaddafi's overtures to Algeria—Hassan abrogated the treaty on August 29, 1986.

With the continuing war in the Sahara, the cycle of unrest motivated by economic privation and followed by harsh security measures continued throughout the 1980s. Unrest was led by both leftists and Islamists, and the government charged that the Polisario was backing leftist efforts to conduct subversive activities among students and labor. Hassan invariably disregarded specific demands regarding political prisoners but maintained his long-established practice of pardons and amnesties, especially on national or religious holidays. In July 1986 he amnestied prominent political exile Mohamed "Fkih" Basri, a founder of the Moroccan Resistance Movement. *Fkih* is a term of reverence ascribed to a religious leader. In 1989, Hassan also released four hundred detainees to mark the 'Id al-Adha celebration.

Although the government has historically been relatively lenient on press freedom, especially in comparison to Tunisia and Algeria, it has suspended newspaper circulation several times in recent decades. In general, papers have been permitted to criticize the government's policies so long as they do not mention the king personally or question Moroccan control of the Western Sahara. Additionally, in 1988 the government banned the Moroccan Human Rights Organization (OMDH) because of its plans to hold a constitutive assembly. Other Moroccan human rights organizations are the Moroccan Association of Human Rights, linked to the USFP; Istiqlal's Moroccan League of Human Rights; and the Association for the Defense of Human Rights in Morocco, based in Paris. After international and domestic pressure, however, Hassan finally approved establishment of the OMDH, which held its assembly in December 1988.

The king also began to secure "contributions" for the construction in Casablanca of the Hassan II Mosque. Completed in the early 1990s, the mosque has a minaret over five hundred feet tall and an internal capacity of 25,000. Many Moroccans take great pride in the mosque's grandeur and beauty, but there were complaints about a cost estimated at US$800 million. Some charge that it would have been much better to devote these resources to development projects than to an edifice devoted to a then living monarch. Additional anxieties have emerged in recent years because of the mosque's majestic location on the Atlantic Ocean; the anticipated rise in sea level associated with climate change will pose challenges for the building's foundation.

The Post–Cold War Era and a Controlled Opening

Despite riots in December 1990 and the Gulf crisis in 1990 and 1991, the country's situation generally stabilized in the early 1990s, due largely to international assistance. The riots began with a general strike protesting price increases for basic commodities and austerity measures under structural-adjustment programs. In quelling the protests, security forces opened fire, reportedly killing thirty-three in Fez alone. The situation remained tense during Desert Storm in early 1991. Hassan sent a contingent of soldiers to the Gulf to join the anti-Iraq coalition, prompting much domestic criticism from a population that generally sided with Saddam Husayn. The king adroitly navigated the criticism by allowing protests, with as many as 300,000 people filling the streets of Rabat. Nonetheless, the king's stance was rewarded with debt relief and enhanced aid from the EU, Saudi Arabia, the United States, and international financial institutions.

Yet, disturbances continued in 1991. Student riots in April and November included Justice and Charity (*al-Adl wal-Ihsan*), a banned Islamist group. In 1992, the king announced that deferred elections would be held, in part to respond to ongoing criticism from the international community about human rights. In September, a referendum approved a revised constitution that allowed the prime minister rather than the king to distribute ministerial portfolios, although the monarch maintained final approval. After several delays legislative elections finally took place in June 1993, the first since 1984. Turnout was relatively low, with only about 63 percent of the electorate voting. This figure reflected an increase in official candor, however, especially after the implausible 97.2 percent turnout reported for the 1992 constitutional referendum.

In the election itself, the USFP and the Istiqlal agreed not to compete against each other; the USFP fielded 104 candidates, and the Istiqlal fielded candidates in 118 constituencies. The election turned on ambiguous concerns such as calls for greater attention to human rights. With characteristic savvy, Hassan undermined the potency of these issues by inviting Amnesty International to visit the country, promoting the efforts of the Consultative Council for Human Rights, ratifying international conventions against torture, granting yet another amnesty to prisoners in June 1993 during 'Id al-Adha, and establishing a Ministry of Human Rights that November.

The 1993 elections provided a clear example of the system's structural bias, much like the experience in 1977 and 1984. Of the 333 seats in the *majlis*, only two-thirds (222) were elected by popular vote. Local councils, chambers of commerce, and official unions elected the remaining third of the members. This system consistently resulted in a pro-palace legislature because of the conservative tendencies of the local bodies. The 1993 elections took place in two stages: In the summer's direct elections, 54 percent of the seats went to loyalist parties, a slight majority; in the indirect vote three months later, however, 79 percent of the seats went to loyalists, cementing their control of the *majlis*. Cries of fraud and manipulation of the 1993 election remained a central component of the political scene until the 1997 election. Finally, in a noteworthy development, women were elected to the chamber for the first time: a USFP candidate from Casablanca and an Istiqlali candidate from Fez.

This period was characterized by a certain *attentisme*, or waiting, that led to paralysis. Hassan was visibly unwell on several occasions and traveled to New York to receive medical treatment in 1996. In July 1995 Hassan permitted USFP leader Fkih Basri to return after thirty years of exile. And in September 1996, a new referendum changed the constitution, creating a bicameral *majlis* with a directly elected Chamber of Representatives and an upper house, the Chamber of Councilors. In turn, in November 1997 the first election under the new constitution was held, inaugurating an *alternance*, or accountable, competitive government. The opposition had argued for years that, if given the opportunity, they would do well in an election, and they did. In March 1998 Hassan appointed the USFP's Abderrahman Youssoufi to the post of prime minister, a move that granted him significant power, albeit hardly omnipotence.

The Post-Hassan Era

In the end, a full assessment of Hassan's ability to rule under *alternance* was rendered impossible by his death on July 23, 1999, and the accession to the throne of his son, Muhammad VI, on July 30. Muhammad quickly distinguished himself by presiding in a less-engaged fashion than his father. Moreover, Muhammad—along with the system of *alternance*—initially began to nurture vibrant discussions of human rights. Most notably, he created a climate that allowed exposés of the human rights violations from the *années de plomb* ("leaden years") during his father's reign. Muhammad was also dubbed the "king of the poor" because of his trips throughout the country and his willingness to wade into crowds. In 2002 he married a commoner, an engineer from Tetouan. Some even called Muhammad "Al Jawal"—the Moroccan word for the ubiquitous cellular phones—because of his high mobility.

After September 11, 2001, however, the gradual opening began to slow, as the palace increasingly circumscribed the power of the *majlis*. To be sure, elections in September 2002 marked a significant moment in the post-Hassan era, with the Justice and Development Party (PJD) performing very well, tripling its presence and becoming the third-largest party after the USFP and the Istiqlal Party. Given the aforementioned exclusion of Justice and Charity, support for Islamists in the country was likely much higher than the elections indicated. Despite a few irregularities and skepticism—particularly on the part of the Spanish media—the elections were trumpeted as the country's first free elections. These elections are discussed further below.

The political and social landscape was profoundly rocked by bombings in Casablanca on May 16, 2003, that killed forty-five people. In a royal discourse on

May 29, 2003, the king declared the "end of the era of leniency." Coupled with attacks on the Atocha train station in Madrid on March 11, 2004—in which Moroccan nationals were implicated—the political system tightened still further.

Concomitant with this tightening were several complicated developments. First, in January 2004 Muhammad created the Equity and Reconciliation Commission (IER) to formally investigate the human rights violations of the past. It was the first such step in the Middle East and North Africa. Unlike its South African analog, it did not come on the heels of significant regime change. Criticized for its circumscribed purview, underestimation of the number of victims, and unwillingness to name perpetrators, the IER nonetheless publicly investigated rights violations from the Hassan years. It released its report in March 2006, stating that several hundred people had been illegally killed and over 9,000 subjected to human rights abuses during the reign of Hassan. It called for reform of the judicial system and compensation for victims. The event offered, perhaps, some closure for the victims and their families.

A second development was the reform of the family code, known as the *Muddawanna*. In a balancing act with conservative interests, a royal commission announced the changes in 2004 after several years of negotiation and deliberation. The new law reduced men's ability to treat their wives as property. It required a man to inform his wife that he was seeking a divorce and stipulated that he must get permission from a judge before taking a second wife. The legal age for marriage was increased from fifteen to eighteen. The implementation of the juridical reforms has been complicated because the legal system is ill equipped to deal with and enforce the changes. Not surprisingly, conservative segments were frustrated by the developments. Yet, some of the reforms have been criticized by women's groups, too. While they welcome the reforms, with four out of five rural women being illiterate and lacking socioeconomic power, the reforms are not altogether meaningful. For example, divorce would likely lead to severe deprivation.

The September 2007 elections marked a significant turning point for the country, demonstrating a consolidation of electoral reforms, even though turnout was below democratic norms. The election results are discussed below.

POLITICAL ENVIRONMENT

Geography

The country's physical geography is remarkably diverse, from the relatively fertile, sun-drenched Mediterranean and Atlantic coasts to the snow-capped Atlas Mountains and deserts in the east and south. The beauty of the country's natural patrimony has impressed Moroccan and foreign travelers for ages. In recent times this has been the source of crucial foreign exchange, as tourists have traveled to Morocco to explore its varied landscape.

Morocco has been plagued by chronic drought in recent decades, undermining efforts to engineer economic growth. In a country where the preponderance of the population works on the land and the government has devoted considerable resources to irrigated agriculture and hydrologically intensive, high-end tourism, the challenges of the water deficit are profound.

The country has enormous phosphate reserves—a key source of foreign exchange during periods of high commodity prices—as well as deep-sea fisheries off the Atlantic coast. The amount of hydrocarbon reserves is a "known unknown." Oil was discovered in Talsinnt in 2000, but it is not easily accessible or of high quality. Many breathed a sigh of relief, as the country seemed to have avoided the "resource curse" that afflicts many petroleum producers.

The existence of oil reserves in the Western Sahara—as well as off the Atlantic coast—is another matter. Reserves are abundant. Yet, oil exploration contracts lack sufficient legal standing given the territory's disputed sovereignty; companies operating in the region have been targeted for protest. The US Department of Energy acknowledges that oil claims in the region are controversial, citing the pullout of most foreign firms from the region, with the exception of Kerr-McGee.

Political Culture

A primary feature of Moroccan political culture is distrust. This is visible both in the attitude of the people toward their leaders and in relations among political elites. For decades Moroccans viewed the political system as a coercive instrument rather than a basis for cooperative action. The inauguration of *alternance* and the accession of Muhammad VI have changed that dynamic to a certain extent, with greater scrutiny of Hassan's *années de plomb*.

A second, related feature is conspiratorial politics. Political authority is derived only secondarily from formal political offices, and the system thus lacks accepted rules by which decisions are reached. Instead, patterns of patrimonialism dominate political life. A third feature of Moroccan political life is political stalemate, or *attentisme*. Morocco's political culture facilitates the monarch's power, wherein *lèse-majesté*, or criticism of the monarchy, is expressly forbidden.

The powerful Ministry of Interior and Information controls domestic affairs. For years, the ministry was headed by Driss Basri, a confidant of Hassan's. Basri was viewed as the country's most powerful man after Hassan because he controlled such a wide array of governmental powers: police, security, human rights, media and information, electoral mechanisms, even foreign affairs. In a celebrated move in September 1999, however, Muhammad VI dismissed Basri.

In recent years, the Ministry of Interior has remained very powerful, especially in the clampdown since the 2003 Casablanca attacks. Despite the ever-close ties between Rabat and Washington, DC, since September 11, the US State Department sharply criticized Morocco in its 2006 Human Rights Report, especially regarding press freedom. Most prominently, Ali Mrabet, an editor with *Demain* and its Arabic-language counterpart, *Douman*, was imprisoned in 2003. The courts charged that Mrabet had libeled the king and supported self-determination for the people of the Western Sahara. He launched a brief hunger strike to protest his treatment. According to Human Rights Watch, he was banned from practicing journalism for ten years.

Judicial and administrative institutions reflect both French and Spanish colonial influences. The country is administratively divided into nineteen provinces and two urban prefectures, Casablanca and Rabat. The provinces are further divided into seventy-two administrative areas and communes. Each administrative region is headed by a governor, who is appointed by the king and responsible to him. There is a supreme court composed of four chambers: civil, criminal, administrative, and social. The king appoints all judges, with the advice of the Supreme Judicial Council. Moroccan courts administer a system that is based on Islamic law but strongly influenced by the French and Spanish legal systems. A separate system of courts administers the Judaic religious laws for Jewish citizens, although today there is only a small remnant of the country's once prosperous Jewish community.

Economic Conditions

Economic growth remains uneven. The early part of the first decade of the twenty-first century saw respectable economic growth: 5.2 percent in 2003, 3.5 percent in 2004 and 2005, 8.0 percent in 2006, and 2.3 percent in 2007. Overall, economic growth improved from an average of 2.6 percent annually in 1987 to 1997 to 4.5 percent in 1997 to 2007. Gross domestic product (GDP) per capita for the country's 30.9 million people stood at US$2,250 in 2007. Half of the population is illiterate, including nearly 80 percent of rural women. Foreign debt as a percentage of GDP fell from a high of 112 in 1987 to 28 in 2006. Most of this debt is bilateral and private, with the World Bank holding only 14 percent of the total.

The 2008 global financial crisis is having profound reverberations in Morocco. Growth is expected to weaken, as European tourists eschew trips abroad and European demand for Moroccan exports falls sharply. Rather than the 7 to 10 percent annual growth considered necessary to reduce poverty and unemployment, projections envision an average growth rate of 4 percent in 2009 to 2013.

Agriculture remains the largest sector in terms of manpower, employing over half of the population. Its economic importance, however, has declined since independence, comprising only 12.4 percent of GDP in 2007. This decline has to do in part with land tenure and exports. Wealthy landlords own the best 10 to 15 percent of the land. Although the productivity of that sector exceeds that of subsistence farming and the government subsidizes it, agricultural exports dropped significantly throughout the 1990s. Traditional markets in Europe were limited by the EU's Common Agricultural Policy. Moreover, with the admission of Greece in 1981 and Spain and Portugal in 1986, the EU has become self-sufficient in citrus, olive oil, and wine, which Morocco had long exported. Intellectuals have lamented ruefully that the country enjoyed better trade ties with Europe during colonialism.

A second factor is drought. As noted above, Morocco experienced some of its worst drought in the 1980s and 1990s. Severe drought struck in 2000, again in 2005, and to some extent in 2007. Rains returned in 2008, contributing to the 5.7 percent growth rate. Drought mostly affects subsistence farmers, particularly those cultivating more marginal lands in the south and southeast.

The principal crops grown by peasant smallholders are wheat, barley, maize, beans, and chickpeas. In addition, there is a large government-owned sugar beet sector to satisfy the domestic market's insatiable appetite for sweets and reduce sugarcane imports. Livestock productivity and crop yields remain low, and the government imports relatively inexpensive food regularly from the EU and the United States to meet domestic requirements.

For its part the fishing sector offers some promise, although export markets for the main product, sardines, are highly competitive. Since the 1970s the government has sought to develop the deep-sea fishing fleet that plies the abundant Atlantic waters. In so doing, however, it has come up against the interests of Spain. European boats want to fish in Morocco's territorial waters, and sharp diplomatic disputes have occurred. In 1995 Rabat and the EU signed a fishing accord, but only after protracted dispute. After the accord expired in 2000, negotiations resumed, only to fall apart in 2001. In 2005 Rabat signed a new fishing agreement with the EU. In addition, chronic overfishing in the world's fisheries raises questions about the long-term sustainability of the deep-sea fishing sector.

Manufacturing and industry accounted for 48 percent of GDP in 2007. The main industries are phosphoric acid, fertilizer production, and oil refining; light manufactures such as textiles and leather are growing rapidly. Most industry is concentrated in the Rabat-Casablanca region along the western seaboard. The mining sector plays an essential role. Morocco holds three-quarters of the world's known phosphate reserves. Its National Phosphate Office has reduced the production of phosphate rock since 1981 because of low prices on the international market.

Also worth mention is the new economic activity in the north, focused on the Tangier Mediterranean Port. Construction was completed in the summer of 2007, with further phases scheduled in the years to come. Hailed as the largest deep-sea port in Africa, it is expected to dynamize not only Morocco's northern economy but the entire Maghribi economy.

Finally, tourism remains an extremely important economic sector. The government aggressively markets a romantic destination to high-end travelers; luxurious world-class hotels and top-notch golf courses are found throughout the country. The government continues to promote tourism and has welcomed direct foreign investment in the sector. The results of this effort have been mildly disappointing in recent years. In 2005, 5.8 million tourists visited, of which 2.7 million were Moroccan expatriates returning home during the annual summer visit known as *Opération Marhaba*. In 2008 the figure increased to 7.8 million, of which 3.6 million were Moroccans. The global financial crisis prompted a downturn in tourism in 2009.

The government has also placed primary emphasis on the manufacturing sector since the 1983 adoption of a structural-adjustment program (SAP). The SAP was adopted with heavy conditionality by the World Bank and the International Monetary Fund (IMF) to alleviate the economic strain caused by the Western Sahara war. The SAP combined austerity with liberalization of the economy. To attract foreign investors, for example, the government lifted barriers to foreign investment, loosened exchange controls, reformed the tax system, and began to privatize state industries. The overall intention was to move away from the import substitution policies of the 1960s and 1970s. In recent years the government has attempted to position Morocco as a newly emerging economy. In pursuit of these efforts King Hassan authorized the creation of a new Ministry of Privatization in 1989 and a Ministry of Foreign Trade in 1990 and made other efforts throughout the 1990s to energize the economy. Muhammad VI has vigorously continued these efforts.

The challenges posed by the 2004 US–Morocco Free Trade Agreement, which began in 2006, as well as freer trade with the EU, remain profound. The free trade agreement with the United States is its first in Africa and the first under its Middle East Free Trade Initiative. The government has developed training programs for its exporters in an effort to improve quality in order to compete in international markets.

The World Bank and the IMF also have applauded the gradual privatization of state-owned industries, such as the 2001 partial privatization of the state-run Itissalat Al Maghrib, or Morocco Telecom, followed by further privatization in 2005. Other privatizations included the 2004 sale of the Banque Centrale Populaire and the state-owned tobacco distribution company Régie des Tabacs.

In terms of meeting basic human needs, in 2008 the country ranked 127th on the UN Development Program's Human Development Index. Much of the population remains impoverished and locked out of an economic system that benefits only a few. Urban overcrowding, inadequate housing, and poverty remain endemic. The official unemployment rate is 10 percent, but this is rather absurd: Urban unemployment is estimated at 30 percent, and college graduates are dramatically underemployed. It is important to note that unemployment is not evenly spread throughout the country. In the twenty-first century's first decade Marrakech enjoyed significant growth tied to its booming tourist and real estate sectors and has a rate of unemployment 6 percent less than the national average.

POLITICAL STRUCTURE

The Palace and Makhzen

The king is the center of the political, economic, and military system, known as the *Makhzen*. He is the supreme authority—the *emir al-mu'minin*, or "commander of the faithful"—as well as commander in chief of the armed forces. The *Dar al-Mulk* (royal palace) and the four "sovereign" ministries (interior, justice, foreign affairs, and Islamic affairs) are at the core of the *Makhzen*. The king appoints ministers to the sovereign ministries.

The Alawite king's moral authority is based on his role as imam of the Islamic community. Because of his noble religious ancestry and the attendant powers ascribed to him, the Moroccan king satisfies the aspirations of rural Muslims who seek the miraculous qualities inherent in the monarch's *baraka*. Muhammad, like his father and grandfather, is thus deeply venerated by the population, who view him as a sharif (descendant of the Prophet) and a dispenser of God's blessing. His legitimacy as a religious leader is said to defuse the potency of political Islamism.

The monarchy's ability to manipulate rival factions—and, when necessary, eliminate them altogether—is an additional source of power. Another source is the fact that the monarch is the nation's most prominent dispenser of patronage. Most notably, the royal family is the lead shareholder in the Omnium Nord Africain, a massive holding company with subsidiaries in virtually every economic sector. Using royal patronage, Muhammad balances and dominates the political and economic elite. Many in his inner circle are "engineers," young and often Anglophone technocrats trained in engineering or business abroad before returning home.

Party Structure

On the loyalist right wing are three parties known as the *Wifaq* ("Covenant"): the Popular Movement (MP), the Constitutional Union, and the National Democratic Party (PND). The MP is a Berber movement, founded by resistance leaders in 1958 to counter the preponderance of the Istiqlal. The PND is a party of rural notables.

Center-right parties include the National Independent Rally (RNI), the National Popular Movement (MNP), and the new Democratic and Social Movement (MDS). The RNI was formed in 1977 and soon splintered off from the PND. Like the PND, the RNI is comprised of rural notables. The MNP was created in 1991, after a 1986 break with the MP, and espouses a more Berber, or Tamazight, authenticity. The MDS was created in 1996, after a break with the MNP, and seems very similar to its MNP parent, except for a greater emphasis on participatory democracy. All of the centrist and right-wing parties support the monarchy without question.

On the opposition side, the venerable Istiqlal and the USFP dominate the Kutla. Each is affiliated with a trade union, the USFP with the Democratic Workers Confederation (CDT) and the Istiqlal with the General Union of Moroccan Workers. Other parties in the opposition include the Progress and Socialism Party (PPS) formed in 1974 out of the former Communist Party; the left-wing Popular Democratic Action Organization, formed in 1983; the Social Democratic Party, which broke from the OadP in 1996 over the OadP's decision to boycott the referendum; the Democratic Forces Front formed in July 1997 after breaking off from the PPS; the Democratic Movement; and the Party of the Socialist and Democratic Avant-Garde, which consistently boycotts elections and referendums.

The Islamist organization Justice and Charity (*al-Adl wal-Ihsan*) remains outside the Moroccan political process. Its leader, the septuagenarian Abd al-Salam Yassin, was placed under house arrest throughout the 1990s for his mocking condemnations of the monarchy as insufficiently Islamic and beholden to Western interests. In May 2000 Muhammad VI released him from house arrest. His daughter, Nadia Yassin, a former French teacher, has emerged as a forceful and controversial spokesperson in her own right.

The 2002 election for the *majlis* saw a proliferation of parties, many of which were one-candidate parties. Twenty-six parties took part in the election, with twenty-two winning seats. The USFP maintained its presence at ninety-four seats. The Islamist PJD increased its presence from nine seats in 1997 to forty-two in 2002, despite standing in only fifty-six constituencies. Muhammad appointed Driss Jettou as prime minister; this was a striking development, as Jettou was a venerable technocrat with no formal party affiliation. The government included six parties: the USFP, Istiqlal, RNI, MP, PPS, and MNP. The PJD did not join the government. The 2002 elections also included a national list of female candidates, guaranteeing that thirty parliamentary seats would be held by women.

In the aftermath of the March 2003 bombing, the PJD took a lower profile in the September local elections. In 2004 the party elected a moderate, Saad Eddine Othmani, as its leader. In contrast to Justice and Charity, the PJD recognizes Muhammad VI as *emir al-mu'minin* and—like its counterpart in Turkey with the same name—runs on a platform of social justice and transparency. In addition to the PJD, there are several smaller Islamist groups committed to nonviolent methods: al-Badil al-Hadari ("Civilized Alternative"), Harakat min Ajli al-Umma ("Movement for the Nation"), and al-Chebiba el-Islamiya el-Maghrebiya ("Moroccan Islamic Youth"). In contrast to Tunisia and Algeria, Morocco has not thrown its Islamist opposition out with the bathwater.

In late 2005 the *majlis* passed a new political-parties law transferring authority to approve new parties from the Ministry of the Interior to the courts; the purpose was to enhance the independence of the party-formation process from the palace. Additionally, the new law limited state funding to parties that receive 5 percent of the vote, a move to reduce the proliferation of single-candidate parties and "political entrepreneurs" who strategically switch parties. Most importantly, the new law banned parties based on religion, ethnicity, or language, a step designed to attenuate the Islamist and Tamazight parties.

The legislative elections of September 2007 appeared to defy conventional expectations. Theoretically, a consolidation of electoral reforms would prompt increased voter enthusiasm and turnout as voters sense a stake in the importance of the elections. By contrast, Morocco's 2007 elections saw a turnout of only 37 percent, a sharp decline from 52 percent in the 2002 election and 58 percent in 1997. In addition, the number of spoiled ballots increased to 19 percent from 17 percent in 2002. Reasons for this likely included ongoing voter disaffection, the *majlis*'s marginal position in the political system, and insufficient media coverage. In addition, legislative fraud in the 2006 municipal elections—for which the government arrested perpetrators—enhanced skepticism.

In terms of the actual outcome, the Istiqlal won 11 percent of the vote to garner fifty-two seats, an increase of four from 2002. The PJD also won 11 percent of the vote, increasing its presence by four seats to forty-six. The pro-government Popular Movement won 9 percent and increased its presence by fourteen seats to forty-one. And the National Rally of Independents earned 10 percent of the vote, resulting in thirty-nine seats. The big loser was the USFP, which lost twelve seats from 2002. It earned 9 percent of the vote to hold thirty-eight seats. It left the governing coalition after the election. The king appointed Istiqlal leader Abbas El Fassi to be the new prime minister.

Radical Islamists

Most analysts tend to place radical Islamism under the rubric of Salafiyya al-Jihadia ("Jihad for Pure Islam"), founded in the early 1990s by Mohammed el-Fizazi. The leader of Salafiyya is the son of a veteran of the Afghan war, Abdelwahab Rafiki, alias Abu Hafs. Abu Hafs refers to his group as al-Sunna wal-Jamaa ("Teaching of the Prophet and the Community"). Estimates of the movement's strength run to around a few thousand members; the number of sympathizers is likely much higher.

One current within the Salafist movement is al-Sirrat al-Moustakim ("The Straight Path"), which claimed responsibility for the 2003 Casablanca bombing. Another current is al-Takfir wal-Hijra ("Exile and Flight"), headed by thirty-year-old Youssef Fikri. The groups target adherents in urban slums and use ganglike enforcement measures to discipline adherents and community members. Inflammatory literature and sermons are also used to disseminate arguments. The government has tried to meet the challenge with some efforts to fight poverty, but much of the response has been coercive. Thousands of suspected Islamist radicals have been jailed since September 11, 2001.

The Moroccan Islamic Combatant Group (MICG) remains salient as well. Tied to Algeria's al-Qa'ida in the Islamic Maghrib, the MICG networks are mysterious to analysts outside the intelligence community. Many speculate that there may be little formal cooperation; the groups instead have "franchised" al-Qa'ida's political philosophy and theology. In either case, the government has taken a resolutely hard line against radical Islamism. Morocco is often mentioned as one of the countries participating in the extraordinary US rendition program.

The Military and Security Structure

The military, once viewed as a staunch pillar of the monarchy, has on occasion been a serious threat to the king—most obviously during the coups. Although Muhammad is the head of the Royal Armed Forces and served in that capacity for years as crown prince, the prospect that the military will remain indifferent to the profound social and economic dislocations occurring in Moroccan society can never be certain. Shortly after assuming the throne in 1999, Muhammad launched an inquiry into corruption within the armed forces, but he backed off when it became apparent that the military would not countenance such examination.

The greatly expanded size and combat experience of the army in fighting the Polisario Front add to the potential military threat to the king. Although resolution of the Western Sahara continues to elude the parties to the conflict, the "military *Makhzen*" continues to resist being diminished. Contending with demobilized military units may be a difficult source of pressure on the economy. The exact number of Moroccan troops in the Western Sahara is not known, although it is estimated at more than 100,000. According to the International Institute for Strategic Studies, the defense budget is US$2 billion, or 3.7 percent of GDP.

Despite these developments, the military will most likely remain supportive of the regime, not only because of the monarch but also because of close ties with NATO. Ties with NATO and relations with Western governments are discussed below under "Foreign Policy."

Civil Society Organizations

Important political institutions include the National Union of Moroccan Students (UNEM) and the various labor unions. Since the 1960s, the UNEM has been extensively involved in radical activities directed against the government. In recent years student activism has taken on a decidedly Islamist cast, with supporters of Yassin's Justice and Charity and other Islamist currents frequently active in protests. Students protested government policies in Casablanca in 1998 and in Marrakech in 2000. Unemployed graduate students regularly protest their status, gaining media attention and highlighting the economy's difficulties in generating employment.

The Moroccan trade union movement acquired extensive organizational conviction and solidarity as a result of its struggles against colonialism. The Moroccan Workers Union was the sole trade-union confederation until 1960, when the Istiqlal organized a rival union, the General Union of Moroccan Workers. In the late 1970s, the CDT, a socialist-oriented union with ties to the USFP, overtook the UMT in prominence and militancy.

Despite the UMT's historic role and the CDT's occasional success in opposing the government, the political and economic climate remains unreceptive to the development of a vigorous labor movement. High levels of unemployment make unions insecure and vulnerable. In the face of the March 2000 implementation of the EU Association Accord, the signing of the 2004 US-Morocco Free Trade Agreement, and Tunisia's success in maintaining a relatively cowed labor movement, the Moroccan government constantly seeks to contain its labor forces in order to make its economy attractive to investors.

The country's nongovernmental organizations proliferated during the early 1990s and have remained salient. Organizations devoted to women's rights, human rights, education, health, AIDS, and Tamazight rights have all staked claims on the political process and the opening of the country's political system. Their political efficacy remains in question, however, and many organizations quickly become programmatically and financially exhausted. But they add up to a relatively vibrant civil society, especially in comparison to many countries in the Middle East and North Africa (MENA) region.

POLITICAL DYNAMICS

The Western Sahara demands special attention in any consideration of Morocco. Despite the rise of Saharawi nationalism in the 1950s and 1960s, Spain did not relinquish control until the Madrid Accord of November 14, 1975. With the accord, Spain ceded the colony to Mauritania and Morocco, setting the stage for King Hassan's *massira*, or "Green March."

Spain withdrew its last remaining troops on February 26, 1976, and the next day the Polisario Front declared that the area was the Saharan Arab Democratic Republic (SadR). It also initiated a guerrilla war against Morocco and Mauritania. Initially Hassan devoted his energies to crushing the Polisario, sending in troops and authorizing a massive defensive sand wall to inhibit guerrilla operations. By the mid-1980s over 80,000 troops were deployed in the Sahara. Nevertheless, victory eluded Hassan. Algeria and Libya supported the Polisario, the former with safe haven across the Algerian frontier. Libyan support ceased in 1984 with its "union" with Morocco.

In 1984 the SadR won a diplomatic victory by becoming a member of the Organization of African Unity (OAU). In 1986 the United Nations and the OAU together hosted indirect talks, with Mauritania (which renounced its claim in 1978) and Algeria invited as observers. Although the SadR was initially successful in diplomatic terms, Morocco continued to dominate militarily. Importantly, although nearly eighty countries now recognize the SadR—most recently South Africa in 2004 and Kenya in 2005—no global power broker does so. The United States does not; nor does any member of the EU, China, or Russia.

This position enabled Hassan to balk at accepting UN Resolution 40/50 advocating direct negotiations between the SadR and Morocco. In addition, Hassan began to receive crucial support from the United States. The United States and Morocco conducted joint military exercises off the coast of the Western Sahara in 1986; in 1987 the United States approved the sale to Rabat of one hundred M-48A5 tanks suitable for desert terrain.

Fighting resumed in February 1987 after a two-year lull during which diplomatic efforts to find a solution to the conflict had been pursued. The Polisario Front attacked Moroccan forces in Mahbes, near the Algerian and Moroccan borders, and claimed victory. Fierce fighting continued as the Saharawis sought to breach the Moroccan defensive wall. The Moroccans responded with the construction of a new defensive fortification that extended to the Mauritanian border in the south of the territory.

By August 1988, both sides had accepted a UN plan for a cease-fire and a referendum in which the Saharawis would choose between independence and union with Morocco. Although the cease-fire suffered intermittent interruptions, both parties agreed that all Saharawis over the age of eighteen would be eligible to vote. The plan was delayed, primarily because the Polisario Front wanted Morocco to withdraw its troops before the vote, which Rabat refused to do. In June 1990, however, the Security Council approved the secretary-general's plan in Resolution 658, and in April 1991 it authorized establishment of the UN Mission for the Referendum in Western Sahara (MINURSO) to monitor the cease-fire and balloting. Since 1991 the cease-fire has held.

Problems had reemerged by the summer of 1991, however. Most significant was a dispute over voting eligibility for the referendum. The Polisario wanted to restrict the voting list to the 74,000 names on the Spanish census of 1974. But Rabat wanted to include those of Saharan birth or parentage, which would have added another 120,000 names to the register—votes that would have ensured Morocco's claims. In September 1991, in violation of UN guidelines, Morocco began to relocate tens of thousands of people who were purportedly Saharawis and who carried what appeared to be old Spanish documents.

Since 1991, the United Nations has tried to get both sides to agree to arrangements for a referendum. Beginning in 1997, former US secretary of state James Baker served as negotiator. Rabat, for its part, devoted its efforts to delaying a vote while consolidating its superior position on the ground. The June 2001 Baker Plan was a significant departure from previous frameworks in that it called for several years of autonomy for the territory, to be followed by a referendum in which Moroccans who had settled in the territory since 1975 would vote along with UN-approved residents. The vote would come down to a choice between independence, integration, and a "third way" (i.e., autonomy under Moroccan sovereignty). Initially the proposal was embraced by Rabat as well as the United States and France, but the "third way" received sharp criticism from Algeria and various international observers. Baker resigned from his efforts in 2004. Yet, while the numbers would be weighted in Morocco's favor, Rabat ultimately resumed its recalcitrance because it could not be confident that the vote would go as it wished. It argued that sovereignty was nonnegotiable.

The question of Moroccan sovereignty of the "Southern Province" will likely remain front and center for years to come. It is the terrain on which intractable questions of decolonization, nationalism, and regional and international diplomacy are played out.

FOREIGN POLICY

Foreign policy decisions are made by the king and a small group of personal advisers within the military, political, and economic *Makhzen*.

The most immediate concern appears to be Europe; Morocco's interests in the Mediterranean stem from geopolitical and economic realities as well as historical conditioning. The country's formal association with the EU dates back to 1969; in 1976 a trade and cooperation agreement gave industrial products privileged access to Europe as well as reasonably generous financial aid protocols. In 1987 Morocco applied to join the EU, an effort quickly rejected by the European Commission. The 2000 Association Accord with the EU brought the country into still closer contact, establishing a free trade arrangement designed to liberalize trade over a twelve-year period, with the crucial exception of agricultural commodities.

Europe's 1995 Barcelona Process was renamed Union for the Mediterranean in 2008. Morocco has held a principal position in the EU's foreign policy; it is the largest recipient of funds under the Mesures d'accompagnement (MEDA) of the Barcelona Process. Under MEDA I (1995–1999), Morocco received €660 million; for MEDA II (2000–2006), Morocco received €812 million.

Not surprisingly, France is a particularly important focus of diplomatic efforts with Europe, given the Moroccan elite's close affinity with the former metropole. In the early 1990s, Franco-Moroccan relations were strained by the 1990 publication of Gilles Perrault's *Notre ami le roi* (*Our Friend the King*), in which Hassan received harsh criticism for his human rights record (and France for its long-term support of the monarch). Hassan castigated Danièlle Mitterrand, the French president's wife, for her visit to refugee camps in southern Algeria. Morocco threatened to sever ties with France and banned French newspapers and television broadcasts. The issue receded in 1993, however, and Rabat continues to enjoy close relations with France's right-wing governments. Former president Jacques Chirac was reported to be a close friend of Rabat. His successor, Nicolas Sarkozy, visited Morocco in 2007 along with French business executives to sign business contracts and jump-start efforts on the Union for the Mediterranean.

France has traditionally viewed Morocco as a lynchpin in its *politique Africaine*. Many French senior citizens are opting to retire in Morocco. Low housing costs, perceptions of a simpler lifestyle, and the sun have all prompted such a trend. Enterprising Moroccans speak of building assisted-living communities for retirees, a potential source of foreign exchange and employment in the health-care sector.

Relations with Spain are another story. Franco and Hassan appear to have had a decent working relationship, with mutual interests in keeping their respective authoritarian structures intact. Despite some tension over competition with Spanish agriculture and fisheries, Moroccan-Spanish relations improved steadily after Franco's death in 1975. Spain is Morocco's second-largest trading partner after France. Spanish-Moroccan relations were cemented by Hassan's visit to Spain in September 1989 and by the signing of a friendship treaty in 1991 during Spanish king Juan Carlos's visit to Rabat. In addition, Madrid and Rabat have collaborated on such projects as underwater electricity links, financial-sector ties, and the Maghrib-Europe Gas (MEG) pipeline. The MEG runs from Algeria through Morocco, across the Strait of Gibraltar, to Spain and Portugal. Gas from the pipeline is being used to power an independent power project in Tahaddart, near Tangier.

On the political front, however, Spanish public opinion has sharply criticized Morocco on the Western Sahara. And as Spain began to experience dynamic economic growth in the 1990s and "reborder" itself as part of Europe, a condescending attitude toward Morocco deepened. For Spanish political culture, Morocco is a foil that represents the past: absolutist, backwards, undeveloped. By the late 1990s, tension became quite palpable on an array of issues: drugs; access to deep-sea fisheries;

security; the status of Ceuta, Melilla, and islands along Morocco's Mediterranean coast; and, above all, immigration. Tensions came to a head in July 2002 when six Moroccan gendarmes set up tents and raised a flag on Leyla, a small, uninhabited island three hundred meters off the coast near Ceuta. In response, Spanish warships deployed special forces and removed the police. Morocco had claimed that its initial action was necessary to fight clandestine migration and drug running to Spain. The Spanish government, however, claimed that the island, known to the Spanish as Perejil, was one of its possessions. After lengthy negotiations involving US Secretary of State Colin Powell, the Spanish forces withdrew, leaving the island once again uninhabited—except by goats and birds.

The election of José Luis Rodriguez Zapatero in March 2004—which removed José María Aznar's Popular Party from office a few days after the Atocha train bombings—restored greater comity between the two countries. Yet, tensions remain over migration and show no signs of abatement. In September 2005, efforts by non-Moroccan migrants to scale fences in Ceuta and Melilla returned the enclaves to the international news and exacerbated tensions. Immigration remains an issue that transcends the domestic-international divide. Europe's demand for immigrant labor is facilitated by restrictive policies that depress wages. For Morocco, emigration provides a valuable opportunity to obtain crucial remittances from overseas workers.

With respect to the MENA region, the 1990–1991 Gulf crisis, the Israeli-Palestinian conflict, and the 2003 Iraq War highlighted the stark discontinuity that exists between elite and popular attitudes about the government's pro-Western orientation. In 1991 mass demonstrations in support of Iraq were held in major cities. Nonetheless, the United States and Europe rewarded Morocco's contribution of a contingent of 6,000 soldiers to the anti-Iraq coalition with military aid and economic assistance. In September 1991, Hassan traveled to Washington, DC, and signed a $250 million agreement securing twenty military aircraft. Shortly after the Algerian military crackdown in January 1992 nullifying the election victory of Algeria's Islamic Salvation Front, a team of US military experts visited Rabat. The United States then delivered twelve more fighters to Morocco ahead of schedule. Throughout the 1990s and into the first decade of the twenty-first century, Morocco has deftly played the "security card," requesting support for its economy and society in order to preclude the emergence of an Islamist threat. Morocco also has bought commercial aircraft from the United States. In 1993 Royal Air Maroc ordered twelve Boeing aircraft worth $525 million, despite heavy pressure from France to buy its Airbus. In 2001 Morocco agreed to purchase four Airbus aircraft, but only after it had purchased twenty-two Boeing planes in 2000.

Since the early 1980s the Royal Armed Forces have maintained close collaboration with NATO, conducting bilateral exercises with France, Spain, and the

United States and securing much-needed military assistance. In a celebrated move in the summer of 2004, the Bush administration proffered non-NATO ally status, elevating the country to an august club that includes Australia, Egypt, Israel, Japan, Jordan, and Pakistan The designation entitles Rabat to priority delivery of defense materiel and access to generous loans. Additionally, the country is a player in Washington's Trans-Sahara Counter Terrorism Initiative.

In regional affairs, the monarchy has also long sought to play a mediating role in Arab politics, hosting a number of important Arab summits. Hassan's July 1986 meeting with Israeli prime minister Shimon Peres in the mountain resort town of Ifrane was the first public meeting between Arab and Israeli leaders since the 1981 assassination of Egyptian president Anwar Sadat. Despite harsh criticism from Algeria, Libya, and Syria, however, Egypt, Jordan, the Palestine Liberation Organization (PLO), and other moderate Arab states backed the move. In January 1989, Syria resumed ties broken off after the Peres-Hassan meeting. Morocco's relations with Egypt also accelerated after Egypt's readmission into Arab League affairs in 1989. Hassan proudly hosted the 1989 Arab League summit in Casablanca.

In the 1990s, Hassan sought to persuade Arab countries, particularly Saudi Arabia, to develop ties with Israel in the context of the peace process. In a striking illustration, he welcomed the Israeli leadership to Rabat the day after the September 1993 PLO-Israeli accord was signed. Morocco was keen throughout the 1990s to encourage Israeli investment in the Moroccan economy, particularly from the large population of Israeli citizens of Moroccan descent. After the collapse of Palestinian-Israeli peace negotiations in the fall of 2000 and the emergence of the second Palestinian Intifada, however, diplomatic and economic relations between Morocco and Israel stagnated. In March 2005, relations improved somewhat, as Muhammad met with Israeli deputy prime minister Peres.

Since 1989, some of Morocco's greatest efforts in the region were for the establishment of the Arab Maghrib Union (UMA). An agreement setting up the UMA was signed in February 1989 in Marrakech. Morocco's energies in the early years of the UMA were devoted to improving relations with Algeria and to a lesser extent Mauritania in connection with the conflict in the Western Sahara, to little avail. In 1994 borders with Algeria were closed again, and relations have remained deeply strained. Even the meeting between Muhammad and Algerian head of state Abdelaziz Bouteflika at the Arab League in March 2005 did little to diminish skepticism. In October 2005, after the conflagration at the fences at Ceuta and Melilla, Morocco accused Algeria of funneling sub-Saharan migrants to the enclaves. Relations with Tunisia are cordial, if not warm, and Libya is regarded with suspicion. The 2006 reestablishment of ties between the United States and Libya might warm Moroccan-Libyan relations.

BIBLIOGRAPHY

Pre-independence Morocco is analyzed in Allal Al Fasi, *The Independence Movement in Arab North Africa* (New York: Octagon, 1970); Robin Bidwell, *Morocco Under Colonial Rule* (London: Frank Cass, 1973); Edmund Burke, *Prelude to Protectorate in Morocco* (Chicago: University of Chicago Press, 1976); Alan Scham, *Lyautey in Morocco* (Berkeley: University of California Press, 1970); and Janet Abu-Lughod, *Rabat: Urban Apartheid in Morocco* (Princeton, NJ: Princeton University Press, 1980). Richard Pennell, *Morocco Since 1830: A History* (New York: New York University Press, 2001); Michel Le Gall, "The Historical Context," in *Polity and Society in Contemporary North Africa*, ed. I. William Zartman and Mark Habeeb, 3–18 (Boulder, CO: Westview, 1993); and Benjamin Stora, "Algeria and Morocco: The Passions of the Past, Representations of the Nation That Unite and Divide," in *Nation, Society and Culture in North Africa*, ed. James McDougall, 14–33 (London: Frank Cass, 2003), are valuable. Jamal Abun-Nasr, *A History of the Maghrib in the Islamic Period* (London: Cambridge University Press, 1987), never fails. French-language works include Abdallah Laroui, *Les origines sociales et culturelles du nationalisme marocain (1830–1912)* (Casablanca: Centre Culturel Arabe, 1993).

For analyses of Morocco's political system, see John Entelis, *Culture and Counterculture in Moroccan Politics* (Boulder, CO: Westview Press, 1996); Azzedine Layachi, *State, Society and Democracy in Morocco* (Washington, DC: Georgetown University CCAS, 1998); Saloua Zerhouni, "Morocco: Elite Change and Regime Maintenance," in *Arab Elites: Negotiating the Politics of Change*, ed. Volker Perthes, 61–85 (Boulder, CO: Lynne Rienner, 2004); and Abdellah Hammoudi, *Master and Disciple* (Chicago: University of Chicago Press, 1997). John Waterbury, *The Commander of the Faithful* (New York: Columbia University Press, 1970), is a classic work on the nature of elite politics in Morocco. Ellen Lust-Okar, *Structuring Conflict in the Arab World* (London: Cambridge University Press, 2005), compares Jordan and Morocco. Gregory White, "The End of the 'Era of Leniency' in Morocco," in *North Africa: Politics, Region, and the Limits of Transformation*, ed. Yahia Zoubir and Haizam Amirah-Fernández, 90–108 (London: Routledge, 2008), analyzes democratic reform in the current decade. French-language works include Remy Levau, *Le fellah marocain: Défenseur du trône* (Paris: Presses de la Fondation Nationale des Sciences Politiques, 1985), and Ali Benhaddou, *Les élites du royaume: Essai sur l'organisation du pouvoir au Maroc* (Paris: L'Harmattan, 1997).

For controversial treatments of the monarchy, see Gilles Perrault, *Notre ami le roi* (Paris: Gallimard, 1992); Malika Oufkir and Michéle Fitoussi, *Stolen Lives: Twenty Years in a Desert Jail* (New York: Hyperion, 2001); and Christine Daure-Serfaty, *Letter from Morocco*, trans. Paul Raymond Côté and Constantina Mitchell (Lansing: Michigan State University Press, 2003). The king's own perspective, as well as much additional information about Moroccan political life, is presented in his memoirs, *The Challenge* (London: Macmillan, 1978) and *Hassan II: La mémoire d'un roi, entretiens avec Eric Laurent* (Paris: Plon, 1993). Guilain Denoeux and Abdeslam Maghraoui, "King Hassan's Strategy of Political Dualism," *Middle East Policy* 5, no. 4 (1998): 104–130, and Abdeslam Maghraoui, "From Symbolic Legitimacy to Democratic Legitimacy: Monarchic Rule and Political Reform in Morocco," *Journal of Democracy* 12, no. 1 (2001): 73–86, are perceptive.

For considerations of the politics of human rights and democratic reforms set in a comparative context, see Susan Slyomovics, *The Performance of Human Rights in Morocco* (Philadelphia: University of Pennsylvania Press, 2005); Susan Waltz, "The Politics of Human Rights in the Maghreb," in *Islam, Democracy and the State in North Africa*, ed. John Entelis, 75–92 (Bloomington: Indiana University Press, 1997); and Sieglinde Gränzer, "Changing Human Rights Discourse: Transnational Advocacy Networks in Tunisia and Morocco," in *The Power of Human Rights*, ed. Thomas Risse et al., 109–133 (Cambridge: Cambridge University Press, 1999).

For analyses of Islam in Moroccan politics, see Henry Munson, *Religion and Power in Morocco* (New Haven, CT: Yale University Press, 1993); François Burgat, *The Islamic Movement in North Africa*, trans. William Dowell (Austin: University of Texas Press, 1993); Dale Eickelman, *Knowledge and Power in Morocco* (Princeton, NJ: Princeton University Press, 1985); and Elaine Combs-Schilling, *Sacred Performances in Morocco* (Chicago: University of Chicago Press, 1989). Accounts of Morocco's Jewish community are provided in Norman Stillman, "The Moroccan Jewish Experience: A Revisionist View," *Jerusalem Quarterly* 9 (fall 1978): 111–123; and Mark Tessler, "Israel and Morocco: The Political Calculus of a 'Moderate Arab State,'" in *Israel After Begin*, ed. Gregory Mahler (Albany: State University of New York Press, 1990). Rahma Bourquia and Susan Gilson Miller, eds., *In the Shadow of the Sultan* (Cambridge, MA: Harvard University Press, 1999), offers an array of discerning essays.

Studies on the role of women include Fatima Mernissi, *Dreams of Trespass* (New York: Addison-Wesley, 1994); Deborah Kapchen, *Gender on the Market* (Philadelphia: University of Pennsylvania Press, 1998); Alison Baker, *Voices of Resistance* (Albany: State University of New York Press, 1998); Mounira Charrad, *States and Women's Rights* (Berkeley: University of California Press, 2001); Laurie Brand, *Women, the State, and Political Liberalization* (New York: Columbia University Press, 1998); Louisa Dris-Ait-Hamadouche, "Women in the Maghreb: Stereotypes and Realities," in Zoubir and Amirah-Fernández, *North Africa*, 202–226; and Loubna Skalli-Hanna, *Through a Local Prism: Gender, Globalization and Identity in Moroccan Women's Magazines* (New York: Rowman & Littlefield, 2006). Katherine Hoffman, *We Share Walls: Language, Land and Gender in Berber Morocco* (New York: Wiley-Blackwell, 2008), examines crucial dimensions of Berber politics, too.

Analyses of Morocco's economic situation are available in Will Swearingen, *Moroccan Mirages* (Princeton, NJ: Princeton University Press, 1986); Serge Leymarie and Jean Tripier, *Maroc: Le prochain dragon?* (Casablanca: Eddif, 1992); and Gregory White, *On the Outside of Europe Looking In: A Comparative Political Economy of Tunisia and Morocco* (Albany: State University of New York Press, 2001), and "Free Trade As a Strategic Instrument in the War on Terror? The 2004 U.S.-Moroccan Free Trade Agreement," *Middle East Journal* 59, no. 4 (2005): 597–616. An intriguing book is Muhammad VI's doctoral dissertation, Mohamed Ben El-Hassan Alaoui, *La cooperation entre l'Union Européenne et les pays du Maghreb* (Paris: Éditions Nathan, 1994). Morocco's position in the global economy is treated by Shana Cohen, *Searching for a Different Future: The Rise of a Global Middle Class in Morocco* (Durham, NC: Duke University Press, 2005). Its experience with immigration is engaged by Laurie Brand, *Citizens Abroad: Emigration and the State in the Middle East and North Africa* (New York: Cambridge University Press, 2006); and David McMurray, *In and Out of Morocco: Smuggling and Migration in a Frontier Boomtown* (Minneapolis: University of Minnesota Press, 2000).

The war with the Polisario Front is carefully documented and discussed by John Damis, *Conflict in Northwest Africa* (Stanford, CA: Hoover Institution Press, 1983); I. William Zartman, *Ripe for Resolution* (New York: Oxford University Press, 1987); and Jacob Mundy, "'Seized of the Matter': The UN and the Western Sahara Dispute," *Mediterranean Quarterly* 15, no. 3 (2004): 130–148.

Finally, Marvine Howe, *Morocco* (New York: Oxford University Press, 2005), provides an accessible overview of the country. And Brian Edwards, *Morocco Bound* (Durham, NC: Duke University Press, 2005), offers a stimulating analysis of America's cultural and political relationship with the Maghreb from World War II until the 1970s.

Useful websites include the government's press agency (www.map.ma/eng) and official website (www.maroc.ma/PortailInst/An/home). The National Company for Radio and Television (www.snrt.ma) began a website in the early 2000s devoted to Moroccans living abroad; it streams daily news clips in Spanish, Amazight, French, and Moroccan Arabic. For news within Morocco from a more critical perspective, *Tel Quel* is available online at www.telquel-online.com. *Le Journal Hebdomadaire* is no longer available online. *Tingis Magazine* is a Moroccan American, English-language weekly at www.tingismagazine.com. *Morocco News Line* (www.morocconewsline.com) has interesting content. *Jeune Afrique* is available at www.jeuneafrique.com.

Different parties have their own newspapers. The Istiqlal publishes news in *Al Alam* (www.alalam.ma), with the USFP's news available in French online at liberation.press.ma. *Al Bayane* is the newspaper of the Communist Party of Progress and Socialism, available in French and Arabic at albayane.ma and albayanalayoum.ma. *La Vie Economique* and *L'Economiste* are independent weeklies available at lavieeco.com and leconomiste.com; *Al Sabah* is independent, too, at www.assabah.press.ma. The pro-government *Le Matin du Sahara* is available at lematin.ma. Finally, the official TV station 2M is available at www.2m.ma. Radio Méditerranée Internationale is a Tangiers-based radio station that broadcasts online at www.medi1.com; it plays an intriguing mix of music as well as official news in Arabic and French.

16

DEMOCRATIC AND POPULAR REPUBLIC OF ALGERIA

Azzedine Layachi

HISTORICAL BACKGROUND

Algeria's political history is both a reflection and a product of its struggle for national identity, a struggle made difficult by the pervasive influence of foreign invaders. Invaded in the early seventh century by the Arabs, Algeria in the twenty-first century reflects both the Arab tradition and the culture of the indigenous Berber (Amazigh) tribes. Its central location on the Mediterranean, making it an outpost for piracy until well into the eighteenth century, has led it to absorb many other cultural traditions. People of French, Greek, Italian, and Spanish descent have constituted a substantial part of the Algerian population throughout its history.

Until the sixteenth century, the Maghrib region of North Africa consisted of a large number of autonomous and independent tribes. The Berbers are its oldest inhabitants. The Phoenicians established themselves there in the 1100s BCE, followed by the Romans in 146 BCE and the Vandals in 439 CE. In 533 Algeria fell under the Byzantine Empire, and in the seventh century the Arabs conquered it and made it part of the Arabo-Islamic Empire. After being ruled by several Arabo-Islamic dynasties, Algeria in 1518 became part of the Ottoman Empire, which united it in a loose configuration of tribes and protected it against the imperial ambitions of the Europeans. In 1830 Algeria was conquered by the French, who controlled it until 1962.

Throughout recent centuries, the Arabo-Islamic tradition served as a powerful unifying tool in Algeria's struggle against foreign domination, most notably in the war for independence against France from 1954 to 1962. Nonetheless, the integrationist policy pursued by France heavily instilled French values and culture into Algeria and is partially responsible for the nature of contemporary Algerian politics, which is split between Western-oriented elites and the masses, who identify more

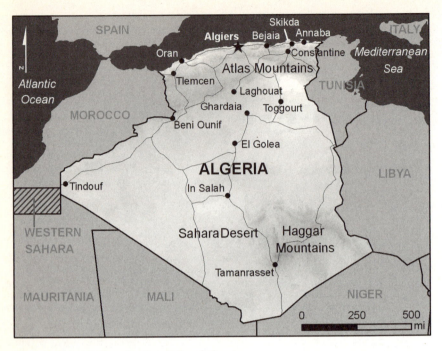

Democratic and Popular Republic of Algeria

with their Arab, Berber, and Islamic cultures. Algerian political culture and tradition continues to reflect the impact of these diverse traditions and their varied effects on the country's history.

France is often credited with the definition and consolidation of Algeria's modern state, but elements of statehood already existed under the Ottoman Empire. It took France more than forty years to conquer and subdue the whole country, and under its "civilizing mission" the entire political and economic structure of the region was dramatically transformed.

In colonial Algeria the European settlers were mostly peasants, working-class people, army officers, and bureaucrats who profited from the prosperous arable land along the coast. Within fifty years of French occupation, more than 150,000 Europeans had settled in Algeria, and the indigenous population had lost its independence, its freedom, and most of its land through seizure, expropriation, and property laws favoring Europeans. Moreover, by 1900 more than 3 million natives had died from mass repression and disease. France's "total colonialism" policy drew the antagonism of the inhabitants and gave rise to a nationalist movement.

The Nationalist Struggle

From 1830 to about 1870, traditional Algerian nationalists resisted colonial rule. The most prominent leader of that era was Amir Abd Al Qadir, who set about establishing a Muslim state in all land in the interior not occupied by the French. However, he was imprisoned and sent into exile in Syria by 1847, and all Algerian territory was soon firmly under French control. In the 1850s the French government declared the territory part of France, and Algerians officially became French subjects, though not citizens. The extension of French authority triggered more nationalist revolts in the 1870s, but these were suppressed and followed by more land confiscations, onerous taxes, and tighter control of the indigenous people. These and other punitive actions were intended to terrorize Algerians into submission and procure land and money for colonization. French atrocities were documented in several eyewitness accounts and in reports such as the one issued by a French royal commission in 1883, which stated,

> We tormented, at the slightest suspicion and without due process, people whose guilt still remains more than uncertain. . . . We massacred people who carried passes, cut the throats, on a simple suspicion, of entire populations which proved later to be innocent. . . . [Many innocent people were tried just because] they exposed themselves to our furor. Judges were available to condemn them and civilized people to have them executed. . . . In a word, our barbarism was worse than that of the barbarians we came to civilize, and we complain that we have not succeeded with them![1]

Early Algerian resistance movements, such as Jeunesse Algérienne and Fédération des Elus Musulmans, wanted full assimilation and the integration of Algerians into the French community without surrendering their Muslim identity. (Existing laws required Muslims to renounce Islamic law in favor of the French civil code.) However, when the demand for equality with Europeans in Algeria remained unanswered and reformist efforts became irrelevant, a number of parties called for independence in the 1920s. In early 1954 the Comité Révolutionnaire d'Unité et d'Action (CRUA) was created by dissidents from earlier movements, ex-soldiers in the French army, and miscellaneous groups of dedicated men disillusioned with the French administration and unafraid of violence. In October 1954 CRUA was transformed into a political organization, the Front de Libération Nationale (FLN), and its military arm, the Armée de Libération Nationale (ALN).

On November 1, 1954, the FLN issued a proclamation calling on all Algerians to rise and fight for their freedom. The revolution had begun. A provisional

ALGERIA

Capital city	Algiers
Chief of state	President Abdelaziz Bouteflika
Head of government	Prime Minister Ahmed Ouyahia
Major political parties *(seats in lower house)*	National Liberation Front (136), National Democratic Rally (61), Society of Peace Movement (52), Workers Party (26), Rally for Culture and Democracy (19), Algerian National Front (13)
Ethnic groups	Arab-Berber (99%), European (less than 1%)
Religious groups	Sunni Muslim (99%), Christian and Jewish (1%)
Export partners	United States (23.9%), Italy (14.9%), Spain (11.1%), Canada (9.6%), France (8.6%), Netherlands (4.5%)
Import partners	France (19.8%), Italy (10.9%), China (9%), Spain (7.6%), Germany (5.4%)

government (GPRA) was formed in 1958, but fighting continued until a cease-fire agreement was signed at Evian, France, on March 19, 1962. The Evian Accords stipulated a national referendum on independence that was to include both European colonists and indigenous Algerians. On July 1 the overwhelming majority voted for independence, and Algeria officially became independent on July 5, 1962.

Postindependence Algeria

Soon after independence, serious divisions within the nationalist leadership and rank and file threatened the success of the revolution and left a weak organization to lead the country. The absence of a unifying revolutionary ideology, the lack of an uncontested leader, and the factional fighting that had characterized the revolutionary years carried over into the postindependence period. The tactical unity that had marked the FLN's military and diplomatic efforts for independence broke down, and a vicious power struggle began. The three major contestants were the

Algerian provisional government, the *wilayate* command councils, and the external army (ALN). Factional rivalries remained an intrinsic feature of Algeria's postindependence politics.

On September 26, 1962, the Algerian National Assembly elected Ahmed Ben Bella premier of the new Democratic and Popular Republic of Algeria. His government was formed from the ranks of the military and close personal and political allies, including Col. Houari Boumediene. The most pressing task of the new government was to restore normality to the war-torn country. The mass exodus of Europeans had caused a severe shortage of highly skilled workers, technicians, educators, and property-owning entrepreneurs; many people had lost their jobs after their French employers left.

A new constitution made the president military commander in chief, head of state, and head of government. It also preserved the hegemony of the FLN as the single political party. Ben Bella became its secretary-general in April 1963 and was elected president in September for a five-year term.

The concentration of power in the hands of Ben Bella caused factionalism within the leadership to resurface. Ben Bella owed his power position to his legacy as "historic chief of the revolution." He had been a key figure in the struggle against French colonialism and spent several years in French prisons. However, in postindependence Algeria, his inability to manage the various rivalries and controversies facing his regime, his ouster of traditional leaders, his repeated attacks on the Union Générale des Travailleurs Algériens (UGTA) labor union, and his failure to transform the FLN into an effective mass party eventually led to his defeat. He was overthrown on June 19, 1965, in a bloodless coup by Col. Houari Boumediene, who had helped put him into office in 1962.

The political transition was smooth and efficient. All political power was transferred to Boumediene and his military-dominated Council of the Revolution, which was the only functioning national political institution. The constitution and the National Assembly were suspended, and Boumediene was named president, head of government, and minister of defense. He relied on the support of the mujahideen (veterans of the war of independence) and a technocratic elite drawn partially from the military. The new regime promised to reestablish the principles of the revolution, end corruption and personal abuses, eliminate internal divisions, and build a socialist economy based on industrialization and comprehensive agrarian reform.

A new national charter, approved by referendum in June 1976, reaffirmed Algeria's socialist orientation, recognized the FLN as the only legal party, and implicitly maintained the authoritarian system. A new constitution, approved by referendum in November 1976, reestablished the national legislature (the Assemblée Populaire Nationale). A month later, Boumediene was elected president with more than 95 percent of the vote on a single-candidate ballot. He was head of state and government, commander in chief, minister of defense, and secretary-general of the FLN. In the parliamentary elections of February 1977, all candidates were FLN members. The diverse membership of the new assembly and its high proportion of industrial and agricultural workers were lauded as the final step in the creation of a socialist state.

Boumediene died suddenly in late 1978 of a rare kidney ailment. His legacy included a consolidated state, a stable political system, a rapidly industrializing economy, an extensive state-centered socialist program, and an expanding petroleum and gas export industry. He also left a political vacuum. His charismatic leadership and political acumen were very much responsible for Algeria's economic and political development during the 1970s. He left no designated successor. Rabah Bitat, the National Assembly president, was named interim president until a special FLN congress, following the army's recommendation, selected Col. Chadli Bendjedid as presidential candidate. He was elected to office in January 1979.

Through a policy of "change within continuity," President Bendjedid consolidated his power and took full control of the state, party, and military apparatus. By the end of his first term in 1984, he had completed a process of "de-Boumedienization," firmly secured his position and powers, and consolidated state authority. Reelected in 1985, he faced many challenges, including a declining economy due to the inefficiency of oversized industrial complexes, neglect of the agricultural sector, rapid population growth, increasing unemployment, and a sharp drop in energy prices.

Bendjedid's initial reforms concentrated on structural change and economic liberalization, including a shift in domestic investment away from heavy industry toward agriculture, light industry, and consumer goods. State enterprises were broken up into smaller units, and several small state-owned firms were privatized. Subsidies were reduced, and price controls were lifted. The fiscal deficit was attacked by cutting government spending, and an important anticorruption campaign was launched. Other changes included opening the economy to limited foreign investment, expanding and revitalizing the private sector, shifting away from the Soviet Union toward the West in strategic considerations, and lowering Algeria's once highly visible profile in global and Third World affairs. These policies allowed Bendjedid to eliminate much of the old guard opposition still loyal to Boumediene's legacy and firmed up his control of the political realm.

However, Bendjedid's economic reforms exacerbated an already dismal situation. They increased unemployment, reduced industrial output, and sharply increased prices, undermining the purchasing power of most Algerians. The upper class profited from economic liberalization while the burden of reform fell mostly on the masses. A wide generation gap increased between the masses—70 percent of whom were under the age of thirty and had no memory of the independence war—and the elites, who based their legitimacy on their war credentials. By the late 1980s Algeria was highly polarized.

In the first week of October 1988, the crisis exploded amid the most violent public demonstrations since independence. Weeks of strikes and work stoppages were followed by six days of violent riots in several cities that targeted city halls, police stations, post offices, state-owned cars, and supermarkets—anything seen to represent the regime and the FLN. It was a demonstration against the leadership, corruption, declining living standards, increasing unemployment, food shortages, and persistent inequality and alienation. The riots were quickly suppressed by the military, and a state of siege was declared. Hundreds of rioters were killed.

On October 10, President Bendjedid promised new political reforms, which were approved in a referendum on November 3 and embodied in a constitutional amendment approved in a referendum in February 1989. The reforms included the separation of party and state, restructuring of executive and legislative authority, strengthening of presidential power, elimination of the ideological commitment to socialism, free local and national elections, freedom of association, and a reduced role for the military in politics.

These riots and the reforms constituted the most important changes in postindependence Algeria. The political system and ruling elite were severely challenged and shaken by the sudden political mobilization of society. Throughout the 1990s, several armed groups contested the legitimacy of the state and sought to overthrow it. Furthermore, the state, bankrupted by failed economic policies, reluctantly turned to International Monetary Fund (IMF)–sponsored structural-adjustment and neoliberal reforms. During that same period, socioeconomic conditions worsened even further, due to the combined effects of the internal war and structural adjustment. Relative peace and stability had returned by early 2000, but the challenges facing the country remain important, and many have not yet been addressed.

POLITICAL ENVIRONMENT

Algeria is located in the center of the Maghrib region. It is only a few hundred miles from the southern coast of France and even closer to Spain and Italy. Its strategic importance stems from several factors, including its vast territory (it is the second-largest country in Africa after Sudan), linking sub-Saharan Africa to the Mediterranean; its 1,200 kilometers of shoreline; its vast petroleum and gas reserves; and its important mineral resources, including phosphate, coal, iron, lead, uranium, and zinc.

Algeria's 91,935 square miles of land is 85 percent desert. Two ranges of the Atlas Mountains divide it into three regions: the Tell, along the Mediterranean lowlands on the coast; the High Plateau, south of the Tell and north of the Sahara; and the Sahara, which is the largest region. Only 3.2 percent of Algeria's land is arable, located mostly in the northern lowlands.

The Tell region has mild, rainy winters and hot, dry summers, though the coast is quite humid. On the High Plateau, summers are hot and dry, and winters are colder, with some rain. Snow falls regularly on some mountains in the winter. The Sahara is hot by day and cool at night. In the spring, a hot, dry wind from the south, the sirocco, blows across the desert and causes strong sandstorms. Rainfall is rare in the Sahara, and some desert areas may not see rain for up to two decades.

More than three-fourths of Algeria's 34 million citizens live in northern cities and towns. The remainder live in desert oases or in the desert itself. The population is young, with 25.4 percent under fifteen years of age and 70 percent below thirty. Most Algerians are Muslims of Arab–Berber stock. Arabic is the official language, though French is widely spoken and used in business. In 2004, under pressure from Berber militants, the government agreed to make the Berber language (Tamazight) a second national language. Berbers live throughout North Africa, with the heaviest concentrations in Morocco and Algeria. Their presence in North Africa goes back 4,000 years. While most Berbers were "Arabized" and converted to Islam following the Arabo-Muslim invasions of the seventh and eleventh centuries, many have maintained the Berber language and cultural traditions. In postindependence Algeria, ethnicity became politicized as a result of the state's control over the country's culture and language, its imposition of Arabic as the sole official language, and its repression of minority culture and language.

Distinctive Political and Cultural Factors

Extensive "Arabization" programs and the masses' identification with Islam and the Arab ethnos also conflict with the elites' secular outlook and ideology. Some of this tension dates from the colonial era, when secularization was used by the French to "divide and conquer." The extensive European presence in colonial Algeria ensured that the minuscule domestic elite controlled the bulk of the Algerian population. The elite-mass divide remains a constant source of hostility and mistrust that reflects historical experience and cultural and ideological values.

One consequence of this is the political and military leaders' pervasive lack of trust in the masses. Distrust of any form of political opposition has led to years of authoritarian rule. That distrust reappeared in response to the emergence of opposition parties in 1989. In addition, personal rivalries and clashes among the leaders themselves have long substituted for legitimate political discourse. Political ambitions are served better by personal loyalties than by purely political objectives and opinions.

Despite the persistence of these elite attitudes, tolerance for limited "legitimate" dissent and discourse has gradually emerged. Since the late 1980s, the leadership has increasingly recognized the validity of popular participation and political discussion. In the 1980s and early 1990s, remarkably open and candid debates occurred over the national charter and the restitution of local and national representative legislatures, evolving into a radical liberalization program that permitted the emergence of competitive political parties. Although tolerance for opposition may be only superficial, achieving "legitimacy" has become increasingly important, even if this means including the opposition.

An even more paradoxical feature of Algerian political culture is an innate distrust of those in power. Tolerance for rebellion and sporadic violence, however, sometimes conflicts with more conformist attitudes about appropriate behavior. The revolutionary experience and authoritarian leadership resulted in a strange dichotomy between populism and centralized rule. On the one hand, the colonial and war experiences exerted a profound impact on perceptions of the "proper" role of government—the need for a strong, centralized state to achieve economic and political development. On the other hand, Algerian political culture remains strongly committed to the populism that fueled the revolution. Algerian populism is a belief in the will of the people, a belief that in part subsumes the purely political. It places justice and morality above all other norms and emphasizes the importance of a direct relationship between the leadership and the people. This relationship, which is not dependent on intermediary political structures, accounts for the phenomenal success of the charismatic leadership of Boumediene.

Nationalism and socialism have long been intrinsic parts of Algeria's political culture. Although there appears to be more commitment to their rhetoric and symbolic content than to their substance, most statist policies appeal heavily to the notion of nationalism to justify interventionist policies and government actions. The entire revolutionary period looms large in the minds of Algerians and reinforces the nationalist cause. The preservation of national unity and the Algerian nation supersedes all other commitments and affiliations. In fact, this commitment to national unity has been used by the military leadership since 1992 to screen opposition groups for legalization. The 1989 constitution legalized all political parties on the condition that they never "violate national unity, the integrity of the territory, the independence of the country or the sovereignty of the people" (Article 40).

Algeria is a Muslim country with a primarily secular state. Islam in Algeria is part of the cultural and political tradition dating back at least to the independence war, when the revolutionary rhetoric of the FLN drew upon the unifying force of Islam to strengthen national cohesion and opposition to colonial rule. Islam directly contributed to a uniquely Algerian form of socialism under Boumediene and a conservative political outlook. Conservative policies regarding personal, family, religious, and moral affairs have predominated, despite sweeping secular and modernizing policies in the economic sphere. The populist Islam that arose in the 1980s and 1990s in virtually every segment of Algerian society finds its roots in the nation's conservative and traditional mass political culture.

ECONOMIC CONDITIONS

Upon assuming office in 1965, President Boumediene began an extensive industrialization program and established government control over most, if not all, of foreign trade, manufacturing, retail, agriculture, utilities, and banking sectors. All major foreign business interests and most domestically owned businesses were nationalized. By the early 1970s, almost 90 percent of the industrial sector and more than 70 percent of the industrial workforce were under state control.

From 1970 to 1973, economic policy was financed entirely by petroleum revenues; nearly 45 percent of capital investment was allotted to the capital-intensive industrial sector, about 40 percent went to social and economic infrastructure, and only 15 percent went to agriculture. The "Agrarian Revolution" aimed to transform the agricultural sector into a system of cooperatives. However, with insufficient funding and infrastructure, agriculture declined as a percentage of gross national product.

In the second four-year plan (1974–1977), which tried to remedy earlier oversights, the agricultural sector and small to mid-sized industries were encouraged, but the emphasis on heavy industry remained unchallenged. However, due to poor design, many large-scale industrialization projects, instead of providing the impetus for national development, eventually became a source of economic drain. Industrialization was driven more by nationalist sentiments than by considerations of economic efficiency. Falling energy prices in the mid-1980s left Algeria with substantial deficits and an underdeveloped agricultural sector, which led to frequent food shortages, dependence on food imports, and urban migration.

President Bendjedid's economic reforms of the early 1980s emphasized that maintaining a high level of industrial development was vital to the economy, despite a dramatic redirection of funds away from heavy industry toward agriculture, light industry, and public services. These changes were aimed at breaking down the massive state enterprises into manageable and efficient entities, with the hope that gradually removing restrictions would help the private sector grow. These early reforms were motivated more by pragmatism and administrative concerns than by a genuine commitment to liberalization.

In 1986, economic reformers recognized the need to consider a postpetroleum economy and include the foreign sector in Algeria's economic revitalization. Foreign investment up to then had been strongly circumscribed or prohibited outright, as it was considered a threat to the country's independence. The restrictions on both foreign and domestic investment were loosened in order to move the economy away from socialism. Money and credit laws were restructured, contract laws were revised, the central bank was given full independence, and a system of banks specializing in trade finance and capital investment was established. The state started disengaging from the economy, making significant progress toward a market-driven economy.

Despite these changes, the economic crisis deepened, threatening political stability. High unemployment, urbanization, an unbalanced industrial sector (concentrated mostly on heavy industries), highly polarized and dualistic economic conditions, and rapidly declining export revenue eroded the state's welfare capacities and its ability to maintain security and stability. A massive foreign debt had also become cause for concern. Unpredictable global prices and a high level of external dependence (on both food imports and petroleum-product exports) left the country dangerously vulnerable.

Bendjedid's reform failure and the sharp drop in hydrocarbon export earnings in the late 1980s worsened the economic situation and further discredited the state, which was no longer able to finance generous services and subsidies. After 1988, the state retreated from more areas. A growing black market made up for the empty shelves of the state distribution networks, corruption and private appropriations of state funds by some officials multiplied, and political and social challenges remained unchecked. Socioeconomic conditions were made even worse by the political instability that followed the cancellation of elections and the overthrow of Bendjedid in January 1992. The resulting conflict disrupted reform attempts, damaged economic infrastructure, hindered internal and external business relations, and stimulated population movements from the areas affected the most by political violence. It was in this context that the government reluctantly opted for a structural-adjustment program to help halt the economic decline, provide temporary debt-servicing relief, and attract foreign investments.

Structural Adjustment

The structural-adjustment program adopted in April 1994 stabilized the economy by 2000, and foreign investors began showing interest in non-hydrocarbon areas. Inflation was brought down from 30 percent in 1995 to 2 percent in 2006. The fiscal budget and trade balance both produced surpluses—due mostly to increased hydrocarbon revenues. Hard currency reserves increased from $1.5 billion in 1993 to $140 billion in 2008. The country's external debt was less than $4 billion in December 2008, down from $33 billion in 1996. After years of poor performance, the gross domestic product (GDP) growth rate improved substantially, rising from –2.2 percent in 1993 to 5 percent in 2008. In 2008, GDP per capita reached $4,681, up from less than $2,000 in the 1990s.

Despite these overly positive aggregate results, the structural-adjustment reforms carried a heavy social cost. The country's currency was devaluated by 40 percent, and the remaining subsidies on primary consumption items were drastically cut.

Since 1994 more than 500,000 workers have been laid off as a result of the restructuring or closing of public enterprises. Overall unemployment climbed to 35 percent in the 1990s, with some 100,000 unemployed school graduates. Because of this, employment in the informal sector has increased significantly, and the number of people living below the poverty line has risen substantially, reaching a high of 12 million in 2000. A 2006 report on poverty issued by Algeria's Security Services indicated that social inequality has increased, as at that time less than 20 percent of the population controlled more than 50 percent of the country's wealth. Socioeconomic conditions led Algeria to be ranked 100 out of 179 countries in the 2008 Human Development Report.

The "shock therapy" sponsored by the IMF and World Bank did not fulfill its overall promises for several reasons. Fear of the social cost and opposition by vested interests created strong resistance to the reforms by the largest labor union (the UGTA), civil and professional associations, public-enterprise managers, small private entrepreneurs hurt by high interest rates and currency devaluation, and the few big private import-export businesses whose informal monopolies reform threatens.

Artificially sustained long past its viability by centralized control and fortuitous energy exports, the economy is, in the first decade of the twenty-first century, trying to rechannel its energies and focus. In 2002 the government initiated a special $7 billion investment plan for economic revival between 2002 and 2004. An additional $145 billion Program for the Support of Economic Growth (2005–2009) was established to build housing, infrastructure (including the East-West Highway, linking Algeria to Morocco and Tunisia), desalination stations, non-hydrocarbon industries, and tourism facilities. It was hoped that these investments would create at least 300,000 new jobs a year in order to absorb current and future employment demand. Even though these numbers have not been reached, the unemployment rate fell from 31 percent in 2003 to 11.8 percent in 2008. However, 75 percent of the unemployed are less than thirty years old.

The privatization of public enterprises picked up speed in the mid-2000s. In February 2005 the government announced that 942 out of 1,055 enterprises would be partially or totally privatized. The privatization plan included even the state-controlled telecommunications and banking sectors. However, the plan to privatize the first bank, Crédit Populaire d'Algérie, was postponed indefinitely in 2007 due to the subprime crisis in the United States. The plan to open Sonatrach, the sole state-owned hydrocarbons company, to private capital was also cancelled due to domestic opposition.

As for agriculture, its long neglect was a costly mistake for Algeria, which has become a big importer of food. However, this sector has gradually taken on more importance in economic policy as state collectives were privatized, a new agricultural bank was established, and funds were allotted for irrigation. The productivity of the agricultural sector has increased sharply since the mid-1990s, producing an average sectoral growth rate of 7.5 percent between 2000 and 2004. In 2008 its share of GDP was 8.1 percent, and it employed 14 percent of the workforce. Its major challenge remains recurring drought, which directly affects its growth capacity.

The transition to market rule seems to be taking hold slowly, but continuing reliance on ad hoc reform is often counterproductive. Non-hydrocarbon industrial output remains dismal, and most public enterprises still run deficits. Hydrocarbons, which dominate the economy and are likely to continue to do so, account for 97 percent of Algeria's export earnings. The fall of international demand and prices in late 2008 and 2009 negatively affected the country's revenues. In January 2009 hydrocarbon income had decreased by 36 percent from a year earlier, while total imports had increased by 9 percent.

Reforms in the areas of taxation, the management of public expenditures and public debt, and the banking system have been moving very slowly. Market-oriented change in these and other areas will certainly come sooner rather than later, as Algeria needs to be ready for accession to the World Trade Organization and implementation of the free trade agreement it signed with the European Union in 2002. These reforms are especially crucial for making Algeria attractive to foreign investment in the non-hydrocarbon sectors. Foreign investment reached $1.8 billion in 2008, but only a small fraction was in non-hydrocarbon activities. The World Bank's 2009 Ease of Doing Business Index ranked Algeria 132nd out of 181 economies.

POLITICAL STRUCTURE

Algeria's war of national liberation left a political legacy in the form of a competitive authoritarian political structure. The main actors in the national liberation controlled the Algerian polity after independence. This tradition evolved into a triangular system of government in which the military, party, and state apparatus share, but continually compete for, power.

The constitution concentrated virtually all important powers of the Algerian state in the executive branch, which remained the supreme institution, both formally and effectively. The president's role as head of state, head of government, commander of the armed forces, defense minister, and head of the FLN ensured that he had virtually unlimited rule. The republican nature of the state was regularly reaffirmed, as were the Islamic character and socialist commitment of the country. The FLN was recognized as the "only authentic representative of the people's will" and controlled all mass associations from 1968 until 1989.

All this changed after the social upheaval of 1989. During the next two years, Algeria's political structure evolved toward a competitive pluralistic multiparty democracy. However, most political institutions have yet to enjoy power of their own. For example, the power of the presidency during Abdelaziz Bouteflika's first term

(1999–2004) was still subordinate to that of the military, but after a showdown with the army, which almost cost him a second term, Bouteflika managed to wrestle some concessions from that institution, notably less interference in politics.

The Military

The Algerian armed forces (Armée Nationale Populaire) has remained a constant, if inconsistent, force in Algerian politics, at some times quite visible, at others more discreet. In the early years of independence, the military, endowed with organizational capacity and technical competency, quickly occupied the power vacuum left by traditional and religious forces whose power bases were almost completely undermined by the revolution.

The Algerian army has always had a valuable asset in its symbolic role as "guardian of the revolution" and guarantor of the country's integrity and stability. Historically it has maintained a discretionary role in politics, interfering only when conditions "necessitated" it to ensure the stability and security of the state. However, following the brutal suppression of the October 1988 riots, the army found its image severely discredited and quickly retreated from politics. Further constitutional change and political maneuvering under President Bendjedid helped keep the army away from politics while the country was moving toward full-scale political liberalization. However, in June 1991 the military saw the civilian leadership crisis as an occasion to reassert its historically predominant role in politics. It had as little faith in the government as it had taste for the Islamists. In January 1992 it overturned the elections, the constitutional framework, and the president's authority. The army remained the ultimate guarantor of the Algerian state if only because it alone decides the country's fate.

The military institution was known for most of its existence as "La Grande Muette" ("the Big Mute") because it communicated very few of its views publicly. However, in the last few years, several high officers—in retirement or in office—have started speaking out about past and present policies and events, such as the massacres committed by the Islamists in the 1990s, which the military allegedly failed to prevent when it could have. The army also was accused of involvement in some of these massacres. New publications and eyewitness accounts accuse high officers of crimes against humanity perpetrated by their troops and then attributed to the Islamists.

Officially, the military establishment is committed to a democratic project and a republican form of government. In the 2004 presidential election it announced for the first time that it would not play a role in choosing the next president. The decision not to support Bouteflika was probably due to a political showdown between the latter and the military over the president's constitutional prerogatives and his decision to authorize international organizations to investigate civilian massacres. Despite this, Bouteflika won with a wide margin against an unorganized and divided opposition. When he sought a third term and a constitutional amendment ending term limits in 2009, the army did not seem to mind. With no real rival candidate and the army's tacit acquiescence, he won a third term with 90 percent of the vote.

With the improved security situation and strong domestic and international pressure to retreat from the political sphere, some army officers began to speak publicly about such a retreat as a "professionalization" of the army. This would mean a return to the barracks, a sharp cut in the number of conscripts, and modernization of training and education for professional soldiers. It would also entail reducing the politicization of the military ranks in order to curtail the temptation to intervene in politics.

There are many signs that the military is eagerly working to professionalize itself and reduce its interference in politics and economics. Its increasing interaction with the US military and NATO may help this transformation. Furthermore, the sudden retirement in August 2004 of Gen. Mohamed Lamari, the military chief of staff, and the appointment of Gen. Larbi Belkheir, the president's chief of staff, as ambassador to Morocco allowed Bouteflika not only to appoint new individuals to top positions but also to start asserting the preeminence of the civilian leadership over the military. This development weakened the army's hard-line tendency toward the Islamists and allowed President Bouteflika to accommodate moderate Islamists and offer amnesty to the rebels.

The Islamists

For the Algerian political leadership, the Islamist movement has been a constant source of agitation. Recognizing the powerful message and capabilities of the movement, the regime has alternated between suppressing and befriending its leadership. The Ministry of Religious Affairs was established to control the mosques and oversee the appointment of imams (prayer leaders). However, urban growth led to a rapid proliferation of mosques and neighborhood associations, which the government could not contain, and created the opportunity for an independent Islamist movement to emerge. The Islamist message was accompanied by extensive voluntary social work and charitable action in areas such as education, garbage pickup, and aiding the poor, the sick, and the elderly. These actions were warmly welcomed at a time of diminishing government services. These social services fostered a loyal and extensive mass political base that the Islamists could draw on once legislation allowed the creation of independent political parties.

Although more than one Islamist organization emerged in the months following the legalization of parties, the Front of Islamic Salvation (FIS) became the only national challenger to the FLN. The FIS, officially recognized on September 16,

1989, was led by Abassi Madani, a moderate and Western-educated university professor, and Ali Belhadj, a high school teacher from a poor urban neighborhood known for his fiery rhetoric and radical views. The contrast in their styles reflected the pluralistic nature of their party.

Despite its victories in the 1990 municipal and 1991 legislative elections, as well as its impressive skills at political mobilization, critics argued that the FIS had profited from the discontent of unemployed youth in the urban slums and that, apart from its dubious sociological roots, it lacked the organizational and technical capabilities to lead an effective government. Most directly, many have questioned its commitment to democracy should it attain national office.

The FIS presented an alternative to the existing regime at a time when there was none. Its electoral success constituted a large protest vote against the existing rulers by those who were less than confident of the party's governing capabilities. To the extent that people were willing to risk the outcome of an FIS electoral victory, even if only as an alternative to the FLN, the FIS seems to have had a "legitimate" sweep at the polls.

Following the state's crackdown in the early 1990s, the Islamist movement became increasingly radical. Splits in the FIS leadership and membership separated moderate "pragmatists" from hard-liners. This division led to the emergence of a number of radical, armed Islamist groups composed of people who had grown impatient not only with the government but also with what they considered the accommodationist tactics of the FIS. After the FIS was banned in 1992, most of its leaders were in jail or in exile, and many others and their followers either defected to more radical Islamist groups or retreated from political activity altogether.

A newly radicalized Islamist opposition emerged to contest by force and terror the authority of the state and to claim power in the name of electoral victory. In actions reminiscent of the most brutal days of the colonial war against the French, the Armed Islamic Group (known by its French acronym as the GIA), the Armed Islamic Movement, the Islamic Salvation Army (the military wing of the FIS), and the Salafist Group for Preaching and Combat (GSPC), engaged in a daily terror campaign, killing not only security personnel but also civilians, including journalists, professors, poets, doctors, union officials, opposition party leaders, citizens suspected of cooperating with the state, women not abiding by the commandments of the Islamists, and foreigners. They also destroyed infrastructure, including telephone centers, public utility vehicles, and schools. State countermeasures also left scores of people dead, hundreds jailed, and thousands unaccounted for. Within a few years, Algeria had descended in a vicious spiral of political violence with no immediate end in sight. By 2001 some 200,000 people had been killed. This led to the flight of most foreigners living and working in Algeria, along with hundreds of intellectuals, artists, and others who feared the Islamist rage or government forces.

The Islamist rebellion failed to achieve its objective, and its crude violence negatively affected the Islamists' standing in people's minds. Support for Islamist parties declined in the 2002 parliamentary elections, due partly to the general irrelevance of opposition parties and to internal conflict within the Society of Peace Movement (MSP), a moderate Islamist party formerly known as Hamas, and Ennahda (Movement for Islamic Renaissance), also a moderate Islamist party. The MSP lost thirty-one of its sixty-nine seats, and Ennahda kept only one of its thirty-four seats. However, a new party—a breakaway from the latter—Harakat al-Islah al-Watani ("Movement for National Reform," known as Islah), obtained forty-three seats. Overall, the number of seats controlled by the Islamists declined from 103 to 82. In the November 2005 elections in 143 municipalities, the Islamists obtained only seven seats.

The Islamists lost more seats in the May 2007 parliamentary elections, losing twenty-two of the eighty-two seats they had won in 2002. The pro-government FLN and National Democratic Rally (RND) parties similarly lost forty-nine seats but remained the dominant parties (see Table 16.1). Between 2002 and 2007 the process had come full circle, with the FLN back in control of parliament and supportive of the executive branch headed by Bouteflika.

Despite this setback, the religious parties continue to take advantage of their inclusion in politics to influence state policies and actions. They have chosen not to confront the state directly in a battle they would lose; instead, they hope to capture society and the state through preaching and by playing the political game. As a protest movement or part of the governing establishment, moderate Islamists will continue to take advantage of the inclusionary opening. Once fully entrenched in political institutions and processes, militant Islamists will work to implement their vision for Algeria from within the system and hopefully within institutional safeguards, which a democratizing polity ought to create.

Civic Associations

Following political legalization in 1989, the FIS was but one of many political parties. By the time campaigning opened for the country's first multiparty elections, sixty-two parties had come into existence, some of which were led by noted exiled political leaders and historic war figures such as Ahmed Ben Bella (Movement for Democracy in Algeria) and Hocine Aït Ahmed ("Front of Socialist Forces," or FFS).

Until that time, Algeria's civil society was sharply inhibited. Civic associations and mass organizations were subordinate to the state-party apparatus and relegated to recruitment, mobilization from the top, and propaganda; they were constrained, though not entirely circumscribed. Strikes were not uncommon, and

Table 16.1   Results of the 1997, 2002, and 2007 Parliamentary Elections

Party	1997 (% of votes)	1997 Seats	2002 (% of votes)	2002 Seats	2007 Seats
Front de Libération Nationale (FLN)	16.1	69	35.27	199	136
Rassemblement National Démocratique (RND)	38.1	156	8.23	47	61
Mouvement de la Réforme Nationale (MRN/Islah)	—	—	9.5	43	3
Harakat Moujtama'a al-Silm (MSP/HMS)	16.7	69	7.05	38	52
Independents	5	11	4.92	30	33
Parti des Travailleurs (PT)	2.1	4	3.33	21	26
Ennahda (MRI)	9.9	34	0.65	1	5
Front des Forces Socialistes (FFS)	5.7	20	—	—	—
Rassemblement pour la Culture et la Démocratie (RCD)	4.8	19	—	—	19

Source: http://www.mae.dz, http://electionworld.org/election/algeria.htm, and
http://www.aps.dz/fr/legislatives2.asp

student associations proved to be a volatile source of opposition, with demonstrations frequently breaking out on university campuses. Most importantly, though, these organizations, however limited in autonomy or independence, provided vital pressure for political liberalization. After 1989, civic associations proliferated and became a vibrant part of Algerian political life. Many organizations—mainly those of journalists, women, and human rights advocates—played a significant role in Algeria's brief democratic experiment and became a source of challenge to the regime and an imposing element of the political dynamics of Algeria.

In the spring and summer of 2001, a series of protests against the regime erupted in the Kabylie region east of Algiers, following the killing of a young man imprisoned by the paramilitary gendarmerie. The violent protests quickly spread across the region and resulted in the death of several more protesters. From these events was born what became known as the "Citizen Movement," which demanded the recognition of Berber as a national language and of the inherent Amazigh (Berber) essence of Algeria's identity. It was a unique movement started by grassroots traditional village and tribal leadership structures called the *aarch*, which were revived because of the failure of institutional outlets for the expression of popular demands and grievances. The movement bypassed two Berber-based parties, the FFS and the Rally for Culture and Democracy.

Notwithstanding its cultural demands, the movement was directed against the entire regime, its repressive nature, and its unresponsiveness in the face of the grave social and economic problems faced by Algeria's youth. The bulk of the Berberist movement has positioned itself in opposition to both Islamism and the regime.

While most demands of the Kabylie movement were not met, its actions led to direct negotiations with the government over popular grievances and a promise by the president to make the Berber language an official national language. Beyond this movement, the civil society incipient in the late 1980s and early 1990s has fallen victim to resilient authoritarian rule, which, after quelling radical Islamism, muzzled most civil society voices through repression, co-optation, infiltration, and control.

POLITICAL DYNAMICS:
FAILED DEMOCRATIZATION, VIOLENCE, AND RECONCILIATION

Political Liberalization

Following the riots of October 1988, President Bendjedid's political reforms significantly altered the configuration of the state and opened the way for political liberalization. Bendjedid may have seen political liberalization as the best way to quell popular discontent. He tried to distance himself from the FLN and the old guard; he dismissed the prime minister, the head of military security, and a number of other officials associated with the most conservative faction of the party and the military. His constitutional reform promised a "state of law" and removed all references to the socialist commitment. The revised constitution deprived the FLN of its single-party status and made it dependent on popular approval. Also, no longer constitutionally recognized as the "guardian of the revolution," the army saw its role limited to defense and external security responsibilities.

Presidential authority, by contrast, was further enhanced. As head of state, head of the Higher Judicial Council, commander in chief of the military, and presiding officer over all legislative meetings, the president was given effective control over all institutions of the state. He has power to appoint and dismiss the prime minister and all other nonelected civilian and military officials; he is the only one authorized to initiate constitutional amendments; and he may bypass parliament by way of national referendum.

The Law Relative to Political Associations of July 1989 extended the right to form political parties to all organizations committed to national unity and integrity and explicitly prohibited parties of a specifically religious, ethnic, or regional character. This last preclusion was laxly enforced.

A new electoral code was designed to preserve the rapidly diminishing hegemony of the FLN, which faced a narrow mandate and a plethora of newly formed political parties. However, in spite of this, the first multiparty elections for local and regional offices, held on June 12, 1990, delivered a decisive blow to the FLN. The changes had favored its greatest rival, the FIS, which secured 853 of the 1,520 local councils (55 percent) and 32 of the 48 provincial assemblies (67 percent). The FLN won only 487 local and 14 provincial constituencies.

Despite the FLN's massive defeat, Algeria appeared to be moving forward with the region's boldest experiment in political liberalization. However, this was short-lived. New changes in the electoral laws, also meant to favor the FLN, caused major public protests by the Islamists in the summer of 1991. On June 1, hundreds of people rallied in the streets and organized sit-ins in Algiers. On June 5 the army intervened to restore order. A four-month state of siege was instituted, the government was dismissed, and parliamentary elections were indefinitely postponed. On June 15, after the FIS daringly called for a general strike and a mutiny within the military, army troops and tanks moved to break the Islamist sit-ins and arrested thousands of protesters, including the two leaders, Abassi Madani and Ali Belhadj. The latter were sentenced to twelve years in prison, which they served fully.

When new parliamentary elections were set for December 26, 1991, and with the FIS leadership in jail, there seemed to be little threat to the FLN at the polls. However, to the surprise of many, the Islamists won another resounding victory. The FIS won 188 seats out of 430 in the first round and was only 99 seats short of achieving a two-thirds majority. In second place, with twenty-five seats, was the FFS, a secular, liberal party whose support base was limited to the Berber-speaking region of Kabylie. The FLN won merely sixteen seats. The runoff was scheduled for January 16, 1992.

President Bendjedid apparently initiated talks with the FIS for a cohabitation agreement, but the military was opposed to giving power to a political party it regarded as a threat to security and stability. As a result the president was forced to resign on January 11, 1992, and the second round of elections was cancelled. The country was to be temporarily ruled by a High State Council headed, at first, by Defense Minister Gen. Khaled Nezzar. From then on, the country descended into its worst crisis since independence. The state pursued a strategy of crackdown, control, and containment of the Islamists and other opposition groups. Besides suspending the constitution, annulling the first-round electoral results of December 1991, disbanding parliament, and banning the FIS, the army initiated a hardline policy toward the Islamists and their supporters. Thousands of alleged militants were imprisoned in makeshift camps in the Sahara, scores were killed, and a state of war set in.

On the political front, the regime was unable to assemble a civilian government that commanded the confidence and respect of all Algerians. President Mohamed Boudiaf, who was invited to return from exile and lead the country in January 1992, was assassinated six months after his appointment. He was followed by Ali Kafi, whose one-year presidency was largely symbolic. The appointment on January 31, 1994, of retired general Lamine Zeroual as president stimulated some hope for improved economic and security conditions. On November 16, 1995, in Algeria's first free presidential election, Zeroual won a six-year term with 61 percent of the vote. It was hoped that his new electoral legitimacy would help solve the crisis. However, violence against civilians increased even more.

Zeroual, who remained defense minister, seemed committed to dialogue with all social forces, including Islamists who renounced violence. However, he had to convince elements in the government and the army, who opposed any compromise with the Islamists. A 180-member National Council of Transition (CNT) was established as an advisory body in the absence of a working parliament. The CNT served as an institutional framework for passing legislation and was filled with representatives of parties, trade unions, managers' associations, professional organizations, and other civic associations.

As attempts at dialog with the jailed FIS leaders failed, the state turned to a firmer repression of radical Islamists while opening up to moderate opposition parties, both religious and secular. In January 1995, most opposition parties (including the banned FIS) met in Rome and agreed on a platform for resolving the crisis. The initiative failed because the government rejected the document.

In 1996, other constitutional amendments reinforced the powers of the president and prime minister and created a second parliamentary chamber, the Council of the Nation, with one-third of its members appointed by the president and the rest elected by indirect suffrage. The amendments also declared Islam the state religion, prohibited the creation of parties on a "religious, linguistic, racial, gender, corporatist or regional" basis, and outlawed the use of partisan propaganda based on these elements. It also officially recognized the Berber culture—along with Algeria's Arabic heritage and Islam—as a fundamental component of the country's identity.

Elections in June 1997 produced Algeria's first multiparty parliament. The main winners were the RND (a party created three months earlier to support the incumbent president), the MSP, Ennahda, and the FLN. The RND, FLN, and MSP constituted a pro-government coalition that controlled an absolute majority and twenty-one ministerial posts, seven of which went to the Islamists.

The political and economic changes initiated by Zeroual did not stop political violence and the rapid deterioration of conditions in the country. President Zeroual, who faced strong resistance from the regime's hard-liners when he attempted a discreet dialogue with the jailed FIS leaders, decided in the fall of 1998 to resign well before the end of his term. Former foreign minister Abdelaziz Bouteflika quickly became the candidate favored by the military and many people. Two days before the vote on April 15, 1999, the other six candidates withdrew, angered by electoral irregularities. Bouteflika, the only candidate, then won by 73 percent of the vote, with support from the military, the FLN, the RND, and the MSP. For him it was a triumphant return from a twenty-year self-imposed exile abroad.

Violence and terror, which had started to subside during Zeroual's tenure, continued to diminish, and security improved markedly after an amnesty program called the National Concord—approved by referendum in September 1999—invited armed Islamists to give up the fight and avoid prosecution. The first to take advantage of this was the Army of Islamic Salvation, which had been observing a unilateral cease-fire since October 1, 1997. The National Concord enacted by Bouteflika was wrapped in total secrecy as to the deals made with the armed groups that surrendered. It was not part of a comprehensive political solution but merely a judicial action that allowed alleged "terrorists" to be freed with impunity.

A national referendum in September 2005 approved another open-ended amnesty program, the Charter for Peace and National Reconciliation, which came into effect in February 2006. It invited the remaining armed Islamists to surrender and avoid prosecution. Many did surrender, and others were released from jail, but a small number remain active, causing occasional violence. Just like its predecessor, this amnesty was widely criticized for not only preventing the prosecution of rebels who had committed grave crimes against civilians but also absolving state agents responsible for similar offenses. Furthermore, many of those who surrendered have returned to armed rebellion by joining the GSPC, which officially declared its allegiance to al-Qa'ida in 2006 and became part of that network, renaming itself al-Qa'ida in the Islamic Land of the Maghrib (AQIM). Since then, AQIM has conducted several violent attacks against foreign personnel in Algeria and a series of bombings in Algiers that killed more than thirty people. Other violent actions attributed to it have taken place in Mauritania, Morocco, and Tunisia.

President Bouteflika also tried to further the return to normalcy by holding regular elections. In the parliamentary elections of May 30, 2002, and to the surprise of many observers, the FLN was the biggest winner with 199 seats, up from 69 in the previous parliament and 15 in the 1991 elections. (See Table 16.1.)

The 2002 elections were marked, however, by people's growing apathy toward the political process in general and political parties in particular, both religious and secular. People lost faith in many of the parties created since 1989 because of their internal dissention and their marginalization within the political process. Some opposition leaders were co-opted through election to parliament or appointment to high office. This reduced both their ability to oppose the regime and their popular appeal. It seemed that because economic and political promises went unfulfilled by the new opposition, people placed their hope back in the most established party, the FLN. This apathy was resoundingly expressed in the 2007 parliamentary election, which had a mere 35 percent voter turnout rate, the lowest in Algeria's history.

Political and Economic Prospects

Algeria appears to be coming out of its long, nightmarish era of unrelenting violence at the hands of both Islamists and the state. Its aggregate economic indicators have improved markedly, and the improved environment has started to attract domestic and foreign investment.

The government's most pressing task undoubtedly is to resolve the country's disastrous socioeconomic problems. A great number of technocrats and members of the political elite share the will to enact serious—albeit stringent and painful—reforms, but a consensus on their form, depth, and timing has been elusive. Also, fears about the potentially negative consequences of severe economic change on an already discontented population have led to hesitation and inconsistency.

The state is caught in the difficult position of having to resolve serious socioeconomic problems while opening the economy to global capital, enacting more austerity measures, and maintaining strict budgetary discipline. Already the implementation of some neoliberal reforms is causing friction between the state and society, as witnessed by a series of strikes in the public sector and recurring unrest in towns and villages throughout the country. This unrest has become a regular occurrence in an environment marked by failure of the institutions of political representation and justice.

A resolution of the crisis would have to include, in addition to sound and timely economic reforms, major changes in the country's political institutions and informal political practices. Many facilitating factors that could help thrust Algeria in the right direction are already in place. They include economic assets such as hydrocarbons, an industrial base, and a large pool of skilled workers and technocrats; a windfall of oil income that could help start the non-oil economy and respond to the most pressing needs of the population; a multiparty system that can help nurture tolerance and compromise; and a thriving independent press that can serve as a forum for public policy debates and push for accountability.

Moreover, the military's role in politics must be curtailed, the powers of the presidency must be weakened, and parliament must be allowed to exercise its legislative, oversight, and investigative functions. The judicial system needs to become independent and made to guarantee basic freedoms and protections against abuses of power. Notwithstanding the power of conservative forces—both secular and religious—a united core of reformist elite, backed by constitutional and popular legitimacy, is needed to get Algeria out of its current predicament. Unfortunately, the prospects for this were not hopeful in 2009, when President Bouteflika managed to amend the constitution to end term limits and win a third term in office despite dismal economic and political performance.

FOREIGN POLICY

Algeria's revolutionary tradition has strongly influenced its foreign policy. Its anti-colonial revolution against France was extended to encompass a challenge to imperialist powers worldwide. This lent Algeria a prominent position in the Maghrib, the Arab and Middle East region, and the Third World more broadly. Pursuing an independent, if often abrasive, course in its foreign policy, Algeria acquired an influential role in world politics, a role which far exceeded its resources and capabilities. Gradually, however, internal economic and political problems and changing global circumstances restricted Algeria's foreign policy. Strategic, economic, and political interests in its region began to take precedence over its ideological commitment to Third World causes. Political liberalization further increased the constraints. Algeria's foreign policy came to reflect the actions of a state accountable to its citizens and their perspectives, as evidenced by the dramatic reversal of the government's position on the Iraqi invasion of Kuwait in 1990.

Despite significant assistance from the other Maghrib countries (Libya, Mauritania, Morocco, and Tunisia) during the revolutionary period, Algeria's relations with its neighbors were strained after independence and remained so throughout the 1970s, especially with Morocco, whose conservative ideological orientation conflicted with Algeria's socialist orientation. In the 1980s, however, political and economic liberalization in Algeria drew the two countries closer, and relations improved dramatically, only to deteriorate again in 1994 after Morocco accused Algeria of supporting an armed Islamist attack in a Marrakech tourist hotel and imposed visa requirements on Algerian visitors. Algeria responded by closing the common border.

A treaty in 1989 established an economic and political Arab Maghrib Union (UMA) between Algeria, Libya, Mauritania, Morocco, and Tunisia. However, regional integration remains elusive and remote as Algeria and Morocco continue to disagree on a host of issues, especially the Western Sahara problem.

Despite its membership and founding role in the Organization of African Unity (OAU), Algeria is still much more closely affiliated with its Arab neighbors and southern Europe than with the African countries to the south. It remains involved in the OAU more out of tactical considerations than genuine commitment and has often utilized the organization to further its distinctly self-informed views. President Bouteflika increased the country's involvement in the OAU. He hosted its 1999 summit, assumed the presidency of the organization for one year, and committed himself to an active role in conflict resolution in Africa—mediating a peace agreement between Ethiopia and Eritrea—and in negotiations with the industrialized countries over African debt. After the OAU gave way to the

African Union in 2001, President Bouteflika became involved in the New African Partnership for Africa's Development. In July 2009, Algeria hosted the second African cultural festival—the first was held in 1968.

Algeria has been an active member of the League of Arab States since immediately after independence in 1962, but its involvement in Middle Eastern and Arab affairs has been limited mainly to supporting the Palestinian cause. Its historical and ideological commitment to self-determination fostered a strong affinity with the Palestinians. The Iraqi invasion of Kuwait in August 1990 and the subsequent retaliation by Western coalition forces produced substantial popular support for Iraq, leading the regime to quickly backpedal from its neutral position.

Political and economic liberalization at home and a moderate foreign policy have substantially improved Algeria's relations with Europe and the United States in recent decades. In January 1981 Algeria mediated the release of the fifty-two US hostages from Iran. Western powers likewise have shown increasing tolerance for the resolutely authoritarian nature of the Algerian state, which has moved toward the West in its economic orientation and affiliation. The West's growing need for energy and the common fight against Islamist violence have led to increased interaction and diplomatic improvement.

France undoubtedly is Algeria's most significant foreign partner. More than 20 percent of all Algerian exports and imports head to or originate from France. There are close to 2 million Algerians living in France, and many Algerians speak French, creating a tremendous cultural overlap. However, French-Algerian relations have not always been cordial. Algeria's high level of dependence on France and its desire to be free of that dependency have complicated relations between the two countries. France's support for Morocco on the Western Sahara issue and "exploitative" French trade and economic initiatives have repeatedly strained their relations. As with many countries, however, diplomatic relations are largely determined by economic ones, in this case by gas and oil exports. Despite problematic political relations, economic ties have persisted since Algeria's independence. Undoubtedly the most sensitive issue in French-Algerian relations is that of Algerian emigration to France. French policies toward Algerian immigrants have been less than consistent, and popular sentiment in France has generally been unfavorable to people of North African origin. Racially motivated flare-ups between migrant workers and French ethnocentrists are common.

In the 1990s and early 2000s, the Algerian government criticized France's relaxed policy toward Islamist networks in France, which channeled money and arms to their brethren in Algeria. Also, in the wake of the Kabylie riots of 2001, the Algerian government accused France of supporting the Berberist movement and encouraging its ambitions for independence. Algerians and their government also were unhappy with a 2005 law passed by the French parliament that described the colonization of Algeria as positive. The Algerian government requested a repeal of the law and a formal French apology for the colonization of Algeria and the brutality that accompanied it. The law, which jeopardized a planned treaty of friendship between the two countries, was later repealed. Algeria agreed in 2008 to support French president Nicholas Sarkozy's proposed Union for the Mediterranean, whose regional cooperation structures and aim remain vague.

Algeria's wide range of contacts qualifies it as one of the few countries in the world to maintain a truly independent position in the international arena. Throughout the most difficult years of the Cold War, Algeria remained actively involved with both the Soviet Union and the United States. Even during times of tension between the United States and France, Algeria similarly has maintained extensive economic relations with both countries.

Since Bouteflika came to power, Algeria has been actively trying to balance its relations with Europe with increasing interaction with the United States. The events of September 11, 2001, provided both the United States and Algeria with a newfound affinity: the fight against Islamist terrorism. Algeria thus became a key partner of the United States in the "war on terror," notably because of its experience in fighting armed Islamists and its intelligence on radical Islamists and their international networks. At the economic level, the traditional American focus on investment in Algerian hydrocarbons has slowly extended to other economic sectors. However, in spite of this newfound friendship between the governments of the two countries, many Algerians still hold a negative attitude toward the United States because of its unconditional support of Israel and its invasion of Iraq.

NOTES

1. Cited in Pierre Nora, *Les Français d'Algérie* (Paris: Julliard, 1961), 88.

BIBLIOGRAPHY

A good analysis of contemporary Algerian history is found in John Ruedy, *Modern Algeria: The Origins and Development of a Nation* (Bloomington: Indiana University Press, 1992). A more polemical account sympathetic to the Boumediene regime and its socialist policies is found in Mahfoud Bennoune, *The Making of Contemporary Algeria, 1830–1987* (Cambridge: Cambridge University Press, 1988).

On Algeria's war of national liberation, the best account remains Alistair Horne, *A Savage War of Peace: Algeria, 1954–1962* (London: Penguin Books, 1979). Competent interpretations also can be found in David Gordon, *The Passing of French Algeria* (New York: Oxford University Press, 1966), and Alf Andrew Heggoy, *Insurgency and Counterinsurgency in Algeria* (Bloomington: Indiana University Press, 1972). The war's psychocultural consequences are evocatively treated in Frantz

Fanon, *The Wretched of the Earth* (New York: Grove Press, 1963) and *A Dying Colonialism* (New York: Grove Press, 1967). An excellent recent publication with French and Algerian contributors is Mohamed Harbi and Benjamin Stora, eds., *La guerre d'Algérie, 1954–2004: la fin de l'amnésie* (Paris: Robert Lafont, 2004). Other works worth consulting are Charles Robert Ageron, *Modern Algeria: A History from 1830 to the Present* (Trenton, NJ: Africa World Press, 1991), and Pierre Nora, *Les Français d'Algérie* (Paris: Julliard, 1961). An excellent reference book is Naylor Phillip Chiviges, *Historical Dictionary of Algeria* (Lanham, MD: Scarecrow Press, 2006).

A good sociological analysis of colonial and postcolonial Algeria is that of Pierre Bourdieu, *The Algerians* (Boston: Beacon Press, 1962). Socialist experiments of workers' self-management are the subject of Thomas L. Blair, *The Land to Those Who Work It* (Garden City, NY: Anchor Books, 1970), and Ian Clegg, *Workers' Self-Management in Algeria* (New York: Monthly Review Press, 1971). Questions of culture, women, and society are treated in Ali El Kenz, *Algerian Reflections on Arab Crises* (Austin: University of Texas Press, 1991); Peter Knauss, *The Persistence of Patriarchy* (New York: Praeger, 1987); and I. William Zartman and William Mark Habeeb, eds., *Polity and Society in Contemporary North Africa* (Boulder, CO: Westview Press, 1993). The following works deal with the Berber question: Amar Ouerdane, *La question berbère dans le mouvement national algérien: 1926–1980* (Sillery, Quebec: Septentrion, 1990); Ernest Gellner and Charles Micaud, eds., *Arabs and Berbers: From Tribe to Nation in North Africa* (Lexington, MA: Lexington Books, 1972); Azzedine Layachi, "The Berbers in Algeria: Politicization of Ethnicity and Ethnicization of Politics," in Maya Shatzmiller, ed., *Nationalism and Minority Identities in Islamic Societies* (Montreal: McGill University Press, 2005), 193–228.

Treatments of Algeria's modern political history from elite perspectives are found in William B. Quandt, *Revolution and Political Leadership* (Cambridge, MA: MIT Press, 1969); David and Marina Ottaway, *Algeria: The Politics of a Socialist Revolution* (Berkeley: University of California Press, 1970); John P. Entelis, *Algeria: The Revolution Institutionalized* (Boulder, CO: Westview Press, 1986); and Rachid Tlemçani, *Élections et élites en Algérie: paroles des candidats* (Algiers: Chihab, 2003).

The role of the military is treated in I. William Zartman, "The Algerian Army in Politics," in *Soldier and State in Africa*, ed. Claude E. Welch (Evanston, IL: Northwestern University Press, 1970); John P. Entelis, "Algeria: Technocratic Rule, Military Power," in *Political Elites in Arab North Africa*, ed. I. William Zartman et al. (New York: Longman, 1982); and Hugh Roberts, *Commanding Disorder: Military Power and Informal Politics in Algeria* (London: I. B. Tauris, 2002).

On the internal war of the 1990s, the following are noteworthy: Habib Souaidia, *La Sale Guerre* (Paris: Découverte, 2001), which presents a strong indictment of the Algerian military in particular and the regime in general; Nesroulah Yous, *Qui a tué à Bentalha* (Paris: Découverte, 2000); Luis Martinez, *The Algerian*

Civil War, 1990–1998 (London: Hurst & Co., 2002); and Hugh Roberts, *The Battlefield Algeria, 1988–2002: Studies in a Broken Polity* (London: Verso, 2002). Regarding the loss of popularity of the Islamist parties, see Mokrane Ait Ouarabi, "Est-ce la déconfiture des partis islamistes?" *El Watan*, November 17, 2005.

Analyses of Algerian political and economic development, including the role of Islamism, can be found in Azzedine Layachi, "Political Liberalization and the Islamists in Algeria," in *Islam, Democracy and the State in Algeria*, ed. Michael Bonner, Megan Reif, and Mark Tessler (New York: Routledge, 2005); Azzedine Layachi, "Algeria: Crisis, Transition and Social Policy Outcomes," in *Social Policy and Development: The Middle East and North Africa*, ed. Massoud Karshenas and Valentine Moghadam (New York: Palgrave Macmillan, 2006); Azzedine Layachi, "Domestic and International Constraints of Economic Adjustment in Algeria," in *The New Global Economy: North African Responses*, ed. Dirk Vandewalle (New York: St. Martin's Press, 1996); Azzedine Layachi, "The Private Sector in the Algerian Economy," *Mediterranean Politics* (summer 2001): 29–50; Azzedine Layachi, "Reinstating the State or Instating Civil Society: The Dilemma of Algeria's Transition," in *Collapsed States: The Disintegration and Restoration of Legitimate Authority*, ed. I. W. Zartman (Boulder, CO: Lynne Rienner, 1995); Azzedine Layachi, "Reform and the Politics of Inclusion in the Maghrib," *Journal of North African Studies* (autumn 2001): 15–47; Azzedine Layachi, "The Algerian Economy After Structural Adjustment," *Middle East Insight* (November–December 1999): 25–28; Andrea Liverani, *Civil Society in Algeria: The Political Functions of Associational Life* (London: Routledge, 2008); Martin Evans and John Phillips, *Algeria: Anger of the Dispossessed* (New Haven, CT: Yale University Press, 2007); Amar Benamrouche, *Grèves et conflits politiques en Algérie* (Paris: Karthala, 2000); John P. Entelis and Phillip C. Naylor, eds., *State and Society in Algeria* (Boulder, CO: Westview Press, 1992); François Burgat and William Dowell, *The Islamic Movement in North Africa* (Austin: University of Texas Press, 1993); Hugh Roberts, "A Trial of Strength: Algerian Islamism," in *Fundamentalisms and the Gulf Crisis*, ed. James Piscatori (Chicago: Fundamentalism Project, 1991); and John P. Entelis and Lisa Arone, "Algeria in Turmoil: Islam, Democracy, and the State," *Middle East Policy* 1, no. 2 (1992): 23–25.

For economic data and analysis, see OECD Development Center, *African Economic Outlook 2008, Country Notes, Algeria*, www.oecd.org/dataoecd/14/40/40573850.pdf. The latest IMF comprehensive report with data can be found at "IMF Country Report No. 06/101 Algeria," March 2006, www.imf.org/external/country/DZA/index.htm. For the most recent report on poverty, see "Pauvreté en Algérie: Rapport alarmant des services de sécurité," *Le Soir d'Algérie*, May 11, 2006, www.lesoirdalgerie.com/articles/2006/05/11/article.php?sid=38197 &cid=2. For an excellent socioeconomic analysis, see Conseil National Economique et Social (CNES), *Rapport préliminaire sur les effets economiques et sociaux du programme d'ajustement structurel* (Algiers: CNES, November 1998).

The best works on Algerian foreign policy include Nicole Grimaud, *La politique extérieure de l'Algérie* (Paris: Karthala, 1984), and Robert Mortimer's articles in *African Studies*, March 1984; *Orbis*, fall 1977; and *Current History*, 1991, 1993, and 1994. The chapter on foreign policy in Helen C. Metz, *Algeria: A Country Study* (Washington, DC: Library of Congress, 1995), is straightforward and comprehensive.

Comprehensive English- and French-language bibliographies can be found in Azzedine Layachi, *Economic Crisis and Political Change in North Africa* (Westport, CT: Praeger, 1998); Helen C. Metz, ed., *Algeria: A Country Study* (Washington, DC: Library of Congress, 1995); and John P. Entelis and Phillip C. Naylor, eds., *State and Society in Algeria* (Boulder, CO: Westview Press, 1992).

17

REPUBLIC OF TUNISIA

John P. Entelis

HISTORICAL BACKGROUND

The history of Tunisia has been marked by continuity and change. Despite nearly 3,000 years of occupation by various foreign forces, empires, and civilizations, the country has remained culturally integrated and politically unified. The country's name derives from Tunis, a city originally settled by conquering Phoenicians from the eastern Mediterranean. But to the Romans and later the Arabs, Tunisia was known as *Ifriqiyah* ("Africa"), a name later extended to the whole of the continent.

The region within which Tunisia is located was called *jazirat al-maghrib* ("island of the west") by its Arab conquerors, who first arrived in 647 CE, referring to the land between the "sea of sand" (the Sahara Desert) and the Mediterranean Sea. Given its size and location, Tunisia has long been considered a bridge between the Arab west (*maghrib*) and the Arab east (*mashriq*), between Africa and the Muslim world, as well as a direct link with Europe, with Sicily located only forty miles from the Tunisian coast.

Although the Arabs initially unified North Africa, in the thirteenth century the Hafsids, a dynasty established by a rebel Almohad governor, founded a Tunisian kingdom over which they ruled for two centuries. Muslim Andalusians migrated to the area after being exiled from Spain in 1492. By 1574 Tunisia was incorporated as an autonomous province of the Ottoman Empire ruled by dynastic Turkish beys (governors). In 1881 France conquered Tunisia, transforming it into a colonial protectorate that lasted for seventy-five years, until independence in 1956.

Colonial Period

The French colonial experience in Tunisia, although not benign, brought less social disruption than in neighboring Algeria. It formally began on May 12, 1881, when the French forced the bey of Tunis to sign the Treaty of Ksar Said. The document

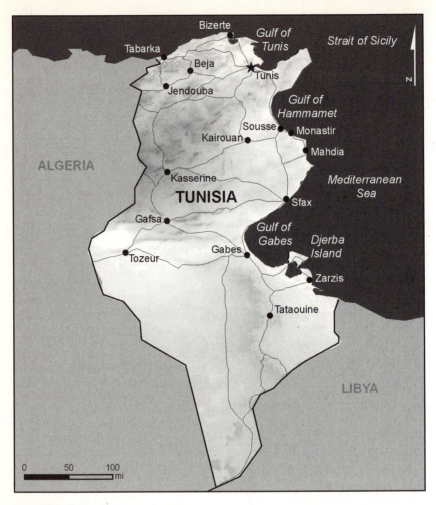

Republic of Tunisia

granted France control over defense and foreign affairs for a "temporary but indefinite period." In 1883 the French gained control over Tunisia's domestic affairs as well in the Treaty of Marsa. The French established a separate parallel "protectorate" administration under a resident-general and quickly acquired effective control over the state.

Although no large-scale colonization occurred, as in Algeria, the French administration placed the European settlers' interests first and subjected Tunisia to reforms that were clearly not in the interest of the Muslim population. Although the settler population remained relatively small, Italian and French settlers bought land, and the dispossessed rural Muslim population sank into destitution.

The French colonial experience in Tunisia also featured some relatively positive reforms, many building on efforts that had been underway for several decades. France's contribution to Tunisia's development was perhaps greatest in the field of education. University training for Tunisians in France reinforced these skills, which were used to great advantage in the nationalist struggle for independence and the subsequent formation of a modern state.

Tunisia was the first Maghribi country to be influenced by modern nationalism. In 1905 the Young Tunisian movement was established by members of the European-educated, professional middle class of Tunis, emulating the Young Turk movement of the decaying Ottoman Empire. The Young Tunisians demanded better education, a combination of French and Arab cultures, and Tunisian access to government. They also sought to modify, but not overthrow, French colonial rule.

The Liberal Constitutional, or Destour (*destour* means "constitution" in Arabic), Party was organized in February 1920 by Shaykh Abdelaziz al-Thaalibi. The emergence of the Destour Party marked a new moment in Tunisian nationalism—that of traditionalistic anticolonialism. In contrast to the bicultural orientation of the Young Tunisians, the Destour called for greater emphasis on Arab culture and Islam and criticized the French for introducing an alien cultural order. The party provided an ideological foundation for opposition to French colonialism and, over the next decade, recruited many well-educated young men who were eventually to take control of the nationalist movement.

In March 1934 these young men broke away to form the Neo-Destour Party. The principal force behind the new party's creation was a thirty-one-year-old French-educated lawyer, Habib Bourguiba, who eventually led Tunisia to independence and, in the process, earned the label "father of his country." Bourguiba was born of middle-class parents in 1903 at Monastir in the Sahel and was educated at the Sorbonne. Like many of his generation who were trained in French universities, he adopted a populist brand of nationalist consciousness. Bourguiba and his contemporaries inherited from the Young Tunisians a strong faith in French liberalism. They also admired the Young Tunisians' economic and cultural innovations. From the old Destour they took the banner of anticolonialism.

The Neo-Destourians were the first Tunisian secular nationalists (although they used Islamic symbols as instruments of political mobilization when seeking mass public support). The party was committed to national independence and economic development via extensive grassroots organization and political education. Unchallenged by rival nationalist groups, it was able to create a mass movement despite occasional French attempts to suppress it.

TUNISIA

Capital city	Tunis
Chief of state	President Zine el Abidine Ben Ali
Head of government	Prime Minister Mohamed Ghannouchi
Major political parties *(seats in lower house)*	Constitutional Democratic Rally Party (161), Movement of Socialist Democrats (16), Popular Unity Party (12), Unionist Democratic Union (9), Liberal Social Party (8), Green Party for Progress (6), Movement for Renewal (2)
Ethnic groups	Arab (98%), European (1%), Jewish and other (1%)
Religious groups	Muslim (98%), Christian (1%), Jewish and other (1%)
Export partners	France (28.4%), Italy (18%), Germany (9.6%), Libya (5.8%), Spain (5%)
Import partners	France (22.4%), Italy (20.1%), Germany (9.4%), Libya (4.8%), Spain (4.6%)

Independent Tunisia

The first three decades of postindependence Tunisian politics were dominated by Bourguiba and the Neo-Destour, renamed the Destourian Socialist Party (PSD) in 1964 and the Democratic Constitutional Rally (RCD) in 1988. Bourguiba's charisma and popular appeal proved durable. He was the country's only president until his forced removal from office on November 7, 1987. At the same time, the party maintained political supremacy over all other national organizations and governmental institutions, and the use of repression against opponents was certainly not unheard of. Despite Bourguiba's increasingly authoritarian character, especially in the latter years of his regime, the "Supreme Combatant" provided crucial national unity and political stability in the years following independence. Indeed, it is not an exaggeration to credit Bourguiba's authoritarian presence and manipulative skills with the evolution of Tunisia into a relatively stable polity. There are nine historical phases in postindependence Tunisia.

Phase I: 1955–1959

In the first period, 1955 to 1959, Bourguiba overcame internal challenges and consolidated power. When Bourguiba signed the internal autonomy convention with France in 1955, the secretary-general of the Neo-Destour, Salah Ben Youssef, denounced it and openly attacked Bourguiba as a moderating collaborationist. Ben Youssef, who called for immediate Tunisian independence within the framework of pan-Arabism, had the support of strongly religious and conservative groups as well as urban elements that sympathized with his radical Arab nationalism. In contrast, Bourguiba, who represented moderation and an attachment to specifically Tunisian national identity, had the support of Western-educated elites from the Sahel and Tunis.

Bourguiba prevailed in the bitter personal confrontation that followed, largely because of overwhelming support from the international arena, the party, and the trade union movement. The union movement was headed by Bourguiba's ally, Ahmed Ben Salah. Ben Youssef organized a guerrilla insurrection after independence, but this was quashed. Although Ben Youssef's uprising failed, it constituted the greatest challenge to Bourguiba and the Neo-Destour during this formative period—crystallizing their authoritarian manner and marking the ascendancy of a Sahelian, pro-Western, secular elite over a conservative, Islamist opposition, a schism that persists to this day.

The defeat of Ben Youssef did not completely eliminate challenges to Bourguiba's leadership. Following independence in 1956, trade union leader Ben Salah broke with his old ally, at least for a while. Ben Salah was a socialist who espoused nationalization of the country's resources, state economic planning, and the transformation of the General Union of Tunisian Workers (UGTT) into the primary instrument for social and economic development. Bourguiba, on the other hand, although he sought to secure a virtual monopoly of power for the party, wanted to create within it the widest possible political base. A believer in the market economy, he wished to avoid risking national unity or foreign investment with radical economic change. Bourguiba prevailed and replaced Ben Salah with Ahmed Tlili, who shared Bourguiba's liberal, reformist political philosophy.

Thus, in Tunisia's first years of independence, Bourguiba was able to establish his supremacy not only in the party but also in the formal machinery of the state. In April 1956 he became prime minister, leading a government in which sixteen of the seventeen ministers belonged to the Neo-Destour. In July 1957 he became head of state as well when his government abolished the powerless and unpopular monarchy and proclaimed Tunisia a republic.

A new constitution, promulgated in June 1959, established Tunisia as an Islamic republic within the greater Maghrib, with Arabic as its official language and a presidential form of government responsible to the president rather than to the legislature. On November 8, 1959, Tunisia held its first elections under the new constitution. President Bourguiba ran unopposed, and all ninety candidates in the unicameral Chamber of Deputies (*Majlis al-Nuwaab*) were backed by the Neo-Destour. Thus, by 1959 Bourguiba and his Neo-Destour Party had placed their indelible imprint on the Tunisian political system.

Phase II: 1960–1964

The second period, 1960 to 1964, was highlighted by a series of crises and by the regime's shift to socialist economic policies dominated by the state. In July 1961, fighting broke out between Tunisian and French troops over the Tunisian demand for France's evacuation of the large naval base at Bizerte on Tunisia's northern coast. The French finally departed in March 1963, but relations with France remained strained until the early 1970s.

Although the confrontation with France enhanced Bourguiba's prestige and popularity at home and in the Third World, an assassination plot against him was discovered in December 1962. Several military officers were tried and executed. In January 1963, Bourguiba also took action against the Communist Party of Tunisia (PCT) and banned it under the pretext that it was attempting to expand its membership among students and workers.

The shift from private enterprise to state socialism began in 1961. To emphasize its commitment to the new policy, the Neo-Destour Party officially changed its name to the Destourian Socialist Party in October 1964. Relatively mild ideologically, "socialism" included a rejection of class struggle and embraced notions such as "cooperation," "freedom," and the "promotion of man." It also sustained a rather consistent effort to suppress and control opposition from organized labor. To implement the new economic policies, Bourguiba appointed his former rival, Ben Salah, as the minister of planning and national economy.

In May 1964, the Tunisian *majlis* enacted legislation authorizing the expropriation of all foreign-owned land, a move that further exacerbated relations with France. The nationalization legislation also signaled a new commitment to socialism. A month later there were new elections. Bourguiba again ran unopposed, and the PSD, which was the only party to present candidates, won all the seats in the *majlis*.

Phase III: 1964–1969

The third period, 1964 to 1969, was dominated by Ben Salah's efforts to collectivize agriculture through cooperatives, with the full backing of Bourguiba and the PSD. The cooperatives were to be developed primarily on nationalized French estates but were also to involve the small landholdings of many Tunisian farmers.

Many peasants opposed the new cooperatives. More importantly, large landowners also saw the policy as a threat; since many wielded influence in government circles, opposition soon became more directly political.

In January 1969 Ben Salah attempted to extend the cooperative structure further, resulting in riots by small landowners. Opposition from such a key constituency of the PSD led Bourguiba to withdraw his support for Ben Salah's socialist economic policies and dismiss him in September 1969. That same month an agrarian reform law was pushed through, affirming the importance of three sectors: the state, the cooperative sector, and most importantly the private sector. Ben Salah was later arrested and sentenced to ten years of hard labor. In February 1973 he escaped to Europe, where he became a vocal critic of the regime.

Bourguiba was chronically ill during this period, which exacerbated the political crisis, as Ben Salah and other political leaders positioned themselves to succeed him. Moreover, Bourguiba's early support for the unpopular socialist policies had become a liability. Nevertheless, his control of the party and the government remained secure, as reflected in the 1969 presidential and *majlis* elections.

Phase IV: 1970–1974

The fourth period, 1970 to 1974, witnessed a brief reemergence of political liberalism, as Bourguiba sought to reestablish his popularity and prestige and stabilize the country's economic and political systems. He reappointed several former high officials to important positions in the party and government. These included Ahmed Mestiri, the leader of a Tunis-based social democratic faction; Habib Achour, who returned as head of the UGTT; Muhammad Masmoudi, who became minister of foreign affairs; and Bahi Ladgham, who served briefly as prime minister before being replaced in November 1970 by Bourguiba's close ally, former Central Bank governor Hedi Nouira. Nouira was from Bourguiba's hometown of Monastir and had been the PSD's secretary-general since 1969. As prime minister he portrayed himself to the *majlis* as a serious technocrat and an impersonal arbiter interested in solving the country's economic and financial problems.

The government's sensitivity to charges of authoritarianism was clearly demonstrated at the 1971 PSD congress, where the regime's characteristic balance between authority and liberalism tipped toward liberalism and reconciliation. Discussion was free, open, and democratic in spirit and practice. Bourguiba, however, chose his own men for key positions in the PSD's political bureau, ignoring the general sentiment at the congress favoring movement toward competitive politics. In the years that followed, the experiment in political liberalism lost momentum. It ended entirely at the 1974 PSD congress, where the delegates unanimously acclaimed Bourguiba party president for life and called for a constitutional amendment to make him president of the country for life as well.

At the same time, within the economic sphere, Nouira and his technocrats engineered a dramatic economic policy reorientation, known in Arabic as *infitah*, or "economic opening." The state dismantled barriers to external investment and trade, pursued export-oriented industrialization, and espoused the "hard law" of the market. Nouira's new economic strategy emphasized developing a private industrial-export sector while expanding the tourism industry. The state remained intensely involved in the economy, but its aim was to encourage the private sector. The *infitah* continues to this day, and Tunisia once again proved to be one of the innovators in the region.

Phase V: 1975–1979

During the fifth period, 1975 to 1979, the PSD continued to become more monolithic while losing much of its early effectiveness as a vehicle for mass mobilization. At the same time, important new political actors emerged, resulting in a weakened PSD and an increasingly heterogeneous and conflict-ridden political environment. Bourguiba and Prime Minister Nouira showed little interest in the policies of social and cultural reform that had been a hallmark of Ben Salah's leadership. With concern for social mobilization diminished, they placed less emphasis on popular participation in the grassroots activities of the PSD. Proclaiming that they were *évolutionnistes*, not revolutionaries, Bourguiba and Nouira continued to devote themselves to expanding the private sector, dismantling most remaining cooperatives, and aggressively encouraging foreign investment.

Under those conditions, the machinery of the PSD was permitted to atrophy. Mass political activity diminished sharply, and the party lost much of its dynamism at the local level. As efforts to foster popular awareness and participation virtually ceased, most local PSD committees did little more than dispense patronage in order to retain the support of area notables. Moreover, the new regime was increasingly intolerant of dissent and more narrowly tied to a single ideological tendency.

During the late 1970s, two new forces emerged to challenge the regime: the labor movement and the nascent Islamist movement. Habib Achour now led the UGTT. Although the UGTT had been an ally of the PSD, it began to defy the government. Following labor strikes in 1976, the government and the UGTT negotiated a "social contract" that gave industrial workers pay raises linked to inflation. Even so, labor unrest continued, and the government was especially disturbed by the presence at demonstrations of many unemployed young people, most of whom were not UGTT members.

The UGTT's response came in January 1978. Achour resigned his position on the PSD political bureau and central committee. Then the union challenged the government directly by calling a general strike for January 26. Extensive rioting in Tunis and several other cities accompanied the strike, demonstrating the anger of the urban poor. The army killed at least one hundred and arrested hundreds more, including Achour and thirty other UGTT leaders. Thereafter, January 26, 1978, became known as Black Thursday.

Another major source of opposition was militant Islamism. Vastly different from the supporters of Ben Youssef, the Islamists of the late 1970s were more explicitly political, calling themselves Harakat al-Ittajah al-Islami ("Movement of the Islamic Way," or MTI). The group was denied legal status by the government.

The MTI attacked a union-supported café in Sfax during Ramadan in 1977. Although most militant Islamist leaders repudiated such violence, they nonetheless spoke out forcefully in opposition to the regime and its policies.

Phase VI: 1980–1986

The sixth period, 1980 to 1986, saw some halting movement toward the creation of a multiparty political system and the continuation and intensification of the political trends of the 1970s. Although the PSD remained dominant, its vitality continued to erode. At the same time, the emergence of rival groups challenging the regime contributed to the complexity of the political scene. Finally, deepening public anger over political and economic grievances brought new violence of a scope and intensity unprecedented in Tunisia.

Early in 1980, Prime Minister Nouira suffered a stroke. Bourguiba replaced him with Mohammed Mzali, a former minister of education, and Mzali's government moved tentatively in the direction of political liberalization.

At a special PSD congress in April 1981, Bourguiba declared that non-PSD candidates would be permitted to participate in November legislative elections and that any group receiving 5 percent of the vote would be recognized as a political party. Furthermore, in July the PCT was officially recognized and exempted from the 5 percent rule. The PSD, operating with the UGTT in an electoral front, won 95 percent of the popular vote and took all the seats in the chamber.

The possibility of increased political pluralism continued when the government recognized the Movement of Social Democrats (MDS) and Muhammad Ben Hadj Amor's faction of the Mouvement de l'Unité Populaire in November 1983. Yet, some within the PSD opposed this move. In any event, many observers saw relatively little substance in what had been accomplished.

Among Mzali's major rivals were Driss Guiga, minister of the interior and an opponent of multiparty politics, and Mohammed Sayah, a former PSD secretary-general who had supported Nouira's hard line in 1978. Mzali's position as heir apparent was also challenged by Bourguiba's wife, Wassila, who used her influence on behalf of several of Mazli's rivals during this period. Adding to the confusion, Bourguiba turned eighty in 1983, and although he remained politically active, his age added to concern about the country's future. The resulting drift and frustration of this period were manifested in widespread rioting in late 1983 and early 1984. The disturbances were sparked by the government's announcement of higher bread and flour prices. The scope and intensity of the rioting showed that public anger was based on much more than the price of bread. Indeed, intense anger appeared to be directed not only at the government but also at the consumption-oriented middle and upper classes, population categories perceived to be prospering from the government's economic policies at a time when the economic situation of the poor was steadily deteriorating. The riots intensified the power struggle within the PSD, forcing a showdown between Mzali and Interior Minister Guiga.

The first military officer to hold high political office in postindependence Tunisia, Gen. Zine al-Abidine Ben Ali, was brought into the government in October 1984 as secretary of state for national security. Bourguiba dismissed Prime Minister Mzali in the summer of 1986. His successor, Rached Sfar, a technocrat, endeavored to resolve Tunisia's economic crises. Having only mixed success, he was replaced in the summer of 1987 by Ben Ali, by then minister of national security. That set the stage for the Supreme Combatant's own removal.

Phase VII: 1987–1990

The seventh period, 1987 to 1990, was marked by spectacular changes. The most significant was the end of Bourguiba's domination of Tunisian politics. There were also economic and political dislocations prompted by Iraq's invasion of Kuwait in August 1990 and the subsequent Gulf War.

Bourguiba's removal from office on November 7, 1987, was, in large part, the culmination of the government's increasingly intractable relationship with the MTI and its leadership, most notably Rachid Ghannouchi. Ghannouchi had studied in Damascus in the 1960s, where he became disillusioned with Arab nationalism and turned to the study of Islamic unity. In the late 1970s Ghannouchi founded the MTI and an Islamist paper, *al-Ma'arifa*, which was banned in 1979.

The crux of the Islamist criticism in Tunisia—as with its counterparts elsewhere in the Muslim world—is that the regime is too pro-Western and too willing to compromise the country's integrity by allowing non-Islamic influences into the country.

Bourguiba had authorized Ghannouchi's imprisonment from 1981 until 1984, and the government accused the MTI of inciting the bread riots of 1984. In 1987 a high court, with Bourguiba's authorization, condemned Ghannouchi to life at hard labor. Ben Ali, realizing that Bourguiba's actions would make martyrs of the MTI leaders, decided to replace the aging president. The ostensible reason for Bourguiba's removal was medical; he was eighty-four years old and in failing health. Under Article 57 of the constitution, and with a medical report signed by seven doctors purportedly treating Bourguiba, Ben Ali proclaimed himself president on November 7, 1987. Ben Ali released Ghannouchi in 1988 and, despite his stated hostility to Islamism, later met with the Islamist leader.

In 1988, Ben Ali and the party leadership also approved the PSD's name change to the Democratic Constitutional Rally and legalized a wide array of political parties. Ben Ali emphasized technical competence in his cabinet appointments and exhibited a willingness to incorporate outspoken opposition figures. Moreover, he pushed through constitutional amendments in July 1988 to limit the president's term of office to a maximum of three five-year terms. Such a limitation should have resulted in Ben Ali's leaving office in 2004, but his supporters crafted a new revision in 2002 that allowed him to run for a fourth term.

A year after Bourguiba's removal, Ben Ali promulgated a national pact— a "code of honor" for the government and legal opposition entities. He also extended presidential clemency to former opponents, pardoning Ghannouchi, 'Abd al-Fattah Mourou, and other Islamists sentenced in absentia, as well as Ben Salah.

Despite these openings, the national elections of April 1989 proved troublesome. New electoral laws instituted a single-ballot-majority formula, making it difficult for small parties to compete. Indeed, Ben Ali won 99 percent of the vote, and the RCD won all seats in the *majlis*.

Phase VIII: 1990–1999

The eighth period, 1990 to 1999, was marked by the Gulf War and the civil war in neighboring Algeria. Opposition to the government in the early 1990s continued to smolder. In January 1990, three legal opposition parties and the unrecognized Islamist al-Nahda Party boycotted the first meeting of the "higher council" of the national pact. In May, three opposition parties—the liberal MDS, the Communist Party, and the unrecognized Popular Unity Movement of Ben Salah (who had returned to Tunisia from exile in 1989)—formed a coalition to criticize the RCD's power monopoly. Meanwhile, unrest continued at several universities in early 1990, involving students from all sides of the political spectrum.

The opposition boycotted the summer 1990 municipal elections, although the RCD pointed to the large turnout (80 percent) as evidence that the boycott was ineffective. Moreover, the elections coincided with the success of the Islamic Salvation Front in the June 13 Algerian municipal election, a cause of tremendous concern for Tunisia's leadership.

Iraq's invasion of Kuwait in August 1990 and the Gulf War of 1991 wrenched Tunisia. Few were enamored of Saddam Husayn and the invasion of Kuwait, but many were equally critical of the US-led coalition against Iraq. The Tunisian government sided with popular anti-Western feelings, and foreigners left the country before and during the war. With the country's development policy based on European (and Middle Eastern) trade and investment, the exodus of the foreign community placed a sharp strain on diplomacy and commerce.

In the spring of 1991, during the turmoil following the Gulf War, Islamist militants allegedly bombed the RCD party headquarters, and unrest broke out in the universities. The government claimed an "Islamic plot" and suspended the Islamist-dominated General Union of University Students (UGET). The following autumn, the government claimed that al-Nahda planned to assassinate Ben Ali and other leaders "to create a constitutional vacuum."

The early 1990s, then, were marked by the emergence of two trends, which obtain to this day: the consolidation of power by Ben Ali and attempts by the government to balance security imperatives in the face of a continuing Islamist challenge with the need to maintain the image of a liberal, democratizing state. The terrorist attacks by Islamist radicals in New York and Washington, DC, on September 11, 2001, served to reinforce the security imperative while further compromising the liberal, democratic image.

In March 1994, Ben Ali was reelected to a second term by an overwhelming majority. Civil war in neighboring Algeria gave the Tunisian government the pretext for a sharp crackdown on Islamists. Moreover, reforms in the electoral code gave the government confidence that it would win in the *majlis*. These reforms included the introduction of a hybrid electoral code that led opposition parties to compete among themselves and become co-opted into the process. The only candidate who challenged Ben Ali for the presidency, Moncef Marzouki, could not obtain sufficient signatures from members of parliament to be placed on the ballot. As a result, the RCD won 97.73 percent of the vote and gained 144 seats in the 163-seat *majlis*. Ben Ali won 99.91 percent of the presidential vote.

In 1995, Tunisia signed an association agreement with the European Union (EU) to create a free trade area over a twelve-year period, opening the Tunisian economy further to European exports and investment. The association agreement was a clear demonstration of Europe's importance to Tunisia. It also illustrated Europe's interest in supporting the economy of a neighboring country dealing with issues of stability.

Phase IX: 1999–Present

The ninth period of Tunisia's postindependence history began in 1999. In October 1999 Ben Ali won election to a third term by an extraordinary margin, and the RCD dominated the *majlis* election. In contrast to previous elections, however, Ben Ali had distinct opposition from two other candidates: the Popular Unity Party's Mohamed Belhaj Amor and the Popularity Unity Party's Abderrahmane Tlili. Thus, the election was touted as the first multiparty election in Tunisia's history. Nonetheless, with 89 percent turnout, Ben Ali's margin was a whopping 99.4 percent.

Since the early 1990s, the government has sought to display a process of gradual opening, undertaking reforms without challenging the RCD position of prominence. In November 1999, shortly after the election, a new reshuffling of the government created a ministerial portfolio in charge of human rights. In May 2000, in the run-up to municipal elections, the RCD stipulated that 20 percent of its candidates would be women and began granting amnesty to political prisoners.

Despite these efforts, Tunisia remains the target of sharp criticism from human rights observers. Since the early 1990s, the internal security services have increased censorship, detained suspected al-Nahda members, and harassed men with beards or women with veils. Foreign researchers are sharply limited in their access to the country, the Internet is monitored closely, undercover police abound, and an independent, vibrant press is nonexistent. Similarly, the Tunisian National Council for Liberties and the Tunisian section of Amnesty International are banned. The press is not allowed to publish releases from al-Nahda or reports by the Tunisian Human Rights League.

The government has consistently responded to the charges of abusing basic civil liberties by arguing that it must maintain public order and that, moreover, without public order, government efforts to attract foreign capital to expand the economy for the good of all Tunisians would fail.

The most distinctive characteristic of the current period has been the reinforcement of a "robust authoritarianism" through the further consolidation of presidential power, privilege, and patronage. Couched in terms of "reinforcing liberty and human rights" while "laying the foundations of a sophisticated political system," the government put to referendum a series of constitutional reforms that were overwhelmingly approved by 99.52 percent of voters on May 26, 2002. Yet, critics at home and abroad dismissed the result as a "masquerade" aimed at prolonging the rule of President Ben Ali.

The reforms abolished the clause that limited presidents to three five-year terms of office, allowing Ben Ali to stand for a fourth term in October 2004 in an election that he won with 94.49 percent of the popular vote, despite the presence of three so-called opposition candidates. The approved reforms also raised the maximum age of presidential candidates from seventy to seventy-five, permitting the incumbent president, who is sixty-eight, to stand for a fifth term in 2009. For many critics of the regime, these changes are intended to establish a "life presidency" for Ben Ali. One of Ben Ali's other reforms also gave presidents permanent immunity from prosecution for all acts carried out in office.

The reformed constitution also provided for an upper house of parliament, the Chamber of Advisers, and extended the powers of the Constitutional Council, whose members are appointed by the president. Other changes were ostensibly aimed at increasing the accountability of parliament and improving human rights. However, these apparently positive steps have limited significance because parliament serves as little more than a rubber stamp for the president's policies, and laws pertaining to human rights are often ignored.

If the constitutional reform efforts had been serious and undertaken in good faith, they would have restrained the president's powers, increased his accountability, and institutionalized the separation of powers. Instead, the changes made have further entrenched Ben Ali in power for the next decade or so and delayed meaningful political progress. Despite the apparent docility of Tunisian civil society, there is danger that these authoritarian measures will radicalize the opposition and provoke a violent reaction. At minimum, they will be viewed by critics at home and abroad as an attempt to maintain a Mediterranean "crony capitalism" for Ben Ali's family and followers. In believing that he alone can effectively govern the country, Ben Ali bears the most responsibility for preventing potential successors from emerging and for delaying the creation of a more pluralistic process in Tunisia.

POLITICAL ENVIRONMENT AND STRUCTURE

Political Culture

Tunisia's political culture has been influenced by a distinct and historically legitimized tradition of national unity, which gave the country an important advantage in the early years after independence. There are both geopolitical and demographic dimensions to this unity. The geographical basis of modern Tunisia appeared in rough outline in Roman times, and with few exceptions the area has been ruled as a unified polity since that time. The various dynasties that governed there possessed centralized and cohesive administrative networks that, for the most part, extended to the whole of the territory. Thus, even though such dynasties were often nominally subservient to the authority of a foreign power, such as the Ottoman sultan, Tunisia's borders remained constant, and the state gained legitimacy in the eyes of those living within it.

Demographically, Tunisia has no significant ethnic and cultural cleavages, in contrast to Algeria and Morocco. Virtually all Tunisians are Arabs and Sunni Muslims. The Berber-speaking population makes up no more than 2 to 3 percent of the total, and even when there was a flourishing Jewish community, it never exceeded 3 percent. Tunisia thus has a degree of homogeneity that is rare in today's world.

Bourguiba and the Neo-Destours instituted a specific set of beliefs about modernity and development. These included a commitment to balancing Tunisia's Arab and Islamic legacy with what they called its Mediterranean personality.

Drawing inspiration from Tunisian history as far back as the Carthaginian and Roman Empires, this balancing act after 1956 involved the regime in both increased Arabization and the construction of a multicultural (Arabo-Islamic and Franco-European) normative order. The emphasis on Tunisia's diversity and unity has continued with Ben Ali. In his declaration of November 7, 1987, broadcast on state radio and television, Ben Ali stressed the Arabic, African, Islamic, Maghribi, and Mediterranean character of Tunisia.

The regime also placed great emphasis on the role and responsibilities of the individual citizen in promoting national development, reflected in the importance given to education and social mobilization. The goal was to carry out a "psychological revolution" that would restructure social and human relationships in a way that would make modernity possible. As defined by Bourguiba himself, the objective was to make each Tunisian "a good citizen, capable of initiative, eager to learn and cooperate, so the battle against underdevelopment will be won."

Social Policies

The social reforms introduced by the regime have touched on many areas. For example, a personal-status code adopted in 1956 was designed in part to promote women's emancipation. It abolished polygamy, established a minimum age of fifteen for women to marry, provided women with the right to sign their own marriage certificates, and permitted them to demand divorce, vote, and hold office. Bourguiba believed in a more liberal interpretation of the Qur'an; he repeatedly denounced the veil as a "dishrag" and viewed traditional Muslim customs for women as "servility, decadence, and bondage." Such an orientation vis-à-vis the status of women has earned Tunisia a reputation as one of the most liberal countries in the Middle East and North Africa. Although Islamist criticism of the personal-status code in the early 1990s pulled Ben Ali and the RCD in more conservative directions, reforms in the 1990s have included extending additional rights to divorced women, especially concerning child support and alimony. Responding harshly to the increasing Islamization of Arab societies, the regime has banned the wearing of the veil and head scarf in all public institutions.

In other realms, the government nationalized Muslim landed estates (*habor*) in 1956 and 1957, arguing that the religious leaders in control of the land failed to encourage its rational exploitation. The Neo-Destour later redistributed these lands as political patronage. In 1958 the government established a new bilingual educational system. Attention was given to the increased use of Arabic, but French was the language of instruction for many subjects from the third grade on. The newly established University of Tunis taught most of its courses in French, although plans were laid for increased Arabization in higher education.

The Neo-Destour was an effective organization for social change during these years. Members of the party's approximately 1,250 territorial and professional units met often to discuss national problems and raise public awareness. The party performed important regulatory and distribution functions at the local level, too, helping citizens to solve personal problems and dispensing patronage. All these activities built loyalty to the political system and helped to foster popular support for the party's reforms. The party claimed to have 400,000 active members in 1965, and auxiliary organizations, such as the Union of Tunisian Women and the UGET, were also active in mobilizing and politicizing the populace.

A major effort was made to expand education, which regularly absorbed 25 to 30 percent of the state budget. In the decade following independence, literacy climbed from 15 percent to 35 to 40 percent, the percentage of primary school-age children attending classes grew from 25 to between 60 and 70, and the percentage completing high school rose from 3 to almost 30. In 1960, Tunisia was third among Arab countries in the percentage of children attending school. By 1965, it had moved into second place, behind Lebanon. The regime also took care to see that women shared in the expansion of education. The proportion of girls in the student population rose steadily during this period, climbing from less than 30 percent at independence to over 40 percent a decade later. Vocational training was also expanded. These positive trends continue into the twenty-first century, making Tunisia one of the most socially advanced and educationally progressive Arab states, with an overall literacy rate of 75 percent and a secondary school enrollment rate of 80 percent.

Although serious opposition was not tolerated in this dynamic but centralized political environment, Bourguiba's exercise of power during the early years was not totalitarian and was directed primarily at national, not personal, advancement. He consulted widely on important policy matters and permitted senior officials to exchange ideas vigorously. He also addressed the people in countless speeches and rehabilitated former opponents willing to work with him in the party. Meaningful competition sometimes existed at nonelite levels, too, as local officials struggled with one another and with the party hierarchy. Thus, despite some abuses of power, the government was genuinely committed to far-reaching social change and was highly popular with the masses.

By the mid-1970s, however, the major structures of government—the *majlis*, the cabinet, and the PSD—had all become little more than appendages to Bourguiba's system of personal rule. Under him was a ruling elite composed of an old guard: longtime associates dating from the pre-independence struggle and younger technocrats, men brought into government by Bourguiba because of their specialized education, technical skills, and modernist outlook. Nonetheless, Bourguiba did not allow any of these groups to achieve an independent base of power strong enough to challenge his rule.

Political Counterculture

A political counterculture began to emerge in the 1970s, accompanying and rein-forced by changes in the ideological orientation of the top elite and the increasing authoritarianism of the government. These new trends, including a reinvigorated labor movement and growing public support for militant Islamism, reflected the unfulfilled expectations of an increasingly mobilized populace and the intensifica-tion of economic problems and inequities. Many Tunisians lost faith in the vision and development strategy articulated by the government—a loss of faith that con-tinues to this day. This is particularly true of the growing ranks of young people whose social origins are modest and whose education does not go much beyond primary school. Tunisia's bicultural orientation also limits opportunities for ad-vancement among persons from traditional backgrounds, whose familiarity with French language and culture is limited. Moreover, rapid industrialization intensi-fies competition for jobs and status and increases the relative deprivation of those who are unable to seize the new opportunities being created.

Internal government operations have changed considerably under Ben Ali, al-though the effect of that change on the general population is still limited. In con-trast to Bourguiba, who had an aloof style and played "musical chairs" with his cabinet ministers, Ben Ali is much more of a "hands-on" leader, surrounding him-self with experienced professionals who have served him for many years. At the same time, Ben Ali is very much in charge, exercising power with an "iron fist in a velvet glove."

Conscious of the declining popularity of Western-inspired images and symbols in some quarters, since the late 1980s the regime has sought to invoke Arab and Islamic symbols as a means of buttressing its rule and undercutting the appeal of opposition groups, particularly al-Nahda. Nevertheless, secular Western values are still an integral part of Tunisian national identity, exemplified by the country's deep ties with the EU and the infusion of French and Italian television broadcasts.

POLITICAL DYNAMICS

State-society relations stand at a crossroads in Tunisia today. The hopeful expecta-tions of the immediate post-Bourguiba period have been replaced by a sense of political gloom and doom in an otherwise promising socioeconomic environ-ment. What happened to create this severe disjuncture?

The actual transfer of power in 1987 seemed relatively smooth, even though the so-called constitutional coup was little more than a legal cover for a straight-forward military takeover by a nonelected former army officer. A team of doctors testified that Bourguiba, then in his mid-eighties, was senile and therefore unable to continue serving as president. The relatively peaceful transition was greeted by

many at home and abroad with a sense of relief, following the last years of Bourguiba's politically destabilizing rule.

The Ben Ali presidency began optimistically, with a series of forward-looking,
corrective measures that seemed to point to greater democracy, not less. Among
the more prominent initiatives intended to overcome his predecessor's excesses
were the abolition of the life presidency, the release of thousands of political detainees, and the ratification of the UN convention against torture. Intending to
overcome the deep political divide, Ben Ali opened a process of "national reconciliation" that encouraged many political exiles to return home. He pushed
through legislation in 1988 that created a multiparty system, although movements,
organizations, and parties based on race, religion, or region were banned. Numerous parties were formed, and harsh press laws were overturned or relaxed. A Tunisian "National Pact" was drafted to create a framework for democracy by bringing
together a wide diversity of civil society, including opposition parties, human
rights groups, women's movements, businessmen, trade unions, and Islamist figures
such as the controversial Rachid Ghannouchi. Ben Ali also undertook a major reform of the ruling party by bringing in younger blood and changing its name to
the Rassemblement Constitutionnel Démocratique (RCD).

Whether by design or default, the authoritarian impulse quickly overcame the
democratic imperative, as Ben Ali and the RCD seemed intent on maintaining
the party's primacy at all costs. The initial political consensus therefore eroded rapidly. The political divide was further widened as the regime was determined to
weaken and ultimately destroy al-Nahda, which it saw potentially paralleling the
rise of the Islamic Salvation Front in neighboring Algeria.

What began as a determined effort by the regime to destroy all vestiges of al-
Nahda soon turned into a greater intolerance for all kinds of dissent, whether sectarian or secular. By the early 1990s, security was tightened, and the media was
strictly controlled, as repression extended far beyond the so-called Islamic radicals
and left-wing extremists to reach members of the legal opposition and, in particular, human rights groups and their families. This massive suppression of dissent
continues today, unhindered by the widespread criticism such policies have engendered.

For its part, the regime continues to espouse the language of "reform" and "democracy," highlighting the Kafkaesque gap between rhetoric and reality. The Tunisian constitution, for example, guarantees citizens the "right of security, dignity
and justice, and freedom of opinion, expression, and association." Although there
exists a Ministry of Justice and Human Rights and the president presents a human
rights prize annually on Tunisia's Human Rights Day, the reality is much more
sobering. Scores of individuals and groups who dare to criticize the regime or Ben
Ali himself are thrown in jail, their passports are confiscated, and their families are
routinely harassed. The government insists that there are no political prisoners,

only common criminals, yet the laws on association and political expression are highly restrictive.

Robust Authoritarianism

The regime has consolidated its power through numerous institutional structures—none more important than the Constitutional Democratic Rally. As the direct descendant of the PSD, the RCD has been revitalized as the country's dominant political organization. With a national reach of 2.5 million members, 80,000 party activists, and 7,800 branches, it dominates Tunisian politics. The party holds 152 of the 189 seats in parliament and 4,098 of 4,366 seats on local councils. Its ideological orientation is ostensibly left of center, and it has made concrete efforts to overcome the economic hardships experienced by poorer members of society, although it has also embraced many free market economic principles.

There are seven legal opposition parties, but all lack a popular base and are riddled with factionalism and internal dissent. Moreover, the ideological and programmatic differences between these parties and the RCD have become blurred. Their occasional efforts to form a "united front" at election time have proven fruitless or had little effect.

The largest of these opposition parties is the MDS, a left-of-center party formed during the Bourguiba era that has become divided over whether to oppose or support Ben Ali. The officially recognized wing has supported Ben Ali in the 1999, 2004, and 2009 presidential elections.

The "dissident" opposition consists of three left-wing parties: the Renewal Movement (*Harakat Ettajdid*, formerly known as the Tunisian Communist Party, or PCT), the Progressive Democratic Party, and the Democratic Forum for Labor and Freedoms, established in 2002 and the first new party to gain legal status for over a decade. These parties formed a loose alliance to fight the 2005 local elections but failed to gain a single seat. Al-Nahda has never been legalized, although its candidates, running as independents, managed to get 13 percent of the vote in the 1989 parliamentary election.

Given the anemic character of opposition politics, and by way of demonstrating its democratic credentials, the regime has modified the electoral laws to permit representation of opposition parties in the Chamber of Deputies, producing a facade of pluralism without threatening the RCD's dominance. The same dominance applies to the upper house created in 2005, the Chamber of Advisers, whose appointees are largely controlled by the RCD. The situation is even more distorted at the local level, which saw only 248 of the 4,366 contested municipal seats in the May 2005 election going to opposition parties.

Under the constitution, candidates for the presidency must have the backing of at least thirty members of parliament; yet, no legal opposition has had anything near this number. In 1999 and 2004, this rule was temporarily suspended to allow more than one candidate to stand for the presidency. However, the presence of two opposition candidates in 1999 and three in 2004 was purely symbolic, as Ben Ali won over 90 percent of the vote in both cases. Only one authentic opposition figure, Ahmed Brahim of Harakat Ettajdid (ex-PCT), ran against Ben Ali in 2009. The electoral law was amended in 2009 to increase the proportion of seats reserved for the opposition parties from 20 to 25 percent and to decrease the voting age from twenty to eighteen, but these changes will have little impact on elections. With constitutional provisions allowing the president to serve unlimited terms until the age of seventy-five, all effective power is now concentrated in the executive branch, with the RCD serving as a direct appendage of the state. The president's powers are all encompassing: He appoints the prime minister, all cabinet members, the members of three key advisory councils, the twenty-three regional and local governors, the heads of the armed forces and police, and all senior judges and civil servants. The presidential and parliamentary elections scheduled for October 2009 are guaranteed to maintain the hegemony of both the president and his party.

Civil Society Rising?

For all intents and purposes, Tunisia is a one-party state governed by an unaccountable autocrat. Yet, for many, if not most, ordinary Tunisians, the absence of genuine democracy seems acceptable as long as political stability and socioeconomic development are sustained. The absence of a significant challenge to Ben Ali can be attributed in great measure to the progressive social policies he has pursued, including giving priority to education and health; taking measures to alleviate unemployment, poverty, and regional inequalities; and passing legislation that has successfully promoted women's rights. The regime continues to provide subsidies on staple foods and has ensured regular increases in minimum wages. Health care and education are free, and welfare payments have been provided to low-income families. By providing such vital social services, the government has succeeded in minimizing the role of Islamist groups, whose provision of welfare benefits unavailable from the government has increased their influence in other Muslim countries.

Despite the surface appearance of political tranquility, a stratum of human rights activists, lawyers, scholars, and journalists has long challenged the regime's autocratic excesses. They are now being joined by a growing number of Tunisia's traditionally passive middle class in questioning the theory that security and prosperity can only be had at the expense of political freedom. The business community also is beginning to complain that the system's political rigidity is stifling innovation and creativity. Equally troubling are the growing accusations being made by a wide range of entrepreneurs that the domination of business by allies of the ruling elite is inhibiting economic opportunity, restricting enterprise, and discouraging risk taking.

The reality of contemporary Tunisia is that an increasingly well-educated population with access to foreign travel, satellite television, the Internet, and other modes of communication is becoming restless with its authoritarian leadership and, in the near future, will demand Western standards of democracy. For their part, the authorities continue to impose harsh restrictions on free speech, assembly, and public contestation, making it almost impossible for Tunisians to express dissent. When such dissent has occurred, it has often been inspired, manipulated, or co-opted by the regime itself, as with the massive anti-US protests during the 1991 Gulf War. The government imposed severe restrictions on the nationwide demonstrations in the run-up to the American invasion of Iraq in March 2003. Similar measures were put into place during the biggest and most prestigious international event ever staged in Tunisia, the second and final phase of the UN-sponsored World Summit on the Information Society (WSIS), held in Tunis from November 16 to 18, 2005.

While the regime thus has demonstrated a keen ability to sustain its authoritarian stranglehold on Tunisia, an increasingly restless and reanimated civil society is beginning to emerge. Paradoxically, the regime's own efforts to advance the economy and promote universal education, progressive social policies, and gender equality have aroused the political consciousness of Tunisians of all ages, who are now at the doorstep of democratic opportunity and demanding entry. Whether that entrance will be peaceful or violent rests in the hands of the incumbent leadership, many of whose members are extremely enlightened but whose ability to influence an otherwise autocratic president remains highly problematic.

FOREIGN POLICY

Tunisia's foreign policy is guided by the need for regional security and the desire to advance its economic interests, especially trade and foreign investment. As with his predecessor, Ben Ali has sought to expand his country's international status and project himself as a statesman by involving Tunisia in a wide range of global activities, international conferences, and diplomatic initiatives, the most visible being the November 2005 WSIS.

Given its small size and demographic vulnerability, Tunisia has worked hard to maintain good relations with its immediate neighbors, especially Algeria and Libya, whose own external ambitions and unpredictable domestic politics have at times threatened regional stability. Beginning with Bourguiba and continuing under Ben Ali, Tunisia continues to pursue a moderate, pro-Western stance in foreign affairs. This has resulted in the establishment of diverse military and security arrangements with powerful outside partners like France and the United States, ties that have been intensified since the terrorist attacks of September 11, 2001.

Maghrib Politics

At the urging of its European and American allies, Tunisia joined its four North African neighbors (Algeria, Libya, Mauritania, and Morocco) in forming the Arab Maghrib Union (AMU) at a formal ceremony in Marrakech in February 1989. Intended as a framework for advancing the regional economic interests of its members, the AMU has struggled to maintain its institutional integrity in the face of chronic personal and political differences among these countries. The Western Sahara conflict has been the greatest source of contention, as Algeria and Morocco vie for regional hegemony. Tunisia has worked hard to revive the AMU by bringing the various parties together through summits and agreements, though these efforts have proven fruitless.

Tunisia's bilateral relations with individual Maghribi countries have ranged from good to disagreeable to threatening. In the case of Algeria, the long, bloody civil war between radical Islamists and the army-dominated government has caused great consternation and concern in Tunis. Indeed, despite the significant attenuation of the conflict in the early 2000s, the Algerian insurgency has been used by the Tunisian regime to tighten security and impose harsh restrictions on civil society through the omnipresent state security apparatus, or *mukhabarat*.

Relations with Libya have been erratic, given the unpredictable style of its leader, Muammar al-Qaddafi. Tunisia's failure to implement the hastily announced January 1974 merger with Libya strained relations between the two countries and led to Libyan economic retaliation, political subversion, and military threats. Since 1995 relations between Tunis and Tripoli have been amicable, and there are moves to expand economic cooperation, notably in the energy sector. However, Tunisian officials and citizens alike do not trust the Libyan leader, whom they continue to view with great suspicion despite Tripoli's newly discovered pro-Western foreign policy. For their part, Tunisian-Moroccan relations have been closer than any other Maghribi bilateral combination. Both countries have a tradition of friendship with the West, similarly moderate views on the Palestinian-Israeli dispute, and a distaste for radical foreign policy.

Despite its pro-Western orientation, Tunisia has been able to maintain its credentials as a loyal member of the Arab community. During the 1960s, Bourguiba alienated most of Tunisia's Arab allies by advocating the then unthinkable recognition of Israel. Aware of the strong emotional identification of Tunisia's population with the Palestinian cause, the country's leaders have been careful to maintain solidarity with the Arab world. For example, Tunisia deepened its involvement in inter-Arab politics by hosting both the League of Arab States in 1979 and the Palestine Liberation Organization's headquarters in the 1980s. However, Tunisia was among the handful of Arab states to establish (and later suspend, following the 2000 Intifada) consular, commercial, and tourist ties with the Jewish state, reflecting a concerted effort to attract back from overseas its native Tunisian Jewish population.

The Western Connection

Tunisia has long had a Western orientation, reinforced by its geographical location and history. This pro-Western perspective deepened under both Bourguiba and Ben Ali. For their part, Europe and the United States have consistently viewed the country as a moderate actor in an otherwise turbulent environment. It is viewed as a reliable friend on NATO's southern flank, a firm supporter of peace between Israel and Palestine, and, since September 11, 2001, an American ally in the "war on terror." The latter position has not been easy to maintain, however, given popular anger over the 2003 US invasion of Iraq. Nevertheless, the regime has managed to appease public anger by identifying with the suffering of the Iraqi people and calling for regional stability, while not directly criticizing the United States. Western governments have also been strong supporters of Tunisia's reformist economic policies, which they see as helping to increase prosperity and limit migration to Europe.

The areas of noticeable disagreement between Western nations and Tunisia revolve around the country's continuing political repression, human rights violations, and absence of democracy. From 1995 to 2001, for example, human rights issues became prominent in Tunisia's dealings with the EU states. Faced with such criticism, the Tunisian regime has made concessions on some high-profile human rights cases without, however, altering the system's basic authoritarianism. These external pressures declined after the September 11, 2001, terrorist attacks, as Tunis portrayed its clampdown on the Islamist opposition as part of the "war on terror." The Islamist terrorist attack on European tourists visiting a historic synagogue on the island of Jerba in April 2002 further hardened the regime's repressive policies. Yet, by now this tactic of using Islamic "terrorism" as justification for maintaining an authoritarian political order has resulted in criticisms of Tunisia's human rights abuses by EU and US officials.

In an age of globalization involving the universalization of personal communications, democratic aspirations, and economic opportunities, it will be increasingly difficult for the Tunisian government both to promote socioeconomic change and to prevent the emergence of political freedom. As domestic and international pressure continues to mount, Ben Ali will be forced to decide fairly soon the ultimate trajectory of a nation that for decades has been evolving into a model of political compromise, adaptive modernization, cultural pluralism, and socioeconomic well-being.

BIBLIOGRAPHY

The best historical overview is found in Kenneth J. Perkins, *A History of Modern Tunisia* (Cambridge: Cambridge University Press, 2004). A useful complement is Kenneth J. Perkins, *Historical Dictionary of Tunisia*, 2nd ed. (Lanham, MD: Scarecrow Press, 1997). A good recent overview is Christopher Alexander, *Tunisia: Stability and Reform in the Modern Maghreb* (London: Routledge, 2010).

On Tunisia's colonial experience, see Albert Memmi, *The Colonizer and the Colonized* (Boston: Beacon Press, 1967); L. Carl Brown, *The Tunisia of Ahmad Bey: 1837–1855* (Princeton, NJ: Princeton University Press, 1974); Lisa Anderson, *State and Social Transformation in Tunisia and Libya, 1830–1980* (Princeton, NJ: Princeton University Press, 1986); and Julia A. Clancy-Smith, *Rebel and Saint: Muslim Notables, Populist Protest, Colonial Encounters (Algeria and Tunisia, 1800–1904)* (Berkeley: University of California Press, 1994). The early years of independence are treated in Charles A. Micaud, Leon Carl Brown, and Clement Henry Moore, *Tunisia: The Politics of Modernization* (New York: Praeger, 1964); Clement Henry Moore, *Tunisia Since Independence: The Dynamics of One-Party Government* (Berkeley: University of California Press, 1965); and Lars Rudebeck, *Party and People: A Study of Political Change in Tunisia* (New York: Praeger, 1969). The cooperative era is analyzed in Lars Rudebeck, "Development Pressure and Political Limits: A Tunisian Example," *Journal of Modern African Studies* 8, no. 2 (1970): 173–198, and John Simmons, "Agricultural Cooperatives and Tunisian Development: Part I and II," *The Middle East Journal* 24, no. 4 (1970): 455–465, and 25, no. 1 (1971): 45–75.

On Bourguiba's political legacy, see L. Carl Brown, "Bourguiba and Bourguibism Revisited: Reflections and Interpretation," *The Middle East Journal* 55, no. 1 (2001): 43–57; John P. Entelis, "L'héritage contradictoire de Bourguiba: modernisation et intolérance politique," in *Habib Bourguiba: la trace et l'héritage*, ed. Michel Camau and Vincent Geisser, 223–247 (Paris: Karthala, 2004); and John P. Entelis, "Reformist Ideology in the Arab World: The Cases of Tunisia and Lebanon," *The Review of Politics* 37, no. 4 (1975): 513–546.

Tunisia's political institutions are analyzed in Derek Hopwood, *Habib Bourguiba of Tunisia: The Tragedy of Longevity* (New York: St. Martin's Press, 1992). The government's declining popular legitimacy and shifting ideological orientation and development strategy are treated by John P. Entelis, "Ideological Change and an Emerging Counter-Culture in Tunisian Politics," *Journal of Modern African Studies* 12, no. 4 (1974): 543–568; Mark Tessler, "Tunisia at the Crossroads," *Current History* (May 1985): 217–230; and Ahmed Ben Salah, "Tunisia: Endogenous Development and Structural Transformation," in *Another Development: Approaches and Strategies*, ed. Marc Nerfin (Uppsala, Sweden: Dag Hammarskjöld, 1977). A valuable compendium from this period is Russell Stone and John Simmons, eds., *Change in Tunisia* (Albany: State University of New York Press, 1976).

Tunisia in the 1980s is treated in Russell A. Stone, "Tunisia: A Single Party System Holds Change in Abeyance," in *Political Elites in Arab North Africa*, ed. I. William Zartman et al., 144–176 (New York: Longman, 1982); I. William Zartman, ed., *Tunisia: The Political Economy of Reform* (Boulder, CO: Lynne Rienner, 1991); and Michel Camau, ed., *Tunisie au present: Une modernité au-dessous de tout soupçon?* (Paris: CNRS, 1987). Other accounts include L. B. Ware, "Ben Ali's Constitutional Coup in Tunisia," *The Middle East Journal* 42, no. 4 (1988): 587–601; Mark Tessler, "Tunisia's New Beginning," *Current History* (April 1990): 169–184; Dirk Vandewalle, "From the New State to the New Era: Toward a Second Republic in Tunisia," *The Middle East Journal* 42, no. 4 (1988): 602–620; and Rémy Leveau, "La Tunisie du président Ben Ali: Equilibre interne et environnement arabe," *Maghreb-Machrek* 124 (1989): 4–17. Politics and political economy in the 1990s are treated by Iliya Harik, "Privatization and Development in Tunisia," in *Privatization and Liberalization in the Middle East*, ed. Iliya Harik and Denis J. Sullivan (Bloomington: Indiana University Press, 1992); Guilain Denoeux, "Tunisie: les élections présidentielles et legislatives, 20 mars 1994," *Maghreb-Machrek* 145 (1994): 49–72; Gregory White, *A Comparative Political Economy of Tunisia and Morocco: On the Outside of Europe Looking In* (Albany: State University of New York Press, 2001); Emma Murphy, *Economic and Political Change in Tunisia: From Bourguiba to Ben Ali* (New York: St. Martin's Press, 1999); Nicole Grimaud, "Tunisia: Between Control and Liberalization," *Mediterranean Politics* 1, no. 1 (1996): 95–106; Stephen J. King, *Liberalization Against Democracy: The Local Politics of Economic Reform in Tunisia* (Bloomington: Indiana University Press, 2003); Melani Cammett, *Globalization, Business Politics and Development: North Africa in Comparative Perspective* (Cambridge: Cambridge University Press, 2007); Eva Bellin, "Contingent Democrats: Industrialists, Labor, and Democratization in Late-Developing Countries," *World Politics* 52 (January 2000): 175–205; Eva Bellin, *Stalled Democracy: Capital, Labor, and the Paradox of State-Sponsored Development* (Ithaca, NY: Cornell University Press, 2002); and Melani Cammett, "Fat Cats and Self-Made Men: Globalization and the Paradoxes of Collective Action," *Comparative Politics* (July 2005): 379–400.

The status of women is treated by Mounira A. Charrad, *States and Women's Rights: The Making of Postcolonial Tunisia, Algeria, and Morocco* (Berkeley: University of California Press, 2001); Emma C. Murphy, "Women in Tunisia: A Survey of Achievements and Challenges," *The Journal of North African Studies* 1, no. 2 (autumn 1996): 138–156; Barbara Larson, "The Status of Women in a Tunisian Village: Limits to Autonomy, Influence, and Power," *Signs: Journal of Women in Culture and Society* 9, no. 3 (1984): 417–433; Laurie Brand, *Women, the State, and Political Liberalization: Middle Eastern and North African Experiences* (New York: Columbia University Press, 1998); Angel Foster, "Young Women's Sexuality in Tunisia: The Health Consequences of Misinformation Among University Students," in *Everyday Life in the Muslim Middle East*, ed. Donna Lee Bowen and Evelyn A. Early, 2nd ed., 98–110 (Bloomington: Indiana University Press, 2002); and Sophie Ferchiou, *Les femmes dans l'agriculture tunisienne* (Marseille: Edisud, 1985). Susan Marshall and Randall Stokes, in "Tradition and the Veil: Female Status in Tunisia and Algeria," *The Journal of Modern African Studies* 19, no. 44 (1981): 625–646, offer a comparison to Algeria.

The political role of Islam is examined by Emad Eldin Shahin, *Political Ascent: Contemporary Islamic Movements in North Africa* (Boulder, CO: Westview Press, 1988); Najib Ghadbian, *Democratization and the Islamist Challenge in the Arab World* (Boulder, CO: Westview Press, 1997); Susan Waltz, "Islamicist Appeal in Tunisia," *The Middle East Journal* 40, no. 4 (1986): 651–670; Marion Boulby, "The Islamist Challenge: Tunisia Since Independence," *Third World Quarterly* 10 (April 1989): 590–614; Mark Tessler, "Political Change and the Islamic Revival in Tunisia," *Maghreb Review* 5, no. 1 (1980): 8–19; Elbaki Hermassi, "La société tunisienne au miroir islamiste," *Maghreb-Machrek* 103 (April–June 1984); John P. Entelis, ed., *Islam, Democracy and the State in North Africa* (Bloomington: Indiana University Press, 1997); Azzam S. Tamimi, *Rachid Ghannouchi: A Democrat Within Islamism* (New York: Oxford University Press, 2001); Robert D. Lee, "Tunisian Intellectuals: Responses to Islamism," *The Journal of North African Studies* 13, no. 2 (June 2008): 157–173; François Burgat, *The Islamic Movement in North Africa*, trans. William Dowell (Austin: University of Texas, 1993); François Burgat, *Face to Face with Political Islam* (London: Tauris, 2003); and Mohamed Elhachmi Hamdi, *The Politicisation of Islam: A Case Study of Tunisia* (Boulder, CO: Westview, 1998). Tunisia's Jewish population and relationship with Israel are treated by Mark Tessler and Linda Hawkins, "The Political Culture of Jews in Tunisia and Morocco," *International Journal of Middle East Studies* 11, no. 1 (1980): 59–86, and Michael M. Laskier, *Israel and the Maghreb: From Statehood to Oslo* (Gainesville: University Press of Florida, 2004).

On human rights in Tunisia, see Ahmed Manaï, *Supplice Tunisien: Le jardin secret du général Ben Ali* (Paris: La Découverte, 1995), and Nicolas Beau and Jean-Pierre Tuquoi, *Notre ami Ben Ali* (Paris: La Découverte, 1999). Andrew Borowiec, in *Modern Tunisia* (New York: Praeger, 1998), and Georgie Anne Geyer, in *Tunisia: A Journey Through a Country That Works* (London: Interlink Publications, 2004), offer effusive praise of Ben Ali.

The Ben Ali presidency and its authoritarian style of governance, along with the social context within which it operates, is the focus of numerous critical studies. The most important are Michel Camau and Vincent Geisser, *Le syndrome autoritaire: Politique en Tunisie de Bourguiba à Ben Ali* (Paris: Presses de Sciences Po, 2003); John P. Entelis, "The Democratic Imperative vs. the Authoritarian Impulse: The Maghrib State Between Transition and Terrorism," *The Middle East Journal* 59, no. 4 (2005): 537–558; Christopher Alexander, "Authoritarianism and Civil Society in Tunisia," *Middle East Report* (October–November 1997): 1–7; Michele Penner Angrist, "Parties, Parliament and Political Dissent in Tunisia," *The Journal of North African Studies* 4, no. 4 (winter 1999): 89–104; Eva Bellin, "Civil Society in Formation: Tunisia," in *Civil Society in the Middle East*, vol. 1, ed. Augustus Richard Norton, 120–147 (Leiden: E. J. Brill, 1995); Mark J. Gasiorowski, "The Failure of Reform in Tunisia," *Journal of Democracy* 3, no. 4 (1992): 85–97; Vincent Geisser, "Tunisie: des élections pour quoi faire? Enjeux et 'sens' du fait électoral de Bourguiba à Ben Ali," *Maghreb Machrek* 168 (April–June 2000): 14–28; Kamel Labidi, "Tunisia: Independent but Not Free," *Le Monde Diplomatique* (March 2006): 1–4; Olfa Lamloum, "Tunisie: Quelle 'transition démocratique?'" in *Dispositifs de démocratisation et dispositifs autoritaires en Afrique du Nord*, ed. Jean-Nöel Ferrié and Jean-Claude Santucci, 121–147 (Paris: CNRS Editions, 2006); Olfa Lamloum and B. Ravenel, *La Tunisie de Ben Ali: la société contre le régime* (Paris: L'Harmattan, 2002); Moncef Marzouki, *Le mal arabe: entre dictatures et intégrismes: La démocratie interdite* (Paris: L'Harmattan, 2004); and François Siino, *Science et pouvoir dans la Tunisie contemporaine* (Paris: Karthala, 2004). An excellent review essay of books critical of North Africa's "desperate regimes," including that of Tunisia, is found in Clement M. Henry, "North Africa's Desperate Regimes," *The Middle East Journal* 59, no. 3 (2005): 475–484.

For analyses of the UMA, see Ahmed Aghrout and Keith Sutton, "Regional Economic Union in the Maghreb," *Journal of Modern African Studies* 28, no. 1 (1990): 115–139; Claire Spencer, *The Maghreb in the 1990s: Political and Economic Developments in Algeria, Morocco, and Tunisia* (London: International Institute for Strategic Studies, 1993); and I. William Zartman, "The Ups and Downs of Maghrib Unity," in *Middle East Dilemma: The Politics and Economics of Arab Integration*, ed. Michael Hudson (New York: Columbia University Press, 1999).

Tunisia's experience with immigration to Europe is treated by Gildas Simon, *L'éspace des travailleurs Tunisiens en structures et fonctionnement d'un champ migratoire international* (Aix-en-Provence/Marseille, France: Edisud, 1979); Jean-Pierre Cassarino, *Tunisian New Entrepreneurs and Their Past Experiences* (London: Ashgate, 2000); and Sarah Collinson, *Shore to Shore: The Politics of Migration in Euro-Maghreb Relations* (Washington, DC: Brookings Institution, 1996). Trade issues are well treated in Béchir Chourou, "The Free-Trade Agreement Between Tunisia and the European Union," *The Journal of North African Studies* 3, no. 1 (spring 1998): 25–56. The most recent, mainly optimistic interpretation of Tunisia's relationship with Europe is Brieg Powel and Larbi Sadiki, *Europe and Tunisia: Democratization via Association* (London: Routledge, 2009).

INDEX

Abbas, Mahmoud, 343, 381, 389
Abbasid caliphate, 125, 207, 234
Abd al-Aziz (Ibn Saud), 94–96, 105–106,
    111–112, 114
Abd al-Ilah, 129
Abdallah, Crown Prince of Saudi Arabia,
    85–86, 97–99, 113, 115
Abdallah, Emir of Transjordan, 298,
    300–301
Abdallah ibn Saud Al Saud, 93
Abdallah II, King of Jordan, 303, 306–307,
    310–316
Abu Dhabi, 100, 185, 187–188, 193. *See
    also* United Arab Emirates
Abu Nidal, 444
Achamenian Empire, 50
Achour, Habib, 515–517
Aden, British occupation of, 207–209
Aden-Abyan Islamic Army (AAIA),
    224–225
Afghanistan, 1, 86, 288
Aflaq, Michel, 272–273
African Union (AU), 443–444
Agriculture
    Algeria, 488, 490–491
    arable land, 6(table)
    Egypt, 398–399, 402–403
    GDP percentage, 6(table)
    Iran, 70, 73
    Iraq, 131, 145–146, 150
    Israel, 328
    Jordan, 305
    Lebanon, 244
    Libya, 435, 437
    Morocco, 455, 461–462

    prehistoric Eastern Arabia, 161
    Saudi Arabia, 106
    Syria, 275
    Tunisia, 514–515
    Turkey, 24, 26
Ahmad Shah Qajar, 51
Ahmadinejad, Mahmoud, 49, 65, 75, 82, 87
al-Ahmar, Shaykh, 212
Al Khalifah (Bahrain), 174, 176
Al Moayad, Muhammad Ali Hassan,
    228–229
Al Thani (Qatar), 181
Al Wifaq (Bahrain), 178
Alawi Sharifian Empire, 448
Alawites, 256, 277, 447–448, 464
Alevi-Shi'a. *See* Shi'a Islam
Alexander the Great, 50, 423
Algeria
    civic associations, 495–497
    demographic indicators and
        information, 8(table), 482, 486, 500
    economic conditions and indicators,
        6(table), 485, 488–491, 501
    fertility rates, 7
    foreign policy, 502–504
    French colonialism, 449, 479–481, 504
    geography, 485–486
    historical background, 479–485
    Islamists, 493–495
    Libya's foreign policy, 440
    map, 480
    Morocco's foreign policy, 473
    nationalism, 480–482
    oil wealth, 6
    Polisario Front, 469
    political and economic prospects, 501

Algeria (*continued*)
  political culture, 480, 486–487
  political environment, dynamics and
    structures, 485–487, 491–501
  political indicators, 11(table)
  political liberalization, 497–500
  postindependence turmoil, 482–485
  social indicators, 9(table)
  Steadfastness Front, 284
  structural reform, 489–491
  Tunisia and, 519–520, 529–530
Algiers Accord (1975), 134, 153
Al-Qa'ida, 1, 98, 116, 138, 156, 212–214,
    224, 227, 230, 314–315, 353, 467,
    500
Al-Qa'ida in the Islamic Land of the
    Maghrib (AQIM), 500
Al-Qa'ida on the Arabian Peninsula
    (AQAP), 230
Aluminum production, 175, 192
Amini, Ali, 54–55
Amnesty International, 457
Amor, Mohamed Belhaj, 520–521
Ancient civilizations
  Algeria and the Maghrib region, 479
  Eastern Arabia, 161
  Egypt, 397
  Jordan, 298–299
  Lebanon, 233–235
  Libya, 423–424
  Persia, 49–51
  Tunisia, 509, 523
  Yemen, 205–206
Andalusians, 509
Anglo-Egyptian Treaty (1954), 403
Aoun, Michel, 254–255, 257–258, 260, 288
al-Aqsa intifada, 353, 386
al-Aqsa Mosque, 118
Arab Empire, 51, 124, 233, 267, 397–398,
    424, 509
Arab League, 262, 371, 439
Arab Maghrib Union (AMU), 440, 473,
    530
Arab-African Federation, 440
Arabia felix, 206
Arab-Israeli War (1947–1949), 368–369
Arab-Israeli War (1967), 97–98, 103, 133,
    250, 273–274, 276, 334, 372

Arab-Israeli War (1973), 164, 277, 284, 302,
    373, 409, 440. *See also* October War;
    Yom Kippur War
Arab-Israeli War (1982), 350
Arafat, Yasir, 251–252, 254, 290, 341, 343,
    353, 372, 380, 386
Arif, Abd al-Salam, 130–133
Armenia/Armenians, 44–45, 69, 241
Arms trading, 62, 84, 164, 358, 472
al-Arzuzi, Zaki, 272–273
al-Asad, Bashar, 257, 259, 262, 278–279,
    283, 290–295
al-Asad, Hafiz, 152, 253–254, 256, 274,
    277–279, 284, 286–290, 352–353
Assassinations and attempts, 41
  Abdallah, King of Jordan, 301, 369
  Egypt's Fouda, 406
  Egypt's Sadat, 405, 410, 417
  Faisal, 97
  Iran's exiles, 85
  Iran's president and prime minister,
    61–62
  Israel's Rabin, 339
  Lebanon's Hariri, 257–259, 262,
    293
  Libya's political enemies, 433
  PLO and Israel, 372–373
  Tunisia's Bourguiba, 514
  Turki ibn Abdallah, 93
  UAE rulers, 188
Association Accord (2000), 470
Assyrian community, 129
Aswan Dam, 408, 414–415
Ataturk, 16–19, 26–27, 31, 35, 39
Authoritarian regimes, 12
  Algeria, 483–484, 486–487, 491
  Egypt under Mubarak, 405
  Iran, 54, 57–59
  Iraq's structured democracy, 156
  Morocco's monarchy, 451–453
  Palestine Authority, 385, 388
  Syria under Asad, 278
  Tunisia, 512, 515, 521–522, 524,
    526–529
  Turkey, 17–19
Azerbaijan, 39, 44, 68, 86

Baghdad pact, 36
Baha'i faith, 49, 51, 69, 77–78
Bahceli, Devlet, 22

Bahrain
  Britain's treaty relationships, 164
  demographic indicators and
    information, 8(table), 174
  economic conditions and indicators, 6,
    6(table), 175
  geography, 173–174
  leadership changes, 164–165
  map, 162
  political environment, dynamics and
    structures, 10, 11(table), 173–179
  population, 7
  Shi'a majority, 69
  social indicators, 9(table)
Baker, James, 39, 470
al-Bakr, Ahmad Hasan, 133
Baku-Tbilisi-Ceyhan pipeline, 39
Balfour Declaration (1917), 321–322, 367
Bandar Report, 178
Bani-Sadr, Abol Hassan, 60–61
Bank of Commerce and Credit (BCCI)
    scandal, 194–195
Banking sector, 22–23, 28, 107, 194–195,
    436–439, 490
Barak, Ehud, 340, 353
Barcelona Process (1995), 471
Barzani, Massoud, 41, 134
Barzani, Mustafa, 131–132, 134
Basel Program, 321
Basri, Mohamed "Fkih," 456, 458, 460
Ba'th Party, 131–134, 138–142, 147–148,
    154, 156, 242, 251, 272–274,
    278–279
Bazargan, Mehdi, 59–60, 75–76, 82
Bedouins, 99–100, 167
Begin, Menachem, 337, 349, 417
Ben Ali, Zine al-Abidine, 518–523, 526,
    528–529, 531
Ben Bella, Ahmed, 483, 495
Ben Salah, Ahmed, 512–516, 519
Ben Siddiq, Ibrahim, 454
Ben Youssef, Salah, 513
Bendjedid, Chadli, 484–485, 488–489,
    497–500
Berber tribes, 447, 449, 464, 479, 486,
    496–498
Biden, Joseph, 433
Bin Ladin, Usama, 98, 138
Birri, Nabih, 253, 255

Bitar, Salah al-Din, 272–273
Black market, Algeria's, 489
Boumediene, Houari, 483–484, 488
Bourguiba, Habib, 511–519, 522–525, 529
Bouteflika, Abdelaziz, 473, 491–493,
    499–501, 504
Bremer, L. Paul, 139–140
Britain
  Baghdad pact, 36
  Balfour Declaration, 321–322
  East India companies, 161–162
  Egypt occupation, 401, 413–414
  Iran, 51, 53, 66, 79, 87
  Iraqi colonial legacy, 123, 127–129
  Jordan, 297, 299–301, 316
  Kuwait and, 169–170
  Lebanon occupation, 238
  Libya, 425–426, 439
  mandate in Palestine, 321–323, 369
  Moroccan free trade with, 448
  Omani reunification, 198
  Ottoman occupation of the Levant, 237
  Saudi foreign relations, 95, 117
  Saudi monetary system, 107
  security in the Eastern Arabian states,
    201
  Suez Canal/Suez War, 399, 407–408
  Syrian revolt against the Ottomans,
    269–271
  Yemen bifurcation and occupation,
    207–210
Buraymi Oasis dispute, 100
Bush, George H.W., 137, 338, 351
Bush administration (George W.), 42, 87,
    138–139
  Arab-Israeli conflict, 343, 353
  foreign policy impact on the GCC
    states, 165
  Syria's hegemony in Lebanon, 257
  Syria's stance on terrorism, 292
Byzantine Empire, 50–51, 365

Cairo Accord (1969), 251
Cairo Conference, 417
Camp David Accords, 98, 285, 349–350,
    353, 379–381, 416–417, 441
Carter administration, 38, 55, 57, 83,
    417–418
Central Intelligence Agency (CIA), 54
Chamoun, Camille, 249, 260
Chemical weapons, 135, 444

Cherikha-ye Fedayan-e Khalq (Iran), 56
Chihabs, 235
China, 86, 104, 131, 283–284, 356, 469
Christian population, 5, 235
    Ba'thism, 138
    Egyptian Copts, 397
    Iran's Christian population, 69
    Iraq's Nestorian Christians, 129, 146
    Israel, 333
    Jordan, 304–305
    Lebanon, 233, 235–237, 239–240,
        250–251
    Ottoman Empire and, 15
    Palestine's Muslim-Christian cleavage,
        383–384
    Spanish conquest of Morocco, 447–448
    Syria, 277
    Yemen, 216
Ciller, Tansu, 21
Circassian population, Jordan, 304–305
Citizenship rights
    colonial Algeria, 481
    Israeli Arabs, 326–327
    Kuwaiti suffrage, 171
    Palestinians in Israel and Jordan, 304,
        370
    Saudi Arabia, 104
    Turkey, 25
Civil conflict, 210, 279, 519–520
Civil society organizations
    Algeria, 495–497
    Bahrain, 178
    Iran, 79
    Morocco, 468
    Oman's free association laws, 199
    Palestine, 385
    Tunisia, 528–529
    UAE's association ban, 191
    See also Political participation
Civilian control, Turkey's, 34
Clinton administration, 85, 289–290,
        352–353, 379–380
Cold War. See Soviet Union
USS Cole, 224, 229
Colonialism
    Algeria, 479–481, 504
    British rule in the Gulf, 163
    Egypt, 399
    Iraq, 123
    Libya, 424–425
    Morocco, 449–451

political systems following, 10–11
Syria, 270–272
Tunisia, 509–511
Comité Révolutionnaire d'Unité et
        d'Action (CRUA; Algeria), 481–482
Communism. See Socialism/communism
Comprehensive Nuclear Test Ban Treaty,
        442
Confessional democracy, Lebanon's,
        248–249
Consensus, constitutional: Israel, 330–331
Constitutional monarchy, Iraq as, 129–130
Constitutions. See Political structures
Consultative participation: Saudi Arabia,
        112–113
Coptic Christians, 397, 406, 409–410
Corruption
    Algeria, 484, 489
    Iran under Ahmadinejad, 65–66
    Israel's Olmert, 346
    Syria, 273
    Turkey's third republic, 21–23
    Yemen's kleptocracy, 221
Council of Guardians (Iran), 76, 80–81
Counterrevolutionary forces: Iran, 61–62
Coups d'état
    Algeria, 483, 489
    Cyprus, 37
    Egyptian Revolution of 1952, 401–403
    Fatah, 389
    Hizballah, 258
    Iran, 52, 54
    Iraq, 130, 132–133
    Libya, 428–429
    Morocco, 453–454
    Oman, 198
    Qatar, 164, 182
    Syria, 273–274
    Turkey, 19–20, 22, 27–28
    See also Rebellions and revolutions
Crimes against humanity: Algeria's military,
        492–493
Cuban Missile Crisis (1962), 36
Cultural revolution, Libya's, 431
Cyprus, 20, 23, 34–38

Date cultivation, 161
De-Ba'thification, 140–142
Demirel, Suleyman, 19–21

Democratization, 28, 38, 63–64, 80, 123, 151–152, 155, 220, 229–230, 248–249, 303, 384, 444, 526
Demographic indicators and information. *See under specific countries*
Dervish orders, 25
Desalination system, 100, 490
Destour party (Tunisia), 511
Destourian Socialist Party (Tunisia), 512, 514–516
Development, economic. *See* Economic conditions and indicators *under specific countries*
Dictatorial regimes, 12
al-Din, Fouad Saraj, 404–405
Druze: Lebanon, 234–235, 237, 239–240, 242–243, 249–251, 253–254, 257, 262
Druze: Syria, 277
Dubai, 186–188, 192
Dutch East Indies, 161–162
Dynastic monarchism, 165

East Indies, 161–162
Eastern Arabian States, 161–165, 200–202. *See also* Bahrain; Kuwait; Oman; Qatar; United Arab Emirates
Ecevit, Bulent, 19–23, 35
Economic conditions and indicators, 5–7. *See also* Oil industry; Political economy; *specific countries*
Economic crises, 28, 187–188, 194, 222–223, 330, 461, 463
Economic diversification, 175, 197
Education
    Iran's social change, 71
    Iraq's social structure, 146
    Libya, 436
    Palestinian university system, 376
    Qatar, 180–181
    Tunisia, 511, 523–524
    Yemeni Islamic control, 225
Egypt
    Arab-Israeli War (1973), 284
    Camp David negotiations, 349–350
    decline of secularism and liberalism, 406–407
    demographic information, 400, 412
    economic conditions and indicators, 411–413
    foreign policy, 407–410, 413–419
    geography, 412
    historical background, 397–403
    Iran's foreign policy, 86
    Iraq's foreign policy, 131–132
    Jordan's foreign policy, 302
    Libya's foreign policy, 439–441
    map, 398
    military-based regime, 407
    nationalism, 4–5
    PLO, 373
    political environment, dynamics and structures, 400–401, 403–406
    political indicators, 11(table)
    political opening, 277
    political system, 10
    Saudi foreign policy, 118
    social indicators, 9(table)
    Syrian foreign policy, 288
    UAE judiciary, 190
    UAR creation, 274
    urbanization rate, 7
Egypt-Israel Peace Treaty (1979), 288, 350, 376–377, 416, 441
Eisenhower, Dwight, 54
El Fassi, Abbas, 466
Election fraud, 49, 54–55, 60, 66–67, 77, 80, 405–406, 455, 457–458
Elections
    Algeria, 484, 492–493, 495, 496(table), 497–500
    Bahrain, 177
    Hamas success, 381, 389–390
    Iran, 61–67, 80–82
    Iraq, 142, 155
    Israel, 336–347
    Jordan, 308–313
    Kuwait, 170
    Lebanon, 259
    Morocco, 452–453, 457, 459, 465–466
    Palestine, 345
    Qatar, 182
    Syria, 272, 274, 279
    Tunisia, 514, 519, 527–528
    Turkey, 18–23, 28–30, 43–44
    US election of George W. Bush, 138
    Yemen, 212–213, 219
Electoral code, Algeria's, 497–498
Elite conflict, Palestinians, 385–387
Embargoes, 37–38, 53–54, 106–107, 118

Emergency law, Syria's, 279–280
Employment. *See* Jobs
Energy sector. *See* Oil industry
Ennahda (Algeria), 495, 496(table), 499
Entrepreneurial talent, 243, 437
Enver Pasha, 17
Environmental degradation, Iraq's, 145–146
Equity and Reconciliation Commission
    (IER), 459
Erbakan, Necmettin, 19, 21–22
Erdogan, Recep Tayyip, 23, 34–35, 41–42
Eritrea, 226, 228
Ethiopia, 228
Ethnic loyalties and divisions, 4–5
    Algeria, 486, 496–497
    Arab Israelis, 325–326
    Iran, 60, 68–69
    Iraq, 123, 142, 144–146
    Israel, 337, 344
    opposition to French rule in Syria, 271
    Persia, 50
    Saudi Arabia, 103–104, 109
    Tunisia, 522–523
    Turkey, 16–18, 24–25, 27–28, 34
    Yemen, 217
    See also Kurds
Ethnocentricity, 109
EU Association Accord, 468
European Union (EU)
    Algeria-EU free-trade agreement, 491
    Iran and, 85, 87
    Israel's relations with, 355–356
    Jordan's foreign policy, 306–307
    Libya's foreign policy, 443
    Morocco and, 462, 470–471
    Saharan Arab Democratic Republic,
      469
    Tunisia's free trade area, 520
    Tunisia's pro-Western policy, 531
    Turkey's candidacy, 23, 28–29, 35, 38,
      40, 43–45
Evian Accords (1962), 482
Evren, Kenan, 20
Executive power. *See* political system *under*
    specific countries
Exile communities, 79, 151, 156
Export-led economic growth, 26

Fahd, King of Saudi Arabia, 97–99, 109,
    112, 117

Fahd Plan for Arab-Israeli peace, 98
Failing state, Yemen as, 231
Faisal, King of Iraq, 298
Faisal, King of Saudi Arabia, 93, 96–98,
    105, 107–108, 119
Faisal, King of Syria, 269–271
Fakhr Al Din Ma'n, 235
Family loyalties and connections, 5, 72,
    103–105, 114, 147, 217, 243, 249,
    459
Family planning, 71
Farouk, King of Egypt, 401–402
Fatah movement, 345, 372, 377, 381, 385,
    387, 389–390
Faysal, King, 128–129
Federalism, 155, 189, 426–429
Federation of Arab Republics, 439–440
Felicity Party (Turkey), 23, 33
Fertile Crescent, 3–4
Fertility rates, 7, 8(table)
Fez, Treaty of (1912), 449
Fikri, Youssef, 467
Fishing industry, 161, 165–166, 216, 462
Foreign investment, 149, 194–195, 223,
    283, 488–489, 516
Foreign policy
    Britain in the Trucial States, 163
    Eastern Arabian States, 200–202
    See also under specific countries
France
    Algerian colonial history, 448, 479–482,
      504
    Iran's nuclear program, 87
    Jordanian territory, 297
    Lebanon and, 237–238, 245–246
    Libya's foreign policy, 425–426, 439,
      442
    Morocco's colonial history, 449–451
    Morocco's foreign policy, 471
    Napoleonic France's designs on the
      Middle East, 162
    occupation of Egypt, 399
    Saudi monetary system, 107
    Suez War, 407–408
    Syrian occupation, 270–272
    Tunisia's colonial history, 509–511,
      513–515
    Turkey and, 32, 43
Franco, Francisco, 449, 471
Franjiyah, Sulayman, 251–252

Frankish peoples, 235
Free French, 238
Free Officers Movement (Egypt), 401–403
Free Party (Turkey), 17
Free-trade agreements, 179, 463, 468, 491
Front de Libération Nationale (FLN;
    Algeria), 481–485, 491, 493–495,
    496(table), 497–500
Front of Islamic Salvation (FIS; Algeria),
    493–495, 498–499
Fuad II, King of Egypt, 401–402

Gas resources, 180–181, 435, 443, 471
al-Gaylani, Rashid Ali, 129
Gaza Strip, 335, 339, 342–346, 349, 351,
    370, 375, 379–384, 389–390. *See also*
    Palestinians
General Union of Moroccan Workers, 465,
    468
Geography. *See under specific countries*
Germany, 43, 87, 328–329
Ghanim, Shukri, 439
Ghannouchi, Rachid, 518–519, 526
al-Ghazal, Daif, 433
Ghazi, King, 129
Global recession, 187–188, 194, 330
Global war on terrorism, 1, 165, 225,
    228–229, 291–292, 316–317, 504
Golan Heights, 275–276, 350
Gorbachev, Mikhail, 288, 358
Government. *See political system under
    specific countries*
Greece, ancient, 50
Greece, modern, 17, 20, 35–38, 40, 439
Greek Catholics: Lebanon, 241
Greek Orthodox Church, 277, 305
Green Book (Qaddafi), 429, 438
Green March, 454–455, 468
Guerrilla organizations, 56, 58–59, 79, 87,
    132, 372, 469, 512–513
Guiga, Driss, 517–518
Gul, Abdallah, 23, 41, 43
Gulenists, 29
Gulf Cooperation Council (GCC), 154,
    164, 227
Gulf War (1991), 21, 84, 98, 141, 182,
    282–283, 306, 338, 351, 379,
    519–520, 529

Hadhrami group, 104
Hafsid dynasty, 509
Hajj pilgrimage, 84, 101–102, 104,
    106–107
al-Hakim, Muhammad Baqr, 145
Hamad, Crown Prince of Qatar, 164
Hamad bin Jasim Al Thani, 181–183
Hamad ibn Isa Al Khalifa, 176–177
Hamas, 1, 42, 86, 312, 354, 380–381, 385,
    387, 389–390
Hanbali school of Islamic jurisprudence,
    91, 106, 180
Haram Mosque, Makkah, 97, 102
Hariri, Rafik, 244–245, 255–259, 262, 293
Hariri, Saad, 259–260
Hashemi, Mehdi, 62
Hashimite kings, 128, 269. *See also* Jordan,
    Hashimite Kingdom of
Hassan, King of Morocco, 452–458, 463,
    469, 471–472
Hassi Mas'ud Treaty, 440
al-Hawrani, Akram, 273
Hawwalah: Bahrain, 174
Helou, Charles, 250
Herzl, Theodor, 321
Hijaz region, 95–96, 101, 104, 116–117,
    206–207, 300, 424
Historical background. *See under specific
    countries*
Hizballah, 1, 83–84, 86, 242, 249, 256,
    258–259, 346–347
Holland, 161–162
Holocaust denial, 87
Hostages, 60, 62, 82–83, 444
al-Houthi, Husayn, 213
Houthi Rebellion (Yemen), 213, 226–227
Hoveida, Amir Abbas, 57–58
Hrawi, Ilyas, 255
Human rights record
    Algeria, 481, 492–493
    Bahrain, 178
    Iran, 57, 67
    Morocco, 456–458, 461, 471
    Oman, 199–200
    Qatar, 185
    Tunisia, 521–522, 526–527, 531
    Turkey, 34, 38
    UAE, 190–191

Husayn, Saddam, 40, 133–138, 147–148, 150, 152–154, 164, 173, 255, 284–285, 288, 519–520
Husayn (Muslim saint), 92, 124
Hussein, King of Jordan, 290, 301–303, 308, 352, 408
Huyser, Robert, 59

Ibadi Islam, 5, 196
Ibn Rashid, 94–95
Ibn Saud, 94–95
Ibrahim, Abdallah, 452
Ibrahim Pasha, 93
Identity, national
    Algeria's political history, 479, 481
    Iran's geography protecting, 67–68
    Iraqi Ba'thists, 139
    National pact threatening Lebanon's, 250
    Saudi Arabs, 116–117
    Tunisia, 524–525
    Turkey, 27–28
    See also Ethnic loyalties and divisions; Tribal loyalties and divisions
Ideology, 30–32, 56, 115–116, 138, 387
Idris al-Mahdi al-Sanusi, 424–428, 439
Idrissids, 424–425, 447
Ikhwan (warriors), 95
Immigrants/immigration
    demographics and social conditions, 7
    Israel, 329, 358
    Jewish Law of Return, 325
    Jews to Palestine, 366–367
    Moroccan-Spanish relations, 472
    Saudi Arabia, 104–105
Import-substituting industrialization, 19, 26
Independence
    Algeria, 481–485
    Iran under Pahlavi rule, 53
    Iraq, 142
    Israel, 368
    Lebanon, 238, 241–242, 286–287
    Morocco, 449, 451–453
    political indicators by country, 11(table)
    Sudan, 413–414
    Syria after French rule, 272, 286–287
    Tunisia, 511, 513
India, 163–164, 356
Indirect rule, Iraq's, 128
Industrialization
    Algeria, 488

industry as percentage of GDP, 6(table)
    Iran, 70
    Iraq, 149–150
    Israel, 328–329
    Lebanon, 244
    Libya, 435–437
    Morocco, 462
    Turkey, 26
Infant mortality rates, 8, 9(table), 71
Infitah (economic opening), 516
Inonu, Ismet, 17–19, 31, 37
Institutional reforms, Algeria's need for, 501
Institutionalism, 12, 114–115
Intermarriage of Alevis and Sunnis, 25
International Atomic Energy Agency (IAEA), 87
International Monetary Fund/World Bank programs
    Algeria, 485
    Egypt, 413
    Iran, 74
    Jordan, 306
    Morocco, 461, 463
    Syria, 283
    Turkey, 20, 23, 26–27, 35
    Yemen, 210–211, 222, 229–230
Internet, 9, 71, 79–80
Intifada, 329–330, 351, 377–379, 386, 441
Iran, Islamic Republic of
    Baghdad pact, 36
    demographic information, 52
    economic conditions and indicators, 6(table), 65, 70, 73–75, 81
    fertility rates, 7
    foreign policy, 82–88
    geography of, 4, 67–68
    Iran-Iraq War, 134–136
    Iraq's foreign policy, 153
    Islamic radicalism, 59–62
    Lebanese factionalization, 259
    map, 50
    moderation, 62–65
    1978–1979 revolution, 57–59, 70–76, 153, 164, 285
    oil wealth, 6
    Pahlavi era, 52–56
    Persian empires, 49–51
    political culture, 71–73
    political environment, dynamics and structures, 60, 63–64, 70–71, 75–82
    political indicators, 11(table)

political system, 10
radical resurgence after moderates,
    65–67
religious and linguistic loyalties and
    divisions, 5
Saddam's invasion of, 285
Saudi-Iranian relations, 120
security in the Eastern Arabian states,
    201
social change, 69–71
social indicators, 9, 9(table)
Turkey's strategic importance, 39
Iran-Contra Affair (1985–1986), 62, 84
Iran-Iraq War (1980–1988), 38–39, 63, 74,
    135–136, 153–154, 164, 254, 288,
    418
Iraq, Republic of
Arab-Islamic conquests, 124–125
Baghdad pact, 36
Ba'th Party rule, 133–134
British mandate, 127–129
colonial history, 123
constitutional monarchy, 129–130
demographic indicators and
    information, 8, 8(table), 126, 142,
    144
economic conditions and indicators,
    6–7, 6(table), 148–151
foreign policy, 131, 152–154
future challenges and options, 155–157
geography, 123–124, 142
historical background, 123–142
Iran-Iraq War, 39, 135–136
Iran's foreign policy, 83–84, 86
Israel as target of Scud missiles, 338
map, 124
non-oil economic sectors, 149–151
Ottoman rule, 125–127
political environment, dynamics and
    structures, 131, 134, 138–152
political indicators, 11(table)
political system, 10
republican period, 131–133
Saddam years, 135–137
Saudi-Iraqi Neutral Zone, 100
Saudis' 19th-century sacking of, 92
Shi'a majority, 69
social indicators, 9(table)
social structure, 146–147
Syrian foreign policy, 288
Turkey's foreign policy, 44
Turkey's Kurdish unrest, 21

US-Turkish relations, 40–42
See also Kuwait, Iraqi invasion of
Iraq, US invasion of, 23–24, 137–142
Algerian position on, 504
GCC states' relationship with US, 165
Iran-US tensions resulting from, 64
Jordan's stance, 316–317
reconstruction, 151
security in the Eastern Arabian states,
    201
Yemeni foreign policy and, 229
Iraq Petroleum Company (IPC), 131
al-Iryani, Abd al-Rahman, 208
Islam. *See* Religious loyalties and divisions;
    Shi'a Islam; Sunni Islam
Islamic Action Front (IAF; Jordan), 311,
    316
Islamic Government (Khomeini), 76
Islamic Salvation Army (Algeria), 494
Islamic Salvation Front (Morocco), 472
Islamic Supreme Council (Iraq), 144–145
Islamism
Algeria, 492–495, 498–499
Bahrain, 178
Egypt's Copts and, 409–410
Iran, 56, 71
Jordan's parliament, 312–313
Kuwait, 172
Morocco, 449, 455–456, 464–467
Qatar, 183
Saudi Arabia's marginalized youth,
    98–99
Tunisia, 517–520, 523, 525
Turkey, 19–20, 23
Yemen, 212
See also Radicalism
Ismail, 51
Israel
alliances and friends, 355–360
constitution, 12
demographic indicators and
    information, 8(table), 324
economic conditions and indicators,
    6(table), 328–330
Egypt-Israel Peace Treaty, 288, 350,
    376–377, 416–417, 441
Egypt's foreign policy, 418
Faisal's Palestinian support, 97–98
foreign and security policies, 347–355
geography, 3
Hamas in Gaza, 381–382, 389–390

Israel (*continued*)
    historical background, 321–324
    Hizballah coup, 258
    Iran's relations with, 66, 79, 84–87
    Jordanian relations, 301, 303, 313,
        315–316
    Lebanese security zone, 256
    Lebanon raids, 244–245
    Lebanon's foreign policy, 261
    map, 322
    Morocco's efforts to develop Arab ties
        with, 473
    1982 invasion of Lebanon, 252,
        286–287, 374, 377, 417
    occupation of West Bank and Gaza
        Strip (1967–1993), 375–379
    Oslo peace process, 380–381
    Palestinian foreign policy, 390–391
    Palestinian intifada, 377–379
    Palestinian-Israeli hostilities causing
        migration to Lebanon, 250–251
    PLO negotiations, 374–375
    political and military crises, 1
    political dimensions, 336–347
    political environment, dynamics and
        structures, 12, 324–327, 330–331,
        333–335
    political indicators, 11(table)
    religion and the state, 327–328
    Saudi-US relations, 118
    social indicators, 9, 9(table)
    South Lebanese Army and Hizballah,
        242
    Suez War, 407–408
    Syria's assertive anti-Israel policy, 274,
        286
    Syria's response to the creation of, 281
    territorial disputes with Syria, 275
    Tunisia's foreign policy, 530–531
    Turkey's diplomatic ties, 38
    withdrawal from Lebanon, 290
Israel Defense Force (IDF), 324, 335, 346,
    354
Israeli-PLO Declaration of Principles
    (1993), 289
Istiqlal Party (Morocco), 451–453,
    456–458, 464–465
Italian Peace Treaty (1947), 425
Italy, 424, 511

Jadid, Salah, 274, 277
al-Jahmi, Fathi, 433

Japan, 86, 306
Jerusalem, Kingdom of, 235
Jews, 5, 69, 146, 216, 277, 366–367, 461,
    522. *See also* Israel
Jobs
    Algeria, 483, 490
    Bahrain, 174–175
    demographic and social conditions, 7
    Iran, 70
    Iraq, 146–147, 149–151
    Saudi Shi'a skilled labor, 104
    Syrian labor force expansion, 283
    UAE human rights abuses, 190–191
Johnson, Lyndon B., 37, 414–415
Jordan, Hashimite Kingdom of
    demographic indicators and
        information, 8(table), 300, 304
    economic conditions and indicators,
        6(table), 305–307
    foreign policy, 315–317
    geography, 303–305
    historical background, 297–303
    liberalization and deliberalization,
        310–315
    map, 298
    Madrid peace conference, 289
    Palestinian refugees, 371
    PLO, 251, 372
    political environment, dynamics and
        structures, 301, 303–305, 307–310
    political indicators, 11(table)
    political system, 10
    Saudi Arabian geography, 102
    social indicators, 9, 9(table)
    Syrian foreign policy, 285–286
    UAE migrant labor, 192
Judicial systems
    Bahrain, 179
    Egypt, 406
    Iran's constitutional reform, 77–78
    Israel, 327–328, 333
    Lebanon, 245–246
    Morocco, 461
    Oman, 199
    Qatar, 185
    Saudi Arabia, 99, 109–110
    Syria, 278–279
    Turkey, 30, 34
    UAE, 190
Jumayyil, Amin, 252–254
Jumayyil, Bashir, 252
Jumblat, Kamal, 249–251

Jumblat, Walid, 253, 257–261
Justice and Development Party (AKP; Turkey), 23, 28–29, 33–34, 42–44

Kabylie region, Algeria, 496–497
Kadima Party (Israel), 344–345, 347
Kazakhstan, 39
Kemal, Mustafa (Ataturk), 16–19, 26–27, 31, 35, 39
Kemalism, 30–32, 35
Kennedy administration, 36, 414–415
Kenya, 356
Khaddam, Abd al-Halim, 293–294
Khalid, King of Saudi Arabia, 97
Khalifah Bin Hamad Al Thani, 182
Khamenei, Ali, 62–63, 66–67, 76, 80, 82, 86
Kharjism, 196
Khatami, Mohammad, 63–66, 73, 75, 79, 81, 85–86
Khobar Towers bombing, 85
Khomeini, Mostafa, 57, 59
Khomeini, Ruhollah, 55–58, 60–63, 72, 75–76, 84, 145, 153, 285
Kidnappings, 224–225, 258, 346, 354
Kissinger, Henry, 415–416
Kleptocracy, Yemen as, 221
Knesset (Israel), 331–337, 339, 341–343, 347, 350, 352
Ksar Said, Treaty of, 509–510
Kurdish Democratic Party (KDP; Iraq), 134, 150
Kurdish Regional Government (KRG; Iraq), 141
Kurdish Workers Party (PKK), 39–40, 42, 44, 154
Kurds
    British mandate in Iraq, 128–129
    Iran, 53, 68
    Iran-Iraq War, 135–136
    Iraq, 132, 134, 137, 141–142, 144–145, 151–152, 154
    Turkey, 20–21, 24–25, 27–28, 31–32, 34, 39–41, 43–44
Kutla al-Amal al-Watani (Morocco), 451
Kuwait
    Arab-Israeli conflict, 277–278
    British treaty system, 163
    demographic indicators and information, 7, 8(table), 166–168

dynastic monarchism, 165
economic conditions and indicators, 6(table)
GCC creation, 164
geography, 165–166
Iraq's future foreign policy options, 157
Iraq's refusal to recognize, 132
map, 162
oil wealth, 6
political environment, dynamics and structures, 165–173
political indicators, 11(table)
political system, 10
Saudi-Kuwaiti Neutral Zone, 100
social indicators, 9(table)
Yemen's foreign policy, 226–227
Kuwait, Iraqi invasion of, 136, 154
    Arab-Israeli conflict and, 351
    Egypt's stance, 418
    GCC states' support of Saddam, 164
    impact on Kuwait, 168
    Jordan's dilemma over, 302–303
    PLO presence, 374
    Saudi concerns over, 98
    Syrian support of the US-UN coalition, 288–289
    Tunisia's response to, 519–520
    Turkey's foreign relations, 39–40
    Yemen's stance, 226

Labor migration, 7, 105, 167, 173, 187, 192, 196–197, 455–456
Labor Party (Israel), 336–339, 341–342, 344, 349, 351–353
Labor unions, 465, 468, 483, 490, 513, 516
Lahoud, Emile, 245, 256–257, 259, 292
Land reform, 402, 454, 523
Language
    Algeria, 486
    Egypt's Copts, 397
    Iran's political and social geography, 68
    origins of Arabic, 116–117
    Persian speakers, 5
    Rosetta stone, 397–398
    Tunisia's social reforms, 523
    Turkey, 25, 34
    Yemen, 217
Law of Return, Israel's, 325
Lawrence, T.E., 95
League of Arab States, 530–531

Lebanon
    Bashar's involvement in Lebanese
        politics, 292–293
    demographic indicators and
        information, 8(table), 236, 239–240
    economic conditions and indicators,
        6(table), 243–245
    fertility rates, 7
    foreign policy, 260–263
    geography, 238–239, 260
    historical background, 233–238
    Iran's radicals attacking American
        targets, 83
    Israel's 1982 invasion of, 252, 286–287,
        350, 374, 377, 417
    Israel's 2000 withdrawal from, 353
    Israel's Second Lebanon War, 354
    map, 234
    Palestinian refugees, 370
    PLO presence, 372–373
    political environment, dynamics and
        structures, 238–243, 245–260
    political indicators, 11(table)
    social indicators, 9(table)
    Trans-Arabian Pipeline (TAPLINE),
        103
    Turkey's diplomatic overtures to Syria,
        42
Legal systems, 110, 173, 185, 190, 248, 308
Levy, David, 340
Liberalism, 30–32, 511, 515
Liberalization
    economic, 26–27, 168–169, 179, 184,
        281–283
    political, 182, 310–315, 406–407,
        497–500
Liberation Movement (Iran), 56–58, 72
Libya
    demographic indicators and
        information, 8(table), 423, 426
    economic conditions and indicators,
        6(table), 433–439
    foreign policy, 439–444
    geography, 423
    historical background, 423–429
    map, 424
    Morocco's foreign policy, 455–456, 473
    oil wealth, 6–7
    Polisario Front, 469
    political environment, dynamics, and
        structures, 427–439
    political indicators, 11(table)

political system, 10
    social indicators, 9, 9(table)
    Steadfastness Front, 284
    Tunisia's foreign policy, 529–530
Life-expectancy rates, 8, 9(table)
Likud Party (Israel), 337–342, 344, 349,
        352, 373, 376, 380
Linguistic loyalties and divisions, 5
Literacy rates, 8, 9(table), 26, 55, 436, 524
Livni, Tzipi, 345–347
Lloyd George, David, 270
Lockerbie, Scotland, 438, 441–442
Lomé summit, 444

Madani, Abassi, 494
al-Madinah pilgrimage, 92–93, 101–102,
        116–117
Madrid Accord (1975), 468
Madrid peace conference (1991), 289, 351,
        379
Maghreb, 3, 509, 530–531. *See also* Algeria;
        Libya; Morocco; Tunisia
Maghrib-Europe Gas (MEG) pipeline, 471
Mahmud II, Sultan, 127
Makhzen (Morocco's political, economic,
        military system), 464, 470
Makkah, 84, 92–93, 97, 101–102, 104,
        106–107, 116–117
al-Maliki, Nuri, 142, 156
Management and Planning Organization
        (Iran), 75
Mandates, British, 128–129, 321–323, 369
Mansur, Hassan Ali, 56
Manufacturing, 26, 435, 462–463
Marhaba, Opération, 463
Maritime industry, 161–162
Maritime Peace in Perpetuity, Treaty of
        (1838), 163
Market-driven economies, 193–194, 209,
        283, 488–489, 491
Maronite Christians: Lebanon, 233,
        235–242, 246, 249, 251, 254,
        260–261, 285, 288
Marsa, Treaty of (1883), 510
Marsh Arabs, 145–146
Martial law, 19, 54, 58–59, 310
Marxist-Leninist ideology. *See*
        Socialism/communism

Mauritania, 469
Media/media independence
    communication media as social
        indicators, 9
    Iran, 64, 77–79
    Jordan, 310, 313–314
    Kuwait, 172–173
    Lebanon, 247–248
    Morocco, 456, 461
    Qatar, 183
    Tunisia, 521
    Turkey, 29, 34
Mehlis, Detlev, 293
Merenids, 447
Merkel, Angela, 43
Mesopotamia, 123
Middle class, 70–71, 146–147
Middle East, defined, 3
Midhat pasha, 127
Migration. *See* Immigrants/immigration;
        Labor migration; Urbanization and
        urban migration
Military forces/military rule
    Algeria, 483, 491–493, 498, 501
    Bahrain, 179
    Egypt, 407
    Iraq, 133, 135–136, 139
    Lebanese Shi'a militias, 242
    Morocco's military and security
        structure, 467–468
    Morocco-US ties, 472–473
    Ottoman Empire, 15–16
    subduing protest in Tunisia, 517
    Turkey, 20–22, 24, 27–28, 30–31,
        33–34, 36
    Yemen, 208, 219
    See also Coups d'état
Military industry, Iraq's, 150
Millet system, 327–328
Modernization, 17, 52–53, 55, 98–99,
        107–108
Mofaz, Shaul, 341–342
Mohammad (prophet), 51, 69, 124, 277
Mohammad Reza Pahlavi, 53–56
Mojahedin-e Khalq (Iran), 56, 61, 71, 79
Monarchies
    Bahrain, 176
    dynastic monarchism, 165
    extended family loyalties, 5
    GCC states, 165
    indirect rule in Iraq, 128

Iraq's constitutional monarchy, 129–130
    Libya, 426–429
    Tunisian kingdom, 509
    Yemen, 207–208
    See also specific countries
Monetary and banking system, 107
Mongols, 51, 125
Morocco
    Berbers, 486
    coups, 453–454
    demographic indicators and
        information, 8, 8(table), 450
    economic conditions and indicators,
        6(table), 454–456, 461–464
    foreign policy, 454, 470–473
    geography, 459–460
    historical background, 447–459
    Iran's foreign policy, 84
    map, 448
    military and security structure,
        467–468
    nationalism, 449–451
    political culture, 460–461
    political environment, dynamics and
        structures, 452–454, 458–470
    political indicators, 11(table)
    political system, 10
    radical Islamism, 466–467
    social indicators, 9(table)
    Tunisia's foreign policy, 530
Mosaddeq, Mohammad, 53–54, 72
Motherland Party (Turkey), 20–22
Movement of Social Democrats (MDS;
        Tunisia), 517
Mubarak, Gamal, 405–406
Mubarak, Hosni, 405–407, 410, 413,
        417–418, 441
Muddawanna (family code), 459
Muhammad Ali, 268, 398
Muhammad Ben Yussuf (Muhammad V of
        Morocco), 451–452
Muhammad ibn Abd al-Wahhab, 91–93
Muhammad (prophet). *See* Mohammad
Muhammad VI, King of Morocco,
        458–461, 464–465, 468
Munich Olympics (1972), 372–373
Musavi, Mir Hossein, 62, 66
Muscat, 163
Muslim Brotherhood, 172, 178, 224, 287,
        311, 405–406, 432

Muwahhidin, 91–94
Mzali, Mohammed, 517–518

Naguib, Muhammad, 401–402
Najd region, 91–95, 101, 104
Napoleon, 397–398, 413
al-Nasser, Gamal Abd, 274, 402–404,
    407–408, 411–412, 415–416, 428
Nasserism, 133, 250
National Front (Iran), 55–59
National Independent Rally (NI), 465
National Liberation Front (Yemen), 209
National loyalties and divisions, 4–5
National Pact (1943; Lebanon), 241,
    246–247, 250
Nationalism, 416
    Algeria, 480–482, 487
    Cyprus, 37
    Egypt, 400–401
    Hussein's resistance to, 302
    Iran, 53, 71
    Iraq, 128, 130–132, 157
    Lebanese sectarianism, 241
    Morocco, 449–451
    Palestinian protest against the British
        Mandate, 367–368
    Syria, 268–269, 284
    Tunisia, 511
    Turkey, 16–17, 32
    Zionism, 321–322, 356–357, 367, 372,
        441
NATO (North Atlantic Treaty
    Organization), 36–38, 253, 467,
    472–473, 493, 531
Natural gas. *See* Gas resources
Neo-Destour Party (Tunisia), 511–512,
    514, 522–524
Netanyahu, Benjamin "Bibi," 332,
    340–342, 346–347, 352, 354
New majority, Lebanon's, 258, 262
New Wafd Party (Egypt), 404–405
Nezzar, Khaled, 498
9/11. *See* September 11, 2001
Nixon, Richard, 119, 415
No-fly zone, 40, 137, 256
Nomadic peoples, 4, 68–70, 99–100, 167
Nouira, Hedi, 515–517
Nour, Ayman, 405–406

Nuclear capability, 36, 87, 137, 150, 157,
    347, 442
Nusayris. *See* Alawites

Obama administration, 43, 88, 260, 294
Ocalan, Abdallah, 22, 28, 40
October War, 416. *See also* Arab-Israeli War
    (1973); Yom Kippur War
October Working Paper, 409
Oil embargo, 118–119
Oil industry
    Algeria's economic crisis, 488–489
    Bahrain, 175
    Baku-Tbilisi-Ceyhan pipeline, 39
    economic disparity among oil-
        producing countries, 6–7
    Egypt, 412
    fuel exports per capita, 6(table)
    Hajj economic impact, 101–102
    Iran, 53–54, 57, 70, 73–75
    Iran-Iraq War, 135
    Iraq, 131, 134, 148–149
    Jordan, 305–306
    Kuwait, 167–169
    Libya, 433–434, 436, 443, 455–456
    Morocco, 455–456, 460
    Oman, 197
    OPEC control, 106–107
    Qatar, 181
    Saudi Arabia, 96–98, 100, 105–108
    Syria, 277–278
    threats to the Gulf States, 164
    Trans-Arabian Pipeline (TAPLINE),
        103
    United Arab Emirates, 186–188,
        191–193
    Yemen, 216, 231
Oligarchy, Yemen as, 220–221
Olmert, Ehud, 345–346, 381
Olympic Games (1972), 372–373
Oman, Sultanate of
    British presence, 162–163
    Buraymi Oasis dispute, 100
    demographic indicators and
        information, 8(table), 195–196
    economic conditions and indicators,
        6(table)
    map, 162
    Muwahhidi defeat of, 92–93
    oil wealth, 6

political environment, dynamics and
    structures, 195–200
political indicators, 11(table)
political liberalization, 165
political system, 10
religious and linguistic loyalties and
    divisions, 5
social indicators, 9(table)
Yemen's foreign policy, 226–227
Omar, Jarullah, 212
Operation Cast Lead, 346, 354, 382
Operation Desert Storm, 98, 136, 164
Operation Peace for Galilee, 350
Operation Provide Comfort (OPC), 40
Organization of African Unity (OAU), 469
Organization of Economic Cooperation
    and Development (OECD)
    countries, 328
Organization of Petroleum Exporting
    Countries (OPEC), 106–107, 200
Oslo Accords and process, 339, 353,
    379–381, 384–386
Ottoman Empire, 15, 24–25, 36, 51
    Algeria's occupation by, 479
    British rule in Palestine, 322
    Egypt, 398–399
    emergence of modern Jordan, 299–301
    Hashimites' alliance with the British
        against, 297–298
    Iraq occupation, 123, 125–127
    Israel's religion-state conjunction,
        327–328
    Lebanese territorial state, 237–238
    Levant conquest, 234–237
    Libyan conquest, 424
    Morocco's resistance to, 447–448
    Muwahhidi defeat of, 92–93
    Palestinian occupation, 365–367
    political system, 15–17
    Saudi occupation, 93–95
    Syrian occupation, 267–270, 280
    Tunisia occupation, 509
    Yemen occupation, 207
Ozal, Turgut, 20–21, 26–27, 38–39

Pahlavi era, Iran, 52–56, 70
Pakistan, 36, 86, 163–164
Palestine Liberation Organization (PLO),
    251–252, 254, 261, 285–286, 290,
    342, 347, 350–351, 371–375,
    378–379, 385, 530–531

Palestinian Authority (PA), 385–388,
    390–391
Palestinians
    British Mandate, 321–324
    demographic indicators and
        information, 8(table)
    economic conditions and indicators,
        6(table), 378
    elite conflict, 385–387
    Faisal's support of, 97–98
    foreign policy, 390–391
    Hamas rule in Gaza, 389–390
    historical background, 365–382
    intifada, 326, 329–330, 351, 377–379,
        386, 441
    Iran's ties to, 86–87
    Israeli-Arab peace negotiations, 340,
        343–344
    Jordanian elections and, 312–314
    Jordan's West Bank annexation, 301
    Lebanon and, 240–242, 251–252, 261
    map, 366
    political economy, 387–388
    political environment, dynamics and
        structures, 382–387
    political indicators, 11(table)
    power imbalance of the PA, 388
    Saudi-US relations, 118
    social indicators, 9, 9(table)
Pamuk, Orhan, 34
Pan-Arabism, 152–153, 406–407. *See also*
    Nationalism
Parallel government, Iran's, 76
Paramilitary organization, Libya's, 432
Parties. *See* Political participation
Partition of Palestine, 118, 368
Pearling, 175
Pelt, Adrian, 425
Peres, Shimon, 332, 336–340, 343–344,
    347, 352, 473
Peretz, Amir, 344, 346
Persia, 10, 49–56, 68, 125–126, 174
Persian Gulf Arab countries, 3, 8. *See also*
    Bahrain; Kuwait; Oman, Sultanate
    of; Qatar; United Arab Emirates
Persian Gulf War. *See* Gulf War (1991)
Personal-status law, Iraq, 147
Philby, H. St. John B., 95, 106
Philosophy of the Revolution (Nasser),
    415–416

Phoenicians, 233, 243, 423–424

Phosphate exports, 454–455, 460, 462

Physical geography, 3–4

Pilgrimage, 84, 92–93, 101–102, 104, 106–107, 441

Pillars of Islamic faith, 110

Piracy, 162–163, 479

Polisario Front (Morocco), 455–456, 468–470

Political culture. *See under specific countries*

Political dynamics. *See under specific countries*

Political economy, 186–188, 191–195, 387–388. *See also* economic conditions *under specific countries*

Political environment. *See under specific countries*

Political Islam
  Egypt, 406–407
  Libya, 432–433
  response to Iran's White Revolution, 55
  Turkey, 27–28, 31–33, 43–44
  Yemen, 224–226
  See also Islamism

Political participation, 12
  Algeria, 486–487, 495
  Bahrain, 176
  Egypt's ban on parties, 402
  Iran, 54–55, 76–79
  Iraq's Ba'th Party, 132
  Israeli parties, 326, 334, 336–347
  Jordan's parliamentary system of representation, 310–311
  Kuwait's ban on parties, 172
  Lebanon, 240–241, 249
  Morocco, 451, 464–466
  Oman encouraging, 198
  political indicators by country, 11(table)
  Tunisia, 511, 527–528
  Turkey, 17–23, 27, 32–33
  Yemen's opposition, 212–213

Political structures, 11(table). *See also under specific countries*

Political systems, 9–12, 11(table). *See also under specific countries*

Population statistics, 7. *See also* demographic indicators and information *under specific countries*

Populism, 400, 487, 511

Poverty: social indicators by country, 8

Powell, Colin, 472

Precolonial political systems, 10

President for life, Tunisia's, 515, 521

Prisoners, political
  Bahrain, 176
  Egypt, 403
  Iran, 58–59
  Libya, 433
  Morocco, 456
  Syria, 258, 291
  Tunisia, 521, 526–527
  Turkey, 34
  Yemen, 227

Privateers, 162–163

Privatization, 75, 438–439, 490

Professional class, Iraq's, 146–147

Progress and Socialism Party (PPS; Morocco), 465

Progressive Republican Party (Turkey), 17

Protest and demonstrations
  Algeria, 485–487, 496–497
  Iran's reformist-centrist coalition, 66–67
  Iraq's constitutional monarchy, 130
  Israeli Arabs, 326
  Khomeini's allies demonstrating against the shah, 58
  Morocco, 454–457
  Palestinian intifada, 329–330, 351
  Tunisia, 516–518
  Yemen, 213
  See also Nationalism

Proto-Arab nationalism, 268

Provisional government, Algeria, 482–483

Qabus, Sultan, 198–199

al-Qaddafi, Muammar, 429–431, 434, 439, 441, 443, 455–456, 530

Qajar dynasty (Persia), 51

Qasim, Abd al-Karim, 130–132

Qatar
  bloodless coup, 164
  Britain's treaty relationships, 163–164
  demographic indicators and information, 8(table), 180
  economic conditions and indicators, 5, 6(table), 184
  GCC creation, 164
  map, 162
  oil wealth, 6
  political environment, dynamics and structures, 179–185
  political indicators, 11(table)

political system, 10
population, 7
social indicators, 9(table)
Yemen's foreign policy, 226–227
Qavam, Ahmad, 53

Rabin, Yitzhak, 289, 336, 338–339,
351–352
Radicalism, Iran's, 59–62, 65–67, 76,
80–83. *See also* Islamism
Radio and television, Saudi, 97
Rafsanjani, Akbar Hashemi, 61, 63, 65–67,
81, 84–86
Raja'i, Mohammad Ali, 61–62
Ras al-Khaymah, 162–164
Rashid Al Maktum, 192
Rebellions and revolutions
Algeria, 481–483, 487, 492–493
Egypt's 1952 revolution, 411–413
Iran, 49, 57–59, 70–76, 153, 164, 285
Iraq, 136, 152
Lebanon's war of liberation against
Syria, 254–255
Morocco's nationalist uprising, 451–453
Palestinian protest against the British
Mandate, 367–368
See also Coups d'état
Reconciliation commission, Morocco's,
459
Reformist movements, 72, 75, 81–82, 130,
290
Reforms
Syria's zigzag approach to economic
reforms, 281–284
Reforms: economic, agrarian, political,
judicial, legal
Algeria, 484–485, 488–489, 497–500
Bahrain's economic liberalization, 177
Egypt's agrarian reform, 403
Iran's constitutional reform, 63–64
Iraq, 131, 156
Jordan's economic adjustment, 306
Lebanon, 244–245, 250
Libya's religious reform, 430
Ottoman Empire, 15–16
Qatar's legal reforms, 185
Saudi Arabia, 97, 99
Syria under Bashar al-Asad, 291–295
Tunisia, 511, 515, 521–524
Turkey's economic and judicial reforms,
23, 29, 34–35, 38

Yemen's economic reforms, 210–211,
222–223, 229–230
Refugees, 39–40, 240–242, 250–251, 261,
304, 369–370, 383
Regional Command (Syria), 279
Religious freedom in Iran, 69, 77–78
Religious loyalties and divisions, 4–5
Ataturk's reforms, 17–19
Iran, 49, 68–69
Iraq, 147, 151–152
Israel, 327–328, 337
Jordan, 304–305
Lebanon, 239–240, 246
Palestine's Muslim-Christian cleavage,
383–384
pre-Islamic Turkey, 15
Tunisia, 522–523
Turkey, 18, 24–25, 27–28, 43–44
Yemen, 216
Remittances, Yemen's, 226
and rents, 219–221
Reparation to Algeria, 504
Republican Guard (Iraq), 136–137
Republican People's Party (Turkey), 17–18,
24
Resurgence Party (Iran), 55, 57–58
Revolutionary Council (Iran), 59–61
Revolutionary Guard (Iran), 78
Reza Khan Pahlavi, 52–53
Rezaie, Mohsen, 66
Rifian republic, Morocco, 449
Roman Empire, 51, 365, 423–424
Roosevelt, Franklin D., 117–118
Rosetta stone, 397–398
Rub' al-Khali ("Empty Quarter"), 3–4, 94,
100
Rural society, Iraq's, 146–147
Rushdie, Salman, 62, 84–85
Russia, 39, 43–44, 86, 288, 357, 469. *See
also* Soviet Union
Russia, imperial, 51

Sa'adeh, Antoun, 240–241
Saadians, 447–448
Sabaeans, 146
Sabah Al Ahmad Al Sabah, Shaykh, 171
Sabah family (Kuwait), 169
Sabri, Ali, 408–409
Sa'd Abdallah, Crown Prince Shaykh, 171

Sadat, Anwar, 349, 373, 404–405, 407–410, 412, 417, 441

al-Sadr, Muhammad Baqr, 144

Safavid Empire, 25, 51, 125

Sahara Desert, 3–4, 440, 444, 455–456, 463, 468–471, 485–486, 509

Saharan Arab Democratic Republic (SadR), 469–470

al-Sa'id, Nuri, 129–130

Salafism, 224, 268–269, 494

Salah al-Din al-Ayyubi, 235, 267

Salih, Ali Abdallah, 208, 210–211, 224–228, 231

al-Sallal, Abdullah, 208

Sampson, Nicos, 37

San Remo Conference (1920), 127–129

San'a Forum for Cooperation, 228

Sanctions, economic, 87, 137, 147

Sanusiya movement, 424–425

Sarkozy, Nicholas, 43, 262, 504

Sassanian dynasty, 50–51

The Satanic Verses (Rushdie), 62

Saudi Arabia
    Arab-Israeli conflict, 277–278, 284
    consultative participation, 112–113
    demographic indicators and information, 8(table), 94, 103–105
    economic conditions and indicators, 6(table), 96–98, 106–108
    foreign policy, 97–99, 116–120
    GCC creation, 164
    geography, 99–103
    Hashimites' expulsion, 297–298
    historical background, 91–98
    Iran's foreign policy, 84–86
    judicial branch, 109–110
    map, 92
    modernization, 98–99
    Moroccan foreign policy, 473
    oil wealth, 6
    physical geography, 4
    political culture, 108–109
    political environment, dynamics and structures, 99–105, 109–113, 115–120
    political indicators, 11(table)
    political process, 113–115
    political system, 10
    postwar era, 96–98
    social indicators, 9(table)

unification of Hijaz and Najd, 95–96
    Yemen and, 208, 210, 220, 227

Saudi Arabian Monetary Agency (SAMA), 107

Saudi-Iraqi Neutral Zone, 100

Saudi-Kuwaiti Neutral Zone, 100

Sayah, Mohammed, 517

Sazeman-e Ettel'at va Amniyat-e Keshvar (SAVAK), 54–55, 58–59

Secessionism, Yemen, 211, 228

Second Lebanon War, 354

Sectarian alliances, Lebanon's, 248–249, 253

Secularism
    Algeria, 487
    Egypt, 406–407
    Iran's 1978–1979 revolution, 57–58, 72
    Iraq's middle class, 147
    Israel, 327–328
    Tunisia, 520
    Turkey, 16, 27–28, 30–31, 43–44

Security policy, Israel's, 347–355

Selective liberalization, Syria's, 281–283

Seljuks, 15, 234

Separatist movements, 16–17, 25, 53

September 11, 2001, 28–29, 64, 86, 99, 118–119, 165, 212, 458, 504, 531. *See also* Terrorist activities and organizations

Shakespeare, W.H.I., 95

Shalit, Gilad, 354

Shamanism in pre-Islamic Turkey, 15

Shamir, Yitzhak, 337–339

Shamir Plan, 351

Shariati, Ali, 56

Sharif Hussein, 95

Sharjah, 187, 193

Sharon, Ariel, 335, 340–346, 353, 380–381

Shi'a Islam, 5
    Bahrain, 174–175, 177–178
    Ba'thism, 138
    Iran, 53, 59, 69, 71–72
    Iraq, 124–125, 129–130, 136–137, 141–142, 144, 151–152
    Kuwait, 166–167, 172
    Lebanon, 234–236, 240, 253
    Ottoman conquest of Iraq, 125–127
    Persia, 49
    Safavid dynasty, 51

Saudi population, 104
Saudis' hostility towards, 92–93
security in the Eastern Arabian states, 201
Sunni Islam and, 69
Turkey, 24–25
Yemen, 216, 242
Shipping, 161–162, 399
al-Shishakli, Adib, 273–274
Shuqayri, Ahmad Al, 371–372
Sinai II agreement, 416
Sinai-Suez War (1956), 414
Siniora, Fuad, 258–259, 262
Sistani, Ali, 145
Six Day War (1967), 348, 356, 358–359, 415
Slavery, 104, 184
Social change, 80–81, 131, 528
Social geography, 3–4
Social indicators, 9(table)
Social market economy, Syria's, 283
Social structure. *See under specific countries*
Socialism/communism, 31, 53–54, 56, 133, 209, 272–273, 278, 411–412, 430–431, 483–484, 487, 513–514
Somalia, 227–228
South Lebanese Army, 242
South Yemen, 209
Soviet Union
   Algeria's foreign policy, 504
   Egypt's foreign policy, 414–415
   Iran occupation, 53
   Iraq's foreign policy, 131, 152
   Israel's relations with, 357–358
   Jordan's policy shift, 315
   Libya and, 425–426, 442–443
   Saudis' antipathy to, 97–98
   Suez War, 408
   Syria's foreign policy, 284, 286
   Turkey and, 27–28, 36, 38–39
   Yemen and, 210, 224
   See also Russia
Spain, 447–449, 454–455, 459, 461, 468–469, 471
Stalemat , political, 460
Sta .ocal information. *See* demographic indicators and information *under specific countries*
Steadfastness Front, 284

Strikes, Algeria's, 495–496, 498
Structural adjustments. *See* International Monetary Fund/World Bank
Structured democracy, Iraq's, 151–152
Student demonstrations, 54, 60–61, 456–457
Succession, political, 133, 171, 188, 198, 231, 290, 484
Succession, royal, 110–111
Sudan, 86, 228, 413–414, 439
Suez Canal, 127, 209, 399, 407–410, 412–413
Suez War (1956), 407–408
Suffrage, 11(table), 171, 428
Sunni Islam, 5
   Bahrain, 174–175, 177–179
   Ba'thism, 138
   Iran's political and social geography, 69
   Iraq, 124–125, 139–140, 144, 151–152, 154
   Lebanon, 239–240, 247, 250–251, 257, 259–260
   Ottoman conquest of Iraq, 125–127
   Saudi Arabia, 91–93, 110
   Shi'a Islam and, 69
   Syria, 271, 277
   Turkey, 24–25
   Yemen, 216
Sykes-Picot agreement, 297
Syria
   Arab-Israeli War (1973), 373
   Ba'thism, 138
   coups, 273–274
   demographic indicators and information, 8(table), 270, 276
   economic conditions and indicators, 6(table), 278, 282
   foreign policy, 284–290
   French rule in, 270–272
   geography, 275
   Hariri assassination, 293
   hegemony in Lebanon, 244–245, 254–257
   historical background, 267–274
   Iran's foreign policy, 84, 86
   Iraq's foreign policy, 132
   Iraq's invasion of Kuwait, 418
   Iraq's resentment of, 124
   Israeli peace negotiations, 352–353
   Lebanon's relations with, 234, 247–248, 254–255, 262

Syria *(continued)*
  map, 268
  Palestinian–Lebanese tensions, 253–254
  PLO, 374
  political environment, dynamics and
    structures, 275–284
  political indicators, 11(table)
  Saddam's foreign policy, 152–153
  Saudi Arabian tribes, 102
  social indicators, 9, 9(table)
  Turkey's diplomatic overtures, 42
  under Bashar al-Asad, 290–295
  United Arab Republic, 403
  withdrawal from Lebanon, 257

Ta'if Agreement (1989), 247, 256
al-Takfir wal-Hijra (Exile and Flight;
    Morocco), 467
Talabani, Jalal, 41, 134, 141
Taliban, 86
Tangier Mediterranean Port, 462–463
Taqi al-Din Ahmad Ibn Taymiyyah, 91
Tawhid (monotheistic doctrine), 91
Telecommunications, 9, 9(table), 490
Term limits, 501, 521
Territorial disputes
  Iraq, 155–156
  Israel-Lebanon-Syria-Palestine,
    256–257, 275, 349–353, 375–376
  Jordan's West Bank annexation, 301
  Lebanon's lack of monopoly of force,
    261
  Morocco, 462, 472
  Western Sahara, 440, 444, 468–471
  Yemen, 226–227
Territorial expansion, 15, 93
Terrorist activities and organizations, 1
  AAIA kidnappings, 225
  al-Aqsa intifada, 343–344
  Algeria, 494–495, 504
  Iran, 58, 66, 83, 85–86
  Israel's Operation Cast Lead, 346, 354,
    382
  Libya, 438, 441–442, 444
  Morocco's bombings, 458–459, 467
  Palestinian attacks on Israel, 353–354
  Qatar's low levels of, 183
  Saudi Arabia, 98–99
  Tunisia's pro-Western policy, 531
  Turkey, 28–29, 42

US expectations of Syria's Bashar
    al-Asad, 291
US tensions with Iran, 64
Yemen, 212, 227, 229–230
See also Al-Qa'ida; Global war on
    terrorism; September 11, 2001
Timur the Lame, 125
Tlili, Abderrahmane, 520–521
Tlili, Ahmed, 513
Torture, 77, 190–191. *See also* Human
    rights record
Tourism, 175, 193–194, 463
Trade partnerships, 18, 43, 161–164, 187,
    306–307, 471, 520. *See also*
    demographic indicators and
    information *under specific countries*
Trans-Arabian Pipeline (TAPLINE), 103
Transitional Administrative Law (Iraq),
    140–141, 143
Treaty of Maritime Peace in Perpetuity
    (1838), 163
Treaty system, British, 163–164
Tribal loyalties and divisions, 4–5
  Algeria and the Maghrib region, 479,
    486
  Iran, 68–70
  Iraq, 137, 147
  Kuwait, 165–166
  Morocco, 447, 449
  Qatar, 184
  Saudi Arabia, 95, 99–100, 102
  tribal warfare in the Eastern areas, 163
  Turkey's Kurds, 25
  United Arab Emirates, 185
  Yemen, 10, 217
Trucial States, 163–164
Truman, Harry, 53, 118
Truman Doctrine, 36
Tudeh Party (Iran), 53, 56
Tunisia, Republic of
  authoritarianism and the PSD, 516–517
  Bourguiba's overthrow, 518–519
  colonial period, 509–511
  demographic indicators and
    information, 8(table), 512
  economic conditions and indicators,
    6(table), 516, 522–523, 528–529
  fertility rates, 7
  foreign policy, 529–531
  Gulf War and civil war with Algeria,
    519–520

historical background, 509–522
Libya's foreign policy, 440
map, 510
Morocco's relations with, 468, 473
multipartyism, 517–518, 520–521
PLO and, 374, 378–379
political culture and counterculture,
    522–523, 525
political environment, dynamics and
    structures, 513–514, 522–523,
    525–529
political indicators, 11(table)
political system, 513–514
post-independence, 512–522
social indicators, 9, 9(table)
social policies, 523–524
socialist system, 514
Turkey
    Armenian reconciliation, 44–45
    Baghdad pact, 36
    civil-military relations, 33–34
    cultural rights, 34
    demographic indicators and
        information, 8(table), 18, 24
    economic conditions and indicators,
        6(table), 20, 23, 26–27, 38
    foreign policy, 34–45
    geography, 24
    historical background, 15–24
    human rights record, 34, 38
    Iran's foreign policy, 86
    Iraq's post-Ba'th foreign policy, 154
    Libya's foreign policy, 439
    map, 16
    political environment, dynamics and
        structures, 19–20, 24–30, 32–35
    political indicators, 11(table)
    political prospects, 43–45
    political system, 15–17, 29–32
    religious and linguistic loyalties and
        divisions, 5
    Saudi alliance, 95
    Seljuk dominance in the Levant, 234
    social indicators, 9
    statistical information, 18
Turkic peoples, 5, 68
Turkmenistan, 39, 68, 154
Twelver Shi'as, 234, 236, 277

Uganda, 444
Umayyad caliphate, 124–125, 267
Umma Party (Kuwait), 172

Unification, Yemen's, 210–211, 219–220,
    226
Union for the Mediterranean, 471, 504
Union Socialist des Forces Populaires
    (USFP; Morocco), 454
United Arab Emirates
    creation of, 164
    demographic indicators and
        information, 8(table), 186
    economic conditions and indicators,
        6(table), 186–188, 192, 195
    GCC creation, 164
    Iran's foreign policy, 86
    map, 162
    oil wealth, 6
    political economy, 191–195
    political environment, dynamics and
        structures, 185–186, 188–191
    political indicators, 11(table)
    political system, 10
    social indicators, 9(table)
    Yemen's foreign policy, 226–227
United Arab Republic (UAR), 132, 250,
    274, 403
United Kingdom. *See* Britain
United Nations
    British Mandate in Palestine, 323
    Israel's relations with, 355
    Lebanese state monopoly of force,
        262
    Libya sanctions, 438
    Libya's Italian Peace Treaty, 425
    Mission for the Referendum in Western
        Sahara, 469–470
    Palestinian refugees in Jordan, 304
    Partition Plan, 357, 368
    Relief and Works Agency, 304
    Saddam's avoidance of, 137
    Saharan Arab Democratic Republic,
        469–470
    Security Council Resolution 338,
        351
    Security Council Resolution 425, 256,
        353
    Security Council Resolution 242, 118,
        348, 351
    Security Council Resolution 1559, 257,
        292–293
United States
    Afghanistan occupation, 1
    Algeria and, 493, 504
    Bahraini free-trade agreement, 179

United States (*continued*)
    Egypt and, 399–400, 405, 418
    GCC states' support of Saddam, 164
    Iran hostages, 60, 62, 82–83
    Iran under Pahlavi, 57
    Iran-Iraq War, 135
    Iran's emerging terrorist movements, 66
    Iran's foreign policy, 82–83, 85–88
    Iran's openness, 59
    Iran's political reform, 55
    Iran's radio broadcasts, 79
    Iran's tensions with, 64
    Iraq's Coalition Provisional Authority,
        139–142
    Iraq's foreign policy, 153–154
    Israeli foreign policy and peace
        negotiations, 352–353, 358–360
    Jordan's foreign policy, 306–307, 315
    Lebanon's relations with, 252–253, 262
    Libya's foreign policy, 438–439, 441
    Libya's Italian Peace Treaty, 425–426
    Morocco and, 460–461, 472
    oil shortage, 106–107
    Operation Desert Storm, 98, 136, 164
    PLO negotiations, 374
    Saharan Arab Democratic Republic, 469
    Saudi foreign relations, 117–120
    Saudi monetary system, 107
    Suez War, 408
    Syrian role in the Gulf War, 289
    Syrian-Israeli peace, 284
    Syria's isolation under Bashar, 293–295
    Tunisia's pro-Western policy, 531
    Turkey and, 23–24, 29, 35–43
    Turkey and Greece's NATO
        membership, 36
    USS *Cole* bombing, 224
    Yemen's foreign policy, 228–230
    See also Iraq, US invasion of
United States of Africa, 443–444
Urbanization and urban migration, 7
    Algeria, 486
    altering tribal loyalties' political impact,
        5
    demographic indicators and
        information by country, 8(table)
    Iran, 70
    Iran's rural-urban migration, 70
    Iraq, 146–147
    Lebanon, 244
    Saudi water resources, 100
    Turkey's rate of, 26
Uzbekistan, 39

Veiling, 110, 523
Virtue Party (Turkey), 22–23

Wafd Party (Egypt), 399–401, 404–405,
    411
Wahhabi Islam, 91–92, 95, 224
War in Gaza (2008–2009), 346, 354, 382
Water resources, 100, 150, 412, 435
Wattasids, 447
Weapons of mass destruction (WMD), 137,
    139, 153, 442
Welfare Party (Turkey), 21–22, 28–29, 33
West Bank, 308–309, 326, 339, 342,
    345–346, 349, 370–371, 373–375,
    379–380, 382–384, 390–391. *See also*
    Palestinians
Western countries and
        influences/Westernization
    Algeria, 479–480, 484–485
    Egypt, 410
    Iran, 57, 73, 84–85
    Iraq's foreign policy, 152–154
    Israel, 325
    Lebanon, 237, 247, 260
    Libya's foreign policy, 439
    Saudi development, 101
    Syria, 291
    Tunisia, 525, 531
    Turkey, 15–17
    Yemen, 210, 213
    See also European Union (EU); United
        States
Western Sahara dispute, 440, 444, 468–471
White Revolution (Iran), 55
Wifaq, 177–178
Wilson, Woodrow, 399
Winograd Committee, 354
Women
    Bahraini representation, 177
    fertility rates, 7
    Iran's politicization, 81
    Iran's White Revolution, 55
    Iraq, 131, 147
    Israel's cabinet, 345
    Jordanian parliamentary elections,
        312–313
    Kuwait's legislature, 170
    Lebanese political participation, 248
    Libya's literacy rates, 436
    literacy rates, 8, 9(table)
    Morocco, 457–459, 465

Oman's Consultative Assembly, 199
Qatari education, 180–181
Saudi government and politics, 105
Tunisia, 521, 523–524
Turkey, 21, 26, 43–44
World Bank. *See* International Monetary
  Fund/World Bank
World Trade Organization (WTO), 179,
  442, 491
World War I
  Arabian Peninsula's power politics,
    95
  Egypt, 399–400
  ending Ottoman rule in the Levant,
    237–238
  Iran's Qajar dynasty, 51
  Jews in Palestine, 367
  Jordanian territory, 297
  Saudi foreign relations, 117
  Syria's economic condition, 280
  Syria's turkification, 269
World War II
  British interests in maritime trade
    routes, 163
  British mandate in Iraq, 127–129
  French occupation of Lebanon,
    238
  Iran occupation, 53
  Italian departure from Libya, 425
  Saudi foreign relations, 117–118
  Syria's economic condition, 280
  Turkey's military and political weakness,
    35–36

Yamani, Zaki, 107
Yassin, Abd al-Salam, 465
Yassin, Nadia, 465
Yazdi, Ibrahim, 60
Yazidis, 146

Yemen, Republic of
  bifurcation of, 207–210
  demographic indicators and
    information, 8, 8(table), 208
  economic conditions and indicators, 5,
    6(table), 211–216, 219–223
  foreign policy, 226–230
  geography, 214–215
  map, 205
  historical background, 205–219
  political environment, dynamics and
    structures, 10, 214–226
  political indicators, 11(table)
  Saudi border dispute, 100
  Saudi migrants, 104
  social indicators and structures, 9,
    9(table), 216–218
  Steadfastness Front, 284
  unification, 210–211
  urbanization rate, 7
Yemen Arab Republic (YAR), 208, 221
Yilmaz, Mesut, 22
Yom Kippur War (1973), 336, 348–349,
  356. *See also* Arab-Israeli War (1973);
    October War
Young Ottoman movement, 15
Young Tunisian movement, 511
Young Turk movement, 15–17, 269,
  366–367, 511
Youth: demographic indicators and
  information by country, 8(table)

Zagros Mountains, 67–68
al-Zaim, Husni, 273
Zaydi imamate, 207
Zeroual, Lamine, 498–499
al-Zindani, Abd al-Majid, 224, 229
Zionism, 321–322, 356–357, 367, 372, 441
Zoroastrians, 5, 49, 69, 146